TWELVE GERMAN NOVELLAS

TWELVE
GERMAN NOVELLAS

Edited and Translated by
Harry Steinhauer

University of California Press
Berkeley   Los Angeles   London

University of California Press
Berkeley and Los Angeles, California
University of California Press, Ltd.
London, England
Copyright © 1977 by The Regents of the University of California
ISBN: 0-520-03002-8
Library of Congress Catalog Card Number: 75-7204
Printed in the United States of America

The Buffoon by Thomas Mann appears here by arrangement with
Random House, Inc. and Martin Secker & Warburg, Ltd. Translated from the German by Harry Steinhauer. Reprinted by permission of Alfred A. Knopf, Inc., publishees of *Stories of Three
Decades*, by Thomas Mann.

The Heretic of Soana by Gerhart Hauptmann appears with the permission of Verlag Ullstein GmbH., Frankfurt/M.-Berlin.

Fräulein Else by Arthur Schnitzler appears by arrangement with Joan
Daves on behalf of the Schnitzler estate.

Ordeal by Fire appears with the permission of Verlag Philipp Reclam
Jun., Stuttgart.

CONTENTS

PREFACE

This anthology is a revision of *Ten German Novellas*, which was published in 1969 by Doubleday & Company in the Anchor Books series. It is designed for the student of comparative literature as well as for the general reader. The novellas selected for this book represent the principal currents in German literature since the late eighteenth century, when the novella emerged as a significant genre in German letters. Each of the included authors has made a major contribution to novella literature. In some cases the piece chosen is the author's acknowledged masterpiece (Kleist, Chamisso, Hauptmann, Schnitzler); in others the story is a work which, despite its excellence, is not as well known as it deserves to be (Wieland, Meyer, Mann, Bergengruen). Like every anthologist, this one is distressed by the scores of notable titles that space has compelled him to exclude, but consoles himself with the thought that the book may serve as an appetizer for the serious student of literature.

The translations aim at fidelity and, it is hoped, some degree of elegance. The case of Kleist is exceptional; the conviction that an attempt to render his involved sentences into an equivalent English would merely alienate the reader persuaded me to break them up into more easily digestible morsels. Kleist has so much more to offer than sentence structure.

The general introduction wrestles with that perennial chestnut in German literary criticism: What is a novella? It seeks an answer by drawing on both theory and practice in non-German literatures. The individual introductory notes offer a brief orientation to the author's total work and throw out a few suggestions about the nature and meaning of the story to follow.

I wish to express my thanks to Robert Zachary and Udo Strutynski of the University of California Press for their encouragement and criticism; to my colleague Stuart Atkins for his help in solving textual problems; and to Ursula Mahlendorf for her valuable suggestions for improving the introductory note on Thomas Mann.

University of California   HARRY STEINHAUER
Santa Barbara

INTRODUCTION

The term "novella" is a fairly recent addition to the vocabulary of
Anglo-American criticism. The dictionaries and handbooks define it
as "a short prose narrative" and refer to Boccaccio's *Decameron* as
the prototype of the genre. This definition would make novella synonymous with short story. The third edition of Webster's says: "a
short novel, a work of fiction intermediate in length and complexity
between the short story and the novel." This is more in line with general Anglo-American usage, which recognizes three subdivisions in
prose fiction: the novel, the short story, and a form intermediate in
length that has been called variously novelette, short novel, and
latterly, novella. One of the first critics to use the term novella was
Henry James. Feeling that the short story did not give him enough
room to carry out his elaborate and refined psychological analyses,
he favored the "blessed nouvelle," which permits the artist "to express
the idea beautifully developed." James distinguished between the
"mere tale," which deals with one central character, and the novella
proper, which is a short novel—that is, presents the more complex
world of the novel in smaller compass; the implication is that the only
difference between novel and novella is that of length. The origin of
the word *novel* (which is derived from the Italian *novella*) indicates
that both long and short fiction were originally regarded as one literary medium, whose basic characteristic was its novelty: it told a new
story and a newsworthy—novel—one, a story that would, in our day,
be reported in the newspapers and on television. Both novella and,
later on, novel referred to content, not to form. As late as the middle
of the nineteenth century British writers still used the term novel to
indicate a short story, and some German critics referred to a novel as
a *Novelle*. It is true that there have been attempts, beginning with

Edgar Allan Poe, to single out special features as characteristic of the short story; but these theoretical works seem to be largely ignored in general studies of literature. Wellek and Warren, in their authoritative *Theory of Literature*, do not even mention the novella or short story as a subgenre of fiction, and there are no entries in their index for these terms. In their chapter dealing with narrative fiction they use short stories to illustrate techniques of fiction, and this is the general practice among scholars and critics. It is therefore fair to say that Anglo-American criticism thinks of novel, novella, and short story as different-sized members of the same literary family.

On the European continent the term novella has been current since the time of Boccaccio. While the Spaniards use the word *novela* for both novel and short story, the Italians and the French very early restricted it to describe shorter fiction only. Moreover, in the Romance literatures there developed at an early date a body of criticism which took upon itself the definition and censure of both the content and form of the genre. The situation is most complex in German criticism. The term *Novelle* did not become popular in Germany until the early nineteenth century, when Goethe and the Romantics began to use it. The novella quickly became *the* genre in which German literature (which of course includes Austrian and Swiss as well) achieved preeminence. With the growth of German *Wissenschaft* it was inevitable that a formidable body of critical and theoretical literature should develop around the novella. That literature is contradictory, confusing, dogmatic, and too often contrary to common sense and common literary experience. Fortunately a small but growing nucleus of skeptics have questioned the assertions of the theorists. But the net result of the controversy is that German scholarship is without a tenable definition of the novella. Possibly some light may be shed on this murky situation by tracing the development of the novella in European literature and then discussing the various German attempts to identify the special characteristics that short fiction supposedly manifests.

HISTORICAL SKETCH

There is an almost continuous tradition of story telling, oral and written, from the most ancient times. Many of these early stories, like

the Book of Ruth in the Old Testament, the parables about Jesus in
the New, or the *Thousand and One Nights*, show a high level of
artistry. A large body of short narrative fiction, in verse and prose,
also exists in medieval literature, such as the *lais* of Marie de France,
the exempla and nova, the *Gesta Romanorum*, the *Cento Novelle
Antiche*. But there is general agreement that the character of
European short fiction has been molded by Boccaccio's *Decameron*,
the publication of which (1438-1353) established the short story as an
art form and exerted an immense influence on its future development. The *Decameron* consists of one hundred stories, most of them
no more than three or four pages long, which are presented as having
been told orally by ten Italian aristocrats over a period of ten days to
while away the time. These stories are held together by a frame,
which opens and closes the whole cycle and introduces each story.
The claim made by Boccaccio that these tales are told orally and
extempore is a fiction; the truth is that he wrote them down over a
period of six years. He called them "novellas" because he wished to
indicate that they were novel, unheard before this telling, and that
they were true, based on real happenings, unlike the old tales derived
from classical mythology or medieval chivalry and romance, which
every cultivated Italian knew. But this claim, too, was a fiction, for
the stories of the *Decameron* were anything but new or real; most of
them were borrowed from various sources, Oriental and medieval—
Boccaccio admits as much in the afterword to his book. What was
new and real about the book was its spirit, its mood and tone, the
great variety of people, events, and ideas, and the delicate irony that
pervades many of the stories, especially the polemical passages in the
frame, where Boccaccio takes on his critics and detractors. The
Decameron is, by common consent, the first projection of the Renaissance spirit of joy in life for its own sake; it presents us with a gallery
of living, individualized people who act out their instincts, ambitions,
and ideals in a secular spirit. It is a work written to entertain, though
some of the stories inculcate an ethical ideal in a broad, humanistic
sense. These tales were meant to counteract the same spirit of
unreality that Cervantes later satirized more consciously in *Don
Quixote*.

Despite the broad spectrum of tone, mood, and form covered by
the stories of the *Decameron*, the book is limited in scope in that it is
not concerned with the depiction (or development) of character, nor

with describing how people lived. These are tales of action and ideas; they tell about piquant and extraordinary events, comic or tragic incidents, physical or intellectual difficulties overcome, about witty sallies and encounters.

The belief, widespread in German scholarship, that Boccaccio created a new art form, which he called novella, is refuted by Boccaccio himself in the *Proemion* and by the contents of the book, which includes fables, parables, legends, anecdotes, love stories, tales of married life, practical jokes, satires, and debates on serious subjects; and it embraces the whole tonal scale from the farcical to the tragic. Boccaccio was an innovator only in this respect: he elevated the art of story telling to a new level. If he was sincere in disclaiming any high literary quality for his stories, he was mistaken, for the *Decameron* is a work of great literature and is fine entertainment too, and it is as alive today as it was four centuries ago when it first appeared.

The followers of Boccaccio—Chaucer, Bandello, Marguerite de Navarre, La Fontaine, among many others—carried on his tradition without introducing any radical innovation. A new note, however, was struck by Cervantes in the *Novelas Ejemplares* (*Exemplary Novellas*, 1613). Cervantes was the first independent and original artist in the genre since Boccaccio; his influence on the development of the European novella is second only to that of the Italian master; on this scholars are generally agreed. While some of Cervantes's stories are Italian in theme and spirit, dealing with adventure, intrigue, and improbable coincidence, eight of the twelve strike a new note. They are considerably longer than short stories, and their greater length enabled the author to paint on a larger canvas, to pay more attention to the depiction of human character, which is moreover shown in development rather than as static. Cervantes also sets the action against the social background from which it arises. He gives us genre pictures, detailed descriptions of places, characters, and manners, not disdaining to mention such inelegant matters as unwashed hands and dirty fingernails. But above all, the author's assurance that he is writing with a moral purpose (as indicated by the title) is no mere sop to the moralists, but may be taken as a sincere statement of intention. The spirit emanating from the *Exemplary Novellas* is wholly different from that of the *Decameron*. With Cervantes the novella became a serious form of high literature in a sense only glimpsed here and there in Boccaccio and his followers. In the opinion of Werner Krause, the extended form that Cervantes gave the novella had some bearing on this development, because it brought this short genre closer to the prose epic (the forerunner of the novel) and thereby raised its status as literature. Cervantes's novellas point the way that fiction was to follow in the coming centuries.

But it is a long way yet. For three centuries, from Boccaccio to La Fontaine, writers of novellas had to fend off the attacks and advice of clerics and critics. It was not until the Enlightenment that the *novelliste* was left alone to follow his artistic conscience. Meanwhile in seventeenth-century France the long novella had developed from the example set by Cervantes. Stories from two hundred to seven hundred pages in length were published as *nouvelles*; these differed in no way from novels, and were indeed sometimes called *petits romans*. During the Enlightenment the *conte philosophique,* a long tale expounding an idea, a moral or metaphysical position, became a vehicle for moral instruction in a secular, generally liberal, spirit. Examples are Johnson's *Rasselas,* Voltaire's and Diderot's *contes* and the moral tales of Marmontel. But the traditional preoccupation of the novella with sexual license was continued; and the new romantic passion that we associate with Rousseau, but which really goes back to the seventeenth century, is represented by *Manon Lescaut* and the many versions of the Abélard and Héloïse story.

It was the fiction of Denis Diderot which, through its realism, showed the direction in which all literature was moving. The early novella had been realistic only in comparison with the medieval tales of chivalry and romance. It had made no attempt to reproduce the world of nature or human behavior and speech with any precision. But this is precisely what Diderot set out to do. He was very much concerned with the problem of artistic illusion: how can the writer make the reader or spectator forget that he is in a fictitious world? Diderot believed that the solution lay in supplying "historical" fiction, that is, recording what has actually happened or could happen around us. Diderot brought the novella into close relationship with the novel, which was developing across the English Channel as an instrument for chronicling the course of real life. To the realism of plot and character he added a *vérisme* of diction: speech that is free from images, metaphors, ornaments, descriptive detail. He favored a dry, sober, flexible, rapid style; and, where the situation became dramatic, he represented it by dialogue in the midst of the narrative, in order to render the spontaneity, tension, vivacity of human speech in society. This is a remarkable anticipation of future developments in fiction and drama. From now on the novella and the novel, even when they are romantic in inspiration, remain in contact with real life as they never had before.

The fiction of the early nineteenth century has a background of reality that foreshadows much of later realism. It is proper to speak of Kleist as a realist, for *Michael Kohlhaas* shows us a real world in a way that Wieland's *Love and Friendship Tested* does not; and, however fantastic the events related in *Mademoiselle de Scudéry* may be, the world presented in that novella is a real picture of Paris under Louis XIV.

In the nineteenth century the novella, like the novel, became an instrument for transmitting serious thought, social criticism and psychological exploration. The example of Cervantes was not lost on Goethe and those who followed him in developing the art of the novella. Goethe's *Unterhaltungen deutscher Ausgewanderten* (*Conversations of German Emigrés*, 1795) pretends to be entertainment for aristocratic ladies and gentlemen; but the spirit of the stories is serious, the atmosphere more realistic than, say, that in Wieland's *Hexameron of Rosenhain*. The direction is away from didacticism and mere play, toward a concern with the serious problems of life. That is not to say that the novella rejected altogether the element of fun that had played so large a role in its earlier history. Of course, there continued to be humorists and satirists who expressed themselves through the medium of the novella. The point is that the novella no longer registered on the popular mind as a bawdy or funny tale. Even a comic fairy story like Keller's *Clothes Make the Man*, for all its pure fun, is a serious criticism of bourgeois ideals.

Looking back historically we see that the novella and the novel underwent the same development: from shallow entertainment and shallow didacticism to high literature that treats the problems of life with ever subtler artistry, which expresses itself as a conscious study of structure, point of view, symbolism, language. Like every art form, the novella reflects the *Zeitgeist*. Now the nineteenth century shows a Janus face: it is the age of both rationalism and irrationalism; the two antithetical attitudes pervade the whole spectrum of mental life. For,

as Whitehead has pointed out, the development of the natural
sciences and inductive reasoning since the seventeenth century has
actually encouraged irrationalism. Thus the nineteenth century
shows a powerful rational bent in religion and an irrational undercurrent in science. It was the physicist Ernst Mach who questioned
the existence of an integrated personality and suggested that the "I"
is nothing more than a bundle of sensations without a solid core. And
it was the neuroanatomist Sigmund Freud who diagnosed the "third
great trauma" of modern man by his assertion that most human
thinking is conducted on the subconscious, irrational level. In literature, too, both currents existed side by side, often turning up where
one would least expect them. The example set by science favored
both the tight, stylized classical structure and the loose, open, relaxed
style that the Romantics had championed and which some of the
naturalists found to be "truer to life" and therefore aesthetically
right. The realists attacked the "well-made play" and advocated a
more amorphous, open-ended drama. The two manners are equally
represented in all genres: in the poetry of Leconte de Lisle versus that
of Whitman; in Ibsen versus Hauptmann and Shaw; in Flaubert ver
sus Hardy; and, for the novella, in Maupassant versus Chekhov.
Chekhov was especially influential in directing literature toward the
expression of suggestion, impression, and atmosphere rather than
toward hard reality, although he worked in the realist-naturalist
tradition. His impact on short fiction has been profound.

The German Novella

German literature felt the influence of Boccaccio at an early date.
In the Age of Humanism and the Reformation the Italian *novellistes*
were translated and imitated. The period showed a predilection for
the various forms of short fiction that had been popular since the
Middle Ages; these were promulgated in broadsheets, folk- and
chapbooks and in almanacs. The collections of Johannes Pauli and
Jörg Wickram are still readable. Grimmelshausen's great picaresque
novel *Simplicissimus* (1668) is studded with numerous anecdotes, farcical tales, learned and didactic allegorical digressions. Grimmelshausen also composed three long novellas, one of which, *Die Land-
störzerin Courage* (*Mistress Courage the Adventuress*, 1670), is the

source of Bertolt Brecht's play *Mutter Courage* (*Mother Courage*, 1939).

In the eighteenth century French short fiction was popular in Germany; Marmontel's moral tales and Voltaire's *contes philosophiques* were widely read and imitated. The English essayists were also influential in the moralistic German lands. The didactic penchant was satisfied by the beast fable and the idyll; Gessner's versified idylls were much in vogue in their day. But while Voltaire's *contes* are as fresh today as they were then, the German short fiction of the Enlightenment has little interest for the general reader of our age.

We tread more solid ground after 1750. Christoph Martin Wieland, who opens our anthology, is a major figure in German, indeed in European, literature. He is a natural storyteller in verse and prose and is perhaps the last important writer of short fiction in the gay tradition of Boccaccio. His novellas are still aesthetic games to be played by cultivated people to while away the time in a pleasant and instructive pursuit. They are intellectually stimulating, urbane in tone, and delightfully written; but the stamp of social sport is clearly on them.

About the same time as Wieland published the cycle of stories that make up the *Hexameron von Rosenhain*, Goethe's *Conversations of German Emigrés* appeared. Following the example of Boccaccio, Goethe provided the cycle with a frame into which he introduced discussions on various topics of interest to the company of storytellers. The novellas themselves cover a wide range of theme, mood, tone, and style. Almost immediately there was a rich harvest of short fiction. Kleist and the Romantics (Tieck, Arnim, Brentano, Hoffmann, Eichendorff, Chamisso) produced both sophisticated fairy tales (*Kunstmärchen*) and "realistic" novellas. Moreover, they nurtured a taste for the novella among the reading public. For during the Restoration Period (1815-48) the German public consumed huge quantities of short fiction, which appeared in the almanacs and albums for ladies, the forerunners of the modern magazine. Most of these stories belong to the sphere of popular or trivial literature. But the best writers, too, published their novellas in these periodicals. By the middle of the century the novella was established as a respectable genre, practiced by the best writers. Its subsequent history merges with the general history of literature; it went through the same changes that the novel and the drama and even lyric poetry experienced: from realism, through naturalism, neo-romanticism, expressionism, and back to a "neo"-realism.

Novella Theory in German Criticism

The frame of the *Decameron* contains a number of passages in which Boccaccio defends himself against the attacks of critics, who find his stories immoral, unhistorical (that is, made up), and original (rather than based on well-worn traditional themes, motifs, and plots). It was not until the Enlightenment that this line of attack vanished and it began to look as if the writer would be left alone to do his work without interference from clergymen and critics. With the rise of the German novella in the nineteenth century a new type of critical concern arose to plague the *novelliste*: criticism became aesthetic. The questions now asked were: What is the true nature of the novella as distinct from other prose genres? What are the criteria that it must observe? Boccaccio was resurrected as the great master and model; his authority, as culled from the *Decameron*, was distilled into a theory of the novella, a theory that developed gradually. The *Decameron* was seen as a unified, monolithic collection of examples of the novella as an art form, although Boccaccio himself states that his book is a potpourri of many literary types. Some zealots even tried to freeze the characteristics of the genre for all time by invoking the authority or supposed practice of Boccaccio, even as the authority of Aristotle's *Poetics* had been invoked for centuries as the source for the theory of tragedy.

The first important contribution to novella theory in Germany was made by Friedrich Schlegel in a group of essays on prose fiction, specifically in his *Nachricht von den poetischen Werken des Johannes Boccaccio* (*Report on the Poetical Works of Giovanni Boccaccio*, 1801). Schlegel believed that the novel should be a purely intellectual *jeux d'esprit*, sheer poetry and fancy, as much an abstraction from reality as the arabesque, which Kant had extolled as the highest form of art, because it does not copy any object in nature but is pure form. Schlegel therefore shifted the task of presenting real life from the novel to the novella. He felt that the depiction of life should be carried out by the writer in an objective, detached, ironic frame of mind, but in a way that allows a subjective (i.e., personal, ideological) position to show through to the discerning reader. He found both types of story in Boccaccio: tales that are pure anecdotes (that is, tales of action, adventure, and situation) and those that have a philosophical core or express a personal, psychological point of view.

Ludwig Tieck, who produced many volumes of novellas, concurred in the general opinion that the novella deals with the real life about us, though his own early novellas are tales of magic and the supernatural. His theoretical legacy concerning the novella is his observation that every true novella has a "turning point," at which the course of events takes a different direction from the one it has been following. Unless he had some arcane literary tactic in mind, he was revealing what writers had practiced for centuries. Is this not the *peripeteia* that Aristotle prescribed for tragedy and which applies equally to all literary genres? But while there is obvious dramatic force in leading an action in a certain direction to a climax and then turning it around, it is not the only possible technique. If the author prefers to develop the action in a straight line, inexorably moving to a tragic or happy conclusion, whether without checks and frustrations or with only minor ones, he has a perfect right to do so, if he can carry it off. But Tieck's doctrine of the turning point remained one of the pillars of novella theory right into the twentieth century.

Perhaps the most celebrated contribution to German novella theory was made by Goethe in a casual remark reported by his secretary Eckermann in 1827. Goethe had just completed an allegorical, moral tale, for which he was seeking a title. Finding none that was suitable, he remarked to Eckermann: "Do you know what? We'll call it *The Novella*; for what is a novella but an unheard of event that has occurred [Denn was ist eine Novelle anders als eine sich ereignete, unerhörte Begebenheit]? This is the basic concept, and so much of what passes in Germany under this name is not a novella at all but merely a tale or whatever else you wish to call it. The novella in *The Elective Affinities* is also used in that original sense of an unheard-of event." Now Goethe's formula is very ambiguous. The word *eine* means both "a" and "one"; *unerhört* usually means "unheard-of," "remarkable," but also "never heard before," "novel"; Goethe may be echoing Schlegel's phrase from his essay on Boccaccio, "an as yet unknown story." Finally, what does Goethe intend by the word "Begebenheit?" Is he endorsing Schlegel's assertion that the novella is essentially an "anecdote," that is, a story of action or adventure, with little concern for metaphysical problems, psychology, social background, and local color? If so, then his choice of *Novelle* as the title for his story is most unfortunate, because his novella is brim full of historical, social, metaphysical, allegorical, symbolical underpinning. Essays and monographs have been written to "explicate" it.

From this time on there has been a steady flow of contributions to the theory of the novella. For a time they came chiefly from writers: Tieck with his turning point, Hebbel and Spielhagen with contradictory views on the role of character in the novella; Heyse with his celebrated but obscure "falcon" theory. Early in the twentieth century the new science of literary theory (*Literaturwissenschaft*) began to generate definitions, regulations, speculations, prescriptions, and proscriptions, most of them threatening to clip the wings of the novellistic Pegasus. Fortunately, as happened in the romance literatures at an earlier date, the creative writers paid little attention to this body of criticism and went on writing novellas according to the dictates of their artistic taste and their literary conscience. Fortunately, too, among the literary theorists there have been some who have taken a latitudinarian position against the legislators and censors.

The following is a summary of the most common demands made by literary theorists on the novella:

1. The novella deals with one central event.

2. This event is extraordinary but falls short of the miraculous and supernatural. The novella is realistic, dealing with everyday life.

3. The novella depicts the intrusion of fate or an irrational force (some say chaos) into an ordered existence.

4. It treats events rather than character, which is the prerogative of the novel.

5. The novella treats fixed, not developing, characters; others claim that it shows character developing.

6. The novella should have a small cast of characters; according to some, one central character.

7. It should not deal with great historical figures but with the fate of ordinary people.

8. It should have a tight, compact structure, rejecting background and local color. Its diction should be plain, spare, taut.

9. The novella should have a turning point.

10. It relies heavily on symbolism, in this respect resembling poetry rather than the novel.

11. The novella should have a falcon, so called after the falcon in *Decameron* V, 9. This falcon is interpreted either as a concrete symbol for the theme of the story or as a clear and concise silhouette of the plot.

12. The narration should not be linear or chronological but dramatic, analytic: it should begin in the middle of the action and reveal prior events through a series of flashbacks, like the Greek epic or an Ibsen drama.

Now it is obvious that every one of these criteria has been violated by one or another eminent novella. Some of the above prescriptions are so vague as to be almost meaningless; others, such as number 9, are as characteristic of the epic, novel, and drama as they are of the novella. Some of the restrictions are so contrary to common sense and our experience with literature that we should be compelled to reject them out of hand as an "ought," even if it could be demonstrated that every extant novella observed them: 7, for instance, and 4, 10, 11, 12; but especially 3. If this last means that a novella should contain an ingredient of pure chance that disturbs the smooth flow of life and the logic of events, it is a truism; any literary work dealing with life seriously must include events that seem to happen by chance. If, however, it means that the author must subscribe to an irrational philosophy and inject this ideology into his novella, it is patent nonsense. Would we make the same demand on the dramatist, novelist, or lyric poet? Such a requirement would eliminate many of the world's finest novellas from membership in the genre.

The most plausible of the twelve criteria is the first: the novella should confine itself to one central event because that is all it can handle effectively in the space at its disposal. But this cannot be a characteristic feature of the novella, because there are many outstanding novellas that narrate a whole life or a large slice of life or the fate of a whole social group: Balzac's *The Curate of Tours,* Flaubert's *A Simple Heart,* Keller's *A Village Romeo and Juliet,* Meyer's *The Sufferings of a Boy,* James' *Daisy Miller,* to cite a few random examples. There are even short stories that are novels in miniature: Heinrich Mann's *Three-Minute Novel,* Hebbel's *Barber Zitterlein,* and, according to Elizabeth Bowen, the short stories of

Thomas Hardy. Johann Peter Hebel's anecdote *Unverhofftes Wie-dersehen* (*Unexpected Reunion*) is a novel in outline; Hoffmann expanded it into a long novella, *The Mine at Falun*, and Hofmannsthal made a full-length drama out of it. It is still waiting for someone to turn it into a novel; the recipe for doing so is given in Hebel's three-page anecdote.

So it is difficult to support the thesis that a novella should confine itself to one central event. The reverse, that a novel should give us a panorama of life, is equally hard to substantiate as a dogma. Many novels do, many do not. There are outstanding novels that are "really" expanded novellas: Richardson's two novels, Flaubert's *Madame Bovary*, whose plot has been condensed into eight lines of print, Camus's *The Stranger* and *The Plague*, and Claude Mauriac's *The Dinner Party*. Beside novellas that are like novels and novels that are "really" novellas, there are novels that were originally conceived as novellas, such as Goethe's *The Elective Affinities*, Thomas Mann's *The Magic Mountain*, and his Joseph tetralogy. Hawthorne has told us that he intended *The Scarlet Letter* to be a tale; and Bertolt Brecht first treated the chalk-circle theme as an anecdote and then developed it into a full-length drama.

Since Percy Lubbock, in *The Craft of Fiction*, made his classic distinction between scenic and panoramic techniques of narration, it has been obvious that the writer of short fiction has a choice between two techniques: he can restrict his subject matter to one central event and treat this intensively, "scenically," or he may take on a larger segment of life, like the novelist, and handle it in a "panoramic," outline manner. The effect produced by the two techniques will of course be different and some readers will find the one or the other more or less to their taste. But there can be no question about the legitimacy of either approach; narrative technique does not determine whether a work of short fiction is a novella or not.

All this suggests that there is no inherent, magical character in literary materials that predestines them to become a novel, a novella, or an anecdote. A writer in *The Times Literary Supplement* asks, "Why are short stories so short?" and replies, "Because the author wants them no longer." It is the author who decides how he will shape the raw material at hand, whether he will present the experience as one single event or a whole life; whether he will create static or dynamic characters; whether his structure will be chronological or analytic; whether he will work with symbols and "falcons," write "obliquely" or "directly," in Tillyard's suggestive terminology. Instead of stating dogmatically that the short story deals with a short subject and the novel with a long one, it would be more fruitful to say that there are two ways of treating any subject, a short way and a long one, and to study the implications of the author's choice in a specific work. And when a scholar characterizes Thomas Mann's *Buddenbrooks* as "an accretion of sketches and short scenes," he may imply that this is a flimsy way of constructing a supposedly great novel; but we may draw the conclusion that here is still another way of composing a great novel.

Definition

Is it then possible to formulate a satisfactory definition of the German novella? The following factors must be reckoned with. In German literature the term *Novelle* is largely confined to the nineteenth century. During this time it was used to describe all short fiction between the novel and the anecdote, except for a few special categories like the fairy tale, legend, and sketch. The long novella was a favorite form of literary expression in this period. In the twentieth century, probably under Anglo-American influence, the short story (called, not surprisingly, *Kurzgeschichte*) displaced the long novella.

Throughout the period under consideration the term *Novelle* was used very loosely by most writers as a fashionable term for short fiction; others preferred the older terms *Erzählung* (narrative, tale) and *Geschichte* (story). However, with the rise of *Literaturwissenschaft*, scholars began to make special claims for the novella and to differentiate it from other short fiction that was labeled *Erzählung, Geschichte,* and, latterly, *Kurzgeschichte*. It is doubtful whether the criteria that have been set up for the novella have any real validity; important German scholars have joined the ranks of the skeptical. Recent German writers have shown little awareness of the academic industry in this area of scholarship and even less concern about novella theory; they (or their publishers) use the various terms for classifying short fiction with anarchic insouciance.

If German culture possessed the equivalent of a French Academy, one would be tempted to recommend to that august body that it should adopt Anglo-American usage, which classifies prose fiction with a yardstick, so to speak. And this suggestion is not to be laughed out of court; for classification by size is widely used both in nature (botany and zoology) and in culture. Such a recommendation would gain the support of the eminent Swiss scholar Emil Staiger, who once defined the *Novelle* simply as "a story of medium length." However, as far as German literature is concerned, such "materialistic" classification is not likely to triumph. Students of German literature should therefore be reminded that there are more fruitful questions to be asked in studying a work of fiction. They are the questions that literary theory of the recent past has taught us to ask of literature in general and of the novel in particular. And the skeptic in the realm of novella metaphysics should be flexible enough to admit that it is legitimate to inquire what artistic qualities result from the fact that a story is three or thirty or three hundred pages long.

Perhaps Goethe said the final word on the subject. His ironical question to Eckermann contains two essential criteria for the novella: (1) it should tell an exciting story, "a tale that holds children from play and old men from the chimney corner," and (2) the story should be told with credibility, as if it had really happened. Goethe was talking essentials; "tout le reste est littérature."

Christoph Martin Wieland

1733 — 1813

Wieland is the most representative literary figure of eighteenth-century Germany. As his life spanned the period extending from the Enlightenment to the Classicism of Goethe and Schiller, so his writings recapitulate the evolution of German literature during this era. Rationalism, the fervent spirituality of Pietism, the Anacreontic vogue, Rococo, Classicism and hellenism, "faery" Romanticism — he tried them all. One mood alone he rejected: that of the turbulent literary current known as *Sturm und Drang*, which swept Germany in the sixties of the eighteenth century, carrying even the young Goethe and Schiller with it. Its addiction to violent passion, a radical break with the humanist tradition in the name of naturalism were antipathetic to his nature.

Wieland was born in a village near Biberach in southern Germany, the son of a Pietist pastor. From the age of three he was taught by his father, then enrolled in a Latin school. He learned quickly and thoroughly; at the age of eleven he was reading the latest literary publications, the heavy works of Gottsched and Brockes. At twelve he composed a Latin poem of six hundred lines and a large body of German poetry, operettas, cantatas, ballets. A year later he was sent to a Pietist boarding school, where he managed to read widely in the profane fields of ancient Greek literature, popular literary magazines like the *Spectator, Tatler, Guardian,* as well as current German literature.

In 1749, aged sixteen, he was sent to an uncle at Erfurt, with whom he studied philosophy. His Pietism melted away suddenly and he emerged, for a brief period, at once a materialist and a disciple of Leibniz. His love for his cousin Sophie Gutermann did not contribute to his serenity, for she became engaged to another man.

He enrolled at the University of Tübingen the following year as a law student, but spent his time reading and writing literature. He had returned to his earlier pietistic views and composed a didactic poem, *Die Natur der Dinge* (*The Nature of things*, 1752), belaboring the materialism of Lucretius. Another poem was directed at Ovid, the erotic Roman poet, and a series of stories celebrated religious enthusiasm as true soulful love. These, and a heroic epic *Hermann*, in the manner of Klopstock, pleased the celebrated Swiss critic Bodmer so much that he invited the young student to Zurich. Under Bodmer's tutelage, Wieland poured out seraphic writings, fictional and critical, in verse and prose. In Zurich, and later in Bern, he made his living as a private tutor and became engaged to a brilliant young woman who exerted considerable influence over him.

He was now ready to throw off his traditional intellectual baggage and become what he was. External forces helped; in 1760 he was elected a senator and member of the city council of Biberach; soon after, he became director of the municipal secretariat. He began to frequent the castle of Count Stadion, where he again met his cousin Sophie, now married to Court Councillor La Roche. This circle opened to Wieland the world of French rococo culture, which responded to his inner need. His first important work heralds the change in its title: *Der Sieg der Natur über die Schwärmerei oder die Abenteuer des Don Sylvio de Rosalva* (*The Triumph of Nature over Enthusiasm or the Adventures of Don Sylvio de Rosalva*, 1765). His municipal post proved to be a source of aggravation to him because he became involved in sectarian political warfare between Protestants and Catholics. Later these petty bickerings were described with serene irony in Wieland's satirical masterpiece *Die Abderiten* (*The Inhabitants of Abdera*, 1774). Their immediate effect was to make life in Biberach intolerable for him. But amid his distress he managed to enjoy the social life at Count Stadion's castle Warthausen, to marry a middle-class girl (who bore him thirteen children) and to write steadily. Between 1762 and 1766 he translated twenty-two of Shakespeare's plays into German prose. He wrote his important *"Bildungsroman"* *Agathon*, which appeared in 1766-67. In it Wieland first formulated his ideal of man: a harmonious balance between the opposing forces of sensuality and puritanical repression, the development of a natural, rational, humane attitude to life. The same ideal is advocated in the verse tale *Musarion* (1768), in which

Wieland's own conversion from a rigid hostility toward the healthy pleasures of life to a serene, tolerant enjoyment in moderation is brought about through the grace of a young girl.

In 1769 Wieland escaped from the poisonous atmosphere of Biberach into the supposed calm of academic life. He became a professor of philosophy at the University of Erfurt. Unfortunately, he was so successful with his students that he incurred the enmity of his colleagues, some of whom conspired against him and made life diffcult for him. So, when the Duchess Anna Amalia of Weimar, impressed by his political novel *Der goldene Spiegel* (*The Golden Mirror*, 1772), invited him to become the tutor of her two sons, he joyfully accepted the invitation.

He remained in Weimar for the rest of his life. They were happy years, after an initial period of isolation and unpopularity. He maintained a warm relationship with the reigning family, established a solid friendship with Goethe (who came to Weimar in 1775) and with Herder, the theologian and writer. Here he founded and for forty years edited the literary journal *Der teutsche Merkur* (*The German Mercury*). His most famous work, *Oberon*, a romance in verse, appeared in 1780 (it was translated into English verse by John Quincy Adams). Wieland had always been an excellent classical scholar. He now began an ambitious work of translating classical writers into German: the letters and satires of Horace, the works of Lucian, plays by Aristophanes and Euripides, the writings of Isocrates and Xenophon and five volumes of Cicero's letters. And he created original works.

In 1797, aged sixty-four, he bought an estate at Osmannstedt near Weimar, and until 1803 played a new role of landed gentleman, living on a pension granted him by the duchess. The death of his wife and his own advancing years prompted him to sell the estate and return to Weimar, where he lived for another decade. It was during these years that he translated Cicero and wrote the stories *Das Hexameron von Rosenhain* (1805), from which the following novella is taken. He died in January 1813.

Wieland was essentially a novelist. He possessed the traditional breadth and objectivity of the epic writer and lacked the emotional note of the lyricist or the rhetorical gestures of the dramatist. His literary assets are his cosmopolitanism, his enlightened philosophy of life, his mental agility and, above all, his light, graceful style. ("His

incomparable sense of form" Friedrich Beissner writes.) It is this
lightness and grace in the presentation of ideas that has given Wieland the reputation among Germans of being superficial and frivolous. It is true that Wieland lacks the rugged manliness of Lessing,
the softer strength of Goethe, the soaring passion of Schiller. He
belongs, rather, to the company of Erasmus, Montaigne, Diderot
and Anatole France. it is a very respectable company.

Das Hexameron von Rosenhain was written when Wieland was in
his seventies; but these stories do not read like the work of an old
man, especially when one compares them — inevitably — with Goethe's
cycle of novellas published a few years earlier under the title *Unterhaltungen deutscher Ausgewanderten.* The *Hexameron* is a collection of six stories, three of them sophisticated fairy tales (involving
magic and the supernatural) and three novellas with purely human
settings. All six deal with ethical, psychological and social problems
arising from the erotic relationship: love and selfishness; the cure of
narcissism; a sure treatment for philandering; the dangers inherent
in erotic infatuation; love and self-sacrifice; capriciousness in love;
love and greed. This bald statement of theme gives no clue to the
atmosphere of the tales; the story reprinted here will perhaps do that,
although it will not convey to the reader the mixture of sophisticated
realism and supernatural allegory that is characteristic of the first
half of the collection.

The six (originally five) stories were published separately between
1802 and 1803; they appeared as a connected cycle in 1805. The title
recalls the *Heptameron* of Marguerite de Navarre and the
Decameron of Boccaccio. All three (and this is true also of Goethe's
collection) use the artificial, conventional framework: a company of
well-to-do or aristocratic ladies and gentlemen meet to while away
the time by telling or inventing stories. But within this contrived situation Wieland aims at and achieves a measure of realism: in disguis-
ing names and places, in alluding to other writers (Mrs. Radcliffe
and Jean Paul Richter, Boccaccio and Marguerite de Navarre), in
allowing the narrative to be interrupted by members of the audience,
in reminding us that the author-editor is not the narrator. In fact, in
the introductory frame the company agree that the stories they are
going to tell shall be such as correspond to real life, thus excluding
moral tales, the supernatural and the miraculous. Finally, the editor
slyly remarks that the manuscript which was sent to him was prob-

ably not intended for publication. But in spite of these assurances to the contrary, the first three stories are definitely allegorical romances, in which a supernatural machinery is introduced to direct the action. Even the three novellas are not realistic in style; our story does not even have that element of everyday realism that characterizes Chamisso's fairy tale. But while the setting is stylized, as that of Voltaire's *contes* is, the problem presented in the story itself and the psychological analysis are real enough. Though the charm of Wieland's style is inevitably lost in translation, the rococo spirit of sportive grace may be felt even through the imperfect vehicle of communication represented by this rendering.

Love and Friendship Tested

Two young ladies from one of the German provinces which had been under French jurisdiction for a long time had grown up in mutual affection almost from their childhood days. In their more mature years this inclination had developed into a friendship so perfect that they were better known in their native town as "the friends" than by their family names. I myself first made their acquaintance in the boarding school run by the English ladies in **, when their time had almost run out and mine was just beginning; for they are both a few years older than I. Young though I still was at the time, I had the good fortune to be liked by them and, since our parents lived in the same city, we promised each other to renew and continue our acquaintance in later years. When I returned home from the boarding school I found them both already married. I had lost my mother early in life, and since my father allowed me a great deal of freedom, I sought out every opportunity to see the two friends; and so there gradually arose such an intimate relationship between us that, in a sense, I became the third partner in their alliance. This close bond furnished me with the opportunity to inform myself more precisely about the anecdote which I do not hesitate to relate to you. But before I proceed to the story of my two friends, I shall have to give you an idea of their character, if only with a few strokes.

Selinde (as I shall name the younger of the two women) unites with the daintiest nymphlike figure a head that would yield the most beautiful model for a Hebe or Psyche. Her temperament is frank, sincere, noble and good; without wearing her virtue like a shield, she bears in herself the germ of all those virtues which lay the foundation for an admirable character; but an excessive vivaciousness and a good dose of frivolity often cast a false light on her; in the consciousness of her ingenuousness and innocence she pays too little heed to this. The desire to please and a no less strong inclination to joy and all those pleasures we are accustomed to call innocent and therefore indulge in with a certain excess, seem to be her only passions, unless we can give the name of passions to inclinations which are as natural to her as breathing and which seldom disturb the inner peace of her mind.

A very lively imagination and an innate, inexhaustible vein of wit, which often makes her see in a ridiculous light objects that demand respect or indulgence, are the outstanding qualities of her mind. To be sure, her intelligence is not uncultivated; but apart from the fact that she has never had enough patience to occupy herself with serious matters for any length of time, she would appear ridiculous in her own eyes if anyone noticed anything akin to wisdom in her manner of talking or behaving. She has put it into her pretty frivolous head that there is a host of amiable little follies which are more appropriate to a beautiful woman than the countenance of a female Socrates, the name with which she is accustomed to tease her friend in her frivolous moments. Nor is Selinde without talents; but since the desire to please through them is no stronger in her than the inclination to all sorts of pleasant diversions and as she has always lacked time (especially since the toilet table takes away a large part of her forenoon), I must confess that she has remained very backward in the fine arts, which are accounted today as part of the education of young people of social standing.

Clarissa (thus we may name the second of the two friends) cannot pass for a beauty, at least beside Selinde. However, her features are intelligent and pleasant; her body, although constructed on a larger scale, is built in such perfect harmony and her health is so pure and blooming that one cannot doubt she could rival her friend with respect to many physical charms if she did not actually make an effort to be noticed as little as possible from this angle, especially in the company of Selinde. The feature through which, as through a hidden magic, unknown to her herself, she gently attracts and permanently grips, is therefore something spiritual rather than sensuous; and whoever sees the two friends together becomes at sight Selinde's lover and Clarissa's friend. It would be difficult to have more right to demand respect and love and to make fewer claims on that right than Clarissa. The formation of her mind, although it is the fruit of her industry and of a wise investment of her time, seems to be a sheer gift of nature; and the large store of knowledge that she possesses peeps out so bashfully from behind the veil of modesty (and only when it would be unseemly to wish to deny it) that neither the ignorance of the women who are put to shame by it nor the presumptuous pride of men is insulted by it. She possesses diverse talents in an uncommon degree; she draws and paints excellently, plays the piano and the harp with as much taste as skill; she even writes pretty little verses, although she scarcely admits this even to her most intimate friends.

It is, if not quite impossible, certainly extremely rare to achieve any degree of perfection in an art without effort and stubborn diligence. Perhaps Clarissa does not possess by nature any more natural gifts than Selinde; but her calm, sedate and more collected mind makes her more apt and more inclined to develop and practice these gifts. She is less fond of diversions than her friend; she always husbanded her time more, divided her day better, and the morning hours, which Selinde allowed to slip through her fingers, partly in superficial perusal of annuals, newspapers, new magazines, partly (and especially) at her dressing table, were always put to a useful and specific purpose by Clarissa. Selinde read to banish boredom or to take pleasure in pleasant pictures and fantasies; Clarissa always read for utility, for she always asked herself: is this true? Do you really think or feel what the author wants you to think and feel? And if not, is the fault yours or his? In this way she learned to compare, differentiate, survey and summarize, discovered the criterion of the true and the beautiful in her person and accustomed herself to a correct evaluation of things. All this gave her clarity of mind, sharpness and correctness of view and freedom from moods, whims, overhasty judgments and frivolous inclinations and antipathies. Everything in her is calm, measured and in harmony with itself. Without passions, without fanaticism, a born enemy of all exaggeration, of everything unnatural, of self-deception and dishonesty toward others and herself, she enjoys an indestructible inner peace, and pure love of the beautiful and the good is in all her circumstances and situations, the soul of her thoughts, inclinations and actions. Naturally, with such a disposition she is always in the mood to sympathize with others, to be thoroughly indulgent toward the failings and weaknesses of others, and in general inclined to select and to do what is most proper in all the

happenings of life. Her seriousness has nothing dour about it, her
sedate nature has nothing heavy or oppressive; serenity and cheerfulness are always spread on her lovely countenance, like sunshine over
a pleasant valley, and universal benevolence seems to be the element
in which she breathes. This is my friend Clarissa, and if the letters of
Aristippus have given me a correct conception of what Socrates was,
I would be greatly mistaken if the name of a female Socrates with
which Selinde teases her were not appropriate to her in all seriousness.

Pardon me if I have unintentionally tarried too long in the description of such a charming woman. I am not an expert portrait painter;
a more skillful hand would perhaps have given the picture more precision and more life with fewer strokes. But I have subjected mine to
the impulse of my heart; and if I finally withdraw it, it is not because
I am satisfied with the portrait, but because I feel that one must
know when to stop.

At first glance it might appear strange that such an intimate
friendship could arise, or at least endure, between two such unequal
people as Clarissa and Selinde. But as soon as one is better acquainted
with both of them, nothing seems to me more intelligible. Selinde's
beauty, frivolity and good nature, on the one hand, and Clarissa's
totally unassuming character on the other, kept even the mere shadow of jealousy from them. It never occurred to Selinde that Clarissa
could contest any one of her advantages; in return, she always willingly recognized her friend's qualities and is even now proud of being
known as the most intimate friend of a woman of so many merits. In
point of fact, Clarissa's love for Selinde (the only thing about her
which approaches a passion) can be nothing but flattering for her;
one might say she permits herself to be loved by Clarissa approximately as the handsome Alcibiades permitted himself to be loved by
Socrates, and Clarissa keeps no more precise accounts than Socrates
did with the son of Clinias, whether her love is returned in equal
measure. For, to tell the truth, the beautiful Selinde is (perhaps unconsciously) too much in love with herself to be able to love in the
same degree as she is loved. But one of her greatest and most deeply
felt needs is to have always a confidante and counselor in her per-
plexities, to whom she can open up completely; and where could she
have found a person who was better suited to this role than Clarissa?
Clarissa's kindness, her indulgence, her apparent sympathy for
Selinde go so far beyond the bounds of the usual friendships among

persons of our sex that Selinde, convinced of Clarissa's complete attachment to her, could suffer even unpleasant truths from her and (what she tolerates from no one else) contradiction and censure. The cases in which they had slight differences were therefore always extremely rare; when something of the sort did occur, Clarissa's gentleness and good sense were able to restore harmony in short order.

As soon as the two friends had come home from the convent, the parents made it their business to spare their beloved daughters the trouble of seeking out husbands after their own eyes or hearts, and they thought they had done everything possible for them by selecting, from among the different suitors who made their appearance, those who might be considered the best match with respect to fortune, age, looks and other perquisites of this sort. Through a strange whim of chance the choice fell on two young men who were united from their earliest youth by a no less intimate friendship than that between Selinde and Clarissa. Wherever they were known, when the topic of friendship came up, Raymond and Mondor (as I shall call them instead of giving them their real names) were cited as a proof of the fact that, even in our degenerate times, there are still friends who may be compared to Pylades and Orestes, Pythias and Damon and others among the heroes of friendship so highly lauded by the ancients.

In order to shed proper light over the story of this double couple, I find it necessary once more to practice my slight skill in portrait painting.

Mondor, who won the charming Selinde, combined with a prepossessing exterior, a very substantial fortune and a fairly recent patent of nobility, almost everything that is demanded from the character of an estimable man: education, talent, good manners and, what is supposed to be rarer today than ever before among people of his class, an unblemished reputation. With all these good qualities it could still happen that a man would not be a proper marriage partner for a lady like Selinde; and this really seemed to be the case after they had for a while drawn the gentle yoke of Hymen together. Mondor was of a serious temperament, slightly tinged with black bile, with a warm intellect and even warmer blood; extremely irritable, vehement and persevering in his passions, and difficult to wean from an idea that he had once put into his head. His imagination, a fairy who exerted a rather tyrannical power over him, was accustomed to paint everything in the world for him either in the most delicate pink or in pitch-black darkness. The object of his love could be nothing slighter than an angel; but woe to the angel if Mondor discovered any dark spot on him — he would then be fortunate if he did not sink in Mondor's opinion and affection deeper than the level of general everyday humanity. In all the ideas, feelings and demands of this young man there was always something excessive and boundless. A natural consequence of this was that he lived more in his own world of ideas than in that of reality and that in the latter world almost nothing was right or good enough. He was therefore no friend of public entertainments; the usual social affairs caused him lethal boredom, and because he had little business to occupy him, he spent the greater part of his day in his library, which was richly stocked with the best works on all subjects and in every language.

His friend Raymond is almost the exact opposite of all this: a light, cheerful, carefree, jovial soul; the most decided lover of all social joys and amusements; somewhat too swift and inconstant in his inclinations and fancies and too sensuous in his pleasures; but basically a good-natured, upright man insofar as no sacrifice of his favorite inclinations is demanded from him, capable of very noble actions and inclined to participate in all good works; in short, one of those happy mortals upon whom everything smiles, who can find pleasure everywhere and who can live with all human beings. He was the son and grandson of a painter and had been directed in his youth toward the art of his fathers. A rich inheritance which came to him unexpectedly liberated him from the necessity of forcing his talent; but the love of art remained one of his dominant inclinations. He possesses a choice collection of paintings, paints himself to his own satisfaction and that of his friends and, as was once said of Apelles, he seldom allows a day to pass without a stroke of the brush.

An intimate friendship between such dissimilar men as Raymond and Mondor may seem to be even more difficult to grasp than that between Selinde and Clarissa; but here too, as everywhere, everything developed quite naturally. Their childhood years, when diversity of temperaments is not yet so strongly pronounced, laid the first foundation; an important service which Raymond subsequently rendered to Mondor at the risk of his life drew the at first loose bond indissolubly tight. They were now friends for life and death. Raymond had done so much for Mondor that the latter could never do too much for him. All their dissonances were always resolved in this pure harmony; each of them made it his duty to conceal as much as possible that side from which he might displease the other. The love of art too, which was common to both, contributed no little to make their association always entertaining. Moreover, Mondor had his hours in which Raymond's superb joyousness was a benefit to him, just as Raymond often laughed heartily at the witty exaggerations in which Mondor was inexhaustible whenever the mood to be malicious about human follies came over him. Even the useful quite often combined with the pleasant in their association; for as often as one of the two came into a situation where the counsel and help of a friend became indispensable to him, he could be certain of finding both in the other: the frivolous Raymond in Mondor's earnest sobriety, the visionary Mondor in Raymond's cold-blooded view of things.

The marriage between Raymond and Clarissa seemed so rational that everyone prophesied a most permanent happiness for them. His feelings for his fiancée possessed everything that could have persuaded anyone but Clarissa to take it for love; she alone could not deceive herself; for she was herself free and had understood Raymond's character too correctly not to see that he was not capable of an enthusiastic love. It was this very thing which made her resolve to favor his courtship. If he had loved her as Mondor loved Selinde, she could scarcely have been moved to give him her hand. For, according to her way of thinking, marriage should not be the work of the blind god of love but of calm reflection, of deliberate approval of each other and of mutual trust; and even then there is always still more or less of a risk on both sides. She had no real objection to Raymond; and since, as she said with a smile, she had to risk it some time or other with one of the uncivilized creatures, she knew of none other for whom she felt more confidence and affection than for him.

Raymond's case was not quite the same. Truly something else had been added to the respect he felt for Clarissa's character and to his pleasure in her person and talents, to make his courtship of her something passionate, although he carefully sought to conceal it from her. In fact, his artistic sense here played the role which is usually assigned to the god of love. He had incurred the slightest suspicion because of the vestal dress which Clarissa favored — unusual at the time — and, by bribing her personal maid, had found a means of ridding himself of his doubts more completely than he had dared to hope. What a discovery for an art lover who is himself an artist! From this moment on he vowed that Clarissa must be his, even if she were to hang from Jupiter's golden chain between heaven and earth.

Mondor's passion for Selinde was of a quite different character. Everything was settled from the first moment; for from his first look into her angelic face, into her heavenly blue eyes, the purest, fairest, most charming of all feminine souls had smiled back at him. What heaven full of superterrestrial bliss did these eyes promise him! Could he hasten enough to assure himself of their possession? If Mondor, as is quite often the case, had had to work for two or three years at the spinning wheel of perfect love, such a long period of time would probably have brought opportunities enough for him to convince himself that his goddess was human after all. However, even in the short time that elapsed between his courtship and the wedding day, the natural, frank Selinde, who was very well contented with her own human qualities, produced such opportunities. But Selinde was Mondor's first love and — as I once heard a very learned gentleman assert, basing himself on some old Latin poet — first love casts a very strange spell over the lover's eyes, gives gentle, palliative and embellishing names to all the faults and failings of the beloved, and transforms them into so many heart-melting charms and perfections. Mondor saw nothing in Selinde which did not fan his fire into a bigger and bigger flame; and Selinde, for her part, as soon as she resolved to become his, obedient to the will of her parents, faced him so pleasantly and obligingly that the honest dreamer regarded all this as the purest harmony between her soul and his and as the pledge of a love which left him no other wish than that it might last forever.

And in truth, during the first days and weeks, no bliss was like his bliss. But of course the sweet delusion could not last forever. Possession imperceptibly weakens the aforesaid charm of first love; his eyes were opened, or rather, restored to their natural state, and he began to perceive all sorts of qualities in his spouse which in no way corresponded to his high-keyed expectations. He had hoped that she would live for him alone, occupy herself with him alone, renounce all distracting amusements, in fact give up most of her social engagements and find her highest bliss in the consciousness of providing his. But this is not what the fair Selinde had intended; she had never promised him this, and the thought of being restrained in her inclinations and pleasures by her marriage had been so far from her mind that she had hoped marriage would give her even more liberty to live after her own heart. She was not aware of any evil; what she asked was the most innocent thing in the world: she merely wanted to please and to have fun. Mondor could complain of no lack of tenderness and complaisance; she loved him as much as she could love; in short, her heart did not reproach her in the least. You may therefore imagine how astonished she was when, from the mouth of the man who a short while ago had still worshiped her like a goddess, believed in her blindly and shown himself infinitely satisfied with everything she said and did, she had to hear the first contradiction and, what was worse still, very soon the first reproaches. Nothing indeed was equal to her astonishment, except the astonishment of her husband to find in this gentle, angelic soul, which he thought was in such pure harmony with his own, a stubbornness, insubordination, indeed even a slight defiance, which (to be sure) was very becoming to her beautiful face and which a lover would have found enchanting, but which, in the eyes of a husband like Mondor, suddenly hurled her down from the height to which he had elevated her in his imagination and put her on the same level as the common daughters of earth.

The marital misunderstandings arising from the mutual error that each had harbored in respect to the other were at first cleared up after an exchange of words and some resistance on both sides, still under the invisible influence of Amor and Hymen. A tender caress, when necessary, a small glistening tear in Selinde's beautiful, gently pleading eyes, were at that time still adequate to melt Mondor's heart to the point of yielding; and more than once she even made a virtue, too, of the fact that she was sacrificing an excursion, a dance or something of this sort at his request in order to give the evening to him, to their marital bliss. But as soon as she noticed, after the lapse of some time, that Mondor wanted to abuse her tender yielding to the jeopardy of her rights, as soon as he assumed a domineering tone and used strong words because his pleas produced the desired effect less and less, Selinde remembered that she was a woman and that she had on her side, if not the universal approval of her own sex, certainly the votes of all nice young men and loyal knights. From this moment on the spiritual bond which had bound Mondor to her was broken; and, although he had to admit to himself at times that everything that he considered to be an outrage would appear in the eyes of a hundred other men to be a matter of total indifference or, at most,

youthful vanity, which could easily be forgiven, he could not bring
himself to pardon her for the shame he felt burning on his cheeks at
the thought that he had so grossly erred about her.

But the consequences of the cleavage that arose between them
through the more and more frequent quarrels, at times insignificant,
at other times very serious, were of unequal character. For poor Mondor, whose tender weakness for his fair partner kept returning from
time to time with all the accidents of a burning spiritual fever, suffered very strongly in his peace of mind through this division in their
temperaments and often felt very badly; Selinde, on the other hand,
who had really never loved the man by whom she considered herself
unforgivably insulted, found herself richly compensated by the freedom to live according to her own fancy which he had to give her
willy-nilly; and in addition she had also the immortal pleasure of
almost driving him to insanity through her cold-blooded politeness
and pleasantness as often as he became unfaithful to his principle of
paying no further heed to what she did or did not do.

I need hardly say that Clarissa, who lived on a very pretty footing
with her own husband, could not approve the conduct of her friend
toward her spouse. In truth, she tried to move them to mutual indulgence and complaisance by every means that could be expected from
her cleverness and the warm sympathy which she felt for them. But
since both partners always wanted to be in the right and only saw
total wrong in the other, she finally left them alone and contented
herself with using her influence to prevent outbreaks that would have
made them the talk of the town.

Because Mondor, as a result of his conjugal distress, often had an
opportunity of becoming more closely acquainted with his friend's
wife, he imperceptibly developed a respect for her which at first
seemed to be the most innocent thing in the world, but subsequently
became very injurious to his peace of mind. Every time he saw her he
wondered the more how he could have been so blind as not to have
perceived long ago Clarissa's striking superiority to Selinde. "What a
woman this Clarissa is!" he often said to himself; "free from all the
weaknesses and bad habits of her sex, she combines with all that is
charming in a woman everything that makes a man highly estimable." And now he reckoned up her total advantages, talents, virtues, pleasant qualities item by item, compared them with everything
about Selinde that was blameworthy or at least unpleasing to him,

and always ended with a profound sigh at the good fortune of the frivolous Raymond, who did not even seem to feel the value of the treasure he possessed and who could have lived just as happily with any pretty and inoffensive wife.

However, a lengthy span of time went by before Mondor surprised himself in thoughts and wishes that did not seem wholly congruent with what he owed his wife and his friend. At first he merely sought from Clarissa what he had always found in her: cheering up, dispersal of his ill humor, entertainment of his mind and easy exchange of ideas. He always left her presence calmer than he had come, and Selinde could always tell from his good mood that he had spent a few evening hours with her friend. Subsequently, when he could no longer conceal from himself the fact that his admiration for Clarissa became warmer and warmer as his visits became more and more frequent, he deluded himself for a while longer with the beautiful chimera of platonic love, a delusion which was all the easier for him because even the keenest and most fault-finding observer could not have perceived in Clarissa's conduct the slightest feature to stir the imagination or that could be interpreted as a quiet encouragement of secret desires. But this very naturalness, this complete remoteness from all those little spiderlike arts of feminine coquetry—from which, as men claim, even those among us who are not conscious of any definite design are not wholly free—had to produce in a man like Mondor precisely the opposite of what Clarissa probably wished to prevent; for it was this very thing which in his eyes made an angel out of a woman. No wonder, therefore, that what for a long time had been the purest friendship became on his part a decided passion which wrought in his mind a desolation that was all the greater because he saw himself forced to conceal it most carefully from Clarissa.

About this time a trifling incident occurred which could not have happened more inopportunely for poor Mondor. Raymond had completed a lifesize portrait for his own pleasure, representing the eternally virgin goddess Pallas accidentally surprised in her bath by young Tiresias. Never had anything more beautiful been seen than that which the young Theban, to his misfortune, did not see here, for at the very moment when he became aware of the goddess the poor man became blind in both eyes. This painting had for some time been hanging in a small chamber adjoining Raymond's room, but Mondor had never seen it. It happened one day that the door of this little room was half open when Mondor visited his friend in his study. A bright morning sun was just then illuminating the main figure of the painting and it stirred Mondor's attention and curiosity. He had to admit that he had never seen so perfect a form, either in nature or in art, and paid his friend lavish compliments on the favor in which he stood among the dwellers on Olympus; for the goddess in person must have sat for him for this portrait. Raymond, swayed by a fit of thoughtless vanity, confessed that as a result of constant begging he had finally persuaded Clarissa to pose as the model for this Pallas. Although his features betrayed nothing, he would have been as blind as Tiresias if he had not noticed that Mondor, upon hearing this intimate revelation, suddenly turned as pale as a marble statue and then just as quickly as fiery red as a setting autumn sun and left the side room as hastily as if he had seen a ghost in it. From this time on poor Mondor's state of mind was truly pitiable.

I confess to a suspicion that Raymond was on this occasion unconsciously moved to play Candaules* before his friend. For I can no longer conceal the fact that at this time, when Mondor's high esteem for Clarissa was moving step by step to the point at which it would be transformed into the most violent passion, something akin to love had developed between Raymond and Selinde too; and this threatened to become more serious than it was at first thought to be. The intimate association between the two ladies provided Raymond with frequent opportunities of seeing Selinde and of even establishing himself imperceptibly on an intimate footing with her.

Now, there were actually many similarities and correspondences between them. Selinde was a very beautiful woman and Raymond a very handsome man. Selinde was very flighty, always gay and had a passionate love for all social entertainments; in addition, she was full of wit and lively ideas, which not infrequently ran ahead of reflection. All this was true of Raymond too. Neither was capable of a love that would make for a happy or unhappy life; like Rosalinde's Narcissus and Narcissa, they were both fundamentally only in love with

---

*Candaules, king of Lydia (seventh century B.C.), was so vain of his queen's physical beauty that he persuaded Gyges, a member of his bodyguard, to see her naked from a concealed spot in their bedroom. The queen caught sight of the intruder and felt mortally insulted. She conspired with Gyges to kill her royal spouse, usurp his throne and marry her. The legend is told in Book I of Herodotus' *History* and by Plato; in modern times by Friedrich Hebbel, *Gyges und sein Ring*, and by André Gide, *Le Roi Candaule*.

themselves. But Selinde's greatest pleasure consisted in weaving webs around hearts, although she did not know what to do with them, and Raymond could not look at a beautiful woman without wishing she were his and, if he had possessed the power and the fortune to do so, he would, out of a purely artistic sense, have kept a more numerous harem than that of King Solomon. With so many points of contact, nothing was more natural than they they should attract each other. Added to this was the disharmony that existed between Selinde and her tyrant (as she jestingly named her husband), designed to make Raymond more interesting to her and her to Raymond. He could not but gain favor with Selinde through the comparison between politeness, graciousness and his good-naturedness and Mondor's dry earnestness, his unsociable nature, his stern demands and extravagant ideas; and Selinde became twice as beautiful and charming in Raymond's eyes when he realized that what made her enchanting to him was, in her husband's eyes, the most displeasing thing about her. How was it possible not to be graciousness itself toward such a woman? Mondor was his friend and would always have found him ready to risk his life for him; "but," he often said to himself in jest, "would it not be a real act of friendship to help him out of a wife who is making him unhappy with all her charm?" He said this to himself so often in mere jest until he finally came to believe it in full earnest. "If we could exchange wives," he thought, "we would both be served." But for all his cleverness, he could not answer the question how this could be done.

By good fortune there appeared about this time in France the notorious law that abolished the indissolubility of marriage and made divorce as easy and arbitrary as the frivolity and fickleness of the most lively nation on earth could but desire. A mass of ill-yoked couples or partners who were surfeited with each other hurried as fast as they could to make use of this liberty and in a short time the example of broken marriages in the larger cities became so common that the fear of public judgment could no longer deter anyone from doing what his heart desired.

These almost daily divorces were for a time the favorite subject of conversation at parties. Our two friends, too, talked often and with pleasure about the new law; and although Mondor took a more serious view of the matter than Raymond, he always ended by agree-

ing with a sigh with his friend, who regarded this law, as long as it
was not abused too much, as the most wholesome of all those which
the Revolution was so fertile in producing.

More than once something seemed to waver on the half-open lips
of the two friends, which they wished to reveal to each other; but just
as often something I cannot explain forced the secret that was working its way upwards back into their hearts, until it was no longer possible for either of them to keep it hidden.

One morning Raymond set out for Mondor's home with the intention of ridding himself of it, when Mondor ran into him when he was
halfway there.

"I was just going to your place, Mondor."

"That was my intention too, my dear Raymond."

"I have something to tell you," Raymond continued, "which has
been on my mind a long time."

"That's just my situation too, my friend."

"Well then, let us find a comfortable spot where we can get it off
our chests without witnesses."

They now proceeded, without saying another word, to the most
secluded walks in a public park, and as soon as they felt they were
alone, Raymond began again:

"You have a very beautiful, very charming wife, my friend—"

Mondor sighed but remained silent.

"—who doesn't make you happy?"

"Unfortunately!"

"But with whom I would be as happy as a god."

"Not impossible!"

"Clarissa is a splendid woman, you know that."

Mondor was silent again.

"How would it be if we made an exchange, Mondor? I would be
totally deceived if Clarissa were not the very woman you need."

"And you could give her up, Raymond?"

"Mondor, we are old friends, let us be frank with each other. I
have no cause for separating from Clarissa; but I will confess to you
openly that I am crazy about Selinde, and you, as I have long
observed, love Clarissa. What in the whole world, then, could prevent us from making use of the new law?"

"I must confess to you too, Raymond, that I worship Clarissa. She feels a certain degree of friendship for me; but will she consent to separate from you? And even if she does agree, will she be willing to become my wife?"

"I hope to persuade her easily to do the former; the latter will then be your affair. Between you and me, she is rather cold; you will have to put up with that."

"Anything in the world, if only she consents to live with me. I desire no greater happiness than to be the first among her friends."

"Listen, my dear Mondor! I know what I am losing in Clarissa; it's a lot—but Selinde will be ample compensation."

"You have saved my life for the second time, my dear Raymond! Then you'll arrange everything with Clarissa? For it seems that you have already reached an understanding with Selinde."

"Not so completely as you think; but if you would like to turn your kindness toward your friend into a virtue in her eyes, she might allow herself to be swayed. For, with all the advantages you have over me—"

"No compliments among friends! If you can only win Clarissa, the rest will fall into place. —Then you'll take the matter up?"

"Here is my hand on it."

"And mine. Weren't we silly to be afraid of each other?"

The two friends now parted, each highly contented with the other, and the impatient Raymond went to see Clarissa that very morning and, after some preparatory remarks he might well have spared himself, presented his and his friend's proposal to her with an assumed light-hearted gaiety, behind which he sought to conceal his embarrassment at making such a proposal to a woman like Clarissa. "It's really just a joke," he concluded with a roguish look on his face; "but perhaps it would not be a bad thing if we took it seriously. What do you think, dear Clarissa?"

"So it's quite easy for you to give me up, dear Raymond?"

"I feel ashamed standing like a little boy before so wise a woman as you are. My proposal really does not make sense. You are the most charming woman I shall ever see. I fully know and feel your worth, although I was never worthy of you. But I cannot bring myself to deceive you. That witch face of Selinde's has simply driven me insane. I must really be under a spell, the devil Amor incarnate has entered my system and I see no way of ridding myself of him except by doing his will."

"You may well be right, dear Raymond," said Clarissa with a laugh; "at least it may be the most pleasant way of driving out this devil."

"I will confess everything to you, my dearest wife," Raymond continued. "I have done everything possible, but alas! in vain, to persuade Selinde to enter into a clandestine agreement."

"You fickle man! To even think of such a thing with a woman like Selinde!"

"Don't be angry with me, Clarissa; it happened only because I hate the thought of losing you."

"I suppose you would prefer to have us both?"

"That would be the best thing, of course," said the irresponsible man, kissing her hand as if in gratitude —

"And then you would still regret that you're not a Muslem, so that you could add a couple of gazelle-eyed Circassian women? — But, jest aside, my spouse, I hope you know me. For your and Selinde's sake I am prepared to do anything, if your friend Mondor is as gracious as I am. But why won't you leave me in a single state? Why should I of all people be Selinde's substitute?"

"As if you didn't know that Mondor worships you, that he can't live without you?"

"That is really more than I know."

"Then I know it all the more surely. I have read his mind a long time. Selinde is not the woman for him. With you he would be the happiest man under the sun, with her he is the very opposite. I must tell you, Clarissa, I have often felt such profound pity for him that there were moments when I could have been capable of renouncing you to him out of sheer sympathy, even to fall at your feet and beg for your consent, even if Selinde had meant as little to me as King Solomon's favorite."

"Raymond, you deserve a kiss for this, unlike any I have ever given you." — She was as good as her word.

"Clarissa, Clarissa," Raymond exclaimed, "if you begin to act like this — "

"Don't say what you wanted to say," she interrupted; "you would be seriously mistaken. It was only meant to be a farewell kiss. It's the last one, you may be assured."

"We part as friends, don't we?" said Raymond half sadly.

"Most certainly. But don't misunderstand, dear Raymond. The

time might come when you would be overcome by remorse — "

"Quite possible."

"I don't want you to get the idea that, in such an event, you need only come back to me and take possession of your old place again. There can be no thought of that now."

"In the project we are planning, such a thing simply must not be anticipated," said Raymond with a smile.

"It is always good, my dear," she replied, "to know what one may expect in every eventuality." — And with that Raymond was dismissed and hurried as fast as he could to inform Mondor and Selinde of the successful issue of his negotiations with Clarissa.

All the necessary steps were now taken without delay to give the proper legality to the strangest exchange that was perhaps ever made.

Clarissa had stipulated two more principal conditions, to which the other three could not deny their approval: first, that Mondor should spend the first six months with Clarissa on his estate, situated four or five miles out of the city; second, that in future Raymond should see and speak to Clarissa and Mondor to Selinde only in public places. Moreover, in consequence of a few words which Clarissa whispered in the ear of her former husband, the bathing Pallas was wrapped and packed up and sent from Raymond's side room to Mondor's country estate.

Confidentially Clarissa revealed to me one more secret article which Mondor had to agree to in her regard and which scarcely anyone but such a platonic lover such as he was would have agreed to. It was the same condition under which, in the well-known little novel *Abbassai*, Calif Harun Al Rashid gives his sister to the Grand Vizir Giafar to wife; but with this commendable moderation: that, inasmuch as Mondor was only renouncing every legally compelling claim on her, he should have full freedom in attempting to see how far he could get to her by the road of kindness. How successful this agreement was, it was not proper for me to inquire, nor perhaps for her to reveal to me.

So far you have no doubt found nothing particularly strange about my anecdote; but the strangest part is still to come.

During the first half year of their new marriage the two friends seemed to be infinitely happy with their exchange. Mondor, in whose

life it had been a rare day that passed without blowing up a storm
between him and Selinde, believed he was living in a veritable Ely-
sium with the gentle, serene, consistently equable Clarissa. In her he
found everything that Selinde could not have given him, even if she
had wanted to: pleasant, varied mental diversion, intimate exchange
of thoughts and feelings, tender sympathy and kind attentiveness.
Her knowledge, her talents, seemed to be inexhaustible sources of
pleasure for the happy man, who was able to draw on them directly.
She lived almost wholly for him alone, and he left her side only rarely,
and then from necessity. For it was simply Mondor's nature to push
everything to its extreme; and the shorter the shrift Clarissa gave him
in other respects, the more eagerly he overtaxed himself in intellectual enjoyments, which she granted him with the most gracious generosity He husbanded every instant and would never have forgiven
himself if, through his own fault, he had forfeited a single moment
that he could have spent in her company.

The natural consequences of this superhuman type of happiness
could not fail to appear for both of them. Even in intellectual enjoyments, satiety and immoderateness bring indifference and a weaken-
ing of the inner senses in their wake. However much Clarissa had to
give, in the end she had given her all; however amiable she was, she
remained, after all, the same person; and it was not in her character
to exert herself to present, in ever new form, the qualities and virtues
through which she had enchanted Mondor. The deceptive charm
was in him, not in her; in her everything was true and unassuming. It
was not her fault that he was a dreamer; nor was she to blame for the
fact that he finally ceased to dream; but for some time she began to
become a matter of indifference to him, he had repelled her only too
often by his extravagant devotion. Imperceptibly he became too bur-
densome to her through the restrictions that his inseparability
imposed on her and, not infrequently, she thought back with some
longing to the days when Raymond's complaisant coldness had left
her unlimited freedom to employ herself and her time in any way she
pleased. But the worst was that gradually a misunderstanding
appeared between their way of looking at things, and this necessarily
became pregnant with unpleasant consequences for both of them.
For Clarissa was a born enemy of all exaggeration and untruth — and
Mondor was constantly exaggerating. Clarissa had no prejudices, no

pet opinions; Mondor, on the other hand, had a host of Dulcineas, whose beauty he was ever prepared to defend against the whole world with his consecrated lance.

It therefore became evident, after they had lived together a few months, that they thought quite differently about many things. At first Clarissa's complaisance always found means to resolve such dissonances through skillful accommodation or through mediating ideas; but with time this indulgent yielding became more and more rare, and in most cases she played out her own score without caring whether his instrument was properly attuned to hers or whether they were actually playing in two different keys. Nevertheless, her wisdom and gentleness would have made all these disharmonies tolerable, if it had not been this very wisdom which drove the vehement Mondor, who was infatuated with his own ideas and whims, on many occasions into impatience. The very fact that she never exposed herself and was fundamentally always in the right stirred the spirit of contradiction in him all the more powerfully, and so he often stated the most irrational things, less to show his intelligence than to hurt her intellect and to make her embarrassed for an answer. No one suffered more than Mondor from the petty unpleasantness which resulted from this. Clarissa, who rarely became excited and never became bitter, was always prepared to make peace at once; her soul was like a serene sky, which is not obscured by the small clouds that quickly blow away. But Mondor's irritability and heat, which always pushed him beyond the bounds of moderation, prevented him from returning to a state of equilibrium as quickly or with as good grace. Disgruntled at himself, disgruntled because he had caused the quarrel, disgruntled by the fact that anything could disturb the harmony between him and Clarissa, his excessive sensitivity and boundless imagination made a big evil out of a little one, and not seldom he pouted for a fairly long time with Clarissa because he could not forgive himself for the fact that he had lost his head. All these and similar petty causes produced a profound effect even before the first year was over: namely, that Mondor, against all his expectation, felt himself even less happy with Clarissa than he had been with Selinde.

When the approaching winter called him back from the country to the city, he had the not wholly pure pleasure of seeing that his friend Raymond was, on the contrary, living in the most edifying harmony with the fair Selinde and that they were generally held to be the

happiest couple in the whole district. They seemed to be made wholly
for each other; the same inclinations, the same tastes, one will, although neither imposed the slightest pressure on the other and each
did what he felt like doing. Not a trace of misunderstandings or cool-
ings. When they were together they seemed to be as enraptured by
each other as if they had not seen each other for a long time; when
they were in different places, as was mostly the case, neither seemed
to miss the other.

For all his friendship for Raymond, Mondor could not resist a
slight attack of jealousy. The memories from the golden days of his
first love became more and more vivid in his imagination; the desire
to see Selinde again, more and more impatient in his breast; and
since he was permitted to see her only in public, he even overcame his
old aversion to large, mixed and noisy parties and sought her out
everywhere in assemblies and at dances. It seemed to him that since
he had committed the folly of separating from her, she had become
twice as beautiful as she was before; she was once more his ideal of all
the graces, and he understood less and less how the possessor of such
a charming wife could ever have been unhappy with her. Added to
this was the fact that she was fundamentally the most innocent creature in the world; for the only things that he ever had against her —
her frivolity, her inclination toward pleasure and her desire to please
— had never brought the slightest blemish on her reputation; and
while she seemed to be laying nets for all men, there was not a single
one who could boast of having received the slightest encouragement
or favor from her. "Her faults," Mondor now said to himself, "make
her all the more lovable and actually do not even deserve such a
name. For it is they which give her these inexhaustible, ever new
charms, which make surfeit and satiety impossible." These reflections led him imperceptibly to the discovery that the fair Selinde,
when everything was considered, was really more suitable for him
than the cold, uniform, self-sufficient Clarissa, with her lofty Socratic
wisdom and her lifeless statuelike form, and that the total guilt for
the former discord with Selinde could be traced to his whimsical,
extravagant demands. If he had not been kept back forcibly by his
sense of shame before Clarissa and by the fear of being ridiculed by
Raymond and rejected by Selinde — he scarcely dared confess to himself what he might have been capable of doing.

However, he tried to approach Selinde more and more, as much as decorum would permit him to do; and since she behaved toward him so naturally and nicely, as if they had only now become acquainted, he felt himself encouraged to allow what was going on in his heart to peep out more and more clearly from his whole behavior, although under the most delicate veil. Selinde's vanity was no little flattered by this and all her friendship for Clarissa could not prevent her from having to make an effort to conceal the joy she felt at such a beautiful triumph of her charms. Imperceptibly there awoke in her, too, the pictures of the first days and weeks of her union with Mondor, and she could not refrain from making silent comparisons between him and Raymond, which always turned out to his advantage. Mondor observed her too sharply not to notice traces of what was going on in her mind, in her eyes and in a thousand trifling remarks that went unnoticed by other people; and the yearning for a restoration of their former relationship now increased daily together with his hopes.

Clarissa, the only wholly natural person among the four friends (for Raymond, too, had his reasons for wishing himself back in his former condition, although he was able to put a smiling face on a bad situation), Clarissa, I say, watched the comedy with a calm expectation of its development, without either encouraging or frightening the actors off, somewhat the way one watches children at play; she was all the more serene since, to her way of thinking, she had more to gain than to lose in the conclusion which she foresaw. For, as we know, she had separated from Raymond not from choice but from mere complaisance toward him and her friend; and since Raymond seemed to have nothing more important to do than to convince her that his means for ridding himself of the amorous devil whom Selinde had charmed into him had succeeded excellently, there was no doubt that it would depend solely on her whether and under what conditions she would risk it again with him.

This is how matters stood between the four friends when Mondor, the most passionate among them, finally resolved to break the ice and to gain certainty about Raymond's and Selinde's frame of mind, whatever it might be. "Our exchange," he said on one fine morning to his friend, "has, as I see, suited you very well, Raymond."

"You think so?" Raymond replied in a rather light tone.

"It seems to me that one couldn't be happier than you are with Selinde."

"At least not happier than you are with Clarissa, I should think."

Mondor sighed.

"Listen, dear Mondor, it would be horrible if I were to trifle one moment longer with a friend whose happiness forces such a deep groan from him. You would be greatly mistaken, brother, if you were to judge my happiness by external appearances or by your feelings. Not all that glitters is gold, Sancho Panza would say in my place, and no one knows where the shoe pinches the other man, however new and dainty the shoe may be. Let us talk frankly to each other and away with false shame! We have both committed a great folly, Mondor! We might have been contented with our lot, we thought we could improve it and are now both convinced that we would have done better if each of us had kept his own. Selinde and Clarissa are both very lovely women in their own way, but for that reason alone they are not suited for everyone. You and I are not the worst among men, each of us, I believe, deserves the best wife. But the best for Raymond isn't necessarily also the best for Mondor, and vice versa. For example, Clarissa is not warm enough, not vivacious enough for you; but I need just such a cold and wise wife, as a counterweight to my frivolity. You are too hot-headed for Clarissa and I am not rich enough for Selinde. Who could be so cruel as to deny so beautiful and good-natured a woman as Selinde any one of her trifling whims, her basically innocent pleasures? But my means are not sufficient to satisfy both without slighting them; and since I can refuse her nothing, she would have ruined me in a few years. You, however, are rich enough for an even far more expensive wife than Selinde. Besides, she too, like you and me, has become wiser through experience; you will be more complaisant toward her and she will reward you for it through her moderation. The less you demand from her, the more she will do for you. So take your Selinde back and give me back my Clarissa, with whom I was formerly contented and happy, so happy that I could never forget her even in Selinde's arms."

Mondor felt that his friend had drawn very valid conclusions; and since nothing was more certain to him than that either one had to be insane (as he admitted he had been) or one could not give up a woman like Selinde without feeling pain, he ascribed to Raymond's meritorious generosity and as the highest proof of his friendship what was in fact merely the work of prudence and concern for his own best interests.

Everything now returned to the old order. Mondor and Selinde had an equal amount to forgive each other and joined again with the intention to make up for it to the other all the more generously, since they had been made wiser by their errors. Both kept their word; and Clarissa, with too sound an intellect to be a sentimentalist and too pure of heart to be either genuinely or hypocritically coy, permitted the disenchanted Raymond, without imposing too heavy a penalty on him, to bring back triumphantly into his house both the picture and the original of his Pallas in the bath.

Both couples have been, since this time, daily more satisfied with their second exchange and (this reveals a great deal about all four of them) never has even a shadow of suspicion or jealousy caused the slightest damage either to their love or their friendship. I therefore believe that I gave my anecdote the right name by entitling it *Love and Friendship Tested;* and now there remains nothing for me but to wish that it may not have displeased my kindly and indulgent audience.

Heinrich von Kleist

1777 — 1811

Heinrich von Kleist was born in Frankfurt on the Oder in what was formerly East Prussia. He came from a family of soldiers and was himself destined for a military career. After the death of his father in 1788 he was sent to Berlin and put under the care of a clergyman, who supervised his education. Four years later he joined the guards regiment in Potsdam. He fought in the Napoleonic Wars in the Rhineland (1793-95) and was given a commission in 1797. Two years later he left the service, which he found extremely boring, and entered the university of his native city, where he studied philosophy, economics and law. It was here that he suffered his first spiritual crisis, occasioned by his study of Kant's philosophy, which he interpreted as denying the possibility of absolute knowledge. Kant's demonstration that absolute knowledge is unattainable was a devastating blow to his extremist mind.

He became engaged to Wilhelmine von Zenge in 1799; but the next year he broke the engagement. He then traveled in Germany, Switzerland and France, where he met some of the eminent Germans of the day. He was at this time an enthusiastic supporter of the French Revolution. In Switzerland he experimented with the simple life recommended by Rousseau. His wish to join the French forces in the war against England was thwarted by the French authorities, who sent him back to Germany. He reached Mainz in a state of mental collapse.

In 1804 he was sufficiently recovered to take a post in the Prussian civil service, but after two years his health broke down again. On the way to Dresden in 1806 he was arrested by the French on suspicion of espionage and imprisoned in France for six months. After his release he settled in Dresden, where he enjoyed the friendship of eminent literary and intellectual figures. Together with Adam Müller, the publicist, he edited the short-lived journal *Phoebus*. He was now imbued with a violent hatred of the French and went to Austria in 1809 to join the fight against Napoleon, but got there after the Austrian defeat at Wagram. He suffered another severe breakdown in Prague; but again he recovered and returned to Berlin, where he once more took up his literary and journalistic activity, editing the very successful periodical *Berliner Abendblätter*. However, this was forced to suspend publication because of harassment and censorship by the government.

His plays, poems and novellas were published and there were performances of his dramas in various German theaters. But the ups and downs of his career, the succession of hopes and disappointments proved too much for him. Kleist's mental state was now desperate. He felt rejected by his family, his friends and his nation. Through Adam Müller he had become acquainted with a young officer's wife, Henrietta Vogel, who was suffering from a fatal disease. They planned a common suicide, which they carried out on the shores of the Wannsee near Berlin.

Kleist was a literary artist of the first rank, a tragic genius who destroyed himself by his inability to compromise with the absolute. He was driven, both in his life and work, to the edge of the abyss by the demon of perfection. He was an extremist in his loves and hatreds, in his search for a way of life and in his literary ambition, which impelled him to try to outstrip Goethe, to unite in himself Sophocles and Shakespeare. Exaggeration and excess is a theme to which he returns repeatedly in his work: excess in patriotism, in sex, in submissiveness, in self-assertion. His will to explore the recesses of the human mind knew no bounds; he dealt with abnormal psychological phenomena like sadism and masochism, erotic cruelty, somnambulism, the occult. His emotions were not recollected in tranquility but burst from him like physical charges. He depicted passion with a naked realism as perhaps no one had done before him, in language and sentence structure which are bold, powerful, intense, hard and metallic.

Kleist's reputation rests equally on his dramas and novellas. Both reveal the same qualities and create the same atmosphere of intensity, passion, breathlessness. He has no time to compose harmonious sentences or even to break up his narrative into paragraphs. His sentences surge like mighty torrents, twisting and turning in all directions, picking up minute details before they come to a stop. His paragraphs run on for pages, mirroring the headlong race of life to its dramatic climax.

Of his eight novellas, *Michael Kohlhaas* (1810) is the longest and the most powerful. It is based on a chronicle from the sixteenth century which records the turbulent career of a quarrelsome fellow, a merchant named Hans Kohlhase, who terrorized the countryside because of a grievance against society. Out of this minor episode, Kleist has created a powerful tale of fate and character which is also a *conte philosophique*, depicting the conflict between the individual and society.

Kohlhaas is a noble man imbued with a nice sense of justice. His crusade against the junker is morally justified, as the elector of Brandenburg fully concedes. But Kohlhaas fails to realize that even a virtue, when carried to extremes, can cause crime. Moreover, the repeated thwarting of his hunt for the culprit junker turns his quest for justice into a search for revenge, and lowers it to the primitive ethic of an eye for an eye. Even so, a just society, represented by the elector of Brandenburg, must grant him his claim: the horses are restored to him in their former condition. But the untold damage caused by this ruthless pursuit of revenge must be punished for the crime that it is. Kohlhaas himself realizes this and accepts his death sentence willingly. The development of his character under the impact of the dramatic and fateful events that befall him, and the depiction of the political action as it changes from day to day and draws into its net an ever wider circle of willing and unwilling participants, are combined by Kleist to fashion one of the masterpieces of shorter prose fiction in world literature.

Michael Kohlhaas

AFTER AN OLD CHRONICLE

About the middle of the sixteenth century there lived on the bank of the Havel River a horse dealer named Michael Kohlhaas. He was the son of a schoolmaster and one of the most upright, and yet most terrible, men of his time. Until the age of thirty this extraordinary man might have been taken for the very model of a good citizen. In the village that still bears his name he owned a farm, from which he made a peaceful living by his trade. The children that his wife bore him were raised in the fear of the Lord and taught industry and loyalty. There was not a man among his neighbors who had not profited from his benevolence and fairness. In short, the world would have been compelled to bless his memory if he had not carried one virtue to excess. But his sense of justice turned him into a robber and murderer.

One day he led a string of sleek, glistening young horses across the border between Brandenburg and Saxony. He was turning over in his mind what he would do with the profit from the sale of the horses in the market: part of it he decided to reinvest, as good businessmen do; the rest he would spend for immediate enjoyment. When he reached the Elbe River and a stately castle that stood on Saxon territory, he found his way blocked by a barrier he had never before seen on this road. It was pouring rain as he halted the horses and called to the gatekeeper. The man soon appeared at the window with a sour look on his face. The horse dealer asked him to open up for him, and after some time the toll collector appeared.

"What new device is this?" asked the horse dealer. "Sovereign's privilege," replied the collector, unlocking the barrier, "granted to our Junker Wenzel von Tronka." "Is that so?" said Kohlhaas, "the junker's name is Wenzel?" And he looked at the castle, whose gleaming pinnacles towered above the field. "Is the old lord dead?" "Died of a stroke," replied the collector as he raised the toll bar. "Hm, too bad," remarked Kohlhaas. "He was a fine old gentleman. He liked people and helped trade and commerce wherever he could. He once had a stone road built because a mare of mine broke her leg out there where the road leads into the village. Well, what do I owe you?" With some effort he took the few pennies that the collector demanded from the pocket of his coat, which was blowing in the strong wind. When the tollman kept muttering, "Hurry, hurry!" and cursed the bad weather, Kohlhaas remarked, "Yes, old fellow It would have been better for both of us if this tree had been left standing in the forest instead of serving as a toll bar." He handed over the money and prepared to ride on.

But he had hardly passed the toll bar when he heard a new voice calling from the castle tower, "Stop there, you horse dealer!" He saw the castle steward bang a window shut and hurry down. "Well, what's up now?" Kohlhaas thought to himself, pulling up the horses again. The steward was buttoning another vest over his ample body as he approached, bending forward to meet the storm. He asked the merchant for his passport. "Passport?" repeated Kohlhaas, feeling puzzled. He said that as far as he knew, he hadn't one; but if the steward would describe the contraption to him, it might just happen that he had such a thing on his person. The steward gave him a sidelong glance and said that no horse dealer could be allowed to cross the border with horses unless he had written permission from the sovereign. The horse dealer assured him that he had crossed the border seventeen times in his life without such a permit and knew all the governmental rules pertaining to his trade. This must be a mistake; he asked for time to reconsider the matter; he had a long journey ahead of him; would they please not detain him any longer to no purpose? The steward replied that he was not going to slip through for the eighteenth time; the regulation had been issued only recently to prevent just such cases; he could either obtain a passport here or go back where he came from. The horse dealer was beginning to feel bitter about this bit of illegal extortion. After a moment's reflection he dismounted, turned his horse over to his servant and said he would take the matter up with Junker von Tronka himself. And he went into the castle, followed by the steward, who muttered something about money-grubbing skinflints who would benefit by a bleeding. The two men entered the great hall, eyeing each other warily.

The junker just happened to be sitting over the wine cups with a company of merry friends. As Kohlhaas approached him to lodge his complaint, the junker and his companions burst into gales of laughter over some joke that had just been told. The junker asked him what he wanted. The knights grew silent when they saw the stranger. But scarcely had Kohlhaas begun to state his petition about the horses, when the whole company cried, "Horses? Where are they?" and hurried to the windows to look at them. Seeing the splendid string of horses, they raced down into the courtyard at the junker's suggestion. The rain had stopped; the castle steward, the estate manager and his men gathered about them, all inspecting the animals. One knight praised the light bay with the blaze; another liked the brown chestnut; a third stroked the piebald with the tawny spots. They all agreed that the horses were like deer and that none better were bred in the land. Kohlhaas replied jovially that the horses were no better than the knights who would ride them and urged them to buy.

The junker, strongly tempted by the powerful light bay, asked the price. But the manager urged him to buy a pair of blacks which he thought he could use on the estate, as they were short of horses. But when the dealer had stated his price, the knights thought it was too high and the junker remarked that if he valued his horses that much, he ought to take them to King Arthur and the Round Table. Kohlhaas noticed that the steward and the manager were whispering together, casting meaningful glances at the black horses. A dark foreboding made him resolve to get rid of the horses at any price. He said to the junker: "Your Lordship, six months ago I paid twenty-five golden guilders for the blacks; give me thirty and you shall have them." Two knights who were standing near the junker said outright that the horses were certainly worth that much. But the junker said he was prepared to spend money for the bay, but not for the blacks; and he turned as if to go. Kohlhaas said perhaps they could make a deal next time he passed through here with his horses. He bowed to the junker and grasped the reins to ride off.

At this moment the steward came forward from the group of bystanders and said, "You heard that you can't leave this place without a passport." Kohlhaas turned to the junker and aksed whether this

was so; such a restriction, he added, would ruin his trade. The junker
answered, as he walked away with a look of embarrassment on his
face, "Yes, Kohlhaas, you'll have to get a passport. Speak to the steward about it and get on your way."

Kohlhaas assured him it was not his intention to circumvent any of
the regulations concerning the export of horses. He promised to get a
passport at the government office on his journey through Dresden,
and asked to be allowed to go on this time, since he had known
nothing about the regulation.

"Well," said the junker, as the weather was getting stormy again,
sending a chill through his skinny shanks, "let the poor devil go.
Come," he said to the knights, and made for the castle.

Turning to the junker, the steward remarked that Kohlhaas
should at least leave some pledge of assurance that he would get a
passport. The junker stopped again under the castle gate. Kohlhaas
asked what amount in money or valuables he should leave behind as
pledge for the black horses. The manager mumbled in his beard:
why couldn't he leave the blacks themselves? "Of course," said the
steward, "that's the most practical solution; when he gets the passport, he can claim them anytime." Kohlhaas was indignant at such
an insolent demand. He said to the junker, who stood there shivering, drawing the skirts of his coat about him for protection, "But I
want to sell the blacks!" At that moment, however, a gust of wind
drove a mass of rain and hail through the gateway. To put an end to
the matter, the junker shouted, "If he won't relinquish the horses,
kick him back over the toll bar!" and walked off.

The horse dealer saw that he must yield to force and decided to
comply with the demand, since he could do nothing else. He unhitched the black horses and led them to a stable that the steward
assigned to him. He left one of his men behind to attend to them,
provided him with money and warned him to take good care of them
until he returned. He then continued his journey with the remainder
of his string to Leipzig, where he intended to visit the fair. He had
become uncertain about this matter of the passport; perhaps, he
thought, the new horse-breeding industry in Saxony had really
needed such a regulation.

Kohlhaas owned a house and stables in a suburb of Dresden and
used this establishment as a center for his trade in the smaller Saxon
markets. Upon his arrival in Dresden he went at once to the govern-

ment office. He knew some of the officials and learned what he had
suspected from the first, that the story of the passport was a fairy
tale. At his request the displeased officials gave him a document that
proved the baseless nature of the demand. Kohlhaas smiled at the
stratagem the lean junker had employed, although he could not
clearly see its purpose. A few weeks later, after selling the string of
horses at a good profit, he returned to Tronka Castle, without any
bitterness in his heart except that which he felt for the general misery
in the world.

The steward, to whom Kohlhaas showed the document, made no
fuss. When Kohlhaas asked him if he might have his horses back, he
told him to go down and get them. But on his way through the courtyard Kohlhaas had already made the unpleasant discovery that the
servant he had left behind to look after the horses had been severely
beaten and driven out of the castle shortly after he had left for Leipzig. The reason given for the beating was improper conduct. Kohlhaas now asked the boy who had given him this information what
wrong the servant had done and who had looked after the horses in
his absence. The boy said he didn't know and opened the door of the
stable where they stood. The horse dealer's heart was already heavy
with foreboding. But how great was his astonishment when he saw,
instead of his two sleek, well-fed blacks, a pair of lean, bedraggled
nags: bones sticking out like racks to hang things on; manes and hair
matted from lack of care—a true picture of misery in the animal
kingdom.

The horses neighed and stirred feebly. Kohlhaas, filled with indignation, asked what had happened to his horses. The boy, who was
standing beside him, replied that nothing special had happened,
they had been properly fed. But as it was harvest time and there was
a shortage of draft animals, they had been used a little in the fields.
Kohlhaas cursed this shameful and deliberate act of violence; but in
his impotence he suppressed his rage. Since there was nothing else he
could do, he was on the point of leaving this robbers' den with his
horses, when the steward, who had heard the exchange, appeared
and asked what was the matter.

"What's the matter?" Kohlhaas replied. "Who gave Junker von
Tronka and his men permission to use my two blacks for field work?"
Was such conduct human? he added. He struck the exhausted nags
lightly with a switch and showed the steward that they did not even
stir.

The steward looked at him defiantly for a while; then he said, "Look at the boorish fellow! Why, you ought to thank God, you lout, that the nags are even alive. Who was supposed to look after them when your servant ran away? Wasn't it right that the horses should earn the fodder they consumed?" He warned Kohlhaas that he had better not start any nonsense or he'd have to call the dogs on him to restore peace in the courtyard.

The horse dealer's heart beat hard against his coat. He felt an urge to throw the bloated rascal into the mud and grind his copper face under his heel. But his sense of justice, which was as delicate as a gold scale, caused him to hesitate. He was still uncertain before the bar of his own heart whether his adversary felt guilty. Swallowing the words of abuse that came to his lips, he went over to the horses. As he untangled their manes, he weighed the circumstances in silence, then asked the steward in a low voice, for what offense the servant had been expelled from the castle. The steward answered, "Because the rascal was insolent in the yard! Because he objected to a necessary change of stable and demanded that the horses of two visiting noblemen should spend the night on the open highway for the sake of his two nags!"

Kohlhaas would have given the value of the horses if he could have had his man there to compare his statement with that of the loud-mouthed castle steward. He was still standing there, smoothing out the tangled manes of the horses, pondering what he should do, when the scene suddenly changed. Junker Wenzel von Tronka, together with a swarm of knights, servants and dogs, rode into the courtyard from a hare hunt. The junker asked the steward what was wrong. The steward spoke up at once that this horse dealer was making an awful fuss because his two blacks had been used for a bit of work. His report, which was the vilest distortion of the truth, was accompanied by a murderous howling from the dogs at the sight of the stranger, with the knights trying to silence them. The man, sneered the steward, refused to recognize the horses as his own. Kohlhaas cried, "These are not my horses, my lord. These are not the horses that were worth thirty golden guilders. I want my well-fed, healthy horses back." The junker turned pale, dismounted and said, "If the — — won't take the horses back, he can leave them. Come, Günther," he cried. "Come, Hans!" He shook the dust from his breeches and shouted, "Bring wine!" as he and the knights reached the door and vanished inside. Kohlhaas said he would rather call the knacker and

sell them for the flaying pit than take them back to his stable in Kohlhaasenbrück in their present condition. He left the horses in the
courtyard without paying any attention to them, mounted his bay
horse and rode off with the assurance that he would see to it that he
got justice.

He was already riding at full speed towards Dresden when, remem-
bering the charges that had been made against his man at the castle,
he slowed down to a walk and, before he had gone a thousand feet
further, turned back to Kohlhaasenbrück, resolved to subject the servant to a preliminary examination. This seemed to him the just and
prudent thing to do; for he well knew how imperfectly this world is
ordered, and in spite of the insults he had suffered, he was inclined to
write off the loss of the horses as a just punishment if his servant was
really in any way culpable, as the steward said he was. But an equally
sound instinct told him that, if the affair had been rigged, as all
appearances seemed to indicate it had, then it was his solemn duty to
obtain satisfaction for the offense that had been committed against
him, and to protect his fellow citizens from similar offenses in the
future. This latter feeling grew in him and struck deeper root as he
rode on and heard, wherever he stopped, of the outrages to travelers
that were perpetrated daily at Tronka Castle.

As soon as he arrived in Kohlhaasenbrück and had embraced his
faithful wife Lisbeth and kissed his children, who clung happily to his
knees, his first question was whether they had heard anything about
his head man Herse.

Lisbeth said, "Yes, dearest Michael, this Herse! About a fortnight
ago the unhappy man arrived here in a most pitifully bruised condition; so battered that he couldn't breathe properly. We put him to
bed, for he was spitting blood. We questioned him repeatedly and
heard a story from him which none of us can make sense of. He said
you had left him at Tronka Castle with some horses that they refused
to let through; that they had forced him, through the most shameful
mistreatment, to leave the castle; and it hadn't been possible for him
to take the horses with him." "Is that so?" said Kohlhaas as he took
off his overcoat. "Is he well again?" "More or less, except for the
blood spitting," she replied. "I intended to send another man to the
castle at once to look after the horses until you got there. Herse has
always shown himself to be so truthful and loyal to us, more so than
any other of our men; so I couldn't bring myself to suspect that he

had lost the horses in some other way, especially as his statements were backed by so much evidence. But he implored me to let no one show himself in that robbers' den, and to give the animals up, unless I was willing to sacrifice a human life for them." "Is he still in bed?" asked Kohlhaas, untying his neckerchief. "He's been walking about the farm for some days now," she replied. "In short, you'll see that it's all true and that this incident is one of the crimes that Tronka Castle has recently dared to commit against strangers." "Well, I must investigate the matter first," replied Kohlhaas. "Call him in, Lisbeth, if he's about." With these words he sat down in the easy chair. His wife, pleased by his calm air, went to fetch the servant

"What did you do at Tronka Castle?" Kohlhaas asked when Lisbeth came into the room with the servant. "I'm not very satisfied with you." A flush appeared on the servant's cheeks when he heard these words. He was silent for a while; then he said, "You are right, sir. For, by some dispensation of Heaven, I carried a stick of sulphur with me and intended to set fire to that robbers' den from which they'd driven me. But when I heard a child whimpering inside the castle I threw the sulphur into the Elbe and thought, may God's lightning reduce it to ashes, I won't do it." "But," said Kohlhaas in perplexity, "what did you do to make them drive you out of the castle?" "I did a wicked thing, sir," replied Herse, wiping the sweat from his brow, "but what's done can't be undone. I wouldn't let them ruin the horses with field work, and told them they were still young and had never drawn." Trying to conceal his perplexity, Kohlhaas said that Herse had not told the exact truth; the horses had actually been in harness for a short time during the previous spring. "You might have accommodated them once or twice at the castle," he continued, "where you were a sort of guest, especially since it was urgent to get the harvest in." "And so I did, sir," said Herse. "After all, I thought, when they all made sour faces at me, it won't ruin the horses. On the third morning I hitched them to a wagon and brought in three loads of grain."

Kohlhaas' heart was pounding; he lowered his eyes and said, "They told me nothing about that, Herse." Herse assured him it was so. "My unfriendliness consisted in this, that I refused to hitch the horses again when they had scarcely finished feeding at noon. Besides, when the steward and manager proposed that I should accept free fodder for the work and pocket the money you had left me for

the purpose, I replied that I'd oblige them in another way, turned my
back on them and went away." "But it was not this unfriendly act
that made them drive you from the castle?" "Heaven forbid!" the servant exlaimed. "It was because of an ungodly crime. For that evening, two horses belonging to newly arrived knights were led into the
stable and mine tied to the stable door. When I took the horses from
the hands of the steward, who had made the arrangements himself,
and asked him where I was to lodge the animals, he assigned them to
a pigsty built of laths and boards against the castle wall." "You
mean," Kohlhaas interrupted him, "it was such a wretched place
that it looked more like a pigsty than a horse stable." "It *was* a pigsty,
sir," Herse replied: "really and truly a pigsty, in which the pigs ran in
and out and I couldn't stand upright." "Perhaps there was no other
shelter to be found for the blacks," remarked Kohlhaas. "In a way,
the knights' horses had preference." Herse replied, lowering his
voice, "The place was crowded. There were now seven knights in all
at the castle. If it had been yourself, you would have moved the
horses in more snugly. I said I'd try to rent a stable in the village, but
the steward replied that he had to keep the horses under his eye, and
dared me to take them out of the courtyard." "Hm!" said Kohlhaas,
"what did you do then?" "Because the manager said that the two
guests would only stay overnight and leave next morning, I took the
horses into the pigsty. But the next day went by and they didn't leave;
and when the third day came, I learned that the knights intended to
stay at the castle for several weeks more." "But, Herse, it really wasn't
as bad in the pigsty as you thought when you first stuck your nose in,
was it?" said Kohlhaas. "Well, that's true," replied the servant.
"When I swept the place out a bit, it was passable. I gave the maid
some money for taking the pigs somewhere else. And in the course of
the day I managed to fix things so that the horses could stand upright, by removing the top boards from the sty by day and replacing
them at night. Now they peered through the roof like geese and
looked in the direction of Kohlhaasenbrück, or somewhere else where
things were more comfortable." "Well then, why in heaven's name
did they drive you out?" "Sir, I tell you it's because they wanted to get
rid of me; because as long as I was there they couldn't ruin the horses.
Everywhere they made sour faces at me, in the courtyard and in the
servants' quarters; and because I thought to myself, 'twist your faces
till they freeze,' they seized the opportunity and kicked me out of the

courtyard." "But the motive!" cried Kohlhaas. "They must surely have had a motive for doing it." "Oh, of course," replied Herse, "the most righteous motive. On the evening of the second day I spent in the pigsty the horses were filthy; so I started to take them to the horse pond. I'd reached the castle gate and was just making a turn, when I heard the steward and manager racing behind me with servants, dogs and clubs, crying, 'Stop the rogue! Stop the gallows-bird!' as if they were possessed. The watchman at the gate blocked my path, and when I asked him and the raging pack pursuing me what the trouble was, the steward said, 'What's the trouble?' and grabbed the reins of my two blacks. 'Where are you going with the horses?' he asked, and took hold of my jacket front. 'Where am I going?' I said, 'to the water, by God! Do you think I . . .' 'To the water?' cried the steward. 'You scoundrel, I'll teach you to swim the highway to Kohl-haasenbrück!' And with a spiteful, murderous blow, he and the manager, who had grabbed me by the leg, threw me off my horse, so that I was stretched out full-length in the mud.

" 'Murder!' I cried. 'Harness and blankets and a bundle of my laundry are still in the stable.' But he and the servants attacked me with feet and whips and clubs, so that I collapsed half-dead behind the castle gate, while the manager led the horses away. And then I said, 'Thieving dogs! Where are they taking my horses?' and I got up. 'Get out of this courtyard,' the steward shouted. And, 'Sic 'im, Caesar! Sic 'im, Hunter! Sic 'im, Pointer! and a pack of more than a dozen dogs attacked me. So I broke a lath, or whatever it was, from the fence and knocked out three dogs beside me. But I was so badly mauled that I had to give way. 'Tweet!' a whistle shrilled, the dogs raced into the courtyard, the gates were shut, the bolt shoved forward and I fell unconscious on the road."

Kohlhaas, his face pallid, forced himself to assume a joking tone. "But didn't you really want to run away from the place?" Herse kept his eyes fixed on the ground, his face a dark red. "Confess," Kohlhaas said, "you didn't like it much in the pigsty; you thought how much more comfortable it was in the stable at Kohlhaasenbrück." "By thunder!" cried Herse, "I left the harness and blankets and a bundle of my laundry in the pigsty. Wouldn't I have taken the three guilders I had hidden in the red silk kerchief behind the manger? Hell and damnation! When you talk this way, I feel like lighting that sulphur taper I threw away!" "There, there," said the horse dealer. "I didn't

mean to anger you. Look, I believe what you told me, every word of
it. In due time I'll take my oath on the truth of what you've told me.
I'm sorry things haven't gone better for you in my service. Go to bed,
Herse, order a bottle of wine and be comforted: you shall have
justice!" And with that he got up, made a list of the articles the servant had left behind in the pigsty, specified their value, asked him
what he thought the cost of his cure would be and dismissed him
after shaking his hand again.

Then he told his wife Lisbeth the whole story with its deeper implications and announced that he was determined to seek public justice
for himself. He was glad to see that she fully supported him in this
intention. For she said that many another traveler, possibly less tolerant than himself, would pass the castle; to stop disorders of this kind
was to do God's work. She would find ways of financing the lawsuit.
Kohlhaas called her his brave wife, spent that and the following day
in the joyful company of his family and, as soon as his affairs permitted, set out for Dresden to bring his suit before the law courts.

With the help of a lawyer of his acquaintance, he drew up a
charge. He gave a circumstantial account of the crime that Junker
Wenzel von Tronka had committed both against himself and against
his servant Herse, demanded punishment of the junker according to
the law, the restoration of the horses to their former condition and
payment of the damages that both he and his servant had sustained.
The legal case was indeed clear. The fact that the horses had been
detained illegally cast a decisive light on everything else. And even if
it was assumed that the horses had fallen sick by sheer accident, the
horse dealer's demand that they be restored to him in a healthy condition would still have been just. Nor did Kohlhaas, while he was
looking about, lack friends in the capital; they promised to give his
cause warm support. The extensive horse trade he carried on and the
honesty with which he conducted his business had won him the
acquaintance and good will of the most important men in the country. Several times he dined in good spirits with his lawyer, who was
himself a prominent man. He deposited a sum of money with the
attorney to defray the cost of the lawsuit, and after some weeks
returned home to his wife Lisbeth, his confidence in the outcome of
his righteous cause fully supported by the lawyer.

Months passed, however, and the year was drawing to a close before he received as much as an acknowledgment from Saxony, to say

nothing of a decision about the lawsuit. After making several new representations before the tribunal, he asked his lawyer in a confidential letter what was causing such an excessive delay. He learned that the Dresden court, acting on word from a high authority, had completely quashed the case. The horse dealer wrote back indignantly to demand the reason for this action. The attorney reported that Junker Wenzel von Tronka was related to two noblemen, Hinz and Kunz von Tronka, one of whom was cupbearer, the other no less than chamberlain, to the prince elector. He further advised Kohlhaas to desist from any more appeals to the supreme court, and to make an immediate effort to get possession of the horses in Tronka Castle; it seemed that the junker, who was now in the capital, had instructed his servants to release them to him. He concluded with the request that, if this advice was not satisfactory, he would like to be spared any further involvement in the matter.

Kohlhaas happened at this time to be in Brandenburg, where the captain of the civic guard, Heinrich von Geusau, in whose jurisdiction Kohlhaasenbrück lay, was establishing several charitable institutions for the sick and needy, from a substantial fund that had accrued to the city for the use of the ailing. He was especially interested in opening up a mineral spring that had been discovered in one of the neighboring villages, the medicinal powers of which seemed to promise more than they later yielded. Kohlhaas was known to him through business contacts at the court. He therefore allowed Herse, who, since that fateful day at Tronka Castle, had had difficulty with his breathing, to try the healing powers of the little spring, which was provided with a roof and fence. The captain just happened to be giving orders at the tank in which Herse was bathing under Kohlhaas' supervision, when a messenger sent by the horse dealer's wife delivered the discouraging letter from his attorney in Dresden. The captain was talking with the doctor of the spa and noticed that Kohlhaas shed a tear on the letter as he read it. He hurried over and asked the merchant warmly what unpleasant news he had received. The horse dealer handed him the letter in silence. The captain knew the story of the monstrous injustice that had been perpetrated on him in the castle, the consequences of which were still affecting Herse's health, and would perhaps affect him for the rest of his life. He clapped Kohlhaas on the shoulder and told him not to lose heart, he would help him obtain satisfaction. He invited the horse dealer to come and

see him that evening in his castle. Kohlhaas went, and the captain
asked him to draw up an appeal to the elector of Brandenburg with a
brief description of the incident, to include the letter from the lawyer, and to ask for public protection against the act of violence that
had been committed against him on Saxon territory. He promised to
add this petition to a packet that was lying ready and was sure to
reach the hands of the elector, who would, without doubt, send it on
to the elector of Saxony when the opportunity to do so should arise.
This was enough to secure justice for him from the law courts at
Dresden, in spite of the wiles of the junker and his friends. With a
buoyant heart Kohlhaas cordially thanked the captain for this new
mark of his favor. He said he regretted that he hadn't taken the matter straight to Berlin, bypassing Dresden altogether. He had the
document drawn up in proper form in the offices of the municipal
court and gave it to the captain. Then he returned to Kohlhaasenbrück, more confident than ever about the final outcome of his
affair.

But a few weeks later an official of the law courts, who was in Potsdam on business for the captain, brought Kohlhass the disturbing
news that the elector had turned over the petition to his chancellor,
Count Kallheim, who had not applied to the court at Dresden for investigation and punishment of the act of violence — which would have
been logical — but had written to Junker von Tronka for more detailed preliminary information. The official stopped his carriage in
front of Kohlhaas' house and seemed to have instructions to give him
this information. To Kohlhaas' perplexed question why this procedure had been adopted, he could give no satisfactory answer. He
merely added that the captain advised him to be patient. He seemed
in a hurry to continue his journey, and only toward the end of the
brief conversation did Kohlhaas surmise, from a few casual words
dropped by the official, that Count Kallheim was related by
marriage to the house of Tronka.

Kohlhaas no longer found joy in his business, his house and farm,
or even in his wife and children. He waited all next month in gloomy
foreboding. Just as he expected, Herse returned at the end of this
period from the spa, somewhat better in health, with a written message from the captain and an enclosed document. The captain
wrote: he regretted that he could not help him in his affair; he was
enclosing a decision of the chancery that had been delivered to him,

and advised him to send for the horses he had left in Tronka Castle and forget the whole matter. The decision read: According to the report of the Dresden tribunal he was a good-for-nothing, cantankerous fellow. The junker with whom he had left the horses was not withholding them in any way. He was to send to the castle for them, or at least inform the junker where they should be delivered. In any case he was to spare the chancery such squabbling and wrangling.

Kohlhaas did not care about his horses; he would have been equally hurt if the matter had concerned a pair of dogs. On receiving this letter he foamed with rage. Every time there was a noise in the farmyard he looked toward the gate with a feeling of repugnance and expectation such as he had never experienced before, to see whether the junker's men had appeared to return the starved, sickly horses to him, perhaps even with an apology. This was the only situation which his mind, properly schooled though it was by the world, was not fully prepared to meet emotionally. But shortly after this he heard from an acquaintance who had traveled the highway that the horses were still being used in the fields, along with others belonging to the junker of Tronka Castle. Mingled with the pain he felt at seeing the world engulfed in such monstrous disorder, there shot through him a feeling of inner satisfaction from the knowledge that his own state of mind was morally right. He had a neighbor, a magistrate, who had long cherished the plan of enlarging his estate by purchasing the adjoining property. Kohlhaas invited this man to his house and asked him what he would give for all the Kohlhaas properties in Brandenburg and Saxony, lock, stock and barrel, fixed or rolling. His wife Lisbeth turned pale at these words. She picked up her youngest child, who was playing on the floor behind her. While the child toyed with the ribbons at her throat, she let her eyes wander past his red cheeks and fixed them, with a look in which death was reflected, on the horse dealer and on a paper he held in his hand.

The magistrate gave him a puzzled look and asked what had suddenly brought such ideas into his head. Kohlhaas replied, with as much cheerfulness in his voice as he could muster, that the idea of selling his farm on the banks of the Havel was by no means a new one. They had both often discussed this subject. Compared to his farm, the house in the Dresden suburb was a mere appendage which was hardly worth considering. In short, if the magistrate would oblige him by taking over both pieces of land, he was ready to sign a con-

tract. He added, in a forced tone of levity, that Kohlhaasenbrück
was, after all, not the world. There might be goals compared with
which the duty of acting as head of a family was of subordinate,
indeed of insignificant, rank. In short, he felt he must tell him that
his mind was set on great things, which he might perhaps soon hear
about. Reassured by these words, the magistrate jokingly told the
woman, who was smothering the child with kisses, that he hoped
Kohlhaas did not expect immediate payment. He put his hat and
cane, which till now he had held between his knees, on the table and
took the sheet of paper that the horse dealer held in his hand, to read
it through. Kohlhaas moved closer to him and explained that the
paper was a contract drawn up to fall due in four weeks' time. He
pointed out that it needed only the signatures and the specification of
the sums of money involved, that is, the purchase price and the penalty if the option were dropped within four weeks. Then he gaily
urged the magistrate once more to make an offer, assuring him that
he would sell at a fair price and not make difficult terms.

Kohlhaas' wife was walking up and down the room. Her breast
heaved, so that her kerchief, at which the child had been tugging,
threatened to fall from her shoulder. The magistrate said he could
not possibly estimate the value of the Dresden property. Kohlhaas
handed him some letters that had been exchanged at the time he
bought it; he estimated its value at one hundred golden guilders,
although the letters showed that it had cost him almost half as much
again. The magistrate read the bill of sale again and saw that it gave
him, too, the right to withdraw from the deal—a most unusual stipu-
lation. Half-decided, he said that after all he couldn't use the stud
horses in the stables. But Kohlhaas replied that he was not willing to
let the horses go; he also intended to keep for himself some weapons
that hung in the armory. Still the magistrate hesitated and hesitated,
and finally repeated an offer that he had recently made for the property, half in jest, half in earnest, while they were out for a walk
together—an offer that was ridiculous compared to the true value of
the estate. Kohlhaas pushed pen and ink toward him to sign. The
magistrate could not trust his senses. He asked again if Kohlhaas was
in earnest, to which the horse dealer replied somewhat testily, did he
think he was merely playing a joke on him? With a dubious look on
his face the magistrate took the pen and signed. However, he first
crossed out the clause that mentioned the penalty incurred by the

seller in case he repented of the transaction. He undertook to loan
the horse dealer one hundred golden guilders, with the Dresden
property as a mortgage (for he had no desire to buy this estate), and
left Kohlhaas complete freedom to withdraw from the deal within
two months. The horse dealer, touched by this act, shook the magistrate's hand warmly. They agreed on a principal condition: that a
fourth of the purchase price was to be paid over immediately, the rest
to be deposited in the Hamburg bank within three months. Then
Kohlhaas called for wine to celebrate a deal so happily closed. He
told the maid who came in with the bottles to instruct his groom
Sternbald to saddle the chestnut; he had to go to the capital on business, he said. He promised that when he returned he would speak
more frankly about matters which he must for the present keep to
himself. Then, as he was filling the glasses, he asked for news of the
Poles and Turks, who were then at war, drawing the magistrate into
various political conjectures on this subject, and drank once more to
the success of their transaction. Then he saw his guest out.

When the magistrate had left the room, Lisbeth fell to her knees
before her husband. "If you harbor the least affection in your heart
for me and the children that I have borne you; if you haven't already
cast us out for some unknown reason, then tell me the meaning of
these dreadful negotiations!" Kohlhaas replied, "My dearest wife, as
matters now stand, it's nothing that should disturb you. I have received a court decision in which they tell me that my suit against
Junker Wenzel von Tronka is a piece of idle cantankerousness. And
since there must be a misunderstanding here, I have decided to
present my suit once more, to the sovereign himself." "Why do you
want to sell your house?" she cried, getting to her feet with a gesture
of agitation. The horse dealer, pressing her gently to his chest,
replied, "Because, dearest Lisbeth, I do not want to remain in a
country in which they are not willing to protect me in my rights. I'd
rather be a dog than a man if I am to be trodden underfoot! I'm sure
that in this my wife thinks as I do." "How do you know," she asked
fiercely, "that they won't protect you in your rights? If you approach
the sovereign modestly with your petition, as you should, how do you
know that he will reject it or refuse to hear you?" "Very well," replied
Kohlhaas, "if my fears in this matter are unfounded, my house isn't
sold yet. The sovereign himself is just, I know; and if only I succeed
in reaching him through the ring of those who surround him, I have

no doubt that I'll get justice for myself and return happily to you and
to my old affairs before the week is out. May I then," he added as he
kissed her, "remain with you to the end of my days! Still, it's advisable," he continued, "to be prepared for every eventuality. For that
reason I should like you to leave this place for some time, if that's possible, and go with the children to your aunt's in Schwerin; you've
been wanting to visit her for a long time anyhow." "What!" she cried.
"I'm to go to Schwerin? Cross the border with the children? To my
aunt in Schwerin?" Horrow choked her speech. "Of course,"
answered Kohlhaas, "and at once, if you can, so that I may not be
hampered by any considerations in the steps I wish to take on behalf
of my cause." "Oh, I understand you!" she cried. "Now you need
nothing but weapons and horses; everything else you'll give away to
anyone who wants it!" And with that she turned away, threw herself
into a chair and wept. Kohlhaas said in perplexity, "Dearest Lisbeth,
what are you doing? God has blessed me with wife and children and
property. Shall I wish, for the first time today, that it were otherwise?" Seeing her turn red, he sat down beside her, and she threw her
arms about his neck. "Tell me," he said, stroking the curls away from
her forehead, "what am I to do? Shall I give up my cause? Shall I go
to Tronka Castle and beg the junker to give me back the horses,
mount them and come back here with them?" Lisbeth did not dare to
say, "Yes, yes, yes." She shook her head as she wept, pressed him
vehemently to her and covered his chest with her passionate kisses.
"Well then," cried Kohlhaas, "if you feel that I must obtain justice if
I'm to carry on my trade, then grant me the freedom I need to secure
it." And with that he stood up and told the servant, who had just
reported that the chestnut was saddled, that tomorrow the bays, too,
would have to be harnessed to take his wife to Schwerin. Lisbeth said
she had an idea. She rose, wiped the tears from her eyes and, as Kohlhaas sat down at his desk, she asked him whether he would give her
the petition and let her take it to Berlin in his place and present it to
the sovereign. Kohlhaas was touched by this suggestion for more than
one reason; he drew her down on his lap and spoke. "My dearest
wife, that's really quite impossible. The sovereign is very strongly
guarded; anyone who tries to approach him is exposed to much
vexation." Lisbeth replied that in a thousand cases it was easier for a
woman than for a man to approach him. "Give me the petition," she
repeated, "and if all you want is the knowledge that it will get to him,

I guarantee that he shall have it." Kohlhaas, who had many proofs of her courage and prudence, asked her how she intended to do it. She looked down shyly and replied that years ago the steward of the elector's castle had been a suitor of hers when he had served in the army in Schwerin. He was by now married, of course, and had several children; still, he hadn't altogether forgotten her. In short, he could leave it to her to gain advantage from this and other favorable factors too complicated to describe. Kohlhaas kissed her happily and said he accepted her proposal. He told her all she needed to do in order to have access to the sovereign was to get lodgings with the steward's wife and give her the petition. He had his bays saddled and sent her off, snugly bundled up, with his faithful servant Sternbald.

But of all the unsuccessful steps he had taken to further his cause, this journey was the most disastrous. For, after only a few days had passed, Sternbald returned to the farm, leading the horses at a slow pace; in the wagon lay Lisbeth, prostrate with a dangerous contusion of the chest. Kohlhaas, pale with fright, went up to the vehicle but could get no coherent account of what had caused the misfortune. The servant reported that the steward had not been at home, so they had been obliged to put up at an inn near the castle. On the following morning Lisbeth had left this inn and instructed the servant to stay with the horses. It was not until that evening that she had come back, in her present state. It seemed that she had forced her way too boldly toward the person of the sovereign. A member of the guard that surrounded him had, in his brutal zeal, through no fault of the ruler, thrust the shaft of his lance against her chest. At least that was the story told by the people who brought her back to the inn that night in an unconscious state; for she herself could say little, being prevented from speaking by a steady flow of blood from her mouth. The petition had subsequently been taken from her by a knight. Sternbald said it had been his intention to mount a horse at once and bring Kohlhaas news of this unhappy event. But in spite of the remonstrances of the surgeon who had been summoned, she had insisted on being brought back to Kohlhaasenbrück without sending any prior report to her husband.

Kohlhaas put her to bed; she was in a state of complete collapse from the journey. She lived a few days longer, struggling painfully for breath. In vain they tried to bring her back to consciousness, to learn from her what had happened. But she only lay there with staring, glazed eyes and said nothing. Not until shortly before her death did she regain consciousness. A clergyman of the Lutheran faith (she had adopted the new religion, following the example of her husband) was standing beside her bed, reading a chapter from the Bible in a loud, solemn, emotional voice. She suddenly gave him a dark look, took the Bible out of his hand — as if there were nothing in it she did not know — and kept turning the pages, seemingly searching for some passage. With her index finger she directed Kohlhaas' attention to the verse: "Forgive your enemies; do good unto them that hate you." With that she pressed his hand, gave him a soulful look and died.

Kohlhaas thought, "May God never forgive me if I forgive the junker." With tears streaming from his eyes, he bent down to kiss her, closed her eyes and left the room. He took the hundred golden guilders which the magistrate had already delivered for the Dresden stables, and ordered a funeral more fit for a princess than for a farmer's wife: a coffin of oak with metal lining, pillows of silk with tassels of silver and gold and a grave sixteen feet deep lined with fieldstones and mortar. Kohlhaas himself stood beside the grave with his youngest child on his arm, watching the work. On the day of the funeral, the body, white as snow, lay in state in a room whose walls he had had draped in black cloth. The clergyman had just concluded a moving oration at the bier when Kohlhaas was handed the official decision on the petition which the deceased woman had presented. It said he was to fetch the horses from Tronka Castle and desist from any further action in this matter, under penalty of imprisonment. Kohlhaas pocketed the letter and had the coffin put on the hearse. As soon as the mound had been erected and the cross planted on it and the guests who accompanied the hearse had left, Kohlhaas threw himself down beside his wife's now desolate bed and undertook the business of vengeance. He sat down and composed a legal judgment in which, by virtue of the power inherent in him, he condemned Junker Wenzel von Tronka to bring back to Kohlhaasenbrück, within three days of receiving this judgment, the black horses he had impounded and ruined on his fields, and to fatten them up personally in his stables till they were restored to their former condition. This decree he sent off to the junker by a messenger on horseback, and instructed the latter to return to Kohlhaasenbrück immediately upon delivering the document. When the three days passed without any sign of the horses, he summoned Herse and revealed to him the ultimatum he had sent the junker concerning the restoration of the horses. He then asked Herse two questions: Would he accompany him to Tronka Castle to fetch the junker personally? Secondly, once the junker was here, if he should show himself to be lazy in carrying out the task of feeding the horses in the Kohlhaasenbrück stables, would Herse help him along with the whip? When Herse caught his meaning, he roared with joy: "Master, this very day!" and, throwing his cap into the air, assured Kohlhaas that he would order a whip with ten knots in it to teach the junker the art of currying. So Kohlhaas sold the house, sent the children across the border in a wagon, and summoned the rest of his servants at nightfall. There were seven of them, each one as true as gold; he armed and mounted them and set out for Tronka Castle.

The little band arrived at the castle on the third evening at nightfall. They struck down the toll collector and gatekeeper, who were standing in the gateway chatting, and entered the castle. They set fire to all the outbuildings in the castle area, and these burst into sudden flame. Herse hurried up the circular staircase to the tower where the steward's quarters were. Here he found the steward and manager, sitting half-undressed at cards, and fell upon them with club and knife. Kohlhaas rushed into the castle in search of Junker Wenzel. Even thus does the Angel of Judgment descend from heaven. The junker was just regaling a troupe of friends by reading them, amid much laughter, the decree the horse dealer had sent him. But he had scarcely heard Kohlhaas' voice in the courtyard below, when he turned deathly pale, cried, "Brothers, run for it!" and vanished.

As he entered the great hall, Kohlhaas met a Junker Hans von Tronka; he seized the knight's jacket front and hurled him into a corner of the hall with such violence that his brains spattered on the stone floor. The other knights made an attempt to seize arms, but they were overpowered and scattered by Kohlhaas' men. Kohlhaas asked where Junker Wenzel von Tronka was, but none of the stunned servants could tell him. He kicked open two doors that led into the wings of the castle and ran through the spacious building in all directions without finding anyone. With a curse he hurried down to the courtyard to block all the exits. By this time the whole castle, including its side buildings, had caught fire from the barracks, sending up dense clouds of smoke to the sky. Sternbald and three busy men dragged together everything that was not nailed down, to be hauled away as plunder. With a cry of triumphant exultation from Herse, the dead bodies of the steward, the manager, their wives and children were thrown out of the window into the courtyard. As Kohlhaas hurried down the castle stairs, the gouty old woman who kept house for the junker threw herself at his feet. He stopped for a moment on the stairs and asked her where the junker was. In a weak, quavering voice she replied that she thought he had fled to the chapel. He summoned two men with torches and, since he had no keys, had the doors of the chapel battered down with crowbars and axes and overturned altars and benches; but to his intense pain he did not find the junker.

It happened that, just at the moment when Kohlhaas emerged from the chapel, a young servant from the castle was hurrying past, making for a large stone stable that was threatened by the flames, to rescue the junker's battle horses. At this moment Kohlhaas noticed his two blacks standing in a little shed with a thatched roof. He asked the servant why he didn't rescue the blacks. The boy put the key into the lock of the stable and replied, "The shed's already on fire, isn't it?" Kohlhaas wrenched the key out of the keyhole and threw it angrily over the wall, drove the boy into the burning shed by raining blows on him with the flat side of his blade, and, amidst the ghastly laughter of the bystanders, compelled him to rescue the two blacks. But when the servant appeared with the horses several moments later, pale with fright, just barely emerging as the shed collapsed behind him, he no longer found Kohlhaas there. He joined the servants who stood about on the castle square; when he saw the horse dealer, who turned his back on him several times, the boy asked what he was to do with the horses. Kohlhaas raised his foot with fearful fury, which would have meant the lad's death if the kick had landed. Without giving him an answer, Kohlhaas mounted his bay horse and sat at the castle gate, waiting in silence for day to come, while his men went on with their work. By dawn the whole castle had burned down except for the walls; not a soul was in it save Kohlhaas and his seven men. He dismounted and re-examined every corner of the square, which was bathed in the rays of the rising sun. However bitter it was for him to admit it, he had to confess that his whole undertaking against the castle had failed. His heart heavy with pain and misery, he sent Herse with several men to gather information about the direction the junker had taken in flight. He was especially disturbed to learn about a wealthy convent for ladies of rank, bearing the name of

Erlabrunn and situated on the banks of the Mulde River, the abbess of which, Antonia von Tronka, was known in the region as a devout, charitable and saintly woman. To the unhappy Kohlhaas it seemed only too probable that the junker, stripped as he was of all necessities, had taken refuge in this convent, as the abbess was his aunt and had given him his first schooling when he was a child. When Kohlhaas had obtained this information, he went up to the steward's quarters in the tower, where there was still a room fit to be used. Here he drew up a so-called "Kohlhaasian Mandate," in which he called upon the whole country to refrain from aiding and abetting Junker Wenzel von Tronka, with whom he was engaged in a just war, and ordered every resident of the region, including friends and relatives of the junker, to deliver him into his hands, upon penalty of life and limb and the inevitable reduction of all their property to ashes. With the help of travelers and strangers he distributed this declaration throughout the district. He gave a copy of it to his servant Waldmann and instructed him to deliver it into the hands of Dame Antonia at Erlabrunn. Then he enrolled some servants from Tronka Castle in his service, men who were dissatisfied with the junker and were tempted by the prospect of booty. He armed them after the fashion of infantry soldiers, with crossbows and daggers, and taught them how to ride behind his mounted men. After converting all the booty into money and dividing the money among his followers, he spent a few hours resting at the castle gate from his wretched labors.

Toward noon Herse returned and confirmed what Kohlhaas' heart, always full of the gloomiest forebodings, had already told him: that the junker was at the convent of Erlabrunn with old Dame Antonia, his aunt. It seemed that he had fled through a back door that led into the open, by way of a narrow iron stairway extending under a small roof, down to a few boats on the river Elbe. At least, Herse reported, the junker had appeared at midnight in a village by the Elbe, alighting from a boat without rudder or oars, to the astonishment of the villagers, who had been attracted to the spot by the flames that came from the distant castle. He had then gone on to Erlabrunn in a farm wagon he had hired in the village. At this news, Kohlhaas gave a deep sigh of distress. He asked if the horses had been fed; the answer was yes. So he ordered his troop to mount, and within three hours they were at the gates of Erlabrunn. As he entered the courtyard of the convent with his men, all carrying torches, which they lit

upon arriving at the spot, there was a rumbling of distant thunder on
the horizon. His servant Waldmann met him with the report that he
had duly delivered the mandate. Immediately he saw the abbess and
the steward of the convent emerge under the portal, engaged in an
agitated exchange of words. The steward, a little old man with snow-
white hair, shot venomous glances at Kohlhaas as he was helped into
his armor. In a bold voice he commanded the servants who surrounded him to ring the storm bell. At the same time the abbess,
white as a sheet, with a silver crucifix in her hand, descended the
ramp and prostrated herself before Kohlhaas' horse, together with all
her nuns. The steward, who carried no sword, was easily overpowered
by Kohlhaas' men and led away a prisoner among their horses. Kohlhaas asked the abbess where Junker Wenzel von Tronka was. She detached a large key ring from her girdle as she replied, "In Wittenberg, Kohlhaas, worthy man!" and added in a trembling voice, "Fear
God and do no evil." Kohlhaas found himself plunged back into the
hell of unsatisfied vengeance. He turned his horse and was on the
point of crying, "Set fire to the place!" when a tremendous thunder-
bolt struck quite close to him. He turned his horse again, so that he
faced the abbess, and asked her whether she had received his mandate. In a weak, scarcely audible voice she replied, "Only now!"
"When?" "Two hours, so help me God, after the departure of the
junker, my nephew." Kohlhaas turned a dark face upon his servant
Waldmann. The latter stammered confirmation of the fact; the
waters of the Mulde, swollen by the rains, had prevented him from
arriving sooner. Kohlhaas regained control of himself; a sudden fearful gust of rain that poured down on the pavement of the yard extinguished the torches and eased the pain in his unhappy breast. He
brusquely doffed his hat to the lady, wheeled his horse around,
shouted, "Follow me, brethren, the junker is in Wittenberg!" gave his
animal the spur and left the convent.

When night came upon them, he put up at an inn on the highway.
He had to rest a whole day for the sake of the weary horses. Realizing
that with a troop of ten men (for that was the number of followers he
now had) he could not defy a place like Wittenberg, he composed a
second mandate, in which, after giving a brief account of what had
befallen him, he summoned every good Christian, as he expressed it,
to espouse his cause against Junker Wenzel von Tronka as the common enemy of all Christians, with the promise of booty and other

advantages accruing from war. In another mandate, which appeared soon after this one, he called himself "a gentleman free in the Reich and in the world, subject only to God." It was a misdirected, morbid fanaticism; yet it brought him droves of rabble, who were left breadless by the peace with Poland and were attracted by the clink of money and the prospect of booty. So he now had some thirty-odd men when he set out for the right bank of the Elbe with the intention of reducing Wittenberg to ashes.

He waited with his men and horses under the roof of an old tumbledown brick barn in the solitude of a dark forest, which at that time surrounded this region. Meanwhile he sent Sternbald in disguise into the city with the mandate. No sooner had the servant returned with the news that the mandate was already known there, than Kohlhaas set out with his troop on the holy eve of Whitsuntide and, while the inhabitants of the city were asleep in their beds, set fire to the four corners of the place. While his men were plundering the suburbs he pasted a sheet of paper to a pillar of a church door with the message that he, Kohlhaas, had set fire to the city, and if the junker were not handed over to him, he would reduce it to ashes so completely that (as he expressed it) he would not need to look behind any wall to find him.

The horror of the inhabitants at this unheard-of crime was indescribable. Since the fire had, fortunately, occurred on a fairly quiet summer night, the flames had razed only nineteen buildings, including, however, a church. Towards morning, as soon as the fire had been brought partly under control, the old Governor Otto von Gorgas sent out a detachment of fifty men to capture the monstrous villain. But the captain who led the band, a man by the name of Gerstenberg, managed the affair so badly that the expedition, instead of overthrowing Kohlhaas, rather helped him gain a most dangerous reputation as a warrior. The captain had divided his band into several small groups in order, as he thought, to surround Kohlhaas and crush him. Kohlhaas, on the other hand, had kept his band together, so that he was able to attack the enemy at several points with full strength and defeat each unit separately. Consequently, by the evening of the following day, not a single man of the city's soldiers, on whom the hope of the country rested, was left in the field. Kohlhaas had lost several men in the skirmishing; on the morning of the following day he was able to set fire to the town once more, and his murderous plans were so well laid that again a large number of buildings and almost all the barns in the suburbs lay in ashes. Once again he nailed up the well-known mandate, at the corners of the city hall itself, adding to it an account of the fate that had befallen Captain von Gerstenberg, whom the governor had sent out against him and whom he had annihilated. The governor was highly incensed by this defiance and set out himself, together with several knights, at the head of a force of one hundred and fifty men. Upon receiving a written request from Junker Wenzel von Tronka, the governor supplied the junker with a guard to protect him from the violence of the people, who flatly wished to drive him out of the city at once. He also posted guards at all the villages in the area and on the wall encircling the city, to prevent a surprise attack. On St. Gervasius' Day he himself set out with his men to capture the dragon who was laying waste the land. The horse dealer was shrewd enough to avoid meeting this band. By skillful marches he was able to lure the governor five miles away from the city. By devious wiles he lulled the governor into the belief that, in view of the superior forces opposing him, he would retreat into Brandenburg. Then he veered suddenly, and at the fall of the third night returned to Wittenberg by a forced march and set fire to the city for the third time. This horrible act of bravado was performed by Herse, who entered the city in disguise. A sharp north wind made the conflagration so devastating that, in less than three hours, forty-two houses, two churches, several convents and schools, and even the building which housed the electoral governor's offices lay in ashes and rubble. At dawn the governor, who believed that his opponent was in Brandenburg territory, was informed of what had happened; he returned by forced marches to find the city in general rebellion. The people had collected in thousands before the house in which the junker was hiding behind barricades of beams and posts. With frenzied shouting they demanded that he be removed from the city.

Two burgomasters, named Jenkens and Otto, who were present wearing their robes of office, together with the whole city council, argued in vain that the people would simply have to wait for the return of a courier who had been sent to the president of the chancery for permission to bring the junker to Dresden, where he himself wished to go for many reasons. The irrational mob, armed with clubs and spears, paid no attention to these words. Several councillors who

advocated strong measures against the mob were given rough treatment; and the mob was on the point of storming the house in which
the junker was lodged and leveling it to the ground, when the governor, Otto von Gorgas, appeared at the head of his force of mounted
men. This dignified man was accustomed to inspire respect and obedience in the people by his mere presence. He had, moreover, succeeded in picking up three of the incendiary's men, who had been
separated from the main body, close to the city gate, as a sort of consolation prize for the failure of his expedition. While the three fellows
were being put in chains before the eyes of the populace, he assured
the councillors in a clever speech that before long he intended to
bring Kohlhaas himself in chains before them, as he was on the man's
trail. With the help of all these reassuring factors he succeeded in
allaying the anxiety of the assembled throng and in pacifying them
about the junker's presence in the city until the courier returned
from Dresden. He and several knights dismounted, had the posts and
barricades removed and entered the house, where he found the junker, attended by two physicians, falling from one fainting fit into the
next, while the doctors tried to revive him with essences and stimu-
lants. Since Otto von Gorgas felt that this was not the moment for exchanging words with the junker about the conduct he had been
guilty of, he merely told him, with a look of silent contempt in his
eyes, to get dressed and to follow him, for his own security, into the
chambers of the knights' prison. A doublet was put on his back and a
helmet on his head; but his chest was left half-bare so that he could
breathe more freely. He was led out on the street, supported by the
governor and his brother-in-law, Count von Gerschau. As he passed
the mob, blasphemous and horrible curses against him were sent
toward heaven. The people, held back by the mercenaries with great
difficulty, called him a leech, a wretched pestilence and tormentor of
human beings, the curse of the city of Wittenberg and the ruin of
Saxony. After a wretched procession through the ruined city, in the
course of which he lost his helmet several times without missing it,
only to have it picked up by a knight behind him and stuck on his
head, they reached the prison, where he vanished into a dungeon
that was put under the protection of a strong guard. Meanwhile the
return of the courier with a decision from the electoral government
threw the city into a new state of alarm. For the citizens of Dresden
had made an urgent appeal directly to the Saxon Government to

prevent the junker from entering the city until the incendiary had been apprehended. The government, therefore, would not hear of the plan to send the junker to the capital. On the contrary, it imposed on the governor the duty of protecting him with all the power at his command, wherever he was, since he had to be somewhere. But it did announce to the good city of Wittenberg, for its pacification, that a detachment of five hundred men under the command of Prince Friedrich von Meissen was already on the way to protect it from further molestation by Kohlhaas.

The governor realized that such a decision could not possibly put the minds of the people at rest. For several slight advantages which the horse dealer had gained in battle at various points near the city had spread some very unpleasant rumors about the strength which his forces had attained. Besides, the type of warfare he waged in the dark of night with a disguised rabble, using pitch, straw and sulphur, was unheard-of and without example. It might have rendered ineffectual an even larger force than the one that was advancing under Prince von Meissen. After brief deliberation the governor decided to suppress the news of the decision he had received. He merely posted the letter announcing the approach of the Prince von Meissen at the city limits. A covered carriage left the knights' prison at dawn, accompanied by four heavily armed mounted guards, and made for the road leading to Leipzig. The guards spread vague reports that the carriage was bound for Pleissen Castle. Having in this way soothed popular sentiment concerning the wretched junker, whose very existence brought with it the dangers of sword and flame, the governor set out with three hundred men to join forces with the prince of Meissen. Meanwhile Kohlhaas had actually increased his following to one hundred and nine men, as a result of the strange position he occupied in the world. In Jessen he had accumulated a supply of arms, with which he had completely equipped his band. He was duly informed in advance of the double storm that was descending on him and decided to meet it with the speed of a hurricane before it broke over him. Accordingly, the very next night he attacked the prince of Meissen at Mühlberg. In this engagement, to his great sorrow, he lost Herse, who collapsed beside him when the very first volleys were exchanged. Embittered by this loss, Kohlhaas pressed the prince so hard in a battle lasting three hours that the latter was unable to collect his men in one spot. The prince was wounded in

several places and his forces were in such disorder that he was com-
pelled to beat a retreat to Dresden at dawn. This advantage made
Kohlhaas reckless. Before the governor could learn of the disaster,
Kohlhaas attacked him at noon in the open fields at the village of
Damerow. The horse dealer's losses were heavy, but his advantages
were equal to those of the governor. The battle raged into the night.
The governor entrenched himself in the churchyard at Damerow.
Kohlhaas would have attacked him here in the morning with the remainder of his forces, but the governor received word through scouts
of the prince of Meissen's defeat at Mühlberg and decided that it was
more prudent to return to Wittenberg and wait for a more propitious
moment.

Five days after these two forces had been routed, Kohlhaas stood
before the city of Leipzig and set fire to it on three sides. In the man-
ifesto he published on this occasion he called himself "the viceroy of
the Archangel Michael, who has come to punish by fire and sword
everyone who took the side of the junker, for the deceit which has
descended upon the whole world." He had overrun Lützen Castle
and established himself there. From here he issued a summons to the
people to join with him in establishing a better order of things. This
mandate was signed in a streak of insanity: "Dated at the seat of our
provisional world government at the arch-castle of Lützen."

It was the good fortune of the inhabitants of Leipzig that a steady
rain which fell from the sky prevented the fire from spreading. The
swift action of the fire fighters reduced the damage to a few shops
situated around Pleissen Castle. Nevertheless the city was seized with
unspeakable dismay at the presence of the raging incendiary and his
delusion that the junker was in Leipzig. Since a troop of a hundred
and eighty mounted soldiers who were sent out against him returned
in defeat, the council, which did not want to endanger city property,
could do nothing but close the gates completely and keep a citizens'
guard day and night outside the walls. In vain the council posted
notices in the surrounding villages, giving positive assurance the the
junker was not in Pleissen Castle. The horse dealer replied with similar notices, insisting that the junker was in Pleissen Castle. Even if he
were not, Kohlhaas would continue to act on the assumption that he
was, until the place where the junker could be found was made
known to him by name. When the elector was informed by a courier
of the distress in which the city of Leipzig found itself, he announced

that he was already recruiting a force of two thousand men, which he intended to lead personally, to capture Kohlhaas. He rebuked Otto von Gorgas severely for the ambiguous and thoughtless stratagem he had employed to rid the Wittenberg region of the incendiary's presence. No one can describe the consternation that seized the whole of Saxony, and the capital in particular, when it was learned that in the villages around Leipzig some unknown person had put up placards addressed to Kohlhaas, informing him that Junker Wenzel was in Dresden with his cousins Hinz and Kunz.

At this juncture Dr. Martin Luther, relying on his prestige, undertook the task of bringing Kohlhaas back into the path of human order by the power of gentle words. Appealing to whatever sanity remained in the incendiary, he published the following message, which was distributed on posters in all the cities and villages of the electoral principality:

Kohlhaas, you who claim that you have been sent to wield the sword of justice, how dare you show such presumption, you arrogant man, in the madness of purblind passion, you who are filled from head to foot with the very spirit of injustice? Because the sovereign, to whom you are subject, has denied you your right, your right in a quarrel about worthless property, you arise, you godless man, with fire and sword, and like the wolf of the desert, you break into the peaceful community which he protects. You who have led men astray by this assertion, full of untruth and guile, do you think, sinner, that you will be able to face God on the day that will shine into the recesses of every heart? How can you say that your right has been denied you? After the first half-hearted abortive attempts, your violent mind, inflamed by the titillation of vile personal vengeance, completely renounced every effort to obtain it for yourself. And who are your "authorities": a bench full of court clerks and sheriffs, who suppress a letter that is brought to them or hold back information that they ought to have passed on? And must I tell you, reprobate, that the authorities know nothing of your affair, indeed, that the sovereign against whom you rebel does not so much as know your name, so that when you come before the throne of God on Judgment Day to accuse him, he will be able to speak with serene countenance: "Lord, I have done this man no injustice, for his existence is foreign to my soul"? Know

that the sword you wield is the sword of plunder and murder: you
are a rebel, not a warrior of the righteous God; your goal on earth
is the wheel and the gallows, and in the beyond: damnation, which
is the punishment for crime and godlessness.

Wittenberg, etc.   *Martin Luther*

At this time Kohlhaas was at Lützen Castle, hatching a new plan
in his tormented brain for reducing Leipzig to ashes. For he paid no
atention to the notices, posted in the villages, that told of the junker's
presence in Dresden, since they had not been signed, least of all by
the city council, as he had demanded. But Sternbald and Waldmann
noticed to their consternation that Martin Luther's handbill had
been nailed one night on the gateway of the castle. For several days
they hoped in vain that it would be noticed by Kohlhaas, whom they
did not like to approach on the matter. He did appear in the evening
with a gloomy, withdrawn look on his face; but he saw nothing and
merely issued a few brief orders. One morning, therefore, when he
was preparing to hang several of his men who had plundered the
region against his orders, they resolved to call his attention to the
poster. He was just returning from the place of execution, passing
through two lines of followers, who retreated timidly before him. He
was surrounded by the pomp that he had assumed since his second
mandate: a large cherub sword on a cushion of red leather, with tassels of gold, was carried before him, and twelve servants with burning
torches followed him. The two men, their swords under their arms,
circled the pillar to which the poster was attached in such a way that
Kohlhaas' attention had to be drawn to it. Kohlhaas was walking
with his hands clasped behind his back, absorbed in thought. When
he came to the entrance gate he raised his eyes and started. The men
drew back respectfully before him. He looked at them absent-
mindedly and took a few swift steps toward the pillar. Who can
describe what went through his mind when he caught sight of the
paper which accused him of injustice, and which was signed by the
most precious and most venerable name known to him, the name of
Martin Luther!

A dark flush spread over his face. Removing his helmet, he read
the poster through twice from beginning to end; then he turned
around with an uncertain look in his eye, as if he wanted to say some-

thing to his men. But he said nothing. He detached the sheet from the wall, read it through once more and cried, "Waldmann, have my horse saddled!" Then, "Sternbald, follow me to the castle!" and vanished. It needed nothing but these few words of Luther's to disarm him suddenly, to show him how corrupt the situation in which he found himself was. He hastily put on the clothes of a Thuringian tenant farmer and told Sternbald that he had to take a trip to Wittenberg on a matter of great importance. In the presence of some of his most trusted men he turned over to Sternbald the leadership of the band, which stayed behind in Lützen. Assuring his followers that he would be back in three days, within which period there was no danger of an attack, he rode off to Wittenberg.

He stopped at an inn under an assumed name. As soon as night had fallen he put on his coat, provided himself with a pair of pistols which he had captured in Tronka Castle and appeared in Luther's study. Luther was sitting at his desk, surrounded by books and papers. He saw the strange man open the door and bolt it, and asked him who he was and what he wanted. The man held his hat respectfully in his hand. In shy presentiment of the terror he would cause, he replied that he was Michael Kohlhaas, the horse dealer. Luther cried, "Begone!" and rising from his desk, hurried over to the bell, adding, "Your breath is pestilential and your presence, destruction!" Without moving from the spot, Kohlhaas drew his pistol and said, "Most reverend sir, if you touch that bell, this pistol will stretch me lifeless at your feet. Sit down and listen to me. You are not safer among the angels whose psalms you record than you are with me."

Luther sat down and asked again, "What do you want?" Kohlhaas replied, "I wish to refute your opinion of me as an unjust man. You told me in your poster that the authorities know nothing of my case. Very well then, procure a safe conduct for me, and I will go to Dresden and put my case before them." "Godless and frightful man!" cried Luther, both confused and calmed by these words. "Who gave you the right to attack Junker von Tronka on the basis of judicial decisions which you made yourself and, when you did not find him in his own castle, to punish with fire and sword the whole community that protects him?" Kohlhaas replied, "Most reverend sir, from this moment on: no one. A report that I received from Dresden deceived and misled me. The war that I am waging against the society of men is a crime if I am not an outcast from that society, as you have assured me I am not." "An outcast!" cried Luther, looking at him. "What madness of thought has taken possession of you? Who has cast you out of the community of the state in which you lived? Indeed, where is there a single case, as long as states have existed, of anyone, whoever he be, being cast out from the state?" Kohlhaas clenched his fist as he replied, "I call him an outcast who is denied the protection of the law. For I require this protection if my peaceful trade is to thrive. Indeed, it is for this protection that I have taken refuge in society, together with everything I own. And whoever denies it to me casts me out among the savages of the desert; he puts into my hand — how can you deny this? — the club that is to protect me."

"Who has denied you the protection of the law?" cried Luther. "Did I not write you that the complaint you submitted is unknown to the sovereign? If servants of the state suppress lawsuits behind his back or mock his sacred name in any other way, who but God may bring him to account for his choice of such servants? Are you, damned, terrible man, authorized to judge him on that account?" "Very well then," replied Kohlhaas, "if the sovereign does not cast me out, I will return to the society which he protects. I repeat, procure for me a safe conduct to Dresden, and I will disband the force of men I have collected at Lützen Castle and bring the rejected suit once more before the courts of the land." With a vexed look on his face Luther rummaged in silence among the papers on his desk. The defiant attitude that this strange man assumed in the state annoyed him. Reviewing in his mind the sentence which Kohlhaas had passed on the junker from Kohlhaasenbrück, Luther asked what he expected from the courts at Dresden. Kohlhaas replied, "Punishment of the junker in accordance with the law; restoration of the horses to their former condition; and compensation for the damages which both I and my servant Herse, who was killed at Mühlberg, suffered through the act of violence committed against us." Luther cried, "Compensation for the damages! You have borrowed thousands on notes and securities from both Jew and Christian to finance your savage private vengeance. Will you add this, too, to the bill of damages?" "Heaven forbid!" replied Kohlhaas. "I do not ask restitution of my house and farm and the prosperity which I enjoyed, any more than I ask for the expenses of my wife's funeral. Herse's mother will submit an account of the doctor's bills and of what her son lost in Tronka Castle; and the loss I suffered through my failure to sell the

black horses can be estimated for the government by an expert."
"Mad, incomprehensible, monstrous man!" Luther said, and stared
at him. "Now that your sword has taken the grimmest vengeance imaginable on the junker, what impels you to insist on a verdict against
him whose weight, when it finally falls, will touch him so lightly?" A
tear rolled down Kohlhaas' cheek as he replied, "Most reverend sir, it
has cost me my wife. Kohlhaas wants to show the world that she did
not perish in an unjust quarrel. Submit to my will on these details
and let the courts speak; on everything else that may still be in dispute, I submit to yours." "Indeed," Luther said, "if public rumor is
right, your demands are just; and if you had been able to bring the
dispute to the sovereign before proceeding to seek justice by your own
powers, I have no doubt that your demands would have been met
point by point. But, all things considered, would you not have done
better to forgive the junker for the sake of your Saviour, to have
taken the black horses by your hand, skinny and worn-out as they
were, and mounted and ridden them home to your stable in Kohlhaasenbrück to restore them there to their former condition?" Kohlhaas walked to the window and replied, "Maybe, maybe not. If I had
known that I would have to get them on their feet again with the
heart-blood of my dear wife, maybe I would have acted as you say,
reverend sir, and not spared a bushel of oats. But because they have
now cost me so dearly, I think the matter should take its course; let
the verdict give me what is my due and let the junker fatten my
blacks." Luther turned back to his papers, various thoughts going
through his mind, and said he would negotiate with the elector on his
behalf. Meanwhile he was to keep quiet at Lützen Castle; if the sovereign should grant him a safe conduct, it would be communicated
to him by way of public placards. As Kohlhaas bent down to kiss his
hand, he added, "Whether the elector will be prepared to practice
mercy instead of justice, I don't know; for I hear that he has collected
an army and is on the point of capturing you in Lützen Castle; however, as I said, I shall spare no efforts." And with that he arose and
prepared to show him out. Kohlhaas said he was perfectly satisfied
with Luther's intercession, whereupon the latter dismissed him with a
wave of the hand. But Kohlhaas suddenly bent one knee before him
and said he had one more request in his heart. He was in the habit of
going to church at Whitsuntide to take communion, but had failed
to do so because of his warlike activities. Would Luther be kind

enough to hear his confession right then and there and administer
the Holy Sacrament to him? Luther pondered briefly; with a sharp
look at Kohlhaas he said, "Yes, Kohlhaas, I will do that. But the
Lord, whose body you desire, forgave His enemies." As Kohlhaas
looked at him dejectedly, Luther continued, "Will you, too, forgive
the junker who has offended you, go to the castle, mount your blacks
and ride them home to Kohlhaasenbrück for fattening?" "Most reverend sir," said Kohlhaas, taking Luther's hand, while the color
mounted to his cheeks. "Well?" "The Lord did not forgive all His
enemies either. Let me forgive the electors, my two sovereigns, the
castle steward and administrator, the knights Hinz and Kunz and
anyone else who may have caused me offense in this matter; but permit me to compel the Junker, if it is possible, to fatten my blacks
back to their normal state." At these words Luther turned his back to
the house door, with a displeased look and pulled the bell. In answer
to this summons a servant appeared in the anteroom with a light.
Kohlhaas rose from the floor, drying his eyes, depressed in spirit. The
servant was trying vainly to open the bolted door. Since Luther had
once more sat down before his papers, Kohlhaas opened the door for
the servant. With a brief side glance directed at the stranger, Luther
said to the servant, "Light his way out." The man was a little puzzled
at the sight of this visitor. He took the house key from the wall and retreated to the half-open door of the room, waiting for the stranger's
departure. Kohlhaas picked up his hat and fingered it agitatedly in
both hands, saying, "And so, most reverend sir, I may not partake of
the grace of reconciliation which I have requested of you?" Luther
answered shortly, "With your Saviour, no; with your sovereign—that
depends on the result of the effort, as I promised you." And with that
he motioned to the servant to carry out the order he had given him
without further delay. Kohlhaas folded both hands on his breast, an
expression of painful emotion on his face; he followed the man who
lighted his way down the stairs, and vanished.

The following morning Luther sent a dispatch to the elector of
Saxony. He began with a bitter denunciation of the prince's close
counselors, the knights Hinz and Kunz von Tronka, chamberlain
and cupbearer who, as was generally known, had quashed Kohlhaas'
suit. He then disclosed to the prince, with the frankness that was
characteristic of him, that in such vexatious circumstances there was
nothing left to do but accept the horse dealer's proposal and, in view

of what had occurred, grant him amnesty for the resumption of his lawsuit. Public opinion, he stated, was on the man's side in a most dangerous way; so much so that even in Wittenberg, which he had reduced to ashes three times, there was a voice that spoke in his favor. If his offers were rejected, Kohlhaas would undoubtedly bring the rejection to popular attention in a malicious light; the people could easily be misled to such a degree that the authority of the state would be powerless against him. He concluded that in this extraordinary instance one should overlook the impropriety of entering into negotiations with a citizen who has had recourse to arms; for in point of fact his treatment had, in a way, put him beyond the reach of state obligations. In short, in order to put an end to the dispute, he must be regarded more as a foreign power which had invaded the country than as a rebel who was attacking the throne. The fact that he *was* an alien subject gave some justification for this view.

The elector received this document in the presence of Prince Christiern von Meissen, generalissimo of the kingdom, uncle of that Prince Friedrich von Meissen who had been defeated at Mühlberg and was still suffering from the wounds received there. Also present were the grand chancellor of the tribunal, Count Wrede; Count Kallheim, president of the chancery; and the two knights Hinz and Kunz von Tronka, the latter chamberlain, the former cupbearer, boyhood friends and confidants of the sovereign. Herr Kunz, the chamberlain who, in his capacity of privy councillor, attended to the sovereign's private correspondence and had authority to use his name and seal, spoke first. He began by repeating the elaborate explanation that he would never, on his own authority, have dismissed the suit which the horse dealer had submitted to the tribunal against the junker, his cousin, if he had not regarded it as a completely baseless and worthless piece of truculence, an opinion he had formed on the basis of false information. He then came to the present state of affairs. He remarked that neither divine nor human law gave the horse dealer authority to take such monstrous vengeance as he had permitted himself for this misdeed. He described the glory that would fall upon his accursed head if one should enter into negotiations with him as if he were a legitimate military power. The disgrace that would fall on the sacred person of the elector seemed to him so unbearable that, in the fire of his eloquence, he preferred to face the most extreme consequences — the possible execution of the mad rebel's sentence — and

to see his cousin, the junker, led away to Kohlhaasenbrück to fatten
the black horses, rather than have Doctor Luther's proposal accepted. Half turning to the chamberlain, the grand chancellor of the
tribunal, Count Wrede, expressed his regret that this tender concern
the gentleman was showing for the sovereign's reputation in the resolution of this unhappy affair had not animated him during its early
stages. He pointed out to the elector that he was dubious about invoking the power of the state to put through a measure that was
patently illegal. With a meaningful allusion to the following which
the horse dealer was steadily acquiring in the country, he remarked
that in this way the thread of crimes threatened to spin itself out end-
lessly, and declared that only a simple act of justice directly and absolutely rectifying the error that had been committed could break this
thread and extricate the government successfully from this nasty
mood. In answer to the sovereign's request for his opinion, Prince
Christiern von Meissen turned deferentially to the grand chancellor
and said his way of thinking filled him with the deepest respect, of
course; but in seeking to secure justice for Kohlhaas, he forgot that
he was jeopardizing the just claims of Wittenberg and Leipzig, and
indeed the whole country that Kohlhaas had laid waste, to repara-
tion or at least to punishment. With respect to this man the social
order had been so radically wrenched out of joint that it could hardly
be set right again by a principle derived from the science of jurispru-
dence. Accordingly he concurred in the chamberlain's opinion that
the existing means for handling such cases should be invoked in this
instance: a military detachment of adequate size should be raised
and used to capture or crush the horse dealer, who was at present stationed at Lützen. The chamberlain took two chairs from the wall,
one for the elector and the other for prince von Meissen, and obligingly placed them in the center of the room. He rejoiced, he said, to
find that a man of the prince's integrity and insight agreed with him
on the means for solving this complex problem. The prince, placing
his hand on the chair without sitting down, looked at the chamberlain and assured him that he had no cause whatever for rejoicing,
since the procedure involved, as a preliminary step, a warrant for the
arrest and trial of the chamberlain himself for misusing the name of
his sovereign. For if necessity demanded that the veil be lowered before the throne of justice over a series of crimes which had become so
hopelessly involved that they could not be brought before that throne,

this was not true of the very first crime that had caused them all. Only the arraignment of the horse dealer on a capital charge could justify the state in demanding the destruction of the man whose cause, as everyone knew, was a very just one, and into whose hand they themselves had placed the sword he was wielding.

At these words the chamberlain looked dejectedly at the elector, who turned very red in the face and walked over to the window. After a pause of general embarrassment, Count Kallheim said that in this way they could never get out of the magic circle in which they were trapped. By the same token, his nephew, Prince Friedrich, could also be brought to trial; for he, too, had in some ways overstepped his instructions during the extraordinary mission he had undertaken against Kohlhaas. If one were to single out the large number of those who had brought about the present state of embarrassment, he himself would have to be included among them and called to account by the sovereign for what had occurred at Mühlberg.

As the elector went over to his table with a look of uncertainty in his eyes, the cupbearer, Herr Hinz von Tronka, took the floor and spoke: He could not understand how men of such wisdom as were assembled here could fail to see the course that was dictated by the situation. From what he understood, the horse dealer had promised to disperse the band with which he had attacked the country, in return for nothing but a safe conduct to Dresden and a renewed investigation of his case. But this did not entail granting him an amnesty for this criminal act of private vengeance, two legal concepts which both Dr. Luther and the council of state seemed to confuse. Slyly putting his finger alongside his nose, he continued, "Once the tribunal at Dresden has passed sentence on the black steeds in one way or another, nothing will prevent us from throwing Kohlhaas into prison for his acts of arson and robbery; this is a clever diplomatic move which combines the advantages of the views held by both statesmen, and is certain to receive the approval of the contemporary world and of posterity as well."

Both the grand chancellor and the prince answered the cupbearer, Herr Hinz, with a mere look. As this seemed to bring the proceedings to a close, the elector said he would like to think over the various opinions which they had brought forward before the council of state met again. It appeared that the preliminary measure Prince Christiern had mentioned had robbed the elector of all desire to send out

the punitive expedition against Kohlhaas, though the force was ready
to start; for he had a heart that was sensitive to friendship. At any
rate he kept with him the grand chancellor, Count Wrede, whose
opinion seemed to him the most practical. The count showed him
dispatches which reported that the horse dealer had now collected a
following of four hundred men, and, owing to the general discontent
that prevailed in the land because of the chamberlain's misconduct
of affairs, one could reckon with the probability that this force would
increase two- or threefold in the near future. Accordingly, the elector
decided without further deliberation to act on the advice given him
by Dr. Luther. He therefore turned over to Count Wrede the conduct of the whole Kohlhaas affair.

A few days later a poster appeared bearing the following message,
the essence of which is given here:

"We, etc., etc., Elector of Saxony, most graciously accede to the
request made to Us through the intercession of Dr. Martin Luther, to
grant a safe conduct to Michael Kohlhaas, horse dealer from the
Mark Brandenburg, to Dresden, for the purpose of reopening his
case; on condition that within three days after this date he lay down
the arms he has taken up. In the event (which is not to be expected)
that the suit regarding the black horses is rejected by the tribunal of
Dresden, the whole weight of the law shall be set in motion against
him for taking justice into his own hands. In the contrary event, however, he and his whole band shall receive grace in lieu of justice and a
full amnesty for the deeds of violence he has committed in Saxony."

Scarcely had Kohlhaas received, through Dr. Luther, a copy of
this poster, which was displayed on every public square in the land,
when he disbanded his men with gifts, words of gratitude and practical admonitions, in spite of the very conditional language in which
the document was couched. He deposited everything that he had collected as booty, whether in the form of money, arms or tools, with
the courts at Lützen, as property of the elector. He sent Waldmann
with letters to the magistrate at Kohlhaasenbrück, to buy back the
farm, if that was still possible; and he sent Sternbald to Schwerin to
fetch his children, whom he wished to have with him again. Then he
left the castle of Lützen and went to Dresden incognito, carrying with
him the remainder of his small fortune in securities.

Day was just breaking and the whole city was still asleep when he
knocked on the front door of the little property situated in the suburb

of Pirna, which remained his because of the magistrate's honesty. The old servant Thomas, who looked after the place, opened the door to him with a look of astonishment and consternation. Kohlhaas instructed him to inform Prince von Meissen at the government building that Kohlhaas, the horse dealer, was here. The prince, upon receiving the message, considered it proper to find out immediately on what footing he stood with this man. He therefore set out with a retinue of knights and retainers to visit Kohlhaas. He found that the streets leading to the horse dealer's house were already jammed by an immense throng of people. The news that the avenging angel who was prosecuting the oppressors of the people with fire and sword was there, had roused all Dresden and its suburbs. The front door had to be bolted against the press of the curious mob; boys climbed up the windows to see the incendiary-murderer at breakfast.

With the help of his guard the prince forced his way through the mob into the room in which Kohlhaas was standing, half-dressed, at a table. The prince asked him if he was Kohlhaas the horse dealer. Kohlhaas took from his belt a wallet with several papers which established his identity; these he handed respectfully to the prince with an affirmative answer, adding that, in accordance with the safe conduct granted him by the sovereign, he had come to Dresden after disbanding his force, to bring before the courts his charge against Junker Wenzel von Tronka in the matter of the black horses. The prince measured him swiftly from head to foot and then glanced at the papers in the wallet. He asked the meaning of a document drawn up by the court of Lützen concerning a deposition in favor of the electoral treasury. He asked Kohlhaas many other questions: about his children, his estate, the type of life he intended to lead in the future. The answers convinced him that the man was completely trustworthy. He therefore returned the wallet to him and assured him that nothing stood in the way of his lawsuit and that he should apply directly to the grand chancellor of the tribunal, Count Wrede, to set it in motion. "Meanwhile," said the prince after a pause, as he went over to the window and surveyed with astonishment the mass of people gathered outside, "you will have to accept a guard for the first few days to protect you both here and when you go out." Kohlhaas looked down in displeasure and was silent. As he left the window, the prince said, "Whatever comes of the matter, it's your own doing." And with that he turned to the door again with the intention of leaving the house. Kohlhaas had had time to reflect. He said, "Most gracious sir, do as you please. Give me your word that you will withdraw the guard whenever I wish it, and I shall have no objection to this measure." The prince said, that was not necessary. He singled out three soldiers and informed them that the man in whose house they were posted was entirely free; when he went out they were to follow him merely for his own protection. He took leave of the horse dealer with a condescending motion of his hand and went out.

Toward noon Kohlhaas, accompanied by the three soldiers, called on Count Wrede, the grand chancellor of the tribunal. He was followed by an immense crowd, which did him no harm, however, because it was warned by the police not to molest him. The grand chancellor received him in his antechamber in a generous and friendly spirit and conversed with him for two full hours After Kohlhaas had narrated the whole history of the affair from beginning to end, the chancellor referred him to a famous lawyer in the city, a man who was in the service of the law courts and who would draw up and submit the charges for him. Kohlhaas went directly to the lawyer's residence; here the claim was set out again in the original terms: the punishment of the junker according to law, the restoration of the horses to their former state, compensation for his damages as well as for those sustained by his man Herse, who had been killed at Mühlberg, the latter damages to revert to Herse's old mother. Kohlhaas then went home again, still accompanied by the gaping mob, determined not to leave his home unless he was called away by important business.

Meanwhile, the junker, too, had been released from his imprisonment in Wittenberg. After recovering from a dangerous erysipelas that had caused an inflammation of his foot, he was peremptorily summoned to appear before the supreme court at Dresden to answer the suit filed against him by the horse dealer Kohlhaas, whose black horses he had illegally seized and ruined. The brothers Tronka, chamberlain and cupbearer, cousins in fief of the junker, received him in their home with the greatest bitterness and contempt. They called him a wretched fellow and good-for-nothing, who was bringing shame and disgrace on the whole family. They told him that he would certainly lose his lawsuit and requested him to take immediate steps to procure the black horses, which he would be condemned to feed back to health, amidst the ridicule of the whole world.

The junker replied in a weak, quavering voice that he was the most pitiable man in the world. He swore he had known very little about the whole cursed quarrel that was the cause of his misfortune. It was all the fault of the steward and the administrator of the castle, who had made use of the horses to harvest the crops without his remotest knowledge or consent; they had ruined them by submitting them to excessive strain, partly on their own fields. As he spoke, he sat down and implored them not to drive him, by wanton insult and injury, back into the illness from which he had just emerged.

Next day the junker's cousins, Hinz and Kunz, who owned estates in the region of the razed Tronka Castle, wrote to their administrators and tenants on the junker's behalf (for what else could they do?) to gether information about the black horses, which had gone astray on that hapless day and had since completely vanished. But because of the total destruction of the place and the slaughter of almost all its inhabitants, they could learn only this: that, urged on by the flat blade of the incendiary-murderer, a groom had rescued the horses from the burning shed in which they had been standing. When the servant asked where he was to take them and what he was to do with them, he was answered by a kick from the maddened villain. The junker's old, gout-ridden housekeeper, who had fled to Meissen, replied, in answer to a written inquiry, that on the morning following that ghastly night the groom had made off with the horses for the Brandenburg border. But all inquiries were fruitless; this report seemed to be based on an error, for the junker had no servant who lived in Brandenburg or on the highway leading to it. Inhabitants of Dresden who had been in Wilsdruff a few days after the fire in Tronka Castle testified that at the time mentioned a servant had arrived there leading two horses by the bridle. The animals had looked miserable and could go no further; he had therefore left them in the cowshed of a shepherd, who undertook to restore them to their former health. For various reasons it seemed highly probable that these were the horses involved in the lawsuit. But people who came from Wilsdruff stated with certainty that the shepherd had already sold them to someone else, no one knew whom. A third rumor, which could not be traced, even asserted that the horses had already joined their maker and were buried in the knacker's pit at Wilsdruff.

Hinz and Kunz, as one may readily understand, were quite pleased with this turn of affairs. For they were now relieved of the duty of fat-

tening the horses in their stables, which they would have been compelled to do, since their cousin the junker no longer had a stable of
his own. However, to be certain, they wished to verify this fact. Accordingly, Herr Wenzel von Tronka, in his capacity as hereditary
feudal and judicial lord, sent a letter to the law court officials at
Wilsdruff. After giving a detailed description of the black horses
which, as he wrote, had been entrusted to his care and had gone
astray through an accident, he enjoined the court officials most duti-
fully to ascertain the current whereabouts of the same and to request
and urge the present owner, whoever he might be, to deliver them to
the stables of Herr Kunz, the chamberlain, in Dresden, in return for
a liberal compensation for all expenses incurred. A few days later the
man who had bought the horses from the shepherd of Wilsdruff
actually appeared with them on the market square of the city. They
were lean and unsteady on their legs, and were tied to the tail bar of
his cart. But the ill luck of Herr Wenzel, and even more, of the
honest Kohlhaas, would have it that the man was the knacker of
Döbeln.

As soon as Herr Wenzel and his cousin the chamberlain heard a
vague rumor that a man had arrived in the city with two black horses
that had been rescued from the fire at Tronka Castle, they hastily
summoned a few servants and went to the square in front of the
castle, where the man was standing. They intended to buy the horses
from him, if they were really Kohlhaas', and to take them away with
them. But one may imagine their chagrin when they found the two-
wheeled cart surrounded by a mob which, attracted by the spectacle,
grew larger from moment to moment. Amidst gales of laughter people were telling each other that these horses, which were shaking the
state to its very foundations, had already been to the knacker's! Junker Wenzel walked around the cart and examined the wretched animals, which seemed on the point of perishing; in embarrassment he
remarked that these were not the horses he had taken from Kohlhaas. But Herr Kunz, the chamberlain, gave him a look of speechless
rage that would have crushed him even if he had been made of iron.
Throwing back his cloak and baring his chain of office and his deco-
rations, he walked up to the knacker and asked him whether these
were the blacks the shepherd of Wilsdruff had turned over to him
and which Junker Wenzel von Tronka, to whom they belonged, had
requisitioned from the courts. The knacker stood with a pail of water

in his hand, watering a stout, well-fed horse that drew the cart. "The blacks?" he asked, and put down the pail, took the bit out of the horse's mouth and explained that the blacks that were tied to the tail bar had been sold to him by the swineherd of Hainichen; where he had got them, and whether they had belonged to the shepherd of Wilsdruff, he didn't know. He took up the pail again and steadied it between knee and wagon shaft; then he remarked that the clerk of the court at Wilsdruff had told him to bring them to Dresden to the house of the knights von Tronka; but the junker he had been sent to was named Kunz. With these words he turned and poured the remainder of the water on the pavement of the square. Surrounded by the jeering crowd, the chamberlain seemed unable to get the fellow to look at him; the knacker was going about his business with phlegmatic diligence. He was the chamberlain Kunz von Tronka, he said; the blacks that were to be delivered to him had to be those that had belonged to his cousin the junker; they had to be the horses that had originally belonged to the horse dealer Kohlhaas and had been brought to the shepherd of Wilsdruff by a servant who escaped with them at the time of the fire at Tronka Castle. The fellow stood there, legs apart, pulling up his trousers. The chamberlain asked him whether he knew anything about this, and whether the swineherd of Hainichen—and this was of the utmost importance—had perhaps bought them from the shepherd of Wilsdruff or from a third party who had bought them from him.

The knacker had turned to his cart to pass water; he replied that he had been sent to Dresden with the black horses to collect the money for them from the house of Tronka. He didn't understand what the man was saying; and whether they had originally belonged to the swineherd of Hainichen or to Peter or Paul or to the shepherd of Wilsdruff didn't matter to him, as they weren't stolen. With these words, holding his whip across his broad back, he strode off toward a tavern that stood on the square, to appease his hunger with some breakfast.

The chamberlain did not know what in the Lord's name he was to do with horses that the swineherd of Hainichen had sold to the knacker of Döbeln unless they were the horses on which the devil was riding through Saxony. He called on the junker to say something; the latter replied with pale, quavering lips that it was advisable to buy the horses whether they belonged to Kohlhaas or not. Cursing the father and mother who had given birth to him, the chamberlain threw back his cloak and stepped back out of the crowd, completely at a loss as to what to do or not to do. He stubbornly refused to leave the square before the mocking, gaping mob which stood there, handkerchiefs in their mouths, seemingly waiting for his departure before they burst into howls of laughter. He beckoned to Baron von Wenk, an acquaintance who was riding by on the other side of the street, to come over, and asked him to call at the home of the grand chancellor, Count Wrede, and request him to send Kohlhaas over to inspect the black horses.

It happened that when the baron arrived, Kohlhaas was in the grand chancellor's office, having been summoned there by a court messenger to make certain explanations about the deposition in Lützen. The grand chancellor rose from his chair with a look of annoyance on his face and left the horse dealer, who was personally unknown to the baron, standing alone for a moment with the papers he held in his hand. The baron told the grand chancellor of the perplexity facing the knights von Tronka. Because of the inadequate requisition made by the court of Wilsdruff, the knacker of Döbeln had turned up with horses in such a wretched and precarious condition that Junker Wenzel was compelled to doubt that they were the ones that had belonged to Kohlhaas. If they were to be bought from the knacker in spite of this, and an attempt made to fatten them in the knights' stables, it was essential that Kohlhaas should inspect them first and establish their identity beyond all doubt. "So will you be kind enough," he concluded, "to send a guard to the horse dealer's house and take him to the marketplace, where the horses are standing?"

The grand chancellor removed his spectacles from his nose and explained that he was under a double misapprehension: first, in believing that the subject under discussion could be determined only through a personal inspection by Kohlhaas; and secondly, in imagining that he, the chancellor, had authority to send Kohlhaas off under guard to any place the junker might think fit. With these words he introduced him to the horse dealer, who had been standing behind him, and asked him to take the matter up with him personally. The chancellor sat down and put his spectacles back on his nose.

Kohlhaas' features betrayed nothing of what was going on in his

mind; he said that he was ready to accompany the baron to the marketplace and inspect the horses the knacker had brought to town.
The baron had turned toward him in embarrassment; Kohlhaas
went to the table at which the grand chancellor was sitting and gave
him several more papers from his wallet concerning the deposition at
Lützen. He then took his leave. The baron, who had turned a fiery
red and walked over to the window, now likewise took his leave from
the chancellor. The two men then went to the castle square, followed
by the three soldiers who had been assigned to Kohlhaas by Prince
von Meissen, and a huge throng of townsfolk. Meanwhile Herr Kunz,
the chamberlain, had insisted upon standing his ground against the
knacker of Döbeln, contrary to the advice of several friends who had
joined him. As soon as the baron appeared with the horse dealer, he
went up to Kohlhaas, and, holding his sword under his arm in a gesture of pride and dignity, asked him whether the horses that stood
behind the cart were his. The horse dealer touched his hat respectfully toward the unknown gentleman who had asked the question.
Without replying, he went up to the knacker's cart, followed by all
the knights who were present. He stopped at a distance of twelve feet
from the horses, which stood there unsteadily with drooping heads,
refusing to touch the hay the knacker had put before them. He examined them briefly, then turned back to the chamberlain and said,
"Most gracious sir, the knacker is quite right! The horses that are tied
to his cart belong to me." And with that he touched his hat again,
looked around the circle of gentlemen about him, and left the
square, followed by his guard.

At these words the chamberlain went up to the knacker, so swiftly
that the plumes on his helmet waved in the air, and threw the man a
purse full of money. The knacker stood there holding the purse in his
hand, combing his hair back from his forehead with a lead comb and
staring at the money. The chamberlain ordered one of his men to untie the horses and lead them home. At the summons of the chamberlain, the servant left a circle of friends and relatives who were in the
crowd, and, somewhat red in the face, went up to the horses, stepping over a large pile of manure that had formed at their feet. But
scarcely had he laid hands on their bridles to untie them when his
cousin, Master Himboldt, seized him by the arm with the words,
"Don't touch those knacker's nags!" and pushed him away from the
cart. Retracing his steps uncertainly over the manure pile, the man

turned to the chamberlain, who stood there speechless at this incident, and added that he would have to get a knacker's apprentice to perform a service of that sort. The chamberlain, foaming with rage, looked at the master for a moment. Then he turned, and, over the heads of the surrounding knights, called for the guard. As soon as an officer with some of the elector's men, summoned by Baron von Wenk, appeared from the castle, he briefly described to the officer the shameful rebellion the inhabitants of the city were permitting themselves and ordered him to arrest their ringleader, Master Himboldt. Taking hold of the master by the chest, he charged him with pushing and maltreating the groom, who had untied the horses upon his orders. The master deftly freed himself from the chamberlain's grip and replied, "Most gracious Sir! To teach a lad of twenty how he ought to act is not rebellion. Ask him whether, contrary to tradition and propriety, he is willing to handle these horses, if he is still willing, it's all the same to me. For all I care, he can slaughter and skin them right now."

At these words the chamberlain turned to the groom and asked him whether he had any objection to carrying out his orders, untying the horses that belonged to Kohlhaas and leading them home. The servant mumbled timidly, as he vanished amid the throng of citizens, that the horses would have to be made respectable before such a thing could be expected of him. But the chamberlain followed him into the crowd, snatched off his hat, which bore the insignia of the house of Tronka, threw it to the ground and trampled on it. He then drew his sword and beat the servant furiously with the flat of the blade, driving him from the square and out of his service. Master Himboldt cried, "Throw the murderous knave to the ground!" and while the citizens, outraged by this scene, joined together to disperse the guard, Himboldt knocked the chamberlain down from behind, tore off his cloak, collar and helmet, wrenched the sword out of his hand and with a furious heave hurled it far across the market square.

As he ran from the scene of turmoil, Junker Wenzel called in vain to the knights to help his cousin. Before they had taken a step to do so they were scattered by the press of the mob, so that the chamberlain, who had injured his head in falling, was delivered up to the fury of the crowd. He was saved only by the appearance of a troop of mounted soldiers who chanced to be passing the square and who were commandeered by the officer in charge of the elector's men to come to his aid. After dispersing the mob, the officer seized the frenzied master and sent him off to prison under guard. The unhappy chamberlain, covered with blood, was helped to his feet and taken home by two friends. This was the sad conclusion of the well-meant, sincere attempt to give the horse dealer satisfaction for the injustice he had suffered.

His business concluded, the knacker of Döbeln did not wish to stay there any longer. When the mob had dispersed he tied the two horses to a lamppost, where they stood all day in complete abandon, the butt of jest for idlers and street urchins. Because they were without shelter or food, the police finally had to take charge of them. Toward nightfall the knacker of Dresden was summoned and asked to lodge the horses in the knacker's pit until further instructions.

Although this incident could hardly be blamed on the horse dealer, it nevertheless produced, even among the moderate and better elements, a sentiment that was most ominous for the outcome of his lawsuit. His relation to the state was found to be altogether intolerable, and both private and public opinion began to form the conviction that it was preferable to commit an obvious injustice against him by quashing the whole case once more than to grant him justice in such a trivial affair, at the price of violence, merely to satisfy his insane obstinacy. The grand chancellor's excessive sense of justice, which stirred in him a hatred of the Tronka family, strengthened and extended this public feeling, thus contributing to Kohlhaas' complete ruin. It was most improbable that the horses which the knacker of Dresden was now caring for would ever be restored to the condition in which they had left the stable at Kohlhaasenbrück. But even if this could have been achieved by skill and constant care, the disgrace that such a course would bring upon the junker's family, which, as one of the first and noblest in the land, enjoyed so much political prestige, was so great that the only proper and practical course seemed to be to pay Kohlhaas the value of the horses in money. A few days later, the president of the chancery, Count Kallheim, wrote to the grand chancellor on behalf of the chamberlain, who was incapacitated by his wounds, and made this very proposal to him; whereupon the grand chancellor sent a communication to Kohlhaas in which he urged the latter not to reject such an offer if it should be made to him. But at the same time he sent a brief, curt note to the president, begging to be excused from interfering in this private matter and urging the chamberlain to make a direct approach to the horse dealer, whom he described as a very decent and modest man. The horse dealer, whose will had indeed been broken by the incident in the market square, accepted the grand chancellor's advice and was waiting for overtures from the junker or his people; he was prepared to meet them with complete good will and forgiveness for all that had happened. But the proud knights could not bring themselves to make these overtures. They were deeply embittered by the grand chancellor's reply, which they showed to the elector the following morning, when the latter visited the sick chamberlain. In a voice that was weakened and rendered pathetic by his physical condition, the chamberlain pointed out that he had risked his life to settle this affair in accordance with the sovereign's wishes. He asked whether he ought now to expose his honor to public censure by begging for arbitration and indulgence from a man who had brought every conceivable disgrace and opprobrium on him and his family. The elector read the letter; then asked Count Kallheim in embarrassment whether the tribunal was not authorized to take the position, without consulting Kohlhaas at all, that the horses could not be restored to health, and to convert the sentence into a money payment as if they were dead. The count replied, "Most gracious sir, the horses *are* dead; they are legally dead because they have no value; and they will be physically dead before they can be brought from the knacker's to the knights' stables." The elector put the letter in his pocket and said he would speak to the grand chancellor about the matter. The chamberlain half sat up and grasped the sovereign's hand in gratitude. The prince soothed the sick man, urged him to take care of his health, rose from his chair with a gracious gesture toward the patient and left the room.

This was the situation in Dresden when a second storm, a more serious one, began gathering over poor Kohlhaas from the region of Lützen; and the crafty knights were skillful enough to direct it toward his unlucky head. Johann Nagelschmidt, one of the men whom Kohlhaas had hired and then discharged when the elector issued his amnesty, had found it profitable to remuster part of the lawless gang on the Bohemian border a few weeks later, men who were ready to commit any outrage, and to continue on his own the trade that Kohlhaas had taught him. This worthless fellow styled himself Kohlhaas' vice-regent, partly to inspire the pursuing constabulary with fear, partly to lure country folk in the usual manner to join in his rascally deeds. With a cunning he had learned from his master, he spread the rumor that the amnesty had been violated in the case of several of Kohlhaas' men who had returned peacefully to their homes. Kohlhaas himself, he continued, had been imprisoned when he arrived in Dresden and placed under guard in the most flagrant breach of faith. Nagelschmidt therefore sent out handbills couched in language very similar to that used by Kohlhaas; they described his gang of incendiaries and murderers as a host which had arisen solely to defend the honor of God, entrusted with the task of safeguarding the amnesty granted by the elector. All this, as we have said, happened neither for the glory of God nor out of attachment to Kohlhaas, about whose fate these fellows cared nothing, but so that they might plunder and burn with impunity under the protection of such dissimulation.

As soon as the first reports of this reached Dresden, the knights could scarcely contain their joy at the new turn of events; for this put a different face on the whole matter. Through sly and disapproving innuendos they called attention to the error that had been committed in granting amnesty to Kohlhaas in spite of their urgent and repeated warnings, as though all sorts of villains had been given a deliberate signal to follow in his path. Not only did they lend credence to Nagelschmidt's pretext that he had taken up arms merely to give his oppressed master support and security; they even expressed the positive opinion that Nagelschmidt's appearance on the scene had been planned by Kohlhaas to frighten the government and to force a decision point by point in accordance with his insane stubbornness. Indeed, Herr Hinz, the cupbearer, went further still. Before a group of hunting pages and courtiers who had gathered about him after dinner in the elector's antechamber, he interpreted the dissolution of the robber band in Lützen as a damnable piece of shadow boxing. He ridiculed the grand chancellor's love of justice and proved, by several skillfully selected details, that Kohlhaas' gang was still very much in existence in the forests of the electoral duchy and was merely waiting for a sign from the horse dealer to storm out of the woods once more with fire and sword. Prince Christiern von Meissen was greatly displeased by this turn of affairs, which threatened to injure the reputation of his sovereign in a most vulnerable spot, and he went at once to consult him in his castle. He saw through the knights' plan to destroy

Kohlhaas by accusing him of new transgressions; he therefore asked permission to institute an immediate investigation into the horse dealer's doings. The latter, somewhat surprised, appeared under guard at the government office. He carried his two young boys, Heinrich and Leopold, on his arms; for only the previous day, his servant Sternbald had arrived with Kohlhaas' five children from Mecklenburg, where they had been living. A train of thought that would be too complex to unravel here had moved Kohlhaas to yield to the boys' tearful entreaties that they should be taken along to the hearing. Kohlhaas put his children on the seat beside him. The prince gave them a kindly look and asked for their names and ages; then he revealed to Kohlhaas the sort of liberties that his former servant, Nagelschmidt, was permitting himself in the valleys of the Erz Mountains. He handed Kohlhaas the so-called mandates that Nagelschmidt had issued and asked him to say what he could to justify himself. Kohlhaas was genuinely alarmed by these shameful and treasonable documents. But to a man as upright as the prince he had little difficulty in demonstrating satisfactorily how baseless the accusations against him were. As matters now stood, Kohlhaas pointed out, his lawsuit was making such excellent progress that he had no need to enlist aid from a third party. He produced letters that he carried on his person which showed how highly improbable it was that Nagelschmidt would show any inclination to give him such aid. For shortly before dissolving his band in Lützen, Kohlhaas had intended to have him hanged for committing rape and other atrocities in the countryside. The fellow had been saved only by the publication of the elector's amnesty, which ended the relation between the two men. The following day they had parted company as mortal enemies.

Kohlhaas proposed that he should publish an open letter to Nagelschmidt, a proposal which the prince accepted. The pretext, the letter declared, that he was carrying on his activity in order to maintain an amnesty that had been violated with respect to himself and his gang was a shameful and unscrupulous fabrication. He said that when he arrived in Dresden he had neither been thrown into prison nor put under guard; his lawsuit was proceeding just as he wished it to; he delivered Nagelschmidt up to the full vengeance of the law in punishment for the arson and murder he had committed in the Erz Mountains after the publication of the amnesty, and as a warning to the rabble that he had gathered about him. Kohlhaas appended to this document a few fragments from the criminal proceedings he had set in motion against Nagelschmidt in Lützen Castle as a punishment for the above-mentioned atrocities, in order to inform the public about this worthless fellow who even then had been destined for the gallows, but, as already stated, had been saved only by the publication of the elector's amnesty. Accordingly, the prince reassured Kohlhaas concerning the suspicion which circumstances had compelled him to express in this interview; he declared that, as long as he was in Dresden, the amnesty granted to Kohlhaas would not be violated in any way. After giving the boys some fruit from the table, he shook their hands, said good-by to Kohlhaas and dismissed him. Nevertheless, the grand chancellor realized the danger in which the horse dealer stood and did his utmost to bring his case to a conclusion before any new incident might complicate and confuse it. But this is precisely what the politically wily knights wished for and schemed to bring about. Whereas until now they had tacitly admitted their guilt and had concentrated their resistance upon obtaining a reduced sentence, they now began to deny this guilt altogether by cunning, twisting and pettifoggery. At one moment they claimed that Kohlhaas' horses had been detained at Tronka Castle by the warden and steward on their own responsibility; the junker had known nothing about it or had been only imperfectly informed. Then again they asserted confidently that the horses had already been afflicted with a severe and dangerous cough when they arrived at the castle; to this effect they cited witnesses whom they promised to produce. When, after extensive investigations and explanations, these arguments were refuted, they were able to produce an edict passed by the elector twelve years before, which had actually forbidden the importation of horses from Brandenburg to Saxony because of a cattle disease that had raged at the time; this was clear proof, not only of the junker's right, but indeed of his duty, to detain the horses which Kohlhaas was taking over the border.

Meanwhile Kohlhaas had bought back his farm from the honest magistrate of Kohlhaasenbrück, after reimbursing him for the slight loss he had suffered by the transaction. He wished to leave Dresden for a few days and return to his home, apparently to conclude the legal arrangements connected with the sale. But it was undoubtedly not so much the business matter that led to this decision, though the winter crop that had to be put in made it urgent enough, as the intention to test his position in these strange and critical circumstances. Perhaps there were also contributing reasons of another kind, which we shall leave for anyone who can look into his own heart to divine. He therefore called on the grand chancellor without his guard. Producing the magistrate's letters, he told the chancellor that, as it seemed he was not needed at court, he wished to leave the city and go to Brandenburg for a period of twelve days, promising to be back within that time. The grand chancellor looked down with displeasure and concern and replied he must confess that Kohlhaas' presence in Dresden was more necessary than ever just now, since the other side had brought up cunning, tricky objections and the court needed his statements and depositions on a thousand unforseeable questions. Kohlhaas, however, referred him to his attorney, who was well informed about the details of the case, promised to cut his absence down to eight days, and persisted in his request with a respectful urgency. The grand chancellor paused for a moment; then, dismissing Kohlhaas, he said curtly that he hoped he would request a passport from prince Christiern von Meissen. Kohlhaas read the grand chancellor's face only too well; it merely strengthened him in his resolve. He sat down right then and there and wrote to prince von Meissen, head of the government office, requesting a passport for an eight-day trip to Kohlhaasenbrück and back. In reply he received a decision of the government office, signed by Baron Siegfried von Wenk, captain of the castle, that his application for a passport to Kohlhaasenbrück would be submitted to His Highness the Elector and the passport issued as soon as His Highness' most gracious permission was obtained. Kohlhaas asked his attorney how it came that the governmental decision was signed by a Baron Siegfried von Wenk and not by Prince von Meissen, to whom he had addressed the application. He was told that the prince had gone to his estates three days ago, leaving the government affairs in the hands of the castle captain, Baron Siegfried von Wenk, who was a cousin of the above-mentioned nobleman of the same name. His whole situation caused Kohlhaas' heart to stir uneasily. For several days he waited for a decision about his petition, which had been submitted to the sovereign with such strange elaborateness. But a week and more passed without a decision being made; nor did the tribunal arrive at a judgment of his case, in spite of the positive tone in which it had been promised him. On the twelfth day, therefore, firmly resolved to learn the government's intentions toward him, whatever they might be, he sat down and once more made urgent representations about the passport he needed. The next day passed without bringing the expected answer. But in the evening, as Kohlhaas was pacing thoughtfully up and down his rooms, pondering his general situation and especially the amnesty which Dr. Luther had worked out for him, he stepped to the window of his small back room and looked at the little house that stood in the courtyard and which had been assigned to the guard as living quarters. He was startled to find no sign of the guard which Prince von Meissen had posted there upon his arrival. He summoned the old janitor, Thomas, and asked him what this meant. The old man replied with a sigh, "Sir, things are not as they should be. There have been more soldiers than usual today; at nightfall they surrounded the house. Two of them are standing at the front door with shields and spears; two are at the rear door in the garden; and two others are lying on a bundle of straw in the vestibule. They say they're going to sleep there." Kohlhaas changed color. Turning away, he remarked that it didn't matter, as long as they were there; would he provide them with a light when he went out into the hall, so that they could see? On the pretext of emptying a vessel, he opened the shutter of the front window and convinced himself that the old man's report was correct; for at that very moment the guard was being silently changed—a precaution no one had thought necessary before. He went to bed, though he felt little desire to sleep. He had swiftly resolved on a course of action for the following day. There was nothing he resented so much as this pretense of justice being made by the government with which he was dealing, when it was actually violating the amnesty it had solemnly promised him. If he was really a prisoner, as he was beyond all doubt, he would compel the government to issue a clear and unequivocal statement to that effect.

The following morning at dawn he sent his servant Sternbald to hitch up his wagon and drive it around to the house. He explained that he intended to drive to Lockwitz to see an old acquaintance, the manager of an estate, whom he had met a few days before at Dresden and who had invited him and his children for a visit. When the soldiers observed these preparations for departure, they put their heads together and sent a secret emissary into the city. In a few minutes a government officer appeared, followed by several policemen; they made for the house lying opposite as if they had business there. Kohlhaas, who was busy dressing the boys, noticed these movements and deliberately let the wagon stand in front of the house longer than was necessary. When he saw that the police were finished with their preparations, he came out with his children, paying no attention to what was going on around him. As he passed the troop of soldiers at the door, he told them in passing that they need not follow him. Then he lifted the boys in the wagon and kissed and comforted the tearful girls, who, according to his instructions, were to remain behind with the old janitor's daughter. But he had scarcely climbed into the wagon when the government officer and his retinue of policemen came over to him from the house across the street and asked him where he was going. Kohlhaas replied that he was going to his friend, the steward at Lockwitz, who had invited him and his two boys a few days ago to visit him in the country. In that case the officer replied, he would have to wait a few minutes; several mounted soldiers would accompany him; these were orders from Prince von Meissen. Smiling down from his wagon seat, Kohlhaas asked whether the officer thought that his person was not safe at the home of a friend who had offered him hospitality at his table for one day. The officer answered in a pleasant and cheerful tone that the danger was of course not great, and added that the soldiers would in no way be a burden to him. Kohlhaas replied earnestly that on his arrival at Dresden, Prince von Meissen had left him the choice whether he would make use of the guard or not. The officer was astonished at this information and referred, in carefully chosen phrases, to the procedure that had been followed as long as he had been there. The horse dealer told him about the incident that had led to the stationing of the guard in his house. The officer assured him that by order of the castle captain, Baron von Wenk, who was at the moment chief of police, he was dutybound to offer Kohlhaas constant protection of his person. If Kohlhaas objected to the escort, he could go to the government office to clear up what seemed to be a misunderstanding.

Kohlhaas was determined to settle the matter once and for all; he gave the officer a significant look and said he would do so. With beating heart he got out of the wagon and had the janitor take the children back into the hall. While his servant kept the wagon waiting in front of the house, Kohlhaas, the officer and his guard walked to the government office. It happened that the captain of the castle, Baron Wenk, was just then busy examining a gang of Nagelschmidt's

men who had been captured in the region of Leipzig and brought to
Dresden the night before. The knights who were with the captain
were interrogating them about various matters they wished to have
explained, when the horse dealer came in with his escort. The knights
stopped their questioning and remained silent. As soon as he saw the
horse dealer, the baron went up to him and asked him what he
wanted. Kohlhaas respectfully informed him that he intended to
have dinner at the home of the steward of Lockwitz and expressed
the wish to leave the soldiers behind, as he had no need of them. The
baron changed color, seemed to swallow something he intended to
say, and replied that Kohlhaas would do well to stay quietly at home
and, for the time being, postpone the banquet at the home of the
steward of Lockwitz. He cut the interview short by turning to the officer and assuring him that the order he had received concerning Kohlhaas was correct, and that he might leave the city only in the company of six mounted soldiers. Kohlhaas asked whether he was a prisoner and whether he was to believe that the amnesty that had been
solemnly promised him before the eyes of the whole world was broken. The baron turned toward him suddenly, his flace a flaming red,
went up close to him, looked straight at him and replied: "Yes! Yes!
Yes!" Then he turned his back to him, left him standing there and returned to Nagelschmidt's men. With that, Kohlhaas left the room.
Though he realized that the only means now left to him to save himself — flight — was made very difficult by the step he had just taken,
he nevertheless approved what he had done, because he felt it relieved him of any further need to abide by the articles of the amnesty.
When he got home he had the horses unharnessed and went to his
room, sad and shaken, followed by the government officer, who, in a
tone that aroused Kohlhaas' disgust, assured him that the whole
thing was a misunderstanding that would be cleared up shortly. At
the same time, the officer ordered his policemen to bolt all the doors
leading to the courtyard and assured Kohlhaas that the front
entrance was open as usual for his use.

Meanwhile Nagelschmidt was being hard pressed on all sides by
the constabulary troops in the forests of the Erz Mountains. He was
wholly without adequate resources to carry through a role such as he
had undertaken. He therefore hit upon the idea of drawing Kohlhaas
actively into the enterprise. A traveler had informed him fairly accurately about the position in which Kohlhaas now stood with regard

to his lawsuit. He believed that, in spite of the open hostility existing between them, he could persuade the horse dealer to enter into a new alliance with him.

Accordingly, he dispatched a man with a letter, written in German that was scarcely intelligible, to this effect: If Kohlhaas would come to the Altenburg region and take over the leadership of the band that had gathered there from the remnants of the dispersed army, he, Nagelschmidt, would undertake to provide horses, men and money for Kohlhaas' escape from his imprisonment in Dresden. He promised to be more obedient in the future and in general more orderly and better behaved. As a proof of his loyalty and devotion, he offered to come in person to the vicinity of Dresden to liberate Kohlhaas from his prison. Now, the fellow who bore this letter had the misfortune of succumbing to a fit of violent convulsions, a lifelong affliction of his, in a village close to Dresden, on which occasion the letter that he carried in his breast pocket was found by the people who came to his aid. As soon as he recovered from his attack he was arrested and taken to the government office under guard, followed by a throng of people. The castle commander, Baron von Wenk, as soon as he read the letter, went to the elector, who had with him the junkers Kunz and Hinz (the former had by this time recovered from his wounds), and Count Kallheim, the president of the chancery. These gentlemen were of the opinion that Kohlhaas should be arrested at once and brought to trial for having a secret understanding with Nagelschmidt. They proved that such a letter could not have been written unless it had been preceded by others from the horse dealer's hand, and unless they were planning a culpable and criminal alliance for the purpose of perpetrating new horrows. The elector steadfastly refused to break, merely on the basis of this letter, the safe conduct he had solemnly promised Kohlhaas. He rather leaned to the opinion that the letter indicated, with some degree of probability, that there had been no previous alliance between the two men. The most he would do in order to be certain on this point was to accept, albeit with great reluctance, the president's proposal that the letter be delivered to Kohlhaas by Nagelschmidt's messenger as if he were still a free man, in order to see whether Kohlhaas would reply to it.

Accordingly, on the following morning the messenger, who had been lodged in the prison, was brought to the government office. The castle governor gave him the letter and asked him to deliver it to

the horse dealer as though nothing had happened; and as a reward
for this he would go free and not pay the penalty he had incurred.
The fellow consented to this vile trick without any objection and appeared in Kohlhaas' room in apparent secrecy under the pretext that
he was selling crabs, which the officer had supplied to him from the
market. Kohlhaas read the letter while his children were playing with
the crabs. Under ordinary circumstances he would have taken the
scoundrel by the collar and turned him over to the soldiers who stood
guard at his door. However, with prevailing tempers, even this step
was subject to differing interpretations; moreover, he had become
completely convinced that nothing in the world could save him from
the conflict in which he was embroiled. So he looked sadly into the
fellow's familiar face, asked him where he lived, and ordered him to
return in a few hours to take back his decision concerning his
master's request. He told Sternbald, who just then appeared in the
doorway, to buy a few crabs from the man in the room. When this
business was completed and both men had left without recognizing
each other, Kohlhaas sat down and wrote a letter to Nagelschmidt
with the following content: first, he accepted Nagelschmidt's offer
concerning the command of his men in Altenburg; therefore, a
wagon with two horses was to be sent to him to Neustadt near Dresden, to liberate him from the temporary arrest in which he and his
five children were being held. In addition, he needed an extra team
of horses on the Wittenberg highway, to make a speedier escape; for
this roundabout way was the only one by which he could come to
him, for reasons too complicated to mention. He believed he could
win over by bribery the soldiers who guarded him; but in case force
should have to be used, he wanted to have a couple of spirited, capable and well-armed men waiting at Neustadt near Dresden. To
defray the costs connected with this affair he was sending along a roll
of twenty gold crowns with the messenger; when the action was completed they would settle the account more accurately. For the rest, he
rejected as wholly unnecessary Nagelschmidt's offer to be present in
Neustadt at the time of liberation. In fact, he gave Nagelschmidt
specific orders to remain behind in Altenburg and to take temporary
command of the band, which could not be without a leader. He
handed this letter to the messenger when he appeared in the late
afternoon, rewarded the man handsomely, and impressed on him the
need to take good care of the letter. His intention was to go to Ham-

burg with his five children and there take ship to the Levant or the East Indies, or wherever else the sky was blue over the heads of any people except those he knew. For, bent with grief, he had renounced the desire to have the horses restored to their former condition and he felt revulsion at having to make common cause with Nagelschmidt in such a matter.

The fellow had scarcely delivered this answer to the captain of the castle when the grand chancellor was removed from office and the president, Count Kallheim, was appointed in his stead as chief of the tribunal. Kohlhaas was arrested on an executive order of the elector and taken in heavy chains to the municipal tower. He was brought to trial on the basis of this letter, which was posted in every corner of the city. Before the bar of the tribunal a counselor, holding the letter up before him, asked him whether he recognized the handwriting; he answered, "Yes." Asked whether he had anything to say in his own defense, he cast his eyes to the ground and said, "No." He was therefore condemned to be clawed with red-hot tongs by knackers, then to be quartered, and to have his body burned between wheel and gallows.

Thus matters stood for poor Kohlhaas in Dresden when the elector of Brandenburg appeared to rescue him from the hands of superior and arbitrary force. In a note sent to the electoral chancery in Dresden the elector claimed Kohlhaas as a subject of Brandenburg. He did this after the excellent city captain, Herr Heinrich von Geusau, had told him the history of this strange, not wholly reprehensible man during a walk on the banks of the Spree River. The astonished prince pressed his companion with questions and learned of the guilt that rested on his own shoulders because of the improper conduct of his grand chancellor, Count Siegfried von Kallheim. In deep indignation the elector confronted the grand chancellor, and, finding that the latter's relationship to the house of Tronka was responsible for the whole catastrophe, dismissed him summarily with various signs of his displeasure and named Herr Heinrich von Geusau to this post.

It happened just then that the crown of Poland and the house of Saxony were living in a state of tension—we do not know why. Poland therefore repeatedly and urgently wooed the elector of Brandenburg to form an alliance in a common cause against the house of Saxony, so that Herr von Geusau, who was not unskilled in such matters, dared to hope that he could satisfy his sovereign's wish to obtain justice for Kohlhaas at any cost, without jeopardizing the general peace any more than was warranted by the interests of an individual. The grand chancellor therefore demanded the unconditional and immediate release of Kohlhaas, who was being held on the basis of a procedure that was wholly arbitrary and contrary to the principles of God and man. If Kohlhaas really was guilty, he would be judged according to the laws of Brandenburg on charges which the court of Dresden could prefer through its counsel at Berlin. He went even further and requested a passport for an attorney whom the elector wished to send to Dresden to secure justice for Kohlhaas in connection with the confiscation of his horses and other outrageous deeds committed on Saxon soil by Junker Wenzel von Tronka. In the reshuffling of diplomatic posts in Saxony, Herr Kunz, the chamberlain, had been named president of the chancery; for various reasons he did not wish to offend the Berlin court in this difficult situation he found himself in. In the name of his sovereign, who was greatly distressed by the note, he replied that they were astonished at the lack of cordiality and reasonableness, which denied the court of Dresden the right to try Kohlhaas for crimes he had committed in the realm according to the laws of that realm, inasmuch as it was well known that the said Kohlhaas owned substantial property in the capital and made no denial of being a Saxon citizen. But the crown of Poland, in support of its claims, was already massing an army of five thousand men on the Saxon border, and the grand chancellor, Herr Heinrich von Geusau, declared that Kohlhaasenbrück, the place from which the horse dealer took his name, lay in Brandenburg territory, and the execution of the death sentence that had been pronounced on him would be regarded as a breach of international law. And so, on the advice of the chamberlain, Herr Kunz, who wished to withdraw from this affair, the elector summoned Prince Christiern von Meissen from his estates, and after a brief consultation with this shrewd gentleman, decided to surrender Kohlhaas to the court of Berlin in accordance with its demand.

The prince was far from satisfied with the improper way in which affairs had been conducted; still, as he was compelled to take over the Kohlhaas case at the wish of his harried sovereign, he inquired what charges would be preferred against the horse dealer at the supreme court in Berlin. It was not possible to cite Kohlhaas' incriminating letter to Nagelschmidt because of the obscure and ambiguous circumstances under which it had been written; nor could the earlier plundering and burning be mentioned, because the handbill had announced that he had been forgiven for them. The elector therefore decided to send a report to His Imperial Majesty in Vienna concerning Kohlhaas' armed invasion of Saxony, to lodge a complaint against the infraction of the public truce he had proclaimed, and to urge His Imperial Majesty, who was of course not bound by any amnesty, to bring Kohlhaas to account before the high court at Berlin through an imperial prosecutor.

A week later the horse dealer, still in chains, and his five children, who at his request had been gathered up from foundling homes and orphanages, were loaded on a wagon and transported to Berlin under guard of the knight Friedrich von Malzahn and six mounted soldiers whom the elector of Brandenburg had sent to Dresden for the purpose. It happened that at the same time the elector of Saxony was on his way to a stag hunt that was being given for his diversion on the large estate of the district magistrate, Count Aloysius von Kallheim, at Dahme on the border of Saxony. Accompanying the elector were his chamberlain, Herr Kunz, and the latter's spouse, Lady Heloise, daughter of the district magistrate, and sister of the president of the state department, as well as other aristocratic ladies and gentlemen, hunting squires and courtiers. A group of tents with flying pennants had been pitched on a hill across the road. At tables in these tents pages and noble squires were serving the whole company, still covered by the dust of the chase, while gay music was played under an oak tree. In the midst of these celebrations the horse dealer slowly rode along the Dresden highway with his mounted escort. The knight von Malzahn, who accompanied him, had been compelled to wait three days in Herzberg because one of Kohlhaas' delicate children had become ill. Malzahn had not thought it necessary to communicate this delay to the Dresden government, as he was responsible solely to the prince whom he served. The elector was sitting beside Lady Heloise, who in her youth had been his first love. His chest was half bared, his plumed hat adorned hunter-fashion with pine twigs. The gaiety of the festival had affected his spirits; turning to the lady, he said, "Let's go and offer the poor wretch, whoever he may be, this cup of wine." Lady Heloise looked at him with her glorious eyes, stood up at once, commanded a silver vessel from a page and filled it with fruit, cake and bread, plundering the whole table

for this purpose. The entire company had already swarmed out of the
tent, carrying refreshments of all kinds, when the district magistrate
came towards them and begged them, with a look of embarrassment
on his face, to go back. The elector asked in astonishment what had
happened to upset him so. Turning to the chamberlain, the district
magistrate stammered that it was Kohlhaas in the wagon. This piece
of intelligence was altogether baffling, for it was common knowledge
that Kohlhaas had set out six days ago. Herr Kunz, the chamberlain,
took his cup of wine and, turning back to the tent, spilled the contents into the sand. The elector, his face a dark red, placed his goblet
on a plate which a page held out to him at a sign from the chamberlain. As he passed the company, whom he did not know, the knight
von Malzahn greeted them courteously and moved slowly on under
the tent ropes that were stretched across the road, in the direction of
Dahme. The hunting party meanwhile returned to the tents at the
invitation of the district magistrate, taking no further notice of the
incident.

As soon as the elector was seated, the district magistrate secretly
sent a messenger to Dahme, requesting the mayor of the town to
speed Kohlhaas on his way at once. However, as the knight insisted
upon spending the night in Dahme because of the late hour, they had
to content themselves with putting him up quietly at a farmhouse
belonging to the mayor, situated in a remote spot, and hidden
among shrubbery.

When evening came, the company, stimulated by wine and a rich
dessert, had completely forgotten the incident. The district magistrate now suggested another expedition to hunt a herd of deer that
had been sighted. The proposal was received with universal acclaim.
In couples and armed with rifles, they set off over ditches and hedges
for the nearby forest, so that Lady Heloise walked arm in arm with
the elector, led by a guide who had been assigned to them. To their
astonishment the guide led them directly to the courtyard of the
house in which Kohlhaas and the Brandenburg troopers were spending the night.

When she heard where they were, the lady said to the prince,
"Come, most gracious sovereign, come," playfully tucking the chain
that hung from his neck into his silken shirt front. "Let's slip over to
the farmhouse before the rest of the company gets here and have a
look at the curious man who is spending the night there." The prince

turned red, took her hand and exlaimed, "Heloise, what an idea!" But she looked at him in surprise, and added that no one would recognize him in this huntsman's garb and drew him away with her. At this moment a couple of hunting squires came out of the house, having satisfied their curiosity; they assured them that, because of the precautions taken by the district magistrate, neither the knight nor the horse dealer knew the identity of the party that was gathered near Dahme. The elector therefore smiled and, pulling his hat down over his eyes, said, "Folly, you rule the world, and your seat is a beautiful woman's lips."

When the couple entered the farmhouse to pay him a visit, Kohlhaas was sitting on a bundle of straw with his back to the wall, feeding rolls and milk to the child that had been taken ill in Herzberg. By way of starting a conversation the lady asked him who he was and what was wrong with the child, what crime he had committed and where he was being escorted. Kohlhaas took his leather cap from his head and gave brief but satisfactory replies to all her questions, continuing meanwhile to feed the child. The elector, who was standing behind the hunting squires, noticed a small lead capsule that hung by a silken thread from Kohlhaas' neck. During a lull in the conversation he asked Kohlhaas what the capsule was and what was in it. Kohlhaas replied, "Well, gracious sir, this capsule"—and taking it from his neck, he opened it and extracted a bit of paper that was sealed with wax—"this capsule has a strange history. It began about seven months ago, on the day after my wife's funeral, as you may have heard, when I set out from Kohlhaasenbrück to capture Junker von Tronka, who had done me a grave injustice. My expedition took me to Jüterbog, a small market town, where the elector of Saxony and the elector of Brandenburg were holding a conference concerning a matter about which I know nothing. Toward evening they had reached an agreement to their mutual satisfaction and were strolling in friendly conversation through the streets of the town, to visit the gay annual fair that was being held there at the time. They passed a gypsy woman who was sitting on a stool, telling fortunes from a calendar. They asked her jokingly whether she wouldn't tell them, too, something they would like to hear. I had just put up at an inn with my troop of men and was in the marketplace when this incident occurred. I stood in the doorway of a church behind a crowd of people, and could not hear what the strange woman told the lords. The people were whispering to each other in amusement that she didn't communicate her knowledge to everyone. A dense crowd had gathered to watch the spectacle that was in the making. Not so much out of curiosity as to make room for the curious, I stood on a bench that had been hewn out behind me out of the church portal. From this vantage point I had complete freedom of vision. But I had scarcely caught sight of the two lords and the woman, who sat before them on her stool and seemed to be scribbling something, when she suddenly stood up, leaned on her crutches, peered about among the crowd, fixed her eye on me—I had never exchanged a word with her, nor did I desire anything of her science—forced her way up to me through the whole dense throng and said, 'There! If the gentleman wants to know, let him ask you!' And with that, gracious sir, she handed me this slip of paper with her withered, bony hands. All eyes were turned on me, and I stood there startled. 'What's this honor you're bestowing on me, mother?' I said. She talked a lot of nonsense that I couldn't make out, but to my great astonishment, in the midst of it all, I heard my name mentioned: 'An amulet, Kohlhaas, horse dealer. Take good care of it, it will save your life some day,' and she vanished. Well," Kohlhaas continued good-naturedly, "to tell the truth, it didn't cost me my life in Dresden, however hard things went with me there. How I shall fare in Berlin and whether it will pull me through there too, only the future will tell."

At these words the elector sat down on a bench. The lady asked him in astonishment what was wrong with him. "Nothing, nothing at all," he replied. But the next moment he fell in a faint on the floor before she could rush to him and catch him in her arms.

At this moment the knight of Malzahn came into the room on a matter of business. "Good Heavens!" he exclaimed. "What's the matter with the gentleman?" The lady cried, "Bring water!" The hunting squires lifted him up and carried him to a bed that stood in an adjoining room. The peak of consternation was reached when the chamberlain, who had been summoned by a page, made several vain attempts to revive him and finally declared that he showed every sign of having had a stroke. The cupbearer sent a mounted messenger to Luckau for a doctor. While they were waiting, the elector opened his eyes; so the district magistrate had him transported into a carriage and moved step by step to his hunting lodge, which was situated nearby. But the journey caused the elector to faint twice more when he arrived at the lodge. Only late next morning, when the doctor arrived from Luckau, did he partially recover, but he showed decided symptoms of an approaching nervous fever.

As soon as the prince regained his senses, he half sat up in bed. His very first question was, "Where is Kohlhaas?" The chamberlain, who misunderstood the question, took his hand and told him he need not feel disturbed about this frightful man; after the strange, incomprehensible incident in the farmhouse at Dahme, the chamberlain had given orders that Kohlhaas be kept there under his Brandenburg guard. He assured the prince of his warmest sympathy, and told him that he had reproached his wife most bitterly for her irresponsible levity in bringing him together with this man. Then he asked what there was in the conversation with Kohlhaas that had moved the elector so strangely and so profoundly. The elector said he must confess that the whole unpleasant incident arose from the fact that he had caught sight of an insignificant scrap of paper in a lead capsule the man carried about on his person. He said much more by way of explaining the matter, but the chamberlain did not understand a word of it. Suddenly the elector took the chamberlain's hand between his own two, assured him that the possession of the piece of paper was of the greatest importance to him, and requested him to go to Dahme immediately and buy the paper from Kohlhaas at any price.

The chamberlain had difficulty concealing his perplexity; but he assured the elector that if the paper had any value for him, nothing in the world was more important than to keep this fact from Kohlhaas. For if the latter should ever discover it through some careless utterance, all the elector's wealth would not be adequate to buy it from the hands of this vindictive fellow, whose lust for vengeance was insatiable. To calm the agitated elector, he added that they would have to think of some other means; perhaps a third, neutral person might get it from him by a stratagem, as the villain probably was not very much attached to the paper that meant so much to the prince.

The elector, wiping the perspiration from his brow, asked whether he couldn't send to Dahme at once and halt the transportation of the horse dealer until the possession of the paper was assured, by any means whatever. The chamberlain, who could scarcely trust his senses, replied that unfortunately the horse dealer had most probably already left Dahme and was by now over the border on Brandenburg soil. Any attempt to hinder his transportation there, to say nothing of

stopping it, would cause the most unpleasant and far-reaching problems—problems that might perhaps never be solved. As the elector
sank back in silence on his pillow with a gesture of utter despair, the
chamberlain asked him what the paper contained and by what
strange and inexplicable accident he had learned that its contents
concerned him. But the elector did not answer these questions, and
merely cast ambiguous glances at the chamberlain, whose compliance in this instance aroused his distrust. He lay there tense, his heart
beating uneasily, looking down at the corner of the handkerchief he
held pensively between his hands. Suddenly he asked the chamberlain to call in hunting squire vom Stein, a young nobleman, skilled
and resourceful, whom he had often employed in affairs of a secret
nature. He had, said the elector, some other business to discuss with
him.

The junker appeared, and the elector explained the situation to
him and impressed on him the importance of the slip of paper that
Kohlhaas had in his possession. He then asked the junker whether he
wished to win his eternal friendship by procuring the paper for him
before it got to Berlin. As soon as the junker had gained a general
picture of this strange situation, he assured the elector of his readiness to serve him with all his powers. The elector then instructed him
to follow Kohlhaas; since offers of money would probably be futile,
he must skillfully lead up to a promise of life and freedom in return
for the paper. In fact, if Kohlhaas insisted, the junker might take
immediate steps, though with the utmost caution, to help him escape
from his Brandenburg captors, supplying him with horses, men and
money.

After obtaining a credential in the elector's own hand, the junker
left at once with a few men. As he did not spare his horses, he had the
good fortune to catch up with the party in a border village as Kohlhaas, his five children and the knight von Malzahn were taking a
midday meal in the open before a village house. The junker introduced himself to the knight as a stranger who was passing through
these parts and was curious to see the singular man he had in his
company. The knight at once introduced him to Kohlhaas and
invited him courteously to join them in their luncheon. The knight
left the table repeatedly to make preparations for their departure;
since his men were eating at a table on the other side of the house,
the junker soon found an opportunity to reveal his identity to Kohlhaas and to state his special mission.

The horse dealer had already learned the name and rank of the man who had fainted in the farmhouse at Dahme at the sight of the capsule. To crown the agitation into which he was thrown by this discovery, he had only to learn the secret of the slip of paper which, for various reasons, he was determined not to open from mere curiosity. He said that, in view of the unchivalrous and unprincely treatment he had received in Dresden, in spite of his complete readiness to make every possible sacrifice, he preferred to keep the slip of paper. The junker asked the reason for this strange refusal, since he was being offered nothing less than life and liberty. To this Kohlhaas replied, "Noble sir! If your sovereign came to me and said, 'I and the whole retinue of those who help me govern the country are prepared to destroy ourselves,' destroy themselves, mark you, which is of course the most fervent wish of my soul, I would still refuse him the slip of paper, which is worth more to him than his very existence, and I would say to him, 'You can bring me to the scaffold, but I can harm you, and I intend to do so.' " With these words, and death on his face, Kohlhaas summoned a trooper and offered him a good-sized portion of the meat that was left on his plate. For the remainder of the hour he spent in the place he paid no attention to the junker, who was sitting at the same table. But just as he was climbing into the wagon he turned around and gave him a farewell look.

On receiving this news the elector became so much worse that for three fateful days his physician feared greatly for his life, which was in jeopardy from so many sides. But after spending several distressing weeks on his sickbed, he recovered by virtue of his rugged constitution—at least to the extent that he could be transported into a carriage, where he was propped up on pillows and well covered with blankets and brought back to Dresden, to return once more to the business of governing. As soon as he arrived in Dresden the elector summoned Prince Christiern von Meissen and asked him how much progress had been made in briefing Judge Eibenmayer, who was to be sent to Vienna to present the case concerning Kohlhaas' violation of the public peace before His Imperial Majesty. The prince replied that, in accordance with instructions which the elector had left when he went to Dahme, Eibenmayer had been sent to Vienna when the jurist Zäuner, representing the elector of Brandenburg in the case against Junker Wenzel von Tronka, had reached Dresden.

The elector flushed, went to his desk and expressed his astonishment at this haste. As far as he could remember, he had requested that Eibenmayer's departure be delayed until a conference had been arranged with Dr. Luther, who had procured the amnesty for Kohlhaas. As he said this, he took a few letters and documents that were lying on his desk and threw them pell-mell over each other as a gesture of controlled displeasure. Prince von Meissen looked at him in astonishment for some moments and said he regretted that he had failed to carry the matter out to his satisfaction, but he could produce the decision of the council of state which had made it incumbent on him to send the attorney to Vienna at the appointed time. He added that the council had made no mention of a conference with Dr. Luther; earlier there might have been some point in negotiating with this churchman because of his intercession with Kohlhaas; but now that the amnesty had been broken before the eyes of the whole world and Kohlhaas had been arrested and delivered up to the Brandenburg courts for sentence and execution, it was meaningless. The elector conceded that the error made in sending Eibenmayer away was not serious; however, he wished that for the present the attorney should not appear as plaintiff in Vienna. He asked the prince to inform Eibenmayer of this wish by express messenger.

The prince replied that this order unfortunately came one day too late, since a report received that very day stated that Eibenmayer had already acted and submitted his brief to the state chancery in Vienna. To the elector's startled question how all this was possible in so short a time, Prince von Meissen replied that three weeks had elapsed since Eibenmayer's departure and that his instructions had been to proceed to a swift settlement of the affair as soon as he arrived in Vienna. Delay, the prince remarked, would in this instance have been all the more inadvisable, as the Brandenburg counsel Zäuner was proceeding against Junker Wenzel von Tronka with the utmost energy and had already submitted to the court a proposal to withdraw the horses temporarily from the knacker with a view to their future restoration, and, despite all the objections of the defense, he had won his point. The elector rang the bell and said no matter, it was of no importance; he asked a number of routine questions about the situation in Dresden and inquired what had happened during his absence. Then he shook hands with the prince, unable to conceal his agitated state of mind, and dismissed him.

That same day, the elector sent him a written request for all the documents in the Kohlhaas case, using the pretext that he wanted to handle the matter himself because of its political importance. The idea of destroying the one man from whom he could learn the content of the mysterious slip of paper was intolerable to him. He therefore composed a letter in his own hand to the emperor, begging sincerely and urgently for permission to drop the charges that Eibenmayer had brought against Kohlhaas. It was a temporary move, he explained, which he was compelled to make for important reasons that he would perhaps be able to communicate shortly.

In a note prepared by the state chancery, the emperor replied that the sudden change of sentiment that seemed to have taken place in his heart was most astonishing. The report submitted to him from the Saxon side had made the case a matter that concerned the entire Holy Roman Empire; accordingly he, as head of the empire, had felt it his duty to appear before the house of Brandenburg as plaintiff. The imperial court counsel, Franz Müller, had already gone to Berlin in his capacity as attorney to call Kohlhaas to account as a disturber of the public peace. The accusation could not possibly be withdrawn; the matter would have to take its course in accordance with the law.

This letter completely crushed the elector. Moreover, after a while a private letter arrived from Berlin, reporting that the trial had begun before the supreme court. The letter also contained the surmise that, despite all efforts on the part of counsel who had been assigned to Kohlhaas, the horse dealer would probably end on the scaffold. This report threw the elector into utter dejection; the unhappy gentleman decided to make one more effort: in a letter written in his own hand, he begged the elector of Brandenburg to spare the horse dealer's life. His pretext was that the amnesty that had been solemnly promised to Kohlhaas did not permit the carrying out of a death sentence on him. He assured his correspondent that, despite the apparent vigor with which he had been proceeding against Kohlhaas, it had never been his intention to let the man die; and he described to him how disconsolate he would be if the protection which Berlin claimed it wished to grant him should finally, by a strange turn of events, be more harmful to him than if he had stayed in Dresden and been tried under Saxon law.

The elector of Brandenburg found much in this document that was obscure and ambiguous. He replied that the energy with which the advocate of His Imperial Majesty was proceeding simply did not

permit of deviation from the strictest prescription of the law in accordance with the wish expressed by the elector of Saxony. He
observed that the anxiety which the elector's letter expressed really
went too far: the accusation charging Kohlhaas with the crimes that
had been pardoned in the amnesty did not stem from the elector of
Saxony who had proclaimed it, but had been brought before the
supreme court in Berlin by the imperial sovereign, who was in no way
bound by the amnesty. He pointed out, moreover, how necessary it
was to set a warning example, in view of Nagelschmidt's continuing
acts of violence, which were now extending into Brandenburg territory with unheard-of insolence. If the elector was not convinced by
these arguments, he must turn to His Majesty, the emperor himself;
for if a decree in favor of Kohlhaas were to be issued, it could come
only through a declaration from this source.

Grief and vexation at all these unsuccessful attempts threw the
elector into a new illness. One day, while the chamberlain was visiting him, the elector showed him the letters he had written to Vienna
and Berlin to spare Kohlhaas' life and in this way at least gain time
for getting possession of the slip of paper. The chamberlain fell on
his knees before the elector and implored him, in the name of everything he held sacred and precious, to tell him what was written on
that slip of paper. The elector asked him to bolt the door and sit
down on the bed; he took the chamberlain's hand, pressed it to his
heart with a sigh and began as follows:

"Your wife has already told you, I hear, that on the third day of
the conference we held at Jüterbog, the elector of Brandenburg and I
met a gypsy woman. You know what a lively man the elector is.
There had been a lot of exaggerated talk at dinner about this strange
woman and her art. So he decided to destroy her reputation through
a joke he would play on her before the eyes of the public. He walked
up to her table with his arms crossed and requested that her prophecy
about him be accompanied by a sign that could be verified that very
day. Otherwise he could not believe her words, even if she were the
Roman sibyl herself. The woman measured us swiftly from head to
foot and replied that the sign would be this: The great-horned roebuck that was being raised in the park by the gardener's son would
come toward us on the market square even before we left it. Now,
you must know that this roebuck, which was being prepared for the
Dresden kitchen, was kept under lock and key in an enclosure that

was fenced in by high boards, overshadowed by the oak trees of the park. Moreover, the park and the garden that led to it were kept carefully locked, because they contained small game and fowl, so that it was simply not possible to imagine how the animal could confirm the gypsy's prophecy by coming toward us in the square where we were standing. However, to prevent any trickery that might possibly be practiced, and to heighten our fun by making everything the gypsy would say absolutely ridiculous, we had a conference, after which the elector sent a messenger to the castle with orders that the roebuck should be killed at once and prepared for a meal in the near future. Then he turned back to the woman, in whose presence the matter had been negotiated in loud tones, and said, 'Well now! What can you tell me about my future?' The woman looked at his hand and spoke: 'Hail, my Electoral Prince and Sovereign! Your Grace will reign long, the house from which you are descended will endure a long time, and your posterity will become great and glorious and attain power above all the princes and lords of the world!' The elector looked at the woman thoughtfully a while; then, with a step in my direction, he muttered in an undertone that he was half sorry he had sent the messenger off to prove the prophecy untrue. Money was meanwhile pouring into the old woman's lap from the knights in the elector's retinue, who were shouting with joy. The elector put his hand in his pocket and added a gold coin to the pile. Then he asked the woman whether the greeting she had for me had the same silver ring as his. The woman opened a box that stood beside her, arranged the coins in it neatly and elaborately according to their denomination and quantity, then locked the box again. She looked at me, shading her eyes from the sun as if it were a burden to her. I repeated the question and, while she was studying my hand, I said jokingly to the elector: 'For me, it seems, she has no pleasant news to impart.' She picked up her crutches, with their help raised herself from the stool, came up to me, cupped her hands mysteriously and whispered audibly into my ear, 'No.' 'Really.' I said in some confusion, and drew back a pace before the creature, who sat down again on the stool behind her, with a cold and lifeless look as though it came from marble eyes. 'What is the source of the danger that threatens my house?' The woman took a piece of charcoal and a paper in her hand, crossed her knees, and asked if I would like her to write it down for me. I was truly embarrassed and, because under the circumstances I had no other choice in the matter, I replied: 'Yes, do that.' She replied, 'Very well then. I'll write down three things for you: the name of the last ruler of your house, the year in which he will lose his kingdom, and the name of him who will wrest it from him by force of arms.' This she did before the eyes of the populace; then she got up, sealed the paper with wax, which she moistened on her withered lips, and pressed upon it a leaden ring she wore on her middle finger. As you may imagine, I was more curious than words can explain; as I was on the point of seizing the paper, she spoke: 'No, no, Your Highness!' She turned, raised one of her crutches and said: 'You may redeem the paper, if you so wish, from that man there with the plumed hat who is standing on the bench at the church entrance behind all the people.' With that she left me standing on the square, speechless with astonishment, before I had properly grasped what she was saying. She shut the box that stood behind her, slung it over her shoulder and disappeared in the crowd that surrounded us, so that I could not see what she was doing.

"To my profound relief the knight whom the elector had sent to the castle returned at this very moment and reported with some amusement that the roebuck had been killed before his eyes by two hunters and carried off to the kitchen. Taking my arm to lead me away from the square, the elector remarked, 'Well now, the prophecy was nothing but a common swindle and not worth the time or gold it cost us.' But how great was our astonishment when we heard, even as these words were uttered, a shout on the market square, with all eyes turned on a big butcher's dog, who had seized the roebuck by the neck in the kitchen, had dragged it away, pursued by servants and kitchen maids, and finally dropped it on the ground three feet before us. And so the woman's prophecy had really been fulfilled, as a pledge of the truth of everything she had predicted for me. The roebuck had really come to meet us, though, to be sure, it was dead.

"The lightning that strikes from heaven on a winter day cannot be more destructive than this sight was for me. As soon as I could shake off the company in which I found myself, my first effort was to seek out the man with the plumed hat whom the gypsy woman had pointed out to me. But after three days of incessant searching, none of my men could give me the remotest clue to his identity. And now, my friend, I saw the man with my own eyes, a few weeks ago, in the farmhouse at Dahme." With these words he let go of the chamberlain's hand and sank back on the bed, wiping the perspiration from his brow.

The chamberlain considered it futile to cross and correct the elector's conception of this incident by his own, so he begged him to try to get possession of the paper in some way and then abandon the fellow to his fate. But the elector replied that he simply saw no way of achieving this, although the thought of doing without the slip of paper, and of seeing the information it contained perish with this man, was driving him to the verge of misery and despair. The chamberlain then asked whether the elector had made any attempt to locate the gypsy woman. The elector replied that, using a false pretext, he had issued an order to the government office to search for the woman in every corner of the electorate; the search was still going on, but in vain. For reasons he refused to divulge, he expressed doubt that the woman was in Saxony at all.

Now it happened that the chamberlain intended to take a trip to Berlin in the matter of some considerable estates that had been left to his wife in Neumark by Count Kallheim, the deposed grand chancellor, who had died shortly after his dismissal from office. The chamberlain felt a genuine affection for the elector; so, after some reflection, he asked him whether he would give him a free hand in the matter. The elector took his hand and pressed it warmly to his heart, with the remark: "Put yourself in my place and secure the paper for me." After turning over his affairs to a colleague, the chamberlain speeded his departure by several days and set out for Berlin, accompanied by a few servants, but leaving his wife behind.

As we said, Kohlhaas had meanwhile arrived in Berlin and been lodged in a prison reserved for knights, upon special orders from the elector of Brandenburg. Here he lived, as comfortably as could be expected, with his five children. As soon as the imperial counsel arrived from Vienna, the horse dealer was brought before the bar of the supreme court and charged with a violation of the public peace proclaimed in the empire. In his defense Kohlhaas claimed that, in view of the agreement made at Lützen between him and the elector of Saxony, it was illegal to proceed against him because of his armed attack on Saxony and the deeds of violence that had accompanied that attack. But he soon learned better: His Imperial Majesty, whose counsel was acting here as prosecutor, could not take cognizance of this arrangement. When the state of affairs was explained to him and he was assured that the Dresden group was ready to give him full satisfaction in his suit against Junker Wenzel von Tronka, he readily accepted the situation.

So it happened that, on the very day on which the chamberlain arrived, sentence was pronounced on Kohlhaas and he was condemned to be brought from life to death with the sword—a sentence that no one believed would be carried out, lenient though it was, because of the complexity of the situation. Indeed, in view of the good will the elector bore Kohlhaas, the whole city hoped that a decree from him would inevitably commute the death sentence into a long, severe term of imprisonment.

The chamberlain realized that if he was to carry out the wish of his sovereign, no time must be lost. He began his quest by appearing before a street window of Kohlhaas' prison in his ordinary court dress. Kohlhaas was standing at the window, looking idly at the passersby in the street. The chamberlain took special pains to show himself clearly and unmistakably; a sudden movement of Kohlhaas' head convinced him that he had been noticed. He was particularly pleased to see Kohlhaas move his hand involuntarily to his chest, where the capsule hung. He felt that the emotions which were stirring in Kohlhaas' breast at that moment were sufficient preparation for the next step in his attempt to procure the paper.

He sent for an old huckster woman who hobbled around on crutches and whom he had noticed on the streets of Berlin in the company of a group of ragpickers; she seemed to him to approximate in age and dress the gypsy woman the elector had described to him. On the assumption that Kohlhaas had not studied very carefully the features of the crone who had fleetingly appeared before him to hand him the slip of paper, he decided to substitute this woman for her and have her, if possible, play the part of the gypsy woman before Kohlhaas.

He trained her for her part by informing her in detail of all the circumstances in the encounter between the elector and the gypsy woman in Jüterbog. Because he did not know how far the original gypsy had gone in her revelations to Kohlhaas, he was careful to impress on her memory the three mysterious items contained in the paper. He instructed her in the stray, half-intelligible phrases she was to let drop before Kohlhaas concerning certain preparations that had been made to get possession of the paper, by trickery or force, be-

cause it was of the utmost importance to the Saxon court. And he
charged her to procure the paper from Kohlhaas, on the pretext that
it was no longer safe in his possession and that she would keep it form
him during the next fateful days. The huckster woman at once
undertook the execution of the matter upon promise of a considerable reward, of which the chamberlain had to pay her a part in
advance.

The mother of Kohlhaas' servant Herse, who had been killed at
Mühlberg, visited Kohlhaas occasionally with the permission of the
government. The old huckster woman had known her for some
months; and so she succeeded, a few days later, in securing admission
to the horse dealer by giving the prison warden a small gift.

When the woman walked into his room, Kohlhaas thought he recognized the old gypsy woman who had given him the paper in Jüterbog by a seal ring she wore on her hand and a coral chain that hung
from her neck. As probability is not always on the side of truth, it
chanced that something had taken place which we report, but permit
anyone who feels so inclined to doubt. The chamberlain had made
the monstrous error of picking from the streets of Berlin none other
than the original mysterious gypsy woman whom he wished to have
impersonated.

At any rate the woman, supporting herself on her crutches,
stroked the cheeks of Kohlhaas' children, who were frightened by her
strange appearance and who clung to the skirts of their father's coat.
She explained that she had returned some time ago from Saxony to
Brandenburg, and had heard that the chamberlain was incautiously
making inquiries about the gypsy woman who had been in Jüterbog
the previous spring. She had therefore gone to him at once under an
assumed name and offered to undertake the business he wished carried out. The horse dealer noticed a strange resemblance between
her and his late wife Lisbeth, so that he felt like asking her whether
she was his wife's grandmother. For not only were her features and
her bony hands still beautiful but the use she made of her hands in
talking reminded him most vividly of Lisbeth; he even noticed that
she had a birthmark on her neck like one that his wife had had.
Absorbed in strange thoughts, he invited the old woman to sit down,
and asked what in the world brought her here on behalf of the chamberlain. Kohlhaas' old dog sniffed about the old woman's knees; she
scratched his back with her hand and he wagged his tail. She replied

that the job the chamberlain had assigned to her was to find out for him the mysterious answers to the three questions that were so important to the Saxon court; she was to warn Kohlhaas of an envoy from Saxony who was in Berlin for the purpose of getting possession of the paper; and she was to procure the said paper from him under the pretext that it was no longer safe on his chest where he was carrying it. But her purpose in coming here was to tell him that the threat to obtain the slip from him by cunning or force was absurd and a sheer fraud. He was under the protection of the elector of Brandenburg, in whose custody he stood, and had absolutely nothing to fear for the slip of paper. In fact the paper was far safer with him than with her; he must beware of letting anyone get it from him under any pretext whatsoever. However, she concluded that she considered it wise for him to use the paper for the purpose for which she had given it to him at the Jüterbog fair. He ought to accept the proposal that Junker vom Stein had made to him at the Saxon-Brandenburg border and deliver the paper to the elector of Saxony in return for his life and liberty, since the paper was of no further use to him.

Kohlhaas, who exulted in the power that had been given him to inflict a mortal wound on the heel of his adversary at the moment he himself was being trampled into the dust, replied, "Not for all the world, mother, not for all the world!" He pressed the old woman's hand and wished to know what answers to these tremendous questions the slip of paper contained. Lifting to her lap the youngest child, who had squatted down at her feet, the woman said, "Not for all the world, Kohlhaas, the horse dealer, but for this lively little fair-haired boy!" And she laughed to the child, caressed and kissed him, while he looked at her wide-eyed, and handed him an apple from her pocket with her withered hands.

Kohlhaas said in some confusion that his children would praise his conduct when they grew up and that he could do nothing better for them and their grandchildren than to hold on to the paper. Moreover, he asked, after the experience he had had, who would safeguard him against a new deception; he might end by surrendering the slip of paper uselessly to the elector, as he had recently done with the troops he had assembled at Lützen. "I don't intend to exchange my word with a man who has broken his to me once already. Only an order from you, a definite and unequivocal one, my good mother, will separate me from this little slip of paper, which has given me such wonderful satisfaction for all my suffering." The woman set the child on the floor and remarked that he was right in many respects and could do as he pleased. And with that she picked up her crutches and started to go. But Kohlhaas repeated his question concerning the content of the strange paper. She answered casually that he could open it himself, although that would constitute idle curiosity. He wished to question her about a thousand other matters before she left him: who she really was, how she came by her knowledge, why she had refused to give the magic paper to the elector, for whom she had after all written it, but had given it to him, Kohlhaas, out of so many thousands of people, although he had had no interest in her science. But just at this moment a noise became audible, made by several police officials going up the stairs. Seized by a sudden fear that she might be found in these rooms, the woman replied, "Good-by, Kohlhaas, good-by! When we meet again, you shall not lack information about all these things!" And turning toward the door, she kissed each child in turn, cried, "Good-by, children, good-by," and went off.

Meanwhile the elector of Saxony, a prey to his wretched thoughts, had summoned two astrologers named Oldenholm and Olearius, who at that time enjoyed great renown in Saxony, and consulted them about the content of the mysterious piece of paper that was so important to him and to the whole race of his posterity. After a profound investigation carried on for several days in the castle tower at Dresden, the two men could not agree whether the prophecy referred to later centuries or to the present time; or whether it referred to the crown of Poland, relations with which were still very strained. This learned disagreement, far from soothing the uneasiness (not to say despair) in which the unhappy lord found himself, merely served to heighten it to a degree that was finally quite unbearable. Added to this was the fact that the chamberlain now asked his wife, who was on the point of following him to Berlin, to inform the elector, as diplomatically as possible, before she left, that he had utterly failed in his attempt to get the slip of paper through the agency of a woman who had since vanished. Kohlhaas' death sentence had been carefully reviewed and signed by the elector of Brandenburg and the execution fixed for the day after Palm Sunday.

Upon receiving this intelligence the elector, his heart rent by grief and remorse, a victim of utter despair, locked himself up in his room and for two days, totally weary of life, touched no food. On the third

day he suddenly vanished from Dresden, merely leaving a brief message for the government office that he was going on a hunting expedition with the prince of Dessau. Where he really went, whether he
made for Dessau, we cannot determine, since the chronicles from
which we have drawn our report strangely contradict and neutralize
each other at this point. This much is certain: the prince of Dessau
was at this time in no condition to go hunting; he lay ill in Braun-
schweig at the home of his uncle, Duke Heinrich. Moreover, on the
evening of the next day, Lady Heloise arrived in Berlin at the house
of her husband the chamberlain, Herr Kunz, accompanied by a
Count von Königstein, whom she announced as her cousin.

Meanwhile, upon orders of the elector, the death sentence had
been read to Kohlhaas, his chains had been removed, and the documents dealing with his estate, which had been confiscated in Dresden, were restored to him. The counsel the court had assigned to him
asked him how he wished to dispose of his property after his death.
With the aid of an attorney Kohlhaas made a will in favor of his children, naming his good friend the magistrate of Kohlhaasenbrück as
their guardian. The peace and contentment of his last days was un-
equaled; for by a special ordinance of the elector, the prison in which
he was kept was opened to all his friends (and he had many in the
city), who had free access to him day and night. He even had the
satisfaction of receiving the theologian Jacob Freising in his prison
cell, bearing a very remarkable letter (which, however, has been lost)
written by Dr. Luther in his own hand. From this churchman, aided
by two Brandenburg deacons, he received Holy Communion.

And now the fateful Monday after Palm Sunday appeared and
found the city still stirred by a hope for an edict of clemency for Kohlhaas. On this day Kohlhaas was to atone to the world for his all too
rash attempt to secure justice for himself in it. As he stepped out of
the prison gateway under heavy guard, with his two boys on his arm
(he had specifically asked for this favor from the court), led by the
theologian Jacob Freising, he was greeted by a mournful throng of
acquaintances, who shook hands with him and bade him farewell.
The keeper of the elector's castle stepped forward, a dazed look on
his face, and gave him a sheet of paper which, as he said, had been
handed to him by an old woman. Kohlhaas gave the man, whom he
scarcely knew, a look of surprise and unfolded the sheet, whose seal,

imprinted in the wax, at once reminded him of the old gypsy woman. But who can describe his astonishment upon reading the following words: "Kohlhaas, the elector of Saxony is in Berlin. He is already at the place of execution and can be identified, if it is of any importance to you, by his hat, which is adorned with blue and white plumes. I need not tell you why he has come; he intends to dig up the capsule after you are buried and learn the contents of the slip of paper concealed on it. — Your Lisbeth."

Kohlhaas turned to the keeper of the castle in utmost consternation and asked him whether he knew the strange woman who had given him the paper. The keeper replied, "Kohlhaas, the woman — " and stopped for some strange reason, trembling in every limb. The surge of people got between him and Kohlhaas, so that the man's words were lost to him.

When he arrived at the place of execution, he found the elector of Brandenburg and his retinue already there, including the grand chancellor, Herr Heinrich von Geusau — all on horseback, surrounded by an immense throng. At the elector's right was the imperial counsel Franz Müller with a copy of the death sentence in his hand; at his left stood Kohlhaas' own counsel, the jurist Anton Zäuner, holding the verdict of the Dresden court of appeals. In the middle of the semicircle formed by the throng of spectators stood a herald with a bundle of effects and the two black horses, sleek with good health and pawing the earth with their hooves. For the grand chancellor, Herr Heinrich, had pushed the suit which he had brought in Dresden on behalf of his sovereign against Junker Wenzel von Tronka, and had won it point by point, without yielding an inch from his original position. The horses had been made honorable by having a flag waved over their heads and been withdrawn from the custody of the knacker who had been feeding them. They had been fed back to their former state by the junker's men and turned over to the attorney on the Dresden market place in the presence of a commission which had been established especially for this purpose.

When Kohlhaas, accompanied by the guard, was brought up the hill to the place where the elector stood, the sovereign spoke: "Well, Kohlhaas, this is the day on which justice is being done to you. Look, I am returning to you everything that was taken from you by force at Tronka Castle and which I, as your sovereign, was duty-bound to procure for you again: the black horses, the neckerchief, the guilders, the linen, even the cost of the medication for your man Herse, who was killed at Mühlberg. Are you satisfied with me?"

At a nod from the grand chancellor, the Dresden verdict was handed to Kohlhaas, who set his two children down on the ground beside him and proceeded to read it with glowing eyes. Since he found in it also a clause which condemned Junker Wenzel to two years in prison, he knelt down at a distance from the elector with his arms crossed over his breast, overcome by emotion. He stood up and, putting his hand in the grand chancellor's lap, assured him joyfully that his dearest wish on earth had been fulfilled. He went up to the horses, patted them and stroked their sleek necks. Coming back again to the grand chancellor, he announced happily that he bequeathed them to his two sons, Heinrich and Leopold.

The grand chancellor, Herr Heinrich von Geusau, looked down at him benignly from his elevated seat and promised in the name of the elector that his last wish would be held sacred. He then asked Kohlhaas to dispose as he wished of the other effects contained in the bundle, whereupon Kohlhaas called Herse's mother, whom he had seen on the square, from the throng of spectators and, handing her the effects, said: "There, mother, this belongs to you!" And he presented her with the sum of money which the bundle contained as damages for himself, to support her in her old age.

The elector cried: "Now, Kohlhaas the horse dealer, you have received satisfaction in this form; make ready to render satisfaction to His Imperial Majesty, whose counsel stands here, for disturbing the peace of the land." Kohlhaas took off his hat, threw it on the ground, and said he was prepared to do so. He raised his two children from the ground, pressed them tightly to his breast and handed them over to the magistrate, who led them away, shedding silent tears.

Kohlhaas then went to the block. He was just untying his kerchief and unbuttoning his doublet, when a hasty glance at the circle of spectators directly in front of him revealed to him the familiar man with the blue and white plumes, half-hidden from view by two knights who stood in front of him. To the surprise of the guard, Kohlhaas suddenly stepped forward, went up close to the gentleman, detached the capsule from his chest, took out the slip of paper, broke the seal and read it. Then, looking directly at the gentleman in the white and blue plumes, who was already indulging himself in sweet expectations, he put the paper into his mouth and swallowed it. At this sight the man in the blue and white plumes fell down in a fit of convulsions. While he was being lifted to his feet by his two astounded companions, Kohlhaas turned back to the block, where his head fell under the executioner's axe.

Here the story of Kohlhaas ends. The body was put in a coffin amidst the general mourning of the populace and given a decent burial in the suburb churchyard. Meanwhile the elector summoned the sons of the deceased and made them knights, explaining to the grand chancellor that he intended to raise them in a school for pages. The elector of Saxony soon returned to Dresden, shattered in body and mind. The rest of his fate is a matter of history. Of Kohlhaas' descendants, however, some were still living in Mecklenburg in the last century, hale and happy.

Ernst Theodor Amadeus Hoffmann

1776 — 1822

He was known as "Gespenster [spook] Hoffmann." The epithet carried a pejorative connotation; it ranked his work as entertainment rather than high literature, and its author as a purveyor of crime and mystery fiction and "Gothic" tales. Today we know that Hoffmann is a major figure in world literature, for his influence has extended far beyond the boundaries of German letters.

Hoffmann was born and raised in Königsberg, East Prussia, the child of emotionally unstable parents. He grew up in the house of his grandmother in a predominantly female and loveless environment. He received his early education from an eccentric uncle. Music played a prominent role in it: he learned to play the organ, the piano and the violin; he had a fine tenor voice and sang in choirs. He also received competent instruction in drawing, for which he demonstrated a superior talent. He studied law while giving music lessons, writing, composing, drawing. When he had completed his legal studies, he held a series of judicial posts in Prussian Poland. Life in the provinces was financially precarious and boring. His relations with women added to his misery; he finally married a Polish girl who was a faithful drag on him to the end of his life. For five years (1808-13) he served as orchestra conductor and musical and stage director of the theater in Bamberg; he also acted as scene painter, stage machinist, and he composed music. Here he began to write and publish is first stories. From Bamberg he went to Dresden as the musical director of a theater. He witnessed the last act of the Napoleonic drama; the disorder of war affected his fortunes but not his creative genius, for throughout the turbulent events around him he went on writing fiction and music. In 1814 he was offered a judicial post in Berlin; he accepted and worked his way up steadily in the Prussian service, ending as a Councillor of the Supreme Court. He devoted all his spare time to literature and produced the bulk of his literary production in these last years.

But misfortune clung to him. Freed from financial care at last, he faced prosecution for refusing to let the government break the law. His health became precarious, aggravated by heavy drinking. He died at the age of forty-six.

This highly gifted, versatile man was an able jurist, exemplary civil servant, and an accomplished virtuoso in several arts — these, however, did not include the art of living. Grotesque in shape and ugly in appearance, he compensated for his physical deficiencies by forming deep romantic attachments. His temperament alternated between exaltation and depression, between a bohemian abandon and a hermit-like withdrawal into the concentration that artistic creativity demands. Dualism or division is the key to his psyche. He was both a *Bürger*,* with a strong sense of order and duty, and a rebellious artist, impatient of regimentation. In him a powerful idealizing imagination was at war with a sharp, abrasive intellect, which expressed itself in satire and grotesque humor, but at times also in the benign humor of Sterne, Jean Paul, and Dickens.

Hoffmann had a Manichaean view of life: good and evil are engaged in perpetual warfare. Evil is "the enemy," an external force or forces (demons, nature spirits) that attack especially noble men in their quest for self-perfection. But the enemy often assumes more concrete form as the bourgeois philistine, the pedantic rationalist, or the pseudoartist. He works through mechanization, atomization of life, by destroying the soul through technology and specialization; and by frustrating the true artist through the intermediacy of philistines, pseudoartists, and snobbish aristocrats.

But the enemy does not always assume the form of an external force; sometimes he is immanent in the psyche of a noble man or woman. An example is Don Juan, whom Hoffmann, in a famous novella, depicts as an excessive idealist who strives to realize the ideal of love in this life and thereby commits the sin against the Holy Ghost, ending as a libertine. It is the syndrome that Goethe treated in *Faust*, and which is a basic motif in romantic literature.

Hoffmann subscribed to Rousseau's myth of cultural pessimism: civilization represents a fall from a pristine, idyllic state of nature into a debased consciousness guided by intellect. In this fallen state

*This term and those in the preceding sentence are explained in the headnote to Thomas Mann, *The Buffoon*.

of culture, children and artists alone represent health and the ideal. But he never yielded wholly to Rousseauism; the other side of him, the realistic, was too strong. So he presents the two antagonistic worlds in conflict. The function of art is to reintegrate the world, to bring harmony out of the prevailing dualism. Sometimes, in his fairy tales, he depicts such ultimate harmony after the inevitable conflict. More often, in his "realistic" tales, the artist-idealist ends in madness or death.

The actual representation of these metaphysical themes takes the form of psychological states that are subtle and modern: ambivalent anxiety, produced by attraction and repulsion in the same person as in *Der Magnetiseur* (*The Mesmerist*); the transformation of sheer negativism into a more productive Christian sense of guilt; a feeling of dread before the uncanny; the irritability, anxiety, fear bordering on despair, caused by the petty frustrations of everyday experience — what the Germans call "the malice of objects" (*die Tücke des Objekts,* as in the opening pages of *Der goldene Topf, The Golden Pot*). It is not surprising therefore that modern psychiatry has found a fertile field of research in Hoffmann's writings.

Much of Hoffmann's fiction deals with the artist in society. It has been a common theme in German literature since Goethe's *Tasso* and was particularly dear to the Romantics, not only in Germany. But Hoffmann gave it a depth and intensity that we do not meet again until Thomas Mann. The artist as the tormented genius, frustrated by ignorant and malevolent society, thwarted by the very forces of nature, which assume the shape of evil demons; the false artist who, like Cardillac, is ridden by greed and driven to commit horrible crimes; the would-be artist who thinks he was called but who was not chosen; the artist who creates an ideal dream woman, only to find that she is a mechanical doll made by her technician father — these are some of the themes he treats. In most of them the supernatural or parapsychological element is joined to the artistic theme. In others the demonic or irrational is the principal motif.

Das Fräulein von Scudery (*Mademoiselle de Scudéry*) was Hoffmann's fifth novella dealing with artists. The first sketches for it date back to March 1818. It appeared in 1820 in an annual literary miscellany. For the historical background Hoffmann read various German and French sources, including Voltaire's *Siècle de Louis XIV*.

The novella belongs to a special category in Hoffmann's work, to those stories in which the supernatural plays at most an incidental role. The influence on Cardillac's character resulting from the experience that his mother had during her pregnancy does border on the supernatural, but essentially the novella is a tale of crime and punishment, of false accusation and the avoidance of a disastrous miscarriage of justice.

This novella has been generally interpreted as portraying *the* artist in conflict with society. Cardillac is an *artiste maudit* who is driven by forces beyond his control to commit heinous crimes against innocent people who admire his genius and are willing to afford him every possibility for expressing it. He is not genius starving in a garret. The finest craftsman of his age, Cardillac could enjoy wealth and prestige, and find domestic happiness through his beautiful, angelic daughter. Nor is he a Robin Hood with a social conscience that has gone out of control. It is a hereditary curse that drives him to crime and to his ultimate destruction. He is even seen as anticipating the kind of artist whom Thomas Mann depicted in his early work, a problematical being who feels inferior to the philistine *Bürger*.

We must ask why Hoffmann called his story *Mademoiselle de Scudéry* and not "Cardillac" or "Olivier Brusson," since all three gifted artists play leading roles in the action. Brusson and Mademoiselle are free from any taint of crime; for Brusson's failure to denounce Cardillac to the authorities has strong mitigating circumstances. Mademoiselle de Scudéry is, of course, an artist of wholly unblemished character. So any interpretation that sees this novella as dealing with *the* artist is untenable.

Suppose we take Hoffmann's title seriously; what then results is a psychological-ethical study of innocence and the loss of innocence — a theme common enough in Hoffmann. Mademoiselle de Scudéry is portrayed as an artist who lives in an ideal world, her own Atlantis in the very worldly-wise, even corrupt, Paris. She has the inner eye of the artist who "sees through" surface phenomena into the deeper reality of things. This vision convinces her that the two young people are innocent of crime and she undertakes to rescue them. But in the face of what seems to be irrefutable evidence she suffers a crisis of conscience much like that experienced by Michael Kohlhaas. For both the world is out of joint, the world order has failed them. For Kohlhaas this disorder stems from the fact that those who are entrusted with the administration of the law are unwilling to punish a monstrous injustice. For Mademoiselle de Scudéry it lies in the fact that one can no longer trust one's finer instincts in judging human conduct. Those who look most innocent are corrupt to the marrow. "Her soul rent [the narrator reports], alienated from the whole world, Mademoiselle de Scudéry no longer wished to live in a world full of diabolical deception. She accused Fate, which had, with bitter scorn, permitted her to strengthen her faith in virtue and loyalty for so many years, and now, in her old age, was destroying the beautiful image that had illuminated her life." It is basically Othello's cry: "and when I love thee not, Chaos is come again." The motif of Mademoiselle's intuitive faith in the innocence of the young people recurs in the later part of the novella. As she contemplates the bliss of the two lovers in the midst of their danger and misery, she says to herself that only a pure heart is capable of such happy forgetfulness. And in the end her intuition and naïve idealism triumph over the logic and "wisdom" of the worldly wise. This is the very essence of the romantic credo.

It is possible that Hoffmann set out to write a psychological study of Mademoiselle de Scudéry but ended by creating the tragic story of Cardillac. Certainly it is Cardillac who holds the center of the stage. As Cardillac's story this novella is the prototype of the crime-mystery tale. One must say that, as a detective story, it is a masterpiece but, as a psychological study, it leaves much to be desired. Certainly, to base Cardillac's pathological behavior on a compulsion that he inherited prenatally is not psychology. There is no attempt to explore or evaluate Cardillac's conduct in the face of the curse that has been laid on him. He is not even given an opportunity to tell us about his state of mind, either directly or in his confession to Olivier. Nor does Hoffmann present Mademoiselle de Scudéry's mental conflict with any of the skill he shows elsewhere in probing the state of mind of his tormented artists. As for Brusson, his scruples of conscience are barely indicated in a sentence or two. But above all, it seems clear that, in this novella, Hoffmann has not dealt with the problematic position of *the* artist in society; for the three artists involved have widely divergent reactions to art and life.

Hoffmann's work was widely admired in Europe and America. French and Russian literature felt his influence most strongly; Baudelaire, Pushkin, Gogol, Dostoevsky, Poe, and Stevenson learned from him; so did the French symbolists and surrealists and Franz Kafka. Offenbach's *Tales of Hoffmann* and Tchaikovsky's *Nutcracker Suite* have become popular classics. In 1926 Paul Hindemith composed an opera *Cardillac*, which he revised in 1952.

Mademoiselle de Scudéry

A TALE FROM THE AGE OF LOUIS XIV

In the rue St. Honoré stood the little house that was inhabited by
Madeleine de Scudéry, who was known for her graceful verses and for
the esteem in which she was held by Madame de Maintenon.

Around midnight, sometime in the autumn of the year 1680, there
was a hard and violent pounding on the front door of this house, so
that the whole entrance hall echoed the noise loudly. Baptiste, who
served in the capacity of cook, servant and doorman in Mademoiselle's small household, had, with the permission of his mistress, left
for the country to attend his sister's wedding; and so it happened that
la Martinière, Mademoiselle's chambermaid, was the only person in
the house who was still awake. She heard the repeated pounding; she
realized that Baptiste had gone away and that she and Mademoiselle
were alone and unprotected in the house. She thought of every crime
—theft, robbery, and murder—that had ever been committed in
Paris and was convinced that the commotion outside was caused by
some gang of thugs who knew that the house was unprotected; once
admitted, they would commit some evil act against the mistress; she
therefore stayed in her room, trembling and fearful, cursing Baptiste
and his sister's wedding.

Meanwhile the pounding on the door continued and Martinière
thought she could hear a voice shouting between the blows: "Open
up, for Christ's sake, open up!" At length, with mounting anxiety,
she snatched up the candlestick with the lighted candle in it and hastened out to the hall; there she quite clearly heard the voice of the
man who was pounding on the door: "For Christ's sake, open up!"
"That certainly isn't the way a robber talks," thought Martinière;

"who knows, it may be a fugitive seeking asylum with the mistress, who has a weakness for doing good. But we must be careful." She opened a window and, making her deep voice sound as masculine as she could, shouted down, who was that down there pounding on the door so late at night, waking everyone out of their sleep. In the moonlight that was just breaking through the dark clouds she perceived a tall figure wrapped in a light gray cloak, with a broadbrimmed hat pulled down over his eyes. In a loud voice that could be heard by the man below, she shouted: "Baptiste, Claude, Pierre, wake up and see what good-for-nothing is trying to demolish our house!" But a gentle, almost plaintive voice called up from below: "Oh, Martinière, I know it's you, dear woman, however you may try to disguise your voice. I know that Baptiste has gone to the country and you're alone in the house with your mistress. Do open up, fear nothing. I must absolutely speak to Mademoiselle, and this very minute." "What are you thinking of?" Martinière replied. "You wish to speak to Mademoiselle in the middle of the night? Don't you know that she went to bed long ago and that I would not wake her at any price from her first sweet slumber, which she certainly needs at her age?" "I know," said the man below, "that Mademoiselle has just laid aside the manuscript of her romance Clélie, on which she has been working tirelessly, and is now writing some verses which she intends to declaim tomorrow at Madame de Maintenon's. I beseech you, Madame Martinière, have mercy and open the door to me. You should know that what is at stake is the rescue of an unfortunate man from destruction; you should know that honor, freedom, indeed the life of a human being depend on this moment in which I must speak to Mademoiselle. Consider that your mistress' anger would be on you forever if she learned that it was you who callously refused admittance to the unfortunate man who came to implore her aid." "But why do you seek Mademoiselle's mercy at this unusual hour? Come back tomorrow at a suitable time," Martinière called down to the man below, who replied: "Does Fate care about time and the hour when it strikes like death-dealing lightning? May help be delayed when rescue depends on a single moment? Open the door to me, fear nothing from a wretched man, defenseless, forsaken by the whole world, persecuted, overwhelmed by a monstrous fate, who seeks to implore your mistress to save him from threatening danger." Martinière could hear the man below groaning and sobbing in profound distress as he uttered these words;

yet the tone of his voice was that of a young man, a gentle tone that pierced the heart. She found herself moved to the depths of her being; without reflecting any longer, she fetched the keys.

But she had hardly opened the door when the figure wrapped in the cloak burst in and, striding past Martinière, shouted in the hall in a wild voice: "Take me to Mademoiselle!" In terror Martinière raised the candlestick; the light fell on a deathly pale, frightfully contorted youthful face. Martinière could have sunk to the floor in terror when the man opened his cloak, revealing the gleaming handle of a stiletto sticking out of his breast pocket. He flashed his eyes at her and cried, even more wildly than before: "Take me to Mademoiselle, I tell you!"

Now Martinière saw Mademoiselle in imminent danger; all her love for her precious mistress, whom she also revered as a pious, devoted mother, blazed up more strongly in her heart and gave her a courage she would not have believed she possessed. She quickly shut the door of her room, which she had left open, took her position in front of it, and spoke with firmness and strength: "Really, your mad behavior inside the house fits ill with your whimpering words out there, which, as I now see, awakened my pity inappropriately. You shall not speak to Mademoiselle now. If you harbor no evil, you have no cause to fear the light of day, so come back tomorrow and state your request. Now get out of the house!"

The man uttered a doleful sigh, fixed Martinière with a terrifying stare and reached for the stiletto. Martinière silently commended her soul to heaven but remained steadfast and looked the man boldly in the eye, leaning more firmly against the door, which he would have to penetrate to get to the mistress. "Let me get to Mademoiselle, I tell you!" the man cried once more. "Do as you please," replied Martinière, "I will not move from this spot; complete the evil deed you have begun; you too will suffer the same shameful death on the place de Grève as your wicked accomplices." "Ha," the man cried, "you are right, Martinière. I look like and am armed like a villainous robber and murderer, but my accomplices have not been executed, have not been executed!" And with that he drew out the stiletto, darting venomous glances at the mortally frightened woman. "Lord Jesus!" she screamed, expecting the death blow; but at that moment the clang of arms and the sound of horses' hooves could be heard on the street. "The mounted police, the mounted police, help, help!" Martinière screamed. "You frightful woman, you want to ruin me—now it's all over, all over—take this, take this; give it to Mademoiselle to night, or tomorrow if you wish." Muttering these words the man had snatched the candlestick from Martinière, blown out the candles and pressed a small casket into her hands. "If you value your salvation, give the casket to Mademoiselle," he cried and dashed out of the house.

Martinière had sunk to the floor; she got up with difficulty and groped her way in the dark back to her room, where she fell into an armchair, completely exhausted, unable to utter a sound. Then she heard the keys that she had left in the front door rattle. The door was being locked, and soft, uncertain steps were approaching her room. She sat spellbound, powerless to move, waiting for something horrible to happen; but to her relief the door opened and in the light of the night lamp she instantly recognized honest Baptiste, who looked as pale as a corpse and quite bewildered. "In the name of all the saints," he began, "tell me, Madame Martinière, what has happened? Oh, what anxiety, what anxiety I felt! I don't know what it was, but last night some power drove me from the wedding. When I came to our street, I thought, Madame Martiniere is a light sleeper; if I knock softly but sharply on the front door, she will hear me and let me in. But then a strong police patrol was marching toward me, some on horse, some on foot, armed to the teeth; they stopped me and refused to let me go on. But fortunately Desgrais, the lieutenant in the mounted police, who knows me well, was among them. When they held the lantern under my nose, he said: 'Oh Baptiste, where have you been this night? You should stay home and keep watch. There's something afoot around here; we expect to make a good catch this very night.' You wouldn't believe, Madame Martinière, how much I took these words to heart. And then I crossed the threshold and a man rushed out of the house wrapped in a cloak, clutching a gleaming stiletto, and he knocked me down. The house is open, the keys are in the lock; tell me, what does it all mean?"

Relieved of her mortal anxiety, Martinière told him what had happened. They both went into the entrance hall; here they found the candlestick on the floor, where the strange man had dropped it as he fled. "It's only too clear," said Baptiste, "that Mademoiselle was going to be robbed, perhaps even murdered. As you say, the man knew that you were alone with Mademoiselle; he even knew that she was still awake, working on her manuscript. He was certainly one of those cursed rogues and thugs, who enter homes, spy out with great cunning for everything that may be useful to them in carrying out their devilish plans. And the little casket, Madame Martinière, I think we'll throw it into the Seine where it's deepest. What assurance do we have that some villainous monster is not plotting to murder our good Mademoiselle; that when she opens the casket, she will not drop dead like the old Marquis de Tournay when he opened the letter he had received from an unknown hand?"

After a lengthy debate the two faithful servants decided to tell Mademoiselle everything next morning and to give her the mysterious casket, which could of course be opened with due caution. They both weighed carefully every circumstance surrounding the suspicious stranger's appearance, and concluded that some special mystery might well be involved, which they should not attempt to control but should leave to their mistress to unravel.

Baptiste's anxiety was based on solid grounds; for at that very time Paris was the scene of the most gruesome horrors; at that very time the most fiendish invention in hell offered the most convenient instrument for committing those horrors.

A German apothecary named Glaser, the foremost chemist of his age, was dabbling in alchemistic experiments, as people of his profession are apt to do. He had set his mind on finding the philosopher's stone. He was joined by an Italian named Exili. But this Exili was using the art of making gold merely as a pretext. He was interested solely in learning how to mix, boil, sublimate poisons which Glaser prepared in the hope of making his fortune; and he finally succeeded in preparing that subtle, odorless and tasteless poison that killed either instantly or slowly, leaving absolutely no trace in the human body, thereby deceiving all the science and art of the physicians who, not suspecting murder by poison, were compelled to ascribe death to natural causes. However cautious Exili was in his labors, he nevertheless came under suspicion of selling poison, and was sent to the Bastille. Shortly after that, Captain Godin de Sainte-Croix was thrown into the same cell. The captain had lived for a long time with the Marquise de Brinvilliers in a liaison that brought disgrace upon her whole family. Since her husband the marquis remained insensitive to his wife's misconduct, her father, Dreux d'Aubray, a civil lieutenant in Paris, felt compelled to separate the adulterous couple by swearing out a summons of arrest against the captain. Passionate, devoid of character, simulating piety while inclined to every sort of vice from the days of his youth, jealous, vengeful to the point of fury, the captain could have found nothing that he welcomed more than Exili's devilish secret, which gave him the power of destroying all his enemies. He became Exili's zealous pupil and soon caught up with his master, so that, when he was released from the Bastille, he was able to continue working on his own.

La Brinvilliers was a degenerate woman; Sainte-Croix turned her into a monster. He persuaded her to poison, in succession, first her own father, with whom she lived, caring for him in his old age with villainous hypocrisy, then her two brothers, and finally her sister; she murdered her father out of revenge, the others for the large inheritance. The story of several poisoners yields a horrible example of the way crimes of this sort become an irresistible passion. Without any other purpose than sheer pleasure in the deed, as the chemist performs experiments for his own satisfaction, poisoners have often murdered people whose life or death was a matter of complete indifference to them. The sudden death of several poor people in the Hôtel Dieu* subsequently aroused the suspicion that there was poison in the bread that this Brinvilliers woman was accustomed to distribute there every week, so that she might pass for a model of piety and benevolence. It is certain, however, that she put poison in the pigeon pies she served to her guests at dinner. The Chevalier du Guet and several other persons fell victim to these infernal meals. Sainte-Croix, his assistant La Chaussée, and the Brinvilliers woman were able to conceal their gruesome crimes for a long time behind impenetrable veils; but what infamous cunning of human reprobates can prevail when the eternal power of heaven has resolved to bring the culprits to justice here on earth?

The poisons that Sainte-Croix prepared were so subtle that, if the powder (*poudre de succession*, the Parisians called them) lay exposed while it was being produced, one single inhalation was enough to cause instant death. For that reason Sainte-Croix wore a mask of thin glass when he was working. One day, as he was on the point of emptying a prepared poison powder into a flask, his mask fell from his face; inhaling the fine dust from the poison, he dropped dead on the spot.

*The oldest hospital in Paris.

Since he left no heirs, the courts stepped in and sealed his effects. They found, locked in a chest, the whole diabolical arsenal of death by poison that the infamous Sainte-Croix had had at his command; la Brinvilliers's letters were found too, leaving no doubt about her crimes. She fled to a convent in Liége. Desgrais, an officer of the mounted police, was sent in pursuit of her. Disguised as a priest, he appeared in the convent where she had sought refuge. He succeeded in drawing the horrid woman into a love affair and in luring her to a secret meeting place in a lonely garden near the city gate. She had barely arrived for the rendezvous when she was surrounded by Desgrais's men; the ecclesiastical lover was suddenly transformed into an official of the mounted police. He forced her to enter the carriage that stood ready outside the garden and the vehicle was driven away to paris surrounded by police. La Chaussée had already been beheaded; la Brinvilliers suffered the same death; after the execution her body was burned and her ashes scattered to the winds.

The Parisians breathed more freely when the world was rid of the monster who could aim that secret weapon at both friend and foe with impunity. But it soon became evident that the frightful art of the villainous Sainte-Croix had found heirs. Like an invisible, malicious specter, murder insinuated itself into the most intimate circles, such as those formed by kin, love, friendship, striking down its unhappy victims swiftly and certainly. The man who had been seen in blooming health today would totter, sick and pining away, tomorrow, and the physician's art was unable to save him from death. Wealth, a lucrative office, a beautiful, perhaps too youthful wife: these were sufficient grounds for persecution to the point of death. The most sacred bonds were sundered by the most inhuman distrust. The husband trembled before his wife, the father before his son, the sister before her brother. The food and wine on the table remained untouched when friends were invited to dine with friends; where formerly pleasure and jest had reigned, savage glances now searched for murder in disguise. Heads of households were seen anxiously purchasing their provisions in remote sections of the city, preparing the food themselves in some dirty restaurant kitchen because they feared devilish treachery in their own home. But even so, the greatest, most circumspect caution sometimes proved to be in vain.

To curb this ever increasing disorder the king appointed a special court of justice, to which he assigned the sole task of investigating and punishing these secret crimes. This was the so-called Chambre ardente,* which met near the Bastille, presided over by La Regnie. For some time La Regnie's efforts, vigorous though they were, remained fruitless; it was left to the crafty Desgrais to discover the most secret nook in which crime lurked. In the Faubourg Saint-Germain there was an old woman named La Voisin, who lived by telling fortunes and raising spirits, and who was able, with the aid of her accomplices Le Sage and Le Vigoureux, to astonish and terrify even people who could not exactly be called weak or credulous. But she did more than that. Like Sainte-Croix she was a pupil of Exili, and like him, she prepared the subtle poison that left no trace; with it she helped unscrupulous sons obtain an early patrimony and degenerate wives find younger husbands. Desgrais discovered her secret, she confessed all, the Chambre ardente condemned her to be burned at the stake; the sentence was carried out on the place de Grève. In her home was found a list of all those who had sought her aid; and so it came about that not only did execution follow upon execution, but that grave suspicion fell even upon persons of great prominence. Thus it was believed that Cardinal Bonzy had obtained from La Voisin the means for removing in a short time all those to whom he had been obliged to pay a pension while he was Archbishop of Narbonne. The Duchesse de Bouillon and the Comtesse de Soisson, whose names were on the list, were accused of conspiring with the fiendish woman, and even François Henri de Montmorency, Boudebelle, Duke of Luxembourg, Peer and Marshall of the Realm, was not spared. He too was prosecuted by the dreadful Chambre ardente. He surrendered to be imprisoned in the Bastille, where he was thrown into a hole six feet long by the vengeful Louvois and La Regnie. Months passed before it could be proved conclusively that the duke had committed no crime except that of having his horoscope cast by Le Sage.

It is certain that President La Regnie was betrayed by blind zeal into committing acts of violence and cruelty. The tribunal took on the character of an inquisition; the slightest suspicion led to harsh imprisonment, and demonstrating the innocence of a man accused of a capital crime was often left to chance. Moreover La Regnie had a hideous face and a malicious character, so that he soon drew on

---

*One of a series of courts set up to judge special cases such as heresy and poisonings. The most famous was the one established in 1679-80 to judge "the affair of the poisonings" referred to in our text.

himself the hatred of those he had been appointed to avenge or protect. The Duchesse de Bouillon, when asked by him in an interrogation whether she had seen the devil, replied: "I believe I see him this very moment."

While the blood of the guilty and the suspected flowed in streams on the place de Grève and the secret poisonings finally became less and less frequent, a new kind of evil appeared, spreading new consternation. A gang of robbers seemed determined to lay their hands on all the jewels in the city. Every precious ornament vanished unaccountably almost immediately after it was bought, no matter how well it was guarded. But what was much worse, anyone who dared to wear jewels on his person in the evening was robbed or even murdered in the public streets or in dark hallways. Those who escaped with their lives testified that a blow on the head had struck them down like a bolt of lightning; when they came out of their stupor they found that they had been robbed and were in a totally different region from the one where they had been attacked. The murdered, who were found almost every morning in the streets or in their homes, all had the same lethal wound: a dagger thrust in the heart, which, in the opinion of the doctors, was delivered so swiftly and with such accuracy that the victim must have sunk to the ground without uttering a sound. Who was not mixed up in some clandestine amorous intrigue at the licentious court of Louis XIV? Who was not making a late stealthy visit to his mistress, bearing an expensive gift on his person? As if they were in league with spirits, the robbers knew precisely when such an event would take place. Often the unfortunate victim never reached the house in which he expected to enjoy the bliss of love; often he fell dead on the threshold, indeed at the very bedroom door of his mistress, who was horrified to find the bloody corpse.

In vain did Argenson, the minister of police, have everyone among the Parisian populace arrested who in any way incurred suspicion; in vain did La Regnie fume and try to extort confessions; in vain were watches and patrols strengthened; no trace of the criminals could be found. Only the precaution of arming oneself to the teeth and being attended by torchlight was of some help; but even so, there were examples of the attendant being harassed by a volley of stones at the moment his master was murdered and robbed.

It was a strange fact that, despite all the investigations carried out in every place that dealt in jewels, not a single one of the robbed gems came to light, so that here too there was no clue that could be followed up.

Desgrais fumed with rage at the way the rogues were able to elude even his traps. The section of the city in which he happened to be working would be spared, while in another, where no evil was suspected, the murderers stalked their wealthy victims.

Desgrais devised the stratagem of creating several doubles of himself, so alike in walk, posture, speech, build, and facial features that even the police did not know which was the genuine Desgrais. Meanwhile he himself spied in the most secret haunts, at the risk of his life, and followed at a distance one man or another who, on his orders, carried an expensive piece of jewelry on his person. But these decoys remained untouched, so the crooks must have known of this strategem too. Desgrais was in despair.

One morning Desgrais came to President La Regnie; he was pale, his features distorted, beside himself. "What's the matter? What's the news? Are you on their trail?" the president asked. "Ah, Your Excellency," Desgrais began, stammering in his rage, "last night, not far from the Louvre, the Marquis de la Fare was attacked in my presence." "Heaven and earth," La Regnie shouted with joy, "we've caught them!" "Oh, listen, please," Desgrais interrupted with a bitter smile on his face; "listen first to what happened. I was standing in front of the Louvre, with all hell in my heart, looking out for the devils who are making a fool of me. A figure walked past me with unsteady steps; he kept looking behind him, without seeing me. In the light of the moon I recognized the Marquis de la Fare. I was expecting him, I knew where he was going. He was hardly ten or twelve steps past me when a form leaped out of the earth, so to speak, struck him down, and fell upon him. Taken by surprise at this moment that might deliver the murderer into my hands, I thoughtlessly uttered a loud cry and took a mighty leap from my hideout, intending to land on him; but I becmae entangled in my cloak and fell to the ground. I saw the man racing away as if on the wings of the wind. I scrambled to my feet and ran after him; as I ran, I blew my horn, to which my men replied on theirs. The street came to life — the clang of arms, the clatter of hooves from all sides. 'This way, this way, Desgrais, Desgrais,' I shouted, and the street echoed my words. I still saw the man before me in the bright moonlight, dodging in and out of corners to confuse me. We came to the rue Nicaise; his strength seemed to ebb. I redoubled my efforts, he was no more than fifteen paces ahead of me—" "You overtook him, seized him, the police arrived," La Regnie cried with flashing eyes, grasping Desgrais's arm as if he were the fleeing murderer. "Fifteen paces," Desgrais continued in a hollow voice and breathing with an effort, "fifteen paces in front of me the man leaped aside into the shadow and vanished through the wall." "Vanished? Through the wall? Are you mad?" cried La Regnie, taking two steps backward and wringing his hands. "You may call me a madman, Excellency," Desgrais continued, rubbing his forehead like a man tormented by evil thoughts, "call me a foolish believer in ghosts, but it happened just as I told you. I stood before the wall, petrified, while several of my policemen came up; with them was the Marquis de la Fare, who had recovered, his drawn sword in his hand. We lit torches, tapped the wall in various places; no trace of a door, window, or opening. It's a strong stone wall, enclosing a courtyard, adjacent to a house in which there live people against whom there is not the faintest suspicion. Today I made a careful inspection of everything. It is the devil himself who is making fools of us."

Desgrais's story became known in Paris. Heads were filled with tales of magic, raising of spirits, pacts with the devil made by La Voisin, Le Vigoureux, the infamous priest Le Sage. And as it is in our eternal nature that the impulse toward the supernatural and the miraculous outweighs our reason, people soon actually believed what Desgrais had uttered only in a peevish moment, that the devil himself was protecting the infamous villains who had sold their souls to him. As may be imagined, Desgrais's story received many embellishments. The tale, illustrated with a woodcut of a gruesome diabolical figure sinking into the ground before the horrified Desgrais, was printed and sold on every street corner. It was enough to intimidate the populace and even to drain the courage of the police, who now roamed the streets at night in fear and trembling, with amulets hanging from their necks and consecrated with holy water.

Argenson saw the efforts of the Chambre ardente failing, and requested that the king appoint a tribunal to deal with the new crime, armed with still wider powers to investigate and punish. The king, who was convinced that he had already vested too much power in the Chambre ardente, horrified by the countless executions that the bloodthirsty la Regnie had carried out, rejected the proposal out of hand.

Another method for stimulating the king's interest in the case was adopted.

In the apartment of Madame de Maintenon, where the king was accustomed to spend his afternoons and to work with his ministers late into the night, he was handed a poem on behalf of all endangered lovers, who complained that, since gallantry commanded them to bring their mistresses an expensive present, they must now do so at the risk of their lives. It was an honor and a pleasure to shed one's blood in chivalrous combat for one's beloved; but the treacherous assault of the murderer against whom one could not defend oneself was another matter altogether. They urged that Louis, the shining polar star of all love and gallantry, dissipate the dark night with his bright rays and thus bring to light the murky mystery that the night concealed. Let the Divine Hero, who had crushed his enemies, now draw his victorious shining sword and, as Hercules had defeated the Lernaean serpent and Theseus the Minotaur, defeat the threatening monster that was causing all the pleasures of love to atrophy and all joy to darken into profound suffering and inconsolable grief.

Serious as the situation was, the poem did not lack clever and witty turns of phrase, especially when it described how the lovers trembled on their stealthy course to their mistress and how their anxiety nipped in the bud all the pleasure of love and every gallant adventure. Add to this that the poem ended with a pompous panegyric on Louis XIV, and it was inevitable that the king should read it with visible satisfaction. Having reached the end, he turned quickly to Madame de Maintenon without, however, taking his eyes from the manuscript, and recited the poem once more in a loud voice; and then he asked her with a gracious smile how she felt about the wishes of the endangered lovers. True to her serious cast of mind, to which was added a certain color of piety, Madame replied that secret forbidden ways deserved no special measures for their extermination. The king, dissatisfied with this inconclusive reply, folded the paper and prepared to rejoin his secretary of state in the next room, when he looked to the side and caught sight of Mademoiselle de Scudéry, who was present, seated in a small armchair near Madame de Maintenon. He walked over to her; the gracious smile that had at first played about his lips and cheeks and then vanished, returned again. Standing close to Mademoiselle, he unfolded the paper again and said softly: "The marquise wholly rejects the gallantries of our amorous gentlemen and evades my question in ways that are perfectly legitimate. But you, Mademoiselle, what do you think of this poetic supplication?" Mademoiselle stood up respectfully; a fleeting blush, like the glow of a sunset, passed over the pale cheeks of the dignified old lady; bowing lightly, she spoke with downcast eyes:

> Un amant qui craint les voleurs
> n'est point digne d'amour.*

The king, deeply astonished at the chivalrous spirit demonstrated by these few words, which disposed effectively of the whole poem with its interminable tirades, cried with flashing eyes: "By St. Denis, you are right, Mademoiselle! No blind measures, which condemn the innocent along with the guilty, shall protect cowardice; let Argenson and La Regnie do their duty!"

The following morning Martinière handed over the mysterious casket in fear and trembling to Mademoiselle de Scudéry, depicting in the most vivid colors all the horrors of the time as she told what had happened on the previous night. Both she and Baptiste, who stood in a corner of the room, pale and twirling his nightcap in his hand in anxiety and nervousness, begged the mistress piteously, in the name of all the saints, to open the casket with the greatest possible caution. Mademoiselle weighed and tested the locked mystery in her hand and spoke with a smile: "You are both seeing ghosts. Those villainous assassins out there who, as you yourselves say, ferret out the innermost secrets of a house, know as well as you and I do that I am not rich, that there is no object here that is worth committing a murder for. Can they be aiming at my life? Who can gain anything by the death of a woman of seventy-three, who has never prosecuted anyone but the villains and disturbers of the peace whom she has created in her novels; who writes mediocre verses that can arouse envy in no one; who will leave nothing after her death except the finery of an old spinster who occasionally visited the court and a few dozen books, handsomely bound with gilt edges? And you, Martinière, no matter how frightening a picture you paint of the strange man, I cannot believe that he harbored any evil against me. So!—" Martinière sprang back three paces and Baptiste half sank to his knees with a muffled "Oh!" as Mademoiselle pressed a protruding knob and the lid of the casket opened with a click.

*"A lover who fears thieves is not worthy of love."

Great was Mademoiselle's astonishment when the casket revealed
to her a pair of golden bracelets richly encrusted with diamonds and
a necklace to match. She took the jewelry out of the box and, while
she lauded the wonderful workmanship of the necklace, Martinière
fixed her eyes on the bracelets and kept exclaiming that even the vain
Mademoiselle de Montespan did not own such jewelry.

"But what is it for, what can it mean?" said Mademoiselle de
Scudéry. At that moment she caught sight of a small folded slip of
paper at the bottom of the casket. She rightly hoped to find in this
note the solution to the mystery. But she had hardly finished
scanning the message when the paper dropped from her trembling
hands. She sent an eloquent look toward heaven and then sank back
into her armchair in a half swoon. The two servants rushed to her in
alarm. "Oh," she cried in a voice half choked with tears, "this insult,
this profound disgrace! Must I endure this at my advanced age? Have
I committed a sin in foolish levity like some thoughtless young girl? O
Lord, are words dropped half in jest capable of such a gruesome interpretation? Can I, who have remained faithful to virtue and blame-
less in piety since my childhood, be accused by criminals of being in
league with the devil?"

Mademoiselle applied her handkerchief to her eyes, weeping and
sobbing convulsively, so that Martinière and Baptiste, confused and
distressed, did not know how to help their good mistress in her deep
trouble.

Martinière had picked up the fateful note from the floor. It contained the following message:

> Un amant qui craint les voleurs
> n'est point digne d'amour.

Your sagacious mind, highly honored lady, has saved us, who practice the right of
the stronger against the weak and cowardly and appropriate to ourselves treasures
that would be squandered unworthily, from intensive prosecution. Graciously
accept these jewels as a token of our gratitude. They are the most precious that we
have been able to lay hands on in a long time, although you, worthy lady, deserve
to be adorned in far more beautiful jewelry than this. We beg that you will not
withdraw your friendship and your gracious memory from us.

> The Invisibles

"Is it possible," exlaimed Mademoiselle de Scudéry when she had
somewhat recovered, "that shameless insolence and villainous

mockery can be carried to such lengths?" The sun was shining brightly through the crimson silken drapes, so that the diamonds lying on the table beside the open casket gleamed in the reddish light. When she glanced at them, Mademoiselle covered her face in horror and ordered Martinière to remove the jewels at once, tainted as they were with the blood of the murdered victims. Martinière promptly locked the necklace and bracelets in the casket and expressed the opinion that it was probably most advisable to hand the jewels over to the minister of police and tell him the whole story of the young man's frightening appearance and the delivery of the casket.

Mademoiselle de Scudéry stood up and slowly paced up and down the room in silence, as if she were reflecting on the best course to take. Then she ordered Baptiste to summon a sedan chair and asked Martinière to help her dress; she intended to call on the Marquise de Maintenon at once.

She had herself conveyed to the marquise at a time when, as Mademoiselle de Scudéry well knew, the marquise was alone in her apartment. She took the casket of jewels with her.

The marquise was of course greatly astonished to see Mademoiselle, who was usually the personification of dignity, indeed of amiability and charm, in spite of her advanced age, appear with uncertain step, her face pale and agitated. "What in the name of all the saints has happened to you?" she exlaimed to the poor, distressed lady who, completely upset, scarcely able to stand on her feet, made quickly for the armchair that the marquise pushed toward her. Finally Mademoiselle regained her power of speech and told about the deep, rankling insult that her thoughtless jest about the petition of the endangered lovers had wrought upon her. After hearing the whole story bit by bit, Madame de maintenon expressed the feeling that Mademoiselle was taking the strange incident too much to heart, that the mockery of such infamous rabble could never affect a pure and noble spirit; finally she asked to see the jewels.

Mademoiselle opened the casket and handed it to her; upon seeing the precious jewels, the marquise could not suppress a loud exclamation of astonishment. She took out the necklace and the bracelets, and went to the window with them, where she allowed the diamonds to play in the sunlight, then held the delicate gold settings close to her eyes, in order to appreciate the wonderful art with which every little link in the intricate chain was wrought. Suddenly the marquise turned quickly to Mademoiselle and cried: "Do you realize, Mademoiselle, that these bracelets and this necklace can have been made by no one but René Cardillac?"

René Cardillac was at that time the most skillful goldsmith in Paris, one of the most artistic and at the same time most eccentric people of his age. Rather short of stature but broad shouldered and of powerful, muscular build, Cardillac, though well into his fifties, still possessed the energy and mobility of a young man. This unusual energy was evidenced also by his thick, curly, reddish hair and his squat, shining face. If Cardillac had not been known in the whole of Paris as the most upright man of honor, unselfish, frank, without guile, always ready to help others, the very peculiar expression of his small, deepset, glittering green eyes might have drawn upon him the suspicion of secret malice and malignity. As noted, Cardillac was the most skilled man in his art, not only in Paris, but perhaps in the world. Possessing an intimate knowledge about the nature of precious stones, he was able to treat and set them in such a way that a piece of jewelry that had been considered ordinary left Cardillac's workshop in shining splendor. He accepted every commission with ardent eagerness and set on it a price so low that it seemed to bear no relation to the labor involved. Then the work gave him no peace; day and night he was heard hammering in his workshop and often, when the work was almost completed, he was suddenly displeased by its form; he doubted whether a setting or a little clasp was delicate enough—reason enough for throwing the whole work into the melting pot and starting afresh. Thus every commission became a pure, matchless masterpiece which astonished the client. But now it was almost impossible to get a completed order from him. Under a thousand pretexts he would put off the client from week to week, from month to month. It was useless to offer him double the price of the work, he would not accept a louis more than the sum agreed upon. When he finally had to yield to the pressure of the client and part with the jewelry, he could not conceal the very deepest annoyance, indeed the inner rage, that seethed in him. When he had had to deliver a more important order, one that was especially expensive, perhaps involving many thousands because of the precious gems or the intricacy of the design, he would run about like a madman, cursing himself, his work, everything around him. But when someone ran after him crying, "René Cardillac, wouldn't you like to make a beautiful necklace for my fiancée, some bracelets for my girl?" and so on, he would stop suddenly, flash his glittering little eyes at the client and ask, as he rubbed his hands: "What do you have?" The other would produce a little casket, saying: "Here are some jewels, they're nothing special, common stuff, but in your hands—." Cardillac would not let him finish his sentence but would snatch the casket out of his hands, take out the jewels, which really were of inferior quality, and cry ecstatically: "Ho, ho, common stuff? By no means—pretty stones—splendid stones—just leave it to me, and if a handful of louis doesn't matter to you, I'll add a few small gems that will sparkle in your eyes like the lovely sun itself." The man would reply: "I leave everything to you, Master René, and will pay you the price you ask." Whether the client was a wealthy burgher or a distinguished nobleman of the court, Cardillac would impetuously throw his arms about the man's neck, hug and kiss him, and say he was now happy again and that the work would be completed in a week's time. He would dash home at breakneck speed, make for his workshop and begin hammering; and a week later a masterpiece had been created. But when the client who had ordered it appeared, joyfully willing to pay the modest price demanded and take the jewelry home with him, Cardillac would become peevish, rude and defiant. "But Master Cardillac, remember, tomorrow is my wedding." "What do I care about your wedding? Come back again in two weeks." "But the work is done; here's the money, I must have it." "And I tell you there are still many changes I have to make and I'm not going to release it today." "And I tell you, if you won't give me the jewelry voluntarily, for which I'm willing to pay you double, you will see me march up here shortly with Argenson's eager helpers." "Well, may Satan torment you with a hundred glowing pincers and may he hang three hundredweights to the necklace so that your bride strangles on it!" And with that Cardillac would throw him out the door so that he would fall down the stairs, and Cardillac would laugh like the devil, watching through the window as the poor young man limped out of the house holding a handkerchief to his bleeding nose.

It was also impossible to explain why Cardillac, after accepting a commission enthusiastically, often suddenly implored a customer with every sign of deep emotional involvement, with the most heart-rending appeals, with tears and sobs, invoking the Virgin Mary and all the saints, to release him from the work he had undertaken. Many people who were most highly esteemed by the king and the nation had in vain offered large sums of money to possess even the smallest product from Cardillac's hands. He threw himself at the king's feet and implored the favor of not being asked to work for him. He likewise rejected every commission from Madame de Maintenon; with an expression of aversion and horror on his face he declined her request to make a small ring adorned with the emblems of the arts, which she intended to present to Racine.

"I wager," Madame de Maintenon said, "that if I summon Cardillac merely to find out for whom he made this jewelry, he will refuse to come, because he will fear that I want to give him an order and he absolutely refuses to work for me. Although his unbending stubbornness seems to have softened recently, for I hear that he is working more industriously than ever and is delivering the goods on time, though still with an expression of profound annoyance on his averted face." Mademoiselle de Scudéry, who was also very much concerned that the jewels be returned soon to their rightful owner, if that was still possible, said that Master Eccentric could be told that he would not be asked to accept an order for work but only to appraise some jewelry. The marquise agreed. Cardillac was sent for; he appeared shortly thereafter, as if he had already been on his way there.

When he caught sight of Mademoiselle de Scudéry he seemed embarrassed and, as someone who has suddenly come face to face with the unexpected forgets to do what propriety prescribes for the occasion, he first bowed deeply and respectfully to that venerable lady and only then turned to the marquise. She asked him quickly, pointing to the jewels that glittered on the dark green tablecloth, whether this was his work. Cardillac scarcely glanced at them; looking at the marquise steadily, he hastily put the necklace and the bracelets into the casket that stood beside them and pushed it vehemently away from him. And now he spoke, an ugly smile lighting up his red face: "Indeed, Madame la Marquise, you cannot be well acquainted with René Cardillac's work if you believe even for a moment that any other goldsmith in the world could create such a setting. Of course it's my work." "Then tell me," the marquise continued, "for whom you executed this commission." "For myself alone," Cardillac replied. As the two ladies looked at him in astonishment, Madame de Maintenon with distrust and Mademoiselle de Scudéry with foreboding as to what turn events might now take, he continued: "Yes, you may find this strange, Madame la Marquise, but it is so. For the sheer joy of doing this beautiful work I collected my best stones and worked more industriously and carefully than ever before. A short time ago the jewelry mysteriously disappeared for my workshop." "Thank heaven," exclaimed Mademoiselle de Scudéry, her eyes shining with joy. She stood up quickly and nimbly like a young girl, went up to Cardillac and placed her two hands on his shoulders. "Master René," she said, "take back your property, which infamous rogues have stolen from you." And now she related to him in detail how the jewels had come into her possession. Cardillac listened to her in silence with downcast eyes; only from time to time he uttered an inaudible "hm — so — ah — ho," and first folded his hands behind his back, then gently stroked his chin or cheeks.

When Mademoiselle de Scudéry had finished, Cardillac seemed to be struggling with very special thoughts that had come to him during the narration of the story and with some resolve that refused to fit the circumstances. He rubbed his forehead, he sighed, he passed his hand over his eyes, apparently to check his tears. Finally he took the casket that Mademoiselle de Scudéry handed him, sank slowly on one knee before her, and said "Fate has destined this jewelry for you, noble, worthy lady. Only at this moment do I realize that while I was working on it, I was thinking of you, indeed working for you. Do not disdain to accept and wear these jewels as the best that I have made in a long time." "My, my," replied Mademoiselle in a tone of gracious banter, "what are you thinking of, Master René? Is it fitting at my age to deck myself out with glittering gems? And what makes you give me such an expensive gift? Come, come, Master René, if I were beautiful, like the Marquise de Fontange, and rich, I would not let the jewels out of my hands; but what business has this vain splendor on these withered arms or this glittering ornament around this covered throat?" Cardillac had meanwhile risen to his feet and, with a wild look in his eyes, as though in a state of distraction, holding out the casket to Mademoiselle de Scudéry, said: "Do me the merciful kindness, Mademoiselle, and take the jewels. You wouldn't believe how deep is the veneration I bear in my heart for your virtue and your noble attainments. Do accept my paltry gift if only as an effort to demonstrate to you my deep feelings."

As Mademoiselle de Scudéry still kept hesitating, Madame de

Maintenon took the casket from Cardillac, saying: "By heaven, Mademoiselle, you are always talking about your advanced age; what have we, you and I, to do with age and its burdens? And aren't you acting like a bashful young thing, who would love to reach out for the proffered sweet fruit if it could only be done without lifting hand or finger? Don't refuse to accept from good Master René as a voluntary gift what a thousand others cannot obtain from him for all their gold, all their begging and entreating."

Madame de Maintenon had been pressing the casket on Mademoiselle de Scudéry, and now Cardillac fell to his knees, kissed Mademoiselle's skirt, her hands, groaned, sighed, wept, sobbed, jumped to his feet and ran out of the room like a madman, upsetting chairs and tables and making china and glass clatter in his insane haste.

Mademoiselle de Scudéry cried in alarm: "In the name of all the saints what has gotten into the man?" But the marquise, in a mood of unusual merriment approaching mischievousness, which was normally alien to her nature, broke into hearty laughter and said: "I've got it, Mademoiselle; Master René is desperately in love with you and is beginning to storm your heart with lavish gifts according to tried tradition and the established custom of true gallantry." She elaborated on this joke, urging Mademoiselle not to be too cruel toward the desperate lover; and Mademoiselle, giving free rein to her natural spirits, was carried down the bubbling stream of a thousand witty conceits. She remarked that, if this was the way matters stood, she she would end up by capitulating and present the world with an unheard-of example of a seventy-three-year-old goldsmith's bride of unimpeachable nobility. Madame de Maintenon offered to weave the bridal wreath and to instruct her in the duties of a good housewife, about which an innocent little girl like herself could not know very much.

When Mademoiselle de Scudéry at length arose to leave the marquise, she became serious, in spite of all the laughter and joking, when she picked up the little casket of jewels. "And yet, Marquise," she said, "I shall never be able to make use of these jewels. Whatever their history may be, they were once in the hands of those diabolical knaves who rob and murder with the impudence of the devil, indeed probably in confounded league with him. I shudder at the blood that seems to cling to the sparkling gems. And now even Cardillac's behavior, I must confess, fills me with a strange anxiety and sense of the uncanny. I cannot rid myself of a dark foreboding that behind all this there lurks some gruesome, horrible mystery; and when I picture the whole situation to myself with all its circumstances, I can't even produce the shadow of an inkling as to what the mystery is, nor how the honest, decent Master René, the model of a good and pious citizen, can be mixed up in something so evil and damnable. But this much is certain: I shall never dare to put on these jewels."

The marquise thought that this was carrying scruples too far; but when Mademoiselle de Scudéry asked her on her conscience what she would do in her place, Madame de Maintenon replied in earnest, decisive tones: "Far sooner throw the jewelry into the Seine than ever wear it."

The scene with Master Cardillac drew some very charming verses from Mademoiselle de Scudéry's pen; she recited them the following evening to the king in Madame de Maintenon's apartment. It may well be that, subduing the horror caused by her uneasy foreboding, she was able to paint in vivid colors, at Master René's expense, the delightful picture of the seventy-three year old goldsmith's bride of ancient noble lineage. Enough, the king was thoroughly amused, and swore that Boileau-Despréaux had found his master, for which reason Mademoiselle de Scudéry's poem was regarded as the wittiest ever written.

Several months had passed when Mademoiselle de Scudéry happened to be crossing the Pont-Neuf* in the Duchesse de Montansier's glass coach. The invention of the glass coach was still enough of a novelty to attract large numbers of curious folk when such a vehicle appeared on the street. So it was that the gaping mob surrounded the Duchesse de Montansier's coach on the Pont-Neuf, almost blocking the progress of the horses. Suddenly Mademoiselle de Scudéry heard a volley of insults and curses and noticed a man fighting his way through the dense throng with his fists and elbows. When he came closer, she saw the piercing eyes of a deathly pale, sorrow-laden young face fixed on her. The young man kept his gaze on her, as he vigorously opened a path for himself with his elbows and fists until he reached the coach door, which he pulled open with impetuous haste. After throwing a piece of paper into Mademoiselle's lap he vanished as he had come, dealing out and receiving blows and punches. When the man had appeared at the coach door, Martinière, who was with

*One of the bridges over the Seine.

Mademoiselle inside, had fallen in a faint on the cushions. In vain
did Mademoiselle de Scudéry pull at the cord and shout at the coachman; he kept whipping the horses as if he were driven by the evil
spirit; they sprayed foam from their mouths, kicked and reared and
finally thundered over the bridge at a brisk trot. Mademoiselle
emptied her flask of smelling salts over the unconscious woman, who
finally opened her eyes and, trembling and shaking, clinging convulsively to her mistress, showing anxiety and horror in her pale face,
moaned with an effort: "By the Holy Virgin, what did that terrible
man want? Ah, he was the one, yes, he was the one, the same one
who brought you the little casket on that awful night!" Mademoiselle
de Scudéry calmed the poor creature by pointing out to her that
nothing evil had occurred and that they need only find out what was
in the note. She unfolded the paper and found on it the following
words: "An evil destiny, which you have the power to avert, is plunging me into the abyss. I implore you, as a son implores his mother to
whom he clings in the full passion of a child's love, to deliver the
necklace and bracelets that you received from me to Master Cardillac
under some pretext, such as that he should make an improvement or
alteration in them. Your welfare, your very life depends on it. If you
don't do it by the day after tomorrow, I will force my way into your
apartment and kill myself before your eyes."

"Now it is certain," said Mademoiselle de Scudéry after she had
read the note, "that this mysterious man, though he may really
belong to the gang of infamous thieves and murderers, harbors no
evil feelings toward me. If he had succeeded in speaking to me that
night, who knows what strange event, what mysterious chain of circumstances might have become clear to me, for which I cannot find
even the faintest clue in my own mind? But no matter what the situation is, I will do what is asked in this note, if only so that I may get rid
of these cursed jewels, which appear to me to be a hellish talisman of
the evil one himself. True to his habit of mind, Cardillac will not
easily let them out of his hands again."

Mademoiselle de Scudéry intended to take the jewels to the goldsmith the very next day. But it was as if all the literati of Paris had
conspired to besiege her that morning with verses, plays, anecdotes.
Scarcely had La Chapelle ended the scene from one of his tragedies
and slyly assured her that he thought this would top Racine, when
the latter himself appeared and floored him with a passionate speech

rendered by some king, until finally Boileau sent up his rockets into the black tragic sky, to escape the eternal chatter about the colonnade of the Louvre foisted on him by the architect and physician Perrault.

It was now high noon, Mademoiselle de Scudéry had to go to the Duchesse de Montansier's house, and so the visit to Cardillac was postponed till the next day.

Mademoiselle was tormented by an unusual uneasiness. The image of the young man stood before her constantly, and from the depths of her memory a faint recollection stirred of having seen this face, these features, before. Even her lightest nap was disturbed by dreams of anxiety about the frivolous, indeed culpable, way in which she had failed to grasp the hand that the unfortunate man, sinking into the abyss, had stretched out toward her, as if it had been within her power to avert some destructive event, some terrible crime. As soon as the light permitted, she had her maid dress her, and set out for the goldsmith's shop, taking the casket of jewels with her.

A throng was streaming to the rue Nicaise, in which Cardillac lived; it gathered in front of the house, screaming and shouting; it wished to storm the house but was held back with difficulty by the mounted police, who had surrounded the place. In the wild, confused din angry voices could be heard: "Crush the cursed murderer, tear him limb from limb!" Finally Desgrais appeared with a large contingent of men, who formed a lane through the dense crowd. The front door burst open; a man, weighed down with chains, was led out and dragged away amidst the most horrible curses of the raging mob.

At the moment when Mademoiselle de Scudéry, half dead from fright and a terrible premonition, witnessed this spectacle, a shrill scream of agony pierced her ears. "Forward—onward!" she cried in extreme agitation to the coachman, who parted the dense crowd with a swift, deft turn and drew up at Cardillac's front door. Here Mademoiselle de Scudéry saw Desgrais and at his feet a young girl, fair as the day, her hair hanging loosely about her, half naked, her face registering wild fear and utter despair. She was clasping Desgrais's knees, crying in a tone of the most terrible, most heartbreaking mortal anguish: "But he's innocent, he's innocent!" In vain were the efforts of Desgrais and his men to pry her loose and raise her from the ground. A strong, rough fellow finally grasped her arms in his burly fists, separated her from Desgrais by force, but stumbled clumsily and let go of the girl, who rolled down the stone stairway and landed in the street below, silent as though dead.

Mademoiselle de Scudéry could not contain herself any longer. "In the name of Christ, what has happened, what is going on here?" she cried, quickly opened the carriage door, and stepped out. The throng retreated respectfully before the worthy lady who, seeing that a couple of kind women had lifted the girl, sat her down on the steps and were rubbing her temples with spirits, approached Desgrais and repeated her question with vehemence. "A dreadful thing has happened," said Desgrais. "René Cardillac was found this morning murdered by a dagger thrust. The murderer is his journeyman Olivier Brusson. He has just been taken away to prison." "And the girl?" cried Mademoiselle de Scudéry. "—is Madelon, Cardillac's daughter," Desgrais interrupted her. "The villainous fellow was her lover. Now she weeps and howls and screams over and over again that Olivier is innocent, wholly innocent. But in reality she knows about the deed, and I must send her to the Conciergerie* too." In saying this he cast such a malicious, cunning look at the girl that it made Mademoiselle tremble. The girl was just beginning to breathe again, gently, but she lay there with closed eyes, unable to utter a sound or make a movement. They were uncertain about the best course of action, whether to take her into the house or to attend to her here until she regained full consciousness. Deeply moved, tears in her eyes, Mademoiselle de Scudéry looked at the innocent angel; Desgrais and his colleagues filled her with horror. At that moment Cardillac's corpse was brought down the stairs with a muffled rumble of footsteps. Making a swift decision, Mademoiselle de Scudéry said in a loud voice: "I'll take the girl with me, you can attend to the rest, Desgrais."

A low murmur of approval ran through the crowd. The women stood the girl up, people pressed forward, a hundred hands offered to assist them, and the girl was carried to the coach as if she were floating through the air, while blessings were showered on the worthy lady who had snatched innocence from the bloody assizes.

The efforts of Seron, the most famous physician in Paris, finally succeeded in restoring Madelon to consciousness after she had lain for hours in a state of rigid coma. Mademoiselle de Scudéry finished what the doctor had begun by shining many gentle rays of hope into

*The prison where suspects were lodged until they were brought to trial.

the girl's heart, until a powerful flood of tears from her eyes brought
back her normal breathing. She was able to relate how everything
had happened; only now and then her words were checked by a par-
oxysm of the most piercing pain.

At about midnight she had been awakened by a gentle tapping on
her bedroom door; Olivier's voice implored her to get up at once
because her father was dying. Olivier, holding a candle in his hand,
his features pale and distorted, the perspiration running down his
face, had gone to the workshop with unsteady steps and she had followed him. There her father was lying with glazed eyes, gasping in
the agony of death. She had thrown herself on him with a cry of
lament and only then noticed his bloody shirt. Olivier had gently
drawn her away and then proceeded to wash a wound on her father's
left breast with balsam and then bandage it. Meanwhile her father
had regained consciousness, the rattle in his throat had ceased, and
he had gazed, first at her, then at Olivier with a feeling look, taken
her hand and put it in Olivier's and pressed them both vigorously.
They had both knelt beside her father's bed; he had raised himself
with a piercing cry but had immediately sunk back again and passed
away with a deep sigh. Then they had both wailed and lamented.
Olivier had told her how the master had been murdered in his presence during a walk at night which he had been ordered to undertake
with Cardillac, and how he had carried the heavy man, whom he did
not believe to be mortally wounded, to the house with the greatest
effort. At dawn other residents of the house had come up, disturbed
by the noise, the weeping and wailing during the night, and had
found the young couple still kneeling in despair beside her father's
corpse. Now an alarm was raised, the mounted police appeared, and
Olivier was dragged off to prison for the murder of his master.

Madelon now added the most touching description of her beloved
Olivier's goodness, piety, loyalty; how he had held the master in high
esteem, as if he were his own father; how her father had returned this
love in full measure; how he had chosen him to be his son-in-law despite his poverty, because his craftsmanship was equal to his loyalty
and to his noble spirit. All this she spoke out of the depth of her
heart, and concluded with the statement that if Olivier had thrust
the dagger into her father's breast in her very presence, she would
sooner take this to be an illusion concocted by the devil than believe
that Olivier could be capable of committing such a dreadful,
gruesome crime.

Mademoiselle de Scudéry, most profoundly moved by Madelon's incomparable suffering and wholly inclined to regard poor Olivier as innocent, made inquiries and found everything Madelon had told her about the personal relationship between the master and his journeyman confirmed. The residents of the house and the neighbors unanimously praised Olivier as the model of polite, devout, loyal, industrious conduct, no one knew anything evil about him; and yet, when the subject of the gruesome deed came up, they all shrugged their shoulders and said, there was something incomprehensible about it.

Brought before the Chambre ardente, Olivier denied the deed of which he was accused with the utmost steadfastness and ringing frankness. He asserted that his master had been attacked on the street and struck down in his presence and that he had carried him home still alive but that Cardillac had died soon after. This too agreed with Madelon's account.

Over and over again Mademoiselle de Scudéry inquired into the minutest details of the dreadful event. She investigated whether there had ever been a quarrel between the master and his journeyman, whether Olivier was perhaps not altogether free from those fits of temper that attack even the best-natured people like a blind madness and lead them to commit acts that seem to deny freedom of the will in action. But the more enthusiastically Madelon spoke about the quiet domestic happiness in which the three lived, bound together in the closest love, the more completely did every shadow of suspicion vanish against Olivier, who was now being tried for his life. Testing every detail precisely, proceeding from the assumption that Olivier, in spite of everything that spoke loudly for his innocence, had nevertheless been Cardillac's murderer, Mademoiselle de Scudéry found no motive within the realm of possibility for the dreadful deed, which, from any point of view, was bound to destroy Olivier's happiness. He is poor but skilled; he succeeded in gaining the affection of the most renowned master; he loves the daughter, the daughter favors his love; happiness, lifelong prosperity are within his reach. But suppose that Olivier did make a murderous assault on his benefactor, his father, provoked by—God knows what, overcome by anger; what diabolical hypocrisy to behave after the deed as he had behaved! In the firm conviction of Olivier's innocence, Mademoiselle de Scudéry decided to save the innocent young man, no matter what the cost.

It seemed to her most advisable, before appealing to the king himself for mercy, to turn to President La Regnie, to acquaint him with all the circumstances that spoke in favor of Olivier's innocence and in this way perhaps kindle in the president's heart an inner conviction that was favorable to the accused, a conviction that might communicate itself to the judges.

La Regnie received Mademoiselle de Scudéry with the high esteem to which that worthy lady, who was highly honored by the king himself, could lay just claim. He listened in silence to everything she said about the dreadful deed, about Olivier's circumstances and about his character. She protested that the judge should not be the enemy of the accused but should heed everything that spoke in his favor. But the only sign he gave that these exhortations did not fall on altogether deaf ears was his subtle, almost mocking, smile. When Mademoiselle was finally silent, totally exhausted and wiping the tears from her eyes, La Regnie began: "It does credit to your excellent heart, Mademoiselle, that, touched by the tears of a young girl in love, you should believe everything she says, indeed that you are unable to conceive the thought of such a horrible crime; but quite different is the situation of the judge who is accustomed to tear the mask from the face of impudent hypocrisy. It is not my office to explain the course of a criminal procedure to everyone who asks me to do so. Mademoiselle, I do my duty and care little for the world's judgment. Let villains tremble before the Chambre ardente, which knows no other punishment than blood and fire. But I would not want you, worthy Mademoiselle, to regard me as a monster of harshness and cruelty; permit me therefore to put before you clearly, in few words, the blood-guilt of the young villain who, thank heaven, has been delivered into the hands of vengeance. Your keen intellect will then condemn the leniency that does you honor but would be wholly inappropriate in me.

"Well now! In the morning hours René Cardillac is found murdered by a dagger thrust. No one is with him except his journeyman Olivier Brusson and his daughter. In Olivier's room we find, among other things, a dagger stained with fresh blood, fitting into the wound exactly. 'Cardillac,' says Olivier, 'was struck down before my eyes in the night.' 'Was there an attempt to rob him?' 'I don't know that.' 'You were walking with him and it wasn't possible for you to stop the murderer, to hold on to him, to call for help?' 'My master

was walking fifteen, perhaps twenty, paces in front of me, I was following him.' 'What business did Master Cardillac have being out in
the street so late?' 'I can't say.' 'But normally he never leaves the
house after nine o'clock in the evening?' At this point Olivier falters;
he is perplexed, sighs, sheds tears, assures us by all that is sacred that
Cardillac really did go out that night and met his death. But now
take note, Mademoiselle. It has been established with complete certainty that Cardillac did not leave the house that night, so that Olivier's assertion that he really went out with him is an impudent lie.
The front door is provided with a heavy lock, which makes a piercing
noise when it is opened or closed; besides, the door creaks and
screeches as it moves on its hinges, so that, as tests have shown, the
sound can be heard even in the topmost floor of the house. Now on
the ground floor, that is the one very close to the front door old
Master Claude Patru lives with his housekeeper, a woman of almost
eighty years, but still nimble and mentally alert. That evening at
nine o'clock precisely these two people heard Cardillac descend the
stairs in accordance with his normal habits, lock and bolt the front
door very noisily, then go up the stairs again, read the evening
prayers in a loud voice and then, as they were able to surmise from
the slamming of the door, go into his bedroom. Master Claude suffers from insomnia, as many old people do. That night too he could
not fall asleep. So at about half past nine his housekeeper struck a
light in the kitchen, which is reached by crossing the main hall, and
sat down at the table beside Master Claude with an old chronicle in
which she read, while the old man, steeped in thought, first sat in the
armchair, then got up again and walked up and down the room
softly and slowly, in order to become tired and sleepy. All was quiet
and calm until after midnight. Then she heard sharp steps above
her, a hard thump, as if a heavy weight were falling to the ground,
and immediately after that a muffled groaning. They were both overcome by a strange anxiety and dread. The horror of the terrible deed
that had just been committed passed over them. Daylight revealed
what had begun in the darkness."

"But in the name of all the saints," Mademoiselle de Scudéry interrupted, "in view of all the circumstances that I have just narrated to
you in detail, can you imagine any reason for Olivier committing this
fiendish act?" "Hm," replied La Regnie, "Cardillac was not poor, he
owned some precious gems." "But wouldn't the daughter inherit it

all?" continued Mademoiselle de Scudéry. "You are forgetting that Olivier was going to be Cardillac's son-in-law." "Perhaps he had to share with others or even murder for others," said La Regnie. "Share, murder for others?" asked Mademoiselle in total astonishment. "You should know," continued the president, "that Olivier would have been executed on the place de Grève long ago, if his deed were not related to the veiled mystery that has hovered so ominously over Paris until now. Olivier is obviously a member of the infamous gang that has been able to carry out its coups with precision and impunity, laughing at all the watchfulness, effort, investigation of the courts of law. Through him everything will — must become clear. Cardillac's wound matches those inflicted on all the people who were robbed and murdered in the street or in their homes. But the most decisive point is that since Olivier's arrest, all the robberies and murders have ceased. The streets are once again as safe at night as they are in the daytime, evidence enough that Olivier was perhaps the head of the gang of murderers. Till now he has refused to confess, but there are ways of making him talk against his will." "And Madelon," cried Mademoiselle de Scudéry, "that loyal, innocent dove?" "Oh," said La Regnie with a venomous smile, "who can vouch that she isn't in the plot? What does she care about her father? She has tears for the assassin only." "What are you saying!" cried Mademoiselle, "it isn't possible; her father! that girl!" "Oh," La Regnie continued, "remember the Brinvilliers woman. You will pardon me if I soon find it necessary to snatch your protégée from you and have her thrown into the Conciergerie."

This terrible suspicion caused a shudder to run through Mademoiselle de Scudéry. It seemed to her that no loyalty, no virtue could survive before this frightful man, that he saw murder and blood-guilt in the deepest, most secret thoughts. She stood up. "Be humane," was all she could say, breathing with effort in her depressed state. She was on the point of going down the stairs, to which the president had accompanied her with elaborate etiquette, when a strange idea entered her mind, she scarcely knew how. "Could I be permitted to see the unfortunate Olivier Brusson?" she asked the president, turning to him quickly. He looked at her thoughtfully, then his face was contorted by that hideous smile that was characteristic of him. "Of course, worthy Mademoiselle," he said, "you wish to test Olivier's guilt or innocence yourself, trusting your feeling, your inner voice rather than the events that have taken place before our eyes. If you don't fear the gloomy abode of crime, if you are not repelled by the pictures of depravity in all its stages, the doors of the Conciergerie shall be open to you within two hours. This Olivier, whose fate awakens your sympathy, will be brought before you."

It was true that Mademoiselle de Scudéry could not convince herself of the young man's guilt. Everything testified against him, no judge in the world would have acted differently than La Regnie in the face of such conclusive facts. But the picture of domestic bliss that Madelon had painted in the most vivid colors for Mademoiselle de Scudéry eclipsed every evil suspicion, and so she preferred to assume the existence of some inexplicable mystery rather than believe what went against her whole inner being. She planned to have Olivier tell her everything that had happened on that fateful night and to penetrate as far as possible into a mystery that had perhaps remained a mystery to the judges because it seemed to them pointless to pursue it any further.

When she arrived at the Conciergerie, Mademoiselle de Scudéry was led into a large, bright room. Not long after that she heard the rattle of chains. Olivier Brusson was led in. But the moment he appeared in the doorway Mademoiselle de Scudéry fainted. When she recovered her senses, Olivier had vanished. She asked vehemently to be taken to her carriage, away from here; she insisted on being removed instantly from the abode of criminal depravity. Alas! At the first glance she had recognized in Olivier Brusson the young man who had thrown the sheet of paper into her coach on the Pont-Neuf, who had brought her the casket of jewels. So now all doubt was at an end, La Regnie's dreadful surmise was fully confirmed. Olivier Brusson was a member of the terrible gang of murderers, he had certainly murdered his master too. And Madelon? Mademoiselle de Scudéry despaired of all truth, for never before had she been so bitterly deceived by her inner feeling, so mortally gripped by the power of hell on earth, in whose existence she had refused to believe. She yielded to the horrible suspicion that Madelon could be involved in the conspiracy and might even have participated in the gruesome blood-guilt. As it happens that the human mind, once it has conceived an image, eagerly seeks and finds pigments to paint it in harsher and harsher colors, so Mademoiselle de Scudéry, weighing every circumstance of the crime, examining Madelon's behavior in its minutest details, found much to support that suspicion. Much that she had until now regarded as proof of innocence and purity became a positive sign of criminal wickedness, of studied hypocrisy. The heartrending laments, the tears of blood might well have been forced from her by her mortal anxiety, not at seeing her lover bleed — no — but at falling under the executioner's hand herself. Mademoiselle de Scudéry got out of the carriage with the resolve to rid herself at once of the serpent she was harboring in her bosom. When she entered her apartment, Madelon threw herself at her feet. Her heavenly eyes (no angel of God had truer ones) fixed upon Mademoiselle, her hands folded over her heaving bosom, she wailed and implored aloud for help and comfort. Controlling herself with an effort and seeking to put as much earnestness and tranquility into her voice as she could, Mademoiselle de Scudéry said: "Come, come, take comfort from the fact that a just punishment awaits the murderer for his shameful deed. May the Holy Virgin avert a heavy blood-guilt from you too." "Ah, now all is lost!" With this piercing cry Madelon fell senseless to the floor. Mademoiselle left the girl in the care of Martinière and went into another room.

Her soul rent, alienated from the whole world, Mademoiselle de Scudéry no longer wished to live in a world full of diabolical deception. She accused Fate, which had, with bitter mockery, permitted her to strengthen her faith in virtue and loyalty for so many years and now, in her old age, was destroying the beautiful image that had illumined her life.

She heard Madelon being removed by Martinière; the girl was sighing softly and lamenting: "Ah, she too, she too has been fooled by those cruel people. How wretched I am — poor, unhappy Olivier!" The words pierced Mademoiselle's heart; once again there stirred from within her deepest being the presentiment of a mystery, the belief in Olivier's innocence. Oppressed by the most contradictory emotions, at her wits' end, Mademoiselle de Scudéry cried: "What demon from hell has entangled me in this dreadful affair, which will be the death of me?" At that moment Baptiste entered, pale and frightened, with the news that Desgrais was outside. Since the gruesome trial of La Voisin, Desgrais's appearance in a house was the certain herald of some criminal accusation; hence Baptiste's fright. So mademoiselle asked him with a gentle smile: "What is it, Baptiste? Has the name Scudéry been found on La Voisin's list?" "Oh, in the name of Christ," replied Baptiste, his whole body trembling, "how can you say such a thing? Desgrais, the terrible Desgrais, is acting so mysterious, so urgent, he can't seem to wait till he sees you!" "Well then, Baptiste," said Mademoiselle de Scudéry, "bring him right in, this man who strikes such fear into you but who can stir no anxiety in me."

"President La Regnie," said Desgrais when he entered the apartment, "sends me to you, Mademoiselle, with a request that he would not hope to see granted if he did not know your goodness and your courage, if a final means of shedding light on an evil blood-guilt did not lie in your power, if you yourself had not already participated in the vicious trial that keeps the Chambre ardente and all of us in suspense. Since seeing you, Olivier Brusson is half insane. Though he seemed ever so ready to confess, he now swears anew by Christ and all the saints that he is wholly innocent of Cardillac's murder; but he is quite prepared to suffer the death that he deserves. Note, Mademoiselle, that that last addition points to other crimes that weigh on his conscience. Yet all our efforts to elicit even a single word more from him, even the threat of torture, have been of no avail. He entreats, he implores us to grant him a conversation with you; to you only, to you alone, he is willing to confess everything. Condescend, Mademoiselle, to hear Brusson's confession." "What!" exlaimed Mademoiselle de Scudéry indignantly, "Am I to serve as an instrument of the bloody assize? "Am I to abuse the trust of the unfortunate man and bring him to the scaffold? No, Desgrais! Even if Brusson is a villainous murderer, I could never play him such a rascally trick. I want to learn nothing of his secrets, which would remain locked in my bosom like a holy confession." "Perhaps, Mademoiselle," Desgrais replied with a subtle smile, "you will change your mind after you have heard Brusson. Didn't you yourself beg the president to be humane? He is being just that by yielding to Brusson's foolish request, and so he is trying the last resort before employing torture, for which Brusson has long been ripe." Mademoiselle de Scudéry shuddered involuntarily. "See, worthy lady," Desgrais continued, "you will not be expected to visit those dark chambers again, which fill you with horror and loathing. In the silence of the night, without any ostentation, Olivier Brusson will be brought to your house like a free man. Without being spied upon, though he must certainly be watched, he can then make a full confession to you of his own free will. I will answer to you with my own life that you yourself have nothing to fear from the wretched man. He speaks of you in tones of fervent reverence. He swears that only the sordid fate that has prevented him from seeing you before this has brought him to his death. And then, it is of course entirely up to you to tell us as much as you please of all that Brusson reveals to you. Can we compel you to do more?"

Mademoiselle de Scudéry sat in deep thought, her eyes fixed on the floor. She felt that she had to obey the higher power that demanded the solution to some dreadful mystery, that she could no longer extricate herself from the extraordinary maze into which she had been lured against her will. Coming to a sudden decision, she said with dignity: "God will give me composure and steadfastness; bring Brusson here, I will speak to him."

Just as on the night when Brusson brought her the casket, there was a pounding on Mademoiselle de Scudéry's door at around midnight. Baptiste, who had been informed of the visit, opened the door. An ice-cold shudder went through Mademoiselle de Scudéry when she gathered from their soft march and their muffled murmurs that the guards who had brought Brusson were stationing themselves in the corridors of the house. At length the door of her apartment was opened very gently. Desgrais entered, behind him Olivier Brusson, freed from his chains, in decent clothes. "Here is Brusson, my worthy Mademoiselle," said Desgrais, bowing respectfully and leaving the room.

Brusson sank down on both knees before Mademoiselle de Scudéry; he raised his folded hands in entreaty, copious tears streaming from his eyes.

Mademoiselle de Scudéry looked down at him, pale of face, incapable of uttering a word. Even these contorted features, which were disfigured by grief and deep pain, shone with a pure expression indicating a most loyal soul. The longer Mademoiselle de Scudéry let her eyes rest on Brusson's face, the more vivid became her memory of some beloved person, whom she could not recollect clearly. All the horror within her faded, she forgot that Cardillac's murderer was kneeling before her, she spoke in the gracious tone of calm benevolence that was characteristic of her: "Well, Brusson, what have you to say to me?" Brusson, still on his knees, sighed with profound, fervent sadness, and then said: "Oh my worthy, my highly revered Mademoiselle, has every trace of your memory of me left you?" Mademoiselle, studying him more attentively still, replied that she had indeed found in his features a resemblance to some person she had loved and that it was only thanks to this resemblance that she had overcome her profound horror of the murderer and was willing to listen to him calmly. Brusson was deeply hurt by these words; he rose to his feet quickly and took a step backward, fixing his eyes gloomily on the floor. Then he spoke in a hollow voice: "Have you completely forgotten Anne Guiot? Her son Olivier, the boy you often rocked on your knees, is standing before you."

"Oh, in the name of all the saints," cried Mademoiselle de Scudéry, covering her face with both hands and sinking back into the cushions of her armchair. Mademoiselle had good cause for this feeling of horror. Anne Guiot, the daughter of an impoverished burgher, had spent her childhood at the home of Mademoiselle, who had raised her in the loyalty and care that a mother gives to her beloved child. When she had grown up, there appeared a handsome, wellmannered youth named Claude Brusson to court the girl. As he was an excellent watchmaker, who was sure to earn a good livelihood in Paris, and since Anne had come to love him warmly, Mademoiselle de Scudéry had no hesitation in agreeing to her foster daughter's marriage. The young couple set up house, lived in quiet, happy domesticity; the bond was made evern stronger by the birth of a beautiful boy, the faithful image of his lovely mother.

Mademoiselle de Scudéry idolized little Olivier, whom she took away from his mother for hours and even days, to caress and fondle. For that reason the boy became wholly accustomed to her and liked to be with her as much as with his mother. After three years, the professional envy of Brusson's competitors had caused his business to decline from day to day, so that he was scarcely able to make a living. Added to this was his yearning for his beautiful native Geneva; and so it came that the small family moved there, despite the objections of Mademoiselle de Scudéry, who promised them every possible support. Anne wrote to her foster mother a few times, then she was silent, and Mademoiselle was forced to conclude that the happy existence in Brusson's native city had suppressed the memory of their former life.

It was now just twenty-three years since Brusson had left Paris with his wife and child and moved to Geneva.

"Oh, horror," cried Mademoiselle de Scudéry when she had recovered somewhat, "you are Olivier, my Anne's son! And now!"

"Indeed," replied Olivier, calm and composed, "you could never have suspected, worthy Mademoiselle, that the boy whom you caressed like the most tender mother, whom you rocked on your lap and fed with candy, to whom you gave the sweetest names, would stand before you one day, grown into a young man and accused of committing a gruesome, bloody deed. I am not above reproach, the Chambre ardente can justly charge me with a crime; but as I hope to die with my soul saved, even though it be at the hands of the hangman, I am innocent of all blood-guilt; the unhappy Cardillac did not die through me, not through my guilt." At these words Olivier began to tremble and shake silently. Mademoiselle de Scudéry motioned him to a small armchair that stood beside him. He sat down in it slowly.

"I have had time enough," he began, "to prepare myself for this conversation with you, which I regard as the last favor that a reconciled heaven will grant me, and to gain as much calm and composure as are needed to tell you the story of my dreadful, incomparable misfortune. Be merciful and listen to me calmly, no matter how deeply surprised, indeed horrified, you may be by the revelation of a secret that I am sure you did not suspect.

"I wish my poor father had never left Paris! As far back as my memory of Geneva reaches, I find myself drenched in the tears shed by my despairing parents, moved to tears myself by their laments, which I did not understand. Later on I had the distinct impression, the full consciousness, of the direst want, the most abject misery in which my parents lived. My father found himself disappointed in all his hopes. Bowed by deep sorrow, crushed, he died at the moment when he succeeded in placing me as an apprentice to a goldsmith. Mother talked a great deal about you, she wanted to tell you her whole lamentable story, but then she was overcome by that despondency that is born of misery. That and probably a false sense of shame, which often gnaws away at a mortally wounded spirit, kept her from carrying out her intention. A few months after my father's death my mother followed him to the grave." "Poor Anne, poor Anne!" cried Mademoiselle de Scudéry, overwhelmed by suffering. "I give praise and thanks to the eternal Power of Heaven that she has passed into the beyond and will not see her beloved son die at the hands of the hangman, branded with shame." Olivier shouted these words, sending a wild, terrible look to heaven. The silence outside was broken, men could be heard walking back and forth. "Ha, ha," said Olivier with a bitter smile on his face, "Desgrais is waking his men, as if I could escape from here. But to continue. My master treated me harshly, even though I was his best worker, indeed eventually far surpassed him in skill. It happened that one day a foreigner came into our workshop to buy some jewelry. When he saw a beautiful necklace I had made, he gave me a friendly pat on the shoulder and said, his eyes on the ornament: 'Why, my young friend, this is really excellent work. I don't know of anyone who can surpass it except René Cardillac, who is of course the finest goldsmith in the world. You should go to him, he will welcome you with joy to his workshop, for you alone can assist him in his highly artistic work, and in return he alone can teach you anything.' The foreigner's words made a deep impression on me. I could no longer find peace in Geneva, I felt a force drawing me out of it. I finally succeeded in freeing myself from my master. I came to Paris. René Cardillac received me coldly and gruffly. But I stuck to him; he would have to give me some work, however paltry it might be. I was to make a small ring. When I brought the work to him, he fixed me with those sparkling eyes, as though he wanted to look into my innermost being. Then he said: 'You are an able, excellent fellow. You can move in with me and help me in my workshop. I'll pay you well and you'll be satisfied with me.' Cardillac kept his word. I had been with him for several weeks but had never seen Madelon who, if I am not mistaken, was at that time in the country, staying with some cousin of Cardillac. Finally she came home. Oh, eternal Power of Heaven, what happened to me when I beheld that angelic figure! Has ever a man loved as I did? And now! O Madelon!"

Olivier could not continue because of the sorrow he felt. He covered his face with his hands and sobbed vehemently. At length he conquered the savage pain with an effort and continued. "Madelon regarded me with friendly eyes. She came more and more often to the workshop. With delight I perceived that she loved me. No matter how strictly her father watched over us, many a stealthy pressure of the hand testified to the bond that held us together. Cardillac seemed to notice nothing. I planned to ask him for Madelon's hand as soon as I had gained his favor and obtained the rank of master craftsman. One morning, as I was about to begin my day's work, Cardillac came up to me, anger and contempt in his stern eyes. 'I don't

need your work any longer,' he began; 'get out of my house within
the hour and don't let me ever set eyes on you again. I don't have to
tell you why I can no longer tolerate you here. You poor wretch are
straining for a sweet fruit that hangs beyond your reach.' I wanted to
speak but he seized me with his powerful fist and threw me out the
door so that I fell, suffering serious injury to my head and arm.

"Indignant, racked by severe pain, I left the house and found a
friendly acquaintance at the extreme end of the Faubourg Saint-
Martin, who took me in to share his attic room. I had no peace, no
rest. At night I prowled around Cardillac's house, imagining that
Madelon would hear my sighs and laments, that she might perhaps
succeed in talking to me from her window unobserved. My brain
hatched all sorts of daring plans, which I hoped to persuade her to
carry out. Cardillac's house in the rue Nicaise stands next to a high
wall with niches containing old, half crumbled stone statues. One
night I was standing close to one of these statues, looking up to the
windows that face the yard surrounded by the wall. Suddenly I perceived a light in Cardillac's workshop, It was midnight; Cardillac was
never awake at this hour, he was in the habit of going to bed on the
stroke of nine o'clock. My heart was pounding with a fearful premonition, I thought of some event that might secure for me an entrance
into the house. But the light went out at once. I squeezed into the
niche against the stone statue, but in horror I bounced back when I
felt a counterpressure, as if the statue had come to life. In the dim
glimmer of the night I saw the stone turn slowly; from behind it a
dark figure slipped out and walked down the street with soft steps. I
rushed up to the statue but it was standing close to the wall as before.
Involuntarily, as though driven by an inner force, I followed the
figure stealthily. At an image of the Virgin the figure turned around,
the full light of the bright lamp in front of the image lit up its face. It
was Cardillac! An indescribable dread, an uncanny horror, seized
me. As though bound by a magic spell I had to go on after the ghostly
somnambulist. That's what I though the master was, in spite of the
fact that it was not the time of the full moon, when this specter con-
fuses sleepers. Finally Cardillac vanished into the deep shadow. The
slight familiar sound of clearing his throat informed me that he had
stepped into the entrance to a house. 'What does it mean? What is he
going to do?' I asked myself in utter astonishment, pressing close to
the houses.

"It wasn't long before a man in a shining plumed hat and jingling spurs came by, singing and warbling. Like a tiger pouncing on his prey, Cardillac rushed out of his hiding place at the man, who fell to the ground instantly, in the agony of death. With a cry of horror I leaped forward; Cardillac was bent over the man lying on the ground. 'Master Cardillac, what are you doing?' I cried aloud. 'Cursed knave!' Cardillac roared, rushed past me with the speed of lightning and disappeared. Completely beside myself, scarcely able to walk, I approached the fallen man. I knelt down beside him; perhaps, I thought, he may still be saved, but there was no trace of life left in him. In my mortal anxiety I hardly noticed that I was surrounded by mounted police. 'Another one laid low by the devils. —Ho there, young man, what are you doing here? Are you one of the gang? Get out of here!' Thus they shouted in confusion and seized me. I could only stammer out that I could never have committed such a horrible deed and that they might let me go in peace. Then one of them shone his lamp in my face and said with a laugh: 'Why, that's Olivier Brusson, the journeyman goldsmith who works for our honest good master Rene Cardillac. *He* murder people on the street? Looks very much like it. Isn't it just like murderous rogues to wail over the corpse till they're caught by the police! How did it happen? Tell us right out!' 'Right in front of me,' I said, 'a man leaped out at this fellow, struck him down and ran away with lightning speed when I raised a cry. I tried to find out if the fallen man could still be saved.' 'No, my son,' said one of the men who had lifted the corpse, 'this one is finished; as usual, the dagger went right through the heart.' 'The devil,' said another, 'we've come too late again, like two nights ago.' And they departed with the corpse.

"I can't describe my state of mind to you; I felt myself to see if it was a bad dream that was plaguing me; I thought I would wake up in a moment and wonder at the crazy delusion. Cardillac, the father of my Madelon, a hideous murderer! I had sat down weakly on the stone steps of a house. The sky was growing brighter; an officer's hat, adorned with many plumes, lay on the pavement before me. Cardillac's bloody deed, committed on this spot where I was sitting, passed clearly before my eyes. In horror I sped away from there.

"In utter confusion, almost senseless, I was sitting in my garret next day when the door opened and in came René Cardillac. 'For Christ's sake, what do you want?' I shouted at him. He paid no heed to me, came up to me and smiled at me with a calm and cordiality that only increased my inner loathing. He pulled up an old, decrepit footstool and sat down beside me. I was unable to rise from the straw pallet on which I had thrown myself. 'Well, Olivier,' he began, 'how are you, my poor boy? I was surely terribly overhasty in throwing you out of my house. I miss you at every turn. Right now I'm working on a project that I simply can't finish without your help. How would it be if you came and worked in my shop again? — You're silent? Yes, I know I have insulted you. I didn't want to hide from you that I was angry with you because of the flirtation you were carrying on with my Madelon. But I thought the matter over later and found that, with your skill, your industry, your loyalty, I could wish for no better son-in-law than you. So come back with me and see how you can win Madelon for your wife.'

"Cardillac's words cut me to the heart, I trembled at this wickedness, I couldn't utter a word. 'You hesitate?' he continued in a sharp tone, his glittering eyes boring into me. 'Perhaps you can't come with me today because you have other plans—perhaps you want to pay a visit to Desgrais or have yourself presented to d'Argenson or La Regnie. Take care, lad, that the claws you plan to thrust out for the destruction of other people don't grasp and rend you yourself.' At that my deeply offended spirit suddenly found expression. 'May those,' I cried, 'who have a gruesome crime on their conscience fear the names you have just mentioned; I don't need to do so, I have no concern with them.' 'Actually,' Cardillac went on, 'it will be an honor for you to work for me, the most famous master of the age, highly esteemed everywhere for his skill, highly esteemed everywhere for his loyalty and honesty, so that any malicious slander would fall back heavily on the head of the slanderer. — Now, as for Madelon, I must confess to you that you owe my compliance to her alone. She loves you with a fierceness that I simply would not have credited to the delicate child. As soon as you left me, she fell at my feet, clasped my knees, confessed amidst a thousand tears that she could not live without you. I thought she was merely imagining things, the way young girls in love are accustomed to do—that they will die on the spot when the first milksop has looked at them with a kind eye. But my Madelon really got sick, and when I tried to talk her out of this nonsense, she called your name a hundred times; so what could I do

if I didn't want her to despair? Last night I told her that I agreed to
everything and would fetch you today. Overnight she blossomed out
like a rose and is now waiting for you, quite beside herself with the
longing of love.' — May the eternal Power of Heaven forgive me, but
I don't know myself how it happened that I was suddenly in Cardillac's house, that Madelon rushed at me, crying in exultation, 'Olivier,
my Olivier, my beloved, my spouse!' threw both arms around my
neck, pressed me firmly to her breast, so that in an excess of the highest rapture I swore by the Holy Virgin that I would never, never leave
her.'"

Deeply agitated by the recollection of this decisive moment, Olivier
had to pause. Mademoiselle de Scudéry, filled with horror at the
crime of a man whom she had regarded as virtue, rectitude itself,
exlaimed: "Dreadful! René Cardillac is one of the murderous gang
that has made a robbers' den of our good city for so long?" "Why do
you speak of a gang, Mademoiselle?" said Olivier. "There has never
been such a gang. It was Cardillac alone, whose villainous activity
consisted in searching out and finding his victims for slaughter in the
whole city. The fact that it was he alone made it safe for him to carry
out his crimes and made it impossibly difficult to get on the trail of
the murderer. — But let me continue; the sequel will reveal to you
the secrets of the most ruthless but also most unfortunate of men. —

"Anyone can easily imagine the position in which I now found myself with regard to the master. The step had been taken, I could no
longer retreat. At times I felt as if I myself had become Cardillac's
assistant in his murders; only my love of Madelon enabled me to forget the inner torment I felt, only in her presence was I able to eradi-
cate every outer trace of my unspeakable grief. When I worked
beside the old man in his workshop, I could not look him in the face
or hardly say a word to him because of the horror I felt near this terrible man who practiced all the virtues of the loyal and tender father
and the good citizen while his crimes were shrouded by the veil of
night. Madelon, the good, angelically pure child, clung to him with
an idolatrous love. It pierced my heart to think that if vengeance
should ever strike the unmasked villain, she who had been deceived
with all the diabolical cunning of Satan would be thrown into the
most frightful despair. That alone was enough to seal my lips, even if
I had to suffer a criminal's death because of it. Although I could

infer enough from the talk by the mounted police, Cardillac's crimes, their motive, his manner of executing them were a riddle to me; but the solution was not long in coming.

"One day Cardillac, who was normally in the best of spirits at work, joking and laughing (and incurring my loathing thereby), was very serious and pensive. Suddenly he threw aside the jewelry on which he was working so that the gems and pearls scattered all over the bench, stood up impetuously and said: 'Olivier, things cannot remain like this between us, this relationship is intolerable to me. What Desgrais and his men couldn't discover with all their subtle cunning, chance has played into your hands. You have observed me at my nocturnal labor, to which I am driven by my evil star and which it is impossible for me to resist. It was your evil star too that impelled you to follow me, that enveloped you in impenetrable veils, giving your footsteps such lightness that you moved as noiselessly as the smallest insect, so that I, who see as clearly as a tiger in the darkest night, who can hear the slightest sound, the hum of a gnat several streets away, didn't notice you. Your evil star led you to me as my accomplice. In your present situation betrayal is out of the question. So you may as well know everything.' I wanted to shout aloud, 'I will never be your accomplice, you hypocritical villain,' but an inner horror that gripped me when I heard Cardillac's words constricted my throat. Instead of words I could utter only unintelligible sounds. Cardillac sat down again at his workbench. He dried the perspiration from his forehead. He seemed to be struggling to recover from the agitation caused by his recollection of past events. At length he began:

"'Wise men say a lot about the strange influences that pregnant women undergo and of the remarkable effect produced on the child by such vivid, involuntary impressions.* I was told a strange story about my mother. During her first month of pregnancy with me she and some other women were watching a splendid court festival that was being staged in the Trianon. Her eye fell upon a cavalier in Spanish costume with a glittering chain of jewels about his neck; she simply could not take her eyes from this necklace. Her whole being became a desire for the glittering gems, which appeared to her to be a supernatural essence. The same courtier had pursued my mother several years before that, when she was still unmarried, but had been

---

*At the time this story was written the subject of prenatal influence was much discussed in medical literature.

rejected by her with loathing. My mother recognized him again, but it seemed to her that now, in the splendor of the radiant diamonds, he was a being of a higher species, the quintessence of all beauty. The courtier noticed the yearning, ardent glow in my mother's eyes. He believed he would have better luck this time. He was able to approach her and even to lure her away from her companions to a lonely spot. There he embraced her passionately. My mother reached out for the beautiful chain; but at that moment he sank down and pulled my mother with him to the ground. Whether he suffered a sudden stroke or because of some other reason—enough, he was dead. In vain did my mother struggle to extricate herself from the stiffened arms of the corpse. His glazed, sightless eyes fixed on her, the dead man rolled on the ground with her. Her piercing cries for help finally reached some passersby in the distance, they hastened to the spot and freed her from the arms of the gruesome lover. The shock threw my mother into a severe illness. Both she and I were given up for lost; however, she recovered, and her delivery was easier than anyone had dared to hope. But the terror of the fearful moment had affected me. My evil star had gained the ascendant and had dropped the spark that kindled in me one of the strangest and most destructive passions. Even in my earliest childhood I valued gleaming diamonds, golden jewelry above everything else. This was taken to be the ordinary fancy of a child. But it turned out to be very different, for in my boyhood I stole gold and jewels wherever I could find them. Like the most skilled expert I could instinctively distinguish genuine jewels from mere paste. Only the genuine article enticed me, I would not touch paste or gold coin. My inborn craving was curbed by my father's most cruel punishment.

" 'In order to be in contact with gold and precious gems, I took up the goldsmith's profession. I worked with passion and soon became the first master of this art. Now there began a period in which my innate impulse, so long suppressed, forced its way into the open and grew in power, consuming everything in its path. As soon as I had finished and delivered a piece of jewelry I fell into a restless, disconsolate state that robbed me of sleep, health and the will to live. Like a ghost, the person for whom I had done the work stood before my eyes day and night, adorned with my jewelry, and a voice whispered in my ears: "But it's yours, but it's yours; take it, what use are the diamonds to the dead man?" So I finally took up the arts of thievery. I had

access to the houses of the great, I swiftly exploited every opportunity, no lock could withstand my skill, and soon the jewelry I had
produced was once more in my possession. But now even that did not
assuage my restlessness. That eerie voice made itself heard again,
mocking me and crying: "Ha, ha, your jewelry is being worn by a
dead person!" I didn't know myself how it came that I conceived a
boundless hatred for those for whom I had made jewelry. Yes, in my
innermost being there stirred against them a lust to murder, which
made me tremble.

"'At the time I bought this house, after I had signed the agreement with the owner, we sat together in this room over a bottle of
wine, happy about the deal we had made. Night had fallen, I wanted
to leave, when my vendor spoke: "Listen, Master René, before you go
I must acquaint you with a secret of this house." With that he unlocked that cupboard that's built into the wall, slid the back wall
open, walked into a small chamber, bent down and lifted a trap
door. We went down a steep, narrow stairway, came to a narrow
gate, which he unlocked, and stepped out into the open courtyard.
Now the old gentleman, my vendor, walked along the wall, pushed a
piece of iron that projected slightly from the wall, and at once a section of the wall rotated, allowing a person to slip through the opening comfortably and reach the street. Someday you will see this clever
device, Olivier, which was probably built upon orders of sly monks
from the monastery that was formerly quartered here, so that they
could slip in and out in secret. It is a piece of wood, covered with
mortar and paint on the outside, into which a statue — it too made of
wood, though it looks like stone — is fitted and which rotates with the
statue on concealed hinges.

"'Dark thoughts arose in my mind when I saw this device; I felt as
if it had been made in anticipation of deeds that were still a secret to
me. I had just delivered an expensive piece of jewelry to a gentleman
of the court who, as I knew, intended it for a dancer at the opera.
The fatal torment did not fail to appear, the specter clung to my
footsteps, Satan kept whispering in my ear. I moved into the house.
Bathed in the bloody sweat of anxiety, I tossed on my bed, unable to
sleep. In my imagination I saw the man going stealthily to the dancer
with my jewelry. In a rage I jumped up, threw my cloak about my
shoulders, went down the secret stairway, out through the wall, into
the rue Nicaise. He passed by, I pounced on him, he uttered a cry;

but holding him firmly from behind, I plunged the dagger into his heart; the jewels were mine. Having done this, I felt a calm, a mental satisfaction such as I had never experienced before. The specter had vanished, the voice of Satan was silent. Now I knew what my evil star wanted from me; I had to yield to it or perish.

"'You now understand all my activity, Olivier. Don't think that, because I must do what I can't help doing, I have wholly renounced that feeling of sympathy and mercy that is said to be part of being human. You know how hard it is for me to part with a piece of jewelry; that I will not accept work from many people whose death I do not wish; that if I know that on the following day only blood will exorcise my ghost, I try to appease it by a vigorous blow of the fist today, which stuns the owner of my jewels and delivers them into my hands.'

"After this Cardillac led me into his secret vault and allowed me to inspect his jewel cabinet. The king does not own a finer one. Every piece was tagged with a small label, which indicated for whom it had been made and when it was taken by theft, robbery or murder. 'On your wedding day, Olivier,' Cardillac said in a hollow, solemn voice, 'you will take a sacred oath with your hand on the image of the crucified Christ that, as soon as I am dead, you will turn all these riches to dust by means that I will make known to you. I don't want any human being, least of all Madelon and you, to come into possession of this treasure, which has been bought with blood.'

"Imprisoned in this labyrinth of crime, rent by love and loathing, by happiness and horror, I could be compared to the condemned man to whom a lovely angel beckons with a gentle smile but who is held fast by Satan with fiery claws; the loving smile of the godly angel, in which all the bliss of high heaven is reflected, turns into the direst torment for him. — I thought of flight, indeed of suicide — but Madelon! Blame me, blame me, worthy Mademoiselle, for being too weak to subdue, by the power of discipline, a passion that kept me chained to crime, but am I not paying for it with a shameful death?

"One day Cardillac came home in uncommonly cheerful spirits. He embraced Madelon, cast the most friendly glances at me, drank a bottle of choice wine at dinner, something he did only on days of high festivity or solemnity, sang and rejoiced. Madelon had left us and I was about to go into the workshop. 'Sit still, my boy,' Cardillac said, 'no more work today; let's drink another to the health of the

most worthy, most excellent lady in Paris.' After I had clinked glasses
with him and he had emptied his, he spoke: 'Tell me, Olivier, how
you like these verses:

> Un amant qui craint les voleurs
> n'est point digne d'amour.'

He then told me what had occurred between you and the king in
Madame de Maintenon's apartment and added that he had always
honored you above all other human beings and that you were
endowed with such lofty virtue, before which the evil star paled in
impotence, that even if you wore the most beautiful jewelry of his
making you would never arouse an evil specter or thought of murder
in him. 'Hear, Olivier,' he said, 'what I have resolved. A long time
ago I was asked to make a necklace and bracelets for Henriette of
England, for which I was to furnish my own stones. The work was
superior to any I had ever done, but it rent my heart to think that I
would have to part with the jewelry, which had become the treasure
of my heart. You know about the princess' unhappy death by assassi-
nation. I kept the jewels and now wish to send them to Mademoiselle
de Scudéry as a token of my respect and gratitude in the name of the
persecuted gang. Apart from the fact that Mademoiselle de Scudéry
will thus receive an eloquent token of her triumph, I shall also be
heaping on Desgrais and his fellows the ridicule they so well deserve.
You will take the jewels to her.'

"When Cardillac mentioned your name, Mademoiselle, it was as if
black veils had been lifted, and the fair, bright picture of my happy
early childhood became visible once more in its gay, resplendent
colors. A marvellous feeling of consolation entered my soul, a ray of
hope, before which the dark ghosts vanished. Cardillac must have
perceived the impression that his words had made on me and given
them his own interpretation. 'My plan seems to please you,' he said.
'I may confess to you that I am acting on the orders of a deep inner
voice, very different from that which demands bloody sacrifices like a
ravenous beast of prey. Sometimes I am overcome by a strange
feeling; an inner anxiety takes possession of me forcefully, the fear of
something dreadful, the horror of which floats into time from a distant beyond. At such times I even feel that what the evil star has committed through me might be charged to my immortal soul, which has
no part in it. In such a mood I resolved to make a beautiful diamond

crown for the Holy Virgin in St. Eustache Church. But the mysterious anxiety came over me with greater intensity whenever I wanted to begin work, and so I gave it up altogether. Now I feel as if, in sending Mademoiselle de Scudéry the finest jewelry I have ever wrought, I am bringing a humble sacrifice to virtue and piety themselves, imploring effective intercession on my behalf.'

"Cardillac, who was most intimately familiar with your way of life, Mademoiselle, detailed to me the manner as well as the time for delivering the jewelry, which he locked in a neat little casket. I was delighted to my core, for heaven itself was showing me, through the criminal Cardillac, the way to save myself from the hell in which I languish as an outcast sinner. So I thought. Contrary to Cardillac's wishes, I intended to reach you in person. I thought of throwing myself at your feet as Anne Brusson's son, as your foster child. I did everything to you. Moved by the boundless misery that would threaten the poor, innocent Madelon if the secret were revealed, you would have kept it, but your lofty, sharp intellect would surely have found positive means for controlling Cardillac's infamous wickedness without revealing it. Don't ask me what these means might be, I don't know; but that you would rescue Madelon and me, of this I was as firmly convinced in the depths of my soul as I believe in the comforting help of the Holy Virgin.

"You know, Mademoiselle, that my plan failed that night. But I did not lose the hope of being luckier another time. Then it happened that Cardillac suddenly lost his good spirits. He prowled about gloomily, stared fixedly before him, murmured unintelligible words, waved his hands about to ward off hostile forces; his mind seemed to be tormented by evil thoughts. He had been carrying on this way for a whole morning. Finally he sat down at his workbench, then jumped up again in irritation, looked out of the window, and said in an earnest, gloomy voice: 'I wish Henriette of England had worn my jewels after all.' These words filled me with dread. Now I knew that his insane mind was once again in the grip of the abominable murderous specter, that the voice of Satan had once more grown loud in his ears. I saw your life endangered by the villainous, murderous devil. If Cardillac could only get his jewels back, you would be safe. The danger grew with every moment.

"Then I met you on the Pont-Neuf, forced my way to your carriage, threw you that note that implored you to return the jewels to

Cardillac at once. You did not appear. My anxiety reached the point
of despair when, next morning, Cardillac spoke of nothing but the
precious jewels, which had appeared to him in a dream that night. I
could only interpret this as referring to your jewels, and I became
certain that he was brooding on some murderous assault that he had
without a doubt planned the previous night. I had to rescue you,
even if it should cost Cardillac his life. As soon as he had locked himself in his room after the evening prayer, as he usually did, I went
into the courtyard through a window, slipped through the opening in
the wall, and took up my position nearby in the deep shadow. It was
not long before Cardillac came out and softly stole away into the
street. I followed him. He went toward the rue St. Honoré and my
heart trembled. Cardillac had suddenly vanished from my sight. I resolved to post myself at your front door. Soon an officer passed, singing and warbling as on that night when chance made me a witness to
Cardillac's murderous act. The officer did not notice me; but at that
moment a black figure leaped out of the shadows and pounced on
him. It was Cardillac. I wanted to prevent this murder; with a loud
cry I reached the spot in two or three leaps. However, it was not the
officer but Cardillac who sank to the ground mortally wounded, with
the death rattle in his throat. The officer dropped the dagger, drew
his sword out of the sheath, took up a fighting position in the belief
that I was the murderer's accomplice. However, when he saw that I
paid no attention to him but busied myself examining the corpse, he
hurried away. Cardillac was still alive. After taking possession of the
dagger that the officer had dropped, I hoisted him on my shoulders
and dragged him home with great effort, and up into his workshop
by way of the secret passage.

"The rest is familiar to you. You see, my worthy Mademoiselle,
that my only crime is that I did not betray Madelon's father to the
courts and thus put an end to his misdeeds. I am clean of every blood-
guilt. No amount of torture will wrest the secret of Cardillac's crimes
from me. I will not allow the eternal Power that veiled the gruesome
blood-guilt of the father from the virtuous daughter to be thwarted,
causing the whole misery of the past, of her whole being, to erupt
over her at this time and deal her a mortal blow; I will not allow that
at this late point worldly vengeance should dig up the corpse from
the earth that covers it; that the hangman should at this late point
brand the moldering bones with shame. No, the beloved of my soul

shall mourn me as the innocent victim. Time will alleviate her pain; but if she discovered the horrible, hellish deeds of her beloved father, her misery would be boundless."

Olivier was silent, then a stream of tears suddenly gushed from his eyes; he threw himself at Mademoiselle de Scudéry's feet and beseeched her: "You are convinced of my innocence, I'm certain that you are. Have pity on me, tell me, how is Madelon?" Mademoiselle de Scudéry called to Martinière and a few moments later Madelon flew to Olivier and threw her arms about his neck. "Now that you are here, all will be well; I knew the most noble spirited lady would save you." So Madelon cried over and over again, and Olivier forgot his destiny and everything that threatened him; he was free and happy. Most touchingly they both lamented what they had suffered for each other, and then embraced once more and went for joy to have found each other again.

If Mademoiselle de Scudéry had not already been convinced of Olivier's innocence, that conviction would have come to her now, as she contemplated the two, who forgot the world and its misery and their unspeakable suffering in the bliss of the deepest bonds of love. "No," she said, "only a pure heart is capable of such happy forgetfulness."

The bright rays of the morning sun broke in through the windows. Desgrais knocked softly on the apartment door and remined them that it was time to remove Olivier Brusson, since this could not be done later without causing a sensation. The lovers had to part.

The obscure forebodings that had dominated Mademoiselle de Scudéry's mind since Brusson's first entry into her house had now taken on life in a terrible form. She saw the son of her beloved Anne innocently entangled in such a way that it scarcely seemed conceivable that he could be saved from a shameful death. She honored the young man's heroic attitude, who would rather die laden with guilt than betray a secret that would certainly mean the death of his Madelon. In the whole realm of possibility she found no means by which she could snatch the poor man from the cruel tribunal. And yet it was clear to her that she must spare no sacrifice to avert the crying injustice that was about to be committed. She tormented herself with all sorts of proposals and plans, bordering on the quixotic, which she rejected as quickly as they were conceived. More and more she lost every glimmer of hope, so that she was ready to despair. But

Madelon's absolutely innocent, childlike trust, the rapture with which she spoke of her fiancé who, soon to be absolved of all guilt, would embrace her as his wife, restored Mademoiselle de Scudéry in spirit to the degree that it touched her heart deeply.

In order to do something, at long last, Mademoiselle de Scudéry wrote a long letter to La Regnie, in which she told him that Olivier Brusson had demonstrated to her most convincingly his total innocence of Cardillac's death, and that only the most heroic resolve to take with him into the grave a secret, the revelation of which would destroy the very embodiment of innocence and virtue, prevented him from making a confession to the court that would free him from the horrible suspicion not only of having murdered Cardillac, but also of having belonged to the gang of villainous murderers. Everything that ardent zeal and brilliant eloquence could achieve, Mademoiselle de Scudéry summoned up to soften La Regnie's hard heart.

After a few hours an answer came back from La Regnie: he was very glad that Olivier Brusson had wholly justified himself before his noble and worthy patroness. As for Olivier's heroic resolve to take with him into the grave a secret related to the crime, he regretted that the Chambre ardente could not honor such a heroic temper but must, on the contrary, seek to break it with every means at its command. In three days' time he hoped to be in possession of the strange secret, which would no doubt shed light on wonders that had been wrought.

Mademoiselle de Scudéry knew only too well what the dreaded La Regnie meant by those means that were to break Olivier's heroic spirit. Now it was certain that the unhappy man was doomed to suffer torture. In her mortal anxiety it finally occurred to her that the advice of a lawyer might be helpful, if only to secure a delay. Pierre Arnaud d'Andilly was at that time the most famous advocate in Paris. His profound knowledge and wide-ranging intelligence were matched by his integrity and his virtue. Mademoiselle de Scudéry went to him and told him everything she could without jeopardizing Brusson's secret. She believed that d'Andilly would eagerly take up the cause of the innocent man; but her hopes were most bitterly disappointed. D'Andilly had listened to her story quietly; he replied with a smile in Boileau's words: "Le vrai peut quelquefois n'être pas vraisemblable."* He demonstrated to Mademoiselle de Scudéry that

*"The truth may sometimes be improbable."

the most striking grounds for suspicion spoke against Brusson, that La Regnie's procedure could in no way be branded as cruel and hasty but was wholly legal, indeed that he could not act otherwise without violating his duty as a judge. He, d'Andilly, did not believe he could save Brusson from torture even through the most skillful defense. Only Brusson himself could do that, either by making a sincere confession or at least by relating the precise details regarding Cardillac's murder, which might perhaps lead to a new investigation. "Then I shall throw myself at the feet of the king and beg for mercy," said Mademoiselle de Scudéry, beside herself with emotion, her voice half choked by tears. "Don't do that," cried d'Andilly, "for heaven's sake, Mademoiselle. Hold this last remedy in reserve, because if it should fail, it would be lost to you forever. The king will never grant a pardon to that sort of murderer; he would incur the most bitter reproaches of the endangered people. It is possible that Brusson, by revealing his secret, or in some other way, will find means for removing the suspicion that militates against him. Then it will be time to invoke the mercy of the king, who will not ask what was proved or not in the courts but will take counsel with his inner conviction."

Mademoiselle de Scudéry had to agree with d'Andilly, the man of wide experience. Sunk in profound grief, thinking and thinking what in the name of the Virgin and all the saints she should do next to save the unfortunate Brusson, she sat in her apartment late one evening, when Martinière entered and announced the Count Miossens, colonel in the Royal Guard, who urgently requested to speak to Mademoiselle.

"Forgive me, Mademoiselle," said Miossens, bowing with military dignity, "for disturbing you so late at such an inopportune hour. This is the way we soldiers act; for the rest, a few words will secure my pardon. I come on account of Olivier Brusson." Tense with expectation as to what was developing, Mademoiselle de Scudéry cried aloud: "Olivier Brusson? The most unhappy person in the world? What have you to do with him?" "I thought," Miossens continued with a smile, "that the name of your protégé would be sufficient to grant me a sympathetic ear. The whole world is convinced of his guilt. I know that you are of a different opinion, based solely, it is said, on the assertions of the accused. My case is different. No one can be more convinced than I of Brusson's innocence in Cardillac's death." "Speak, oh, speak," cried Mademoiselle de Scudéry, her eyes shining with joy. "It was I myself," said Miossens emphatically, "who struck down the old goldsmith in the rue St. Honoré not far from your house." "In the name of all the saints—you? you?" cried Mademoiselle. "And I swear to you, Mademoiselle," Miossens continued, "that I am proud of my deed. You should know that Cardillac was the most outrageous and most hypocritical villain; it was he who treacherously murdered and robbed at night and escaped every snare for such a long time. I don't know how it happened that an inner suspicion against the old villain arose in me when he brought me, in obvious agitation, the jewelry I had ordered from him, when he inquired in precise detail for whom the jewels were intended and when he interrogated my valet very artfully at what time I am in the habit of visiting a certain lady. I had noticed long ago that the unlucky victims of this most abominable robber all bore the same lethal wound. I felt certain that the murderer was well practiced in delivering a blow that would kill instantly and relied on his skill. Once this blow failed, he faced an equal combat. This led me to take a precautionary measure so simple that I can't understand why other people didn't think of it long ago and save themselves from the murder that threatened them. I wore a light breastplate under my vest. Cardillac attacked me from behind. His arms encircled me with tremendous strength but the precisely aimed thrust slipped on the metal plate. In the same instant I broke his grip and drove the dagger I held in readiness into his breast." "And you kept silent?" Mademoiselle de Scudéry asked, "you didn't report to the authorities what had happened?" "Permit me to remark, Mademoiselle," Miossens continued, "that such a report might have implicated me, if not exactly in my own destruction, at least in a most detestable trial. Would La Regnie, who scents crime everywhere, have believed me if I had accused the upright Cardillac, the model of all piety and virtue, of attempted murder? Suppose the sword of justice had turned its point against me?" "That wasn't a possibility," cried Mademoiselle de Scudéry; "your birth, your position—" "Oh," Miossens replied, "just remember the Maréchal de Luxembourg, who conceived the idea of having Le Sage cast his horoscope and incurred the suspicion of committing murder by poison, and was imprisoned in the Bastille. No, by St. Denis, I would not give up an hour of my freedom, not the tip of my ear, to that madman La Regnie, who would love to put his knife to all our throats." "But in this way you will bring the innocent

Brusson to the gallows!" Mademoiselle de Scudéry interrupted him. "Innocent Mademoiselle," replied Miossens, "you call Cardillac's insidious accomplice innocent? who assisted him in his crimes? who has merited death a hundred times? No indeed, his blood will be shed with justice; and I have only revealed to you, my highly honored Mademoiselle, the true facts of the case, on the assumption that you would be able to use my secret in some way in the interest of your protégé without turning me over to the Chambre ardente."

Mademoiselle de Scudéry, delighted to find her conviction of Brusson's innocence so decisively corroborated, had no hesitation in revealing the whole story to the count, who already knew about Cardillac's crimes. She urged him to accompany her to d'Andilly. They would tell him everything under the seal of silence and he would advise them what to do next.

After listening to Mlle. Mademoiselle de Scudéry's most precise account, d'Andilly inquired again about the minutest circumstances. He asked Count Miossens specifically whether he had been attacked by Cardillac and whether he could recognize Olivier Brusson as the man who had carried away the corpse. "Apart from the fact," Miossens replied, "that I clearly recognized the goldsmith in the moonlit night, I have seen in La Regnie's office the very dagger with which Cardillac was struck down. It is mine, identifiable by the delicate carving on the handle. I was only one pace distant from the young man, whose hat had fallen from his head and whose features I perceived; I would certainly recognize him again."

D'Andilly was silent for a few moments, gazing into space; then he spoke: "Brusson cannot possibly be rescued from the hands of justice in any ordinary way. For Madelon's sake he refuses to identify Cardillac as a robber and murderer. He may as well maintain this position, for even if he were to succeed in establishing Cardillac's guilt by revealing the secret exit through the wall, and the treasure that he has accumulated through robbery, he would still be sentenced to death as an accomplice. The same situation prevails if Count Miossens were to reveal to the judges the encounter with the goldsmith as it really took place. Delay is the only hope we have. Count Miossens will go to the Conciergerie, confront Olivier Brusson and identify him as the man who took away Cardillac's corpse. He will then hasten to La Regnie and say: "I saw a man struck down in the rue St. Honoré. I stood close to the corpse when a man rushed over, bent down over the corpse and, seeing that there was still life in him, hoisted him over his shoulder and carried him away. I have identified this man as Olivier Brusson. This statement will cause Brusson to be questioned again and confronted by Count Miossens. torture will not be applied but further investigation instituted. Then will be the time to appeal to the king. It will be up to your intellectual acuity, Mademoiselle, to do this in the most adroit way. In my opinion it would be best to reveal the whole secret to the king. This statement by Count Miossens supports Brusson's confession. A secret search in Cardillac's house will perhaps confirm it. No judicial sentence can bring this about, but the king's decision, based on an inner feeling that, where the judge must punish, the king may practice mercy." Count Miossens did exactly as d'Andilly had advised and things went as the lawyer had predicted.

Now the time came to appeal to the king, and this was the most difficult point, since he held Brusson in such horror, regarding him as the sole abominable robber and murderer who had kept all Paris in a state of anxiety and terror for so long, that the mere mention of the notorious trial threw him into a violent temper. Madame de Maintenon, true to her principle of never mentioning anything unpleasant to the king, declined to intervene, and so Brusson's fate was entirely in the hands of Mademoiselle de Scudéry. After long reflection she came to a swift decision, which she carried out as swiftly. She put on a robe of heavy black silk, adorned herself in Cardillac's precious jewels, threw a long black veil over herself, and appeared in Madame de Maintenon's apartment at the hour when the king was present. The noble figure of the venerable Mademoiselle in this solemn garb possessed a majesty that was bound to arouse profound respect even among the frivolous populace who were accustomed to idle away their trivial existence in the antechambers of royalty. When she entered the apartment, they all made way for her; the king himself stood up in astonishment and went toward her. When the precious diamonds of the necklace and bracelets flashed in his eyes, he exclaimed: "By heaven, this is Cardillac's jewelry!" And then, turning to Madame de Maintenon, he added with a charming smile: "Look, Marquise, how our fair bride mourns her bridegroom." "Ah, Your gracious Majesty," Mademoiselle de Scudéry interrupted, as though pursuing the jest, "would it be proper for a suffering bride to adorn herself in such splendid garb? No, I have completely freed myself from this goldsmith and would no longer give him a thought if I were not visited at times by the dreadful image before my eyes of his murdered body being carried past me." "What," the king asked, "you saw the poor devil?" Mademoiselle de Scudéry now related briefly how chance had brought her past Cardillac's house just when his murder was discovered (she made no mention of Brusson's involvement as yet). She described Madelon's anguished suffering, the profound impression made on her by the angelic child, the way she had rescued the poor girl from Desgrais's hands, amidst the jubilation of the populace. With ever increasing interest there followed the meetings with La Regnie, with Desgrais, with Olivier Brusson himself. The king, carried away by the power of this most vivid tale from real life, which glowed in Mademoiselle de Scudéry's words, did not notice that they were talking about the ugly trial of the abominable Brusson; he could not utter a word, but could only, from time to time, give vent to his inner emotion by some exclamation. Before he realized what was happening, distracted by the unheard-of nature of the events and unable as yet to put any order into them, he saw Mademoiselle de Scudéry at his feet, begging mercy for Olivier Brusson. "What are you doing, Mademoiselle?" the king exclaimed as he took both her hands and forced her back into her armchair. "This is an extraordinary surprise. Why, that is a dreadful story. Who will vouch for the truth of Brusson's fantastic tale?" To this Mademoiselle de Scudéry replied: "Miossens's statement, the investigation in Cardillac's house, my inner conviction and—ah!—Madelon's virtuous heart, which recognized a matching virtue in the unhappy Brusson."

The king was on the point of making a reply when a noise at the door made him turn around. Louvois, who was working in the adjoining room, was looking in with an anxious expression on his face. The king stood up and followed Louvois out of the room. Both Madame de Maintenon and Mademoiselle de Scudéry regarded this interruption as dangerous; for having been surprised once, the king might be wary of being caught in the trap a second time. But a few minutes later the king returned, walked swiftly up and down the room several times, then stopped close to Mademoiselle de Scudéry with his hands behind his back and, without looking at her, said almost in an undertone: "I would really like to see your Madelon." To this Mademoiselle replied: "Oh, my gracious Sire, what great good fortune do you bestow on the poor, unhappy child; only a nod from you is needed to bring her to your feet." And she pattered to the door as fast as her heavy clothes would let her and called out that the king had summoned Madelon Cardillac, and came back and wept and sobbed with delight and emotion. She had foreseen such favor and had therefore brought Madelon with her; the girl was waiting in the care of a chambermaid of Madame de Maintenon with a brief petition in her hand, drawn up by d'Andilly. In a few moments she lay speechless at the king's feet. Anxiety, confusion, timid reverence, love and pain forced the poor child's seething blood more and more swiftly through her veins. Her cheeks glowed a deep red, her eyes shone with bright pearly tears, which now and then fell through her silken lashes upon her beautiful lily-white bosom.

The king appeared to be struck by the wonderful beauty of the angelic child. He raised the girl gently, then made a motion as if to kiss her hand, which he held in his. But he let it go and looked at the lovely child with moist eyes, testifying to his very deep emotion. Softly Madame de Maintenon whispered to Mademoiselle de Scudéry: "Doesn't the little thing look like the image of La Vallière?* The king is reveling in the sweetest memories. You have won your game."

Softly though Madame de Maintenon had spoken, the king seemed to have heard what she had said. His face reddened, his eyes swept past Madame de Maintenon, he read the petition that Madelon had handed him and then said kindly and warmly: "I can well believe that you, my dear child, are convinced of your beloved's innocence, but we must hear what the Chambre ardente will say about it." A gentle motion of his hand dismissed the child, who was dissolved in tears.

Mademoiselle de Scudéry perceived to her terror that the recollection of Madame de la Vallière, however favorable it had appeared to be at first, had changed the king's mind as soon as Madame de Maintenon had mentioned her name. Perhaps the king found himself rudely reminded that he was about to sacrifice strict justice to beauty, or perhaps he was undergoing the same experience as the dreamer who is awakened abruptly and finds that the beautiful magic forms he was about to embrace dissolve swiftly. Possibly he no longer saw his La Vallière before him but was thinking only of Soeur Louise de la Miséricorde (her convent name among the Carmelite

*The Duchesse de Lavallière (1644-1710), one of Louis XIV's mistresses, was supplanted by Mme de Montespan and became a Carmelite nun in 1675.

sisters), tormenting him with her piety and penitence. What else was there to do now but wait calmly for the king's decision?

Meanwhile Count Miossens's deposition before the Chambre ardente had become known; and, as the populace is easily driven from one extreme to the other, the same man who had been cursed as the most villainous murderer, and whom they threatened to tear limb from limb even before he could reach the scaffold, was now mourned as the innocent victim of barbarous justice. Only now did the neighbors recall his virtuous life, his great love for Madelon, his loyalty, his devotion with body and soul to the old goldsmith. Popular processions appeared often before La Regnie's palace, shouting threats: "Release Olivier Brusson, he's innocent." They even threw stones at the windows, so that La Regnie found it necessary to seek protection from the angered mob by the mounted police.

Several days passed without Mademoiselle de Scudéry receiving the slightest intelligence about Brusson's case. Utterly disconsolate, she called on Madame de Maintenon, who assured her that the king was maintaining silence about the matter and it seemed inadvisable to remind him of it. When she added, with a strange smile, how was little La Vallière, Mademoiselle de Scudéry became convinced that, deep within the proud woman's heart, a vexation was stirring concerning an affair that might lure the susceptible king into a region whose magic spell she could not control. There was therefore no hope of receiving help from Madame de Maintenon.

At length, with the aid of d'Andilly, Mademoiselle de Scudéry succeeded in finding out that the king had had a long confidential conversation with Count Miossens; further that Bontems, the king's most trusted valet and chargé d'affaires, had called at the Conciergerie and talked to Brusson; and finally that one night the same Bontems and several other men had been in Cardillac's house and spent a long time there. Claude Patru, who lived on the floor below, reported that there had been a banging above his head all night; he was sure that Olivier had been there, for he had recognized the young man's voice. This much therefore was certain, that the king himself was having the matter investigated; but the long delay in arriving at a decision was not to be explained. Probably La Regnie was making every effort to hang on to the victim he held between his teeth. This nipped every hope in the bud.

Nearly a month had passed when Madame de Maintenon sent

word to Mademoiselle de Scudéry that the king wished to see her that evening in her, Madame de Maintenon's, apartment.

Mademoiselle de Scudéry's heart beat high, she knew that Brusson's fate would now be decided. She informed poor Madelon, who prayed fervently to the Virgin and to all the saints to awaken in the king the conviction of Brusson's innocence.

And yet it seemed as if the king had forgotten the whole matter, for as usual he carried on a pleasant conversation with the two ladies, not spending even a syllable on poor Brusson. At length Bontems appeared, approached the king and spoke a few words to him so softly that the ladies could not make out what was said. Mademoiselle de Scudéry trembled inwardly. Then the king stood up, went up to her and said, his eyes flashing: "I congratulate you, Mademoiselle; your protégé is free!" Mademoiselle's eyes filled with tears; she was speechless and was about to throw herself at the king's feet. But he checked her, saying: "Come, come, Mademoiselle, you should be an advocate in the Parliament and fight my lawsuits for me, for by St. Denis, no one on earth can resist your eloquence. —However," he added more seriously, "when Virtue herself has taken someone under her protection, shall he not be secure against every evil accusation, before the Chambre ardente or any other tribunal in the world?"

Mademoiselle de Scudéry now found words to pour out her most ardent thanks. The king interrupted her, informing her that in her own house a far more ardent gratitude was awaiting her than any he could ask from her, for probably at that very moment the happy Olivier was embracing his Madelon. "Bontems," the king concluded, "will pay you a thousand louis; present them to the child as her dowry in my name. Let her marry her Brusson, who simply does not deserve such good fortune, but then let both of them leave Paris. Such is my will."

Martinière hastened to meet Mademoiselle de Scudéry, Baptiste following behind her, both with radiant faces, exulting, shouting: "He's here, he's free! Oh, the dear young people!" The happy couple fell at Mademoiselle de Scudéry's feet: "Oh, I knew it, you, you alone would save my husband," cried Madelon. "Ah, my trust in you, my mother," cried Olivier, "was firm in my soul," and both kissed the worthy lady's hands and shed a thousand ardent tears. And then they embraced again and declared that the unearthly bliss of this moment outweighed all the unspeakable suffering of the past days, and swore not to part from each other till death.

A few days later they were united by the blessing of a priest. Even if it had not been the king's will, Brusson could not have remained in Paris, where everything reminded him of that dreadful period of Cardillac's crimes; where some hostile chance might reveal the evil secret, already familiar to several more people, and destroy his domestic peace forever. Immediately after the wedding he left with his young wife for Geneva, accompanied by Mademoiselle de Scudéry's blessings. Richly endowed by Madelon's dowry, gifted with rare skill in his art, possessing every civic virtue, he enjoyed a happy, carefree existence there. He realized the hopes that had eluded his father right up to the grave.

A year had passed since Brusson's departure when a public announcement appeared, signed by Harloy de Chauvalon, archbishop of Paris, and by the advocate of the Parliament, Pierre Arnaud d'Andilly, stating that a repentant sinner had, under the seal of the confessional, handed over to the Church a large treasure in stolen jewels and gems. Anyone who had been robbed of jewelry up to the end of 1680, especially as a result of a murderous attack in the open street, was asked to report to d'Andilly. If his description of the stolen jewels tallied with any of the extant items and if there was no other reason to doubt the legitimacy of the claim, he would receive the jewelry in question. Many who were on Cardillac's list as not having been murdered but only stunned by a blow of his fist gradually reported to the advocate of the Parliament and received their stolen jewelry, to their considerable astonishment. The rest was added to the treasury of St. Eustache Church.

Adelbert von Chamisso

1781 — 1838

Adelbert von Chamisso was born into an aristocratic French family in Champagne. His parents left France during the French Revolution and settled in Berlin, where there was a Huguenot minority dating back to the seventeenth century. At the age of fifteen Chamisso became a page-in-waiting to Queen Luise of Prussia, and two years later entered the Prussian Army as an ensign. He rose to the rank of lieutenant and fought on the German side against Napoleon.

An interest in botany relieved the monotony of garrison life. Chamisso also wrote and published verse and edited a literary journal. In 1807 he retired from the Army and for the next three years lived an aimless and despondent life in Berlin; an association with Madame de Staël in Switzerland (1810-12) provided temporary relief. Chamisso then returned to Berlin, where he continued his botanical studies and wrote his novella *Peter Schlemihl*. In 1815 he was appointed botanist to the Russian ship *Rurik*, then setting out on a scientific expedition around the world. The voyage took three years and one of its fruits was Chamisso's valuable diary, published in 1821. On returning to Germany he was appointed custodian of the botanical gardens in Berlin and elected a member of the Academy of Sciences.

His interest in literature revived and he wrote ballads, narrative poems and political and social poetry. His cycle of love poems *Frauenliebe und -leben* (*The Love and Life of Women*) was set to music by Schumann. His scientific work included some original contributions to biology. He died at the age of fifty-seven.

Chamisso is one of those literary figures whose fame, enduring and deserved, rests on a single work. *Peter Schlemihl*, written in 1813, held the attention of the Western world throughout the nineteenth century. Though present-day readers of Joyce, Hemingway, Mann and Faulkner have become accustomed to radically different fiction, *Peter Schlemihl* is as fresh and enjoyable today as it was for the Victorians. The secret of its appeal lies in its fusion of fairy tale and realism, which lends it the same fascination as Kafka's mixture of the fantastic with detailed, photographic representation of everyday reality. The *Märchen* element comprises the two principal motifs: selling one's shadow to the devil, a common theme in folklore and literature, and selling one's soul to the devil. Added to those are such fairyland staples as the moneybag of Fortunatus, the magic bird's nest, the vanishing cap and the seven-league boots. These elements are, however, embedded in the rich soil of reality, from which they draw their natural coloration. As a third ingredient, Chamisso, rooted in French culture, has added social satire such as one finds in eighteenth-century French literature.

The central symbol is shrouded in ambiguity. What does the shadow "stand for"? In folklore there is a close association between invisibility and the divine or its opposite, the satanic, as there is between the shadow, the soul, the mirror and truth. To cast no shadow is a sign of non-corporeality; it is an attribute of saints, of Mohammed, of God — and of the devil. People who have been allied with the devil cast no shadow; they have lost their souls. At a more sophisticated level the shadow is a mystery; it always accompanies the person who casts it, it is a part of him, yet it is impalpable and most of the time invisible. It may symbolize the family, society, class, nation, or social position; it is what Yank, in Eugene O'Neill's *The Hairy Ape,* calls "belonging," that element of "appearance," as opposed to "essence," which is so important to the life of civilized man. Those who prefer to relate a work of literature to the author's personal experience will point to the fact that, in 1813, Chamisso was a Frenchman living in a country at war with France; that he found it difficult to live in society because he was incapable of acting the role of a well-adjusted man, with all its pretense and hypocrisy. Certainly Chamisso thought of himself as a "Schlemihl" — he picked the term up from his Jewish compatriots in Berlin — that is, an unlucky fellow who fails in everything he undertakes, for whom everything goes wrong, who feels himself an outsider, but who still needs the society of men. For Chamisso's ideal was not to retire from the world; Chamisso was driven to cultivate his own garden, as was Candide, by bitter experience. He did find solace in nature and science, but would really have preferred to be part of the company that surrounded Herr John if he could have done so without compromising his ideals. But he was an enemy of mere "appearance"; what harm was there in trading appearance for something more substantial, like money, which opened so many avenues to an authentic life?

This identification of the shadow with appearance has the sanction of Chamisso himself. In a poem, *To His Old Friend, Peter Schlemihl*, he wrote

> Die wir dem Schatten Wesen sonst verliehn,
> Sehn Wesen jetzt als Schatten sich verziehn.

> We who once to our shadow substance lent,
> Now see our substance like a shadow spent.

A careful study of the text shows that the shadow is not to be interpreted as a basic trait of human character: it does not represent the soul. Only later, when Schlemihl tries to get his shadow back from the gray man, is the Faustian motif of selling one's soul to the devil introduced. Moreover, Herr John, the millionaire merchant, has sold his soul to the devil but apparently still has his shadow, for no one shuns him the way poor Schlemihl is shunned by the respectable. The vain and not too scrupulous merchant whom Peter Schlemihl ruins in the competition for social display casts a "broad, though somewhat pale, shadow." And even the rascally Rascal retains his shadow. On the other hand, in the dream that Schlemihl has after his great act of renunciation, all the ideal figures that float past him are without shadows, "and this did not look bad at all." The sale of the shadow has nothing to do with basic ethics. All the people Schlemihl meets instinctively recoil from him in an unreasoned, unexamined aversion. It has nothing to do with Peter's virtue, for the shadowless Schlemihl remains honest, generous, and concerned for the salvation of his soul when tempted by the devil to barter it away in return for his shadow. The respectable forester is shocked by Schlemihl's lack of a shadow, but he is prepared to let his daughter Minna marry the villainous Rascal, of whose true character he is aware. Minna herself does not have enough strength of character to ignore the fault in Schlemihl, but after Peter has gone out of her life, she repents of her treatment of him and dedicates her widowed life to the memory of the noble man. And the faithful Bendel, the soul of honesty, decency and generosity, stays with his master and defends him against all his detractors and assailants, although his first instinctive reaction, too, was one of shock and aversion.

To the end, Schlemihl remains what he has been since his fateful visit to the estate of Herr John: a man without a shadow. Yet he redeems himself; for his present shadowless existence is lived in the interest of science, philosophy, philanthropy, though his state was originally incurred for money and power. Moreover, his present existence without a shadow is a mark of his basic goodness. Were he to reacquire his shadow, he would have to forfeit his soul, since to affect the social graces would involve him in a permanent life of hypocrisy and artificiality. Too honest to consent to such a life, he prefers to accept the curse of isolation.

Chamisso once wrote a friend that the "moral" of his tale was: *songez au solide*. The solid element is that regular rhythm of daily activity which fills out the lives of butcher, baker and banker alike, and which the artist-intellectual is apt to look down on as trivial compared to his flights of intellect and art, as a life which is a mere shadow of the authentic existence provided by science or art. This superiority is what Chamisso contests; what is mere appearance to Schlemihl is actually solid reality, which one disregards at one's peril. The closing paragraph of the story leaves no doubt as to Chamisso's interpretation of the shadow symbolism. Anyone who wants to live in society must learn to respect his shadow above money. But the man who wants to live for himself alone "and for his better self," needs no counsel; the tale has no moral for him.

Schlemihl is the romantic, isolated man, but in reverse. The romantics depicted the intellectual-artist who is a social misfit as a hero who scoffs at the Philistines. Schlemihl is the first modern "outsider," the ancestor of the ambivalent artist-intellectual as we know him from Thomas Mann. He, too, is a "clown" (see p. 397 ff.) who envies the solid bourgeoisie, though another side of his being impels him to rebel against its standards and mores. The difference between Chamisso's Schlemihl and Mann's clown is that Chamisso's hero ends in constructive resignation, Mann's, in despair. It is perhaps not only the difference between the two writers, but also between the nineteenth and twentieth centuries.

The Strange Story of Peter Schlemihl

(1)

After a successful but for me very difficult, even voyage, we finally reached port. As soon as I got off the tender, I loaded all my posessions on my back and, pushing my way through the teeming crowd, entered the first humble house that had a sign in front of it. I asked for a room. The clerk sized me up with a single glance and took me to the attic. I asked for fresh water and for precise instructions as to where I could find Herr Thomas John. "At the north gate, the first country house on the right, a large, new hourse built of red and white marble, with many columns." Good. It was still early, I undid my bundle at once, took out my black coat, which I had newly turned, dressed in my best clean clothes, put the letter of recommendation in my pocket, and immediately set out on the road to the man who was to help me realize my modest plans.

After I had walked up the long North Street and reached the gate, I soon saw the columns gleaming through the green foliage. "So this is it," I thought. I wiped the dust from my feet with my handkerchief, arranged my cravat and pulled the bell rope for good or ill. The door sprang open. In the entrance hall I had to undergo an examination; but the porter had me announced, and I had the honor of being summoned to the park, in which Herr John was strolling with a small company. I recognized the man at once by his aura of corpulent self-satisfaction. He received me very well, as a rich man receives a poor devil; he even looked at me, but without turning away from the rest of the company, and took the letter from my outstretched hand. "So, so, from my brother; I have heard nothing from him for a long time. He's in good health, I hope?" "There," he continued to the company without waiting for an answer, and pointing with the letter to a hill, "that's where I'm going to have the new building erected." He broke open the seal without breaking off the conversation, which was turning to the subject of wealth. "A man who isn't master of at least a million," he interjected, "is, if you'll pardon the word, a rogue." "Oh, how true!" I exclaimed, with full, overflowing emotion. This must have pleased him, because he smiled at me and said, "Stay here, dear friend, I may perhaps have time later on to tell you what I think about this" — he pointed to the letter, which he then put in his pocket, and turned to the company again. He offered his arm to a young lady; other gentlemen addressed their attention to other fair ones; all who belonged together found each other; and they made a pilgrimage to the hill blooming with roses.

I stole along behind them without burdening anyone; for not a soul paid any more attention to me. The company was in good spirits, there was sporting and jesting. At times they spoke with importance of frivolous matters, more often, frivolously of important ones; and gradually their wit was directed especially to absent friends and their affairs. I was too much a stranger to understand a great deal about all this, too concerned and introverted to have a mind for such puzzles.

We had reached the copse of roses. The beautiful Fanny, who seemed to be the mistress of the day, wanted to break a branch herself, out of sheer stubbornness; she pricked herself on a thorn and a deep red flowed down her delicate hand as if it had come from the dark roses. This event threw the whole company into confusion. A search was made for English plaster. An elderly man, tall and thin, who was walking beside me and whom I had not noticed before, immediately put his hand into the tightly fit back pocket of his old-fashioned gray taffeta coat, took out a little portfolio, opened it and, with a humble bow, handed the lady what she wished. She received it without thanks and without glancing at the donor. The wound was bandaged and the company went on up the hill, from whose ridge they wished to enjoy the spacious view extending from the green labyrinth of the park toward the boundless ocean.

The sight was truly grand and glorious. A bright point appeared on the horizon between the dark water and the blue of the sky. "A telescope here!" cried John, and even before the servants who had answered the call had started out, the gray man, bowing modestly, had already put his hand in his coat pocket. He drew a handsome Dollond telescope from it and handed it to Herr John. The latter at once put it to his eye, and informed the company that it was the ship that had set out yesterday being held back within sight of the harbor by adverse winds. The telescope went from hand to hand but not back into those of its owner. I looked at the man in astonishment, failing to understand how such a big instrument had come out of that small pocket. But it seemed not to have surprised anyone else, and they paid no more attention to the gray man than to me.

Refreshments were served, the rarest fruits from every part of the world in the most costly dishes. Herr John did the honors with a light grace, and at that point addressed a second sentence to me: "Do eat. You didn't have this at sea." I bowed but he did not notice, for he was already talking to someone else.

Had it not been for the damp ground, they would have liked to lie down on the lawn, on the slope of the hill facing the panoramic land-scape. It would be heavenly, one of the guests said, if they had Turk-ish carpets to spread out there. The wish had hardly been uttered when the man in the gray coat already had his hand in his pocket and, with a modest, indeed humble, gesture, busied himself with drawing out an expensive Turkish carpet embroidered with gold thread. Servants took hold of it as if this was the most inevitable and natural thing to do, and spread it out at the desired place. The com-pany took their places on it without ceremony. Once more I looked in astonishment at the man, his pocket and the carpet: it was more than twenty feet long and ten feet wide. I rubbed my eyes, at a loss about what to think, especially since no one else found anything remark-able about it.

I wanted very much to learn something about the man and to ask who he was, but I did not know to whom I might turn, for I was almost more afraid of the lordly servants than of the lords they served. I finally mustered my courage and approached a young man who seemed to be less important than the others and who had frequently stood alone. I asked him softly to tell me who the obliging gentleman in the gray suit was. "That one, who looks like an end of thread that has escaped a tailor's needle?" "Yes, the man standing by himself." "I don't know him," he replied and, apparently in order to avoid a lengthy conversation with me, turned away and spoke to another man about some trivial matter.

The sun now began to shine more intensely and became a nuisance to the ladies. The beautiful Fanny addressed the gray man, who had not yet been acknowledged by anyone, and asked him casually if he had a tent with him too. He replied with a very deep bow, as though an undeserved honor had been bestowed on him. He already had his hand in his pocket, from which there soon emerged tools, poles, ropes, hardware, in short, everything necessary for the most splendid pleasure-tent. The young gentleman helped open the tent, which extended over the whole area of the carpet. Still no one found anything extraordinary in this.

By that time I had long felt queer, in fact faint at heart. How much more so when, at the next wish that was expressed, I saw him pull three black horses — I tell you, three beautiful, large horses with saddles and harness — imagine, in Heaven's name! three saddled horses out of the same pocket out of which a portfolio, a telescope, a twenty-by-ten-foot Turkish carpet, a pleasure-tent of the same dimensions, with all the hardware pertaining to it, had come! — If I didn't swear that I saw it with my own eyes, you would certainly not believe it.

However embarrassed and humble the man himself seemed to be, however little attention the other paid him, his pale figure, from which I could not tear my eyes, became so gruesome to me that I could no longer bear it.

I decided to steal away from the company, which, in view of the insignificant role I was playing there, seemed to me an easy thing to do. I wanted to return to town, try my luck with Herr John again the next morning, if I found the courage to do so, and question him about the strange gray man. If only I had been lucky enough to get away!

I had actually succeeded in stealing through the rose copse, down the hill, and was on an open lawn when, afraid that I might be seen walking through the grass beside the path, I cast a searching glance behind me. Imagine my terror when I saw the man in the gray coat coming behind me and toward me. He lifted his hat to me at once and bowed lower than anyone had ever done to me. There was no doubt about it, he wanted to talk to me, and I could not avoid him without being rude. I took my hat off, too, returned his bow, and stood there bareheaded in the sun, as though rooted to the spot. I looked at him, rigid with fear, and felt like a bird charmed by a snake. He himself seemed to be deeply embarrassed; he did not raise

his eyes, kept bowing repeatedly, came closer to me and addressed
me in a soft, uncertain voice, somewhat like that of a beggar:

"I hope you will excuse my importunity, sir, for daring to seek you
out in this way without knowing you; but I have a request to make of
you. Will you most graciously grant . . ." "But in the name of Heaven,
sir," I exclaimed in my anxiety, "what can I do for a man who . . ."
We both stopped and it seems to me that we turned red.

After a moment of silence he resumed: "During the short time in
which I enjoyed the pleasure of being near you, I was able, sir, to
study — allow me to say so, several times — really in inexpressible admiration, the beautiful, beautiful shadow you cast in the sun, with a
certain aristocratic disdain, so to speak, without any effort, this
splendid shadow here at your feet. Pardon my bold presumption; but
would you possibly feel not disinclined to let me have your shadow?"

He was silent and my head began to spin like a mill wheel. What
was I to make of this strange proposal of his to buy my shadow from
me? He must be insane, I thought, and in an altered tone of voice,
which better fitted the humility of his, I therefore replied:

"Oh, oh, my good friend, isn't your own shadow enough for you? I
call this a most unusual bargain." He continued at once: "I have in
my pocket many things that might not appear unworthy to you, sir.
For this invaluable shadow I consider the highest price too small."

Now a cold shudder seized me again as I was reminded of his
pocket, and I could not understand how I could have called him a
good friend. I spoke again, trying, if possible, to rectify my error with
the utmost politeness:

"But, my dear sir, pardon your most humble servant. I don't really
understand your attitude. How could I possibly sell my shadow?" He
interrupted me: "I ask Your Honor's permission to pick up this noble
shadow, here on the spot and pocket it; how I do it is my business.
But in evidence of my gratitude to you, sir, I permit you to choose
from among all the treasures which I carry with me in my pocket:
spring root, mandrake, change pennies, robber dollar, the napkin of
Roland's page, a mandragora at your own price: but I don't suppose
these are things for you. The wishing cap of Fortunatus, new and
durably restored, would be better. Also a moneybag like his." "Fortunatus' moneybag," I interrupted him, and great though my anxiety
was, he had with this one word captured my whole mind. I became
dizzy, and objects like double ducats danced before my eyes. "Will

you be kind enough, sir, to examine and test this bag." He put his hand in his pocket and drew out a moderately large, firmly sewn pouch of strong cordovan leather, held shut by two stout leather cords, and handed it to me. I put my hand in and drew out ten gold coins, and ten more and ten more and ten more. I quickly held out my hand to him. "Agreed; it's a bargain; for this pouch you have my shadow." He clasped it, and then without further delay knelt down before me and I saw him gently loosen my shadow from head to foot out of the grass with an admirable dexterity, lift it up, fold it and finally put it in his pocket. He stood up, bowed once more to me and then withdrew to the rosebushes. It seemed to me that I heard him laughing softly to himself there. But I held the pouch tightly by the cords; round about me the world was bright in the sun and I had not yet come to my senses.

(2)

I finally regained my senses and hastened to leave that place, with which I hoped I would have no further concern. First I filled my pockets with gold, then I tied the cords of the pouch tightly about my neck and hid the pouch itself on my chest. I got out of the park un-noticed, reached the highway and made my way back to the city. As I was approaching the gate, lost in thought, I heard someone shouting behind me: "Young man, hey, young man, stop a moment!" I looked around. An old woman called after me: "Do look out, sir, you've lost your shadow." "Thanks, mother." I threw her a gold coin for her well-intentioned advice and stepped under the trees.

At the city gate I had to listen to the same words from the sentry: "Where did you leave your shadow, sir?" And immediately after that, from several women: "Good Lord! The poor man has no shadow!" This began to annoy me and I took great care not to step into the sunlight. But it couldn't be managed everywhere. For instance, on Broad Street, which I had to cross immediately, and moreover, to my misfortune, at an hour when the boys were going home from school. A confounded hunchbacked rascal — I can still see him — noticed at once that I had no shadow. With a mighty shout he betrayed me to all the literary street urchins of the suburbs, who promptly began to criticize and throw dirt at me. "Regular people usually take their shadows with them when they go into the sun." To keep them at bay I threw handfuls of gold among them and, helped by some sympathetic souls, sprang into a cab.

As soon as I found myself alone in the moving vehicle, I began to weep bitter tears. The suspicion was already forcing itself upon me that, in the same degree as gold outweighs merit and virtue on earth, the shadow is valued above gold; and just as I had formerly sacrificed wealth to my conscience, so I had now given away my shadow for mere money. What was going to happen to me on earth?

I was still in a very disturbed state when the cab pulled up in front of my hotel; I was frightened at the idea of going up to that poor attic room. I had my things brought down to me, was handed the wretched bundle with contempt, threw down a few gold coins and gave orders to be taken to the most expensive hotel. The place had a northern exposure, so I had no cause to fear the sun. I dismissed the cabdriver with gold, asked to be shown the best room facing the front of the hotel and locked myself in it as soon as I could.

What do you think I did now? Oh, my dear Chamisso, it makes me blush to confess it even to you. I drew the unlucky bag from my bosom and, with a sort of fury which grew within me by its own power like a flaring flame, I drew out the gold and gold and gold and still more gold and scattered it over the carpet and walked over it and let it clatter and kept throwing more and more of the metal against the metal, feasting my poor heart on the glitter, until I fell back in exhaustion on the luxurious couch and rolled over and over in it in revelry. In this way the day and the evening passed. I did not open my door. Night found me lying on the gold, and then sleep overpowered me.

Then I dreamed of you; it was as if I were standing behind the glass door of your little room, and I saw you sitting there at your desk between a skeleton and a bundle of wilted plants; Haller, Humboldt and Linnaeus were open before you, and on your sofa lay a volume of Goethe and the *Magic Ring*. I studied you a long time and then every object in your room, and then you again; but you did not stir, nor did you breathe; you were dead.

I awoke. It still seemed to be very early. My watch had stopped. I felt crushed and thirsty and hungry too. I had eaten nothing since the previous morning. Peevishly and with a feeling of surfeit, I thrust away this gold with which I had shortly before satiated my foolish heart; now in my annoyance I did not know what to do with it. It could not remain lying there, so I tried to see whether the pouch would swallow it again. No. None of my windows opened out to the sea. I had to yield and drag the gold painfully and with bitter sweat to a large clothespress which stood in a closet and pack it in there. I left only a few handfuls lying about. After I had finished this task, I stretched out in exhaustion on an easy chair and waited till the people in the hotel began to stir. As soon as it was possible I had some food brought me and called for the landlord.

With him I discussed the future arrangement of my apartment. For personal service I selected a certain Bendel, whose loyal and intelligent face won my trust at once. It is he whose attachment has since then accompanied me and given me comfort through the misery of life and who has helped me to bear my sad lot. I spent the whole day in my rooms with temporary servants, shoemakers, tailors and merchants. I set my apartment in order and, merely to get rid of some of the stored-up gold, bought many precious objects and jewels, but it did not seem to me as if the pile of gold could be diminished.

Meanwhile I was in a state of great anxiety about my condition. I did not dare to step out of my room, and in the evening I had forty wax candles lit before I dared to emerge from the shadows. I recalled in horror the fearful scene with the schoolboys. I decided to test public opinion once more, though it required considerable courage to do so. — At that time the nights were moonlit. Late in the evening I put on an ample cloak, pressed my hat down over my forehead and stole trembling out of the house, like a criminal. Only when I reached a distant square did I venture to step out of the shadow of the houses, in whose protection I had come this far, into the moonlight, prepared to hear my destiny from the lips of the passers-by.

Spare me, dear friend, the painful repetition of all that I had to endure. Women often showed the very deep sympathy that I inspired in them; there were remarks that pierced my soul no less than the mockery of youth and the arrogant contempt of men, especially those stout, corpulent men who themselves cast a broad shadow. A beautiful sweet girl apparently accompanying her parents, who were cautiously looking down at their feet, turned her shining eyes on me by chance. She was visibly frightened when she noticed that I had no shadow, hid her beautiful face in her veil, let her head droop and walked silently by.

I could bear it no longer. Salty rivers burst from my eyes, and with my heart sundered I withdrew, tottering into the dark. I had to hold onto the houses in order to steady my steps, and reached my apartment slowly and late.

I spent a sleepless night. The next day my first concern was to have the man in gray searched for everywhere. Perhaps I might succeed in finding him again, and how lucky it would be if he should regret the foolish bargain as I did. I sent for Bendel, for he seemed to have skill and dexterity. I gave him an exact description of the man who had in his possession a treasure without which my life was only a torment. I told him the time and the place where I had met the man in gray, described to him all the people present and even added the clue that he was to make precise inquiries about a Dollond telescope, a Turkish carpet embroidered with gold, a splendid pleasure-tent and finally, black horses, whose history was somehow intertwined with that of the mysterious man, who had seemed to be insignificant to everyone, but whose appearance had disturbed the peace and happiness of my life.

When I had finished talking I brought out some money, as heavy a pile as I could carry, and added jewels and precious stones to it to give it greater value. "Bendel," I said, "this will smooth many paths and will make much that looked impossible easy. Don't be stingy with it, as I am not, but go and bring your master the joyful news on which alone his hope now rests."

He went. He came back late and dejected. None of Herr John's people, none of his guests—he had spoken to them all—could even remotely remember the man in the gray coat. The new telescope was there, but no one knew where it had come from. The carpet, the tent were still there, spread out over the same hill; the servants boasted of their master's wealth and not one of them knew how these new treasures had come to him. He himself enjoyed them and was not in the least concerned about their source. The young gentlemen had the horses, which they had ridden, in their stables, and they praised the generosity of Herr John, who had given them the horses that day. That much was clear from Bendel's detailed account. Though he had failed, his swift zeal and intelligent management received their merited praise from me. I motioned sadly for him to leave me alone.

"I have," Bendel began again, "given you a report, sir, about this matter which was so important to you. There still remains a message for me to deliver, which was given me early this morning by someone

I met outside the door when I went out on the business in which I failed. The man's very words were: 'Tell Herr Peter Schlemihl that he will not see me here again, because I am going overseas and a favorable wind calls me to the harbor now. But at the end of a year I shall have the honor of seeking him out myself and proposing another bargain, which will perhaps be acceptable to him. Give him my most humble regards and assure him of my gratitude.' I asked him who he was, but he said you 'would know who he was.'"

"What did the man look like?" I cried, full of foreboding. And trait by trait, word for word, precisely as he had described the man when he was looking for him, Bendel described to me the man in the gray coat.

"Unhappy man!" I cried, wringing my hands. "That was the very man himself!" and the scales fell from his eyes. — "Yes, it was he, it really was!" Bendel exclaimed in fright. "And I, blind, stupid fool, did not recognize him, did not recognize him, and have betrayed my master!"

Shedding tears, he broke into the bitterest reproaches against himself, and fell into a despair which inspired me with sympathy. I comforted him, assured him repeatedly that I did not doubt his loyalty in the least, and soon sent him to the harbor to pursue the man's steps if possible. But that very morning many ships, which had been held back in the harbor by adverse winds, had sailed each in a different direction, each destined for some other coast, and the gray man had vanished like a shadow, leaving no trace behind him.

(3)

What good would wings be to a man bound in iron chains? He would be in despair, in terrible despair. I lay there, like Fafner beside his treasure, far from all human intercourse, starving amidst all my gold; but my heart was not with the gold; and I cursed that for the sake of which I saw myself cut off from all life. Nursing my gloomy secret all by myself, I was afraid of my lowliest servant, whom I was compelled to envy; for he had a shadow and dared to show himself in the sun. I passed the days and nights in my rooms in lonely mourning, and grief gnawed at my heart.

Another person was wasting away under my very eyes. My loyal

Bendel did not stop tormenting himself with silent reproaches for having betrayed the confidence of his kind master by failing to recognize the man he had been sent out to find and with whom he must think my sad destiny stood in a close bond. But I could not blame him; I recognized in the event the fabulous character of that unknown man.

To leave no stone unturned, I once sent Bendel with a precious diamond ring to the most famous painter in the city, whom I invited to visit me. He came, I sent my servants away, locked the door, sat down beside the man, and after I had warmly praised his art, I came to the point with a gloomy heart—but not until I had sworn him to the strictest secrecy.

"Professor," I asked, "could you possibly paint an imitation shadow for a man who in the most unlucky way in the world has lost his own?" "You mean a shadow cast by light?"

"Precisely." "But," he asked, "what clumsiness, what negligence made him lose his shadow?" —"How it happened," I replied, "is a matter of no importance. But this much," I lied to him shamelessly, "I must say. In Russia, where he was traveling last winter, his shadow once froze to the ground in an unusual cold spell, so that he was unable to tear it loose again."

"The imitation light-shadow that I could paint for him," the professor replied, "would really be only of the sort which he would lose again at the slightest movement. Especially a man who was so little attached to his own natural shadow, as would appear to be the case from your story. A man who has no shadow does not go into the sun—that's the most sensible and safest course." He got up and went away, after giving me a piercing look which I was unable to meet. I sank back in my easy chair and hid my face in my hands.

This is the state Bendel found me in when he entered. He saw his master's grief and wanted to withdraw silently, reverently. I looked up. Crushed beneath the burden of my sorrow, I had to share it with him. "Bendel," I cried to him, "Bendel, you incomparable man, you who see my suffering and respect it, you who don't seek to probe into it but seem to sympathize silently and piously, come to me, Bendel, and be the person closest to my heart. I have not locked the treasures of my gold from you, nor will I lock the treasures of my grief from you. Bendel, the world has judged and rejected me, and you, too, will perhaps abandon me when you learn my terrible secret. Bendel,

I am rich, generous, kind, but—in God's name!—I have no shadow!"

"No shadow?" the good youth exclaimed in fright, and the tears poured from his eyes. "Woe is me that I was born to serve a master without a shadow!" He was silent and I covered my face with my hands.

"Bendel," I added after some time, trembling, "now that you have my secret, you can betray it. Go and give testimony against me." He seemed to be passing through a severe inner struggle, until finally he fell down before me and took my hand, which he moistened with his tears. "No," he exclaimed, "whatever the world may say, I will not forsake my kind master for the sake of a shadow, I will act justly, not prudently. I will stay with you, lend you my shadow, and help you where I can. And where I cannot help you, I will weep with you." I threw my arms about his neck, astonished by such an unusual attitude; for I was convinced that he was not doing it for money.

After that my fate and my way of life changed somewhat. It is unbelievable how zealous Bendel was to conceal my failing. Everywhere he was in front of me and beside me, anticipating everything, making arrangements and, where danger threatened unexpectedly, covering me swiftly with his shadow, for he was bigger and stronger than I. So again I ventured into society and began to play a role in the world. Of course, I had to assume many peculiarities and eccentricities. But these suit man, and as long as the truth remained concealed, I enjoyed all the honor and respect my gold merited. I looked forward more calmly to the visit promised by the strange unknown man at the end of the year.

I knew very well that I must not stay long in the place where I had already been seen without my shadow and where I might easily be betrayed. Perhaps I only remembered the figure I had cut before Herr John and the memory of it depressed me. For that reason I merely wanted to hold a rehearsal there, so that I might play the role elsewhere more easily and with more confidence. However, what kept me here for a time was my vanity: this is the element in man in which the anchor finds the most solid ground.

None other than the beautiful Fanny, whom I met again in another house, granted me some of her attention, without realizing that she had met me before, for now I possessed wit and intelligence. When I talked, people listened; and I myself did not know how I had acquired the art of carrying on or dominating a conversation with such ease. The impression I realized I had made on the beautiful woman made a fool of me, which is just what she wished, and after that time I followed her wherever I could, with a thousand efforts through shadow and twilight. I was vain only in order to make her vain about me, and with the best will in the world I could not force the intoxication out of my head and into my heart.

But why repeat to you at length the whole commonplace story? You yourself have told it to me often enough about other worthy people. But, to be sure, the old, well-known drama, in which I had good-naturedly taken a stale role, was given a denouement made especially for it, unexpected by me, by her and by everyone else.

One beautiful evening when, as usual, I had invited some people to an illuminated garden party, I was strolling arm in arm with the lady at some distance from the other guests, working hard to turn pretty phrases for her. She looked modestly down at her feet and gently returned the pressure of my hand. At that point the moon unexpectedly emerged from the clouds behind us and she saw only her own shadow cast before her. She started, looked at me in consternation, and then gazed down at the ground again, her eyes searching for my shadow. What went on in her mind was painted so strangely on her features that I would have broken into loud laughter had not an ice-cold shudder run down my back.

I released her from my arm and she fainted. Like an arrow I shot through the rows of horrified guests, reached the door, threw myself into the first carriage I found stationed there, and rode back to the city, where this time, in anticipation of my misfortune, I had left the cautious Bendel. He was frightened when he saw me and one word revealed everything to him. Post horses were fetched on the spot. I took only one servant with me, a weathered scoundrel named Rascal, who had been able to make himself indispensable to me through his cleverness, and who could have no suspicion of what had happened that day. I drove thirty miles that same night. Bendel remained behind to liquidate my household, to give out gold and to bring me what I needed most. When he caught up with me the following day, I threw myself into his arms and swore to him, not that I would commit no more follies, but that I would be more cautious in the future. We continued our journey without delay, over the border and the mountains, and only in a nearby, little-frequented bathing spot on the other side of the mountains, separated from that unlucky place

by that lofty bulwark, did I allow myself to be persuaded to rest from
the distress I had experienced.

(4)

I shall have to pass rapidly over a period on which I should like to
dwell, if I could conjure up its living spirit in my memory. But the
color which animated it and which alone can reanimate it, has faded
within me; and when I try to find again in my heart what moved it so
powerfully at that time — both pain and happiness, the pious illusion
— I strike in vain at a rock which no longer yields a living spring, and
God has forsaken me. How different it looks to me now, that past
time! — Badly rehearsed, and a novice on the stage, I was supposed to
play a tragic role in that bathing place. I gape at a pair of blue eyes
and forget the play. The parents, disappointed by the game, stake
their all on setting the whole action swiftly, and the common farce
ends in derision. And that is all, all! — It seems silly to me and in bad
taste, and again it seems frightful that something that once moved
my heart so luxuriously and grandly can now appear to me in that
light. Minna, as I wept then, when I lost you, so I weep now for having lost you in myself as well. Have I then become so old? O mournful
reason! Only one more pulsebeat from that period, one moment of
that delusion — but no! Alone on the high, desolate sea of your bitter
flood; out of the last cup of champagne, the elf has vanished long
ago.

I had sent Bendel ahead with some golden sovereigns to arrange an
apartment for me according to my needs. He had thrown much
money about and some vague information about the distinguished
stranger whose servant he was, for I did not want my name to be
known, which caused the good people to have strange thoughts. As
soon as my house was ready, Bendel came to take me there and we set
out on our journey.

About an hour from the place, on a sunny field, our road was
barred by a crowd in holiday dress. The carriage stopped. Music, the
music of bells, and cannon shots were heard; a loud *hurrah* penetrated the air; and before the door of the carriage there appeared a
chorus of maidens of exceptional beauty in white dresses, but who
faded before one of their group as the stars of the night fade before

the sun. She stepped out from amidst her sisters; the tall, delicate figure kneeled down before me, blushing modestly, and held out to me on a silken cushion a wreath, twined from laurel, olive and roses, while she spoke a few words about majesty, reverence and love, which I did not understand but whose magical silver sound intoxicated my ears and heart—it seemed to me that this heavenly figure had already passed me once before. The chorus joined in and sang the praise of a good king and the happiness of his people.

And this scene, my dear friend, in full sunlight! She was still kneeling two feet from me and I, without a shadow, could not bridge the abyss, could not in turn fall on my knees before the angel. Oh, what would I have given at that point for a shadow! I had to conceal my shame, my anxiety, my despair, deep in the recess of my carriage. Bendel finally took thought on my behalf; he leaped out the other side of the carriage. I called him back and, from the little box which lay beside me, handed him a diamond-studded crown which had been meant to adorn the beautiful Fanny. He stepped forward and, in the name of his master, who could not and would not accept such signs of honor, said there must be a mistake. However, the good inhabitants of the city were thanked for their good will. Meanwhile he took the wreath from her hands and put the diamond crown in its place; then he reverently gave the beautiful maiden his hand, helped her to her feet, and with a gesture dismissed the clergy, the magistrates and all the deputations. No one was admitted beyond that point. He commanded the crowd to part and make way for the horses, mounted the carriage again, and we went on at a steady gallop, under a gateway made of foliage and flowers, toward the town. The cannon was fired energetically over and over again. The carriage stopped before a house. I leaped swiftly to the door, parting the crowd that had collected with the desire to see me. The mob shouted "Hurrah" under my window, and I let double ducats rain out of it. In the evening the city was spontaneously illuminated.

And still I did not know what all this was supposed to mean and whom I was taken for. I sent Rascal out to inquire. He learned that the townsfolk had reliable news that the good King of Prussia was traveling through the country under the name of a count; that my adjutant had been recognized and that he had betrayed himself and me; that their joy had been great when they were certain that I was there personally. Of course they realized now, since I obviously wished to preserve the strictest incognito, how wrong they had been to lift the veil so importunately. I had been so benignly, so graciously angry; I would certainly have to pardon their good hearts.

My scamp was so amused by the affair that he did his utmost, by words of blame, to strengthen the people in their belief for the present. He gave me a very comical account of the matter and, seeing me cheered by it, regaled me with an account of his own tricks. Must I admit it? I was really flattered to be taken for the reverend sovereign, if only under these circumstances.

I had a party arranged for the next evening under the trees which shaded the ground in front of my house and invited the whole town to it. The mysterious power of my purse, Bendel's efforts and Rascal's nimble inventive skill even succeeded in conquering time. It is truly astonishing how magnificently and beautifully everything arranged itself in those few hours. The splendor and luxury which were created there and the ingenious illumination were so wisely distributed that I felt myself quite secure. There was nothing left for me to add. I had to praise my servants.

The evening grew dark. The guests appeared and were presented to me. The phrase "Your Majesty" was heard no more, but with deep reverence and humility they addressed me as "Count." What was I to do? I accepted the title of count, and from that moment on I was called Count Peter. In the midst of the festive whirl my soul yearned only for one person. She appeared late, she who was the crown and wore it. She followed her parents modestly and did not seem to know she was the most beautiful woman there. The forest inspector, his wife and their daughter were presented to me. I was able to say many pleasant and obliging things to the old man; but before the daughter I stood like a boy who has been spanked, unable to stammer a word. Finally I begged her hesitatingly to dignify this festive occasion, to wield the office whose symbol adorned her. With a touching look in her eyes she modestly begged to be excused; but more abashed in her presence than she was herself, as her first subject, I brought her homage in profound reverence. The nod of the count became a command to all the guests and everyone joyfully strove to obey it. Majesty, innocence and grace, allied to beauty, dominated the happy festivity. Minna's happy parents believed that their child was being exalted only in their honor; I myself was in an indescribable state of intoxication. Everything I still had of the jewels I had brought along—to get rid of the load of gold, all the pearls and all the diamonds — I had put in two covered bowls and distributed at dinner in the name of the queen among her friends and all the other ladies. Meanwhile gold was being constantly cast among the exulting crowd in amounts exceeding all reasonable bounds.

Next morning Bendel revealed to me confidentially that the suspicion he had long nursed about Rascal's honesty had now become a certainty. Yesterday Rascal had embezzled full bags of gold. "Let us not begrudge the poor rogue the little bit of plunder," I replied, "I gladly give to everyone, why not to him too? Yesterday he and all the new people you gave me served me honestly, they helped me celebrate a happy festivity."

We talked no more of the matter. Rascal remained the first of my servants, but Bendel was my friend and confidant. He had grown accustomed to regard my wealth as inexhaustible, and he did not snoop about as to its source; but rather, entering into my spirit, he helped me invent opportunities to show it off and to squander gold. Of the unknown gray man, the pale sneaky fellow, I knew only this much: he alone could release me from the curse which weighed on me, and I feared the man upon whom my sole hope rested. For the rest, I was convinced that he could find me anywhere, but I could find him nowhere; for this reason I stopped all useless searching and waited for the promised day.

The splendor of my party and my behavior at it at first confirmed the very credulous inhabitants in their preconceived notion. It was soon learned from the newspapers, of course, that the whole fabulous journey of the King of Prussia had been a mere unfounded rumor. But I was a king once and for all, and a king I simply had to remain; and, moreover, I was one of the wealthiest and most royal kings there ever was. Only they did not really know which. The world has never had cause to complain of a lack of monarchs, least of all in our days. The good people, who had never seen one with their own eyes, guessed now this one, now that one, with equal success — Count Peter remained what he was.

Once there appeared among the bathing guests a merchant who had gone bankrupt to enrich himself, who enjoyed general respect, and cast a broad, though somewhat pale, shadow. Here he wished to display the fortune that he had accumulated, and it even entered his mind to compete with me. I applied myself to my bag and soon had the poor devil at a point where, in order to rescue his reputation, he had to go bankrupt again and retreat beyond the mountains. In this way I got rid of him. I created many good-for-nothings and idlers in this region.

Amidst the royal splendor and squandering by which I made everyone subject to me, I lived very simply and in retirement in my house. I had made it a rule to observe the greatest caution; no one beside Bendel was to enter the rooms I inhabited, under any pretext whatsoever. As long as the sun shone I kept myself locked up there with him and it was believed that the count was working in his study. This labor was connected with the frequent couriers whom I sent out and received concerning every trifle. I received company only in the evening under my trees or in my drawing room, which was, under Bendel's direction, lavishly and skillfully illuminated. When I went out, on which occasions Bendel constantly had to watch me with the eyes of an Argus, it was only to the forester's garden and for the sake of her alone; for the innermost heart of my life was my love.

Oh, my good Chamisso, I will hope that you have not yet forgotten what love is. I leave much here for you to fill in. Minna was really a good, lovable, pious child. I had tied her whole imagination to myself. In her humility she did not know what she had done to deserve my interest in her, and she repaid love with love, with the full youthful power of an innocent heart. She loved like a woman, sacrificing herself completely, devotedly loving only him who was her life, unconcerned even if she herself should be destroyed; that is, she really loved.

But I—oh, what frightful hours—frightful and yet worth longing for again—I spent weeping on Bendel's shoulder when, after my first senseless intoxication, I reflected, looked at myself sharply, I without a shadow, who was destroying this angel with malicious selfishness, stealing this pure soul with lies. At such times I resolved to reveal myself to her; then again I vowed with solemn oaths to tear myself from her and to flee; and finally I broke into tears again and arranged with Bendel how I was to visit her in the forester's garden that evening.

At other times I deceived myself with great hopes of the impending visit of the unknown gray man, and wept again when I sought in vain to believe it. I had calculated the day on which I expected to see the frightful man again, for he had said in a year, and I believed him.

Minna's parents were good, respectable old people who loved their only child very much. The whole relationship took them by surprise when it was already in existence, and they did not know what to do about it. They had not dreamed that Count Peter could even think about their child, and now he actually loved her and was loved in return. The mother was probably vain enough to think of the possibility of a union and to work toward one; but the common sense of the old man left no room for such hairbrained notions. Both were convinced of the purity of my love; they could do nothing but pray for their child.

A letter has fallen into my hands, which I still have from Minna from those days. Yes, it is her writing. I will copy it for you.

"I'm a weak, silly girl and I would like to think that my lover, because I love him deeply, deeply, would not hurt a poor girl like me Oh, you are so good, so inexpressibly good; but don't misunderstand me. You must not sacrifice — or wish to sacrifice — anything for me; oh Lord, I could hate myself if you did that. No, you have made me infinitely happy, you've taught me to love you. Go thou forth! I know my fate, Count Peter belongs not to me but to the world. I'll be proud when I hear: that was *him*, and that was *him* too, and *he* did that; there they worshiped *him* and there they idolized *him*. Behold, when I think this, I am angry with you for forgetting your lofty destiny for a simple-minded child. Go thou forth, else the thought will yet make me unhappy, I who am so happy, so blissful through you. Have I not twined an olive branch and a rosebud into your life, too, as into the wreath that I was permitted to present to you? I have you in my heart, my beloved, do not fear to leave me — I shall die, ah, so happy, so unspeakably happy through you!"

You can imagine how deeply these words cut into my heart. I explained to her that I was not what people seemed to take me for; I was only a rich but infinitely miserable man. A curse rested on me, which was to be the only secret between her and me, because I was not without hope yet that the curse would be lifted. This was the poison of my life: that I might drag her down with me into the abyss, she who was the only light, the only happiness, the only heart of my life. Then she wept again because I was unhappy. Ah, she was so full of love, so good! To spare me but one tear, she would have sacrificed everything, and with what happiness!

However, she was far from interpreting my words correctly. She

merely surmised that I was some prince upon whom a severe exile
had been imposed, some loftly, outlawed brigand, and her imagination vividly pictured her lover in heroic colors.

Once I said to her: "Minna, the last day of next month may change
and decide my destiny. If it does not, then I must die because I don't
want to make you unhappy." Weeping, she hid her face on my
breast. "If your destiny changes, just let me know that you are happy.
I have no claim on you. But if you are wretched, then bind me to
your misery so that I may help you to bear it."

"Darling, darling, take back those rash, foolish words which
escaped your lips. Do you know this misery, do you know this curse?
Do you know who your lover . . . what he . . . ? Don't you see me shud-
dering convulsively before you, hiding a secret?" She fell sobbing at
my feet and repeated her request, swearing an oath.

The forest inspector entered and I declared to him that it was my
intention to ask for his daughter's hand on the first day of the following month. I fixed that time because much might happen before
then that could influence my destiny. Only my love for his daughter
was unalterable.

The good man was properly frightened upon hearing such words
from the lips of Count Peter. He threw his arms about me and then
was quite abashed at having forgotten himself. Now it occurred to
him to doubt, to weigh and to inquire. He spoke of a dowry, of security, of a future for his dear child. I thanked him for reminding me of
this. I told him that I wished to settle in this region, where I seemed
to be liked, and to lead a carefree life here. I asked him to buy the
finest estates that were available in the country in the name of his
daughter and to send the bill to me. In this way a father could best
serve the suitor. This gave him much trouble, for everywhere some
stranger had anticipated him, and so he only bought estates for
about a million.

Occupying him in this way was basically an innocent stratagem to
get him out of the way, and I had already used similar devices with
him, for I must confess that he was something of a nuisance. The
good mother, on the other hand, was a little deaf and not, like him,
eager for the honor of entertaining the count.

The mother arrived and the happy people urged me to spend more
of the evening with them. I dared not stay another minute: I already
saw the rising moon half lighting the horizon. My time was up.

Next evening I went to the forester's garden again. I had thrown my cloak loosely over my shoulders and pushed my hat far over my eyes; I was walking toward Minna. As she looked up and caught sight of me, she made an involuntary gesture; once more there stood clearly before my mind the scene of that gruesome night when I had shown myself in the moonlight without a shadow. It was really she. But had she, too, recognized me now? She was silent and thoughtful. A hundred-pound weight lay on my chest. She threw herself on my breast weeping silently. I went.

Now I found her frequently in tears. My heart grew more and more somber, and only the parents swam in excessive bliss. The fateful day was approaching, fearful and dull as a storm cloud. The next to last evening was there and I could scarcely breathe any longer. By way of precaution, I had filled a few chests with gold and I sat up waiting for the twelfth hour. It struck.

Now I sat there, my eyes fixed on the hands of the clock, counting the minutes, the seconds, like dagger thrusts. At every sound I started. Day broke. The leaden hours crowded each other, midday came, evening, night; the handle of the clock moved, my hope faded; it struck eleven and no one appeared, the last minutes of the last hour came and no one appeared, the first stroke of the twelfth hour struck and I sank back on my couch shedding hopeless tears. Tomorrow I was to ask for the hand of my beloved — I who was permanently without a shadow. Toward morning an anxious sleep closed my eyes.

(5)

It was still early when I was awakened by voices raised in a violent altercation in my anteroom. I listened. Bendel refused access to my door, Rascal asserted adamantly that he would not take orders from the likes of him and insisted on getting into my room. The kind Bendel reproved him: such words, if they should come to my ears, would lose him his profitable job. Rascal threatened to lay hands on him if he barred the entry to me any longer.

I had half dressed, pulled the door open in anger and advanced on Rascal. "What do you want, you rogue?" He took two steps backward and answered quite coldly: "To ask you most humbly, Count, to let me see your shadow. The sun is shining so beautifully on the courtyard right now."

I stood there thunderstruck. It was a long time before I could speak again. "How dare a servant!" Calmly he interrupted me: "A servant can be a very honest man and not be willing to serve a man without a shadow. I demand to be dismissed." I had to pluck other strings. "But Rascal, dear Rascal, who put this unhappy idea into your head, how can you believe...?" He continued in the same tone: "People are saying you have no shadow. Show me your shadow or give me my discharge."

Bendel, pale and trembling but more collected than I, made a sign to me. I tried gold, which soothes everything; but gold, too, had lost its power and he threw it at my feet. "From a shadowless man I take nothing." He turned his back on me and, whistling a ditty, with his hat on his head, went slowly out of the room. Motionless, my mind a blank, as if turned to stone, I stood there with Bendel, looking after him.

With a deep sigh and death in my heart I prepared to redeem my promise and to appear in the forester's garden like a criminal before his judges. I arrived in the dark arbor, which was named after me, and where she must have expected me this time too. The mother came toward me, carefree and joyful. Minna sat there, pale and beautiful like the first snow which sometimes kisses the last flowers in the autumn and at once melts into bitter water. The forest inspector was walking up and down excitedly, holding a written paper in his hand. He seemed to be suppressing many emotions which painted themselves on his normally impassive face in alternating flushes and pallor. He came up to me as I entered and in halting phrases asked to speak to me alone. The walk on which he invited me to accompany him led to an open, sunny part of the garden; I sat down silently on a chair and a long silence followed, which even the good mother did not dare interrupt.

The forest inspector was still storming up and down the arbor at an uneven pace. Suddenly he was standing before me, looking at the paper he had in his hand. He asked me with a searching look: "Is it possible, Count, that you are not unacquainted with a certain Peter Schlemihl?" I was silent. — "A man of excellent character and of special gifts—" He expected an answer. — "And suppose I were that man myself?" — "Who," he added vehemently, "has lost his shadow!" "Oh, my foreboding, my foreboding!" cried Minna. "Yes, I've known a long time, he has no shadow!" And she threw herself into the arms of her mother, who was terrified and clasped her convulsively to her breast, reproaching her for keeping such a secret to her own misfortune. But she, like Arethusa, had been transformed into a spring of tears, which flowed more copiously at the sound of my voice and burst into a storm at my approach.

"And you," the forest inspector began again furiously, "you have not hesitated, with unheard-of insolence, to deceive her and me; and you pretend to love the girl whom you have brought so low? See how she weeps and wrings her hands. Oh horrible, horrible!"

I had so completely lost control of myself that, talking as in a fever, I began: "After all, a shadow is nothing but a shadow; one can get along without it and it isn't worth raising such a fuss about it." But I myself felt so keenly what nonsense I was talking that I stopped of my own accord and he did not think I deserved an answer. I added: "What one has lost once, one can find another time.

He burst out angrily. "Confess, my dear sir, confess. How did you lose your shadow?" I had to lie again: "A rough man one day stepped so heavily on my shadow that he tore a big hole in it. I've merely sent it in for repairs, for gold can accomplish much; I was supposed to get it back yesterday."

"Good, my dear sir, very good!" the forest inspector replied. "You are courting my daughter. Others are doing the same. As a father it is my duty to look after her. I give you three days' time to look about for a shadow; if you appear before me within three days with a well-fitted shadow, you will be welcome. But on the fourth day—this much I can tell you—my daughter will be another man's wife." I wanted to say a word to Minna, but she clung tighter to her mother, sobbing more vehemently, and the mother silently motioned to me to go. I staggered away, feeling as if the world were closing behind me.

Separated from Bendel's loving care, I roamed through the woods and fields in confusion. The sweat of anxiety was dripping from my forehead, a hollow groan was wrung from my breast, madness raged within me.

I don't know how long this had lasted, when I suddenly found myself on a sunny heath with someone tugging at my sleeve. I stopped and looked about me. It was the man in the gray coat and he seemed to have lost his breath running after me. He began to speak at once: "I had announced my arrival for this day, but you could not wait. However, things can still be remedied. Take my advice, trade your shadow in again—it's at your disposal—and turn right back. You'll be welcome in the forester's garden and the whole thing will have been only a joke. I shall take care of Rascal, who betrayed you and who is courting your fiancée. The fellow is ripe."

I still stood there as though in sleep. "Announced yourself for today?" I reviewed the chronology again; he was right, I had been out by one day all the time. I searched for the little bag on my chest with my right hand. He guessed my intention and retreated two steps.

"No, Count, it's in good hands. You keep it." I looked at him with staring, wonder-filled eyes. He continued: "I ask for only a trifle as a memento. You will be good enough to sign this note." On the parchment were the words:

"By virtue of this, my signature, I bequeath my soul to the bearer after its natural separation from my body."

In mute astonishment I gazed alternately at the document and at the unknown gray man. I had scratched my hand on a thorn; from this scratch he caught a drop of blood on a freshly cut pen, which he now held out to me.

"But who are you?" I finally asked him. "What does it matter?" he replied. "And can't you tell from looking at me? A poor devil, a sort of scholar and doctor, who reaps poor thanks from his friends for excellent services, and has no other joy on earth except a bit of experimentation. But do sign. Down below at the right: Peter Schlemihl."

I shook my head and said: "Excuse me, sir, I'm not going to sign that." "No?" he repeated in astonishment. "And why not?"

"It really seems to me a bit risky to stake my soul on a shadow." "That so? That so? Risky," he repeated, and he broke into loud laughter. "And, if I may ask, what is this thing, your soul? Have you ever seen it, and what do you expect to do with it when you are dead? You should be happy that you have found an amateur who is willing to pay you while you are still alive for the bequest of this X, this galvanic force or polarizing effect or whatever else the silly thing may be, with something real, namely with your bodily shadow, through which you may obtain the hand of the girl you love and the fulfillment of all your wishes. Would you rather deliver the poor young creature to that rogue Rascal? No, you really must see it with your own eyes. Come, I'll lend you this vanishing cap here"—he pulled something out of his pocket—"and we'll make an unseen pilgrimage to the forester's garden."

I must confess that I felt very much ashamed at being ridiculed by this man. I hated him from the bottom of my heart, and it was this personal repugnance rather than principles or prejudices that kept me from buying my shadow, however much I needed it, with the signature he desired. Besides, the thought of undertaking the journey he proposed in his company was unbearable. It revolted my deepest feelings to see this ugly sneak, this sneering kobold, step mockingly between me and my beloved, between our two torn, bleeding hearts. I looked on what had happened as an act of fate, my misery as unalterable, and, turning to the man, I said to him:

"Sir, I have sold you my shadow for this little bag, which is in itself most excellent, and I have regretted it enough. Can the deal be canceled, in Heaven's name?" He shook his head and made a very gloomy face. I continued: "Then I will not sell you anything else that I possess, even if it is at the price of my shadow, and so I will sign nothing. I may conclude from this that the disguise you have invited me to assume would turn out to be incomparably more amusing for you than for me. So consider this a refusal, and since it just can't be otherwise, let us part."

"I regret, Monsieur Schlemihl, that you stubbornly reject the proposal I have offered you as a friend. However, I may be luckier another time. I'll see you again soon. By the way, do permit me to show you that I don't allow the things I buy to grow moldly, but respect them, and that they are well taken care of with me."

He promptly drew my shadow out of his pocket and, skillfully unfolding it, threw it on the heath, and spread it out at his feet on the sunny side in such a way that he walked between the two attendant shadows, mine and his; for mine had to obey him also, and direct and accommodate itself to his movements.

When I saw my poor shadow once again after such a long time, and found it being humiliated into doing such base service, I was in boundless distress. My heart was sore and I began to weep bitterly. The hated man strutted about with the plunder he had snatched from me and renewed his insolent proposal:

"You may still have it; one stroke of the pen and you will deliver poor, unhappy Minna from the claws of the rogue into the arms of the highly honored count. As I said, only one stroke of the pen." My tears flowed with renewed force, but I turned and beckoned to him to leave.

Bendel, who in great anxiety had followed my steps to this spot, appeared at this moment. When the faithful, good soul found me weeping and saw my shadow — for it was unmistakable — in the power of the gray stranger, he resolved at once to restore my property to me, even if it required force to do so. Since he did not know how to attack the delicate thing, he attacked the man himself with words, and without much questioning he ordered him peremptorily to let me have at once what belonged to me. Instead of answering, the man turned his back on the innocent boy and went. Bendel raised the buckhorn club he carried and, following on his heels, let him feel the full force of his sinewy arm accompanied by repeated commands to give up the shadow. The other bowed his head as if he were used to such treatment, arched his shoulders and silently went his way over the heath with calm steps, abducting both my shadow and my faithful servant. For a long time still, I heard the muffled sound echo through the wilderness, until finally it was lost in the distance. As before I was alone with my misfortune.

(6)

Left on the desolate heath, I gave rein to my boundless tears, relieving my poor heart of a nameless, anxious burden. But I saw no limits, no end, no goal to my excessive misery, and with especially grim fury I sucked at the new poison which the stranger had poured into my wounds. When I conjured up Minna's image in my mind and the beloved, sweet figure appeared to me pale and in tears, as I had last seen her in my disgrace, Rascal's phantom insolently and mockingly stepped between her and me. I hid my face in my hands and fled through the desert, but the ghastly phantom would not give me rest, but pursued me at a run, until I sank breathlessly to the ground and moistened the earth with a new spring of tears.

And all this for a shadow! And this shadow I could have regained by a stroke of the pen. I thought over the strange proposal and my refusal. I was desolate — I had lost all sanity and judgment.

The day passed, I stilled my hunger with wild fruits, my thirst in the nearest mountain stream. Night descended and I lay down under a tree. The damp morning awakened me from a heavy sleep, in which I heard myself panting as though in a death rattle. Bendel must have lost track of me and I was glad to think that he had. I didn't want to go back among human beings, from whom I had fled in terror like the frightened mountain game. In that way I lived for three anxious days.

On the morning of the fourth I found myself on a sandy plain on which the sun shone. I sat on some rocky ruins bathed in its rays, for I was now eager to enjoy the sight of the sun after being so long without it. Silently I nourished the despair in my heart. Then I was frightened by a gentle noise. Ready for flight, I cast my eyes about me but saw no one, except that a human shadow, not unlike my own, came gliding by me on the sunny sand; walking by itself, it seemed to have lost its master.

At that a mighty impulse stirred within me. "Shadow," I thought, "are you seeking your master? I will be he." And I leaped over to take possession of it; I thought that if I succeeded in stepping into its traces, so that it met my feet, it would remain attached to them and in time become used to me.

At my movements the shadow took flight, and I had to begin a strenuous hunt for the nimble fugitive; only the thought of being delivered from my fearful predicament supplied me with enough strength to pursue it. It was fleeing toward the forest some distance away, in whose shade I would surely lose it. As I saw this, terror shot through my heart, kindled my desire and gave wings to my feet. Clearly I was gaining on the shadow, I was gradually coming closer to it, I must reach it. Now it suddenly stopped and turned toward me. Like the lion at his prey, I sprang at it with a mighty leap, to take possession of it. Unexpectedly I met with hard, physical resistance. Invisibly I received the most violent blows in the ribs that it was ever the lot of man to feel.

The effect of my terror was to make me lower my arms convulsively and to press firmly whatever it was that stood invisibly before me. In the swift action I fell forward, stretched out on the ground; but below me, on his back, was a man, whom I held in my embrace and who only now became visible to me.

And now the whole phenomenon became intelligible to me in a very natural way. The man must have carried and then thrown away the invisible bird's nest which renders the person who holds it, but not his shadow, invisible. I peered about me and soon discovered the shadow of the invisible nest itself. I leaped up and seized the precious booty. Invisible and shadowless, I held the nest in my hands.

The man stood up swiftly, looked about for his successful conqueror, but on the spacious sunny plain saw neither him nor the shadow, for which he was especially searching. He had not had time to observe before this that I was without a shadow, nor could he have suspected such a thing. When he had convinced himself that every trace was lost, he turned his hand against himself in the greatest despair and tore his hair. But this treasure which I had gained gave me the opportunity and the desire to mingle among men once more. I lacked no pretexts for justifying my vile robbery, rather, I needed no such pretexts, and in order to avoid any such problem I hurried away, not looking back at the unfortunate man, whose anxious voice echoed behind me a long while. At least that is how all the circumstances of this event appeared to me at that time.

I burned with the desire to go to the forester's garden and learn for myself the truth of what the hated gray man had told me; but I did not know where I was. To get my bearings I climbed the nearest hill. From its peak I saw the nearby town and the forester's garden lying at my feet. My heart pounded and tears of another sort than those I had shed before came into my eyes: I was to see her again. Anxious longing hastened my steps down the best path. Unseen, I passed several farmers who were coming from the city. They were talking about me and Rascal and the forester; I wanted to hear nothing and hurried by.

I came into the garden, all the thrills of expectation in my heart. Something like laughter came toward me and I shuddered; I cast a swift glance about me, but I could discover no one. I went on; I thought I heard the sound of human steps near me, but I could see nothing and I believed my ears were deceiving me. It was still early, there was no one in Count Peter's arbor, the garden was still empty. I roamed through the well-known paths and approached the house. The same sound pursued me more audibly. With an anxious heart I sat down on a bench in the sunny space opposite the house. I seemed to hear the unseen kobold sit down beside me with a mocking laugh. The key was turned in the lock, the door opened and the forester came out, holding some papers in his hand. I felt a sort of mist over my head. I looked about and—horror—the man in the gray coat was sitting near me, studying me with his satanic smile. He had pulled his vanishing cap over his head and mine. At his feet his shadow and mine lay peacefully alongside each other. He was playing carelessly with the familiar parchment he held in his hand and, while the forester was walking up and down the arbor, absorbed in his papers, he bent over confidentially and whispered in my ear:

"So you did accept my invitation and here we are, two heads sitting under one cap. Very good, very good. But now give me back my bird's nest. You don't need it any longer and you're too honest a man to want to keep it from me. But you needn't thank me, I assure you, for I was glad to loan it to you." He took it out of my hand without any resistance from me and put it in his pack, once more laughing at me so loudly that the forester looked about for the source of the noise. I sat there as though petrified.

"You will surely admit," he continued, "that such a cap is much more convenient. It covers not only the man but his shadow, too, and as many others as he wants to take with him. Look, today I have two more with me." He laughed again. "Mark this, Schlemihl, what you refuse to do voluntarily at first, you are finally compelled to do. I should think you'd buy the thing from me, take your fiancée back, for there is still time, and we'll let Rascal swing on the gallows. That will be easy, as long as there's no shortage of rope. Listen, I'll throw in my cap into the bargain."

The mother came out and the conversation began. "What's Minna doing?" "She's crying." "Simple child! The situation can't be altered." "Of course not. But to give her to another man so soon. Oh, my husband, you are cruel to your own child." "No, Mother, you see things in a false light. Even before she's through shedding these childish tears, she'll find herself the wife of a very rich and honored man, and she'll awaken out of her pain, comforted, as though from a dream, and thank God and us, you'll see." "Heaven grant it." "True, she has a considerable estate right now; but after the sensation caused by the affair with the adventurer, do you believe another match as suitable as this Herr Rascal will turn up? He has property here in the country worth six millions, free from all encumbrances, paid for in cash. I have had the deeds in my own hands. He was the man who snatched everything from me; and besides, he has in his portfolio notes against Thomas John for about three and a half millions." "He must have stolen a lot." "What sort of talk is this again?

He saved wisely where others squandered." "A man who has worn livery." "Nonsense! And he has an impeccable shadow." "That's true, but..."

The man in the gray coat laughed and looked at me. The door opened and Minna came out. She was leaning on a maid's arm. Silent tears rolled down her beautiful pale cheeks. She sat in an easy chair which had been set up for her under the linden trees, and her father took a chair beside her. He took her hand tenderly and talked to her gently as she began to sob vehemently:

"You are my good, dear child, and you will be sensible too. You won't wish to sadden your old father, who wants only your happiness. I can well understand, dear heart, that you've been deeply shaken, you've miraculously escaped from your misfortune. Before we discovered this shameful deception you were deeply in love with this unworthy fellow. Look, Minna, I know it and don't blame you for it. I myself, my dear child, loved him too, as long as I took him to be a prominent man. But now you yourself realize how everything has changed. Why, every poodle has his shadow, and my only precious child shall marry a man...? No, you're not even thinking of him any more. Listen, Minna, now you're being courted by a man who is not afraid of the sun, an honored man, who is, to be sure, not a prince, but who owns ten millions, ten times more than you do, a man who will make my precious child happy. Don't answer me. Don't resist. Be my good, obedient daughter. Let your loving father care for you. Dry your tears. Promise me you'll give your hand to Herr Rascal. Say it, will you promise me this?"

She answered in a faint voice: "I have no will, no further wish on earth. Let the will of my father be my fate." At that moment Herr Rascal was announced and insolently joined the party. Minna lay in a swoon. My hated companion looked at me angrily and whispered to me swiftly, "And you can bear this? What substitute for blood do you have in your veins?" With a swift movement he scratched a slight wound in my hand; some blood flowed, and he continued: "Real red blood! Then sign!" I had the parchment and the pen in my hand.

(7)

I shall expose myself to your judgment, dear Chamisso, and not attempt to prejudice it in my favor. For a long time I have judged myself sternly, for I have nourished the gnawing worm in my heart. This earnest moment perpetually hovered before my mind, and I was able to face it only with a dubious eye, with humility and contrition. Dear friend, anyone who lets his foot wander frivolously from the straight and narrow path is led unexpectedly into other paths, which draw him downward, ever downward. In vain he sees the guiding stars shine in the sky; there is no choice left him, he must continue irresistibly down the slope and sacrifice himself to Nemesis. After the precipitate error which had put the curse on me, I had through love flagrantly forced my way into the destiny of another being. What was left for me but to jump blindly in to rescue where I had sowed destruction, where swift help was demanded of me? For the final hour had struck. Don't think me so base, Adelbert, as to believe that any price demanded of me would have seemed too high, that I would have been stingy with anything I had, more than with mere gold. No, Adelbert; but my heart was filled with an unconquerable aversion for this mysterious sneak on crooked paths. Perhaps I was doing him an injustice, but all association with him was revolting to me. Here, too, as so often in my life, and as so often happens in history, an event took the place of an action. Later I became reconciled with myself. First I learned to respect necessity, and what is more substantial than the deed which has been done, the event which has occurred, which is the property of necessity? Then I learned to revere that necessity as a wise providence which permeates the whole great machine of which we are mere driving and driven wheels: what must be, must be; what was to happen, happened; and not without that Providence which I finally learned to revere in my own destiny as in those affected by mine.

I don't know whether to ascribe it to the tension of my mind under the stress of such powerful emotions, or to the exhaustion of my physical powers, weakened by unaccustomed starvation during the last days, or finally to the disturbing turmoil which the presence of this gray monster aroused in my whole being. In any case, as I reached to sign the paper, a deep swoon came over me and I lay for a long time as though dead.

The stamping of feet and cursing were the first sounds that reached my ears as I regained consciousness. I opened my eyes. It was dark. My hated companion was angrily busying himself about me. "Isn't this behaving like an old woman! Pull yourself together and do what you've resolved to do! Or have you changed your mind and

prefer to whine?" I sat up with difficulty and looked silently about
me. It was late evening. From the brightly lit forester's house festive
music could be heard. Groups of people were walking along the
garden paths. A few approached, engaged in conversation, and sat
on the bench where I had been siting. They were talking about the
union, solemnized that morning, of the rich Herr Rascal with the
daughter of the house. So it had happened.

I brushed the vanishing cap from my head, so that the stranger
promptly vanished, and, silently plunging into the deepest darkness
of the bushes, I took the road through Count Peter's arbor and hurried toward the garden gate. But, invisibly, my tormenting spirit
pursued me with sharp words. "So, Monsieur with the weak nerves,
this is the way you thank me for the trouble I've taken to look after
you the whole day long. And I'm to act the fool in the play. Very
well, you stubborn fellow, just you try to run away from me; we're inseparable. You have my gold and I, your shadow. That will leave
neither of us in peace. Has anyone ever heard of a shadow aban-
doning its master? Yours will draw me after you until you accept it
again with grace and I'm rid of it. What you have failed to do energetically and willingly, you'll have to make up for, only too late, in
surfeit and boredom. One does not escape one's fate." He went on
and on in the same tone. I fled in vain; he did not yield but was always there, talking sneeringly of gold and shadow. I was unable to be
alone with my own thoughts.

I had taken a path to my house through streets empty of people.
When I stood before it I could scarcely recognize it. Behind the shattered windows no lamps were lit; the doors were shut; there were no
servants stirring within. Beside me the stranger gave a loud laugh:
"Yes, yes, that's the way it is. But you'll find your Bendel at home indeed. Recently he was providentially sent home so tired that he's
probably been guarding your house ever since." He laughed again.
"He'll have tales to tell. Well then, good night for today. See you
again soon."

I rang the bell repeatedly until light appeared. From inside Bendel
asked who was ringing. When the good man recognized my voice, he
could hardly control his joy. The door flew open and we stood weeping in each other's arms. I found him greatly altered, weak and ill;
but then my hair had turned quite gray.

He led me through the desolate rooms to an inner chamber which

had been spared; he brought food and drink, we sat down and he began to cry again. He told me that he had thrashed the lean man
dressed in gray whom he had met with my shadow, so long and for
such a distance that he himself had lost trace of me and had collapsed
with weariness. Later, unable to find me, he had returned home,
where the mob, at Rascal's instigation, had soon stormed the house,
smashed the windows and satisfied its lust for destruction. That is
how they had behaved toward their benefactor. My servants had
scattered and fled. The local police had banned me from the city as a
suspicious character and given me twenty-four hours to leave the
region. Bendel was able to add much to what I already knew about
Rascal's wealth and his betrothal. This villain, who had prompted all
the mischief done to me here, must have known my secret from the
beginning. Apparently, attracted by the gold, he had been able to
force his way to me and, even at that early time, had procured a key
to the safe full of gold, where he had laid the foundation for the fortune which he could now scorn to increase.

All this Bendel told me with frequent tears, and then wept to see
me once more and to have me back again, and because, having long
suspected to what state my misfortune might have reduced me, he
saw me bear it calmly and resolutely. For this is the form which despair had taken in me. I saw my misery before me, gigantic, unalterable; I had shed tears until they would flow no more. Not another cry
would be pressed from my heart; I now met my misfortune with
bared head, cold and indifferent.

"Bendel," I began, "you know my lot. A severe punishment has
been visited on me, not without former guilt on my part. You shall
not, innocent man, tie your fate to mine any longer; I won't have it.
I'm going to leave this very night. Saddle a horse for me. I'll ride
alone. You stay here. I insist. There must be a few more chests of
gold here. Keep them. I'll wander alone in the world. But whenever a
serene hour smiles upon me again, and fortune looks upon me in
reconciliation, I'll think of you loyally, for I have wept on your faithful breast in heavy, painful hours."

With a broken heart the honest fellow had to obey his master's last
order, which pained his soul. I was deaf to his requests and entreaties,
blind to his tears. He brought my horse, I pressed the weeping boy
once more to my breast, leaped to the saddle and, under the cloak of
night, left the grave of my life, heedless of what road my horse might

take, for I had no further goal on earth, no wish, no hope.

(8)

I was soon joined by a pedestrian who, after walking beside my
horse for a while, asked if I would let him put his cloak on my horse's
back, since we were going the same way. I allowed him to do so in
silence. He thanked me with easy grace for the slight favor, praised
my horse, and took the opportunity to laud the fortune and the
power of the rich and, I hardly know how, entered upon a sort of
soliloquy, in which I was merely the audience.

He developed his views about life and the world and very soon
turned to metaphysics, from which he demanded the solution to all
riddles. He analyzed the problem with great clarity and went on to its
solution.

You know, my friend, that I have clearly recognized, ever since I
went through the school of the philosophers, that I have no aptitude
for philosophical speculation, and I have completely abandoned this
field. Since then I have left many things alone, have renounced the
hope of knowing and understanding much and, as you yourself
advised me to do, I have as far as possible followed the voice within
me on the road it took, trusting my common sense. Now, this word
artist seemed to erect, with great talent, a tight structure which rose
by itself on its own foundation and stood up as though through an
inner necessity. Only, I wholly missed in it the very thing I would
most have liked to find; so the structure became for me a mere work
of art, whose graceful compactness and perfection served to delight
the eye alone. But I listened gladly to this eloquent man who had di-
verted my attention from my sufferings to himself, and I would
cheerfully have yielded to him had he claimed my soul as well as my
intelligence.

Meanwhile time had passed and imperceptibly the dawn had
brightened the sky. Startled, I suddenly looked up and saw the splendid colors unfolding in the east, announcing the approach of the sun.
Against it there was no protection at this hour, when shadows preen
themselves at their full length; no rampart was visible in the open
country. And I was not alone. I cast a glance at my companion and
was startled again. It was none other than the man in the gray coat.

He smiled at my confusion and, without giving me a chance to speak, continued: "Do let our mutual interests unite us for a while, as is the custom in the world; we always have time to part. This highway along the mountain range is, after all, the only one you can sensibly take; though this may not have occurred to you, you must not go down into the valley, and you will want even less to return over the mountains from which you have come. This happens to be my road too. I see you already blanching before the rising sun. I will lend you your shadow for the time we are together, and in return you will put up with my presence. Since you don't have your Bendel with you any more, I'll serve you well. You don't like me, I'm sorry about that, but you can use me all the same. The devil isn't as black as he is painted. It's true you annoyed me yesterday, but I don't resent that today; and I have already shortened the way for you as far, you must admit that yourself. Why don't you try on your shadow once more?"

The sun had risen and people were passing us on the road, so I accepted his offer, though with inner revulsion. With a smile he let my shadow glide to the ground, and it soon assumed its place by the horse's shadow and merrily trotted along beside me. I felt very strange. I rode past a troop of country folk, who respectfully made way, their heads bared, before a man of means. I rode on and with eager eye and pounding heart looked down sideward from my horse at what had formerly been *my* shadow. I had now borrowed it from a stranger, from an enemy in fact.

The latter walked along beside me unconcerned, whistling some ditty. He on foot, I on my horse. I was seized with a dizziness, the temptation was too great, and I suddenly jerked the reins, dug my spurs into the horse and took a side road at full speed. But I did not take my shadow away with me, for, as I turned, it glided from the horse and waited on the road for its lawful owner. I had to turn back in shame; after he had finished his tune the man in the gray coat laughed at me, put my shadow back in place again, and informed me that it would only consent to cling to me and stay with me if I possessed it as my legal property. "I'm holding on to you by your shadow," he continued, "and you can't escape me. A rich man like you simply must have a shadow, there's no other way; your only fault is that you haven't recognized this before."

I continued my journey on the same road; all the comforts of life and even its splendors returned to me; I could move freely and easily now that I possessed a shadow, though it was only a borrowed one; and I inspired respect everywhere, the respect which wealth commands. But I had death in my heart. My strange companion, who announced himself as the unworthy servant of the richest man in the world, was extraordinarily helpful, exceedingly dexterous and skillful, the very model of a valet for a rich man; but he would not leave my side and talked incessantly, always manifesting the greatest confidence that in the end I would conclude the bargain about the shadow, if only to get rid of him. He was as much a nuisance to me as he was objectionable. I was really afraid of him. I had made myself dependent on him. After leading me back to the glory of the world from which I was fleeing, he clung to me. I had to suffer his eloquence and almost began to feel that he was right. A rich man must have a shadow in this world, and if I wanted to maintain the position which he had again seduced me into assuming, there was only one possible outcome. But on this point I stood firm; after sacrificing my love, after my life had turned stale, I was not going to sell my soul to this creature, even for all the shadows in the world. I did not know how it was to end.

One day we were sitting in front of a cave which is visited by tourists who travel in the mountains. You can hear the roar of subterranean rivers rising from boundless depths, and when you throw a stone, no bottom seems to check it in its reverberating fall. As he often did, the man in gray painted for me, with exaggerated imagination and the iridescent charm of the most brilliant colors, careful, detailed pictures of what I might achieve in the world by virtue of my little bag, if only I had my shadow in my power again. Supporting my elbows on my knees, I hid my face in my hands and listened to the perfidious fellow, my heart divided between his blandishments and the stern will within me. I could not last with such an inner cleavage and began the decisive struggle.

"You seem to forget, sir, that while I have allowed you to remain in my company under certain conditions, I have reserved full freedom for myself." "If you give the word, I'll pack up." This was his usual threat. I was silent. He sat down at once and began to roll up my shadow. I turned pale but let him go on. A long silence followed. He spoke first:

"You can't bear me, sir, you hate me, I know; but why do you hate me? Is it perhaps because you attacked me on the open highway and tried to rob me violently of my bird's nest? Or is it because you thievishly sought to snatch my property, the shadow, which you thought was entrusted to you on your honor alone? I for my part don't hate you for this; I find it quite natural that you should try to make the most of your advantages, cunning and force; besides, the fact that you have the very strictest principles and think like the very soul of honesty is a whim I have nothing against. In point of fact I don't think as strictly as you; I merely act as you think. Have I ever applied my thumb to your throat to take possession of your most valuable soul, which I happen to fancy? Have I ever let a servant loose against you to regain my bartered purse? Have I attempted to abscond with it?" I had no answer to this. He continued: "Very well, sir, very well. You can't bear me; I can understand that very well too, and I don't resent it. We must part, that's clear, and you, too, are beginning to bore me. To rid yourself completely of my humiliating presence, I advise you once more: buy the thing from me." I held the purse out to him: "At this price." "No." I gave a deep sigh and spoke again: "Well then. I insist upon it, sir, let us part; don't block my path any longer in a world which I trust has enough room for both of us." He smiled and replied: "I am going, sir, but first I want to inform you how you may ring for me if ever you should feel the need for your most humble servant. You need only shake your purse so that the everlasting gold coins in it jingle; the sound will attract me instantly. Everyone in the world thinks only of his own advantage; but you see that I am concerned with yours too, for I am obviously making new power available to you. Oh, this purse! And even if the moths had already eaten your shadow, that purse would still form a strong bond between us. Enough, you control me through my gold. Command your servant even from a distance; you know that I can show myself helpful enough to my friends, and that the rich are in especially good standing with me. You've seen this yourself. But your shadow, sir — let me tell you — will never again be yours save on one single condition."

Figures out of the old days appeared before my mind. I asked him quickly, "Did you have a signature from Herr John?" He smiled. "With such a good friend it wasn't necessary." "Where is he? By heaven, I must know." He slowly put his hand in his pocket and from it dragged out by the hair the pale, crippled form of Herr Thomas John; his blue, corpselike lips moved to form the heavy words: "*Justo*

judicio Dei judicatur sum; justo judicio Dei condemnatus sum." (By
the just judgment of God I am judged; by the just judgment of God I
am condemned.) I was horrified and, swiftly throwing the ringing
purse into the depths, I spoke my last words to him: "I beseech you in
God's name, frightful man, get thee hence and never let me set eyes
on you again." He arose morosely and promptly disappeared behind
the masses of rock which formed the boundary of the savage, overgrown place.

(9)

I sat there without a shadow and without money; but a heavy
weight had been lifted from my chest and I was serene. If I had not
lost my love as well, or if I had had no guilt about the loss, I believe I
could have been happy, but I did not know what to do. I searched my
pockets and found a few more gold coins in them; I counted them
and laughed. My horses were down below at the inn, and I was
ashamed to return there; I had at least to wait for the sunset, and the
sun was still high in the sky. I lay down in the shadow of the nearest
trees and fell quietly asleep.

In a sweet dream, pleasant pictures merged into a merry dance.
Minna, a wreath of flowers in her hair, floated past and gave me a
friendly smile. The honest Bendel was adorned with flowers too, and
hurried past with a friendly greeting. I saw many more figures and it
seems to me I saw you too, Chamisso, in the distant crowd; a bright
light shone but no one had a shadow, and what is stranger still, this
did not look at all bad—flowers and songs, love and joy, under palm
groves. I would neither detain nor interpret the mobile, lovely forms
that flitted quickly by; but I know that I enjoyed dreaming this
dream and took care not to awaken. I was really already awake, but
still had my eyes closed in order to retain the vanishing forms a little
longer.

I finally opened my eyes; the sun still stood in the sky, but in the
east; I had slept through the night. I took this as a portent not to return to the inn. I lightly gave up the possessions I had there and decided to go on foot along a side road that led through the densely
wooded base of the mountain, leaving Fate to decide what to do with
me. I did not look behind me and did not think of turning to Bendel

—whom I had left behind me a rich man—as I could, of course, have done. I reflected on the new character that I was to assume in the world. My clothes were very modest. I had on an old black Russian jacket I had worn in Berlin and which had turned up again on this journey, I don't know how. In addition I had a traveling cap on my head and a pair of old boots on my feet. I got up, cut a knotty stick at that spot as a memento of it and set off at once on my wanderings.

In the forest I met an old peasant, who greeted me in a friendly way and with whom I fell into a conversation. Like a curious traveler I inquired from him first about the way, then about the region and its inhabitants, the products of the mountains and so on He replied to my questions talkatively and with intelligence. We came to the bed of a mountain stream which had spread desolation over a large strip of forest. I shuddered inwardly at the sunny expanse. I let the peasant precede me. But in the midst of the dangerous spot he stopped and turned around to tell me the story of this desolation. He soon noticed what I was lacking and broke off in the middle of his sentence: "But how does it happen that you have no shadow, sir!" "Alas, alas!" I replied with a sigh. "During a long, serious illness, I lost my hair, nails and shadow. You see, father, at my age, the hair that I have gotten back is quite white, and my nails are short, but my shadow still refuses to grow back." "Oh, oh!" the old man replied, shaking his head, "no shadow, that's bad. That was a bad illness you had, sir." But he did not resume his story and, at the next crossroad we came to, he left me without saying a word. Bitter tears once more trembled on my cheeks and my serenity was gone.

I continued my way with a sad heart, and no longer sought any man's company. I kept to the darkest forest. Sometimes I had to wait for hours at a sunny spot until there was no human eye to forbid my passage. In the evening I sought shelter in the villages. I was really making for a mine in the mountains, where I thought I would find work underground; for, apart from the fact that my present situation made it necessary for me to support myself, I had realized that only strenuous work could now protect me from my destructive thoughts.

A few rainy days helped me considerably on my way, but at the cost of my boots, whose soles had been made for Count Peter, not for the servant on foot. I was already walking on my bare feet. I had to get myself a pair of new boots. The following morning I attended to this business with due solemnity in a spot where there was a church fair, and where one of the booths had old and new boots for sale. I chose a pair and haggled about them for a long time. I had to give up the idea of a new pair, which I very much wanted; the high price frightened me off. I therefore contented myself with some old boots, which were still good and strong. The handsome, fair-haired boy who ran the booth handed them to me with a friendly smile in return for cash payment, wishing me luck on my way. I put them on at once and left the place by the northern gate.

I was deeply absorbed in my thoughts and scarcely saw where I set foot; for I was thinking of the mine, which I hoped to reach that evening, and where I did not really know how to announce myself. I had not gone two hundred feet when I noticed that I had lost my way; I looked about for it but found myself in a desolate, ancient pine forest, which seemed never to have been touched by an axe. I pressed forward a few more feet and saw that I was in the midst of desolate rocks, which were overgrown with moss and lichens and between which lay snow and ice fields. The air was very cold. I looked about me, the forest had vanished behind me. I took a few more steps; around me the stillness of death prevailed; the ice on which I stood extended as far as the eye could reach. A heavy mist hung over it; the sun stood bloody on the edge of the horizon. The cold was unbearable. I did not know what had happened to me; the congealing frost compelled me to hasten my steps, and I heard only the roar of distant waters; one step more and I was at the icy shore of the ocean. Countless herds of seals hurled themselves noisily into the waters. I followed this shore again; I saw naked rocks, land, forests of birch and pine; I continued straight ahead for some minutes more. I was stifling hot. I looked about me; I was standing under mulberry trees between beautifully cultivated rice fields. I sat down in the shade of the trees and looked at my watch; I had left the marketplace not more than fifteen minutes before; I thought I was dreaming and bit my tongue to wake myself; but I was awake. I shut my eyes in order to compose my thoughts. Before me I heard strange, nasal syllables. I looked up and two Chinamen, whose Asiatic features would have made them unmistakable even if I had utterly disregarded their clothing, addressed me in their native tongue with the traditional greetings of their country. I stood up and took two steps backward. I saw them no more; the landscape was totally altered: trees and forests instead of rice fields. I studied these trees and the vegetation around me; the ones I knew were southeastern Asiatic plants. Wanting to go up to one tree, I took a step and again everything was changed. I now marched like a recruit at drill and strode along with slow, measured steps. Strangely changing lands, fields, meadows, mountain ranges, steppes and dunes rolled past my astonished eyes. There was no doubt about it, I had seven-league boots on my feet.

(10)

I fell to my knees in mute devotion and shed tears of gratitude, for my future suddenly was clear to me. Cut off from human society by a youthful guilt, I had by way of compensation been thrown back on nature, which I had always loved. The earth had been given me as a rich garden; study was to be the direction and strength of my life, with science as its goal. It was not a resolve I made. What appeared before my inner eye then as a clear and perfect model, I have since then merely sought to depict faithfully with quiet, strict, unremitting diligence, and my satisfaction has depended on the congruence of what I have depicted with that model.

I roused myself to take immediate possession of the field which I was to harvest in the future by making a rough survey of it. I was standing on the heights of Tibet, and the sun, which had risen a few hours before, was already setting in the evening sky. I wandered through Asia from east to west, overtaking the sun in its course, and entered Africa. I looked about curiously, measuring it repeatedly in all directions. In Egypt, as I was gazing at the old pyramids and temples, I saw in the desert, not far from Thebes and its hundred gates, the caves in which Christian hermits had formerly dwelt. Suddenly it struck me: here is your house. As my future abode I chose one of the most hidden caves, which was at once spacious, comfortable and inaccessible to jackals. Then I continued on my way.

I crossed over to Europe at the Pillars of Hercules and, after viewing its southern and northern provinces, I went from northern Asia over the polar glacier to Greenland and America, and roamed through both parts of that continent. The winter, which had already set in in the south, drove me north from Cape Horn.

I lingered until day came in eastern Asia and continued my wandering only after a period of rest. Through both Americas I followed the chain of mountains which constitutes the highest known irregularity on our globe. I walked slowly and cautiously from peak to peak, now over flaming volcanoes, now over snow-covered domes, often breathing with difficulty. I reached Mount Elias and jumped across the Bering Straits into Asia. There I followed the eastern coast in its manifold windings and studied with special attention which of the islands situated there were accessible to me. From the Straits of Malacca my boots carried me to Sumatra, Java, Bali and Lamboc; by way of the smaller islands and rocks which teem in this sea, I attempted, often in the face of danger but always in vain, to find a northwest crossing to Borneo and other islands of this archipelago. I had to abandon hope. I finally sat down on the extreme point of Lamboc and, my face turned toward the south and east, I wept as if I had firmly locked the gate of my prison, because I had reached my limit so soon. New Holland, that remarkable country, so essential for an understanding of the earth and its sunwoven cloak, of the plant and animal world, and the South Sea with its zoöphyte islands, were forbidden to me; and so everything that I was to collect and cultivate was condemned from its very inception to remain a mere fragment. Oh, my Adelbert, how vain are man's efforts!

Often in the severest winter of the Southern Hemisphere I attempted to take those two hundred steps which separated me from Van Diemen's Land and New Holland, from Cape Horn westward by way of the polar glacier, quite unconcerned about my return, or whether that land should close over me like the lid of my coffin. I took desperate steps with foolish daring over the drifting ice and braved the cold and the sea. But all in vain. I have not been in New Holland to this day; I always came back to Lamboc and sat down on its extreme point and wept again, my face turned toward the south and the east, as though at the securely locked gate of my prison.

I finally tore myself away from this spot and went once more with a sad heart into the interior of Asia; I continued to roam through it, following the morning twilight westward, and arrived that very night at my predetermined house in the Thebaid, which I had touched the previous afternoon.

As soon as I had rested a little and it was day over Europe, I made it my first concern to procure everything I needed. First of all, brakes; for I had learned how inconvenient it was not to be able to shorten my steps in order to investigate nearby objects comfortably, except by taking off my boots. A pair of slippers over them did the job. Later on I even carried two pairs about with me, because I often threw a pair off when lions, humans or hyenas frightened me during my botanizing and I had no time to pick them up. My very good watch was an excellent chronometer for the short duration of my walks. In addition I needed a sextant, some instruments and books.

To obtain all these things, I took a few wretched walks to London and Paris, which were conveniently covered by fog. When the remainder of my magic gold was used up, I produced as payment some African ivory, which I easily found, though I had to choose the smallest tusks so as not to overtax my strength. I was soon provided and equipped with everything, and immediately began my new way of life as a private scholar.

I roamed about the earth, one time measuring its height, another time, the temperature of its springs and of the air, now observing animals, or again investigating plants. I hurried from the equator to the pole, from one world to the other, comparing experience with experience. My usual food was the eggs of African ostriches or northern sea birds, and fruits, especially bananas and those of tropical palms. In lieu of happiness I enjoyed nicotianas, and in place of human bonds and sympathy, the love of a faithful poodle, who watched over my cave in the Thebaid and, when I returned to him laden with new treasures, leaped up at me in joy and gave me the human feeling that I was not alone on earth. One more adventure was to lead me back among men.

(11)

One day, when I was collecting lichens and algae on the shores of Norway, with the brakes on my boots, a polar bear unexpectedly came toward me from behind a rock. I threw my slippers away and was about to step on an island that lay before me; a naked rock projecting from the water formed a transition to it. I stepped firmly on the rock with one foot, but fell into the sea on the far side of it, because the slipper was still on that foot.

The intense cold gripped me; I survived with great effort. As soon as I was on land again, I rushed as fast as I could to the Lybian desert to dry myself in the sun. But the sun was so hot and beat so strongly

down on my head that I staggered back north very ill. I tried to find
relief in vigorous movement and ran with swift, unsteady steps from
west to east and from east to west. I was in daylight at one moment,
in the dark of night the next, sometimes in summer and soon in the
cold of winter.

I don't know how long I staggered over the earth this way. A burning fever raged in my veins, and I feared that I was losing my sanity.
My bad luck would have it that in my careless running about I
stepped on someone's foot. I may have hit him; for I received a
powerful blow and fell down.

When I regained consciousness, I was lying comfortably in a good
bed among many others in a spacious and handsome room. Someone
was sitting at my head; people were going through the room from
bed to bed. They reached mine and talked about me. They called me
Number Twelve, and yet on the wall at my feet there was certainly a
black marble tablet — it was no illusion, I could read it clearly! — with
large golden letters which spelled my name

PETER SCHLEMIHL.

On the tablet under my name there were two more rows of letters,
but I was too weak to make them out. I closed my eyes again.

I heared something, in which Peter Schlemihl was mentioned,
being read loud and clearly, but I could not grasp its meaning. I saw
a very friendly man and a very beautiful woman in black appear before my bed. The forms were not alien to me, yet I could not recognize them.

Some time passed and I regained my strength. My name was Number Twelve, and Number Twelve was taken for a Jew because of his
long beard, though he was cared for no less because of that. No one
seemed to have noticed that he had no shadow. My boots, I was assured, were with everything that had been found on me when I was
brought here; they were in good and secure custody and would be returned to me after my recovery. The place in which I lay ill was
called the *Schlemihlium*; what was recited daily about Peter Schlemihl was an exhortation to pray for him as the founder and benefactor of this institution. The friendly man whom I had seen at my bed
was Bendel; the beautiful woman was Minna.

I recovered in the *Schlemihlium* without being recognized and
learned still more. I was in Bendel's native city, where he had built
this hospital in my name with the remainder of my otherwise unlucky

gold and supervised the place himself. Minna was a widow; a criminal trial had cost Herr Rascal his life and most of her fortune. Her parents were no longer alive. She lived here as a devout widow, doing works of mercy.

She once had a conversation with Herr Bendel at the bed of Number Twelve: "Why, noble lady, are you willing to expose yourself so often to the bad air here? Is it possible that Destiny is so harsh to you that you want to die?" "No, Herr Bendel, ever since my long dream came to an end and I awoke to my true self, I have been satisfied; I no longer wish death, nor do I fear it. I think of past and future with serenity. Don't you, too, now serve your master and friend in a blessed way with a quiet, inner happiness?" "Thank Heaven, yes, noble lady. Things have gone strangely for us; we have heedlessly drunk much good and much bitter woe from the full cup. Now it is empty, now one would like to think that all of it was merely a rehearsal and that, equipped with true insight, one may expect the beginning of reality. The beginning of reality is something different; one does not wish the earlier hocus-pocus to return and yet, on the whole, one is glad to have experienced it. Also I am confident that things must be better for our old friend than they were then." "I too," replied the beautiful widow, and they went on.

This conversation had made a profound impression upon me; but I did not know whether to reveal my identity or to leave the place unrecognized. I made my decision. I asked for paper and pencil and wrote the words:

"Your old friend, too, is now better off than then, and if he is atoning, it is the atonement of reconciliation."

After this I asked permission to dress, as I felt stronger. They brought the key for the little closet that stood near my bed. I found in it everything that belonged to me. I put on my clothes, hung my botanical box, in which, to my joy, I found my northern lichens again, about my neck over my black Russian jacket, put on my boots, placed the note on my bed and, as soon as the door opened, I was already far on the road to the Thebaid.

As I was traveling the road along the Syrian coast which I had taken the last time on my way from home, I saw my poor Figaro coming toward me. This excellent poodle seemed to want to follow the track of his master, whom he may have long been expecting. I stopped and called to him. He leaped up at me, barking with a thousand touching expressions of his innocent, high-spirited joy. I took him under my arm, for of course he could not follow me, and brought him home with me.

I found everything in order and gradually, as I regained my strength, I returned to my former occupations and to my old way of life. Except that for a whole year I kept away from the polar cold, which had become unbearable to me.

And so, my dear Chamisso, I live to this day. My boots do not wear out, as the very learned work of the famous Tieckius *De Rebus Gestis Pollicilli** had at first led me to fear. Their power remains unimpaired; only my strength is fading, but I am comforted by the fact that I have used it for a steady purpose and not fruitlessly. I have, as far as my boots would allow, explored more thoroughly than any man before me the earth, its shape, its elevations, its temperature, its atmospheric changes, the phenomena of its magnetic power, and the life on it, especially the plant kingdom. In several works I have noted and arranged the facts with the most painstaking precision and I have set down my desultory conclusions and views in a few treatises. I have established the geography of the interior of Africa and of the northern polar regions, of the interior of Asia and of its eastern coasts. My *Historia stirpium plantarum utriusque orbis*† stands as a large fragment of the *Flora universalis terrae* and as a part of my *Systema naturae*. I believe that I have not only increased the number of known species by more than a comfortable third, but have also contributed something to the knowledge of nature and the geography of plants. I am working very diligently at my fauna. I shall see to it that before my death my manuscripts are deposited with the University of Berlin.

And I have chosen you, my dear Chamisso, to be the trustee of my strange story, so that it may perhaps serve as a useful lesson for many of the earth's inhabitants when I have vanished. But you, my friend, if you want to live among men, learn to respect first your shadow, then your money. But if you want to live only for yourself and for your better self, oh, then you need no counsel.

---

*In Ludwig Tieck's play *The Life and Deeds of Little Tom Thumb* a character remarks that seven league boots carry the wearer one mile less every time they are repaired.

†The Latin titles mean respectively: *History of the Stems of Plants of Either World; Flora of the Whole Earth; System of Nature.* Chamisso published a work entitled *Ansichten von der Pflanzenkunde und vom Pflanzenreich* (*Views on the Science of Plants and the Realm of Plants*).

Gottfried Keller

1819—1890

Keller was born in Zurich, Switzerland, the son of a self-educated artisan. He lost his father at the age of five; so it remained for the practical, stern mother to bring up her two children, which she did on very slender means. Gottfried was a wayward boy and experienced the stresses that go with the period of adolescence. Expulsion from school for a minor prank brought an abrupt end to his education. He decided to become a painter and spent two and a half years in Munich proving to himself that he was not a painter. An unsuccessful love affair and the turbulent political situation in the forties brought him to maturity. He fought on the side of progress and democracy against reaction and acquired an ideal for which he could live. The publication of his first volume of poems in 1846 established him as a writer of promise.

The city of Zurich now offered him financial aid to further his education. He studied at Heidelberg and later at Berlin, profiting greatly from his intellectual contact with men like Ludwig Feuerbach and Hermann Hettner. But above all, he was writing.

When he returned to Zurich he settled down to a literary career. This was interrupted by a ten-year stint as secretary of the canton, a post he filled with credit. He lived in Zurich until his death in 1890.

Keller has left a considerable body of lyric poetry, but his fame rests on his fiction. His novel *Der grüne Heinrich* (*Green Henry*) is one of the most important in German fiction, belonging to the category of *Bildungsromane* (novels of education or development). He wrote three cycles of novellas, two describing the vagaries of the inhabitants of his imaginary Seldwyla, the "Gopher Prairie" of nineteenth century Switzerland, and the third, *Das Sinngedicht* (*The Epigram*), representing the most intricate cycle of stories ever contrived around a single idea: the relation between sensuality and modesty in love.

He is best remembered for his Seldwyla tales, which, taken together, constitute a critique of bourgeois society. Most of them are humorous and satirical and include elements of farce; but there is always a serious undercurrent in them—one or more social vices are castigated amid the merriment.

Keller was not a fancy littérateur; his style was "of the man": simple, unaffected, concrete, earthy. It is his love of solid detail which permits him to carry off the strong element of the grotesque and farcical, the fantastically improbable, that crops up everywhere in his tales, without, however, antagonizing the sophisticated reader. One comes away from his stories with a sense of sheer delight.

Clothes Make the Man, published in 1874, grew out of a newspaper account that came to Keller's attention. The theme of the plebeian impostor who passes himself off as an aristocrat was not new to literature. But Keller's genius enabled him to give body, life, and depth to the skeletal newspaper account of a piquant imposture. The title—a proverb in both English and German—says that men judge by appearances rather than by essences. Thus an unemployed tailor who looks like a count and rides in a count's carriage is taken for a count. But this is only possible because the people of Seldwyla want to be fooled. They need illusion. Being prosperous, they have become smug, self-satisfied and bored; they need sensation and romance. Moreover, being prosaic bourgeois, they hanker for an aristocracy to adore, like M. Jourdain in Molière's comedy, and feel honored to be fleeced, insulted and trodden under foot by this aristocracy. But when they are exposed as dupes, they react with cruelty against the half-innocent deceiver.

But the title may be interpreted in another sense too, as a satire on the idea of aristocracy, which gives a man nothing that is more than skin deep. The same thesis was presented by Shaw in *Pygmalion*, by Barrie in *The Admirable Crichton*, by Carl Zuckmayer in *The Captain of Köpenick* and by Beaumarchais in his Figaro comedies.

The title has still another meaning. It is clothes, not the conduct of a confidence man, that "make" the man Strapinski. He goes back to his tailoring, becomes a successful bourgeois, thus beating the Seldwylers and Goldachers at their own game. He raises a family and lords it over his fellow citizens by virtue of the real talent he possesses rather than because of his spurious aristocracy. Appearance has turned into essence.

This motif of appearance versus reality dominates the story: through the symbol of clothes; through the Homeric catalogue of house signs which lead Strapinski to conclude that these signs really indicate what goes on inside the houses they describe; above all through the "Bovarysme" that is characteristic of this whole bourgeois society and which is happily outgrown by the two principal characters in the novella—Strapinski and Nettchen. But "appearance versus reality" is a theme that lends itself to tragic treatment too; witness *Othello* and *King Lear*. Because Keller has revealed it to us in its comic aspects does not alter the fact that there is a serious undercurrent in this farcical, fairylike tale. Keller the solid, liberal, democratic republican depicts in *Clothes Make the Man* the dangers that threaten a prosperous bourgeois society of basically good people. The "moral" is stated by Nettchen during her interview with Strapinski after his unmasking: "No more romances."

Clothes Make the Man

On an unfriendly November day a poor tailor was strolling along the highway to Goldach, a small, wealthy town only a few hours distant from Seldwyla. The tailor carried in his pocket nothing but a thimble, which, for lack of a coin, he kept twirling between his fingers whenever he put his hands into his pockets because of the cold. His fingers were quite sore from this turning and rubbing. The bankruptcy of a master tailor in Seldwyla had compelled him to forfeit his wages and his job and to leave town. He had had nothing for breakfast except a few snowflakes which had flown into his mouth, and he saw even less ahead of him for lunch. Begging was something he found extremely difficult to do; in fact he felt it to be utterly impossible, because over his black Sunday suit, which was the only suit he had, he wore a full, dark-gray cape, faced with black velvet; and this gave him an aristocratic and romantic appearance, especially since his long black hair and small mustache were carefully groomed and he possessed pale but regular features.

This type of dress had become a necessity for him, without his intending anything evil or deceptive by it; on the contrary, he was satisfied to be left alone to do his job quietly. But he would sooner have starved than be parted from his cape and Polish fur cap, which he also wore with style.

He could therefore work only in larger towns, where such things did not attract too much attention; when he was on the road and carried no savings with him, he fell into the direst need. When he approached a house, people looked at him in astonishment and curiosity and expected anything but that he would beg. And so, since he was not a glib talker either, the words died on his lips; so that he was the martyr of his cloak and suffered hunger as dark as its velvet facing.

As he was climbing a hill, worried and weakened, he came up beside a new and comfortable coach, which the coachman of a nobleman had fetched in Basel and was delivering to his master, a foreign count living somewhere in eastern Switzerland in an old manor house that he had rented or bought. The carriage was fitted with all sorts of devices for holding baggage and therefore seemed to be heavily packed, although it was completely empty. Because of the steep road, the coachman walked beside the horses; when he got to the top of the hill he mounted his box again and asked the tailor whether he did not want to get into the empty carriage. For it was just beginning to rain and he had seen with one glance that the pedestrian was making his weary and wretched way through the world.

The tailor gratefully and modestly accepted the offer, whereupon the carriage swiftly rolled away with him and, in little under an hour, rode stately and rumbling through the gateway of Goldach. The elegant vehicle pulled up suddenly in front of the first hotel, called the Scale, and at once the bellboy gave such a violent tug at the bell that the wire almost snapped in two. Thereupon the landlord and his help rushed out and pulled the carriage door open; children and neighbors were already surrounding the splendid vehicle, curious to see what sort of kernel would emerge from such an unheard-of shell. And when the astonished tailor finally came out, pale and handsome in his cloak, and looking mournfully at the ground, he seemed to them to be at least a mysterious prince or young count. The space between the carriage and the door of the hotel was narrow, and moreover, the way was virtually blocked by the spectators. Whether it was because he lacked presence of mind or courage to break through the crowd and simply go on his way, at any rate he did not do so, but passively allowed himself to be led into the house and up the stairs; and he did not really grasp his new, strange situation until he saw himself transpanted into a comfortable dining room and solicitously helped out of his dignified cloak.

"You wish to dine, sir?" he was asked. "Dinner will be served at once, we've just finished the cooking."

Without waiting for an answer, the landlord of the Scale rushed to the kitchen and cried: "The devil take it! Now we have nothing to serve except beef and leg of lamb. I daren't cut into the partridge pie, because it's reserved and promised to the gentlemen who are coming this evening. That's the way it goes. The only day we don't expect a guest and have nothing on hand, a gentleman like this one has to appear! And the coachman has a coat of arms on his buttons, and the carriage is like a duke's. And the young man can scarcely open his mouth from sheer nobility!"

But the calm cook said: "Well, sir, what is there to lament about? You can safely serve him the meat pie; he isn't going to eat it all! The gentlemen coming this evening will then get it in individual portions; we can certainly get six portions out of what's left."

"Six portions? You forget that the gentlemen are in the habit of eating till they're full," said the landlord. But the cook continued imperturbably: "And so they shall, too. We can send out quickly for half a dozen cutlets. We need these for the stranger anyhow, and what's left I'll cut into little pieces and mix with the meat pie. You just let me attend to it."

But the good landlord said earnestly: "Cook, I've already told you before this that we don't do such things in this town or in this house. We live solidly here and honorably, and we can afford to do so!"

"For Heaven's sake, yes, yes!" cried the cook in some excitement. "If we can't handle such a situation, we may as well give up. Here are two snipe which I just bought from the hunter; perhaps we can add these to the meat pie. The gourmets won't object to a partridge pie adulterated with snipe. Then there's the trout too. I threw the largest one into the boiling water when that remarkable carriage arrived, and the broth is already boiling in the pan; so we have a fish, the beef, the vegetables with the cutlets, the leg of lamb and the meat pie. Just give me the key so that we can get the preserves and dessert out. And, sir, you might with all honor and confidence let me have the key for good, so that I don't have to run after you everywhere and suffer the greatest embarrassment."

"Dear cook, don't be annoyed; I had to promise my late wife on her deathbed that I would always keep the keys in my hands; so it's a matter of principle, not of mistrust. Here are the pickles and cherries; here, the pears and apricots; but the old pastry must not be served again. Let Lizzie run out quickly to the confectioner's and get some fresh pastry, three plates of it, and if he has a large cake he can send it along too."

"But, sir, you can't charge all that up to the one guest; you can't make money that way, not with the best will."

"No matter, it's for the honor of the thing! It won't ruin me; on the other hand, such a grand gentleman shall be able to say he found a

decent meal when he passed through our city, although he came
quite unexpectedly, and in winter too. I don't want it to be said, as
they say about the innkeepers of Seldwyla, that we gobble up all the
good things ourselves and serve the bones to strangers. So step on it,
get going, hurry up, everybody!"

During these elaborate preparations, while the table was being set
with glistening silver, the tailor found himself in the most painful
anxiety. And, however passionately the starving man had yearned a
short while before for some nourishment, all he wanted now was to
escape from the threatening meal. Finally he gathered courage, put
his cloak about his shoulders and his cap on his head, and walked out
of the dining room looking for an exit. But as, in his confusion, he
did not find the stairway in the spacious house at once, the waiter,
who was constantly driven by the devil thought he was looking for a
certain convenience and cried: "Your most gracious permission, sir,
I'll show you the way!" and led him through a long passage, which
ended nowhere else than before a beautifully lacquered door on
which an artistic inscription was affixed.

So the owner of the coat went in without objecting, meek as a
lamb, and modestly locked the door behind him. Inside he leaned
against the wall, sighing bitterly, and wished once more to share in
the golden freedom of the highway, which now appeared to him as
the highest good fortune, bad though the weather was.

But instead, he now involved himself in his first deliberate lie, because he waited a while in the locked room and thereby set out on the
precipitous road of evil.

Meanwhile the landlord, who had seen him walking around in his
cloak, cried: "The gentleman is freezing! Put on a bigger fire in the
room! Where's Lizzie, where's Annie? Quick, throw a basketful of
wood into the stove and a few handfuls of chips, so that it'll burn
properly! The devil! Are people in the Scale to sit at dinner in their
overcoats?"

And when the tailor emerged again from the long passage, as
melancholy as the ancestral ghost of a family castle, the landlord accompanied him into the cursed dining room, rubbing his hands and
paying him a hundred compliments. He was invited to the table
without further delay, his chair was moved into place behind him;
and as the fragrance of the nourishing soup, the like of which he had
not smelled for a long time, completely robbed him of his will power,

he sat down resignedly and at once dipped the heavy spoon into the golden brown broth. In profound silence he refreshed his faint spirits and was served in respectful calm and quiet.

When he had emptied his plate and the landlord saw how much he had enjoyed the soup, he courteously encouraged him to take another spoonful, saying it was good in this raw weather. Then the trout was served, garnished with greens, and the landlord helped him to a handsome portion. The tailor, tormented by anxiety, did not dare, in his timidity, to use the gleaming knife but toyed shyly and fastidiously with the silver fork. The cook, who was peeping through the door to observe the grand gentleman, noticed this and said to those who stood about her: "Heaven be praised! he knows how to eat a delicate fish properly; he doesn't saw about in the tender creature with his knife as if he wished to slaughter a calf. This is a gentleman from a great family; I'd be willing to swear to it if it weren't a sin to swear. And how handsome and sad he is! I'm sure he's in love with a poor girl whom they won't let him marry. Yes, yes, the great have their sorrows too!"

Meanwhile the landlord saw that is guest was not drinking and said respectfully: "You don't like the table wine, sir? Would you like to order a glass of good Bordeaux, which I can recommend most highly?"

Thereupon the tailor committed his second deliberate sin, by obediently saying yes instead of no. At once the landlord of the Scale went down to the cellar personally to fetch a choice bottle; for it meant everything to him that people should be able to say there was something really good to be had in the place. When the guest, out of a bad conscience, again took very small sips from the wine that was poured out for him, the landlord joyfully ran into the kitchen, clicked his tongue and cried: "The devil take me, that man is a connoisseur! He sips my good wine on his tongue the way you put a ducat on the gold scale!"

"Heaven be thanked!" said the cook. "I told you: he knows."

So the meal took its course, but very slowly, because the poor tailor kept eating and drinking daintily and undecidedly; and the landlord let the dishes stand long enough to give him time. However, what the guest had consumed so far was not worth mentioning; only now did his hunger, which was being steadily and dangerously stirred, begin to overcome his terror. When the partridge pie appeared, the tailor's

mood took a sudden turn and a firm resolve began to take shape in
his mind. "Things are now as they are," he said to himself, warmed
and stimulated by a new drop of wine. "I would be a fool if I were
willing to bear the coming disgrace and persecution without having
had a good meal for it. So make hay while the sun shines. That little
tower they've set up before me may easily be the last food they'll serve
me; I'll make the most of it, come what may. What I once have inside
of me, not even a king can take from me."

No sooner said than done. With the courage of despair he plunged
into the dainty meat pie without a thought of stopping, so that in less
than five minutes it had half disappeared and things began to look
very dubious for the evening guests. Meat, truffles, dumplings, bottom, crust, he swallowed everything indiscriminately, concerned
solely with filling his belly before fate overtook him. He drank the
wine moreover, in vigorous draughts, and crammed large bits of
bread into his mouth. In short, it was as hasty and lively a hauling in
as when, in a rising storm, the hay is rescued by being pitched on the
fork from the meadow into the barn. Once more the landlord ran
into the kitchen and cried: "Cook! He's eating up the meat pie, while
he's scarcely touched the roast beef. And he's drinking the Bordeaux
by the half-tumblerful!"

"May it agree with him," said the cook. "You just leave him alone;
he knows what partridge is. If he were a common fellow, he would
have kept to the roast."

"I think so too," said the landlord. "Of course, it doesn't look very
elegant; but when I was traveling during my apprenticeship I saw
only generals and canons eat like that."

Meanwhile the coachman had had the horses fed and had eaten a
solid meal in the dining room reserved for common people; being in
a hurry, he soon had the horses hitched up again. The staff of the
Scale could no longer contain themselves and asked the nobleman's
coachman straight out, before it was too late, who his master up
there was and what his name was. The coachman, a sly, jocular fellow, replied: "Hasn't he told you himself?"

"No," they said, and he replied: "I can well believe it; that man
doesn't say much in one day; well, he's Count Strapinski. But he's
going to stay here today and perhaps a few more days; for he ordered
me to ride ahead with the carriage."

He made this bad joke to get revenge on the tailor, who, as he

thought, instead of repaying his favor with a word of thanks and a
good-by, had gone off into the house without turning around and
was playing the lord. Carrying his prank to an extreme, he climbed
up on his carriage without requesting the bill for himself or his
horses, cracked his whip and drove out of the city, and everything
was found to be in order and added to the tailor's account.

Now, it just so happened that the tailor, who was a native of
Silesia, was really called Strapinski, Wenzel Strapinski. This may
have been a coincidence; or perhaps the tailor had taken his guild
book out in the carriage, forgotten it there, and the coachman had
taken possession of it. In any case, when the landlord, beaming with
joy and rubbing his hands, stepped up to the tailor and asked
whether Count Strapinski would take champagne or a glass of sea-
soned Tokay with his dessert, and announced that his rooms were
just being prepared for him, poor Strapinski turned pale, became
confused again and made no reply.

"Most interesting!" the landlord grumbled to himself, hurrying to
the cellar once more and taking, from a special locker, not only a
small bottle of Tokay but also a little jug of Bocksbeutel and a bottle
of champagne, which he put under his arm. Soon Strapinski saw a
young forest of glasses before him, the champagne glass standing out
like a poplar tree. These glasses glittered, rang and gave out a strange
fragrance, and what was stranger still, the poor but elegant man
reached into the little forest not unskillfully, and when he saw the
landlord put a little red wine into his champagne, he put a few drops
of Tokay into his. Meanwhile the town clerk and the notary had
come to drink their coffee and play their daily game for it. Soon the
older son of the House of Häberlin and Company, the younger son of
the House of Pütschli-Nievergelt, and the bookkeeper of a large spin-
nery, Herr Melcher Böhni, also arrived. But instead of playing their
usual game, all these gentlemen, their hands in their back coat
pockets, walked around behind the Polish count in a wide arc, winking to each other and laughing up their sleeves. For although these
members of prominent families stayed home all their lives, they had
relatives and associates scattered all over the earth, and therefore believed they had adequate knowledge of the world.

So this was supposed to be a Polish count? Of course they had seen
the carriage from their office chairs; besides, they didn't know
whether the landlord was entertaining the count or the count the

landlord; however, the landlord had done nothing stupid till now; on the contrary, he was well known as a fairly sharp fellow; and so the circles which the curious gentlemen drew about the stranger became smaller and smaller, until they finally sat down familiarly at his table and skillfully, but in an off-hand manner, invited themselves to the banquet simply by beginning to throw dice for a bottle.

However, they did not drink too much, as it was still early; the idea was to take a sip of excellent coffee and to wait on the "Polack," as they were already secretly calling the tailor, with good cigars, so that he might smell more and more where he really was.

"May I offer you a decent cigar, Count? I got it direct from my brother in Cuba," said one.

"You Polish gentlemen also like a good cigarette; here is some genuine tobacco from Smyrna my business partner sent it to me" cried another, thrusting a little red silken pouch at him.

"This one from Damascus is finer, Count," said the third, "our agent there got it for me himself."

The fourth stretched out a big ungainly cigar, crying: "If you want something quite excellent, try this planter's cigar from Virginia, home-grown, homemade and absolutely not to be had for money."

Strapinski smiled a sickly smile, said nothing and was soon enveloped in fine fragrant clouds, which turned beautifully silver as the sun broke through them. In less than a quarter of an hour the sky cleared and the most beautiful autumn afternoon set in. The general opinion was that they should make the most of the favorable hour, as the year might perhaps not bring many more such days; so it was decided that they should drive out to visit the jovial district councillor on his estate and taste his new wine, the red must; for he had pressed grapes only a few days before. Pütschli-Nievergelt, Junior, sent for his dogcart and soon his young iron-gray horses were pounding the pavement in front of the Scale. The landlord himself also got a carriage ready, and they courteously invited the count to join them and get to know the region.

The wine had warmed his wits; he made a rapid calculation that this would give him the best opportunity for disappearing unnoticed and continuing his journey on foot; the expense would be borne by these foolish and insistent gentlemen. He therefore accepted the invitation with a few polite words and got into the dogcart with young Pütschli.

238   GOTTFRIED KELLER

Now, it also happened that the tailor had occasionally worked for
the lord of the manor in his native village as a young boy, had done
his military service with the hussars, and therefore possessed an adequate knowledge of horsemanship. When, therefore, his companion
asked him politely whether he would like to drive, he at once took
hold of the whip and reins and drove through the gate and along the
country road at a swift trot in a professional manner, so that the
gentlemen looked at each other and whispered: "It is true, he certainly is a gentleman."

In half an hour they reached the councillor's estate; Strapinski
drove up in a magnificent half-arc and let the fiery horses pull up
short in the best style. The guests jumped from the carriages, the
councillor came out and led the company into the house, and soon
the table was loaded with half a dozen carafes full of carnelian-
colored wine. The fiery, fermenting beverage was first tested, praised
and then cheerfully attacked, while the master of the house spread
the news that a distinguished count had come, a "Polack," and gave
orders for a more elegant reception.

Meanwhile, to make up for the card game they had missed, the
company divided into two parties. In this country men simply could
not come together without gambling, probably from an innate urge
for activity. Strapinski, who for various reasons had to decline to participate, was invited to look on; for even this seemed to them worthwhile, because they were accustomed to display much cleverness and
presence of mind at cards. He had to sit down between the two
games, and the participants now took pains to play cleverly and skillfully and to entertain the guest at the same time. And so he sat there
like an ailing prince being entertained by his courtiers with a divert-
ing spectacle depicting the course of the world. They explained to
him the most significant changes, tricks and events, and when the
one party had to turn its attention for a moment exclusively to the
game, the other carried on a conversation with the tailor all the more
solicitously. The best topic for this seemed to them to be horses, hunting and the like. Strapinski was perfectly at home in this area too; for
he merely had to dig out the phrases he had once heard around officers and the landed gentry, and which had pleased him uncommonly
even then. He produced these phrases only sparingly, with a certain
modesty and always with a melancholy smile, and thereby achieved
an effect that was only the greater. Whenever two or three of the

gentlemen got up and stepped aside, they said: "He's a perfect squire!"

Only Melcher Böhni, the bookkeeper, the born doubter, rubbed his hands in glee and said to himself: "I see it coming, there will be another Goldach putsch; in fact, in a way it's here already. But it's time for one too; it's two years since the last one. That man has strangely pierced fingers; perhaps he's from Praga or Ostrolenka.* Well, I'll take good care not to disturb the course of events."

The two card parties had now come to an end, and the gentlemen's thirst for must had been satisfied. They preferred to cool off a little on the councillor's old wines, which were now served; but the cooling off was of a rather passionate nature, for, in order not to fall into base idleness, the guests proposed a general game of chance. The cards were dealt, everyone threw in a Diabantine taler, and when Strapinski's turn came, he could not very well put his thimble on the table. "I don't have such a coin," he said, turning red. But Melcher Böhni, who had been watching him, had already put in a stake for him without anyone's noticing; for they were all far too comfortably fixed to entertain the suspicion that anyone in the world could be without money. The next moment the whole pot was moved toward the tailor, who had won; in confusion he let the money lie and Böhni managed the second round for him, which another man won, as well as the third. But the fourth and the fifth were again won by the Polack, who gradually woke up and got into the spirit of the thing. By keeping quiet and calm, he played with changing fortune; once he came down to one taler, which he had to risk, won again, and finally, when they got tired of the game, he had a few louis d'or, more than he had ever owned in his whole life. When he saw that they were all pocketing their gains he took these, not without dreading that it was all a dream. Böhni, who was watching him carefully all the time, was now clear in his mind concerning him and thought: "The devil he rides in a coach-and-four!"

But because he observed, too, that the enigmatic stranger had shown no greed for the money and had in general conducted himself with modesty and sobriety, he was not ill disposed toward him, and decided to let the matter take its own course.

But while they were taking a walk in the open air before dinner, Count Strapinski collected his thoughts and considered that the right

*Two towns in the vicinity of Warsaw.

moment had come to take a noiseless departure. He now had a tidy sum of money for traveling and planned to pay the landlord of the Scale from the nearest town for the dinner that had been forced on him. So he put on his cape, pressed the fur cap farther down over his eyes and strode slowly up and down in the evening sun under a row of tall locust trees, contemplating the beautiful landscape, or rather, spying out which road he should take. He looked superb with his troubled brow, his attractive but melancholy mustache, his glistening black curls, his dark eyes and his pleated coat blowing in the wind. The evening light and the rustling of the trees above him heightened the impression, so that the company studied him from afar with attention and benevolence. Gradually he got further and further away from the house, and strode through a clump of bushes behind which a field path ran. When he saw that he was protected from the eyes of the company, he was on the point of moving into the field with firm step, when suddenly the councillor and his daughter Nettchen came toward him from around a corner. Nettchen was a pretty young lady, dressed most splendidly, perhaps overdressed, and decorated with much jewelry.

"We've been looking for you, Count," cried the councillor, "first of all, because I want to introduce you to my child here, and secondly to ask you if you'll do us the honor of taking a bit of supper with us. The other gentlemen are already in the house."

The wanderer quickly took his cap from his head and made reverent, indeed timid, bows, blushing deeply. For matters had taken a new turn; a young lady now occupied the theater of events. But his shyness and excessive reverence did not hurt him with the lady; on the contrary, the shyness, humility and reverence of such a distinguished and interesting young nobleman appeared to her to be truly touching, indeed enchanting. You see, the thought went through her mind, the more aristocratic they are, the more modest and unspoiled; mark this, you rude gentlemen of Goldach, who scarcely tip your hats to a young girl any more!

She therefore greeted the knight most graciously, blushing adorably too, and at once said many things to him hastily and rapidly, in the manner of smug, small-town women who want to show off to strangers. Strapinski, on the other hand, became transformed in a short time; while so far he had done nothing to enter into the role that was being thrust on him, he now involuntarily began to speak a little more affectedly and mixed all sorts of Polish scraps into his talk; in short, the tailor blood in him began to cut capers in the presence of the woman and to carry off its rider.

At dinner he received the place of honor near the daughter of the house; for her mother was dead. But he soon became melancholy again when he reflected that he would now have to return to town with the others or force himself to escape into the night, and when he further considered how transitory was the fortune that he now enjoyed. But he felt this fortune nevertheless, and told himself in advance: "Ah, once in your life, at least, you will have been somebody and sat beside such a higher being."

It was indeed no trifling matter to see a hand gleaming beside him on which three or four bracelets tinkled, and to perceive, at every fleeting side-glance that he took a daring, charming coiffure, a lovely blush, a full glance. For no matter what he did or did not do, everything was interpreted by this young lady as unusual and aristocratic, and his very awkwardness was charmingly interpreted as remarkable ingenuousness — though usually she could chat for hours abut social faux pas. As they were in good spirits, a few guests sang songs that were in fashion in the thirties. The count was asked to sing a Polish song. The wine finally overcame his shyness, although not his anxiety; he had once worked on Polish territory for a few weeks and knew a few Polish words; he even knew a Polish folk song by heart, without being aware of its meaning, like a parrot. So he sang in Polish with an elegant air, timidly rather than loudly, in a voice which quavered gently as though with a secret sorrow:

> "A hundred thousand pigs are quartered
> From the Desna to the Vistula,
> And Katinka, that filthy wench
> Walks in dirt up to her ankles.
>
> A hundred thousand oxen roar
> On Volynia's green pastures
> And Katinka, yes Katinka
> Thinks I am in love with her."

"Bravo! Bravo!" all the gentlemen cried, clapping their hands, and Nettchen said with emotion: "Ah, national songs are always so beautiful!" Fortunately no one asked for the translation.

After this high point in the entertainment, the company broke up;

the tailor was packed into the carriage again and carefully brought back to Goldach; but first he had to promise not to go away without taking leave. At the Scale they had another glass of punch; but Strapinski was exhausted and wanted to go to bed. The landlord himself took him to his rooms, whose splendor he scarcely noticed, although he was accustomed to sleep only in poor hostel rooms. He was standing, bereft of all personal belongings, in the middle of a beautiful carpet, when the landlord suddenly noticed the absence of all baggage and clapped his palm to his forehead. Then he ran out quickly, rang the bell, summoned waiters and bellboys, exchanged words with them, came back and said: "It's true, Count, they forgot to unload your luggage. Even the most essential things are lacking."

"Even the little package that was lying in the carriage?" asked Strapinski anxiously, because he was thinking of a little bundle the size of his hand, which he had left lying on the seat and which contained a handkerchief, a hairbrush, a comb, a little box of pomade, and a stick of wax for his mustache.

"That's missing too; there isn't a thing here," said the good landlord in fright, because he suspected it was something very important. "We must send a special messenger after the coachman at once," he cried eagerly. "I'll attend to it."

But the count grasped his arm in equal fright and said with emotion: "Don't! You mustn't! All trace of me must be lost for some time," he added, startled by this invention.

The astonished landlord went to the punch-drinking gentlemen and told them about the incident and concluded with the assertion that the count must undoubtedly be a victim of political or family persecution; for just about that time many Poles and other refugees had been expelled from their country for acts of violence; others were watched and ensnared by foreign agents.

But Strapinski enjoyed a good sleep, and when he awoke late, the first thing he saw was the landlord's splendid Sunday dressing gown hanging over a chair, and farther on, a small table covered with every imaginable toilet article. Then he saw a number of servants waiting to deliver, on behalf of his friends of yesterday, baskets and chests filled with fine linen, clothes, cigars, books, boots, shoes, spurs, riding whips, furs, caps, hats, socks, stockings, pipes and flutes and fiddles, and to make the solicitous request that he be gracious enough to use these conveniences for the present. Since his benefactors invariably spent their mornings at their places of business, they announced their visits for the period after lunch.

These people were anything but ridiculous or simple-minded; they were prudent businessmen, smart rather than dense. But since their prosperous town was small and they sometimes felt bored in it, they were always eager for a change, an event, a happening, which they could embrace without restraint. The coach-and-four, the alighting of the stranger, his luncheon, the statements of the coachman were such simple and natural things that the people of Goldach, who were not in the habit of harboring idle suspicions, built an event on them as on a rock.

When Strapinski saw the assortment of merchandise spread out before him, his first impulse was to put his hand in his pocket to find out whether all this was a dream. If his thimble still nestled there in concealment, he was dreaming. But no, the thimble sat their cosily among the coins he had won at gambling and was rubbing sociably against the talers; so its master bowed to circumstance once again and descended from his rooms to the street to inspect the town in which things were going so well for him. Behind the kitchen door stood the cook, who made a deep curtsy to him and looked at him with new pleasure; in the hall and at the front door stood other domestics, all with their caps in their hands, and Strapinski strode out with dignity and yet modesty, gathering his cloak chastely about him. Destiny was making him greater with every moment.

He studied the town with an entirely different mien than if he had gone out to look for work in it. It consisted mostly of fine, solidly built houses, all adorned with stone or painted symbols and supplied with names. In these names the customs of the centuries could be clearly discerned. The Middle Ages were mirrored in the oldest houses or in the new buildings that had taken their place but had retained the old names from the age of the warlike mayors and fairy tales. On them one could read: the Sword, the Iron Helmet, the Armor, the Crossbow, the Blue Shield, the Swiss Sword, the Knight, the Flint, the Turk, the Sea Monster, the Golden Dragon, the Linden Tree, the Pilgrim's Staff, the Nymph, the Bird of Paradise, the Pomegranate, the Camel, the Unicorn and so on. The Age of Enlightenment and Philanthrophy was clearly to be read in the moral precepts which shone over the front doors in beautiful golden letters, such as: Harmony, Uprightness, Old Independence, New Independence, Civic Virtue A, Civic Virtue B, Trust, Love, Hope, Au Revoir 1 and 2, Joy, Inner Righteousness, Outer Righteousness, National Prosperity (a neat little house in which, behind a canary cage covered entirely with cress, a friendly old woman with a peaked bonnet sat spinning yarn), the Constitution (below lived a cooper who zealously and noisily bound little pails and kegs with hoops, hammering incessantly). One house bore the gruesome name Death; a faded skeleton stretched from bottom to top between the windows. Here lived the justice of the peace. In the house of Patience lived the clerk of debts, a starved picture of misery, since in this town no one owed anyone anything.

Finally, the newest houses announced the poetry of the industrialists, bankers and forwarding agents and their imitators in the euphonious names: Rosedale, Morningdale, Sunny Mount, Violet Castle, etc. The valleys and castles attached to ladies' names always indicated to the initiated a handsome dowry.

At every street corner there stood an old tower with an elaborate clock, a colorful roof and a prettily gilded weather vane. These towers were carefully preserved; for the people of Goldach rejoiced in their past and in the present and were justified in doing so. All this splendor was encompassed by the old circular wall, which, although it no longer served any purpose, was nevertheless retained as decoration; it was completely overgrown with thick old ivy and surrounded the little town with a wreath of evergreen.

All this made a wonderful impression on Strapinski; he thought he was in another world. For when he read the inscriptions on the houses, the like of which he had never seen before, he assumed that they referred to the special secrets and habits of life in each house, and that behind every front door things really were what the sign indicated, and that he had fallen into a sort of moral utopia. Thus he was inclined to believe that the remarkable reception he had been given was related to this correspondence — for example, the symbol of the scale under which he lived meant that here uneven destiny was weighed and balanced and that occasionally a traveling tailor was transformed into a count.

On his stroll he came to the city gate, and as he looked over the open field, his conscience prompted him for the last time to continue on his way at once. The sun was shining, the highway looked fine and

firm, not too dry and not too wet either, as if made for walking. He
now had traveling money too, so that he could stop and get comfortable lodgings anywhere he wished to and no obstacle was discernible.

There he stood like the youth at the crossroads, and on a real crossroads; hospitable columns of smoke rose above the linden grove
which surrounded the town; the golden knobs of the towers sparkled
enticingly through the treetops; happiness, pleasure and guilt, a mysterious destiny beckoned from there. But from the direction of the
fields there gleamed open space; work, deprivation, poverty, obscurity awaited him there, but also a good conscience and a serene way
of life. Feeling this, he firmly resolved to turn into the field. But at
the same moment a swift vehicle rolled by; it was the young lady of
yesterday, who sat all alone in a trim light carriage; she was wearing
a fluttering blue veil and driving a handsome horse toward the town.
Strapinski immediately reached for his cap in surprise, and humbly
held it before his chest; the girl bowed to him in an altogether
friendly manner, her face reddened quickly, and she drove away in
great emotion, whipping her horse to a gallop.

Strapinski, however, involuntarily made a complete turn and confidently went back to the city. On that very day he was galloping on
the best horse in town, at the head of a large equestrian company,
through an avenue that led around the green circular wall, and the
falling leaves of the linden trees danced like golden rain about his
transfigured head.

Now the devil took hold of him. With every day he became transformed, like a rainbow which becomes distinctly more colorful in the
triumphant sun. He learned in hours, in moments, what others did
not learn in years, since it had been latent in him, like the spectrum
in the raindrop. He studied the manners of his hosts thoroughly and
shaped them into something new and foreign, even as he studied
them. He was especially anxious to learn what they really thought of
him and what sort of image they had formed of him. This image he
developed further to his own taste, to the contented entertainment of
some, who wanted to see something new, and to the admiration of
others, especially the ladies, who thirsted for edifying stimulation. So
he swiftly became the hero of a pretty romance, at which he devotedly
worked together with the town, but whose main ingredient was still
mystery.

With all this, Strapinski spent one sleepless night after another, something he had never known previously in his obscurity, and it must be emphasized as a point of censure that what robbed him of his sleep was not merely his conscience, but his fear of being shamefully exposed as a poor tailor. His innate need to represent something elegant and extraordinary, if only in the choice of his clothes, had led him into this conflict and now produced that anxiety; and his conscience had only enough power over him to make him harbor the unwavering intention of finding some reason for leaving the place when a good opportunity arose. Then he planned to regain, through lotteries and the like, the means for repaying to the hospitable folk of Goldach, from a mysterious distance, the money he had cheated them of. In fact, he was already sending for tickets, at more or less modest stakes, from all the cities where there were lotteries or agents for them, and in the correspondence which ensued, the receiving of letters was again noted as a sign of important connections and relationships.

He had already won a few guilders several times and had promptly used these to purchase new tickets, when he received one day a substantial sum from a foreign lottery agent who called himself a banker; the sum was enough to permit him to carry out the plan of saving himself. He was no longer astonished at his luck, which seemed to be a matter of course; nevertheless he did feel relieved, and especially at ease concerning the good landlord of the Scale, whom he liked very much because of his good meals. But instead of putting a quick end to the matter, paying his debts outright and departing, he thought of using the pretext of a short business trip, and then announcing from some large city that inexorable fate forbade him ever to return again. At the same time he would meet his obligations, leave a good memory behind him and devote himself once more, and with more prudence and luck, to his trade as a tailor, or hunt out some other respectable vocation. Of course he would have liked best of all to remain in Goldach as a master tailor and would now have had the means for establishing a modest livelihood for himself there; but it was clear that he could live here only as a count.

Because the beautiful Nettchen treated him on every occasion with obvious preference and pleasure, many comments were already circulating, and he had even noticed that the young lady was now and then called the countess. How could he now prepare such a sequence of events for this creature? How could he so criminally give the lie to the destiny which had forcibly elevated him to such heights, and disgrace himself into the bargain?

From the lottery man, called banker, he had received a draft which he cashed at a Goldach bank; this transaction strengthened even more the favorable impressions about his person and his affairs, since the solid businessmen did not have the slightest suspicion that it might be a lottery matter. On the same day Strapinski went to a grand ball to which he had been invited. Dressed in deep, simple black he appeared and promptly announced to those who welcomed him that he was obliged to take a trip.

In ten minutes the news was known to the whole assembly and Nettchen, whose eye Strapinski was seeking, seemed stunned and avoided his glance, turning first red, then pale. She danced several times in succession with young gnetlemen, then sat down absently and breathed rapidly. When he finally did come up to her, she rejected the Pole's invitation with an abrupt bow, without looking at him.

He went away strangely worried and excited, draped himself in his famous cloak and walked up and down a garden path, his locks flowing in the wind. It now became clear to him that he had really stayed here so long only on account of this creature, that the vague hope of seeing her once more inspired him unconsciously, but that the whole affair was simply an impossibility of the most desperate kind.

As he was striding along he heard swift steps behind him, light but disturbedly agitated. Nettchen went past him and, to judge by some words she called out, seemed to be seeking her carriage, although it was standing on the other side of the house, while here only heads of winter cabbage and wrapped-up rosebushes were dreaming away the sleep of the just. Then she came back again, and since he now blocked her way with pounding heart and imploringly stretched out his hands toward her, she threw her arms about his neck without further ceremony and began to weep pitifully. He covered her flushed cheeks with his delicately fragrant dark locks and his cloak encircled the slender, proud, snow-white figure of the girl as though with black eagles' pinions; it was a truly beautiful picture, which seemed to carry its justification wholly in itself.

But in this adventure Strapinski lost his reason and won fortune, which quite often smiles on the simple-minded. That very night on their way home Nettchen revealed to her father that she would have no other man but the count; the latter appeared early next morning looking charmingly shy and melancholy as usual, to ask for her hand. The father made the following speech:

"And so destiny and the will of this foolish girl have been fulfilled. Even when she was a schoolgirl she constantly asserted that she would marry only an Italian or a Pole, a great pianist or a robber chieftain with beautiful locks, and now we're in for it. She has refused all serious local offers; only recently I had to send home that excellent Melcher Böhni, who will be a big businessman someday, and she even made terrible fun of him because he has reddish whiskers and takes snuff from a silver box. Well, Heaven be thanked, here is a Polish count from far away. Take the goose, Count, and send her back to me if she feels cold in your Polackland and if she ever becomes unhappy and howls. Ah, how happy her late mother would be if she had lived to see her spoiled child become a countess!"

Now there was great commotion; the engagement was to be celebrated in but a few days; for the councillor asserted that his future son-in-law must not allow himself to be held back in his business and planned journeys by matrimonial affairs, but must expedite the latter by advancing the former.

Strapinski brought to the engagement bridal gifts which cost him half his earthly wealth; the other half he spent on a banquet he wished to give for his fiancée. It was just carnival time and the late winter weather was wonderful beneath a bright sky. The country roads offered the most splendid sledding, the kind that occurs but rarely and never for any length of time; and so Herr von Strapinski arranged for a sleighing party and a ball in the stately hotel that was popular for such festivities; it was about two hours distant, situated exactly halfway between Goldach and Seldwyla on a high plateau that afforded the most beautiful view.

It so happened that about this time Herr Melcher Böhni had business to attend to in Seldwyla and therefore went there a few days before the winter banquet in a light sleigh, smoking his best cigar. And it happened further that the people of Seldwyla had arranged a sleighing party for the same day as the people of Goldach, and at the same place; it was to be a costume or masked sleigh ride.

The sleighing party from Goldach rode through the streets of the town at about noon amid the tinkling of bells, the sounding of pos-

tilions' horns and the cracking of whips, which made the signs of the
old houses look down in astonishment, and left by the city gate. In
the first sleigh sat Strapinski with his fiancée. He was wearing a Polish
overcoat of green velvet, trimmed with cord and heavily edged and
lined with fur. Nettchen was completely enveloped in white furs;
blue veils protected her face from the fresh air and the glare of the
snow. A sudden development had prevented the councillor from
going along; however, it was his team of horses and his sleigh in
which they were riding, with its gilded image of a woman representing Fortune decorating the front; for the councillor's town house was
named Fortune.

They were followed by fifteen or sixteen vehicles with a gay gentleman and lady in each, all dressed up, but none as handsome and
stately as the betrothed couple. Just as all vessels have their figure-
heads, so each sleigh bore the insignia of the house to which it belonged, so that the people cried: "Look, here comes Bravery! How
handsome Efficiency is! Perfectibility seems to be newly lacquered
and Thrift is freshly gilded. Ah, Jacob's Well and the Pool of
Bethesda!" In the Pool of Bethesda, which closed the procession as a
modest one-horse vehicle, Melcher Bohni drove quietly and contentedly. The figurehead in front of his carriage was a picture of that
little Jewish man who had waited for his salvation at the said pool for
thirty years. So the squadron sailed along in the sunshine and, approaching their goal, soon appeared on the plateau, which gleamed
from a great distance. At the same time gay music was heard coming
from the opposite direction.

From a fragrant forest covered with hoarfrost there erupted a confusion of gay colors and forms which developed into a train of sleighs,
delineating itself against the blue sky high up on the white edge of
the fields. It, too, was gliding towards the center of the region, a grotesque sight. The procession seemed to consist mostly of large peasant freight-sleds, joined in twos to serve as the bases for extraordinary
structures and displays. On the first vehicle a colossal figure towered,
representing the goddess Fortune, who seemed to be flying out into
the ether. She was a gigantic straw puppet full of shimmering gold
tinsel, her gauze robes fluttering in the air. On the second vehicle,
however, rode an equally gigantic billy goat, a black and gloomy
contrast, pursuing Fortune with lowered horns. This was followed by
a strange structure, which turned out to be a fifteen-foot pressing

iron; then there was a mighty snapping pair of shears, which was
opened and closed by means of a cord, and which seemed to regard
the sky as a bolt of blue silken waistcoat material. Other such current
allusions to the tailoring trade followed, and at the feet of all these
structures, on the spacious sleighs, each drawn by four horses, sat the
society of Seldwyla in the gayest clothes, indulging themselves in loud
laughter and song.

When both processions drove up at the same moment on the
square before the inn, there was a noisy scene and a great press of
men and horses. The people of Goldach were surprised and astonished at this strange meeting; the Seldwylers, on the other hand, behaved good-naturedly and with friendly modesty. Their leading
sleigh, the Fortune, bore the inscription "People Make Clothes," and
so it was natural that the whole company represented nothing but
tailors from all nations and all ages. It was, so to speak, a historical,
ethnographic tailor festival, which closed with the converse and complementary inscription: "Clothes Make People." For in the last sleigh,
with this sign, with the utmost gravity, there sat exalted emperors
and kings, councilmen and staff officers, prelates and canonesses, as
the products of the heathen and Christian knights of the needle who
had preceded them.

This world of tailors was able to extricate itself skillfully from the
confusion, and modestly allowed the ladies and gentlemen from
Goldach to walk into the house, with the bridal couple at their head.
The Seldwylers subsequently occupied the lower rooms of the inn,
which had been reserved for them, while the Goldachers noisily
trooped up the broad stairway to the large banquet hall. The count's
company found this behavior proper; their surprise turned to merriment and approving smiles at the imperturbable good mood of the
Seldwylers. The count alone experienced very obscure emotions
which he did not at all like, although in his present state of mind he
felt no definite suspicion and had not even noticed where the other
people came from. In a loud voice, so that Strapinski could hear,
Melcher Böhni, who had parked his Pool of Bethesda carefully at a
side spot and found himself the tailor's attentive neighbor, named an
entirely different place as the origin of the masked procession.

Soon the two companies were sitting at set tables, each on its own
floor, and they gave themselves over to merry conversation and jokes
in expectation of further joys.

These joys soon came for the Goldachers when they went in couples to the dance hall, where the musicians were already tuning their violins. But when they were all standing in a circle and were about to take their positions for the round dance, a delegation from the Seldwylers appeared, presenting the friendly and neighborly request that they be allowed to pay a visit to the ladies and gentlemen of Goldach and to give a dance recital for their pleasure. This offer could not well be refused; moreover, they promised themselves some real fun from the merry Seldwylers, and so, at the request of the delegation, they sat down in a large semi-circle, in the midst of which Strapinski and Nettchen glowed like princely stars.

The aforesaid groups of tailors came in gradually, one after the other. In an elegant pantomime, each one acted out the sentence "People Make Clothes" and its converse, first by pretending to make some stately articles of clothing: a prince's cloak, a priest's gown and the like; and then by dressing some needy person in it, who, suddenly transformed, stood up with the greatest dignity and solemnly marched about in time to the music. Fable, too, was staged in the same way: a tremendous crow appeared, decking itself out in peacock's feathers and hopping about and quacking, or a wolf who was tailoring a sheepskin, and finally a donkey that wore a fearful lion's skin made of cotton waste, draping himself in it heroically as if it were a Carbonari cape.

All who appeared in this way stepped back when they had finished their turn and thus transformed the semicircle of Goldachers into a wide ring of spectators, whose center finally became empty. Then the music went into a sad, serious tune and at the same time a final pantomimist walked into the circle, the focus of all eyes. He was a slender young man in a dark coat, with handsome dark hair and a Polish cap; it was none other than Count Strapinski as he had walked on the highway that November day and climbed into the fateful carriage.

In silent suspense, the whole assembly looked at the performer who, solemn and melancholy, took a few steps in time to the music, then strode to the center of the circle, spread out his cloak on the floor, sat down on it tailor fashion and began unpacking a bundle. He drew out a nearly finished count's coat exactly like the one Strapinski was then wearing, sewed tassels and cords on it with great speed and skill and ironed it professionally, testing the seemingly hot iron with a moist finger. Then he slowly stood up, took off his threadbare coat and put on the elegant garment, drew out a little mirror, combed his hair and finished dressing, so that he finally stood there the spit and image of the count. Unexpectedly the music changed into a swift, spirited air; the man wrapped up his belongings in his old coat and threw the bundle far over the heads of the assembled company into the depths of the hall, as though he wanted to separate himself from his past for good. After this he skirted the circle in stately dance steps as a proud man of the world, bowing graciously here and there to the company, until he came to the betrothed couple. Suddenly he fixed his eyes steadily on the Pole, who was immensely astonished, and stood before him immovable as a pillar, while simultaneously and as though by prearrangement, the music stopped and a fearful silence ensued like a mute flash of lightning.

"Oh! Oh! Oh! Oh!" he cried in a voice that was audible at a great distance, and stretched his arms toward the unhappy man. "Behold our brother Silesian, our water Polack, who ran away from his job because he believed, on the basis of a slight business fluctuation, that it was all up with me. Well, I'm happy that things are so merry for you and that you are celebrating such a happy carnival here. Do you have employment in Goldach?"

At the same time he held out his hand to the young count, who was sitting there pale and smiling; the latter took it unwillingly, like a glowing iron bar, while his double cried: "Come, friends, behold here our gentle journeyman tailor, who looks like Raphael and was so much admired by our maids, including our pastor's daughter, who is, to be sure, slightly mad."

Now all the people from Seldwyla came past and crowded around Strapinski and his former employer, shaking the tailor's hand innocently, so that he swayed and trembled on his chair. At the same time the music started up again with a lively march; the Seldwylers, as they passed the betrothed couple, lined up for departure and marched out of the hall singing a well-rehearsed diabolical laugh chorus, while the Goldachers, among whom Melcher Böhni had been able to spread the explanation of the miracle with lightning speed, ran about in confusion, crossing the ranks of the Seldwylers, so that a great tumult resulted.

When the commotion finally subsided, the hall was almost empty; a few people stood against the walls whispering to each other in embarrassment; a few young ladies stood at some distance from Nettchen, uncertain whether to approach her or not.

The couple, however, sat motionless on their chairs like a stone Egyptian royal pair, silent and lonely; one could almost feel the endless, glowing desert sand.

Nettchen, as white as a marble statue, slowly turned her face to her fiancé and gave him a strange sidelong glance.

Thereupon he got up slowly and, weeping great tears, went away with heavy steps, his eyes fixed on the ground.

He went through the ranks of the people from Goldach and Seldwyla, who lined the staircase, passing them like a dead man who steals away spectrally from an annual fair, and strangely enough, they allowed him to pass like such a ghost, avoiding him silently, without laughing or calling harsh words after him. He also walked past the sleighs and horses from Goldach, which were getting ready to depart, while the people of Seldwyla were having a really merry time of it in their quarters; and he walked down the same highway towards Seldwyla by which he had come a few months before, half unconscious, with the sole intention of never coming back to Goldach. Soon he disappeared in the darkness of the forest through which the road ran. He was bareheaded, for his Polish cap, together with his gloves, had been left on the window sill of the dance hall; and so he strode forward with bowed head, hiding his freezing hands under crossed arms, while his thoughts gradually collected themselves and attained some degree of reason. The first distinct feeling he became aware of was that of a monstrous sense of shame, as though he had been a real man of rank and prominence and had now become infamous through the irruption of some fateful misfortune. But then this feeling dissolved into a sort of consciousness of having suffered an injustice; until his glorious entrance into the cursed town he had never been guilty of a misdemeanor; as far back into childhood as his thoughts could reach, he could not remember ever having been punished or scolded because of a lie or deception; and now he had become a deceiver because the world's folly had overwhelmed him in an unguarded and, so to speak, defenseless moment and had made him its playmate. He saw himself as a child who has been persuaded by another wicked child to steal the chalice from an altar; he now hated and despised himself, but he also wept for himself and his unhappy aberration.

When a prince conquers a country and its people; when a priest professes the teaching of his church without conviction and proudly consumes the goods of his benefice; when a conceited teacher holds and enjoys the honors and advantages of a lofty profession without having the least conception of the dignity of his discipline or advancing it in the slightest; when an artist without virtue makes himself fashionable through superficial activity and empty jugglery and steals bread and fame from the true worker; or when a swindler, who has inherited or obtained by fraud the name of a great merchant, robs thousands of their savings or their emergency funds through his folly and unscrupulousness — all these do not weep at themselves but rejoice in their well-being, and they do not remain for one evening without cheering company and good friends.

Our tailor, however, wept bitterly over himself; that is to say, he suddenly began to do so when his thoughts unexpectedly returned to his abandoned fiancée by the heavy chain of associations from which they were suspended; and he writhed on the ground in shame before the invisible girl. Misfortune and humiliation showed him with one clear ray of light the happiness he had lost, and out of the confused, enamored venial sinner they made a rejected lover. He stretched out his arms towards the coldly glittering stars and staggered rather than walked along the road; then he stood still and shook his head, when suddenly a red gleam lit the snow about him and at the same time the sound of sleigh bells and laughter resounded. It was the Seldwylers riding home by torchlight. The first horses were already approaching him; he pulled himself together, took a mighty leap over the ditch and ducked into the foremost trees of the forest. The mad procession rode by and finally died away in the dark distance without the fugitive's having been noticed; but he, after listening for a good while, motionless and overcome by the cold as well as by the fiery beverages he had enjoyed earlier and by his grievous stupidity, stretched out his limbs unthinkingly and fell asleep on the crackling snow, while an ice-cold breath of air began to blow in from the east.

Meanwhile Nettchen, too, had stood up from her lonely seat. She had looked attentively after her departing lover, had sat motionless for more than an hour and now got up, shedding bitter tears, and walked helplessly to the door. Two friends joined her with dubious words of consolation; she asked them to fetch her coat, shawl, hat and such things, which she put on silently, drying her eyes vigorously with her veil. But, when you cry, you always have to blow your nose; so she found herself obliged to take out her handkerchief after all and to give her nose a vigorous blowing, after which she looked about

proudly and angrily. Into her view came Melcher Böhni, who approached her kindly, humbly and smilingly and pointed out to her
the necessity of having a guide and companion on her way back to
her father's house. The Pool of Bethesda, he said, he would leave behind here at the inn while he guided Fortune securely back to Goldach, together with the venerated unhappy lady.

Without replying, she walked ahead with a firm step toward the
courtyard, where the sleigh with its impatient, well-fed horses stood
ready, one of the last vehicles still there. She swiftly took her place in
it, seized the reins and whip, and while the unsuspecting Böhni,
bustling about with happy officiousness, was getting a tip for the
stable boy who had held the horses, she unexpectedly whipped up the
animals, which dashed out on the highway with vigorous leaps that
soon settled into a steady lively gallop. And to tell the truth she was
not riding home but along the road to Seldwyla. Only when the light-
winged vehicle had already vanished from his sight did Herr Böhni
discover the fact, and he ran in the direction of Goldach with cries of
"Whoa! Whoa!" and "Stop!" then rushed back, jumped into his sleigh
and raced after the beauty who had fled, or, as he thought, had been
carried off by the horses, until he reached the gate of the excited
town, in which the vexatious event already had all tongues busy.

Why Nettchen had taken that road, whether out of confusion or
intentionally, cannot be reported with certainty. Two circumstances
may cast a little light on the matter. For one thing, Strapinski's fur
cap and gloves, which had been lying on the window sill behind the
couple's seat, were now, strangely enough, in the sleigh Fortune beside Nettchen; no one had noticed when and how she had taken these
objects and she herself did not know; she had done it as though in a
somnambulistic state. Even now she was not aware that the cap and
gloves were lying beside her. More than once she said aloud to herself: "I must speak a few words with him, just a few words."

These two facts seem to prove that the fiery horses were not entirely guided by chance. It was also strange that when Fortune got
into the road in the woods, where the full moon was now shining,
Nettchen pulled the reins tighter, so that the horses slowed up and
almost pranced along at a walk, while the driver fixed her sad but
sharp eyes on the road, and did not miss the slightest striking object
to the left or right of her.

And yet it was as though she were in a deep, heavy, unhappy

oblivion. What are fortune and life? What do they depend on? What are we ourselves, that we become happy or unhappy because of a ridiculous carnival lie? What guilt have we incurred, to harvest shame and despair because of a happy, credulous affection? Who sends us such silly, deceptive figures, which erupt destructively into our destiny, while they themselves dissolve in it like weak soap bubbles?

Such questions, dreamed rather than thought, were occupying Nettchen's mind when her eyes were suddenly drawn to a longish dark object that stood out from the moonlit snow at the side of the highway. It was Wenzel stretched out full length; his dark hair mingled with the shadows of the trees, while his slender body lay clearly in the light.

Nettchen involuntarily pulled up the horses, whereupon a deep silence came over the forest. She stared fixedly at the dark body, until it became almost unmistakably clear to her eye. She gently tied the reins fast, got out, stroked the horses for a moment to calm them and then approached the figure cautiously and noiselessly.

Yes, it was he. The dark green velvet of his coat looked beautiful and aristocratic even on the night snow; the slim body and the supple limbs, taughtly laced and clothed; everything about him, even in his numbness, at the brink of ruin, in his helplessness, still cried out: Clothes make the man!

When the lonely beauty bent over him and recognized him beyond doubt, she immediately saw the danger that threatened his life and feared that he might already be frozen. And so she instinctively seized one of his hands, which appeared to be cold and without feeling. Forgetting everything else, she shook the poor man and shouted his Christian name in his ear: "Wenzel! Wenzel!" In vain: he did not move, but only breathed weakly and sadly. Thereupon she threw herself on him, moved her hand over his face and, in her anxiety, flicked her finger against the pale tip of his nose. Then a bright idea struck her; she took handfuls of snow and vigorously rubbed his nose and face and fingers with all her strength until the lucky unhappy man recovered, awoke and slowly sat up.

He looked about him and saw his rescuer standing before him. She had thrown her veil back; Wenzel recognized every feature in her white face, which was looking at him with wide eyes.

He fell down before her, kissed the hem of her cloak and cried: "Forgive me! Forgive me!"

"Come, stranger!" she said, suppressing the trembling in her voice. "I'll talk to you and send you away!"

She motioned to him to get into the sleigh, which he did obediently; she gave his his cap and gloves just as instinctively as she had taken them with her, took the reins and whip and drove on.

Beyond the forest, not far from the road, was a farmhouse, in which there lived a farmer's wife whose husband had died not long before. Nettchen was the godmother of one of her children, and the councillor, Nettchen's father, was her landlord. Only recently the woman had visited them to wish the daughter luck and to get all sorts of advice; but she could not as yet know anything about the course which events had taken.

To this farm Nettchen now drove, turning off the highway and halting in front of the house with a vigorous cracking of her whip. There was still light behind the little windows; the farmer's wife was awake and was still bustling about the house, although the children and servants had long been asleep. She opened a window and peered out in astonishment. "It's only me, it's us," cried Nettchen. "We have lost our way because of the new upper road, which I have never traveled before. Make some coffee for us, mother, and let us come in for a moment before we go on."

Very pleased, the peasant woman hurried out, recognizing Nettchen at once; she was apparently both delighted and overawed to see the "big shot," the foreign count, too. In her eyes the happiness and the splendor of this world had crossed her threshold in these two persons; vague hopes of winning a small part of this splendor, some modest gain for herself or her children, animated the good woman and gave her every agility in serving the young masters. She quickly woke a young servant to hold the horses, and soon she had also prepared some hot coffee, which she now brought in to Wenzel and Nettchen, who sat facing each other in the half-dark room, a weakly flickering little lamp between them on the table.

Wenzel sat with his head in his hands, not daring to look up. Nettchen leaned back in her chair and kept her eyes closed tight, and her bitter, beautiful mouth too, from which it could be seen that she was by no means asleep.

When the woman had set the coffee on the table, Nettchen stood up quickly and whispered to her: "Now leave us alone for a little while; go and lie on your bed, dear woman; we've had a bit of a quarrel and have to talk matters over, and there's a good opportunity to do it here."

"I understand; you're doing the right thing," said the woman, and soon left the two of them alone.

"Drink this," said Nettchen as she sat down again, "it will do you good." She herself touched nothing. Wenzel Strapinski, who was trembling slightly, straightened up, took a cup and drank it, more because she had told him to do so than to refresh himself. He looked at her now, and as their eyes met and Nettchen's gazed searchingly into his, she shook her head and then said: "Who are you? What do you want with me?"

"I am not entirely what I appear to be," he replied sadly. "I am a poor fool; but I'll make everything good and give you satisfaction and not stay alive much longer." Such words he uttered with conviction and without any affectation, so that Nettchen's eyes flashed imperceptibly. However, she repeated: "I wish to know who you really are and where you come from and where you're going."

"Everything has happened as I'm now going to tell you in accordance with the truth," he replied, and he told her who he was and how things had happened on his entrance to Goldach. He emphasized especially how he had wanted to escape several times but had finally been prevented from doing so by her appearance, as though in a bewitched dream.

Nettchen was overcome by an impulse to laugh; however, the situation was too serious to permit such an outburst. Instead, she asked: "And where did you intend to go with me and what did you plan to do?" "I hardly know," he replied; "I looked forward to further remarkable or lucky events; also I sometimes thought of death in such a way that I would bring it on myself, after —"

Here Wenzel stopped and his pale face turned quite red.

"Well, continue!" said Nettchen, also turning pale, while her heart beat strangely.

Then Wenzel's eyes flamed up big and sweet and he cried:

"Yes, now it is clear to me how it would have happened. I would have gone with you into the great world, and after living a few brief days in happiness with you, I would have confessed the deception to

you and committed suicide. You would have returned to your father,
where you would have been well cared for and would have forgotten
me easily. No one need have known about it; I would have disappeared without leaving a trace. —Instead of pining away all my
life, yearning for a dignified existence, for a kind heart, for love," he
continued sadly, "I would have been great and happy for one
moment and high above all those who are neither happy nor unhappy and yet never want to die. Oh, if only you had let me lie there
in the cold snow, I would have fallen asleep so gladly!"

He had grown silent again and looked ahead of him gloomily.

After a while, when the beating of her heart, stirred by Wenzel's
words, had somewhat subsided, Nettchen, who had been studying his
face silently, said:

"Have you played the same or similar tricks before, and deceived
strangers who have done you no harm?"

"I have asked myself this question this bitter night and can't remember that I've ever been a liar. I have never yet begun or experienced such an adventure. Yes, in those days when the impulse awoke
in me to be or appear to be something decent, when I was still half a
child, I controlled myself and renounced a happiness which seemed
destined for me."

"Tell me about it," said Nettchen.

"Before she married, my mother had been in service with a neighboring squire's wife and had accompanied her on journeys and to
large cities. From this she had acquired a more refined manner than
the other women in our village, and I suppose she was somewhat vain
too; for she dressed herself and me, her only child, more attractively,
and more carefully than was the custom there. But my father, a poor
schoolmaster, died early, and so, living in direst poverty, we had no
prospect of enjoying the happy experiences my mother liked to
dream about. Rather, she had to devote herself to hard work to keep
us alive and make sacrifices so that the most precious thing she had
might have better clothes and a somewhat better standard of living.
Unexpectedly, when I was about sixteen years old, the squire's wife,
who had recently become a widow, said that she was moving to the
city permanently; she asked mother to send me along too; it would be
a pity for me to become a day laborer or farmhand in the village; she
would have me learn a refined trade that I fancied, and in the meantime I could live in her house and do various light chores. This

seemed to be the most glorious thing that could happen to us. Accordingly, everything was discussed and ready, when mother became pensive and sad and suddenly begged me one day, with many tears, not to leave her but to remain poor with her; she would not live long, she said, and I would certainly still find something good after she was dead. The squire's wife, to whom I reported this gloomily, came over and protested to my mother. But mother now became quite excited and cried over and over that she would not allow herself to be robbed of her child; anyone who knew him—"

Here Wenzel Strapinski stopped again and did not know how to go on. Nettchen asked: "What did your mother say—'anyone who knew him—?' Why don't you continue?"

Wenzel turned red and replied: "She said something strange, which I didn't really understand and which I have never heard since; she said that anyone who knew the child could never part from him again. I suppose she meant that I was a good-natured lad or something of the sort. In short, she was so excited that, in spite of all urging, I refused the lady's offer and stayed with mother, for which she loved me doubly, begging my pardon a thousand times for standing in the way of my happiness. But when I had to learn to earn my living, it turned out that there was not much else to do but become an apprentice to our village tailor. I didn't want to, but mother cried so much that I yielded. That is the story."

When Nettchen asked why and when he had finally left his mother, Wenzel replied: "Military service called me away. I was put among the hussars and was quite a handsome red hussar, although perhaps the most stupid in the regiment, and certainly the quietest. After a year I was finally able to get a few weeks' furlough and hurried home to see my good mother; but she had just died. So when my time came, I went out alone into the world and finally met my misfortune here."

Nettchen smiled and observed him attentively as he mournfully talked. Then the room was quiet for a while; suddenly a thought seemed to occur to her.

"Since you were always so esteemed and so charming," she said suddenly, yet in a hesitating, pointed manner, "you have no doubt had the usual love affairs or the like at various times, and probably have more than one woman on your conscience—to say nothing about me?"

"Oh Lord," Wenzel replied, turning very red, "before I came to you I never so much as touched the fingertips of a girl, except—"

"Well?" said Nettchen.

"Well," he continued, "it was the same woman who wanted to take me with her and have me educated; she had a child, a girl of seven or eight, a strange, passionate child, and yet as sweet as sugar and fair as an angel. On many occasions I had to play servant and protector to her and she had become accustomed to me. I had to bring her regularly the long distance to and from the parsonage, where she was given instruction by the old clergyman. At other times, too, when no one else was available, I had to take care of her. When I was leading her home for the last time over the field in the evening sun, the child began to talk of her approaching departure, declared that I must really come with them and asked me whether I would, I told her it couldn't be. But the child continued to plead with deep emotion and persistence, clinging to my arm and hindering me in my walking, as children will do, so that I unthinkingly freed myself from her, probably somewhat harshly. At that the girl's head dropped, ashamed and sad, she tried to suppress the tears that now welled up in her eyes, and she could scarcely control her sobbing. In dismay I wanted to appease her, but she turned angrily from me and left in displeasure. Since then the beautiful child has always remained in my mind, and my heart has always clung to her, although I have never heard from her again."

Suddenly the speaker, who had fallen into gentle agitation, stopped as though frightened and, turning pale, stared at his companion.

"Well," said Nettchen in a strange tone, also growing somewhat pale, "why do you look at me like that?"

But Wenzel stretched out his arm, pointed at her as though he were seeing a ghost and cried: "I've noticed this before. When that child was angry, her beautiful hair stood up slightly about her brow and temples, as yours does now, so that you could see it move. That's the way it was that last time in the field in the evening glow."

Indeed, those of Nettchen's locks that were closest to her temples and over her forehead had stirred gently, as though a breath of air had blown into her face.

Mother Nature, always somewhat coquettish, had made use of one of her secrets here to bring the difficult affair to an end.

After a brief silence, during which her bosom began to heave, Nettchen got up, walked around the table toward the man and threw her arms about his neck with the words: "I will not leave you! You are mine and I will go with you despite the whole world!"

So she celebrated her engagement only now, with a profoundly resolute mind, by keeping faith and taking a destiny upon herself in sweet passion.

However, she was by no means so full that she did not want to guide this destiny a little herself; on the contrary, she made new resolutions swiftly and boldly. For she said to the good Wenzel, who was dreaming, lost in this new change of fortune: "Now we'll go straight to Seldwyla and show the people there, who planned to destroy us, that they have united us more than ever and have made us happy!"

The good Wenzel could not see it that way. He wished rather to move to unfamiliar distant parts and to live there in a mysterious romantic manner, in quiet bliss, as he said.

But Nettchen cried: "No more romances! As you are, a poor wanderer, I will accept you and become your wife in my native city in defiance of all these proud and scoffing people. We'll move to Seldwyla and there, through our energy and intelligence, make the people who have mocked us dependent on us."

And they did as they had said they would. After the farmer's wife had been summoned and rewarded by Wenzel, who began to assume his new role, they continued on their way. Wenzel was now holding the reins. Nettchen leaned against him contentedly as if he were a church pillar. For heaven is the fulfillment of our wishes and Nettchen had come of age exactly three days before and could follow hers.

In Seldwyla they stopped before the Rainbow Inn, where a number of the sleigh riders were still sitting over their drinks. When the couple appeared in the drawing room, the word spread like fire: "Ha, ha, we have an abduction here; we have initiated a beautiful story!"

Wenzel, however, walked through the room with his bride without looking about him, and after she had disappeared in her rooms, he went to the Wild Man, another good inn, and there walked proudly through the ranks of the Seldwylers, who were still carrying on, into a room which he ordered, leaving them to their astonished deliberations. They felt obliged to drink themselves into the most furious hangovers about this affair.

In the town of Goldach, too, the cry "Abduction!" was making the rounds.

Very early the next morning, the Pool of Bethesda was riding towards Seldwyla, with the excited Melcher Böhni and Nettchen's perplexed father in it. In their haste they almost drove through Seldwyla without stopping; but just in time they saw the sleigh Fortune standing intact in front of the inn, and surmised to their consolation that the handsome horses would at least not be far away. And so, when their surmise had been confirmed and they had learned of Nettchen's arrival and her presence there, they had their sleigh unhitched and went into the Rainbow.

But it took a little while before Nettchen sent word to her father to come to her room for a private talk. It was said that she had already summoned the best lawyer in town, who would appear in the course of the morning. The councillor went up to his daughter somewhat heavy of heart, deliberating in what way he could best lead the desperate child back out of her confusion, and he was prepared for desperate behavior.

But Nettchen came towards him with calm and gentle firmness. She thanked her father with emotion for all the love and kindness he had shown her, and then declared in determined sentences: first, after what had happened, she did not want to live in Goldach any longer, at least not in the next few years; second, she wished to take possession of her substantial maternal inheritance, which her father had long held in readiness in the event of her marriage; third, she wanted to marry Wenzel Strapinski, and on this she was absolutely inflexible; fourth, she intended to live with him in Seldwyla and help him establish a thriving business there; and fifth and last, everything would turn out well, for she had become convinced that he was a good man and would make her happy.

The councillor began his task by reminding her that she knew, of course, how very much he wished to place her fortune in her own hands as the foundation of her true happiness, and the sooner the better. But then, with all the concern that had filled him since the first news of the catastrophe, he explained how impossible the relationship she wanted to perpetuate was. And finally, he showed how the serious conflict could be resolved with dignity. It was Herr Melcher Böhni who was prepared to put an end to the whole matter by stepping in promptly to fill the breach with his person and to protect and maintain her honor before the world with his irreproachable name.

The word honor finally succeeded in throwing his daughter into a state of greater excitement. It was honor, in fact, she cried, which commanded her not to marry Herr Böhni, because she couldn't stand him, and to remain faithful to the poor stranger to whom she had given her word and whom, moreover, she loved.

There now ensued some fruitless talking back and forth, which finally brought the steadfast beauty to tears.

Wenzel and Böhni burst into the room almost at the same time, having met on the staircase, and a great commotion threatened to ensue, when the lawyer, a man well known to the councillor, came in and urged peaceful cool-headedness for the present. When he heard in a few preliminary words what the issue was, he gave orders that Wenzel should withdraw to the Wild Man and remain there quietly; that Herr Böhni, too, should not interfere but go away; that Nettchen, for her part, should observe the amenities of good tone until the matter was settled; and that the father should renounce any exercise of coercion, since his daughter's freedom was legally incontestable.

So there was an armistice and a general separation for some hours.

In town, where the attorney scattered a few words about the large fortune that might come to Seldwyla through this affair, there now arose a great commotion. The sentiment of the Seldwylers suddenly veered in favor of the tailor and his fiancée, and they decided to protect the lovers with all their power and to guarantee them the right and freedom of person in their town. And so, when the rumor spread that the beauty of Goldach was to be taken back by force, they banded together, placed armed protective and honor guards before the Rainbow and the Wild Man, and in general carried out another of their great adventures with tremendous merriment, a remarkable continuation of yesterday's event.

The frightened and irritated councillor sent his Böhni to Goldach for help. The latter rode off at a gallop, and the next day a number of men drove over from there along with a substantial police detachment to help the councillor, and it began to look as if Seldwyla was to become a new Troy. The parties faced each other threateningly; the town drummer was already tightening his tuning screw, practicing individual taps with his right drumstick. Then some higher officials appeared on the square, both ecclesiastical and worldly gentlemen, and negotiations were carried on on all sides. Since Nettchen remained firm and Wenzel did not allow herself to be intimidated, encouraged as they were by the Seldwylers, it was decided that their marriage banns would be published formally after all the necessary documents had been collected, and that they would wait to see what legal objections might be raised during this procedure and with what success.

In view of the fact that Nettchen was of age, such objections could be raised only in regard to the dubious character of the spurious Count Wenzel Strapinski.

But the attorney who was handling his and Nettchen's case learned that, until now, not even the shadow of evil reputation had touched the strange young man, either in his native village or during his travels; from everywhere there came only good and well-wishing testimonials about him.

As far as the events in Goldach were concerned, the attorney proved that Wenzel had never really represented himself as a count, but that this rank had been forcibly bestowed on him by others; that he had signed all existing documents with his real name, Wenzel Strapinski, without any addition; accordingly there existed no other misdemeanor, except that he had enjoyed a foolish hospitality, which would not have been offered him if he had not arrived in that carriage and if the coachman had not played a bad joke.

And so the war ended with a wedding, at which the Seldwylers fired off their powerful so-called mortars to the annoyance of the Goldachers, who could hear the thunder of the cannon quite well, since a west wind was blowing. The councillor handed over Nettchen's whole fortune to her and she said that Wenzel must now become a big *marchand-tailleur* and cloth master in Seldwyla; for there the draper was still called a cloth master, the iron merchant an iron master, etc.

And this really happened, but quite differently from the way the Seldwylers had dreamed. He was modest, thrifty and diligent in his business, which he was able to build up substantially. He made their velvet vests for them, violet-colored or with white and blue checks, formal dress coats with gold buttons and cloaks faced with red; and they all owed him money, but never too long. For to get new, still more attractive clothes, which he imported or made for them, they had to pay their bills, so that they complained among themselves that he was squeezing the blood out of them.

With all this he became round and stately and almost stopped looking dreamy. He became more experienced and skilled in business from year to year and, in conjunction with his father-in-law, the councillor, who had soon become reconciled to him, he was able to invest his money so well that his fortune doubled, and after ten or twelve years, with as many children which Nettchen had meanwhile borne him, he moved with her to Goldach and there became a prominent man.

But in Seldwyla he did not leave a stiver, either from ingratitude or revenge.

Conrad Ferdinand Meyer

1825 — 1898

Conrad Ferdinand Meyer was descended from a leading patrician family of Zurich, Switzerland. His father was a distinguished jurist and government official and his mother, a highly cultured and refined woman, but high-strung and fanatically religious. The early death of his father and his mother's aggressive, domineering nature aggravated the boy's melancholy temperament so that his mental faculties were temporarily paralyzed. For years he lived in a private world of unreality and finally had to enter a mental hospital. The suicide of his mother in 1856 released him from his anxieties. He traveled extensively and gradually emerged from the state of inadequacy and indecision that had hindered him for years.

Part of Meyer's dilemma stemmed from his inability to choose between the French and German cultural heritages and, in particular, since he was bilingual, between the French and German languages. The Franco-German war and the personality of Bismarck, whom he greatly admired, decided him in favor of the German. From then on — he was forty-five years old — the well of his inspiration began to flow. In the next twenty years he wrote all his original work: distinguished lyric narrative and poetry, and the series of historical novellas on which his reputation rests.

Meyer's artistic world is a stylized one, quite out of tune with the prevailing realism of the time. He wrote about strong, ruthless, amoral men of the past, whose will to power and conflicts of conscience, whose passions, ambitions and loneliness he depicted with subtle skill in a refined, jeweled diction. His novellas are elaborately set in frameworks which are themselves masterly works of fiction.

The Sufferings of a Boy, written in 1883, anticipates modern analytical psychology with its profound understanding of the retarded

boy who is crushed by his environment and an overdemanding
father. While the story is based on an entry in the memoirs of the
Duc de Saint-Simon, who wrote at the court of Louis XIV, the character of Julien owes much to Meyer's recollections of his own mental
state during adolescence. Rarely have so much experience and
artistry been compressed into a novella: a rich and exciting plot, a
varied gallery of characters, a telling portrait of the age of the Sun
King and subtle symbols and leitmotifs that recur throughout the
work—the priest's wolf face, the abbé's enormous nose, the crucial
myth of the frustrated Pentheus.

The elaborate framework in which the story is set, interrupting at
fixed points the flow of the physician's narrative, is characteristic of
Meyer's art.

The Sufferings of a Boy

The King had entered Madame de Maintenon's chamber; feeling in need of air and being insensitive to the weather, he had in his sovereign manner unceremoniously opened a window, and through it the damp autumn air streamed in so penetratingly that the delicate, shivering woman nestled into her three or four afghans.

For some time now Louis XIV had begun to extend the span of his daily visits to the wife of his old age; he often appeared when the evening was still young and stayed until his late dinner was served. At such times, when he was not working in conference with his ministers, he sat beside his taciturn friend, who buried herself in her armchair, attentive and silent. When the weather forbade hunting or walking, when the concerts, consisting mostly of sacred music, had been repeated too often, it was a problem how the monarch could be entertained or amused for four full hours. The impudent muse of Molière, the delicacies and swoons of Mlle de Lavallière, the bold conduct and original witticisms of Mlle de Montespan and many other such diversions had had their day and were now definitely past, withered like a faded tapestry. Temperate and almost contented as he had become, diligent as he had always been, the King had won a wife who also loved restraint and semi-darkness.

Obliging, ingratiating, indispensable and full of charm in spite of her years, the granddaughter of Agrippa d'Aubigné had a pedantic, governess-like disposition, a tendency to give advice in matters of conscience with an authority she was able to exercise fully in Saint Cyr among the young noblewomen whom she educated there; but before her sovereign, this authority changed into a modest accommodation to his higher wisdom. So when Louis was silent, she was too, especially when, as was the case today, the King's young granddaughter, who was wife to the King of Savoy, for some reason failed to appear — she who was the most delightful creature in the world and who brought life and laughter everywhere, with her childlike behavior and her complimentary patter.

Mme de Maintenon, who, in these circumstances, had heard the King's approaching steps not without slight anxiety, felt relieved when she read in the preoccupied and slightly amused expression of the royal countenance, with which she was thoroughly familiar, that Louis himself had something to tell, and indeed something delightful.

The King had closed the window and settled himself in an easy chair. "Madame," he said, "at noon today Father Lachaise brought me his successor, Father Tellier."

Father de Lachaise had been the King's confessor for many years; in spite of the aged Jesuit's deafness and complete debility, the King had been unwilling to part with him and had used him till he was, so to speak, threadbare; for Louis had become accustomed to him, and — incredible though it may sound — he believed, from vague and yet real fears, that he could not choose his confessor from any other order. And he preferred this wreck of a man, who was at any rate honorable, to a younger and more ambitious member of the Society of Jesus. But everything had its limits. Father Lachaise was visibly tottering toward his grave, and Louis did not want to commit parricide against his spiritual father.

"Madame," the King continued, "my new confessor has neither beauty nor form: a sort of wolf's face, and he is cross-eyed too. His appearance is positively repulsive but he is recommended to me as a man who is strict toward himself and others; a man to whom one may entrust one's conscience. That, I suppose, is the main thing."

"The meaner the trough, the more precious the heavenly water that flows through it," the marquise remarked sententiously. She did not like the Jesuits, who had opposed the marriage between Scarron's widow and His Majesty and, by virtue of their elastic sense of morals, had declared that, in this royal instance, the sacrament of marriage was superfluous. So she occasionally took pleasure in hurting the pious fathers, if she could quietly dig her claws into them. Now she was silent, and her dark, soft, melancholy, almond-shaped eyes were fixed with modest attention on the lips of her spouse.

The King crossed his feet and, gazing at the gleam that came from the diamond buckle of one of his shoes, remarked casually, "That man Fagon! He's becoming unbearable. The things he permits himself!"

Fagon was the very old personal physician of the King and the protégé of the marquise. They were both in the company of the King daily and, in case he should die before them, they had selected places of asylum—she, Saint Cyr; he, the botanical gardens—where they would lock and bury themselves.

"Fagon is infinitely devoted to you," said the marquise.

"Of course, but he is definitely taking too many liberties," the King replied with a slight, half-comical wrinkling of his brow.

"Why, what happened?"

The King told her, and was soon finished with his story. At his audience that day he had asked his new confessor whether the Telliers were related to the Le Telliers, the family of the chancellor. But the humble father had quickly denied this and frankly revealed himself as the son of a peasant in lower Normandy. Fagon had been standing not far from there in a bay window, his chin resting on his bamboo cane. From there, behind the bent back of the Jesuit, he had whispered in an undertone but audibly enough, "You good-for-nothing!" "I raised my finger to Fagon," the King said, "and warned him."

The marquise was astonished. "Fagon could not have insulted the father because of this honest denial, he must have had another reason," she said shrewdly.

"In any case, madame, it was a piece of impropriety, if not worse. Good Father Lachaise, in his present state of deafness, did not hear it, of course, but my ear heard it distinctly, syllable after syllable. 'Vile fellow!' Fagon whispered to the father, and the abused man winced."

From this variant the marquise concluded with a smile that Fagon had used a coarser expression. There was also a quivering at the corners of the King's mouth. He had made it a rule from his youth, following a natural inclination, never to utter a vulgar or abusive word, in short, an unkingly word, not even in reporting what someone else had said; and to this rule he adhered to the end of his life.

The high room had grown dim, and as the servant placed the two modest candelabra on the table and left the room walking backward, an auditor who had entered silently became visible, a queer figure, a venerable cripple; a crooked, misshapen, strangely twisted little old man, supporting his fleshless hands under his extended chin on a long bamboo cane with a golden knob, his delicate head bent forward, a white face with ghostly blue eyes. It was Fagon.

"Sire, I said plainly, 'You scoundrel, you rascal!' and I was only speaking the truth." A weak voice could now be heard, trembling with excitement; Fagon bowed respectfully before the King and gallantly to the marquise. "If I treated a clergyman this way in your presence, sire, then I have either remained a hot-headed youth in the face of vileness, or the dignity of old age justifies me in speaking the truth. Was I merely incensed at the spectacle presented by the father when the coarse-grained and hard-boned yokel with his wolf's snout, turned and twisted before you, sire, and in answer to your gracious question about his kinship, could not find enough words to emphasize his insignificance in conceited self-abasement? 'What does Your Majesty think?'" Fagon imitated the father. "'Related to such a distinguished gentleman? Not at all. I am the son of a common man, a peasant from lower Normandy, a very common man...' This contemptible talk about his own father, this crawling, hypocritical, absolutely untrue humility, this fundamental falseness fully deserved to be called rascally. But Madame la Marquise is right: there was something else, something utterly horrible and devilish which I avenged, though only in words, alas; an evil deed, a crime which the unexpected sight of this malicious wolf once more brought so vividly before my eyes that the scant dregs of my blood began to boil. For, sire, this villain murdered a noble boy."

"I beg of you, Fagon," the King said, "what a fairy tale!"

"Let us say: he brought him to his gave," the personal physician softened his accusation with a sneer.

"What boy?" Louis, who liked straight talk, asked in his matter-of-fact way.

"It was young Boufflers, the son of the marshal by his first marriage," Fagon replied sadly.

"Julien Boufflers? He died at the age of seventeen in the Jesuit college, if I'm not mistaken," the King recalled (and his memory seldom betrayed him), "from meningitis the poor child may have contracted through overwork; and since Father Tellier may have been prefect of studies there in those years, he certainly, in a very figurative sense," the King mocked, "brought the boy, who was ungifted though stubborn in his will to learn, to his grave. The boy simply exceeded his powers, as his father the marshal told me himself." Louis shrugged his shoulders. That was that. He had expected something more interesting.

"The ungifted boy. . ." the physician repeated thoughtfully.

"Yes, Fagon," the King replied, "amazingly ungifted, and moreover shyer and more timid than a girl. It was on a Marly day that the marshal, to whom I had granted the reversion to his *gouvernement* for this his oldest child, presented him to me. I saw that the trim, handsome boy, on whose lips the first down was already sprouting, was moved and wanted to thank me cordially, but he began to stutter and blush so painfully that I turned away from him with a 'very good,' more curt than I wanted it to be for the sake of his father, merely to calm him, or at least leave him in peace."

"I, too, remember that evening," the marquise interjected. "The boy's late mother was my friend, and after his fiasco I drew the boy to me, and he appeared, at least outwardly, to be calm and sad but grateful and charming, without feeling too deeply the humiliation he had suffered. He even gathered enough courage to speak about ordinary, every-day matters in a tone of voice that won my heart, and my attachment to him made people envy him. It was a bad day for the child, that Marly day. A nickname—of course everyone at court who is not named Louis must have one" (the sensitive marquise knew that her very antipode, the good but terrifying Palatinate woman, the Dowager-Duchess of Orleans, had given her the most horrible nickname of all) "—one of those dangerous nicknames which can poison a life and which I have most strictly forbidden my girls at Saint Cyr to use, was found for the modest boy; as it circulated from mouth to mouth, it was whispered even by innocent and blooming lips which would certainly not have denied themselves to the attractive boy a few years later."

"Which nickname?" asked Fagon curiously.

"*Le bel idiot*. . .and the twitching of a pair of arrogant eyebrows revealed to me who had bestowed it on the boy."

"Lauzun?" the King guessed.

"Saint-Simon," the marquise corrected him. "Isn't he the listening ear at our court and the watchful eye which observes us all"—the King's face darkened—"and the practiced hand which, at night, behind bolted doors, commits to paper passionate caricatures of us all? This noble duke, sire, did not scorn to brand the most innocent boy with one of his gruesome epithets because I, whom he abhors, in perfect innocence found a fleeting pleasure in the boy and addressed a kind word to him." In this way the gentle woman let her tongue play and aroused the King without wrinkling her brow or letting her voice lose its euphonious tone.

"The handsome idiot," Fagon repeated slowly. "Not bad. But if the duke, who possesses some good qualities along with his bad ones, had known the boy as I got to know him and as he has remained un-forgettably in my mind, upon my word, the rancorous Saint-Simon would have felt remorse! And if he had been present at the child's death, as I was, when, in the delusion of fever, he believed he was charging into the enemy's fire with the name of his King on his lips, the secret judge of Hades of our age — if legend tells the truth, for no one has seen him at his desk — would have admired the boy and wept a tear for him."

"No more about Saint-Simon, Fagon, I beg of you," the King said, contracting his brows. "Let him write down what seems to him to be the truth. Shall I look down on people's desks? World history, too, has a pencil in her hand and will judge me with indulgence within the bounds of my age and my character. No more of him. But tell me much, everything you know, of young Boufflers. He must have been a fine boy. Sit down and tell." He motioned cordially to a chair and leaned back in his own.

"And tell your tale at a really comfortable and deliberate pace, Fagon," the marquise requested, with a look at the dainty hands of her pendulum clock, which were moving forward with astonishing speed.

"Sire, I obey," said Fagon, "but make a humble request. When I abused Father Tellier in your presence today, I took a liberty; and knowing myself from experience, I realize that, once I am on this path, I may easily slip back into it on the same day. When Madame de la Sablière dug the good, or perhaps not so good, La Fontaine, her 'fable-tree' as she called him, out of the bad soil into which he had thrust his roots and transplanted him back into good society, the fabulist agreed to live among decent people again, but on condition that he be permitted a minimum of three liberties, or what he called liberties, every evening. In a similar yet different way I request three liberties if I am to tell my story — "

"Which I grant you," the King finished for him.

Three heads moved closer together: the impressive head of the physician, the Olympian curly head of the King and the delicate profile of his wife, with her high forehead, the charming lines of her nose and mouth and the slight double chin.

"In the days when Your Majesty still possessed your greatest poet," the private physician began, "and he, with Death already taking aim at his ailing chest, made merry by ridiculing him on the stage, that masterpiece, *The Imaginary Patient*, was performed here in Versailles before Your Majesty. Though I would normally rather spend a dignified hour with Homer or Virgil and listen to the rhythmic wave of a classical poem under the starry sky than see the present brought on the stage by distorted faces above the harsh lamps, I dared not stay away when my profession was being ridiculed and, who knows, when perhaps I myself and my crutch"—he lifted his bamboo cane, on which he continued to support himself even when sitting down— "might be depicted. It was not so. But if Molière had immortalized me in one of his farces, I really could not have held it against the man who observed and recorded his own most painful emotions in his comedies. These final plays of Molière, there is nothing to surpass them. This is sovereign comedy, which to be sure not only presents in a mocking light what is perverse, but even depicts with cruel pleasure the most humane aspects of life, so that they begin to leer. For instance, what is more pardonable than that a father should delude himself about his child, that he should be somewhat vain about the virtues and somewhat blind toward the weaknesses of his own flesh and blood? It is ridiculous, of course, and provokes mockery. So in *The Imaginary Patient* the silly Diafoirus praises his even sillier son Thomas, an utter blockhead. But Your Majesty knows the passage."

"Do me the favor, Fagon, of reciting it to me," said the King, who had refrained from attending spectacles of the comic muse ever since family losses and severe public reverses had rendered life serious for him, but whose facial muscles involuntarily twitched at the memory of the good companion whom he had once liked to have near him and in whose masks he had taken delight.

"'It is not because I am hs father'"—Fagon assumed the role of Dr. Diafoirus, which, strangely enough, he knew by heart—"'but I dare say I have reason to be satisfied with this my son, and everyone who sees him speaks of him as a youth without guile. He has never possessed a very active imagination nor that fire that one perceives in some people. When he was little, he was never what is called alert and high-spirited. He was always seen as gentle, peace-loving and taciturn. He never spoke a word and never took part in so-called children's games. It was a difficult task to teach him to read, and at the age of nine he still did not know his alphabet. Good, I said to myself, late trees bear the best fruit; it is harder to dig into marble than into sand...' and so on. This slow, dribbling mockery turned, through the incredibly simple face of the lauded boy, into derision on the stage and into irresistible laughter on the faces of the spectators. Among these I noticed a fair woman of touching beauty, who held my attention by the slowly changing expressions on her simple features: at first joy at the just praise given to a child who was learning zealously though with difficulty, however unimpressive the youth on the stage might appear; then an expression of sad disappointment when the spectator, without realizing it fully, became aware of the fact that the writer, who seemed to be serious with his simple words, was really having cruel fun at the expense of parental self-deception. Of course Molière, that superb mocker, had depicted everything so true to nature and so objectively that one could not become angry with him. A tear of profound pain, which had been held back long and with difficulty, finally rolled down the tender cheek of the grief-stricken woman. I knew then that she was a mother and had an ungifted son. From what I had seen and observed, this was a mathematical certainty.

"She was the first wife of Marshal Boufflers."

"Even if you had not known her, Fagon, I would have recognized my sweet blonde from your description," the marquise sighed. "She was a marvel of innocence and simpleheartedness, without suspicion or guile, indeed without an idea of cunning or deceit."

The friendship between the two women, which had left such a touching imprint on the marquise, had been a true one and of benefit to both. For during the long and hard years of her rise, when the quietly ambitious woman had conquered a king, and the greatest king of his age at that, with the most persistent flexibility and the most patient consistency, always serene and ready to serve anywhere, Mme de Maintenon had with her clever eyes distinguished the innocent noblewoman from among the other court ladies, who looked upon her with disfavor and hostility; and she had bound the lady to her with a few cordial words and engaging favors. The two women complemented and protected each other, the one with her rank and the other with intelligence.

"The marshal's wife had virtue and dignity," the King said in praise of her, as he saw in memory a well-proportioned figure, a lovely face and a head of curly ash-blond hair.

"The marshal's wife was stupid," Fagon supplemented his remark bluntly. "But if I, cripple that I am, ever loved a woman—apart from my patroness"—he bowed in homage toward the marquise— "and if ever I would have sacrificed my life for a woman, it was this first Duchess of Boufflers.

"I soon came to know her better, unfortunately in my capacity as physician. For her health was uncertain, and all this loveliness went out unexpectedly like a candle that is extinguished. A few days before her end she called me to her and declared to me in the simplest words in the world that she was going to die. She felt her condition, which my science had not been able to recognize. She submitted to her destiny, she said, and had only one concern: the future and the fate of her boy. 'He is a good child but completely ungifted, like myself,' she lamented to me, concerned but frank. 'I have had an easy life, as I needed only to obey the marshal, who would have left me no responsibilities beyond the simplest household duties, even if I had been a clever woman. You know him, of course, Fagon; his way is to keep everything in his own hands; he is meticulous and controls everything himself. When I kept quiet in company or confined my remarks to the most obvious things, so that I would not say anything ignorant or embarrassing, this suited him perfectly, for a witty or brilliant woman would only have made him uneasy. So I came off well. But my child? Julien is expected to cut a figure in the world as his father's son. Will he be able to do so? He learns with such incredible difficulty! He has no lack of zeal, really not, for he is a brave child.... The marshal will marry again and some clever wife will present him with abler sons. Now, I don't want Julien to become anything extraordinary, which would of course be impossible; I only hope that, if he remains behind his brothers and sisters, his humiliations will not be too harsh. That's your mission, Fagon. You will also see to it that he is not overworked physically. Don't neglect this, I beg you. For the marshal does overlook it. You know him, of course. His mind is on war, boundaries, fortifications.... Even at mealtime he

is preoccupied with his affairs; this man, who is indispensable to the
King and to France, will suddenly send for a map, if he does not
jump up to get one himself, or he will be annoyed about some careless act of his secretaries which he discovered that morning; in the
general neglect of duty that is spreading everywhere, you cannot
trust them with the slightest task. At such times, if a cup or saucer
breaks by accident, the irritated man forgets himself to the point of
scolding. Usually he sits at meals silent or monosyllabic, with knitted
brows, paying no attention to the child, who watches his every look
intently; for the marshal assumes that a Boufflers does his duty of his
own accord. And Julien will go to the utter limits of his powers. . . .
Fagon, don't let him be hurt! Take an interest in the boy. Bring him
through his tender years safely. Don't hesitate to interfere. The marshal thinks well of you and will accept your advice. He calls you the
most honest man in France. . . . You promise, then, to take my place
with the boy. . . . You will keep your word and more. . . .'

"I promised this to the marshal's wife and her death was not a hard
one.

"Before the bed on which she was lying I observed the boy who had
been entrusted to me. He was dissolved in tears, his chest was heaving, but he did not throw himself on the dead woman in despair or
touch the lifeless lips, but kneeled down beside her, took her hand
and kissed it as he was normally in the habit of doing. His pain was
profound, but chaste and restrained. I concluded that he had a
manly character and self-control which had begun at an early age,
and I was not deceived. Julien was at that time a handsome boy of
about thirteen, with his mother's soulful eyes, her winsome features,
the low brow under tangled blond curly hair and a flawless body,
which enabled him to gain mastery in every physical activity.

"The marshal buried the wife of his youth and a year later married
Marshal Gramont's youngest daughter, the lively, very clever, olive-
skinned, ardent, slender woman we know. He consulted me on his
own initiative about the school to which we should send Julien; for it
was no longer advisable that he should remain in his father's house.

"I had a talk with the ecclesiastical tutor who had supervised and
instructed the child up to that time. He showed me the boy's note-
books, which testified to a touching diligence and a brave persever-
ance, but also to an incredibly mediocre mind, a complete deficiency
in reasoning and dialectic, an absolute lack of intellect. What is

called wit, in the broadest sense of the term, all the emotional illumination of discourse — whether warm or mocking — all the surprises of
shrewdness, all play of the imagination, were lacking. Only the simplest concepts and the most meager words were at the boy's command. At most a phrase pleased one now and again by its innocence
or produced a smile by its naïveté. Strangely and sadly enough, the
ecclesiastical tutor unwittingly spoke of his pupil in the words of
Molière: 'a boy without guile, who takes everything in good faith,
without fire and imagination, gentle, peace-loving, taciturn and,' he
added, 'with the finest qualities of the heart.'

"The marshal and I knew then — there wasn't a great choice — of
no better school for the child than a Jesuit college; and why not the
one in Paris, if we did not wish to separate Julien from the boys of his
social class and age? It must be admitted that the fathers are not
pedants and deserve praise for teaching in a pleasant spirit and treating their pupils in a friendly way. We could not favor a school of Jan-
senist coloring, the marshal because he was a loyal subject who knew
of Your Majesty's dislike for the sect and did not want to forfeit Your
Majesty's favor wantonly, and I for the same reason" — Fagon smiled
— "and because I considered the harsh strictness and the gloomy
basis of this doctrine unsuitable for the boy, who was depressed
enough by his lack of talent. In this instance I regarded the pleasant
earth and accessible heaven of the Jesuits as beneficial, or at least
completely harmless; for I knew that the basic law of this boy's soul
was honor.

"Moreover, I was supported by the natural assumption that the
pious fathers would never be insulted by the marshal, and there was
no danger of this happening, since he did not concern himself with
ecclesiastical quarrels and, as a soldier, actually took a certain pleasure in the principle of subordination, which is carried out so strictly
in the order.

"But how was this naturally inferior boy to keep pace with the
class? On this point the marshal and I counted on two different factors. The marshal relied on the sense of duty and the ambition of his
son. He, who had only moderate gifts himself, had achieved fame in
his field by virtue of his moral qualities, not through brilliant talents.
Without knowing or wanting to know that Julien was far from possessing these moderate gifts which he had exploited through iron
zeal, the marshal believed that nothing was impossible for a strong

will, that even nature could be forced. Indeed his aides accused him of criticizing the sweat that rolled down their faces during parades as being contrary to regulations, because he never sweated himself.

"I, on the other hand, relied on the general humanity of the Jesuits, and especially on the consideration and respect of personality which distinguish these fathers. I conversed with several of them and made them familiar with the boy's characteristics. To bring the child even closer to their hearts, I spoke to them of his father's position, but I saw at once that they cared nothing about that. The marshal, moreover, is a soldier first and last, virtuous and above intrigue, and honor pursues him like his shadow. So the fathers had nothing to hope or fear from him. Under these conditions I believed I had to give Julien a stronger recommendation and dropped a hint to the pious fathers—" The narrator stopped.

"What are you glossing over, Fagon?" asked the King.

"I'll return to it," Fagon stuttered in embarrassment, "and then, sire, you will have something to pardon me for. Enough, the stratagem worked. The fathers competed with each other to make learning easier for the boy, who felt that he was in a warm atmosphere; he became less rigid, his scant talents unfolded, his courage increased and he was well taken care of.

"Then everything changed.

"About half a year after Julien's entry into the Jesuit college, a nasty incident occurred at Orléans, in the precincts of which the fathers had property and a school, both of which they wished to enlarge. Four brothers of the minor nobility owned an estate there, which bordered on the Jesuit property and which they managed jointly. All four served in your army, sire, and, as often happens, consumed their short supply of cash in paying for their equipment, and even more, in their association with wealthier companions, so that they were compelled to mortgage their fields. Now, it came about that, by buying up these mortgages, the Jesuit house had become the sole creditor of the four noblemen; it had voluntarily advanced them a round sum of money on top of this for a period of three years, and after that, on the basis of an annual renewal. In addition, however, the fathers gave the noblemen the most solemn oral promise to let the whole sum stand against the estate; the rule of their order, to loan out money for a maximum of three years, they said, was a mere formality.

"It then came about that the fathers of that house were all unexpectedly sent to the end of the world, actually to Japan I believe, and those who took their place conceivably knew nothing of that oral promise. The three-year term came to an end, the new fathers called in the debt, at the end of the year the noblemen were unable to pay and legal proceedings were instituted against them.

"The pious house had already taken possession of their fields when a storm broke. The dogged brothers pounded on every door, including that of Marshal Boufflers, who knew and esteemed them as brave soldiers. He investigated the dispute with the seriousness and thoroughness that were characteristic of him. The decisive point was the brothers' assertion that they had received from the pious fathers not only oral assurances but at the same time, on repeated occasions, letters to the same effect, which had completely allayed their anxiety. These documents had been inexplicably lost. True, there existed papers folded like letters, with broken, empty seals, which were remarkably like the letters of the fathers, but these papers were blank, devoid of all content.

"So one day, when I entered the marshal's private office, I found him turning those blank squares over in his precise way and examining them from front and back under the magnifying glass. I proposed to him that he entrust me with the papers for an hour, to which he agreed with a serious look in his eyes.

"You granted science and me, sire, a botanical garden, which does you honor, and you built me a quiet home in the country for my old age. Not far from it, at its northern end, I have set up a spacious chemical kitchen, which you once promised to visit. There I subjected the questionable papers to effective chemical agents which were perhaps still unknown to the learned fathers. And behold, the faded writing came out black in the light and revealed the rascality of the Jesuit fathers.

"The marshal hurried at once to Your Majesty with the incriminating documents"—the King stroked is brow slowly—"and found Father Lachaise with you, most profoundly astonished at the aberration of his brothers of the order in the provinces; at the same time he made representations to Your Majesty, saying what a crying injustice it would be to make such a great, benevolent and morally pure society pay for the thoughtlessness of a few or of one single person and this single person, the former head of that house, had, as he knew from reliable sources, recently suffered martyrdom at the stake at the hands of the heathen in Japan.

"It was the four noblemen who profited most from this turn of affairs. The bewildered fathers canceled half the debt, the other half was paid by a generous person."

The King, who may well have been that person, did not alter his expression.

"Father Lachaise then thanked the marshal particularly for having undertaken to establish the truth in the troublesome affair and for having spared his order the sin of burdening itself with property obtained unjustly. Then he asked him, as nobleman to nobleman, not to withdraw his good will from the fathers and to keep their secret, which of course was superfluous for a man like Marshal Boufflers.

"The flattered marshal promised, but, strangely enough, would not hear of handing over the incriminating documents or of destroying them. Father Lachaise first plied him with the most delicate hints, then attacked him with the most definite demands; it was of no use. Not that the marshal would have thought, even remotely, of using these dangerous letters against the pious fathers; but he had once and for all deposited them among his papers, the sorting and registering of which takes up a third of his time. Whatever once gets into this archive, as he calls it, lies buried there. And so, by virtue of the marshal's love of order and his precise habits, a constant threat hovered over the order, and for this threat the order did not forgive the imprudent man. The marshal had no suspicion of it and believed he was on the best terms with the fathers, whom he had spared.

"I was of a different opinion and was not remiss in making urgent representations to him. I pressed him hard to take his boy away from the Jesuits without delay, since the sullen hatred and the swallowed rancor which cheated greed and unmasked rascality invariably feel against the person who has exposed them, would necessarily spread throughout the order, seek a sacrifice and perhaps, indeed probably, find it in his innocent child. He looked at me in astonishment, as if I were talking irrationally and telling him fables. To put it bluntly, either the marshal is short on intelligence or he wanted to keep his given word with pomp and glory, even at the expense of his child.

" 'But Fagon,' he said, 'what in the world has my Julien to do with this affair, which happened in the provinces? What sensible connection is there between the two? For that matter, if the fathers keep a stricter eye on him, it can't hurt. They've pampered him rather badly. Take the boy away from them now? That would be ignoble. People would talk, look for reasons, perhaps dig out the nasty story, and I would stand as a man who had broken his word.' So the marshal saw only the halo of his honor, instead of thinking of his child, to whom he had perhaps never granted an attentive look as long as he lived. I could have beaten him with my crutch for his noble-mindedness.

"Things then happened as they were bound to. Not in any surprising way, without suddenness and without committing any real injustice, the father-professors let the boy sink; they began to hate him as the son of the man who had insulted the order. Not all among them, the better ones least of all, knew the pretty story, but they all knew this: Marshal Boufflers has disgraced and harmed us. And they all hated him.

"A subtly poisonous atmosphere of creeping revenge filled the rooms of the college. Not only all friendliness but every just consideration for Julien had stopped. The child suffered. Every day and every hour he felt humiliated, not through open censure, least of all through scolding words, which are not used by the fathers, but subtly and impersonally, for they no longer supported the deficiency of the fair-headed boy in a friendly way, but exposed his mental inadequacy to shame after refusing him help. And now the child, goaded by a desperate ambition, began to lengthen his vigils, to shorten his sleep brutally, to torture his brain, to undermine his health — I don't like to talk about it, it incenses me — "

Fagon paused and drew a deep breath.

The King filled this pause by remarking calmly: "I wonder, Fagon, how much reality there is in all this. I mean this silent conspiracy of learned and intelligent men to injure a child, and this brooding hatred of a whole society toward a man who was basically of so little danger to them, and who had, moreover, behaved quite chivalrously toward them. You are seeing ghosts, Fagon. You are partisan in this and may perhaps have some personal animosity toward the deserving order, besides that which you have inherited."

"Who knows?" Fagon stammered. He had grown pale, insofar as he could still do so, and his eyes were blazing. The marquise became anxious and secretly touched the arm of her protégé, without his feeling the warning hand. Madame de Maintenon knew that when he was irritated, the impetuous old man was quite beside himself and dared to say incredible things even to the King, who to be sure tolerated from the man who had for many years had an intimate knowledge of his body, what he would not so easily have tolerated from anyone else.

Fagon was trembling. He stuttered disconnected sentences and his words tumbled over each other, like warriors rushing for their arms.

"You will not believe, Your Majesty, you who know human hearts, you will not believe that the Jesuit fathers hate, to the point of destruction, everyone who has insulted them whether knowingly or unknowingly? You will not believe that these fathers know neither true nor false, neither good nor evil, but only their society?" Fagon gave a grim laugh. "You *will* not believe it, Your Majesty.

"Tell me, King, you who know reality," Fagon raved on in a digression, "since we are talking of the credibility of things, can't you believe, either, that in your realm force is being applied in the conversion of Protestants?"

"This question," replied the King very earnestly, "is the first of your three liberties for today. I will answer it. No, Fagon. With the exception of a negligible number of cases, no force is being applied in these conversions, because I have explicitly forbidden it once and for all, and because my orders are obeyed. There is no forcing of men's consciences. The true religion is at present winning over hundreds of thousands through its inner power of conviction."

"Through the sermons of Father Bourdaloue!" Fagon sneered in a shrill voice. Then he was silent. Horror stared from his eyes at this summit of delusion, this wall of prejudice, this total destruction of the truth. He contemplated the King and his wife a while with a secret horror.

"Sire, do not think," he continued, "that I am biased and that the blood of my Protestant ancestors speaks from me. I have defected from a noble church. Why? Because, save for God, whom I will not abandon and who, I hope, will not abandon me in my old days, I think of religions and creeds, one and all, as I do of that verse of Lucretius..."

Neither the King nor Madame de Maintenon knew of this verse, but they were able to surmise that Fagon meant nothing pious by it.

"Do you know how my father died, sire?" Fagon whispered. "It has remained a secret, but I will confide it to you. He was a gentle man, and from the sale of his patent medicines he made an honest but meager living in Auxerre for his wife and children, of whom I was the crippled sixth and last. Auxerre has a healthy climate and threescore pharmacies. The zealous inhabitants, who loved my father, wished him well and would have liked to return him to the Church, but not through violence; for you have said it, sire, one does not force the consciences of men. So they banded together to avoid the Calvinist pharmacy. My father lost his bread and we starved. As everywhere else, the Jesuit fathers were the most active in the matter. From there on, he was at odds with his conscience. He renounced his faith. But because the sharp Calvinist doctrines do not so easily leave a brain on which they have been imprinted since childhood, the poor man soon appeared in his own eyes as a Judas who betrayed his Lord, and like Judas he went and did likewise."

"Fagon," the King said with dignity, "you insulted Father Tellier because of a tasteless remark he made about his father, and yet you talk so nakedly and gruesomely about your own. Unpleasant things ask for a veil."

"Sire," replied the physician, "you are right and are for me, as for every Frenchman, the law in matters of decorum. Of course one may allow oneself to be carried away by certain moods in this world of untruth and, in defiance of that world, may unexpectedly remove the concealing cloth from a bloody fact, even if it is the most painful. . .

"But, sire, how prematurely I have used the first of my liberties, and in truth I have a desire to use my second one at once." The marquise read in the physician's altered features that his anger was over, and knew that after such an outburst there was no cause to fear a relapse that evening.

"Sire," said Fagon almost frivolously, "did you know your subject Mouton, the animal painter? You shake your head. Then I shall take the great liberty of introducing to you this artist, who was not presentable at court, but who belongs to our story; not in person, of course, with his hat riddled with holes, his stump of a pipe between his teeth — I can still smell his cheap tobacco — in his shirt sleeves and with his hose hanging down. Besides, he is lying in his grave. You do not like the Dutch, sire, neither their kermesses on canvases nor their own unrestrained persons. Your Majesty should know, you had a painter, a man from Picardy, who by far outhollanded the Hollanders, both by his objective brush and his unconstrained manners.

"This Mouton, sire, lived among us, painting his grazing cows and his herds of cloudlike sheep without having the faintest idea of all the great and sublime things which your era, Majesty, has produced. Did he know your writers? Not even remotely. Your bishops and preachers? Not even by name. Mouton had never been touched by baptismal water. Your statesmen: Colbert, Lionne and the others? He cared nothing about them. Your generals: Condé with the bird's face, Turenne, Luxembourg and the fair Gabrielle's grandson? Only the latter, for whom he filled a drawing room at Anet with stag hunts of incredibly insolent skill. Vendôme liked Mouton, and by way of praise the latter called his ducal patron a beast of a fellow, if I may utter this word before Your Majesty's ears. Did Mouton know the Sun of our age? Was he aware of your existence, Majesty? It may sound incredible, but perhaps he did not even know your name — the name which fills the world and history, though your golden coins may have passed through his hands once in a while. For Mouton was no more able to read than his favorite, the other Mouton.

"This second Mouton, a wise poodle with a spacious cranium and very intelligent eyes, over which the black shaggy hair from his forehead hung down in tangled tufts, was without doubt — within the limits of his nature — the most gifted of my three guests; I say this because Julien Boufflers, whom I am describing, Mouton the man and Mouton the poodle often sat together contentedly for hours at my place.

"You know, sire, that the Jesuit fathers give generous vacations, because their pupils, though by no means all, come from aristocratic, indeed from the highest, circles, and are often asked to return home or to go elsewhere for hunting expeditions, theatrical performances or other amusements. So I occasionally took Julien with me to your botanical garden, since he was seldom, as a matter of principle, asked home by his father the marshal. There I was from time to time visited by Mouton, who felt at home among plants and animals; he sketched for me on paper, with energetic chalk marks, a learned owl or a comical monkey or possibly, when diligence and the proper mood prevailed, he might populate a quiet room for me with his shying horses or drinking cows. I had given Mouton the key to an attic and a key to the nearest little garden gate, so as to give the tramp a place where he could house his easels and portfolios. So he appeared and vanished in my house at his pleasure.

"On one of those cool and refreshing rainy summer days, those days of silent but swift growth for nature and the mind, I was sitting in my library, looking through the tall window over my spectacles and over an open folio volume at the adjacent building, right into the attic facing me, which was Mouton's den. There I saw a slender boyish blond head bending over an easel in happy tension. Behind him Mouton was nodding his sturdy head and his hairy hand was guiding the boy's slender one. There was no doubt about it, he was giving the boy a lesson in painting. Mouton the poodle was sitting nearby on a high chair with red cushions, wise and approving, as if he were highly in favor of this excellent form of entertainment. I put a marker in my book and went over.

"In my felt shoes I was not audible to the two merry painters and was perceived only by Mouton the poodle, but he confined his greeting to a vigorous wagging of his tail, without leaving his cushion. I sat down quietly in an easy chair to witness the strangest conversation, sire, that was ever carried on in your botanical garden. But first I studied, from my corner, the picture that stood on the easel, breathing in the smell of the oil paint that was being applied easily and generously. What did the picture represent? A mere nothing: an evening mood, calm on a river, and in it the reflection of some dissolved little red clouds and of the moss-covered arch of a bridge. In the river stood two cows gazing in contemplation, the one drinking, the other with water still dripping from the corners of its mouth. Naturally the best part of the picture was Mouton's share in it. But the boy, too, possessed a certain ability with the brush, which could only be the result of many an hour spent painting with Mouton, without my knowledge. However much or little he may have learned, the mere illusion of success, his participation in a highly gifted activity, in something that came happily and without effort, something bold and free that emerged from a creative hand, something which the unimaginative boy had probably had no conception of before and which he looked at in astonishment as at a miracle, made him experience a great happiness after so many blows to his self-confidence. The blood reddened his chaste cheeks and zeal gave wing to his hand, so that nothing could surpass it, and I too felt a bright, fatherly joy.

"Meanwhile Mouton was explaining to the boy the broad contours and heavy gestures of a cow in movement, and closed with the assertion that there was nothing superior to it except the form of a bull.

The latter was the peak of creation. Actually he said 'Nature,' not Creation, if I am to be precise, for Creation was unknown to him, both the word and the thing, as he had grown up neglected and without benefit of the catechism.

"It required little happiness to lure the boy's innate merriment out of him like a gushing spring. Finding Mouton's respect for horned cattle amusing, Julien told him innocently: 'Father Amiel taught us this morning that the ancient Egyptians revered the bull as divine. I find that funny.'

"'By Jove,' the painter replied with passion, 'they were right in that. Smart people, they, real beasts. Don't you agree, Mouton? Eh? I ask you, Julien, isn't a bull's head in its power and threatening size more divine—to use that stupid word—than a triangle or cockpigeon or a flat human face, for that matter? Don't you agree, Mouton? You feel that yourself, don't you, Julien? When I say "flat human face" I am speaking without detracting from the nose of your Father Amiel. All due respect for that!' Without intending any ridicule, Mouton drew a nose on the pine frame of the easel with an insolent stroke of his brush, but what a nose, a monster of a nose, of fabulous size and overwhelmingly comical.

"'You see,' he then continued in complete seriousness, 'Nature does not stand still. It would delight her to produce something new occasionally. But it's too late; the hag has lost her fire.'

"'Father Amiel,' the boy said shyly, 'will not thank Nature for his nose, for it makes him ridiculous and he has a lot to endure from my schoolmates because of it.'

"'They're just boys,' said Mouton generously, 'who lack a sense of the sublime. But by the way, how does it come, Julien, that when I recently paid a visit to your school to bring you the sketches, I found you surrounded by pip-squeaks? Lads of thirteen and fourteen? Is that fitting company for you, who already have down on your lip and a girl friend?'

"This sudden onslaught brought two opposing expressions to the youth's countenance: a happy but profound shyness and a fundamental misery, which prevailed. Julien sighed. 'I was kept back,' he whispered with an unintentional ambiguity.

"'Nonsense!' Mouton scolded. 'Kept back in what? Haven't you grown with your years and become a slim, handsome fellow? If knowledge doesn't appeal to you, that shows your common sense.

Upon my word! I wouldn't have let them put me among the kids when I had a beard or at least down; I would have run away on the spot.'

" 'But Mouton,' the boy said, 'my father the marshal requested of me that I should stay another year among the small boys. He begged me to do him this favor.' He said this with a tender expression of obedience and respectful love which touched me, although I was at the same time annoyed by the marshal for abusing the child's respect for him. I was also very annoyed by the fact that Julien, who preserved a stubborn silence toward me and everyone else, had shown confidence in a Mouton, had opened up before a mere half-human. But I was wrong. Don't we adults, too, tell our deepest troubles to a loyal beast which puts its paws on our knees? And isn't it a sensible instinct in all those who have been deprived by nature to seek their company, not among their equals but below them, where they feel that they are being spared and pitied?

" 'Do you know what?' Mouton continued after a pause, and the other Mouton pointed his ears at the word. 'Your animal drawings are not bad right now, and you're learning more every day. I'll take you south with me as my assistant. I have a commission there at Grignan Castle. That—you know, what's her name, that fat, jolly female? oh, I know, that Sévigné—is sending me to her son-in-law, who's governor round about there. You'll come with me and we'll live luxuriously on olives, you'll be a free bird on the loose, who can flutter and peck at whatever pleases him, you'll never look at a printed word again all your life and will let the marshal severely alone. Your blue, cool, distinguished lady-love will stay behind too. You think I didn't see you, you rascal, only the day before yesterday, when the old quack was in Versailles, before the monkey cage, in the company of the old frump of an herb-woman and the big blue doll? She'll find some brown, tanned substitute, don't you worry.'

"This last remark, which was actually a little more cynical still, shocked me, although it could not hurt the boy as I knew him. I now cleared by throat loudly, and Julien rose in his respectful way to greet me, while Mouton, showing no embarrassment whatever, contented himself with muttering in his beard: 'That one!' Mouton was a fundamentally ungrateful man.

"I took the boy out with me into the garden, while Mouton went on painting merrily, and asked him whether the cynic had really sought

him out at the college, which was unpleasant for me for obvious reasons. Julien confirmed it. It had been an effort, he said frankly, to return Mouton's handshake in the schoolyard among his schoolmates,
because the painter's naked elbows had shown through the holes in
his sleeves and his toes stuck out of his shoes; 'but,' he said, 'I did it
and accompanied him across the street too; for I am indebted to him
for my instruction and some pleasant hours, and I really like him
very much, except for his untidiness.'

"The boy talked on this way without making anything more of it,
and he reminded me of a scene I had witnessed a short time before
from the upper arcades of the college overlooking the playground,
when I was called to attend a sick pupil; I had not been able to tear
myself from that scene for a long time. Down below, a fencing lesson
was being given and the fencing master, an old scarred sergeant who
had served under the marshal for many years, treated the commander's son, who had just shortly risen from his schoolbench among
children, with almost abject reverence, as if he were expecting to receive commands instead of giving them.

"Julien fenced excellently; I had almost said 'nobly.' The boy was
in the habit of turning his wrist mechanically during the long hours
he spent in memorizing, so that it became uncommonly supple. He
had, besides, a precise eye and a sure thrust. So he became, as I said,
a first-class fencer, and he also rode well and intelligently. One might
have expected that the boy, who was humiliated in everything, would
have let his comrades feel this one superiority, so as to gain position.
But no, he scorned this. He treated both those who were skilled and
those who were unskilled in this physical exercise with the same courtesy as he faced them blade in hand, never entering a heated contest
with the skilled, nor making fun of the unskilled, whom he generously allowed to pierce him at times in order to encourage them. In
this way he reestablished on the fencing floor, in a subtle and un-
obtrusive manner, that equality which he missed so painfully in the
schoolroom; and among his companions he enjoyed not the respect
that one gains with one's fists but a respect, mingled with reserve, for
his inexplicable kindness, a respect which, to be sure, dissolved in a
sincere sympathy for his general ungiftedness, a sympathy not usually
found in youth. The adversity of fortune, which embitters so many
souls, educated and ennobled his.

"I had strolled with Julien, sire, to that part of your garden where

the wild beasts are kept behind bars in cages. They had just put a
wolf into one of them and he was pacing his prison with flashing eyes
and a diagonal, hurried gait. I pointed him out to the boy, who,
after casting a hasty glance at the restless beast, turned away with a
slight shudder. The flat skull, the deceiving eyes, the repulsive snout,
the teeth bared in malice, were enough to frighten one. But I was
completely unused to seeing fear in the boy, who had already gone on
hunting expeditions. 'Why, Julien, what's wrong with you?' I smiled,
and he replied with embarrassment, 'The animal reminds me of
someone—' but then he dropped the thread, for we noticed, at a
slight distance from us, a distinguished couple which claimed our attention: a roly-poly old lady and a young girl; the first was the Countess Mimeure—you remember her, sire, even though she has been
avoiding the court for decades, not out of negligence, for she reveres
you boundlessly, but because, as she says, she does not want to insult
your sense of beauty with her wrinkles. Horrible and witty and supporting herself on a crutch like myself, a striking and lively creature,
she was a pleasant sight to me.

"'Good day, Fagon,' she called to me. 'I have been studying your
plants and have come to ask you for a few rhubarb shoots for my
garden at Neuilly. You know I'm a bit of a physician,' and she took
my arm. 'Say hello to each other, you young people! Why, they act as
if they had never seen one another!'

"Julien, the shy boy, greeted the girl, who offered him her fingertips, with no great embarrassment, which both astonished and delighted me. 'Mirabelle Miramion,' the Countess named her to me, 'a
splendid name, isn't it, Fagon?' I studied the beautiful child, and at
once I thought of that 'blue sweetheart' with which Mouton had
teased the boy. She really had big, blue, imploring eyes; a cool,
transparent complexion and a figure that was scarcely full-grown,
yet expressing so far no more than a delicate soul.

"When the countess had introduced me as the King's personal
physician, she began in a childlike voice that was as clear as a bell
and penetrated to the heart in the following way: 'Foremost of physicians and natural scientist, I bow before you in this world-famous
garden, which the homage of the mightiest ruler, who gives his name
to this century, has built for you in his populous and remarkable
capital.' I was so astonished by this elaborate, antique rhetoric from
the small, spring-fresh mouth that I was speechless. The old lady

began to scold her in a good-natured, vexed manner: 'Enough of
that, Belle dear; Fagon will spare you the rest. Among friends, child
— for Fagon is one and not a cynic — how many times have I begged
you in the three weeks I've had you with me to abandon these cursed,
stilted, provincial speeches? People don't speak like that. This man
here is not the foremost of physicians but simply Monsieur Fagon.
The Botanic Garden is simply the Botanic Garden or the Vegetable
Garden or the Royal Garden. Paris is Paris and not the capital, and
the King is satisfied to be King. Note that.' The girl's lips opened
painfully and a single tear trickled down the blooming cheek.

"Then, to my astonishment, Julien turned against the old lady in
great excitement: 'I beg your pardon, Countess,' he said boldly and
vehemently. 'Rhetoric is a required, indispensable subject and difficult to learn. I must admire the young lady, she speaks so elegantly,
and Father Amiel, if he heard her—'

" 'Father Amiel!'—the Countess broke into wild laughter, until her
diaphragm ached—'Father Amiel has a nose! What a nose! A global
nose! Just imagine, Fagon, a nose that puts that of Abbé Genest to
shame! What was I doing at the college? I was fetching my nephew
there—you know, Fagon, I have the children of my two deceased sisters on my back, my nephew Guntram, poor, poor boy!—and I was
taken to Father Amiel's rhetoric class till Father Tellier, the prefect
of studies, returned. O Lord! O Lord!' The countess held onto her
shaking stomach. 'How I suffered from suppressed laughter! First the
Roman woman who commits suicide. The father stabbed himself
with his ruler. Then he pouted sweetly and breathed: "O Paetus, it
doesn't hurt!" But that was nothing compared to the dying Cleopatra
and the adder. The father put the ruler against his left breast and let
his eyes grow misty. If you could have seen it, Fagon! . . . Eh!' she suddenly screamed, so that it went right through me. 'Why, there's
Father Tellier!' and she pointed to the wolf, which we had not left
more than twenty feet behind us. 'Truly, Father Tellier, his spit and
image! Let's get away from these horrid beasts of yours, Fagon, to
your fragrant plants. Give me your arm, Julien.'

" 'Excuse me, Countess,' the boy asked, 'why do you call Guntram
a poor boy, when he is now following the fleur-de-lis, or may even
have the honor of bearing the King's flag himself?'

" 'Oh, oh!' the Countess groaned, the expression on her face
changed suddenly, and tears of laughter were followed by those of

misery. 'Why did I call Guntram a poor boy? Because he no longer even exists, Julien, he's blown away. That is why I came to the garden, where I suspected you were, to tell you that Guntram was killed in battle, just imagine, one day after he joined the forces. He was mustered in at once and led a patrol so daringly and uselessly that a cannonball shattered him, no more and no less than the erstwhile Marshal Turenne. Imagine, Fagon: the boy had not reached his sixteenth birthday yet, but made efforts to get out of the college, where he learned quickly and happily, thinking of the musket by day and in his dreams. And he was near-sighted too, Fagon, you have no idea how much so. So near-sighted that at twenty feet he saw nothing but mist before him. Of course I and every other sensible person tried to dissuade him from taking up the sword—but it was no use, for he was as stubborn as they come. I quarreled with the boy as a mother does, but one fine day he ran away to your father, Julien, who was just getting into his carriage to take over his command in the Netherlands. He questioned the child, as he has just written me himself, whether he was under the authority of a father, and when the boy said no, the marshal allowed him to ride with him in the carriage. Now the brave lad is rotting over there'—she pointed north—'in a Belgian hamlet. But the meager properties of his five sisters have increased a little in size.'

"I read on Julien's face how deeply and differently the death of his playmate was affecting him. The marshal had taken *him* along to the war and was letting his own child sit on a wretched schoolbench. But the boy believed so blindly in his father's sense of justice, even if he did not understand it, that the cloud on the young brow vanished quickly and made way for a clear expression of joy.

"'You're laughing, Julien?' the old lady cried in horror.

"'I am thinking,' he said thoughtfully, as if he were savoring every word on his tongue, 'death for one's King is always good fortune.'

"This chivalrous, though hardly cheerful, maxim and the unnaturally happy tone in which the boy uttered it, made the good countess wretched. A half-suppressed sob testified to the fact that she understood perfectly the boy's suffering and the pain he found in living. 'Go on with Mirabelle, Julien,' she said, 'and keep ahead of us, toward those palms, but not too close, for I have something to say to Fagon; but not too far, so that I may keep you in sight.'

"'How gracefully they walk,' the old lady whispered as they moved away. 'Adam and Eve! Don't laugh, Fagon. Though the girl wears powder and a crinoline, they are walking in paradise just the same, and they are innocent too, because a youth filled with suffering weighs on them and allows them to savor pure love without the sting of their years. I am not offended, as I usually am, by the fact that the girl is a few years older and some inches taller'—she was exaggerating —'than the boy. If *they* don't belong together—

"'It is ridiculous about the girl, Fagon, and I saw how astounded you were to be addressed by the beautiful child in such a tasteless way. And yet she has come quite naturally by this horrible deformity. My sister the viscountess, may God have mercy on her, was a *précieuse* who had come into the world half a century too late; she raised the girl in Dijon, where her husband headed the *Parlement* and she presided over a Poetical Garden, with the circumlocutions and phrases of the erstwhile Mademoiselle de Scudéry. She succeeded in thoroughly corrupting the taste of the poor, obedient child. I wager' —and she pointed her crutch at the two young people, who were enjoying a moment of bliss, to judge by the tender but modest position of the two figures—'now she is chatting quite innocently with the boy, for she has a simple soul and a chaste heart. The air she exhales is purer than that she breathes in. But if she goes with me into society tomorrow and gets to sit near some great gun, an archbishop or duke, she will be overcome by a mortal fear of being thought silly or insignificant, and will deck out her shining nature, out of sheer anxiety, with the rags of patched, empty phrases. In this way the charming girl becomes the very thing she fears to be, a ridiculous figure among us who speaks clearly and concisely. Isn't that a misfortune? What efforts I'll need to correct the child! And Julien, the stupid fellow, actually confirming her in her folly!

"'Oof!' the Countess panted, tired out from walking on her crutch; she sat down heavily on the stone bench in the rondel of myrtle and laurel where, sire, your bust stands.

"'To get back to the boy, Fagon,' she began again, 'you must get him off the schoolbench without delay. It was horrible, I tell you, horrible, Fagon, to see him sitting among the boys. The marshal, that terrible pedant, would let him get moldy among the Jesuits. Just to make him finish his schooling. Among the Jesuits, Fagon! I've sounded out Father Amiel. I tickled him with his interest in rhetoric. He is a vain ass but he has some feeling. He felt sorry for Julien and very cautiously but clearly enough dropped the hint that the boy was badly off among the fathers. They were the best people in the world, but somewhat sensitive and must not be irritated. The marshal had trodden on their toes, but the new prefect of studies did not allow the honor of the Order to be trifled with and was making the child pay for his father's guilt. Then he became frightened by his frankness, looked about him and put his finger to his lips.

"'I took the boys along with me: Guntram, our Julien, who shared some sort of secret with him, and a third friend too, Victor Argenson, the latter for my own pleasure, for he is full of mischief and laughter.

"'That evening he behaved too wildly. Victor and Guntram tormented Mirabelle unbearably, after I had already scolded her at noon for one of her yard-long phrases. "Beautifully expressed, Mademoiselle Mirobolante," they mocked, "but still not beautiful enough. One note higher still." and so on. Julien defended the girl as well as he could but only increased their ridicule. Suddenly the maltreated girl broke into a stream of tears and I drove the young scamps into the large drawing room, where I began to play a game of ball with them. After a while, looking for Julien and Mirabelle, I found them in the garden sitting together on a quiet bench: Amor and Psyche. When I surprised them, they did not blush too much.

"'Mark you, Fagon, Julien is now my adopted child, and if you don't free him from the fathers and make a tolerable life for him, upon my word! I'll limp to Versailles on this crutch and bring the matter to this one here in spite of my wrinkles!' And she pointed to your laurel-crowned bust, Your Majesty!

"The old lady chattered to me about a hundred other matters, while I resolved to have a thorough talk with the boy as soon as she had taken her leave.

"He and the girl appeared again soon, quietly radiant. The countess' carriage was announced and Julien accompanied the ladies to the gateway, while I sought out my favorite bench in front of the orange grove. I savored the delicate scent. Mouton strolled past me without a greeting, his hands in his pockets, smoking some obnoxious tobacco. He was in the habit of concluding his evenings in a tavern outside the garden. Mouton the poodle, on the other hand, paid his respects to me by wagging his tail vehemently. I am certain the clever animal guessed that I would gladly have snatched his master from destruction, for Mouton the man was a heavy brandy drinker, which I have forgotten or felt ashamed to report to Your Majesty.

"The boy came back, tender and happy. 'Let me have a look at your drawing and painting,' I said. 'I suppose it's all lying in Mouton's room.' He agreed and brought me a full portfolio. I examined sheet after sheet. A strange sight, this mixture of two unequal hands: Mouton's insolent lines stammeringly imitated by the modest hand of the boy — and gently ennobled. For a long time I held a blue sheet on which Julien had copied, with unbelievable care, a few bees which Mouton had sketched in various wing positions with the help of a magnifying glass. Obviously the boy had fallen in love with the shape of the little creature. If anyone had told me that the drawing of a little bee would kill him!

"At the bottom of the portfolio there lay a formless scrap of paper on which Mouton had smeared something that held my curiosity. 'That isn't mine,' said Julien, 'it got attached.' I studied the sheet, which contained the remarkable parody of a scene from Ovid: that scene which tells of Pentheus running, pursed by the maenads, and Bacchus, the gruesome god, causing a vertical mountain range to appear in front of him in order to destroy the fugitive. Probably Mouton had heard the boy, who sometimes did his lessons in the painter's room, painfully translating Ovid's verses and had derived his subject from them. A youth — unmistakably Julien in his physical appearance, which Mouton's painter's eye easily knew better than the boy himself — a slender runner, was fleeing, his head turned backward to a few pursuing spectral figures, with an expression of mortal anxiety on his face. They were not bacchantes but ageless women, embodied ideas, anxieties, tormenting thoughts — one of these monsters wore a long Jesuit hat on her cropped skull and had a folio volume in her hand — and then the wall of rock, desolate and insurmountable, which seemed to grow before one's eyes, like a sinister destiny.

"I looked at the boy. He was studying the sheet without revulsion, without any inkling of its possible meaning. Even Mouton may not have realized clearly what dream of an evil omen he had conjured onto the paper with the obscure instinct of a genius. Involuntarily I put it in the middle of the pile of sheets to hide it, before I thrust the papers into the portfolio.

"'Julien,' I began in a friendly tone, 'I must complain to you for preferring Mouton to me, making him your confidant, while you shut yourself off in an incomprehensible silence from my good will, of which you are aware. Are you afraid to tell me of your unhappiness because I can set clear limits to it and judge it correctly? You prefer to consume yourself in hopeless brooding? That doesn't show courage.'

"Julien contracted his brows in pain. But once more a ray of the bliss he had enjoyed that day played over his face. 'M. Fagon,' he said with half a smile, 'I have really told my grief only to Mouton the poodle.'

"This *bon mot*, which I would not have thought him capable of, surprised me. The boy misinterpreted the look of astonishment on my face. He thought he had said something improper. 'Ask me, M. Fagon,' he said. 'I will tell you the truth.'

"'You find life difficult?'

"'Yes, M. Fagon.'

"'People consider you backward, and so you are, but perhaps in a different way than people think.' The harsh word was spoken.

"The boy lowered his fair head into his hands and broke into silent tears, which I did not notice until they ran between his fingers. Now the spell was broken.

"'I will tell you my grief, M. Fagon,' he sobbed, raising his head.

"'Do so, my child, and be certain, now that we are friends, that I will defend you as I would myself. No one will harm you in the future, neither you yourself nor anyone else. You will once more find pleasure in the air and the sun and begin your day's work without horror.'

"The boy believed in me and his eyes filled with hope and confidence. Then he began to tell of his sorrow, as if it were already half in his past.

"'I have had one bad day and the rest were not much better. It was on an autumn day when I rode with Guntram to his uncle the commander at Compiègne. We wanted to practice our markmanship there, a new pleasure for us both and a test of our eyesight.

"'We had a light, two-horse carriage and Guntram entertained me in a cloud of dust by talking about his future. This future could only be a military one. He had no desire for any other. The commander received us expansively but Guntram found no peace until we stood before the target at the standard distance. He did not score a single shot. For he was near-sighted as no one else I know. He bit his lips and grew terribly excited. This made his hand unsteady too, while I hit the bull's-eye because I could see and take proper aim. The commander was called away and Guntram sent his man for wine. He drank a few glasses and his hand began to tremble. With bulging eyes and distorted face he hurled his pistol to the grass, but then picked it up again, loaded it, loaded mine, too, and lost himself with me in the thicket of the park.

" 'At a clearing he raised one pistol and offered me the other. "I'm going to end it!" he shouted in despair. "I'm a blind man and the blind are no good for battle, and if I am no good for battle, I don't want to live! You will accompany me. You, too, are no use in life, although your marksmanship is to be envied, for you are the biggest idiot, the butt of the whole world!" "And God?" I asked. "A fine God," he sneered, shaking his fist at heaven, "who gave me the love of battle and blindness, and you a body without a mind." We wrestled, I disarmed him and he plunged into the bushes.

" 'Since that day I have been unhappy, for Guntram spoke aloud what I knew but concealed from myself as best I could. I always kept hearing the word idiot whispered behind me, in the street as well as in school, and my ears strained to hear the gruesome word. It may also be that my schoolmates, about whom I have no other complaint to make, call me this for short when I am beyond earshot. Even the woman who sells rolls in front of the college, Lisette with the sly wrinkles, tries to cheat me, often very crudely, and thinks she has a right to do so because she hears me called an idiot. And yet on the outer wall of the college hangs God the Savior, who came into the world to teach justice toward all and gentleness to the weak.' He was silent and seemed to be thinking.

"Then he continued, 'I don't want to present myself, M. Fagon, as better than I am. I, too, have my bad hours. But I would not distribute sunshine and shadow unjustly in any game, and how can God, in the contest of life, hang lead weights on an individual and then say to him: "There is the goal, run with the others." Often, M. Fagon, I have clasped my hands before falling asleep and fervently prayed to the good Lord to allow what I had just learned with great pain to grow and be strengthened in my head during sleep, a thing which is after all granted to others by Nature. Then I wake up and have forgotten everything and the sun terrifies me.

" 'Perhaps,' he whispered nervously, 'I am doing God an injustice. He would like to help, kind as He is, but I don't suppose He always has the power to do so. Isn't that possible, M. Fagon? When things got to be too bad, my mother visited me in a dream and said to me: "Stick it out, Julien! Everything will turn out well yet!" ' '

"These incredibly naïve statements and childish contradictions forced a smile to my face; it may even have been a grin. The boy was frightened of himself and of me. Then, as if he had already talked too much, he said, not without some bitterness, for his confidence had once more left him in the course of his narrative: 'Now everyone knows that I'm stupid, even the King, and I would so much have liked to conceal it from him'—Julien may have been referring to that Marly—'everyone except only my father, who refused to believe it.'

"'My son,' I said, putting my hand on his slender shoulder, 'I am not philosophizing with you; but if you will believe me, I will carry you through the waves. Just as you are, I will bring you into port. True, you will not lead an army or navy, in spite of your fine name, but neither will you lose a battle irresponsibly to the detriment of your King and country. Your name will not stand in our annals like your father's, but it will be inscribed in the book of the just, for you know the first beatitude: that the Kingdom of Heaven belongs to the poor in spirit.

"'Mark this. The first point is: you will go into battle and fight in our ranks for the King and for France, which is now so sorely threatened. In the rain of bullets you will learn whether you have a right to live. I will see to it that you get there soon. You will stay or return home with the self-confidence of a good man. Without self-confidence there is no man! No one will lightly make fun of you to your face. Then you will become a simple servant of your King and fulfill your duty most rigorously, as it is in you to do. You possess honor and loyalty, and His Majesty needs these qualities. Among those who surround him, there is no surplus of them. The King's stables, the hunt or the guards, some service which you are able to perform will be found for you. In place of your own merit your birth will favor you over others; this should make you humble. His Majesty, when he is tired from his labors in council, likes to direct a few natural words to a taciturn and absolutely loyal subject. You are too simple to take part in an intrigue; to offset that, you will never be destroyed by an intrigue. The world being what it is, they will sneer and mock behind your back, but you will not turn around. You will be kind and just to your servants and never finish a day without a good deed. For the rest, you must renounce!'

"The boy looked at me with faith in his eyes. 'Those are words from the gospel,' he said.

"'Does not everyone have to renounce,' I jested, 'even your patroness, Madame de Maintenon, even the King — some piece of jewelry or a province? Haven't I, Fagon, also renounced, perhaps more bitterly than you, though in my own way? An orphan, poor, with a wretched body, which became more crippled and bent from day to day at the very age you are now, did I not choose a strict muse: Science? Do you think I had no heart, no senses? A tender little heart, Julien! — and I renounced once and for all the greatest charm of existence: love, which is a natural gift to you with your slender figure and your empty fair head!' " Fagon was declaiming what had perhaps been a heavy burden to him in his youth, with such comical, exaggerated feeling that it amused the King and flattered the marquise.

"I accompanied Julien to the gate and teased him about Mirabelle. 'That was fast work,' I said. 'It just happened,' he replied unselfconsciously. 'They tormented her in spirit, she was crying, so I gained confidence. Besides, she resembles my mother.'

"Warbling an aria from some extinct opera of my youth, the only one I know, I returned to my bench before the orange grove. He must go to the battlefield at once, I said to myself. I was near the point of proposing to him that he saddle one of my horses right then and there and race out to the border to join the Army; but this bold disobedience would not have suited the boy. Besides, it was known that, for the present, the marshal was merely making the boundaries secure and getting the fortifications in Flanders ready. He would return to Versailles before a decisive battle was fought and receive Your Majesty's final orders. I would catch him then.

"I again opened the portfolio, which had been left lying there, put the contents in order, and behold! the Pentheus with the gruesome wall of rock lay on top, although I could have sworn I had slipped it in the middle of the pile of sheets. . .

"A little later it happened that Mouton the poodle, seeking his master in a crowd on the rue Saint Honoré, was run over by a cart. He sleeps in your garden, Majesty, where Mouton the man buried him under a catalpa and cut into the bark of the tree with his pocket knife: II Moutons.

"And in fact he was soon lying beside his poodle. It was time. Drink had undermined his constitution and his mind began to wander. I observed him occasionally from the window of my library as he sat in his room before his easel and not only chatted out loud with the ghost of his poodle but yawned like a dog or snapped his mouth open for flies, altogether in the manner of his deceased friend. A dropsy dragged him down. Things moved swiftly, and one day, when I stepped up to his couch with a spoonful of medicine in my hand, he turned his back on his benefactor and his face to the wall with an unmentionable word and was finished.

"It happened further that the marshal returned home to Versailles from the battlefield. Since his stay could not be a long one, I seized the opportunity. I was determined to approach him with Julien beside me and tell him the whole truth.

"I drove to the Jesuits. Near the main gate the marshal's spirited four horses, barely held in check by the servants, were waiting for Julien, to bring the boy to Versailles at once. The gate of the Jesuit house opened and Julien came staggering out, in what a condition! His head drooping, his back doubled over, his whole figure bent on unsteady legs, his eyes dead, while the eyes of Victor Argenson, who was leading his friend, were flaming torches. The amazed servants in their rich liveries were assiduous in lifting their young master into the carriage swiftly but carefully. I jumped out of mine, thinking that the boy had been stricken by some vicious disease.

"'For Heaven's sake, Julien!' I cried, 'what's wrong with you?' No answer. The boy stared at me with a vacant look in his eyes. I don't know whether he recognized me. I realized that the normally uncommunicative boy would not talk to me now, and since the groom was urging us: 'Inside, sir, or back!' for the impatient horses were rearing up, I let the child go, promising myself that I would soon follow him to Versailles. A crowd had already formed around the exciting scene in front of the Jesuit house; I sought to escape its curiosity and, catching sight of Victor, who, with a passionate gesture, called after the playmate who was being carried away in the storm: 'Courage, Julien! I shall avenge you!' I thrust the boy before me into my carriage and got in after him. 'Where to, sir?' my coachman asked. Before I replied, the alert boy cried: 'To the cloister Faubourg Saint-Antoine!'

"As you know, sire, your ideal minister of police has set up a quiet corner in the above-named cloister, where he is not overrun and can care in secret for the public security of Paris. 'Victor,' I asked above the noise of the wheels, 'what's wrong? What has happened?'

"'A monstrous injustice!' the boy raged. 'Father Tellier, the wolf, has chastised Julien with a strap, and he's innocent. I am the instigator! I am the culprit. But I will get justice for Julien, I will challenge the father to pistols!' This absurdity, together with Victor's confession that he was responsible for the calamity, angered me so much that I gave him a juicy slap on the ear. 'Very good!' he said. 'Coachman, you're crawling like a snail!' He gave the coachman his full purse, 'Fast! Use your whip! Race on! M. Fagon, you may be certain that father will get justice for Julien. Oh, he knows the Jesuits, these rogues, these scoundrels, and their dirty linen. But they are afraid of him as of the devil!' I did not find it necessary to question the raving boy any further, as he would of course lay his confession before his father, and the flying horses were already pounding the bad pavement of the suburb with their hooves so that the sparks were flying. We had reached our destination and were admitted at once.

"Argenson was leafing through a pile of documents. 'We are disturbing you, Argenson,' I excused myself.

" 'No, no, Fagon,' he replied, shaking my hand and moving a chair forward for me. 'What is wrong with the boy? Why, he's glowing like a stove.' 'Father—' 'Shut your mouth! M. Fagon is talking.'

" 'Argenson,' I began, 'a serious accident, perhaps a great misfortune has occurred. Julien Boufflers'—I looked at the minister questioningly—'I know about the poor boy,' he said—'was thrashed in the Jesuits' school and the boy went to Versailles in a state which, if I observed rightly, is the beginning of a dangerous illness. Victor knows all about it.'

" 'Describe what happened!' the father ordered. 'Clearly, calmly, in detail. Even the smallest point is important. And don't lie!'

" 'Lie?' cried the indignant boy. 'Am I going to lie when the truth alone can help? Those rogues, the Jesuits—'

" 'The facts!' the minister commanded with a Rhadamanthine look on his face. Victor pulled himself together and narrated with astonishing clarity.

" 'It was before Father Amiel's rhetoric class and we were putting our heads together to plan what joke we would play on the nosy one. "Something new!" came from all sides. "Something we haven't tried yet! A new invention!" Then it occurred to us—'

" 'Then it occurred to me—' his father corrected him.

" '—to me, to ask Julien, who draws so well, to draw something on the blackboard for us in chalk. I put my arm about his neck as he was sitting on his bench bent over his books, learning his lesson—he learns with such unbelievable difficulty. "Draw something for us," I coaxed him, "a rhinoceros." He shook his head. "I see," he said, "you merely want to annoy the good father by it and I will not take part in that. It's cruel. I will not draw a nose for you."

"'"But a beak, a barn owl, you draw such funny owls."

"'"Not a beak either, Victor."

"'So I thought for a bit and had an idea.' The minister wrinkled his pitch-black eyebrows. Victor continued with the courage of despair: '"Draw a little bee for us, Julien," I said, "you can do it so beautifully." "Why not?" he replied obligingly, and he drew a cute little bee on the blackboard with meticulous lines.

"'"Write something for it."

"'"All right, if you wish," he said, and wrote in chalk: *abeille*.

"'"Oh, you have no imagination at all, Julien. That sounds so dry."

"'"Well then, what should I write, Victor?

"'"At least write: little honey beast, *bête à miel*."

"The minister at once understood the silly pun: *bête à miel* and *bête Amiel*. 'Here's something for that idea!' he exclaimed indignantly and gave the inventor of the pun a slap on the ear, compared to which mine had been a caress.

"'Very good!' said the boy, whose ear was bleeding.

"'Go on, and make it short!' the father commanded. 'I want to get you out of my sight.'

"'—At this moment Father Amiel came in, walked up and down, peered at the blackboard, understood, but acted as if he did not understand, the rogue. But: "Bête Amiel! Stupid Amiel!" came first from a single boy, then from several benches, then from the whole class, "Bête Amiel! Stupid Amiel!"

"'Then—oh horror!—the door was pulled open. It was the raging wolf, Father Tellier. He had been spying in the corridors and now showed his devilish, ugly face.

"'"Who drew that?"

"'"I," answered Julien in a firm voice. He had put his hands over his ears as he continued to study his lesson and understood nothing of what was going on, as, you know, he finds it so hard to grasp anything.

"'"Who wrote that?"

"'"I did," said Julian.

"'The wolf took a leap toward him, yanked the astonished boy up, pressed him to his body, seized a book strap and—' Words failed the boy.

"'And you were silent, you wretched coward?' the minister thundered at him. 'I despise you! You're a scoundrel!'

"'I was screaming like a man who is being murdered,' the boy cried. '"I was the one! I! I!" Father Amiel, too, clung to the wolf, asserting Julien's innocence. He heard it, all right, the wolf. But he did not hurt a hair on my head, because I am your son and the Jesuits fear and respect you. But they hate the marshal and are not afraid of him. So Julien had to pay for it. But I'll put my knife' — the boy reached into his pocket — 'between the ribs of that wolf if he does not —'

"The stern father seized him by the collar, dragged him to the door, opened it, threw him out and pulled the bolt. The very next moment fists were hammering against the door and the boy was screaming: 'I'm going along to Father Tellier! I'll appear as a witness and say to him: "You're a monster."'

"'Basically, Fagon' — the minister turned to me coldbloodedly, paying no attention to the pounding — 'the boy is right: we two will seek out the father without delay, attack him with the naked truth, spread it out on the table before him and compel him to go with us to Julien, this very day, at once, and apologize to the maltreated boy in our presence.' He looked at a mantel clock. 'Half past eleven. Father Tellier adheres to his peasant hours. He has lunch at twelve sharp on black bread and cheese. We'll find him.'

"Argenson took me along with him. We got into the carriage and rolled away.

"'I know the boy,' the minister repeated. "There's only one thing about his story that is not clear to me. It is a fact that the fathers began by coddling him and wrapping him in cotton. His schoolmates, including my rascal, have talked about it often. I can understand that the fathers, being what they are, have hated the child ever since the marshal had the misfortune to unmask them. But I cannot understand why they, to whom the marshal must be a thing of indifference, found any advantage in favoring the boy at first, beyond the indulgence which is due to the weak.'

"'Hm,' I said.

"'And I must know just that, Fagon.'

"'Well then, Argenson,' I began my confession — I must make it to you too, Majesty, for I have offended you most — 'I wanted to make a warm bed for Julien with the fathers at any price, and knew of no

effective recommendation for him. —But people gossip at times—
and so I told Fathers Rapin and Bouhours, whom I met at a ladies'
party, that Julien's mother had been pleasant company for your Majesty. The pure truth. Not a word beyond this, upon my honor,
Argenson!' He made a wry face.

"Your Majesty is showing me a dark and ungracious countenance.
But, sire, am I to blame if the imagination of the Jesuit fathers
changes the purest thing into an ambiguity?

" 'Then,' I continued, 'when they began to hate the marshal and to
take an interest in him, they spied and searched in their way but
learned nothing except that Julien's mother was the purest creature
on the earth before she became the angel who now smiles down on it.
Unfortunately the fathers arrived at the conviction of their error just
as the time when the boy had most need of it.' Argenson nodded."

"Fagon," the King said almost sternly, "that was your third and
greatest liberty. If you gambled so flippantly with my name and with
the reputation of a woman whom you worship, you might at least
have kept this offense from me, even if your story had become less
intelligible because of it. And tell me, Fagon: did you not act in
accordance with the infamous maxim that the end justifies the
means? Have you joined the Order?"

"We all have, a little, Your Majesty." Fagon smiled and continued:

"Halfway there we met Father Amiel, who was wandering about
like a derelict, and, recognizing my carriage, he made such desperate
gestures that I halted it. At the coach door he gave a demonstration
of his foolish rhetoric and was immediately surrounded by a circle of
street urchins laughing wildly. I told him to get in.

" 'May the Mother of God be thanked that I find you, M. Fagon.
An injury has been done to Julien, whose protector you are, and he is
as innocent as the shattered little Astyanax!' the big nose declaimed.
'If you had seen the strange look, M. Fagon, which the boy directed
toward his hangman, that look of horror and mortal anxiety!' Father
Amiel took a breath. 'If I were to flee beyond the seas, that look
would pursue me! If I buried myself in a dark tower, it would penetrate through the wall! If I were to crawl—'

" 'If only you do not crawl away now, Professor,' the minister inter-
rupted him, 'now, when we need face-to-face testimony for Father
Tellier—for we are now going to him, and you are coming with us.
Have you the courage?'

" 'Certainly, certainly!' Father Amiel asserted, but he grew visibly pale and began to shake in his soutane. Father Tellier is feared as a coarse and violent man even in his Order.

"When we got out at the Order house, giving Father Amiel precedence, Victor jumped down from the footboard, where he had made the journey with us standing upright beside the groom. 'I'm coming along,' he said defiantly. Argenson knitted his brows but permitted it, not averse to having a second witness.

"Father Tellier did not refuse to receive us. Argenson indicated that the father and the boy should remain behind in the waiting room. They obeyed, the former feeling relieved, the latter, displeased. The father rector lived in a meager, in fact wretched room, just as he wore a threadbare soutane, the same garment day and night. He received us with his back curved and a bogus smile on his uncouth, wild features. 'How may I serve you, gentlemen?' he asked with a sweet grin.

" 'Your Reverence,' Argenson replied, declining the proffered chair that was covered with dust and had one broken arm, 'a life is at stake. We must hurry if we are to save it. Today young Boufflers was punished at the college in error. In error. A sly scamp made the backward boy draw and write something on the blackboard which turned into a silly mockery of Father Amiel, without Julien Boufflers having the slightest inkling of how he was being exploited. It can easily be shown that he was the only one in his class who was against such pranks and prevented them as much as he could. If he had invented the questionable prank in his fair head, his punishment would undoubtedly have been deserved. As it is, it is a fearful injustice, which cannot be rectified quickly and fully enough. There is something more, something infinitely grave. The victim of the erroneous chastisement, a child in mind, has the soul of a man. You thought you were punishing a boy but you were manhandling a nobleman.'

" 'Oh, oh,' the father said in feigned astonishment, 'what is all this Your Excellency is saying? Can a simple matter be twisted in this way? I walk through the halls. That is my duty. I hear a noise in the rhetoric class. Father Amiel is a scholar who is an ornament to the Order, but he does not know how to win respect. Our fathers do not like to inflict corporal punishment, but this could not go on any longer, an example had to be made. I enter. There is an insult on the blackboard. I investigate the matter. Boufflers confesses. The rest was natural.

" 'Ungifted? backward? On the contrary, he's a sly one, a sneak. Still waters run deep. What he lacks is sincerity; he is a hypocrite and a dissembler. Did it hurt him? O what a tender skin! A pampered aristocrat, eh? I am sorry, we fathers of Jesus are no respecters of persons. Besides, the marhsal himself asked us not to spoil his child. I was older than he is when I received my last and best physical chastisement, in the seminary, forty strokes less one, like Saint Paul, who was also a nobleman. Did I go to pieces? I rubbed the spot, if you'll excuse my mentioning it, and I felt the better for it. And I was innocent, but no one will convince me of the innocence of this hardened fellow!'

" 'Perhaps we can, Your Reverence,' said Argenson, and summoned the two people who were waiting.

" 'Victor,' the Jesuit bleated at the entering boy, 'you did not do it. I'll vouch for you. You are a good-natured boy. You would be an idiot to declare yourself guilty when no one accuses you.'

"Victor, who was approaching him in a defiant stance, looked boldly into the monster's face, but his courage sank. His heart trembled before the increasing savagery of these features and the flashing wolf's eyes.

"He spoke swiftly. 'I induced Julien to do it, he didn't understand a thing about it,' he said, 'I shouted this into your ears but you would not hear, because you are a villain.'

" 'Enough!' Argenson commanded, and showed him the door. He went not unwillingly. He was beginning to feel afraid.

" 'Father Amiel.' The minister turned to the priest. 'On your word of honor, could Julien have made that pun?'

"The father hesitated, with a frightened look at the rector. 'Courage, Father,' I whispered, 'you are a man of honor.'

" 'Impossible, Your Excellency, if Achilles was not a coward and Thersites a hero,' Father Amiel asserted, gathering courage from his rhetoric, 'Julien is as innocent as the Savior.'

"The earth-colored face of the rector became distorted with rage. He was accustomed to blind obedience in the college and did not tolerate the slightest contradiction.

" 'Do you mean to criticize, Brother?' he foamed. 'Criticize first your mad grimaces, which make you the butt of the most stupid. I treated the boy justly.'

"This denigration of his rhetoric made the father lose complete control of himself and caused him to forget all fear for a moment.

'Justly?' he wailed. 'God help us. How often have I begged to consider the boy's backwardness and not to destroy him? Who replied to me: "As far as I'm concerned, he may croak!" who said this?'

"*'Mentiris impudenter!*' howled the wolf.

"*'Mentiris impudentissime, pater reverende!*' the long nose out-shouted him, trembling in every limb.

"'Out of my sight!' the rector commanded, pointing his finger at the door, and the little father ran as fast as he could.

"When the three of us were alone again, the minister spoke earnestly, 'Your Reverence, you have been reproached with hating the boy. A serious charge! Refute and dispel it by coming with us and making Julien an apology. No one will be present except the two of us.' He pointed to me. 'That will suffice. This gentleman is the King's personal physician and is gravely concerned about the boy's health. You grow pale? Calm yourself and reflect: He whose name you bear commands that you shall not let the sun go down over your anger, much less over an injustice.'

"To confess and atone for an injustice!" The Jesuit gnashed his teeth in fury.

"'What have I to do with the Nazarene?' he blasphemed, rearing up in wounded pride, and the ugly man seemed to grow toward the ceiling like a demon. 'I belong to the Church — no, to the Order.... And what have I to do with the boy? I do not hate him, but his father, who has slandered us, slandered us shamefully!'

"'Not the marshal,' I said in astonishment, 'but my laboratory — slandered the fathers.'

"'Forgery! Forgery!' the rector raged. 'Those letters were never written. A devilish deceiver substituted them!' And he cast a murderous look at me.

"I admit that I was confounded at this violence and power to destroy facts, to transform truth into lies and lies into truth.

"Father Tellier rubbed his brazen brow. Then he altered his expression and bowed before the minister, half abjectly, half mockingly: 'Your Excellency, I am your obedient servant, but you will understand that I cannot humiliate my Order to the extent of begging a boy's pardon.'

"Argenson changed his tone with no less skill. He stood beside Tellier with an imperceptible smile of contempt at the corners of his mouth. The father lent his ear.

" 'Are you certain,' the minister whispered, 'that you have chastised the marshal's son and not the noblest blood of France?'

"The father started. 'There's no truth in it,' he whispered back. 'You are fooling me, Argenson.'

" 'I have no certainty. In such matters there is none. But the mere possibility would — you know what I mean and what post you have been proposed for — make you impossible.'

"I thought, sire, I could see arrogance and ambition struggling on the sinister face of your father confessor, but I could not guess which would triumph.

" 'I believe I will accompany you, gentlemen,' said Father Tellier.

" 'Come, Father!' the minister urged him, and stretched out his hand toward him.

" 'But I must change my soutane. You see, this one has patches in it and I might meet His Majesty in Versailles.' He opened the door of an adjoining room.

"Argenson looked over his shoulder into a low, tiny room with a bare trestle couch and a worm-eaten shrine in it.

" 'By your leave, gentlemen,' the Jesuit whispered bashfully, 'I have never yet changed my clothes before worldly eyes.'

"Argenson took hold of his soutane. 'You will keep your word?'

"Father Tellier stretched out three dirty fingers against something sacred which hung in a dark corner and closed the door, which Argenson's foot kept open a crack.

"We heard the clothespress open and close. Two silent minutes went by. Then Argenson pushed the door open. Father Tellier was gone. Had he not believed Argenson's whispered remark and merely seized the opportunity of escaping from our presence? Or had he believed it, but the one demon of his Order had overcome the other: pride over ambition? Who can look into the abyss of that sinister soul?

" 'Perjurer!' the minister cursed, opened the shrine, saw a stairway and rushed down it. I stumbled and fell after him with my crutch. Down below, we stood before the highly astonished countenance of an aristocratic novice with the finest manners, who modestly replied to our question about the father that, as far as he knew, he had gone to Rouen on business a quarter of an hour ago.

"Argenson gave up the idea of pursuit. 'I could sooner drag Cerberus out of hell than this monster to Versailles. . . . Besides, where am I to find him in the hundred hideouts of the society? I'm going. Send for fresh horses, Fagon, and hurry to Versailles. Tell His Majesty everything. He will give his hand to Julien and say to him: "The King respects you, you have suffered too much," and for the boy the scourge will be removed. I agreed with him. That was the best plan, the only really helpful plan, if it was not already too late."

Fagon studied the King from under his ancient bushy eyebrows to see what impression had been made on him by the exposure of his confessor. Not that he flattered himself that Louis would revoke his choice. But he had wanted to warn the King against this enemy of mankind, who was to cast the shadow of his demon's wings over the end of a splendid reign. But Fagon read in the features of His Most Christian Majesty nothing but a natural sympathy for the lot suffered by the son of a woman who had been a passing fancy and pleasure in a narrative whose paths like those of a garden, met at the same central point: the King, always the King.

"Continue, Fagon," His Majesty requested, and Fagon obeyed, irritated and in a more acerbated mood.

"As the horses could not arrive before another quarter of an hour, I entered the house of a bather, a client of mine, who lived opposite the house of the Order and ordered a lukewarm bath, for I was exhausted. While the water was reviving my spirits I reproached myself most harshly for having neglected the boy who had been entrusted to me and for having postponed his liberation. After a while I was disturbed by an immoderate chatter coming through the thin wall. Two girls of the lower middle class were bathing nearby. 'I'm so unhappy!' the one chattered, and unfolded some stupid love tale, 'so unhappy!' A minute later they were giggling together. While I was accusing myself of negligence and bearing a hundredweight burden on my conscience, two fickle nymphs were dallying and splashing nearby.

"In Versailles—"

King Louis now turned to Dubois, the marquise's chamberlain, who had come in softly and whispered: "His Majesty's table is set." "You are disturbing us, Dubois," the King said, and the old servant withdrew with a slight expression of astonishment on his trained features, for the King was punctuality itself.

"In Versailles," Fagon repeated, "I found the marshal at dinner with a few of his peers. There was Villars, every inch a braggart, an *héros*, as people say—an opinion I do not contradict—and the most

shameless beggar, as Your Majesty knows; there was Villeroi, the
loser of battles, the most insignificant of mortals, who lives from the
refuse of your grace, with his indestructible conceit and his grandiose
manners; Gramont, with the distinguished head, who cheated me
yesterday in your salon, Your Majesty, at your gaming table, with
marked cards; and Lauzun, a thoroughly embittered and malicious
man beneath his gentle mien. Pardon me, I saw your courtiers in a
distorted light in the harsh illumination of my anguished heart. The
Countess Mimeure was invited, too, and Mirabelle, seated near
Villeroi, who was frightening the child with his antics of a seventy-
year-old fop.

"Julien had been ordered to the table by his father and sat there
pale as death. I saw that he was shaken by chills and I looked at the
victim steadily with deep dread.

"The conversation — are there accelerating demons who stormily
lift up those who rise and kick the falling into the depths with their
cruel feet? — the conversation was about disciplinary punishment in
the army. Opinions differed. It was debated whether there should be
corporal punishment at all and, if so, with what object it should be
administered: with a cane, strap or the flat of a blade. The marshal,
a humane man, opposed all corporal punishment except in misde-
meanors that were absolutely dishonorable, and Gramont, the cheat
at cards, agreed with him, since honor, as Boileau said, is an island
with jagged shores which, once they have been left, cannot be
climbed again. Villars, if I may say so, behaved as if he were half
mad and told how one of his grenadiers who had been flogged, probably unjustly, had put a bullet through himself and he — Marshal Villars — had inserted into the order of the day: Lafleur had possessed
honor in his own fashion. The conversation became involved. The
boy followed it with dazed eyes. 'Blows,' 'honor,' 'honor,' 'blows,' he
heard from this direction and that. I whispered into the marshal's
ear: 'Julien is ill, he should go to bed.' 'Julien must not pamper himself,' he replied. 'The boy will pull himself together. And dinner will
be over in a moment.' Now the gallant Villeroi turned to his shy
neighbor. 'Young lady,' he said through his nose in his stilted way,
'speak and we shall hear an oracle.' Mirabelle, already sitting on fiery
coals and moreover frightened by Julien's wretched appearance,
naturally fell into her customary manner and replied: 'No subject of
the proudest of kings wil endure corporal punishment; a person so

branded will not continue to live.' Villeroi applauded and kissed the nail of her little finger. I got up, took hold of Julien and dragged him away. This departure passed almost unnoticed. Perhaps the marshal excused it before his guests.

"While I was undressing the boy—he was no longer able to do so himself—he said: 'M. Fagon, I feel very strange. My mind is confused. I see figures. I suppose I'm ill. If I should die—' He smiled. 'Do you know, M. Fagon, what happened today in the Jesuit house? Don't let my father know about it! Never! Never! It would kill him!' I promised him and kept my word, although it was an effort for me. Even now, the marshal has no inkling of it.

"His head already on the pillows, Julien gave me his feverish hand. 'I thank you, M. Fagon . . . for everything . . . I am not ungrateful, like Mouton.'

"To bother Your Majesty now was useless. Before another quarter of an hour had passed, Julien was delirious. The trial and the sentence lay in the hands of nature. The fever became violent, his pulse raced. I had a field bed set up for myself in the spacious bedroom and remained at my post. The marshal had had his papers and maps carried into the adjoining room. He left his desk every hour to visit the boy, who no longer recognized him. I cast hostile looks at him. 'Fagon, what have you against me?' he asked. I simply did not want to answer.

"The boy talked much in his fever but in the sphere of his inflamed vision there hovered only friendly figures and such as had already passed beyond life. Mouton appeared, and Mouton the poodle, too, jumped on his bed. On the third day his mother sat beside him.

"He received three visits. Victor scratched on the door and, when I admitted him, he broke out into such an agonized lamentation that I had to hustle him away. Then Mirabelle's finger tapped. She came to Julien, who was lying in a restless half-sleep just then, and observed him. She wept little but pressed a passionate kiss on his dry lips. Julien was conscious neither of his friend nor of his beloved.

"Unexpectedly Father Amiel came, too, and I did not refuse him admittance. Since the sick boy looked at him with unseeing eyes, he hopped about the bed comically and cried: 'Don't you know me any more, Julien, your Father Amiel, your little Amiel, your nosy Amiel? Just tell me in one little word that you love me.' The boy remained indifferent. If there are Elysian Fields, I believe I shall find the father there, without his long hat, with a well-proportioned nose, and I will walk with him, hand in hand, through the heavenly gardens.

"On the fourth evening Julien's pulse was racing. Meningitis could develop at any moment. I went over to the marshal's room.

" 'How are things?'

" 'Bad.'

" 'Will Julien live?'

" 'No. His brain is exhausted. The boy has overworked himself.'

" 'I'm astonished at that,' the marshal said. 'I didn't know it.' I really believe he did not know it. My patience was at an end. I told him the truth without sparing him, and reproached him with having neglected his child and contributed to his death. I said nothing about the Golgotha he had suffered at the hands of the Jesuits. The marshal listened to me silently, his head slightly bowed to the right, as is his way. His eyelashes trembled and I saw a tear. Finally he recognized his injustice. He controlled himself with the self-control of the warrior and went into the sickroom.

"The father sat down beside the boy, who was now afflicted by horrible dreams. 'I will at least,' the marshal murmured, 'make his death easier for him, as much as I can. Julien,' he said in his precise way. The boy recognized him.

" 'Julien, you will simply have to make a sacrifice and interrupt your studies for my sake. We are going off to the army together. The King has suffered losses on the border and even the youngest must now do their duty.' This speech doubled the dying boy's desire for travel . . . purchase of horses . . . departure . . . arrival in the camp . . . entrance into the line of battle. . . . His eyes shone, but in his chest the death rattle began. 'The death agony,' I whispered to the marshal.

" 'There is the English flag! Capture it!' his father commanded. The dying boy put his hand out into the air. '*Vive le roi!*' he cried, and sank back as though pierced by a bullet."

Fagon had finished and got up. The marquise was moved. "Poor child," the King sighed and stood up too.

"Why poor," asked Fagon serenely, "since he passed away like a hero?"

Theodor Fontane

1819—1898

Fontane came from a line of French Huguenots. His father was an apothecary in Neuruppin, Prussia; an urbane, witty, sociable, and somewhat irresponsible man, he transmitted his more admirable traits to his eldest son, whose early education he personally supervised. The son followed his father's profession, serving his pharmaceutical apprenticeship in various cities, forming friendships, joining literary and political clubs, publishing poems and works of travel, living from journalism. He was actively associated with the liberal political writers of the pre-1848 years (*Vormärz*) and his sympathies were with the rebels in the Revolution of 1848; he even fought briefly on the barricades in Berlin. After the failure of the revolution he took a position in the Prussian Ministry of the Interior. He married a girl of Huguenot descent. In the fifties he lived in England, officially attached to the German embassy as press agent to the ambassador, but acting also as foreign correspondent for various German newspapers, both conservative and liberal. This journalistic activity was continued after his return to Berlin in 1859. It allowed him time to explore Brandenburg and to fix his impressions in *Wanderungen durch die Mark Brandenburg* (*Wanderings Through Brandenburg*, 1862-82), a miscellany of geographical, historical, and social notes and sketches of people and places. He acted as war correspondent during the Prussian campaigns of 1864, 1866 and 1870-71; during the latter war he was taken prisoner by the French because he was suspected of being a German spy. The experience as war correspondent was exploited in his technically expert accounts of these wars.

From 1870 until his retirement in 1889 he was drama critic for the liberal *Vossische Zeitung*. For a few months during 1876 he acted as secretary of the Academy of Arts in Berlin, but the internecine fight-

ing disgusted him and he resigned. Two years later, at the age of
sixty, he published his first novel *Vor dem Sturm* (*Before the Storm*).
This was followed by a series of novels and novellas on which his fame
as a writer rests. It is an astounding phenomenon that a man of his
age should produce a body of fiction of the greatest distinction,
which has won him a place in the front rank of European novelists.

Fontane's intellectual development was from romanticism to realism, aptly symbolized by his movement from ballads and balladlike
novellas, which breathe piety toward the Prussian past and Prussian
ideals, to his later novels, which, for all their objectivity and detachment, are unmistakably the work of a liberal mind. He kept growing
younger, wrote Thomas Mann in a brilliant essay; indeed, his late
letters, his critical essays and his fiction show him to have been in the
vanguard of progressive ideas represented by the young generation of
writers. He combined serentiy — *heiteres Darüberstehen* ("standing
serenely above it all") he called it — with strong convictions, and these
were not favorable to the establishment. While he recognized certain
virtues in the Prussian aristocracy, he condemned them as a class because he found them unable to meet the demands of modern society.
They continued to live in an unreal world, lacking the education and
the will to play a leading role in government and society. Nor did
they any longer possess the economic power they had once had by virtue of the land they owned. Money, the modern key to power, had
passed to the middle class, which had that confidence in its own
future that the aristocracy had once possessed. Specifically, Fontane
condemned the Prussian nobility for their materialism, their arrogance and conservative intransigence, their antiquated and purely
external code of honor. They had lost their nerve but did not know
it; so they blustered and bullied to convince themselves that they
were still in control of things. But the more intelligent among them
were objective enough to realize the ineffectiveness of their social
class, only they lacked the heroic fiber to do anything about it.

After 1870, in the so-called "foundation years" (*Gründerjahre*),
which witnessed Germany's rapid rise to power and wealth, Fontane's
pessimism extended to embrace the whole of German society. He was
in good company, of course; many of Germany's finest spirits were
sorely troubled by the *Zeitgeist*. The materialism of the middle class,
their mad chase after luxury and status, disgusted him. He saw a decline in general culture through the century; industrial society had

been unable to create a culture of its own to replace that of the Enlightenment and the age of Goethe. He felt more sympathy for the
working class and for the social democracy that was the ideal of its
leaders. He believed that the proletariat was at least more genuine,
more sincere than the other social classes. But he was not one to flatter the dispossessed merely because they were impoverished and exploited. Realist that he was, he was convinced of the influence that
heredity and environment exercised on character. He saw life too
clearly to idealize even the class on which he staked the future of
society. He was an old man; serene, yes, but unhappy with what he
saw about him.

He had his share of contradictions, like so many great minds. He
once wrote in a theater critique that he could just as well have said
the opposite of what he actually had written. This was true of his
political and social positions as well. He was a combination of conservative and revolutionary, of romantic and realist. And so he was
ready to praise where he could; he hailed the new generation of
young writers, who condemned established society.

More than any other German writer of fiction of the nineteenth
century Fontane can stand in the company of the great European
masters. As a realist, he tended to depict man as a social animal,
largely determined by his environment, unable to break away from
the culture that had nurtured him. He showed the practical effects of
the great intellectual upheaval that had been occurring in nine-
teenth-century society, arising from the advance of science, the
growth of liberal and democratic thought, the industrialization of
economic life and the involvement of literature with these extra-
literary matters.

But Fontane's novels are not heavy with erudition, he writes with a
wonderfully light touch. Fontane characterized himself as a *causeur*;
it is an apt description of his particular artistic strength. He is unsur-
passed in composing natural dialogue, in conveying the impression of
lifelike conversation at all social levels. An example is the conversations between young Count Haldern and his uncle (chapter 12), the
baron (chapter 11), and Stine (chapters 8, 14). Of course, people do
not really talk like that; but one feels that they do. The dialogue is so
natural, so right, that it creates that perfect illusion that is the hall-
mark of great art. And in these marvellously natural dialogues Fontane detonates his intellectual blockbusters on the effete state of the

Prussian nobility, on the corruption of the bourgeoisie, on the degraded position of woman in our society, on the general hypocrisy rampant in Western civilization. Thomas Mann, an ardent admirer of Fontane, rightly singles out the quality of mellow wisdom that emanates from his pages. Fontane is for him the "classical old man" who brings before us the virtues of gentleness, kindness, justice, humor and deep wisdom, in a chatty, effortless manner.

Fontane is a master of irony, in the double sense in which Mann uses the term: as a literary device for recording understatement or of saying the opposite of what one means; and as a philosophical position of detachment, neutrality, relativism. Irony implies self-criticism, mental flexibility, humor, a readiness to see the other side of a problem or situation and to switch attitudes in the light of deeper insight. These qualities Fontane's work possesses to an eminent degree.

Stine (short for Ernestine) was begun in 1881, then put aside for some years, while Fontane wrote and published several major novels, including *Cécile* (1887) and *Irrungen Wirrungen* (*Errors and Confusions*, 1888), which deal with a related theme and form a triptych with *Stine*. The novella was completed in 1888 and offered to a number of literary journals and to the *Vossische Zeitung*. It was rejected by all of them because of the unfavorable reception that had been given to the "immoral," "lewd" novel *Errors and Confusions*. The Czech writer and scholar Fritz Mauthner published it in the journal *Deutschland* in 1890; it appeared in book form in that same year. The fears felt for its reception proved to be unfounded; perhaps the initial shock of *Errors and Confusions* had immunized, even educated the public. The novella received some warm reviews by important critics and went into a second printing before the year was out.

"Realistic romanticism" was the term one friendly critic used. The phrase was pejorative and Fontane accepted it as justified. He was ready to concede too much. The realists were, of course, the enemies of romance, as we saw in Gottfried Keller's *Clothes Make the Man*. When a realist did treat romanticism seriously, as Flaubert in *Madame Bovary*, it was to demonstrate that it led to disaster. In *Errors and Confusions* the aristocrat Botho floats on the magic carpet of romance with the seamstress Lene, without paying much heed to the consequences; but when a decision has to be made, he remains loyal to the traditions of class and marries an aristocratic girl whom he regards as in every way inferior to the seamstress. But the lower class girl, brought up in the school of hard knocks, is the stronger character of the two. While she too enjoys the liaison, she is clear-headed enough to realize that this experience can only be momentary in this society, and marries a man of her own class, who has none of the romantic charm of her aristocratic lover. But the romance between young Count Haldern and Stine is a very different kind of relationship. This is a serious love that is ready to break down all social barriers, at least on his part; for the count is prepared to leave the old world with its narrow social prejudices and begin life anew in egalitarian America. And Stine is carried away by romantic longing as deep and as naïve as his. Has Fontane then reverted to roman-ticism and written another *Werther*? Not really; he has merely re-jected the conventional wisdom of the realistic tradition, that the upper classes think only of their respability reputation and the masses only of food, sex and circuses. It is the business of realism to treat romance realistically, not to deny its very existence or its power over young people. What Fontane wanted to show was the contrast be-tween establishment thinking and that of uncorrupted youth. For this he needed a young couple who were still capable of feeling romantically, of being swept off their feet by sentiment. He sur-rounded the lovers with other characters who represent the ethical and social standards or prejudices of society: the widow Pittelkow and the actress Wanda; the two old aristocratic roués; the stiff, re-spectable, hypocritical Halderns; and the priceless Polzins, a sort of proletarian Greek chorus. The plot concocted by Pauline and the old count to get Stine out of the way is really unnecessary; for Stine, like Lene, knows how impossible such an alliance would be. The only in-corrigible romantic is young Count Haldern, and Fontane has moti-vated his behavior by making him a sick and hopelessly lonely man. There are physiological reasons why he cannot make the same renun-ciation as Botho. But Stine? Critics have asserted that the last sen-tences of the novella indicate that she will follow the count in death. But this is by no means certain; it is not in the spirit of Fontane. It is quite possible that she will recover, cherish the memory of this romantic episode in her young life, but marry a worker or petty shop-keeper—the locksmith's nephew, perhaps—and bear him children, to whom she will give the same sound advice that her dying mother gave to her.

It is surely significant that the novella is entitled *Stine* and that it

ends with Stine. Fontane seems to underscore that she is the main
character, despite the disparaging remarks he made about her. She
is, indeed, an exceptional girl, who resists her environment and the
temptation of her social class to snatch at happiness at any price.
(We can't afford the luxury of morality, says the widow Pittelkow,
anticipating Doolittle the dustman in Bernard Shaw's *Pygmalion*.)
For she recognizes that this happiness would ruin the man she loves
and might turn into a disaster for her too. So much insight is more
than intelligence, it is character. Stine's realism is of a higher order
than Pauline's. She is the stronger character of the two. Significantly
Fontane made her speak High German with impeccable grammar.
He wished to underline her special quality.

Stine

Chapter 1

Everything was normal in the Invalidenstrasse: the horsecars clanged their bells and the machine-shop workers went to their dinner, and anyone who insisted on finding something remarkable in the scene would have discovered nothing except that in No. 98e on the second floor the windows were being cleaned with a sort of flourish, in spite of the fact that it was neither Easter nor Pentecost and not even Saturday.

It is hard to believe but this remarkable fact was really noticed, and old Frau Lierschen, who lived directly across on the corner of Scharnhorststrasse, grumbled to herself: "I don't know what that Pittelkow is thinking of. But she don't care about nothing. And as for her sister Stine, with her little room upstairs at the Polzins and her separate key so that nobody'll notice nothing, well, she's getting to be just like her. It's bad enough. But it's the fault of that Pittelkow. The way she's standing there again, slaving and drudging away! If it was at least at night, but in the bright sunny noon hour, when the men from Borsig and Schwarzkoppen is just walking down the street. Makes you think she wants all the menfolk to look up at her; a disgrace and a sin."

So Frau Lierschen grumbled to herself and, however unfriendly her reflections were, they were not wholly unfounded; for up there on the windowsill, with her skirts tucked up knee high, stood a beautiful, black-haired woman with a coquettish and elaborately marcelled coiffure, washing and rubbing the windowpanes on one side with a chamois cloth which she held in her hand, while her left arm was placed over the other crosspiece for better support. Occasionally she granted herself a pause in her work and looked down on the street below where, beyond the car tracks, a three-wheeled, almost elegant baby's pram stood in the harsh midday sun. The apparently very unruly child who was sitting in the pram was dressed in aristocratic white lace; it was attended by a ten-year-old girl who, after all her begging and persuading had proved useless, gave the squalling brat a vigorous slap. But at the same moment the ten-year-old girl who had dared to administer this disciplinary measure peered up fearfully to the window and, sure enough, it had all been noticed upstairs, and the beautiful, dark-haired person, who regarded "slapping and educating" as her prerogative, waved her chamois cloth threateningly at the girl she had caught in the act of exceeding her authority. An angry verbal outburst seemed about to follow, in spite of the great distance; but a mailman of their acquaintance was just coming up the street, waving a letter to indicate that he was bringing news. She got the message, stepped from the window ledge onto a chair, and vanished in the background of the room, to receive the letter in the hall. A minute later she returned to the window and sat down in the light to read in greater comfort. But what she read seemed to afford her more annoyance than joy, for her brows knitted in vexation and, opening her mouth, she said with a sneer: "Disgusting old man! Always messing things up." But she was not one to take anything unduly to heart and so, still holding the letter in her hand, she leaned far over the window railing and shouted across the street in that hoarse alto voice that is characteristic of the lower classes in our capital, though scarcely to their advantage: "Olga!"

"What do you want, ma?"

"'What do you want, ma!' You dumb brat. When I call you, you come. See?"

A lorry, loaded with an old steam boiler, which rumbled past the house, roaring and shaking, prevented the immediate execution of the command; but scarcely had the wagon rolled by, when Olga took hold of the handle of the pram and crossed the road, making straight for the house and into the entrance hall with a push. She took the child out and, leaving the baby carriage below for the time being, went upstairs to her mother's apartment.

The mother had meanwhile calmed down, the lines on her forehead had smoothed out and, taking Olga by the hand, she said in that excessively confidential tone that ordinary folk seem to use in dealing with the most intimate matters: "Olga, the old man's coming again tonight. He always comes when it ain't suitable. Just like he wanted to annoy me. Yeah, that's how he is. Well, it can't be helped and thank God he don't come before eight. And now you go to Wanda and tell her . . . Nah, skip it . . . You can't give her the message; it's too long. It's better if I give you a note."

And with these words she walked from the door where this conversation had taken place to an exceedingly elegant (far too elegant for this house and this apartment) rococo secretary, on which lay an even more surprising pressed leather writing kit. In this stationery kit the woman, her skirts still tucked up to her knees, began to hunt for a sheet of stationery, at first calmly; but when, after going through the red blotting sheets three times, she had still found nothing, her irritation erupted again, and as usual turned against Olga: "You've taken it again to cut dolls out of."

"No, ma, honest and true, no; I can swear, ma."

"Ah, go away with your everlasting swearing. Don't you have none at all?"

"I got my notebook."

And Olga ran as fast as she could to the adjacent back room and returned with a blue notebook. Without saying a word her mother tore out the last sheet, at the head of which was a line of *ch*'s in Olga's hand, and scribbled a note with relative speed, folded the sheet in two, and sealed it with a piece of gummed selvage from a sheet of postage stamps (she always saved these, remarking: "Better than English tape"). "There, Olga dear. Now go to Wanda and give her this. And if she ain't there, give it to old Schlichting. But not to his wife and not to Flora neither, she always pokes her nose in and don't need to know everything. And when you come back, you'll go to Bolzanis and order a cake."

"What kind?" asked Olga, her face suddenly lighting up.

"Orange . . . And you'll pay for it. And when you've paid, you'll say he's not to put nothing on it, nor orange slices neither, which is after all only skin and pits . . . And now go, Olga darling, and make it fast and when you're back again you can get six pennies worth of barley candy for yourself at Marzahn's."

Chapter 2

Olga wasted no time but went into the back room to fetch her red
and black checkered shawl which, together with a somewhat tattered
hat with ribbons to tie under the chin, was her usual street attire.

But the widow Pittelkow, after placing the child, still howling, into
a very luxuriously appointed canopy crib and sticking a bottle with a
pacifier in its mouth, personally walked up a flight of stairs to the
Polzin apartment, where her sister Stine had a furnished room.

The Polzins were comfortably off, had no need to rent out a room;
but they rented everything, or as much as they could, out of sheer
greed, so that they themselves could live rent free, or as Frau Polzin
expressed it, "squat for free." Polzin proclaimed himself a "carpet
manufacturer" (though to be sure of the lowest grade) and limited
his production to weaving together narrow strips of cloth, straw or
rush, scarcely a finger's breadth, in studied contempt of all the laws
of complementary colors; these woven confections he sold as "Polzin
carpets." "You see," he concluded every one of his sales talks, "this
'Polzin creation'" (he treated himself as a historical person) "never
wears out; when one spot is worn through or the dining table with its
caster has torn a hole through it, I take out a couple old strips and
put in a couple new ones and everything's ship and shape, fine and
dandy again. You see, that's what the 'Polzin creation' is all about.
But when your Smyrna rug has a hole in it, it's had it, and even God
hisself can't help you with it."

As may be seen from the above speech, Polzin inclined to philosophical reflection, a trait that was considerably enhanced by the second métier he carried on. During the evening hours, when the opportunity arose, he served as a waiter in private homes and was univer-
sally popular in the district between the Invalidenstrasse and the
Chausseestrasse because of his skill and care in serving, a fact that
Frau Polzin always emphasized in her conversations with the widow
Pittelkow: "You see, dear Pittelkow, my husband is an orderly and
genteel person who knows quite well, because we ourselves began in a
very small way, that not everybody has money to throw away. And
you know, he waits on table according to that principle; and he won't
even touch gravy boats as won't stay still but keep sliding back and
forth. And if Polzin has ever ruined a single velvet bodice, I'll be fit

to die. And he's just as gallant and genteel about taking leftovers home. He's my husband, but this I must say, there's something refined and modest about him and altogether something as the others don't have. Yes, I have to give him that. And he's told me a hundert times and more: 'Emilie,' he says, 'today I had to feel ashamed of my colleagues again. Of course it was the fellow with the flat feet from the Charitéestrasse again. Do you think he as much as felt embarrassed and showed any concern for appearances and propriety? Heavens no! Quite insolent, as much as to say, "Yes, ma'm, there's the red wine and now I'm taking it home with me."' "

Such were the Polzins, at whose front door the widow Pittelkow now knocked, although there was a bell at the door, as a signal (so they had agreed between them) that it was only a "friend" calling. And immediately Frau Polzin appeared and opened the door.

The Polzin apartment, consisting of only three rooms, enjoyed the privilege of a hall which, however, was no larger than a folding card table and apparently served no other purpose than to lead to three doors, the one at the left leading to the room occupied by Frau Kahlbaum, the widow of a private secretary, the middle one to the room in which the Polzins themselves lived, and the right one to Stine. She had the best room in the apartment, bright and cheerful, facing the street, whereas the widow Kahlbaum had to content herself with the meager light from the courtyard, and the Polzin couple, with the rays that fell from a slanting skylight on the ceiling, as in a photographic studio.

"Dear Polzin," said the widow Pittelkow when the two women had exchanged polite greetings, "your place smells so strong of petroleum again. Why don't you use coke? With that petroleum cooker of yours, you'll cook all your tenants out of the apartment. And your dear husband! What does he think of it? He must have developed a delicate nose from his turkeys and pheasants. I don't know, but if I was a paid waiter for the gentry, I wouldn't stand for something like that. In company always something delicate, and at home this here. Well, it ain't no business of mine. Is Stine in?"

"I think so. I haven't heard her go out. And besides, you know, dear Pittelkow, we sees nothing and hears nothing."

"Of course, of course," laughed the widow Pittelkow, "sees nothing and hears nothing. And that's the best way too."

This conversation would very probably have continued if the door on the right had not opened at that moment and Stine had not come out into the hall.

"Lord, Stine," said the widow Pittelkow with an expression of joy on her face. "Why, that's just great. It's lucky you're here. You must come down today and give us a hand."

Frau Polzin withdrew politely but with a grin on her face, and the two sisters entered Stine's room and walked toward a couple of small chairs that stood on a footboard on either side of the window. Outside the window a revolving street mirror was attached to the wall; years ago, when he installed it, the practical and sly Polzin had said to his wife, "Emilie, as long as that mirror is there, we'll rent that room."

The widow Pittelkow sat down facing the revolving mirror, which once again, as if to corroborate Polzin's words, became a source of genuine pleasure to the attractive widow, not out of vanity (for she did not even see herself), but out of mere curiosity and playfulness. Stine, to whom this was a familiar game, smiled to herself; she too wore her hair in waves, but her hair was flaxen yellow and the rims of her exceedingly friendly eyes were slightly reddened, which, notwithstanding an otherwise blooming appearance and a certain resemblance to the widow Pittelkow, did point to a more delicate constitution. And so it was too. The brunette widow was the picture of a southern beauty, while the younger sister could pass for the prototype of a Germanic blond, though to be sure, a somewhat ailing one.

For a while Stine watched her sister, who was still preoccupied with the mirror; then she stood up, covered the sister's eyes with her hand and said: "Now you've had enough, Pauline. By this time you must surely know what the Invalidenstrasse looks like."

"You're right, child. But that's the way people are; they're always drawn to the most stupid things and spend their time with 'em, and when I look in the mirror and see all the people and horses in it, I think it's really quite different than when you look at it with your eyes. And it *is* a bit different too. I believe the mirror makes things look smaller, and to make smaller is almost as good as to make 'em nicer. But *you* don't have to get smaller, Stine, you can stay like you are. Yeah, sure thing. But what I've come about . . . Lord, you can't have an hour's peace."

"Why, what's up?"

"He's coming again tonight."

"Well, Pauline, that's certainly no misfortune. Don't forget that he takes care of everything. And how good he is and not that sort at all."

"Well, I could handle him. And he's bringing the old baron along and another one."

"Another one? Who's that?"

"Read."

And she handed the letter she had just received to Stine, who read it half aloud:

My dear black devil:

I'm coming today, but not alone; Papageno* is also coming and a nephew of mine too; still young, of course, and somewhat pale. "But pale and pallid, the ladies find it valid." Arrange for Wanda and Stine to be there too. I'll send wine and a salad bowl. But you must supply everything else. Nothing special, nothing grand, just the usual

Your Sarastro

"Who is the nephew?" asked Stine.

"Don't know. Who can keep track of all the nephews? D'you think I care about his family tree? Lord, I wonder what it looks like. Well, family trees in general . . ."

"Don't let him hear you say that!"

"Oh, he'll hear other things from me too. Or do you think because of an apartment on the second floor with a piano and a couch and a secretary that always wobbles on account of it has such thin legs, I'm gonna muzzle myself? No, Stine darling, if you think that, you don't know your sister. Or on account of the pale nephew? I imagine he looks like this." And she elongated her face and pressed thumb and index finger against both cheeks.

Stine laughed. "Yes, I think you've hit it right. And in any case, I think it's unfitting and uncultured of him to bring the young man along. An uncle is always the sort of person you should respect. As far as he's concerned, he can do as he pleases; but such a young person . . . I don't know, Pauline. Don't you agree?"

"Well, do I agree! Of course, do I ever! But child, if we start on that subject, there'll be no end to it. That's the way things are, they're all no good and that's like it should be, at least for the likes of us (it's different in your case) and for all those who are deep into it

---

*Papageno, Sarastro, and later, Queen of the Night are characters in Mozart's opera *The Magic Flute*. In this story Sarastro is old Count Haldern, uncle of the young count, Papageno is the baron, whose real name we never learn.

and don't know where to turn. For in the long run, how are we gonna
live?"

"By working."

"Oh Lord, working. Are you ever naïve, Stine! Sure, work is good,
and when I roll up my sleeves, I always feel best. But you know, a
person sometimes feels sick and miserable, and Olga has to go to
school. Where's a body to get it? Ah, that's a long story, Stine. Well,
you'll come, won't you? Round eight o'clock, or better still a little
before."

Chapter 3

While the widow Pittelkow was upstairs with Stine to assure her
presence for the evening, Olga was walking up Invalidenstrasse to
deliver the letter, and then, on her way back, to order the cake at the
Bolzani Pastry Shop. She had been told to hurry, but she paid no
attention to the order; rather, she rejoiced in being free from maternal control for an hour or so, and comforted herself with the thought
that it was still a long time till evening. She stopped at every shop,
longest of all in front of a milliner's; from the varied contents in the
window she selected for herself, as the most beautiful, first a red sash
with gold fringes and then again a brown beaver hat adorned with
heron feathers. To be sure, there was little prospect of realizing this
dream; but that didn't matter much, because under any circumstances her immediate future had to be a pleasant one. Wanda, as
she knew from Aunt Stine, mostly had pound cake in her cupboard,
in fact sometimes even chocolate squares, and if neither of these
should pan out, there was always the barley candy.

Absorbed in such reflections, Olga reached the Chausseestrasse, a
region studded with churches, where as usual some large funeral
blocked traffic. Far from objecting to this obstruction, Olga hoped it
would last as long as possible and, in order to have a better view, took
up her position on a stone staircase in front of an oil and spirit shop.
The hearse had already passed some time ago, so that she saw only
the painted silver cross swaying back and forth above a sea of black
hats. There were no carriages in the procession (at least that seemed
to be the case), but to make up for that deficiency, there were all
sorts of wagons with banners and music, and while from the front of

the cortege the funeral march of the carpenters could be heard far to
the rear, a second and third funeral march came from the center and
from Oranienburg Gate, so that Olga did not know which one she
should listen to. Beside the funeral procession proper large masses of
people surged forward, leaving only a narrow lane open for mounted
police to ride through the cortege from the tail end to the front and
back again. "I wonder who it is," thought Olga, in whose heart something like envy formed at the prospect of getting a beautiful funeral;
but no matter how carefully she listened to the people who stood beside her on the stone steps, she could not find out for certain. One
man was sure it was a bricklayers' foreman, another that it was a rich
member of the master carpenters' council, while a woman, completely covered with brown peat-dust, who had obviously been interrupted by the procession while she was unloading, refused to settle
for anything less than a cabinet minister for masons and carpenters.
"Nonsense," interrupted the shopkeeper, who lived nearby, "there
ain't no such thing." But the peat woman refused to be intimidated
and merely said: "Why not, why shouldn't there be such a thing?"
And so the debate went on. But finally the procession was over and
Olga crossed the street and a hundred feet further on turned into the
Tieckstrasse.

No. 272 was the third house from the corner: five windows in the
facade, three stories, and a little mansard. The owner, a copper-
smith, had transformed the yard into a semi-open-air workshop, in
which all day long workmen hammered away at brewing vats the
height of two men; in the midst of this booming and hammering
Wanda memorized her roles. It didn't matter to her; indeed, she preferred this to any other place to live in, and the journeyman copper-
smith who rode the boiler top for hours at a stretch, consuming himself in Platonic love (the only kind Wanda permitted such common
folk), was always her good friend. Her apartment, which she sublet
from the master glazier Schlichting, faced the yard and could be
entered from it by a staircase, where one found her bell and her card
bearing the legend, "Wanda Grützmacher, actress at the North End
Theater."

She had as much right to boast of this title as many a more famous
colleague. For she was the darling of any stage that had the good fortune to possess her, and not only a darling of the public but of the
director too, who, to say nothing of personal relationships, valued in

her above all the fact that, except for salary, she was utterly without pretensions and played any role that turned up. "Ever bravely into the breach," was one of her favorite sayings. She thoroughly subscribed to the principle of "live and let live," treated delicate events from a certain higher point of view, and had certain stereotyped phrases, gleaned from the most ancient store of Berlin wit, by which she expressed her attitude toward the "ideal." Accordingly, she preferred "a good salary to bad treatment"; during suppers with middleclass widowers (a social stratum she was especially fond of), when she was handed the menu, she pointed to what was obviously the best and most expensive item with a seriousness that suited her admirably and which never failed to produce an effect, adding solemnly: "I'm just dying for some of that."

That was Wanda Grützmacher, 27a Tieckstrasse.

Olga who, strangely enough, had never run a message to the actress before this, rang the bell at the Schlichting apartment and Fräulein Flora Schlichting appeared at the door, half asleep, and opened up.

"Is Fräulein Wanda at home?"

"She's at home. I think she's asleep. Have you got something for her?"

"Yes, but I'm supposed to give it to her myself."

"Here, just hand it over . . ." And she snatched at the letter.

But Olga drew it back energetically. "No, I'm not supposed to . . ."

"Well, then you can come again tomorrow."

Although she did not live wall to wall with the front room of the Schlichtings, Wanda must have heard something of this conversation; for just as the door was about to be slammed, she was there, as if she had grown out of the ground, and said: "Lord, Olga dear, what do you bring me, child? Mother isn't sick, I hope?" Instead of an answer, Olga held out the letter to her. "Oh, a letter. Well then, come to my room, so I can read it. It's pitch dark here; you wouldn't believe you were living in a glazier's home."

She took the child by the hand and drew her through the Schlichting apartment, which grew darker with every step, into her own back room. Here she had to laugh when she saw the strange seal her friend Pauline had improvised; then she opened the glued section with a hair pin that she took from her thick black plait and read with visible joy:

Dear Wanda:
   He's coming again today, which is very anoying for me because this is my cleaning
day. Lord, I'm upsett and only ask you: come. Without you, it's nothing. Stine is coming too. Come at eight aclock but no later and love
                          your friend
                          Pauline Pittelkow
                          née Rehbein.

Wanda put the leter under her bodice, cut off a piece from a traditional German pound cake that was kept in a covered porcelain
tureen, and then said: "And now say hello to mother and tell her I'll
come at eight sharp, on the stroke. For us theater folk are punctual
or it wouldn't work. And when you come again, Olga dear, you can
come right up the stairs in the yard, just three steps, so you don't
have to go through the front and there won't be no Fräulein Flora to
shout at you and try to send you away. Do you hear?" And in a sort of
monologue, she added: "Lord, that Flora; the less they know, the
more they blow. I don't understand these people."
   Olga promised to deliver the message and hurried outside with her
booty. When she got out on the street she looked back once more,
then bit into the cake with vigor and smacked her lips with pleasure.
But base ingratitude was already germinating in her heart, and while
she was still enjoying the cake immensely, she was already grumbling
to herself: "Really, it ain't a real cake at all . . . no raisins . . . I'd rather
have one with raisins."

Chapter 4

   When Olga came home after attending to all her assigned duties,
including of course the call at Marzahn's Pastry Shop at the corner,
she found everything changed and Aunt Stine busy hooking up the
red woolen cord of the lace curtains to the brass holders. Everywhere
cleanliness and order reigned — only the adjacent room was not quite
ready — and the only thing that could be regarded as a disturbing element was a recently delivered basket of wine bottles and lobster
mayonnaise that had been temporarily placed on a chair nearby.
   Olga reported that Wanda would come; this intelligence was received by the widow Pittelkow with obvious joy. "When Wanda ain't
there, it's always only half the fun. I wouldn't like to stand up every

day and play the princess; but this must be true, all the theater people have got something and they get a certain chick* and know how to talk. I don't know where they get it, least of all Wanda. She was always the laziest one among us and not the smartest neither and let others tell her what to do, and without her teacher Kulike . . . well, she was stuck on him. Altogether she was a sly toad, something the fat ones ain't customarily. But always decent and not jealous and she always shared."

During this speech, which was only half directed to Stine, the widow Pittelkow had been standing on the sofa, straightening three pictures on the wall; when she was finished, she got down from the sofa and walked back to the threshold of the door so that she could survey the whole scene from this vantage point and convince herself that her arrangements were successful. To be praised for such an achievement was a genuine emotional need for her, given her basic appetite for order and good housekeeping, and if she had ever had a claim to be praised for this quality, it was surely today. Everything that could be done with the material at her disposal had been done, and one could for the moment forget how very much — and to a degree also, how comically — the objects collected in this room clashed with each other. A buffet, a sofa and an upright piano stood parallel to each other, at right angles to a wall that was unbroken by a door, and could have graced the room of a privy councillor; but the three pictures that the widow Pittelkow had just straightened jeopardized the ensemble effect at which the other pieces of furniture aimed. Two of these pictures, *Duck Hunt* and *Tell's Chapel* were nothing more than badly colored lithographs of very recent date, whereas the third picture, which hung between the other two, a huge portrait in oils strongly darkened with age, was at least a hundred years old and immortalized a Polish or Lithuanian bishop who, Sarastro swore, was a direct ancestor of the widow Pittelkow. Such disharmony was revealed in the total furnishings of the room, indeed it seemed to have been desired rather than avoided; and while on one pilaster a splendid pier glass with two projecting golden sphinxes showed off in splendor, two wretched plaster figures stood on the bookcase: a Polish couple, both dressed in national costume, coquettishly beginning a dance. But most interesting of all was the bookcase just mentioned; its four middle shelves were empty, while the top

*Her pronunciation of "chic."

shelf contained a set of twelve volumes of Hume's *History of England* in splendid leather binding, and eighteen volumes of the *OEuvres posthumes de Frédéric le Grand*, forming a strange contrast to the *Berlin Penny Magazine* that was piled up in two heaps on the bottom shelf. All these furnishings, great and small, art and science, had been bought on one and the same morning and had been delivered in the Invalidenstrasse by a secondhand dealer from the Mauerstrasse in a handcart, which had to make several trips. The gentleman who paid for all this had insisted with particular emphasis on the strange inclusion of the splendidly bound books so that, as he liked to put it in his mocking yet admiring manner, the world might find out who Pauline Pittelkow really was.

These were the treasures that were now subjected to a final scrutiny from the doorway, and when the fringes of the Brussels rug in front of the sofa had been smoothed out, the widow Pittelkow said: "There, Stine, now come, we'll make some coffee for ourselves, some real coffee. And Olga will get us something to go with it. Would you like streusel cake or just with sugar and cinnamon?"

"Oh, Pauline, you know—"

"Well, streusel then . . . Olga!"

And Olga, who had heard every word through the open door and was only pretending to be looking after her "dear little brother" with assiduous and loving care, now came racing in from the back room, as though possessed, all eyes and ears.

"There, Olga. Now go. But get it from Katzfuss, not Zachow. And don't nibble again and then make excuses about the crumbs."

"And now, Stine," the widow Pittelkow continued, while Olga vanished instantly and slid down the banister, which had long ago been polished by this exercise, "it's time for us to get ready. But don't come in your green camlet again. You know he can't stand it. And as long as things are the way they are, we have to do what he wishes. And then, he's bringing the sucked-out eggshell too. And I know their kind, they always make the biggest demands, and if there's nothing doing, they at least want to see something and make eyes. And Wanda knows that too. Mark my words, she'll come in her black velvet dress again, with a rose in front. It always makes me want to laugh."

And Wanda did indeed come in black velvet and looked very stately. Her head had nothing of the striking beauty of her old schoolmate and friend of her youth, but she was far superior to her in dash, as Pauline herself admitted. "In dash I can't measure up to Elizabeth." That was the last role in which she had seen Wanda and had admired her almost against her will.

"Ah, Wanda," she now greeted her friend, "it's nice of you to come; always on time."

"Yes, dear Pauline, that's the way we are, we learn it like the soldiers. When the cue falls, we must step forward, even if it should cost us our lives."

The widow Pittelkow laughed heartily, which however did not prevent her from ushering Wanda with a certain solemnity to her proper place on the sofa. Stine, who looked very good in her dotted "guinea fowl" dress, which she was wearing to satisfy her sister's wish, was supposed to sit beside Wanda; but she stubbornly insisted on sitting in an easy chair opposite the actress. Between them stood a huge bouquet that had been cut at the Veterans' Garden for this party: a dozen roses, from the center of which tall tiger lilies stood out. Wanda, who wanted to smell them, bent over too far and came out with a yellow beard, which caused Pauline unusual merriment. Even Olga was called in. "Look, Olga, look; Aunt Wanda's got a mustache. And what a mustache! I'll betcha, children, the young count don't have one at all."

At this moment the bell rang and the widow Pittelkow went to open in person. Stine followed her because she did not wish to play the grande dame by remaining seated. But Wanda, out of a deep conviction of what she owed to herself and to art, did not stir from the spot but kept sitting on her throne. Only when the company entered did she rise and return the greetings of the two older gentlemen casually, making a curtsy before the young count.

"May I do the introductions?" Sarastro now asked in a cordial tone and with an apparently very serious expression on his face. "My newphew Waldemar," who bowed, "Frau Pauline Pittelkow, née Rehbein, Fräulein Ernestine Rehbein, Fräulein Wanda Grützmacher. There is no need to introduce our friend Papageno; he enjoys the privilege of being known to all those present."

The way in which this introduction was received by the three ladies showed the radical difference in their characters: Wanda found everything natural, Pauline mumbled something about nonsense and monkey business, and only Stine, feeling the insult intended by the little scene, turned red.

"Did Borchardt send the stuff?"

"Of course he did . . ."

"Well then, please . . ."

The unusual matter-of-factness with which Sarastro said all this vexed the widow Pittelkow not a little; but she considered it proper to store up her annoyance for another occasion and went out with Stine to carry the table that was all set from the back to the front room.

Meanwhile the old count, who had very delicate nerves, had been severely inconvenienced by the scent of the tiger lilies; he therefore took them out of the bouquet without ceremony, opened the window, and threw them out. "A smell I can't endure; half cemetery, half parsonage. And I don't think much of either."

Before five minutes had passed the company was seated around the oval table: the old count at the head, beside him Wanda and Stine, then Papageno and Waldemar; but at the foot of the table, that is, facing the old count, his friend Pauline. Her position forced her to look into the pier glass every time she raised her head, which elicited from the old count, when he noticed it, the remark, made half in jest, half in homage: "Honor to whom honor is due!" But the widow Pittelkow took pleasure tonight in deprecating such expressions of homage and said: "Lord, honor! I find nothing more revolting than to see my face all the time."

"Then I ask my fair friend to cast her eyes somewhat lower, she will then see me."

This amused her. "Then I'd rather have things as they were. I prefer to look after my own interest."

Sarastro and Papageno were delighted and drank a toast to their dark friend.

"She doesn't change, does she, Fräulein Wanda?" said Sarastro.

Wanda agreed, if only because she had to, but began to tug at her rose, as a sign that she had not come here to have herself hitched up to the widow Pittelkow's triumphant chariot. Then she leaned back and looked at *Tell's Chapel.*

Papageno took this mood into account and favored the artiste, who had to be mollified at any price, with a conversation about art, which was all the more feasible since the old count took a healthy interest in all theater gossip and made no distinction between Lucca or Patti or the last chorine in the *Bat.**

---

*Die Fledermaus, the well-known operetta by Johann Strauss the younger.

"My dear lady," Papageno began, "what new offerings may we expect from your Art Institute in the near future?"

"Our old man," Wanda replied, "wants to try a revue. He thinks it's the only thing left . . ."

"He's quite right. Is it a journey to the moon or to the center of the earth?"*

Wanda smiled. The ice was broken, and from this moment on it became difficult for her to continue with a wretched conversation about art, because it would have to remain impersonal, at least in the immediate future. But she controlled herself and said, throwing an occasional understanding look at the old count: "Of course, the old man didn't get any gray hairs worrying about a text. He persists in his dislike of having to pay for things he can have for nothing and believes, as my colleague Pötrig, a college man, says, that he can encroach upon the realm of literature without hesitation. Our old man is in every way a man of encroachment, a thought which fills me with annoyance."

"Revolting!" said the old count. "For the rest, I have a suspicion on whose door he knocked. I mean, of course, at what poet's door. I'll wager ten to one: Shakespeare . . ."

"You always hit the bull's eye, Count, Yes, *The Winter's Tale*, and the principal role has fallen to me, that of Hermióne; and all I know about her for the present is that I stand on a pedestal for a whole scene, without any ornamentation except a white wrap."

Sarastro smiled. "This assignment of the role can surprise no one, and you least of all, my dear young lady, if you are not blind to your gifts and advantages, which are so clearly in evidence. Nature has endowed you too well to pass you over for the role of the marble bride, which is almost exclusively what we are concerned with here.†
When I see you in my imagination, all stone, and suddenly you are transfused by warm, pulsating life, everything in you surges, and in a reddish illumination you descend from the pedestal to be once more a human being among humans—a sublime thought . . ."

"You flatter me, Count. It is a role that absolutely demands youth; indeed more than youth; I should like to put it this way: youth and delicacy . . ."

---

*Allusion to two plays that were being performed in the Circus Renz at the time. They were based on novels by Jules Verne.

†King Leontes brings the supposedly dead queen, who stands before him as a statue, back to life with a kiss.

"Qualities which you deny yourself in excessive modesty only in order to be assured of our most vehement contradiction. Hermióne, as I remember, is already a wife and mother at the beginning of the play, beside being accused of infidelity — events which occur only exceptionally before the age of fourteen. I ask you, what does 'young' mean, and above all 'delicate'? This word delicate is being constantly misused, everything that is pale and consumptive is sure of being designated as delicate. One of the many aberrations of our modern taste. Delicate, delicate; delicate is something that is inward, spiritual, which can exist even within the most ample forms. Ask my nephew. He has been traveling around Italy for five years, visiting churches especially, and knows, to take a rough figure, five thousand saints of the female sex. And what is holy must of course also be delicate. And now let him give us an account of the concept of delicacy. I don't wish to anticipate his superior judgment, but I dare assert in advance that, whatever he has seen in the line of Saint Cecilias and Barbaras and of course Genovevas too, who always get top billing, they were all ladies with your constitution, my dear; ladies who were devoid of all moonlighty features; ladies in black velvet with a red rose. Waldemar, I urge you to support me in a matter that is dear both to my heart and to my artistic sensibility."

He touched glasses with Wanda and was pleased to hear Waldemar fall in with the tone he had struck, assuring them with a cordial smile that his uncle was right; all the saints were well-proportioned ladies and even the most delicate thing could still be subsumed under the waving line* . . .

"Fine, fine," the count interrupted him at this point. "And so I ask you to fill your glasses and drink to the health of Hermióne, a shift in accent favored by Fräulein Wanda, which promises a whole new conception of the role. For it is the accents that count in life and art. Long live art, long live delicacy, long live the waving line, above all long live Hermióne-Hermíone, long live Fräulein Wanda, long live the red rose!"

Wanda bowed and handed the red rose to the old count, who had put so much meaning into the end of his speech. But the old baron touched glasses with both of them from the other side.

There now followed toast upon toast; Papageno drank to Stine, and after Waldemar, turning to Stine, had said a few words too, Wanda spoke as usual in doggerel that she had adapted very simply

*I.e., the curves of the female body.

for occasions like that of tonight from an old verse album by substituting "love" for "friendship." Finally the old count spoke again, proposing a toast to his friend Pauline. But he did not mention her
name; he spoke only in general terms of the charm and the advantages of widowhood and ended with the peroration: "Long live my
Moorish Queen, my Queen of the Night!"

They all stood up and Baron Papageno assured them that that was
a genuine Sarastro toast and that the series of toasts could not have
ended more worthily.

They all agreed, except the person to whom the toast had been
made. She could accept the drastic aspects of the words (didn't she
herself ridicule everything she called "putting on airs?"), but the
mockery that came through the words and a complacent indulgence
in witticisms that she only half understood and which therefore
appeared to her to be worse than they actually were — this ruined her
mood, and so she said, coloring: "Well, Count, not like that, not too
much high spirits. I don't care for that. And before the whole company too! What's the young count to think of it?"

"Only the best."

"Well, I'd prefer the good." And while she poured herself a glass of
water, she repeated: "Queen of the Night. I don't believe it."

Chapter 5

The displeasure that was stirring in the heart of the widow Pittelkow would in any case have dissipated very soon in the merriment
that prevailed around the table; but the old count, who was only too
familiar with the incomparable vehemence of his "Queen of the
Night," considered it advisable to prevent even the mere possibility of
a storm. "I think," he said, "we need some fresh air and will have our
coffee in the next room."

"Can't be done," replied the widow Pittelkow. "All the curtains are
down, everything's at sixes and sevens."

"Very well then, we'll stay here. Snug and warm has its advantages
too . . . May I . . ." And with that he took Wanda's arm, indicating
that the repast was over, and led her to the place on the sofa where
she had been sitting when the gentlemen arrived. The young count
escorted Stine, while the baron, who was long familiar with the ritual
of these Pittelkow evenings, took an elegant liqueur chest and a box

of cigars from the buffet and placed them on the table beside the sofa. The old count nodded approval, struck a sulphur match on the sole of his patent leather boot, and lit a carefully selected Havana cigar. When he had taken the first puff and blown away the cloud of smoke, he turned to Wanda and Stine with chivalrous courtesy:

"No objection, ladies?"

Pauline had gone directly from the table to the kitchen and returned after a few minutes with the coffee; this speed was due to the fact that Olga had carried out her double task—that of keeping the child quiet and the water boiling—with a conscientiousness that was equally motivated by fear and hope. The coffee was served, the old baron too took a cigar from the box, and a moment later the clouds of smoke curled up through the air from two sides of the room.

"There isn't another such cigar anywhere else in the world," Papageno assured them.

"Agreed," the count replied. "And besides, a cigar here, in my friends's home, is for me like smoking opium, which brings happiness, and every time I take a puff, I see before me the Elysian fields* or, what amounts to the same thing, the houris in paradise."

"Now, now," said the widow Pittelkow, who possibly feared some new ridicule to come, if it was not already there.

But the old count did not allow the interjection to disturb him, but continued: "Absolutely everything is wonderful, and I miss only one thing: the liqueurs. To be sure, Papageno has provided the chest (that's why he's Papageno) but not the key . . . Ah, behold, Fräulein Stine is bringing it. I believe she wants to . . . And now, ladies, leave the choice to me. I'll bet I hit it right for every one of you."

"I wonder," said Wanda, "I'm really curious."

"It's easier than you think. Everyone's preference can be read from her brow: my friend here is for curacao" (the widow Pittelkow nodded), "which formerly had a not undistinguished career under the less pretentious name of "orange"; Fräulein Stine is of course for anisette and Fräulein Wanda for a Benedictine or two. Taste it, dear lady. What do you think of these monks? Not bad, what?"

Things now became more and more animated, and the denser the narcotic cloud that permeated the room, the more enigmatic the language became. The old count took over the direction, seconded by Papageno. But both aimed their intimacies exclusively at Wanda,

---

*Allusion to a painting with that title by the Swiss painter Arnold Böcklin. It aroused much criticism because of the nude nymphs it represented.

because they felt a certain timidity in the face of the two sisters, the older because of her unpredictable temperament, the younger because of her innocence. Wanda, who had long ago forgotten her neglect during the early part of the repast, naturally saw in this constant turning toward her person a triumph that was her due and became intoxicated with the abundance of ovations that were pressed on her with increasing assiduity. And what the ovations failed to achieve was accomplished by the Benedictine. All formality had long been abandoned, and after opening with a few backstage scandals, particularly a sketch of the old director in his most characteristic sphere, that of the harem, she had sufficiently advanced to accede to the old count's wish that she supply some samples of her art. A few scruples that still persisted were swept aside by the baron, who related at the right moment that Rachel, draped only in a lace veil, had played Phaedra on Peacock Island and had inspired the Emperor Nicholas to enthusiasm; he had no doubt that Wanda could achieve as much, no matter whether she declaimed "The Knight Toggenburg" or "The Walk to the Iron Hammer" or even "The Glove."* But someone must stand behind her and perform the pantomime; without pantomime it would be only a half success. This question was elaborated on, and after they had reviewed the various forms and additions that would enhance the effect of the Schiller ballad, they finally agreed to drop it altogether, since declamation depended wholly on the dramatic effect, and to perform a play in place of it — a shadow play or, best of all, a potato puppet play. This word had scarcely been uttered when it was greeted with enthusiasm, and Wanda, after finishing the small liqueur glass in front of her, stood up as a sign that she was now ready to begin a dramatic offering.

"But what? What? . . . Comedy or tragedy?"

"Tragedy, of course . . ." came from all sides, and even the young count and Stine, who had been quiet until then, became animated. Wanda herself, however, bowed and said, not without a touch of humor: "The esteemed audience will in due time be informed about the details concerning the content and title."

"Bravo! Bravo!"

---

*Elisa Rachel, famous French actress. Peacock Island, near Potsdam, is the site of a small castle in which Rachel played the role of Phaedra before King Friedrich Wilhelm IV of Prussia and Emperor Nicholas of Russia. The three poems mentioned are ballads by Friedrich Schiller.

Thereupon she actually withdrew and went into the kitchen, where she hoped to find the barest necessities for the play. The widow Pittelkow followed her. But soon they both reappeared in the front room and began to unfold a checkered plaid in the open door-way and to fasten it at the level of a man's height. Behind this plaid Wanda now took her place and pushed the curtain down far enough to look over it conveniently. And now she announced: "*Judith and Holofernes*, a tragedy in two acts by Tussauer, without music. We begin the first act ("very good" — "remarkable"), or what amounts to the same thing, with the row of tents in Holofernes's camp."

After this announcement the plaid bounced back and in place of Wanda's brunette face there appeared a potato princess dressed in white with a red turban and a mouth of sealing wax. Judith, of course, who bowed to the audience, skillfully manipulated, looked alternately to left and to right, as though she were expecting some-one, and then began in a slightly hoarse voice:

> "It is himself, is Holofernes, hero worn with care,
> Girt with his mighty sword: I see a tassel dangling there."

At this moment there appeared from the right side a gaunt figure in a red cloak, wearing a paper crown:

> "Who are you, lady fair, from where have you been rushing?
> In wartime men will tend to do a little pushing."

"In peace, too," Sarastro whispered to the baron. But Judith continued:

> "Respectful pushiness, you know, I will not spurn;
> My name is Judith, and I seek one Holofern."
> "Then I am whom you seek ... Oh, has my life been lonely ..."
> "But through your fault alone ..." "You'll be my one and only."

And motioning with eye and finger, half commanding, half woo-ing her, he strode to his tent, followed by Judith, while the extin-guished light in the adjacent room indicated that the curtain had fallen.

The young count was about to applaud, but his uncle restrained him and explained that in this sphere, too, one must not rattle away one's fire power too soon. All this was only a prelude, which offered the prospect of something far more complex. He, for his part, was above all curious to see how Fräulein Wanda would handle certain scenic difficulties, the bed scene, for instance, and second, the decapitation. True, nowadays people questioned the existence of scenic difficulties, but after all, everything has its limits.

Sarastro would have said more if the light that went on in the next room had not indicated the resumption of the action. The next moment Judith appeared again, this time to deliver her decisive monologue:

> "Now he shall die . . . but must he? I myself feel sad,
> He spoke of jewels, promised I'd be finely clad,
> But will he keep his word? I know the likes of men
> Who, like the wind when the storm has passed, will turn again.
> He even spoke of marriage — but was that not deceit? . . .
> So come to my breast, my sword, accomplish his defeat;
> He brought it on himself — now I approach his bed,
> He dared to overcovet me, and I will have his head."

And at the same moment (the figure of Holofernes had meanwhile risen out of the depths), the act of decapitation was consummated, and the head of Holofernes flew over the curtain into the front room and fell at the baron's feet. They all applauded the play and even more the virtuoso swordthrust, but the old baron picked up the head that was lying at his feet and said: "Really, only a potato . . . Not Holofernes. And yet I felt as if he were alive. Which isn't really surprising; for sooner or later such a decapitation is the lot of every one of us. Some Judith whom we overcovet — incidentally, a marvelous word — decides our fate and kills us one way or another."

"Drop it, Baron," said the old count. "Why these melancholy reflections? I find it simply superb. And happy is the poet who was able to create such a work. Fräulein Wanda, you mentioned a name before, but perhaps only to divert attention from yourself . . . Your own creation?"

"Oh, no, Count."

"Well, if not by you, my dear, by whom then?"

"By a young friend."

"That means an old admirer."

"No, Count, really by a young friend, a student."

"So are we all. What is he studying? That's the question."

"I've forgotten the word, and his visiting card only half mentions it. And his museum is in the Königgrätzstrasse. There they try to find out, if I get it right, how the world came into being and from what and when."

"And perhaps also why. A very interesting subject ... And he writes too?"

Wanda affirmed it, adding that it had not been easy to draw a play like *Judith and Holofernes* from his serious bent in art. He would not desecrate his Muse, had been his words. But thank heaven, she had had means in her hand for compelling him.

"Ah, I understand — "

"No, not that, Count. He's a very bashful young man and only reads me his great tragedies, always supplied with a prelude. And he hopes that I'll intercede for him. That's my hold over him. To be sure, I must say he'll get nowhere. But he's a good boy, who does anything I want."

"I well believe it," laughed the baron. "But my dear, who would want it otherwise? And now I think we'll play a game of whist."

A card table was brought and set up, and the three gentlemen and Wanda took their places. A Champagne cooler was placed on a small low table nearby, and the old count personally played the host. As a matter of fact only Wanda drank, although she would much have preferred a glass of Spatenbräu. Stine stood behind Papageno's chair and had to listen to his assurance that a pure virgin brings luck. The widow Pittelkow bustled about in the kitchen and was already polishing the silver forks.

In this way a good slice of time passed by. But at length the old count threw down his cards and said: "This is leading nowhere. A game of cards is only worthwhile when it's a question of *la banque ou la vie*.* I believe I've lost seven marks and have been tormenting myself for an hour by the clock. Wanda, are you in good voice? Of course you are; why do I ask? A lady like you always carries her props on her person. *Omnia mea mecum portans* ..."†

Papageno laughed.

But the old count continued: "*Omnia mea* ... What a prospect! To your health, Wanda. And yours, Fräulein Stine. Pauline doesn't need our health, she's healthy from herself."

"Come, come, Count. Don't talk like that. From myself? From what? Lord knows it ain't always fun."

"Oh, excellent, Pauline. You take the prize. Let's touch glasses, child. But now a song, Wanda."

"Yes, who'll accompany me?"

---

*"Either I win or I commit suicide."
†"Carrying all my belongings with me."

"Why, the only one who can, of course: Papageno."

"Good, good."

And the old baron moved a chair to the piano, turned the little key, and opened the instrument. "What shall it be?"

"Well," said the old count, "we owe you this much at least, friend, that we should begin with the Papageno aria. Well then:

> Pamina: No man who feels the pangs of loving
>   Can fail to show a generous heart.

But that's a platitude, of course, it's something obvious. The real thing is what follows:

> Papageno: Such sweet emotion likewise suffering
>   Must ever be the woman's part.

The baron nodded agreement and repeated the closing verse: "Must ever be the woman's part." But Wanda who, like most women of her sort, suffered from quite unmotivated relapses into dignity and virtue, said suddenly: "No, gentlemen, it's still too early. I think this song really goes too far."

The gentlemen looked at each other, because none of them knew what to make of this nonsense; but the widow Pittelkow, who was honestly annoyed by the "Wanda act," interrupted vehemently and said: "Lord, Wanda, no theater, please. Too far! When a person hears the likes of it! You're either over the line or you're not. And when you're over, it's all one whether it's ten o'clock or eleven o'clock. No, Wanda, no airs. Always decent is my motto; but I can't stand airs."

It looked as if a quarrel was in the making which, given the reckless character of the widow Pittelkow, for whom everything had to bend or break, might easily have led to an unpleasant debate. No one knew that better than the old count, from the most personal experience. He therefore vaulted swiftly over the point at issue by saying: "If it can't be *The Magic Flute*, then I'm for *The Old Commander*.* But in costume."

This suggestion was received with general acclaim, and after a short retreat into the adjoining room, Wanda appeared draped in red, with a curtain rod in her hand instead of a flag.

"Sing, sing!"

*Der alte Feldherr, a Singspiel (musical) by Karl Holtei (1798-1880).

"I'll sing, all right," said Wanda, bowing to the audience, "but what? *The Old Commander* has two numbers."

"Well then, the principal number: 'Let No One Ask to Hear My Fate.' A wonderful song and as true as it is gripping. It really is a song that fits everyone, especially such old commanders like us. Isn't that right, Papageno? But now, begin. Quick. Quick."

And the next moment the storm broke and could be heard through the three floors of the house, so that the Polzins above heard it too: the recurring refrain:

> Nothing, nothing at all is left me
> But honor and my aging head.

The widow Pittelkow had been standing behind the chair occupied by the old count, beating time with her index finger on his bald spot.

Wanda was happy and kept giving more and more treats, with the widow Pittelkow, who had a good ear, singing second voice, while Sarastro joined in with his bass, and Papageno, still playing the accompaniment on the piano, assisted with his ruined baritone.

Only the young count and Stine were silent, exchanging looks.

Chapter 6

In this way another hour passed. Then the party broke up and Sarastro and Papageno, with strong insistence, requested from Fräulein Wanda the honor of accompanying her home together, so that no harm might come to her. The young count joined them willy-nilly. The lady who was being celebrated doubly, even triply, in this way, urged in turn a simplification of the procedure, assuring them over and over again that one escort would be enough. But she saw that she was outvoted. The responsibility was too great, they said.

When they had all left, the widow Pittelkow put her arm around her sister's waist, waltzed three times around the room with her and then said: "There, Stine, now things'll be great. I've put aside a brown can full for ourselves and a few rolls are left over too. Of course they'll be rather tough, but they'll do with butter, they'll slide down . . . Well, that Wanda! You wouldn't believe it. And a voice like a street singer."

Stine tried to see the good side of things and reproached her sister with being too stern as usual. Besides, she was betraying herself; everything she said was merely said in envy. But she had no need to be envious, for all three of them had accompanied her and three were always better than one. Dear Wanda! Well, if you tried, you could find something against everyone (including themselves); but all in all that Grützmacher was a nice person and certainly a good-natured one.

"Yeah," said Pauline, "she is that; only she's so important and puts on airs. And when she's exhausted that, she don't put on airs enough and there's something so loud and embarrassing about her."

"You're in fine form today," Stine laughed. "So that's Wanda. And now tell me, what am I really like? But no, I'd rather you didn't tell me . . ."

"Don't intend to . . ."

"I'd rather you told me something about the three men. What's the old count like?"

"Disgusting."

"And the baron?"

"A dumb ox."

"And the young count?"

"A poor, sick chicken."

Chapter 7

The following day passed without the two sisters even seeing each other; the widow Pittelkow had to put the apartment into shape again and Stine was supposed to deliver a large frame embroidery by Saturday evening.

And the second day seemed destined to pass like the first, quietly and without a meeting between them. No one came up to Stine's room, and when Olga brought the key, Stine knew only that her sister Pauline had gone to town with both children. The hours passed slowly and the setting sun was already hanging low between the two towers of the Hamburg Railway Station when an elegantly dressed gentleman walked up the Invalidenstrasse and began to inspect the houses near the one in which Stine lived. It was the young count who, to judge by his looking and searching, must have forgotten the number of the Pittelkow house with its *a*, *b*, and *c*, but who nevertheless was confident that he would find the right place. And whether it was by accident or with the aid of certain little details, he really found it; and when he read the sign "Widow Pittelkow" on the second floor, he continued to climb one more flight, now sure of himself, and rang the bell. Stine, who may have been expecting her sister, came and opened quickly.

"Lord, Count; it's you."

"Yes, Fräulein Stine."

"You want my sister; she'll be back at once. I have the key and can open up for you."

"No, I don't want to see your sister; I want to see you, Fräulein Stine."

"That's impossible, Count. I'm alone, and a single girl must be careful or there'll be talk. People see everything."

He smiled. "If that's the situation, Fräulein Stine, then the safest thing is to enter swiftly."

"Very well, Count . . . Please come in . . ."

And with that she stepped back from the door and led the way to her room.

As long as the conversation lasted, Frau Polzin had stood at her peephole watching them. But the moment Stine led the count to her room, she too returned to her half-dark room, in which the evening meal for her husband was already laid out on a folding table: a kipper and a round loaf of country bread, which she bought two loaves at a time because fresh bread was more wasteful to slice.

"Well," said Polzin, "what do you say, mother? I don't suppose three marks is too much?"

"Three . . . ? What are you thinking of? Five at least. It's only that it ain't certain yet. He was so trembly and shook so."

At these words she put her ear to the wall once more, while Polzin, who did not want to interfere with her listening by hammering, left his work and applied himself to his evening meal.

Chapter 8

The unexpected visitor had meanwhile stepped into the front room and, as Stine returned to the window and to the embroidery

frame that was set up beside it, she invited the count to be seated on
the sofa that stood at right angles to the wall. But he declined to do
this; instead he moved a chair close to Stine, who for her part resumed her work, although visibly agitated. Her needle flew, and the
orange-colored thread of fleece silk flashed with every stitch she
made.

"Well, Count," she began, as she lowered her head closer and
closer to the embroidery, "what brings me this honor? What brings
you to me?"

But before the man to whom the question was directed could
reply, she continued with an animation that was foreign to her
nature: "I think you misjudge me. You may laugh, but I'm a decent
girl, and there's no one in the world who could come up to me and
say, 'You're lying.' Of course, I see the way things are . . . no, no, let
me finish . . . but the sort of life my sister leads doesn't seduce me; it
merely scares me off, and I would rather spend my whole life in
misery and die in the hospital than have old gentlemen about me
every day and have to listen to indecent remarks or sarcasms and
jokes, which are perhaps even worse. I can't and won't stand for that.
So now you know where you're at."

"Fräulein Stine," said the young count, "you say I was mistaken
about you. I don't think I was mistaken about you. But even if it were
so, let me tell you that you are mistaken about me too. I come to you
because I like you and you've inspired me with sympathy, or to put it
plainly, because I feel sorry for you. I clearly read in your face that
not everything that occurred the other evening was in accord with
your ideas or your taste, and so I resolved to see how you are, Fräulein Stine. Yes, that was my resolve; and if I can help you, I *will* help
you and give you back your freedom and release you from this
environment. I believe I can do it, though I'm not a prince and even
less a miracle worker. And you need not fear that I will appear one
day with the intention of being thanked by you for what I've done.
No, nothing of the sort. I'm a sick man and have no feeling for what
the happy and healthy people call their amusement. It's a long story,
I don't want to annoy you with it, at least not today."

In speaking these last words he had stood up, and, leaning his
hand on Stine's chair, he looked at the ball of the sun that was just
then setting between the trees that faced west in Veterans' Park.
Everything swam in a golden shimmer and the silence into which he
fell showed that for some moments he was totally absorbed by the

beauty of the picture unfolding before him. But after a time he took Stine's hand in his and said: "What have I been talking about, giving you freedom and releasing you from your environment! Don't give me an answer; it's all wrong, and vain and foolish into the bargain. Because I feel myself to be in need of help, I assumed that you are in need of help too. But suddenly I feel that you're not, that you can't be."

Stine smiled to herself. But the young count, who did not or would not notice it, continued in the elegiac tone that was characteristic of him: "Yes, Fräulein Stine, being sick, which has been my real voca tion in life since my youth, has its advantages too; you develop all sorts of nerves in your fingertips and feel whether people and situations are happy or not. And sometimes even from the rooms in which people live. And here my senses tell me that you can't be unhappy. It's not chance that such a picture lies spread out before you here, and a room into which the sun takes such a friendly look every evening is a good room."

"Yes," said Stine, "it is that. Of course you shouldn't boast of your happiness, if only to avoid bad luck. But it's true, I am happy."

At these words the young count gave her a sidelong glance that was searching and almost astonished. He had been pleased to grant her happiness without further thought, because of the friendly environment in which he found her, contrary to his expectation; and yet he was amazed to hear her confirm what he had himself just told her. Stine saw this and therefore added: "Of course I don't want you to think that I don't know which way to turn out of sheer happiness. That's not the way it is. I'm happy, but not like those who don't know what privation is, and have nothing but good days always. Nor am I as happy as the Catholic sister who nursed me last winter when I was ill. Such a pious soul, who wants nothing other than to do God's will; yes, she has more, of course, and her condition is a better one. But I'm as well off as ordinary people are, who are grateful to God if only no evil befalls them."

"And living together with your sister? Isn't it a burden and a care to you?"

"No. I love my sister and she loves me."

"But you're so very different."

"Not as much as you think. You misjudge my sister; my sister is very good."

"But the kind of life she leads! Surely there must be a lot of talk

about it and much opposition from people who still have their catechism and keep the ten commandments."

"Yes, they have objections of course, and my sister must often hear
angry words when she meets such people. But sharp as she is normally, she takes it calmly. For she has a good intelligence and a great
sense of justice, and when she hears such talk, she says: 'Yes, Stine, it
just can't be any different; if you hang in the chimney, you're bound
to get black.'"

"Very well then. But the better your sister's intelligence is and the
more she admits that her way of life provokes the judgment and gossip of people, the more she must suffer under the contempt that is
heaped on her."

"Perhaps it would be so," Stine replied, "if all people thought
alike. But that's not the case. Those who condemn her (and who
should sometimes be silent) are always only individuals; most merely
rattle off their lessons and reproaches and mean no harm by it and
often have quite a different feeling about it in their hearts."

"How is that?"

"Well, it's difficult to say; but it is so and can scarcely be any different. For those who suffer need wish to escape from their need and
misery more than anything else, and do nothing but think and plan
how it can be done. To be good and upright, that's all very fine and
beautiful, but after all it's only a luxury for the rich and nobly born,
and anyone who is poor and would like to enjoy the luxuries too, gets
picked on (and most of all by those who were the strictest only yesterday); they talk and sneer that you want to be someone special. 'She
thinks she's it.' Oh, how often have I had to hear these words."

"What a confused way of thinking."

"Well, that's what *you* call it and I don't want to contradict you.
But these same people who seem to be so confused are also very clear
minded and believe in duty when they have accepted a duty of their
free will. And that balances many things. Besides their mere talk,
which is one thing today and another tomorrow, there is also something that remains firm in their minds and that is their word and
their promise. By 'being good' as long as you're free, you can in the
long run act the way you want to; but you have to keep a contract.
What I accept as valid is valid, and honesty has become the main
thing. And so it can happen that a poor woman lives in a situation
that is not admirable and still gets praise for it."

"And this advantage is enjoyed by your sister?"

"Yes. The situation she's in is not admirable, but with the great majority it isn't a disgrace either. The poor woman, they say, she'd rather have a different life; but she's forced to it. And it's a hard nut to crack. And so they don't make her pay for it and only ask one thing from her, that she should keep her promises. Wanda can do or leave whatever she wants to; my sister must not. She has to keep her obligations; and I can assure you she does keep them."

"And your sister has adjusted herself to all that? Perhaps even easily?"

"Well, not easily; rather with difficulty. But to tell the truth, the difficulty is not from her virtue (she'll have none of that), but only because by nature she doesn't like the kind of life she is forced to lead. My sister is industrious and orderly and quite without passion. At least she has assured me of that a hundred times."

"Sincerely?"

"Who can look into her heart? But I believe she's quite sincere. And when you know my sister as well as I do, you will believe it too."

"And yet, the day before yesterday, when I asked her about Olga, she told me: 'You mustn't ask about that. She has a father, that's for certain. But I can't tell you any more.'"

Stine smiled to herself with embarrassment. But at length she said: "Yes, she likes to speak in this tone, it's true; but not because of loose morals but from high spirits. She knows that she is still very attractive and, out of vanity and a desire to please, which I can't deny she has, she feels a constantly tormenting desire to cause astonishment in men, just in order to laugh at them afterward. I know her better because I know her life. She was hardly twenty when Olga was born. There was the child, the product of a commonplace seduction, the details of which I will spare you; and because her claims were laid to rest with a tidy sum of money, she became a 'good catch' and married soon after. And, as in most such cases, a thoroughly decent man. But I must say, she deserved him. She was an excellent wife. There wasn't a breath of scandal in her conduct; and when her husband got sick, she nursed him faithfully, with all she had in her, till he died. To be sure, when he lay in his grave, her last penny was gone, and your uncle, who lived in the same house, took her under his protection. And so it happened — well, you know how. It's now the third year and she doesn't want it to be any different, in spite of the fact that she wails and rages, without thinking very deeply about it, by the way. She regards her present life as a service in which she has no worry about her daily bread. And now I beg you, when you see her again, look at her activity in the light of my words and you will find that I haven't said too much."

"And what does she ask of you?"

"Ask? Nothing. She loves me and is wonderfully decent to me and is glad that I respect myself and encourages me to do so. 'It's always the smartest thing,' these are her words. But if things turned out different, she wouldn't make much of it but would merely say: 'I know quite well, Stine, you can't always do the right thing.' You see, what she calls the right thing, she regards as something desirable but not necessary; she would like me to have it, but no more than that."

During the course of this conversation the sun had gradually been setting and now a last fading red glow still shimmered between the branches of the trees in the park. Stine had long ago laid her embroidery aside and the young count, who was now sitting facing her, saw in the mirror at the window how the gas lamps were being lit all along the street. He was so overcome by the sight that he was silent for a while, watching the unusual street scene.

"I see," said Stine, "the mirror has got you too. I know, it's the same with everybody."

The young count nodded. Then he took Stine's hand as if to say goodbye and, standing up quickly, said: "I may come again, Fräulein Stine?"

"It would be better if you didn't come. You only disturb my peace of mind."

"But you don't forbid it, you don't say no?"

"I don't say no because I mustn't. My sister would find it unwise and I know that I owe her some consideration."

"Well then, till next time, Fräulein Stine."

Stine accompanied him to the small hallway but then, returning swiftly to her room, went to the open window and breathed in the fresh air that came from the park. But there was a fear in her heart, and she had a decided feeling that this acquaintanceship would bring her only hard and painful experiences. "Why didn't I say no? I have now put myself in his hands . . . And yet, I don't want to, don't want to. I had to give her my oath on her deathbed. 'Stine,' she said, don't let go of yourself; it don't pay. You're not as pretty as your sister

Pauline, that's a comfort to me. Ah, those good looks . . .' I was still half a child then; but I'll keep the promise I made to her."

At the same moment when the young count left the room and stepped into the hall, accompanied by Stine, Frau Polzin left her listening post and went over to the folding table, where a brief but intimate dialogue ensued between the couple.

"He really stayed a long time," said Polzin, sitting down at the loom once more. "What was it like?"

"It wasn't like nothing. And it won't be neither."

"Oh, go on," said Polzin. "It'll come out all right Everything takes time. But you always think . . ."

"Oh, get out with your thinking: I don't think at all. I just say, if anything's to happen, it'll happen right off And if it don't happen right off it don't happen at all . . . And I know menfolk too."

"Yeah, yeah," said Polzin with a leer, "you know them all right."

"Listen Polzin, don't get on that line again."

"Eh, I'm not . . . I only meant . . ."

Chapter 9

The young count repeated his visits. During the first week he came every other day, then daily; but he always stayed only till late afternoon; then he left.

Once, by way of exception, evening descended on them, and they opened the windows and looked out. The heavy air caused the street traffic below to make a different impression on the senses than the usual one; the lights burned more dimly and the sound of the horse-car bell was more muffled. Above the park in the distance the moon stood in the sky and cast its shimmer on an obelisk that stood out between the trees; the nightingale sang and the linden trees bloomed in full splendor.

The young count pointed to the scene and said: "Now that's a park and that's what we call it. But isn't it really like a churchyard? The fact that everything is in bloom — why, you find that in the churchyard too. And the obelisk looks like a tombstone."

"And it is something of the sort too."

"How so? Is someone buried in it?"

"No, not buried. But it's a monument that was erected to the memory of the men who went down with the Amazon.* A hundred or more; and I've read their names at one time. It's touching; all young people."

"Yes," said the young count, "I remember now, all young people." Then he lapsed into silence and the tone in which he had spoken almost sounded as if he envied them more than he pitied them.

He left soon after, visibly moved by the turn the conversation had taken, and Stine saw, as he stepped into the street, that he did not, as usual, turn left to the station bridge, but walked straight across the street to the enclosed park. There he stood at the gate, leaning forward, and it seemed that he was trying to read the names on the obelisk in the half light.

That day his visit had lasted somewhat longer; usually he stayed only till sunset, and took pleasure in watching Stine at her work and in hearing her chat. He was interested in all the happenings; but he liked most to hear her tell stories from her life, about her childhood and school days, of her mother's early death, and her confirmation, which had occurred shortly after that, and how the people in the house had taken up a collection to buy her a confirmation dress. And how that same year she had entered the wool and embroidery house for which she still worked; mostly at home, but occasionally in the place of business; and how they lived there and made friendships and during the Christmas week sat together half through the night, and each one read aloud in turn. This was not only permitted but even encouraged; for the head of the business was smart and kind and knew what it was worth to keep those who had to work satisfied and friendly. And that was why they had no turnover in the personnel, or only rarely, and they were all content to stay there, except when they got married. In general, one must say, there was so much talk about exploitation and torment and oppression, but from her experience she could not agree with such talk at all. On the contrary. In the winter they had masked balls and theater parties; for their employer, as she must repeat, never forgot that the poor people, too, liked to escape from their everyday existence occasionally. But the best thing of all was the country picnics in the summer. They rented a few Krems coaches and drove out to the country, even before the dew

*The first training vessel of the Prussian navy. It sank in a storm off the Dutch coast with the loss of all its crew.

had fallen and day broke, to Schildhorn and Grunewald or to Tegel
and Finch Inn. Or an excursion on the water which, however, had
occurred only once as long as she worked there but which remained
an unforgettable experience for her. A steamboat had been leased
and they had sailed up the whole length of the Spree River, past
Treptow and Stralow and past Köpenick Castle and Grünau right
out into the solitude, to a place where there was only one single house
with a high roof of rushes close to the river bank. They had landed
there and played hoops. But her heart had been so full to bursting
that she had been unable to join in the game, at least not right away;
so she had sat down under a beech tree that stood near the house and
had sat there for a good hour, looking out through the hanging
branches at the river and a meadow beyond it that was full of sorrel
and ranunculus, with a black strip of forest behind it. And it had
been so still and lonely as she had never thought God's earth could
be. There was only an occasional fish that leaped out of the water
and a heron that flew above the surface of the river. And when she
had had her fill of the solitude, she had sought out the others again
and joined in their game; and she could still hear the laughter and
still see how the hoops had shone in the sunlight.

The young count liked nothing better than to listen to such stories
and, happy as he was with every word he heard, he found them instructive too. He had grown up in the belief that the large city was a
Babylon, in which popular entertainments were synonymous, if not
with immorality and coarseness, at least with noise and uproar; and
now he had to learn from Stine's lips that this Babylon loved to camp
out in the green and play tag. Such stories did not fail to turn his
thoughts more and more in a direction that was natural to him and
alien to all social prejudices, and when Stine had talked him into a
good mood with such descriptions, both serious and merry, he finally
became communicative himself and even chatty, and told about his
own life: about his private tutor, the theological student, who had
forced him to learn an excessive number of hymns and Biblical quotations because this had been most convenient for the teacher; about
his preparations for the examinations, which he had passed by a
miracle (for he hadn't learned a thing); and finally, after his entry
into the regiment, about his batman and ensign days. That had been
the best time for him, the only happy time, in spite of the fact that
his pious and bullying commander had a firm conviction that "an

ensign is a good-for-nothing." And then suddenly there was war; a general exultation had broken out, and three days later he was sitting in a railway coach, squeezed in among others, deliriously happy to be free from the monotony of the garrison. Deliriously happy. But not for long, of course. For after only three days he was lying on the ground, shot out of his saddle, and had been carried away half dead. And while his comrades had gone from victory to victory, he lay in some hole on the border, torturing himself, not knowing whether he would live or die. And Nature did not really know either and wasn't able to decide. But at last she did decide and he recovered. Or half recovered. Was it for his good? He didn't know. "It's most beautiful when the sun sets and takes a rest from its daily labors."

Stine understood him quite well and begged him not to talk like that. He had a double reason for hoping; for anyone who had been saved from death would have a long life. That's what the proverb said and proverbs were always right.

He smiled at these words and then proceeded to talk of pleasant things. And soon after they parted cordially and in good spirits.

Chapter 10

It was the third week of their acquaintance, a Friday evening, and less than ten minutes had passed since the young count had left the house, when there was a knock on the hall door above. That was the signal for Frau Polzin, who appeared at the door at once and exchanged greetings with the widow Pittelkow.

"Was there a visitor here, dear Polzin? I mean a visitor for Stine?"

"I really can't say, dear Frau Pittelkow. You know, we see and hear nothing."

Frau Polzin seemed desirous of expanding on this her favorite theme; but Stine, who had heard the conversation in the hallway and had recognized her sister's voice, prevented this from happening. "Oh, that's nice of you to come, Pauline." And with that she turned and went back to her room and, groping about cautiously in the dark, she took down the lamp from the corner cupboard that was already enveloped in total evening shadow.

"Never mind, Stine dear," said her sister. "It's so mysterious here, and mystery is just my favorite, and it's always like an old black

crepe-chine shawl where you can wrap yourself and lean against
something and don't need to sit stiff and straight. No, just leave it,
Stine; we got enough light from below. Just look, there's the moon
peeping right over the smokestacks of Sieboldt's factory."

Amid such chatter the widow Pittelkow had taken a seat on the
sofa and, as she snuggled comfortably into the cushions, said: "Well,
what I was gonna say, Stine, the little count was here again just now?"

"Yes, Pauline."

"Lord child, how your cheeks are burning."

"Yes, they're burning; but I really don't know why. It's almost
annoying; I've turned red and don't need to."

"Ah, my darling Stine, you just keep on turning red; sometimes
too much is better 'n too little. But what was I gonna say, the little
count... I don't like his always climbing these stairs at sunset, just
like he had to toll the prayer bell."

"He's the best man in the world, Pauline. I would never have believed that such a good man existed. The first day we exchanged
views and I talked about respectability and dignity and that I'm a
decent girl. But now I almost feel ashamed that I said such things.
For to be anxious all the time isn't good either, and merely shows that
you don't really trust yourself and that you're weaker than you should
be."

The widow Pittelkow smiled to herself and seemed to want to
reply, but Stine continued: "Yes, Pauline, the best person, without
deceit and without arrogance, but without happiness too. When we
sit facing each other, I oftentimes feel as if we had switched roles,
and as if I was a princess and could make him happy. He always looks
at me and listens to every word I say, not merely from make-believe
and because he takes himself seriously. No, I'm no longer such a
dumb creature to imagine such things if it really wasn't so. Nothing
about him of pretense; I can see from looking at him that he's all
attention and that he really likes my chatter. Of course, you'll think
I'm vain and won't believe me."

"Oh, why not, Stine? Why shouldn't I believe it? I believe all of it.
But there's a reason for everything, a good reason even. And I know
what it is."

"And I think I know it too and what's at the bottom of it. You see,
the reason is that he's seen so few people and got to know even fewer.
In his parents' house there weren't many of them (they're all proud

and hard, and his mother is his stepmother), and then he had comrades and superior officers and he heard how his comrades and superiors talked, but he never heard how human beings talk, he doesn't really know that. I'm not thinking this up, I have it from him, these are his own words. Yes, Pauline, that's at the bottom of it. That's the reason why a poor creature like me pleases him; it's no more than that. He's unhappy in his house and family. But above all, don't imagine that he worships me or is my lover or whatever you care to call it. I see clearly that he likes me, but that's something different and I can tell you this: so far not a word has crossed his lips that would make me feel ashamed before God or man or myself."

"I believe it," said the widow Pittelkow. "I believe it all. But my dear Stine, that's just it. That's just the way I imagined it to myself. The very first time I saw him, when the two old gents were with him and Wanda beheaded Holofernes, I knew it. You see, child, I've seen so many men; and when I see some, well, I know 'em at once through and through and can pick 'em out like gloves according to size, and I know at once what's up. And there ain't much up with the young count. He's just a weakling and weaklings are always like that and cause more harm than the wild ones."

Stine looked at her sister.

"Yes, you look at me, child. But it's really and truly so. You think it's a great relief to me when you say 'It isn't a love affair.' Oh, my dear Stine, that's no relief to me at all; the opposite *au contraire*. Love affair, love affair, Lord, love affair is by no means the worst. Today it's still on, tomorrow it's no more and he goes in one direction and she goes in the other and on the third day they both sing, 'Off with you, I got my share.' Ah, Stine, love affairs, believe me, a body don't die from 'em, not even when they turn sour. What's the big fuss about? Well, there's one more Olga running about in the world, and two weeks later nobody gives a tinker's dam anymore. No, no, Stine, love affairs ain't much, a love affair's really nothing. But if it gets lodged here" and she pointed to her heart, "then it becomes something, then it gets to be disgusting."

Stine smiled.

"You laugh and I know why too. You laugh 'cause you think, Pauline knows nothing about love and can't know nothing about it, 'cause it never lodged with her here. And that's correct too. I still managed to get round it. But my dear Stine, you get experience not only from yourself but from other folks too. And I tell you, from the sort of thing you're planning with the count or the count with you, no good has ever come. Everybody's got his place and *you* can't change that, and the little count can't change it neither. I let off steam against the counts, old and young, you know that, you've seen it often enough. But I can blow as long's I wish, my wind ain't gonna blow them away nor the difference between us neither; they're just there and they are what they are and are coddled different from us and can't change their natures. And when one of 'em wants to do it, the others won't put up with it and don't leave off till he's back again as he was. And then you can sit here looking at the sun till it comes back again in the morning in Polzin's room or the widow's room, but he won't come to you, he'll be sitting in a first-class railway carriage with plush seats and an air cushion too and she's wearing a blue veil on her hat and they're going to Italy, hey ho! And that's what's known as a honeymoon."

"Oh, Pauline, it won't happen like that."

"Yes, it will happen like that, my poor little Stine. And if it don't happen like that, then it'll happen even worse; for if he's a stubborn one and insists on running his head through the wall, then you'll have a real mess. Believe me, child, a person can recover from an unhappy love and start over again, but never from an unhappy life."

Chapter 11

For many years Baron Papageno had lived on the fourth floor, with no one above his head, partly because he did not wish to be without the ozone, even in its weak Berlin concentration, which, in his opinion, did not begin until about this level, partly because he had an aversion to hearing half a dozen people and chairs rumbling above him at every meal. He had a mortal hatred of the scraping which, according to his previous experience in the apartments he had rented, was rife wherever children joined the family at the dinner table, that is, children who were not yet old enough to draw up their chairs in a well-bred way and were therefore compelled to supplement their efforts by pushing them toward the table. Besides the screech of slate pencils on slates there was nothing that made him as nervous as such scraping and rumbling over his head.

But to be sure, his concern with the total problem of a dwelling place was not confined to the question of air and domestic tranquillity, but revealed itself even more in the subtlety with which he had gone about choosing the quarter in which he would live, finally settling on Zieten Square at the corner of Mohrenstrasse. As one can imagine, he regarded this, his castle corner, as no more and no less than the most beautiful spot in the city and carried on a perpetual feud on the subject with the old count. The latter for his part much preferred the Behrenstrasse, but he lost every one of the disputes that arose on this subject because he was in the unenviable situation of having to spar against facts with mere sentiments of legitimacy. "I ask you, Count," Papageno would say with a superior air that suggested the futility of all argument, "cross your heart, what is there in the Behrenstrasse? For seven years you have been looking down on the portal of the little Mauerstrasse without ever seeing anything emerging from it except a carriage with an old princess or an even older lady-in-waiting. But to be frank with you, I don't find that attractive enough as a *point de vue*, despite the fact that the carriages are closed. And now would you compare my Mohrenstrasse corner with that? Is it too much to say that from my vantage point the whole of Berlin, or that part of it that counts, lies at my feet? First thing in the morning I am in the position to greet old Zieten on his pedestal. Of course, when he was still white, I liked him even more, and when I used to see him standing there, shining so white in the morning sun, I thought at times that he would begin talking like the late Memnon from his pillar. Well, he never did so even then, and since he has turned bronze and olive color this is wholly impossible; his best days are behind him and behind others too. But best days or not, old Zieten is merely the vanguard on this spot; behind him — it must be because of their large number — I see with every new day old Dessauer's gaiters shining from the left and the tip of old Schwerin's flag glittering from the right. Perhaps it's his sword too. And *en arrière* of my generals the ministries tower, and the palaces of Pless and Borsig, and if I bend forward still more, I can even see the gate of Radziwill, now Bismarck,* and I am filled with the noble patriotic feeling: here

*Zieten, Schwerin, Dessauer — heroes from Frederick the Great's Silesian Wars. Memnon, a statue at Thebes in Egypt; when struck by the rays of the rising sun it supposedly emitted musical tones. The palace of the prince of Pless stood next to that of the Borsig family, owner of the machine works mentioned in the opening paragraph of the story. The palace of Prince Radziwill was bought by the government for Prince Bismarck as the official residence of the Reich chancellors.

is Prussia under old Frederick, there is Prussia under the Iron Chancellor."

In this way Baron Papageno loved to perorate, usually ending with quotations from the first stanza of Schiller's "Ring of Polycrates," which was as much as he, and most people, remembered of this ballad.

Today the baron was leaning out of the window again, but he was looking out at the Mohrenstrasse, not at Zieten Square, watching the sparrows who sat directly opposite him in an eavestrough, keeping up a steady chirping and hopping about, followed by a flapping of their wings, indulging themselves in the extravagances of an orderly (or perhaps disorderly) family existence. He was just pondering whether he should not, for moral and pedagogical reasons, procure for himself a small peashooter and develop a little more asceticism in the birds by shooting small clay pellets at them, when he heard the bell ring. Judging from the time of day that his housekeeper should still have been in the apartment, he continued to remain at his observation post, until repeated ringing of the bell moved him to see who it was.

Baron Papageno had expected to find the mailman at the door and was no little astonished to see instead the young count before him. "Ah, Waldemar, you are cordially welcome. How time and youth change! I was always still in bed at eleven, and you are already up, booted and spurred, paying visits. But please give me your overcoat. Or if you scorn my help, that's all right too; the old motto 'Man helps himself' has its advantages too. On this hook here, please. And now permit me to precede you and be your guide . . . Shall I close the window?"

"I think," said the young count, "we might leave it as it is."

"Good. Or rather, so much the better. Nothing like fresh air. I was just engaged in making observations about natural history, specifically concerning the love life of a family of sparrows in the eavestrough over there. There's nothing more interesting than such observations. And why? Because they permit us to conclude that the most intricate aspects of animal life find their parallel in our own lives. Believe me, Waldemar, there is nothing more false than the idea that there is something special about the species Homo."

The young count nodded agreement. But the old baron, showing not the slightest interest in agreement or skepticism, continued in the jovial tone that was characteristic of him: "Look at these sparrows,

Waldemar. They are my passion. Every age has its passions, and the sparrows are not the worst, when all's said. True, my friends over there aren't pretty, nor are they choosy—about anything; on the contrary, always *frère cochon;** but they're also always amusing, and for me that's the decisive thing. For most animals are—again after a higher analogy—heartily boring, including some that are considered to be privileged and which, I might say, almost receive preference. Take the rooster, for instance. He thinks God knows what of himself and is, after all, nothing but a fop. Apart from the office that he is supposed to perform and which I would not like to discuss at this early hour, what else does he do that is worth talking about? Nothing. In the summertime he keeps office hours from three o'clock in the morning. But that's too little to suit me. And now compare him to the sparrow. Always in a good mood, chatty, jolly. Pokes his nose into everything, wants to know everything, wants to have everything —your pure Prussian in the universal history of birds... But I'm talking a blue streak. Sparrows are simply my hobbyhorse, something of a mixed metaphor. And now please be seated... Cigarettes? Or a cognac?"

And he roamed about the room, to place before the young count first a small box of cigarettes, then an ashtray and matches. But when he was finally finished, he sat down himself and studied his visitor with his friendly gray eyes, which looked out at the world artfully but significantly.

"I have come," the young count began, "concerning a somewhat difficult affair..."

"Ah, a matter of money," Papageno interrupted and attempted to laugh. For his financial situation was not of the best.

"No, it isn't that, my dear Baron. It rather concerns an affair of the heart and social rank. To put it bluntly, I plan to get married."

"Oh, charming. A wedding. Truly, Waldemar, I know of nothing more pleasant that you could tell me. I allowed it to pass by me and am now a confirmed bachelor. But when I hear of someone else who is willing to risk it, I am always gripped by a strong envy and I hear nothing but an organ and dance music, and see nothing but bouquets and tiny white satin slippers. They too are one of my passions, almost stronger even than sparrows. And then cakes are taken out of every baking oven, and in the evening rockets are sent up to the dark

*"Brother pig," i.e., pals.

blue sky from the park and, what I find most interesting of all, the
tavern is filled with frieze skirts, pinafores, and stockings with
clocks."

"My wedding, dear Baron, if it takes place at all, will presumably
be much simpler. I have not chosen among the countesses of the
land, but have, from our point of view, gone down a steep step . . ."

"That too has its advantages. A young middle-class girl?"

"No, Baron. You must descend still another step. I plan, assuming
the girl consents, to become engaged to the widow Pittelkow's sister
Stine."

The baron had jumped up. But he quickly regained control of
himself and said as he sat down: "I'm sure you had your reasons. Besides, I know from a hundred experiences, not to say from my own
experience, what whims the god Amor is subject to and what capers
and deviations he enjoys making. One might almost say that he has a
preference for the exceptional case. But your uncle? Your family?"

"That's precisely, Baron, why I come to you. I'm certain that my
family will never give their consent, it doesn't even enter my mind to
make an effort to obtain it. I respect the prevailing attitudes. But one
can come into the position of being actually opposed to that which
one recognizes as being wholly valid. That is my situation. My family
can never sanction the step that I plan to take, need not, should not,
do so; but they can accept it and pardon it. And this pardon I should
like to have, I ask for nothing more. I don't want to hear any good
words but, if possible, no bad ones either. It is enough for me to be
sure of a certain degree of sympathy which, in the final analysis, always conceals a small remnant of love. And in order to win this
sympathy I need an advocate. Do you think my uncle would consent
to be that advocate? You know him better than I do. He is said to be
proud to the degree of haughtiness; on the other hand I have seen
him in situations that showed the reverse of this. You know what situations I refer to, Baron. And now tell me, what can I expect from my
uncle? If it's your opinion that I am walking into a violent scene filled
with unpleasantness and perhaps full of insults, I shall give up any
attempt to make him my spokesman before my parents."

The baron gazed into space as he twirled his gray, somewhat
scraggly mustache. At length, realizing that he had to say something
for good or ill, he threw himself back into his rocking chair and said,
looking up to the ceiling as fixedly as he had stared at the floor

before: "Dear Haldern, he who gives advice, is easily locked into the vise. And I don't like to get into the vise, any vise. But you seek my opinion, so I must give it and throw my caution to the winds. Well then, it seems essential to me that you should talk to your uncle."

"I'm glad to hear my own view confirmed."

"I say you must certainly speak to him, in spite of the fact that I know he is an absolutely incalculable gentleman and a bundle of contradictions, or at least of characteristics that look like contradictions. He is up to his ears in vanity and class prejudice, and to that extent things don't look too favorable for you; and yet is is just possible that he will hug you and invite himself forthwith to be the godfather of your child. On my honor."

Waldemar smiled to himself, but it was a smile that expressed more doubt than agreement.

"Yes, Waldemar, you smile. And when I judge your uncle by his everyday average moods, I can only say that you are justified in smiling. But to repeat, he is also capable of a diametrically opposite reaction, and I have heard him, in the club and elsewhere, say things that made the blood in my veins turn cold."

"But on questions of this sort?"

"As you put it, precisely on questions of this sort. Was it before or after the war?* No matter, but it's less than ten years ago that the youngest Schwilow became engaged to la Duperré, *balleteuse comme-il-faut*.† You must surely remember her and you must have heard of the affair at the time. Well Waldemar, when I say that la Duperré had a crack in her reputation, it's a gross understatement; for she was one crack from head to toe (her toe was of course the best part of her), and all society was beside itself and the club blackballed poor Schwilow, whom they took to calling Schmilow‡ and I don't know what other names. Nothing but black balls. But what did your uncle do? He gave him a white ball—ostentatiously. And when I asked him on the way home why he had done this, he stopped before the ramp of Prinz Georg Palace, down there where the planks lie, or at least still lay at that time, and made such a loud peroration into the Behrenstrasse that the sentry came up to the iron gate of the ramp and looked down to see what was the matter. And what did he say? That this was the first sensible act of the house of Schwilow in

*The Franco Prussian War of 1870-71.
†"A model of a ballet dancer."
‡Possibly an allusion to the Jewish name Schmil, Samuel.

five hundred years. One of them had been killed at the Cremmer Dam* in the so-called 'first Hohenzollern battle' for the newly created Nürenbergery, which was not exactly the most sensible thing to do; but since that time history had been silent about them, which was truly a piece of good luck, for it would have had to report about a lot of *imbéciles* and at best about all sorts of mediocrities who kept on forming alliances, becoming cousins and in-laws, with the neighboring in-laws (who were just like the Schwilows), and who set themselves the perpetual goal of extending the sixteen ancestors they already had in the age of Albrecht the Bear** to thirty-two, sixty-four and one hundred and twenty-eight. Which they had succeeded in doing long ago, and there was no need to assure anyone of this. For the number had been attained as early as the accession of the Great Elector.† And the same gigantic growth as their ancestral tree had was shown by Stultitia,†† the sole historically authentic ancestress of the family. 'And now, mark my words, Papageno,' he concluded, 'we won't experience it ourselves and can only observe it from some other star—perhaps from Venus, which I like best—but I tell you this, this *balleteuse* will bring the whole tribe to its feet once more; the whole family tree, which is so withered for us and for humanity at large because it greens and blooms so wonderfully for itself, will acquire a new aspect, and where until now there were only county presidents or dikegraves,‡ there will be, from the year 1900 on, young geniuses, generals and statesmen, and some scribbler will write a thick book, which will prove through epitaphs and baptismal certificates that la Duperré was the daughter or granddaughter of Admiral Count Duperré, the same splendid old Duperré who bombarded Algiers in 1830, took the Dey of Tunis captive, and was almost as aristocratic as the Montmorencys and the Lusignans. Believe me, Baron, I know families and family histories, and I pledge you my word, where the old blood is not freshened, the whole clan may as well lie down and die. And for the purpose of freshening blood there are only two legitimate means: illegitimacies or *mésalliances*. And, moralist that I am, I naturally prefer *mésalliances*.'"

*Scene of a battle in which the Elector of Brandenburg defeated the nobles in 1412. The Elector had been the Burggraf of Nürnberg.
**Albrecht the Bear conquered and settled Brandenburg in the 11th century.
†Friedrich Wilhelm of Brandenburg (1620-88).
††"Stupidity."
‡Dikegrave, local official on the north German coast who supervises the maintenance of the dikes.

Waldemar gazed into space. Then he spoke: "I could indeed derive comfort and hope from these words and assume that a friendly reception by my uncle is at least a possibility. But I must remind you, dear Baron, of the old adage that has become such a commonplace with our whole nobility: 'Well, peasant, that's another story.'* It's always the other fellow, the other fellow. What holds for the Schwilows does not hold for the Halderns. Everything may happen to the other fellow, so everyone thinks, but not to himself. It's a remarkable phenomenon with what indifference ancient families judge each other mutually, and what an arsenal of mockery is expended to ridicule competing powers who think of themselves as being our equals. But this ridicule, I must repeat, is always for the other fellow only. What does my uncle care about the Schwilows? The more *balleteuses* the better; for with every new *balleteuse* he not only gets new material for club gossip but a constantly new occasion for becoming conscious, with ever increasing pride, of the abysmal difference between the beduperréd Schwilows and the high-priestly Sarastro† Halderns, who have remained pure. This runs through all the stories of the nobility, is repeated in every family: the freer they are in theory, the more constrained in practice, the narrower and more anxious in the application to their own egos."

"It's as you say, Waldemar, and I will not guarantee that things are different with your uncle. But no matter what his attitude may be, you must grant him the opportunity to express himself. There is always the possibility that he will consent; and if he refuses his consent, it was after all only an uncle, a person deserving half respect, from whom, if worse comes to worst, you can withold respect. And that is the difference between an uncle and a father. Face to face with your father you must keep silent, even when he says the most terrible things to you, and accept the most terrible things from him; the fourth commandment demands it. But the fourth commandment makes a sharp distinction; as far as I know, it does not presume to add the admonition, 'Thou shalt honor thy uncle and thy aunt.' And that's a very lucky thing. Lord, aunts! I had one too once, a remarkable woman, who demanded God knows what from me, but not that I should honor her. The contrary almost. No. Uncles and aunts are

---

*The last line of a poem by Karl Wilhelm Ramler (1725-98), "Der Junker und der Bauer" ("The Squire and the Peasant").
†Sarastro in *The Magic Flute* is a high priest.

hors de concours.* You can defend yourself against an uncle, you can answer him and contradict him and when the situation becomes very bad, stand up to him man to man, even with a pistol in your hand. So forward march, Waldemar, forward march."

The young count stood up, but the baron would not hear of his leaving yet and gently forced his guest back into the sofa. "Surely, Waldemar, you're not leaving without tasting my Lafitte. I know you don't care much for it, and in any case the hour is too early for you. But I will not let you go; if you won't drink, well, you can at least sip. We must touch glasses, if only to bring an unbusinesslike and, if possible, genteel, ending to the business."

While he was talking he had stepped to a wall chest, the bottom section of which was also his wine cellar; he returned with two glasses and a bottle. From the way he pulled the cork one could tell that he was an experienced gourmet. He poured out the wine and they touched glasses. "Listen how they ring. May everything ring with such harmony. Yes, harmony is the right word. And now to your health, Waldemar. I won't keep you much longer, but do stay another five minutes. For I have to make a declaration of love to you, which I'm sure you will permit me to do. A *vieux*† like me is permitted certain liberties. See, you have such a good face, a trifle sad, but that doesn't matter, that only adds to its charm, and I would bet my life on it that you've never hurt anyone in your life. I took you to my heart that first evening . . . And now I'll drink another toast but without mentioning any names. Why should I? The name is locked in your heart . . . And do you see, since then I have become even fonder of you. In the first moments I was scared, I won't deny it, and when I was asked to give advice too, it was a bit too much for me. But the diplomatic and official matters are now behind us and I can now speak bluntly. And so I will tell you frankly but strictly *entre nous* — don't quote me please — I'm always glad when there is someone who has the courage to break through the whole nonsense. What is true of every rule is also true of the rule of noble birth: it is valid until an exceptional case occurs. And thank heaven there are exceptional cases. Long live the exceptional case. Long live . . . Another half glass, Waldemar. And what I wanted to, indeed must tell you in parting: the youngest Schwilow about whom I told you before was right, and

*Out of the running."
†"Old man."

your uncle was doubly right, and society calmed down about la
Duperré. It isn't three months since I met the current Baroness
Schwilow at Tzschazschow, a bit hard to pronounce, in the French
theater, where la Subra played the role of Froufrou.* She looked
charming, I mean the Baroness (Subra did too, of course), and when,
during the intermission, she tossed her little head, causing the diamonds in her earlobes to ring as they jiggled, she rang together the
whole aristocratic society. And do you know who paid most court to
her? Your uncle, of course, who looked as if he himself felt an inclination to write that thick book about the admiral's daughter which
he had foretold someone would write. Yes, Waldemar, yes, success
and courage. Or let us begin with courage. Success depends on
courage. And now, God be with you."

Waldemar had risen and taken his hat. He thanked the baron and
requested permission to repeat his visit if a serious rift should develop.

Chapter 12

In calling on Baron Papageno, Waldemar had wished to hear the
baron's views on a matter that was important to him; but he had, for
the rest, no intention of making a hasty decision. On the contrary,
his plan had been to behave in accordance with his nature, which
was to wait and postpone, if only for a few days. It was the encouraging tone in which the Baron had spoken that had stirred in him the
idea of paying his uncle a visit on the spot, to exploit the good mood
in which he found himself. So he turned from Zieten Square to the
Mauerstrasse and, as he passed the Königsmark Palace, he looked up
to the third floor, behind whose little windows he had chatted away
many a happy hour years ago with a friend who lived there and, after
turning one more street corner, stood before the old-fashioned but
clean and well-preserved house in which his uncle had been occupying the upper story for some years. There were no doormen, but in
their stead a whole system of barred doors; if you rang the bell below
or, what amounts to the same thing, in front of a ground floor barri-
cade, which was richly supplied with all sorts of illegible tin name-
plates, the whole system of doors sometimes sprang open, as though

*Subra was a popular French actress, who played the role of Froufrou in the play of
that title by Ludovic Halévy.

in response to a mysterious pressure on a spring; at other times it did
not, in which latter case there was no end to the individual bells ringing from floor to floor, leading to the appearance of owlish old cooks
on every floor, whose inspection procedure was all the more painful
and thorough, since it was conducted by eye only. Waldemar was too
well and too long acquainted with this ancient Berlin institution to
be offended by it normally; but today this lockout system had a certain symbolic significance for him and every barred door that had to
be passed appeared to him to be an admonition not to try it. But the
good spirits he had brought with him overcame all his doubts and
finally deposited him before the third and last barred door, where he
was received with somewhat surprising friendliness by an old servant
(from the country, of course) with a pudding face; his transformation
into a nobleman's butler was very spotty. The count was at home, he
said, and would be very pleased. "He's looking at his engravings," he
concluded, "and when he's busy with them, he's always in a good
mood."

The servant preceded to announce him, and the first impression
that Waldemar received upon entering was a most favorable one.
The uncle's drawing room always created a sense of comfort based on
good taste in furniture and decoration; today this comfort was enhanced to the point of geniality. The windows were open and from
Unter den Linden came the music of a battalion marching to mount
guard. But that was not all; lights flashed back and forth on the
walls, and on a large and elegant mahogany stand, whose walls
folded downward, there lay a portfolio of copper engravings in which
the count seemed to be browsing busily and with absorption. He
wore Scottish plaid trousers, a velvet jacket, and a fez with a tassel,
all in a rather strange combination which, however, agreed totally
with his assurance that the world belonged to eclecticism.

"Ah, Waldemar. *Soyez le bienvenu.* Heartily welcome, my boy.
Have a chair or come over here . . . Whatever is most comfortable for
you. You find me in a somewhat excited state: Amsler has just sent
me this portfolio of Italian engravings and I am reveling in reminis-
cences. Look . . ."

"Mantegna . . ."

"Yes, Waldemar, Mantegna. You have, of course, seen the original in the Brera. Superb. How pleasing it is to find an understanding

soul. Everyone talks about art but no one knows anything about it, and the few who know, feel nothing, or at least not enough. I should like to know, or rather not know, what the baron would say about this crucified and so strangely foreshortened Christ. Mantegna, for whom incidentally I have a special passion (I hope you have seen his frescoes in the Gonzaga Palace?), Mantegna, I say, has painted the corpse of Christ from the angle of his soles, a marvel of foreshortening, something classical, something unique—of its kind, of course. I'll wager ten to one the baron would assure me that, in this rendering, Christ looks like a bathtub doll. And if he could rise to this level, it would not be the worst thing that could happen. For this much must be admitted: the whole figure has something dwarflike, something koboldlike about it; and as I talk, I am reminded of another comparison, which almost coincides with that of the bathtub doll. Truly, this dwarf Christ reminds me of the Christ child carved in wood in Aracoeli, the bambino doll.* Don't you agree?"

"It does indeed remind one of that," replied Waldemar. "But I fear, dear uncle—"

"—that I've disturbed you. No, Waldemar. An *Italianissimus*† like you can never disturb me when I revel in Italian memories. None of that talk. But these things are disturbing you. At least today. You're distraught, you have something on your mind. And it can't be anything trivial, for I see something like a feverish color in your face and I don't quite like it. Let me tell you, Waldemar, what you know, of course, without my saying so, that your life hangs by a silken thread. So, steady! Let those who can and want live a life of debauchery, but each according to his powers, and roistering nights are not for everyone, and certainly not for you. No harm meant. Hang morality, I'm no moral judge, and certainly the last person to try to recruit you for the Boy Scouts.‡ I pay my dues. But health, Waldemar, health; you are inscribed forever in virtue's register of debts or, to put it more explicitly and yet hardly less poetically, you must live like an immured nun; I don't really trust the others. And now tell me, if it bears the telling, why the hectic spots?"

Waldemar laughed. "From a too early breakfast, dear uncle. I was

*Santa Maria in Aracoeli, in Rome, has a carved icon of the Christ child, the "santo bambino," an object of great veneration.

†An ardent admirer of Italian art.

‡The German text has *Jünglingsverein*, "youth organization," a Protestant chain of youth clubs popular in the 19th century.

at the baron's and when I wanted to leave, he held on to me with a
glass of Lafitte."

Now it was the old count's turn to laugh. "The dear baron. He
calls it Lafitte, God forgive him, and even imagines that he has a
tongue for wine. And why? Because he proceeds from the assumption
that a gourmand must develop into a gourmet, a proposition that is
basically wrong and reminds one of physicians who proudly talk
about their fifty years of experience, during which every one of their
patients who could possibly die did die. Believe me, Waldemar, anyone who shuttles back and forth between Hiller and Dressel* may re-
fine his tongue, and then again he may not. And the latter case is the
rule. But then, at the baron's at eleven o'clock, what's the meaning of
that? There must be something up. And now, out with it!"

"I was there to get his advice.

"From the baron? Advice? Well, I'd rather stick to his Lafitte. If
worse comes to worst, it can be counteracted by pepsin pills, but
there is no way to recover from his advice. Waldemar, I should have
thought... Advice! Well, I'm not one of the seven wise men of
Greece either, but compared to the baron... But perhaps the good
Papageno was only a preliminary stage. Let us hear. Is it a matter
about which I'm permitted to know, about which I can help with
counsel or deed?"

"Yes, uncle. And that's why I'm here. It's as you say, the baron was
only a preliminary stage."

"Well then?"

"Well, in brief, I plan to get married."

The old count struck the table with the palm of his hand.

"You're alarmed..."

"I'm not alarmed. That's not the right word; and if I struck the
table with my hand just now, it was only a vivid, perhaps too vivid,
sign of my interest. Nervousness, nothing more. You are in every way
the object of my concern, Waldemar; I like you immensely, and if I
didn't hate the word because it is so much misused, I would come
right out with it and talk about my love. Truly, my boy, you're the
best of all the living Halderns (perhaps we can include the dead too)
and I don't know what I wouldn't do for you. That you will be my
heir goes without saying; I wish you every conceivable good fortune.
But there is one thing, if it is a thing, that I don't wish for you. A

*High-class restaurants in Berlin on Unter den Linden.

man like you doesn't marry. You owe that to three parties: to yourself, to your offspring (they never fail to be born to people in delicate
health like yourself), and thirdly to the lady you have chosen."

"She's not a lady."

The old count flushed. Among the half-dozen possibilities that
raced through his brain there was one . . . No, no . . . And he composed himself and said, as he regained his calm: "Noy a lady. What
then? Who?"

"Stine."

The old count jumped up, pushed his chair a step behind him,
and said: "Stine! Are you mad, my boy?"

"No, I'm sane. And I ask you if you are willing to listen to me?"

The count said neither yes nor no, sat down again, and looked
questioningly at Waldemar.

"I assume," the latter continued, "that you are willing to listen to
me. And when you have heard my first sentence, you'll be calmer. I
am old enough and in a position to act independently and I *shall* act
independently. There's nothing that can be done about that; illness
makes people stubborn and the Halderns are stubborn by nature. I
haven't come to seek permission from the family, for this permission
would be refused me if the law permitted a refusal. Since this is not
the case, there is no point in asking questions and getting answers.
And so, once more: my mind is made up. You are not to act as my
advocate, least of all for what I plan; I don't come to you with such
matters; and when I nevertheless request a good word from you, it is
because everything hateful is against my nature. Hatred is ugly to
me. I request a good word from you because I feel a need for reconciliation and would like to leave this Old World in peace."

"What does that mean? What do you intend to do? Waldemar, I
beg of you, surely you're not going to stage one of these modern suicide acts for me and, after copulating—the word sticks in my crop—
with your Stine, throw yourself on a railway track or jump into a village pool in the style of Jack and Jill? I beg of you, Waldemar, at least
spare us a debut in the police records."

"That isn't it. I simply intend to call it quits with the Old World
and begin a new life across the sea."

"And end your days as a backwoodsman. Association with Chin-
gachgook, alias *le gros serpent*, marriage of your oldest daughter,
Countess Haldern, with some Uncas or a grandnephew of Leather-

stocking. What do you say to that? And if not a backwoodsman, at least a cowboy, and if not a cowboy, then perhaps a waiter on a Mississippi riverboat. I congratulate you, Waldemar; I don't understand you. Isn't there a trace of Haldern blood in you? Is it so easy to leave a world of clear-cut and legitimate attitudes and to begin again with Adam and Eve?"

"You've hit it, uncle. Yes, to begin again with Adam and Eve, that's what I want, there it is. What terrifies you delights me. I have been persuaded that all things are ruled by the law of opposites, which is also a law of balance, a new theory by someone or other — its authorship is a matter of dispute, I believe. But no matter where its origin, my own experience and the bit of knowledge I possess tell me that it's perfectly true. Old Fritz* hated the Old Testament because he had been tortured with it mercilessly in his youth, and the fat king† liked women and overestimated them because they had been banished from the Prussian Court for half a century. Everything at the bottom rises to the top again at some time, and what we call history and life runs like a wheel; *la grande roue de l'histoire,*‡ the French say. And now permit me to make the application. The Halderns have helped build the feudal pyramid long enough, at long length they have a right to expect the opposite or the balance or whatever you wish to call it. And so Waldemar von Haldern arrives and shows an inclination to begin again with Adam and Eve."

The old man was not insensitive to such propositions, which would very likely have won his approval if their application had not involved a member of his own family. A smile crossed his face, indicating, perhaps, "see, he's supporting his case ably"; indeed, perhaps he even remembered that he himself had more than once, in high spirits and in a mood brought on by wine, proclaimed the same principles. And so it was that he answered in a much calmer tone: "Waldemar, let's talk sensibly. I'm not such an old fogey as you think. I can accept all that, and my conception of the divine world order is not that it coincides fully with the State calendar and the roster of peers. Yes, I will tell you more: I have hours when I feel a fairly strong conviction that they do *not* coincide. And the regulating periods of which you just spoke will come, and perhaps in the not too distant

---

*The popular name for Frederick the Great of Prussia (1712-86).
†Friedrich Wilhelm II of Prussia (1744-97).
‡"The great wheel of history."

future, and perhaps the Adam and Eve times as well. Let them
come, why not? I was never terrified of Adam, even less of Eve. But
are *we* the people to give this historical revolutionary wheel, this
grande roue de l'histoire that you mentioned just now, such an energetic push forward—or backward, if you will? Leave that to others.
At present we are still only the *beati possidentes.** 'Be in possession
and you'll be in the right,' is for the time being still written for our
benefit. Why should we deprive ourselves of this possession and conjure up, at our own expense, a future from which perhaps no one will
profit, certainly not we? Adam, a new beginning for humanity, paradise and Rousseau—all these are wonderful themes, about which
those should feel enthusiasm who in practice only stand to gain and
can lose nothing; but the Halderns will do well to leave this in the
theoretical state and do nothing about it personally."

The young count smiled to himself. "Yes, uncle, that's the general
reaction, the everyday rule of thumb. Of course I know it. In this
situation what you say is valid. And let me assure you: I am far from
wanting to play the role of the world reformer or even merely the
social reformer. I don't have the shoulders for it. But in this particular case, this particular case . . ."

"What particular case?"

"Stine."

"Oh yes, that one," said old Haldern, revealing that in the course
of the conversation he had virtually forgotten its point of departure.
"Yes, Stine . . . It's nonsense. I know that. A bachelor who is more
than fifty years old has been more than once in danger of being ship-
wrecked on that cliff. But these are attacks, bouts of fever. While
they last you interpret world history in the light of the petty emotion
that happens to dominate you at the moment; but by the time tomorrow comes or, in cases of powerful emotion, by next year, you have
had time to think better of it and no longer view things through the
magic and distorting glass of your overheated imagination but
through the windowpane of the everyday. Stine! You should not
break it off abruptly; on the contrary, visit her as long as you feel the
urge to do so; continue having your regular chats with her; but the
moment must come when you have talked yourself out and feel your

*"The happy haves." The quotation that follows is from Schiller's drama *Wallen-
stein.*

error. One fine day the scales will fall from your eyes and you will be looking down into a chasm."

"What chasm?"

"I don't venture to predict that, perhaps merely into the chasm of boredom, perhaps into a worse one. And the day after you will write her a farewell note and start out on your third trip to Rome. Rome is a good match for the Halderns in any case, old with old. But not America. Frankly, I find even Stine too good for the diggings or for a gold-grubber's camp. By the way, what Stine needs from America is a Singer sewing machine."

Waldemar stood up. "From your point of view, uncle, you have a right to talk as you do; yes, perhaps even more harshly and roughly. You have no intention of hurting me, I can hear that from your tone, and I thank you for it. But everything you say cannot change my mind; things must remain as they are. I feel myself not merely attracted — that's an understatement — but actually held by chains to this lovely creature, who is nothing but truthfulness, naturalness and kindness, and a life without her no longer has any value for me and has become unthinkable to me. It need not be America; we could probably find some corner here..."

"May God forbid that..."

"Well then over there. And I beg you to procure for me from my parents in Gross-Haldern, if nothing more, at least the omission of a massive, obdurate protest. I should like to avoid a family excommunication against me if it's at all possible, however little terror all bans and excommunications have held for me. I don't expect a yes or a blessing from them; I renounce it, simply because I must. I only wish to hear that they have accepted the inevitable, that they submit to it as if it were an act of Fate or whatever pious phrase they may choose for it. The young pastor can give them some words to choose from. If old Buntebart were still living, it would be better. The estate will pass on to my younger brother, although Gross- and Klein-Haldern are held in primogeniture; I'll make the renunciation public through the courts. I ask only for a legal share, so that I can satisfy my most essential needs. And now once more: will you be my spokesman, who will at least avert the most painful aspects from me and keep the possibility of a future reconciliation open for me, however distant that future may be?"

The old count shook his head.

"So it's no. And even that is good, because it's something definite. I thank you for listening to me and sparing me phrases about social position, and above all that French word* that is so much tossed about in our circles on occasions like this. And now farewell, I shall not see you again. Everything that still remains to be done or said will happen through others."

The old count had risen too and was pacing up and down the room on the carpet. But then he stopped and spoke to himself, not without emotion: "And this is my fault . . . mine."

"Fault? Yours? Fault for my happiness? No, uncle, only thanks and thanks again." And with that he took his hat to go, but stopped once more, apparently in doubt whether to shake his uncle's hand or not.

The old count saw it and likewise took a step back.

And so the nephew merely made a formal bow and strode to the door that led to the hallway.

In the hall Johann, who had been listening, stood with Waldemar's topcoat in his hands and was not remiss in obsequiousness. But the emphatic silence in which he persevered seemed designed to express disapproval on his part too. For he had been in the service of the Halderns long enough to think even more sternly on the subject of misalliances than his master.

Chapter 13

Only when he was alone again did the old count become fully aware of what he had heard. To be sure, in the very first moment the blood had rushed to his head; but Waldemar's calm demeanor, and perhaps even more an inclination toward the offbeat and the adventurous, had repressed his displeasure. But this state could not last, and now that Waldemar was gone and the discussion concerning the irritating question was at an end, the moment had come for his first repressed emotions—indignation and terror—to burst into flame.

Truly, actual terror. He was the ground and cause of all these confusions, which would not have occurred if he, for his part, had suppressed the foolish whim of introducing Waldemar to the ménage of the widow Pittelkow. This faux pas of his would have to reach his

*Noblesse oblige, aristocracy imposes obligations.

older brother, the lord of the manor of Gross- and Klein-Haldern, sooner or later, and if he should then find himself accused, in words or in silence, how would he meet the accusation? And even if he could face *him*, his brother, how could he face *her*, his sister-in-law? She was the proudest woman far and wide, a Courland lady* supported by her memories of St. Petersburg, before whom even the Halderns could maintain face only with difficulty and for whom a daughter-in-law in the style of Stine Rehbein would simply mean shame and death. What use was it for Waldemar to leave the country and expatriate himself for good? The fact remained that a Haldern had debased himself, and with it the scandal, the disgrace, the ridicule. And the last was the worst.

"No, it won't do," the count reflected as he paced up and down his room, getting more and more excited and nervous. "I interfere with force. It's my fault; yes, yes, yes and yes again ... I will not shake it off. But it wasn't my stupidity alone that brought the matter so far, my good friend is behind it, that black witch, my good Pittelkow, who is becoming more hare-brained every day. For, however much *bon sens* she may have, she is possessed by the devil of arrogance, and while with her left hand she believes she can do what she pleases with me, with her right she wants to insinuate her blond sister, with that boring, virtuous face, into our family. But I will show the House of Pittelkow and all its annexes that it has reckoned without its host. Ungrateful creature. I fished her out of the gutter, and as a reward for my good deed she repays me in this coin."

While he was thus speaking to himself, he happened to look into the mirror. He went up to it, adjusted his red neckcloth and laughed. "So that's the way a man of honor, a savior of widows and father to orphans, looks ... Pleased to meet you." And he bowed to himself. "Same old story. When you're in the soup, you begin to play the innocent, abuse your accomplices, who are mostly far less to blame than you, and let others pay for the stupidities that your honorable self has committed. And in my case this base whitewashing even calls itself aristocratic attitude and elevates itself above the Pittelkows, who at least don't go through life affecting the principle of noblesse oblige. Pitiful. Wherever you look, you see cause for feeling ashamed. And

*Courland, Lettish territory settled by the Teutonic Order, containing a strong German minority. From 1795 to 1918 it was a Russian province. St. Petersburg was the capital of the Russian Empire.

yet something must be done, even if my guilt were ten times greater."

At these words he reached for the bellpull. "A cab, Johann." And while Johann went to the nearest cab stand, the old count spruced up carefully before his mirror but with the speed of an old soldier.

Half an hour later the cab stopped at the entrance to Veterans' Park; the old count got out, crossed the road, and walked to the familiar house, which stood there as if dead in the harsh light of the midday sun. Pauline was standing at the window; she recognized the count as he made for her apartment with hasty steps. "Lord," she said, "now he comes in the daytime too!" But all the same she smoothed her collar and threw her kitchen apron behind the stove. And then she heard the bell.

"Mama at home?"

Olga was going "to find out"; but the count was not in the mood to submit to all sorts of ridiculous formalities about being announced; and so, following Olga, he arrived at the front room at the same time she did.

"Good day, widow."

The widow Pittelkow saw that he was in a bad mood and therefore replied in a tone of utter indifference, without moving from her position at the window: "Good day, Count... A shameful heat..."

The old count showed no desire to engage in a conversation about the weather, but threw himself into the sofa without ceremony and said, as he fanned himself with his handkerchief: "I'm here today about a serious matter, Pauline... What is this about Stine?"

"About Stine?"

"Yes. She's had an affair with my newphew. And now he's gone mad and wants to marry her. And whose fault is it? Yours, Pauline. You've brought this on me. You, you alone. Stine doesn't take three steps, doesn't go from here to the window, without asking you; she's never done anything that you didn't want or didn't approve, and this scandal falls on your shoulders. I ask you whether I deserve such treatment. Well, we shall see what happens. You may want what you want, I want what I want. The world has become insane enough, but we haven't reached the point where the Houses of Haldern and Pittel-kow, arm in arm, will challenge this century in the lists.* No, Pauline, I refuse to tolerate such nonsense and what I demand from you is this: that you put an end to this childish situation."

*Approximation of a line in Schiller's drama *Don Carlos*.

"Can't."

"Because you won't."

"Oh, I want to, all right. I wanted to as soon as I saw the affair starting off. It's a misfortune for my Stine."

"What?"

"It's a misfortune for my Stine. Yes, Count. Or do you think I'm stupid enough to think that such a thing is a stroke of luck? Oh, goodness me, then you hail from Errland, Count. And now listen to me a mite. Over there lives a locksmith, a master craftsman, and he had a nephew, a very dear person, who served with the 'Cockchafers' — but now he's back in the business again. Well, last summer he was always buzzing around Stine, and if he weds the girl, I'll go to the cathedral next Sunday and have myself a good cry and thank the good Lord for His great benevolence and mercy, which I ain't done for a good long time. Yes, Count, that's the situation. My Stine ain't the girl to latch on to anybody or put her claws into a man with force, count or no count. She's healthy and decent and there's never a flaw about her, which not everyone can say about himself. Eh?"

"Don't give me that talk. Those are evasions and phrases to get around the business. That's not the point. Flaws! What do you mean flaws? I haven't said a thing against Stine physically, I know she's a good kid. But what do you mean with your 'flaw' and 'which not everybody can say about himself'? Do you mean me? Let it go; it doesn't bother me; I'm beyond that. But you mean my nephew, and that irritates me and annoys me, because it once more shows up your bad character. Or if not your bad character, at least that you are hard and without real kindness. What's the meaning of that sarcastic reproach, and the sneering face with which it was made? Waldemar is a poor, unhappy person; to be sure he can't swallow a sword or support an anvil on his chest. If you want to call that a flaw, you may do so. But his illness and his misery, they are precisely a source of honor to him before God and man. For where did he get them? He got them in the war. He wasn't nineteen yet and a frail, skinny ensign in the dragoons and looked like a milksop. I have to admit that. But he was a Haldern. And because he was one, he was the first in the squadron to meet the enemy, and before they could break through the French square formation, he collapsed with two bullets in him and a bayonet wound, and his horse on top of him. And that was too much for the young lad. He was on his back for two years, being doctored and sickly, and now he's dragging himself through the world weak and sick; and because he doesn't know what to do, he visits Stine and wants to marry her. That's nonsense. But don't give me any of your jabs and sarcasms, which don't apply to the poor lad. He has the Iron Cross and I insist that you talk about him respectfully."

Pauline laughed. "Lord, Count, when a person listens to you, she'd have to think really and truly that I want to make fun of a person because he's been a good boy. But that's just another of those notions of yours, that you always think we understand nothing about it and know nothing about our country and precious little about courage. But what's the truth of it? Dammit all, I'm for my country too and for Wilhelm; and any man as has taken his bones to market gets my respect and I don't need nobody to tell me to respect him. And then, Count, don't you bring up them Halderns all the time — I've known some that was only nineteen too, and they weren't no Halderns and they didn't sit horseback; no, but they moved about on their own two pins and they too had to keep going forward. And in the end, when the going was uphill and they couldn't make it no more, they hung on to the shrubbery 'cause they would have fallen backwards and always those damn things all round that screeched so and made a noise like a coffee grinder. No, no, Count, the Halderns didn't do it by theirselves and the young count neither. But he done his duty and gave his health for it and so I won't say a thing against him — aah, I'd sooner bite my tongue off. I only meant to say that there was no fault in Stine. And I'll stick by that. And now we're on the subject, I stick by this too, that counts suffer from this more often than the likes of us folk, 'specially the likes of Stine. I don't know what the doctors call it, but I know this much, there's faults that go back to the great great granfathers. And the great granfathers, from the time of the fat king, well, they were a bad lot. And the Halderns weren't no different from the others, I bet."

"That's all right," the count said, his equanimity restored. "What you said at first about the locksmith across the street and his nephew, that's the main thing, that convinced me. I now believe that you're innocent in the matter and must admit that it wouldn't be in your character. You're far too clever and understanding to set such nonsense in motion. For you yourself say so: it's nonsense, and a misfortune too. And for both of them."

Pauline nodded agreement.

"A misfortune, I say. And now let's consider how we can get out of

it or at least keep it in check and restore order to the affair. Waldemar is stubborn (all sick people are) and will not abandon his plan,
of that I'm convinced. So we can only gain anything by winning some
influence over the other party, your sister."

The widow Pittelkow shrugged her shoulders.

"You mean that she too has no lack of stubbornness. And I almost
believe you. Besides, no persuasion will be of any use as long as there
is still a possibility for Stine to see Waldemar and talk to him. Of
course, she'd rather listen to him than to us. Everyone likes to hear
what flatters and pleases him. So I see only one way: she must leave
this place. And I'll give you my full help in bringing this about.
Think. She must have a friend or relative somewhere in the world, in
the Priegnitz or Uckermark,* and if not, we must invent one. She
must go to that friend or relative. Away from here, away. Time
gained means everything gained. And once they have been separated
and they both realize for two weeks that life can go on even without a
kiss in the moonlight, we've at least made a good beginning. And
then we'll see what to do next."

The widow Pittelkow agreed on the essentials and, when Haldern
told her that Waldemar wanted to emigrate to America, she quickly
reverted to her everyday good-natured tone of voice. "I was against
the thing from the start. And now he wants to go to America yet!
Lord Almighty, what'll he do there? They really have to pitch hay
there, seven hours under the blazing sun, he'll just collapse. Only this
morning they carried a man past here from the construction job, and
him a stone carrier with a mustache and a soldier's helmet, which are
always the strongest chaps. And now this poor invalid. Count, I'll fix
the matter and go see Wanda this minute, she'll make up a story for
us. And when I have the story, we'll pack up our Stine and send her
on to Alt-Landsberg or to Bernau with its stork nest or to Fürsten-
wald. She's always ready to help people out, so we must tell her a
story about helping and aiding someone."

The count was delighted, and so they parted.

Chapter 14

After leaving his uncle, Waldemar had gone first to Bellevue
Castle and from there to a summer place situated a few hundred feet

*I.e., in some remote town or region.

further downstream, which he usually sought out on the late afternoons when he went to see Stine. IIe loved to sit there in the shade of
the old trees and to think and dream. The owner of this place and his
wife had known him for years; he was also the intimate friend of the
numerous sparrows domiciled there, which hopped around the table
as soon as he sat down and pecked at the scraps and crumbs of cake
that he ordered especially for them. All this happened today as usual;
only the waiters put their heads together out of curiosity and considered what could have made their guest, who regularly came late in
the afternoon, come so early today. For it was only two o'clock. Waldemar took some pleasure in observing this petty curiosity and read
with certainty in the features of the waiters the course of their conversation, as if he were listening to them from the nearest tree. Nothing
whatever escaped him and, after watching for a while the clouds of
smoke rise from the Borsig ironworks — which were situated directly
opposite him — and disappear toward the Jungfernheide, he suddenly
directed his gaze once more to the side and counted the piers or the
boats on the Spree, which swam down the river from the city. He felt
not a trace of excitement and, what was moreover characteristic of
him, he scarcely thought of the conversation he had just had with his
uncle. Even though he was unable to find peace, to have wanted it
honestly and sincerely was a lot for him. And that was indeed the
case. From this consciousness he derived something like comfort and
resignation, and if resignation was not absolutely the best thing, not
peace itself, still it came closest to peace.

He stayed there about an hour. Only then did he stand up and
walk toward the exit. But from outside he looked back once more
over the picket fence into the garden. There was the platform for the
orchestra with its rickety music stands, and immediately behind it
the primitive buffet with the inlaid crossbars from which numerous
white beer coasters hung like small signs. And close beside it, half
overgrown by a conically shaped acacia, stood the table he had just
left, on whose green top the lights and shadows were now dancing.
He could not tear himself away from all this and impressed it on his
memory, as if he had a definite feeling that he would never see it
again. "Happiness, happiness, who will say what you are and where
you are? In Sorrento, with the view toward Capri, I was wretched and
unhappy; and here I have been happy." And now he walked downstream to the Moabit Bridge, because he intended to walk back on

the other bank. But when he reached the other side he slowly took the road to Humboldt Harbor, making occasional stops, and finally the way to Veterans' Park. There he paused and studied the house facing him. Stine was standing at the upstairs window. He waved to her and then went up to her apartment.

Stine was waiting for him at the door, happy to see him, but with a touch of anxiety on her face because he usually did not come before the twilight hour.

"What is it?" she said. "You look so different."

"Possibly. But it's nothing. I'm perfectly calm."

"Oh, don't say that. When we say we're calm, we never are."

"How do you know that?"

"I believe everyone learns it life soon to that. And then I know it from Pauline. When she says to me, 'Stine, now I'm calm again,' things are always still pretty bad. But now tell me, what's up?"

"What's up? A trifle. Really nothing. I always stood alone among my family, and now I shall stand a little more alone still. It affects you for a moment but not for long."

"You're keeping something from me. Speak."

"Of course; that's why I'm here. And so hear me. I visited my uncle to tell him...yes, tell him what, Stine? To tell him that I love you..."

Stine began to tremble.

"...and that I want to marry you... Yes, marry; not to make a Countess Haldern out of you, but simply a Stine Haldern, a little woman who is precious to me; and that we then intended to emigrate to America. And for this step I was asking for his consent, or at least for his intercession with my parents."

"And?"

"He refused me this intercession."

"Oh, what have you done?"

"Shouldn't I have done it?"

"What have you done?" repeated Stine, adding: "And I, poor creature, am to blame for it. Am to blame, because I let the thing happen and never really asked myself: What will come of it? And when the question did come to me, I repressed it and didn't let it arise and only thought: be happy as long as you can. And that wasn't right. I knew it wouldn't last forever; but at least I counted on a long time. And now it's all been wrong and our happiness is over, far, far sooner than was necessary, only because you wanted it to last."

Waldemar wanted to contradict her; but Stine would not let him and replied, her voice becoming more imploring and urgent with every moment: "You want to go to America because it won't work out here. But believe me, it won't work out there either. It might work for a while, perhaps for a year or two, but then it would be over, even there. Don't think that I wouldn't see the difference between us. Look, I was proud to be allowed to love such a good heart as yours; and when my love was returned, it gave me the greatest happiness in my life. But I would feel silly and childish if I wanted to play the part of Stine Haldern. Yes, Waldemar, that's how it is, and because you wanted something like that, this has come to such a swift end. Years ago — I was still a child — I once saw a fairy play in which two people were happy; but the fairy had told them that their happiness would vanish forever if a certain word or a certain name were spoken. Do you see, so it was with us too. Now you've spoken the word and now it's gone, gone because people know about it. Forget me; you will. And even if you don't, I don't want to be a chain that you have to drag around all your life. You must be free, you of all people."

"Oh, my dear Stine, how little you know me. You speak of a chain and that I must be free. Freedom. Well yes, my life has been free, what people call being free, since I left my parents' house, and in some respects even earlier. But what was the course of my life with all this freedom? What was it since my youth? We've talked so much about it and I've told you about my childhood and about the boring tutor, who had to play the role of the pious man because he was instructed to do so and who tortured me with proverbs and commandments and the everlasting 'What is that?' and with the credo, which I never understood and neither did he. But this poor, sad man (perhaps I shouldn't mock him, I least of all), who always suffered from a catarrh and a love affair, was far from the worst evil. The worst was that I was a stranger in the house itself, with my own parents. And why? I thought about it later on, and observed in more than one family how harsh parents are to their children if the children don't measure up to certain quite precise wishes and expectations."

Stine, who had possibly made the same observation in her modest sphere, nodded agreement, and Waldemar, who rejoiced in this acquiescence, continued: "I suppose it's the same everywhere, at least

it was so in our family. And add to this the whims and ill-humor of a
woman who, because a Grand Duke had once written her a note that
was almost a declaration of love, therefore imagined that her marriage was nothing but a misalliance — there you have the portrait of
my stepmother. Throughout the summer she was in a bad humor
because of the boring life in the country and because of the ladies in
the neighborhood, who were not ladies at all, at least not in her eyes;
and when she went to the court in the winter, she was in an even
worse humor, because there were more beautiful and more distinguished women there, who offered her competition. And I had to
pay for this ill humor; these resentments she took out on me, whom
she disliked from the outset. And when I grew up and wanted to show
in turn that I wasn't pleased with everything, my life was hardly a
bed of roses. And so it went until at the age of nineteen I joined up
and went into battle and got a bullet or two, about which I've told
you. Then things improved for a moment, to be sure, and for about
three months I was the hero and center of interest in the family, especially when telegrams came from the prince asking about my condition. Yes, Stine, that was my greatest period. But I should have died
or molted swiftly back to health and a good career; but because I did
neither the one nor the other but just vegetated, a burden to many
and a joy to none, my fame was soon over. My father might perhaps
have changed things if he had dared to intercede firmly on my behalf
and had not placed his marital and domestic peace above my happiness. As it was, he was unable to assert himself, and so I lived on for
many years without really knowing what a heart and love can mean.
Now I know. And now that I do know it and want to hold on to my
happiness, I am asked to let it slip out of my hands. And all that
merely because you talk of claims and perhaps really believe in them,
claims that are supposed to be in my blood and that cannot be renounced because they are in the blood. Oh, my dear Stine, what is it
I'm giving up? Nothing, nothing at all. I yearn to plant a tree or to
see a brood of hens grow up or perhaps merely to see a hive of bees
swarm."

He was silent and gazed straight ahead of him; but Stine took his
hand and said: "How little you know yourself. The son of the day-
laborer in your village may perhaps live this way and be happy, but
not you. You are not without claims merely because you want to be,
and it's one thing to imagine a poor and simple life and another to

lead such a life. And all that's lacking is to be supplied by the heart! It can't do that, and you will suddenly feel how small and poor I am. Ah, the fact that I'm talking like this at this moment is in itself perhaps a weakness and shows poverty of feeling; but I don't resist it, because I believe that everything you're planning will only bring misfortune, disappointment, and misery. The old count is against it and your parents are against it (you say so yourself), and I have never seen anything turn out happily which from the beginning had no blessing on it. It's against the fourth commandment, and anyone who acts against that hasn't a peaceful hour ahead of him and will be pursued by misfortune."

"Ah, my dear Stine, that's just talk, and now you bring up the fourth commandment. Believe me, the fourth commandment has its limits too. Father and mother are not merely father and mother, they're human beings too, and as human beings they can be as mistaken as you and I. No, let me tell you what it is and why you think you have to talk this way. I have some knowledge of the human heart; for you see, a person who spends years on a sickbed has a lot of time to pursue many matters, and the most alluring are the serpentine courses of the heart, one's own and other people's. And now listen, I'll tell you what it is. It's an arrogance in your family, enough for three counts, something defiant and challenging and a tendency to tell the truth, and sometimes even more. Your sister has a strong dose of it and you have it too; you have your share of it. And you see, in this false pride of yours you don't want me to believe even for a moment that you have as much as thought of a Stine Haldern. It's against your honor. Am I right, is it so?"

"No."

"Good. I believe you. I know with certainty that you would say 'yes' if you could. And that you can say this honest 'no' is a beautiful thing about you, and shows me once more what a good choice I made. And now we are to founder on delusions. *I* have put my prejudices behind me, and now *you* want to keep yours. I implore you, Stine, liberate yourself from them and above all get rid of your anxieties."

Stine shook her head.

"Then nothing is to come of it?"

"It can't."

"And the whole thing has been nothing more than a summer game?"

"It must be so."

"And doesn't the possibility occur to you that all this could cost me my life?"

"For heaven's sake, Waldemar!"

"I don't want exclamations, I want an answer. A 'yes,' brief and definite and then let's go, go. Speak, Stine, you know what I ask. Will you?"

"No."

And she rushed past him in tears. But he held her fast and said: "Stine, we're not going to part this way. 'No' is not to be your last word. Sit down and look at me. And now tell me: Did you really love me?"

"Yes."

"With your heart?"

"With all my heart."

And the convulsive sobbing with which she spoke became a fainting fit. When she regained consciousness she was alone.

Chapter 15

Waldemar turned right in the direction of the Oranienburg Gate because he wished to transact several items of business in a bank that was situated on the corner of Unter den Linden and the Friedrichsstrasse. But near the Weidendamm Bridge it occurred to him that offices were probably already closed for the day, so he gave up his walk to the city and returned to his apartment, which was located very close to the General Staff Building. This location made him a neighbor of Count Moltke; he liked to mention this proximity and to assure people both seriously and in jest: "One can't be better taken care of than at this spot. The man who can look after our national security looks after our private security too."

The clock in the Dorotheenstadt Church struck five when our friend, who was only too inclined to make such reflections, turned into the Schiffbauerdamm, and before the tower clock had ceased its tolling, the small clocks, which existed in fairly large numbers on the waterfront and at the rear of the factory buildings on the other side, were striking the hour too. He counted the strokes, scanned the quays on both sides of the river, and rejoiced in the lively and yet quiet life

that surged everywhere around here. Nothing escaped him, not even
the activity on the boats, on whose ropes and rope ladders, and occasionally on rowing poles laid transversely, all sorts of washing hung
out for drying, and only when, after slowly strolling along, he had
the Graefe Clinic behind him, did he cease observing and walk more
swiftly to the Unterbaum Bridge. Here he paused again and observed
the bronze candelabra which, because they had not formed a patina
yet, flashed and glittered dazzlingly in the slanting rays of the sun.
"How pretty all this is. Yes, better days are coming. But — whoever
will live to see them. *Qui vivra, verra* . . ." and he broke off, and
from the arches of the bridge looked at the willow trees that lined the
quay far below; from their gray-green foliage a few dead branches
stood out like brooms. These trees were his favorites. "Half dead, but
still green."

Finally he came from the Kronprinz bank and the Alsenstrasse to
the charming square, adorned with shrubbery and flower beds and
between these, with marble statues and fountains; situated next to
the Königsplatz, it forms a part of it and yet is separated from it. A
cool breeze was blowing, bringing relief from the heat, but from the
flower beds came a delicate scent of mignonette, while over at Kroll's
the concert had just begun. Our invalid breathed all this fragrance
and melody in deep draughts. "How long since I have breathed so
freely. 'My Queen, life *is* beautiful,'† the immortal words of an opti-
mistic marquis, and a pessimistic little count babbles them after
him."

Now the music in the distance was silent and Waldemar, strolling
up and down between the large round beds, studied the figures that
were formed in the lawns out of starwort and red verbena. But finally
he went up to a bench that was thickly overgrown with all sorts of
shrubbery planted immediately behind it and therefore afforded full
shade. On this bench he sat down, for he had grown tired. His long
walk in the heat had sapped his strength, and so he involuntarily
closed his eyes and fell to dreaming and forgetting. When he awoke
again he did not know whether it had been sleep or a fainting fit. "I
believe Death comes like that"; he regained full consciousness only
gradually, and now noticed that a ladybug had settled on his hand.
It remained there, crawling back and forth, no matter how hard he
shook his hand and blew on the insect. "What a fine instinct animals

*"He who will live will see."
†Quotation from Schiller's *Don Carlos,* spoken by Marquis Rosa.

have; they know that they're secure." But at length the insect did fly away and Waldemar, bending forward from his bench, began to draw all sorts of figures in the sand without quite knowing what he was doing. But when he gathered his wits together he saw that they were semicircles that extended around the tips of his boots, narrow at first but growing wider and larger. "An involuntary symbol of my days. Semicircles! No end, no rounding, no completion . . . Half, half . . . And now, when I draw a transverse line," and he really drew such a line, "the half comes to an end all right, but it won't ever be fully rounded."

Lost in such thoughts, he sat there a while longer. Then he stood up and walked to his apartment. Located at the beginning of Zelten-strasse, it consisted of a front and back room on the third floor; the front room faced the park area of the Kroll Garden, the other looked on a building site overgrown with grass and extending to the edge of the Spree. Behind it were the red roofs of the Moabit district, and further to the left the green border of the Jungfernheide. Waldemar loved this view, and for that reason had made this room, his bed-room, into a living room and study, and had set up an old German rolltop desk in it.

He did not remain in the front room today either; he exchanged his tight-fitting coat for a lightweight jacket and stepped to the win-dow of his bedroom. The sun was setting, and he remembered the day on which he had enjoyed the same sunset picture from Stine's window . . . "Just as it was then," he said to himself. And he looked at the glow which grew redder until the globe of the sun had sunk and full twilight surrounded him.

On his stationery kit lay a small revolver, beautifully decorated and furnished with an ivory handle. He took it in his hand and said: "A toy. And yet it will do the job. With good will much can be achieved; 'with a bare bodkin'* says Hamlet and he is right. But I can't do it. I feel as if everything here were still painful and raw, or that a scar had only just formed. No, I shrink from doing it, though I feel that it would be more appropriate to my class and more Haldern-esque. But what does it matter? The Halderns already have so much to forgive me, they'll have to forgive me this too. I haven't the time to grieve over points like these."

And he put the revolver down.

*The German text has "with a bare [or mere] needle," which is the rendering of Shakespeare's phrase by Tieck and Schlegel in their Shakespeare translation.

"So I must try another way," he continued after a while. "And after all, why not? Is it such a great disgrace? Hardly. No doubt very distinguished comrades can be found. But who are they? I was never brilliant in history (was I in anything?) and now I can't think of any examples. Hannibal . . . I can't get beyond him. However, he is sufficient. And there must certainly be a few others."

While he was speaking he opened one of the lower drawers of his desk and looked for a little box. When he found it he began to reflect again. "Small, too. Even smaller than the toy there. And yet adequate. Saved up from long ago, and my premonition was sound when I held on to it then."

At these words he stood up, trimmed a Roman lamp that he had brought with him from the south and, after lighting its four small wicks, extracted some envelopes and sheets of paper from a portfolio that lay before him.

Then he wrote:

My dear Uncle:

When you receive these lines all my confusions will be resolved. Somewhat violently. But that doesn't matter. It will be your task, and in any case I beg you, to report the event to Gross-Haldern. What decided my course of action, as you will perhaps already know when these lines reach you, but in any case will learn very soon, was resistance from a very different and very unexpected quarter. And so what happened, happened. I accuse no one; if there is any guilt, it is mine. The good child was only too right in refusing me, but I was no longer strong enough to accept it. On the last page of my notebook I have disposed of my inheritance from my mother. I hope I can say: disposed with due consideration for the Halderns. Give the sheet to Solicitor Erbkamm; he will execute my will. Of course I know that she who will profit by the settlement, which is meant to express my gratitude to her, will refuse it; but see to it that a certain part of it will remain hers even against her will. A will can change, and I am happy in the thought that I may perhaps, even if it is only many years later, be able some day to help and benefit a person whose heart I was destined to sadden and hurt, though unintentionally. I shall not write to my father; I wish to avoid quarrels. I cannot put my affairs into better hands than yours, for I well know what you were to me, in spite of everything. However little of a Haldern I was, I yet wish to be buried in the Haldern vault. This is my last wish. I am assured of your kind memory.

Your Waldemar

He put the sheet to one side, laid his pen down, and ran his hand over his eyes and forehead. "And now the last one."

And he took a second sheet of paper and wrote:

My dear Stine:

You did not want to take the long journey with me, and so I am taking the longer one. I believe what you did was right and I hope that my concluding act will be right too. Often there is only one way of restoring order. Above all, don't accuse yourself. The hours we spent together were, from the very first day, sunset hours, and that is what they remained. But they were happy hours all the same... I thank you for all your kindness and love. My life did have some substance after all. "Forget me"—I mustn't say that; it would not come from my heart and would be foolish too, for I know you won't and can't forget me. So: remember me. But remember me kindly and above all, do not give up hope and happiness because I gave them up. Farewell. I owe you the very best.

Your Waldemar

When he had sealed both letters, he leaned back in his chair and the pleasant pictures that this summer had brought him passed through his mind once more. At least so it seemed, for he was smiling. But then he took the little box that was lying before him in readiness and pushed out the inner box from the enveloping cover. It was a tight fit; one could see that he had been collecting capsules for a long time, adding new ones to the crowded box. "Sleeping powders! Yes, I knew your hour would come." And now he broke the capsules open one by one and emptied their content slowly and carefully into a small ruby-colored glass half filled with water. "There, that's it." And as he raised the glass and set it down again, he went to the window once more and looked out. The moon, a faint sickle, had risen and shed its light over the river and far beyond it over field and forest.

"It's bright enough... And I don't want to let the lamp burn and sputter and go out with the dawn, as if I had ended with a banquet and intoxication. *My* life a bacchanal!"

And he extinguished the lights and drank. And then he resumed his seat and leaned back and closed his eyes.

Chapter 16

On the third day after that, beginning at noon, there was a quiet but lively activity at the railway station of Klein-Haldern. A gate near the station house was draped in fir branches; oleander and laurel trees stood in front of the gate, forming a hedge, and on the crossbeam hung a large wreath of immortelles, with the Haldern coat of arms filling the center. Behind the station house several manorial carriages were waiting, the coachmen wearing crepe bands on their hats; but in a stretch of garden that served as an extension of the platform, a dozen people dressed in black, middle-aged villagers, walked up and down, talking seriously in soft tones.

At 3:30 the train arrived. "Haldern, Klein-Haldern," the conductors called and opened several doors, from which various people emerged: first an old clergyman of marked dignity, who was given priority because of his position and his age; then a colonel with his adjutant; and finally several gentlemen copiously adorned with braid, who were unknown even to the stationmaster of Klein-Haldern. But the plumes on their hats, and still more the studied respect they received even from the colonel, left no doubt that they must be, if not princes, at least gentlemen of the court or perhaps high officials of the ministry. They all went to the exit, before which the carriages appeared at that moment, and a minute later one could see only a cloud of dust which, growing thicker all the time, moved along the half-paved road that led to the next village.

While this scene was being enacted in front of the railway station, further down the line the large sliding door of the last railway coach was opened and a coffin lifted out and taken over by six pallbearers from the group of people who had been walking in the garden. They raised the coffin to their shoulders, while the other six men walked beside them to act as relief for them; all the other people in the railway station followed. As long as this procession kept to the road that ran parallel to the railroad for a short stretch, total silence reigned; but at the moment when the coffin and the pallbearers turned from this road into an avenue lined with cherry trees, which led in a straight line to Klein-Haldern, only five hundred feet distant, the school bell of Klein-Haldern began to toll, a little tinkling bell, which sounded anything but solemn, but whose short, sharp strokes were felt to be a comfort, because they interrupted the oppressive silence that had prevailed till then.

So the procession moved to Klein-Haldern without a sound being heard except the tolling of the school bell; but they had scarcely passed the blacksmith's shop, which marked the end of the village on the other side, into the avenue of elms that led from Klein- to Gross-Haldern, its trees intertwining to form almost an arbor, when a general ringing of bells set in, with the whole region participating. The tolling was begun by the Gross-Haldern bell, called the Turkish bell because it was poured from cannon that Matthias von Haldern had brought home from the Turkish wars; but before it had finished its first strokes, the bells of Krampnitz and Wittenhagen joined in, followed by those of Orthwig and Nassenheide. It was as if the bells of heaven and earth were tolling.

Halfway between the two villages there ran a boundary ditch that was crossed by a stone bridge. Beyond this bridge the common of Gross-Haldern began, and here too began the cordon formed by old and young for this last stretch of road. First came the school children, then the veterans' associations with a corps of trumpeters from the nearest small garrison; and whenever the pallbearers passed a section, the trumpeters fell in behind them in a formation of threes and followed with "Jesus, Thou Our Trust."

At the end of the procession a few veterans of 1813 marched, wearing their commemorative medals, all of them in their eighties, shaking their heads, no one knew whether from age or at the state of the world. And so they marched into Gross-Haldern, past the old gabled castle and directly to the church built of field stones, which was situated on higher ground than the surrounding village and was flanked by rows of graves rising in terraces, and at this season rich in flowers. Before the small, Norman gateway stood the village pastor, with two colleagues beside him, to receive the deceased on a consecrated spot. The pallbearers put the coffin down, on which some palm branches were now placed, and then carried it up the central aisle to the altar. Here stood the old general superintendent, who had come from Berlin to make the peroration; the tall candles were burning and the thin smoke they emitted curled up near the large altarpiece, which was half obliterated by smoke. It depicted the prodigal son, not when he returned home, but in his misery and abandonment.

When the coffin was lowered directly over the vault, every seat in the church was occupied; and even the manorial pew, which had mostly been empty on Sunday since the death of Friedrich Wilhelm IV, was filled today. In the front row one could see the old count, Waldemar's father, in a gray toupee and wearing his Cross of St. John; beside him, in deep and elegant mourning, the stepmother of the deceased, a woman who was still beautiful and who regarded the event solely from the angle of the "affront," and with the aid of this

point of view endured the prescribed degree of sadness with almost
more than the dignity appropriate to her social class. Behind her the
younger son (her own), Count Konstantin, for whom his older
brother had made room in a not unwished-for manner, to put it
mildly. His demeanor was faultless and likewise showed a remarkable
composure, without quite attaining that of his mother. A long hymn
was sung, which in the strongest terms sought to put a stop to all
earthly vanity; then the old general superintendent spoke some beautiful, deeply felt words — deeply felt because his own household had
been struck the heaviest blows of Fate — then he came forward and
spoke the blessing, and after the singing of the last verse the organ
gave out its last quavering sounds and the coffin was lowered into the
vault with all the wreaths that had been heaped on it in the last
moments.

A profound silence ensued, and the out-of-town guests were just
putting on their hats after the final prayer, when a vehement and
almost spasmodic sobbing was heard coming from behind one of the
pillars. The countess looked with mortification at the source from
which the sobbing came; but fortunately the cover offered by the pillar did not disclose who had had the presumption to wish to be more
moved than she.

Stine had come to Klein-Haldern by the morning train. To while
away the hours before the funeral, she had spent an hour or more at
the outer edge of Gross-Haldern Park and then in the nearby
meadow, where she watched the cattle grazing. She was among the
last to leave the church. She kept to one side, walked up and down
between the graves for a while, and then slowly began to walk back to
the railway station at Klein-Haldern. There was total silence in the
area; bells were no longer tolling and she heard nothing but the larks
which, warbling their tirili, rose into the air out of the sheaves of
grain that stood round about. One lark flew higher than the others
and Stine watched it until it disappeared high up in the sky. "To
Heaven...oh, if only one could follow it... To live, to have to
live..." And in an excess of painful excitement and on the verge of
fainting, she sat down on a stone beside the road and hid her brow in
her hand.

When, after a while, she stood up and wanted to continue walking
down the middle of the road, she heard a carriage coming at a swift

trot behind her from Gross-Haldern. Turning around, she saw that its occupants were the same people who had sat in the manorial pew during the funeral service. In the last carriage sat Waldemar's uncle, his summer topcoat thrown back over his shoulders, so that one could clearly discern the large blue ribbon of the order he wore, the Swedish Seraphim Order. Stine did not wish to be seen and made a half turn sideways; but the old count had already recognized her from a distance. Swiftly conquering the embarrassment he felt for a fleeting moment, he stood up in the carriage and, with a friendly, welcoming motion of the hand, invited her to get in. Stine's features were bathed in a glow, which expressed her warmest thanks for the old count's chivalry, which never failed him in moments like these. But she shook her head and walked on to Klein-Haldern, making occasional stops and deliberately coming late to the cherry lined avenue, from which she saw the white cloud of steam rising from the train that was speeding to the capital. She knew that there was a second train an hour later, and to be alone till then was by no means unwelcome to her, indeed the very thing she longed for.

But she got more than she had bargained for. Time refused to end, and she kept looking up the long piece of track, always in the direction from which the train must come. In vain; it seemed determined not to come. And yet she was dead tired from excitement and strain, and was cold, and her legs would scarcely carry her weight. But at length she saw the signals being hoisted, and soon after that the great fiery eyes coming closer and closer. And then, halt! One coach-door was opened, and climbing in swiftly she squeezed into a corner for warmth, drawing her mantilla more tightly about her shoulders. But it was of no help, she was shaken by a fever while the train steamed on to Berlin.

"Stine, child, how dreadful you look! Why, the mark of death is on your face." With these words the widow Pittelkow, who had been waiting long on the first hall landing, received her beloved Stine and refused to let her climb another flight of stairs to the Polzin apartment.

"Come, child, lie down right here on the bed. Well, I'll be . . . Was it really that bad? Or did they give you the shove? Or did they want to heave you? Or was it him? Well, I'll teach him a thing or two. I'll send him to the devil. Olga, child, where are you? Get up, I say, and light a fire. And when it's going good, call me, d'you hear?... Lord, Stine, but you're shaking so. What've they done to you?" In saying this she unbuttoned her sister's dress and thrust pillows under her head and covered her with two comforters.

Half an hour later Stine had recovered sufficiently to be able to speak.

"Well, now things is picking up," said Pauline. "When the mill is turning once more, there's wind for it too. Child, your wind was all gone and I was thinking, now this one's gonna die on me too."

Stine took her sister's hand, patted and stroked it and said: "I wish it was so."

"Oh, don't talk like that, Stine. You'll make a comeback, all right. Some good'll come out of it for us all. Lord, he was all right as men go, and really a decent fella, not like the old man who's to blame for the whole thing; why'd he bring him along? But he really wasn't up to much; he was just a sad sack."

The ministrations of her sister brought Stine relief and tears ran down her face.

"Cry, Stine darling, have a good cry. When the dripping begins it's half over, just like in a storm. And now drink another cup... Olga, where are you? I do believe the brat's snoring again... And next Sunday is Sedan,* we'll go to Find Inn and ride the merry-go-round and roll the bones. And then you'll roll a twelve again."

Frau Polzin had been listening from the landing upstairs and, with her only too practiced ears, had taken in every word with which the widow Pittelkow had received her Stine on the landing below. As soon as she heard the door close, she went back to her room, where Polzin was making his nightly toilet. One could really use this term, because, suffering from a chronic dry cough, he wore a military cravat, lined with thick cloth, even in bed.

"Well?" he asked, as he tightened the leather clasp on his necker-chief. "Is she back safe again?"

"Safe? What d'you mean safe? She'll never make it."

"A pity, really."

"Nah, ain't so. That's what you get."

---

*The day on which the French army capitulated at Sedan in 1870 was a national holiday in Germany until 1918.

Thomas Mann

1875 — 1955

Both Heinrich and Thomas Mann placed considerable stress on their mixed blood: a North German, patrician, merchant father and a part Creole, South American, artistically gifted mother. The family had risen to wealth and prominence and had declined as a mercantile dynasty, so that the family business had to be dissolved at the death of their father in 1891. Henceforth the Mann clan became writers, actors, musicians and scholars.

After an unhappy schooling, Thomas joined his widowed mother in Munich and entered an insurance office as an unsalaried clerk, but left the business world after a few months. He had been writing since his school days; now, in the mid nineties, his first stories began to appear in the better journals. A trip to Italy grew into a sojourn that lasted three years; it was in Italy that he began work on his first novel, *The Buddenbrooks* (1901), a chronicle of his family's fortunes. For two years (1898-1900) he worked on the staff of the journal *Simplicissimus*; this was his last regular employment until 1938, when he became a lecturer at Princeton University, a post he held for three years.

Thomas Mann's personal life was uneventful. He lived by his pen as a free-lance writer. His literary fame grew from work to work, culminating in the award of the Nobel Prize for Literature in 1929. However, the drama lacking in his external life was supplied by the many controversies in which he was involved. During the First World War he was engaged in a bitter feud with his brother Heinrich, who opposed the German cause in the name of liberal democracy, while Thomas defended the German ideology in a book titled *Betrachtungen eines Unpolitischen* (*Reflections of a Nonpolitical Man*, 1918). After the German defeat he grew out of his original political credo and moved closer to the liberal, democratic ideals embodied in the Weimar Republic. He foresaw the danger of National Socialism for Germany and the world at large, and did not tire of warning against that danger by pen and word of mouth. When the Nazis seized power in 1933, he and his family chose the hardship of exile. Between 1933 and 1952 they lived briefly in Switzerland, then in the United States. After the Second World War, the wave of intolerance and repression known as McCarthyism was so distressing to Thomas Mann that he returned to Switzerland, where he remained until his death.

Mann's literary work consists almost wholly of prose: a series of massive novels, many novellas, an impressive body of political essays and literary criticism, and hundreds of short occasional pieces that reveal him as a compassionate and generous colleague to young and less known artists, in whose behalf he was always ready to intercede.

Looking back on that life filled with intellectual achievement, one finds it difficult to grasp the state of mind of the young fledgling writer, struggling against feelings of inadequacy, self-doubt, dividedness. One is reminded of the young Goethe, a neurotic groping for integration and identity, attempting suicide and writing *Werther* as an act of liberation. Mann, too, contemplated suicide; his early letters are full of self-deprecation and a search for identity; they show him deeply troubled by the place of art in the scheme of things. The most striking documentation of this condition is furnished by *Der Bajazzo* (*The Buffoon*), *Tonio Kröger*, and *Im Spiegel* (*In the Mirror*. In them Mann paints a very harsh portrait of the artist, especially the writer.

A writer is a fellow who is absolutely useless for any serious activity, who cares only for nonsense, who is not only of no use to the State but actually rebellious against it, who need not even possess any special intellectual gifts but may be as slow and obtuse-witted as I have always been, a charlatan who is at heart a child, given to excess and totally disreputable, who should — and on the whole does — receive from society nothing but silent contempt.

The sketch *In the Mirror,* from which this quotation is taken, is one of the most radical denunciations of the artist as a social type; but it is even surpassed by other passages, in which the artist is compared to a confidence man and swindler. Of course, we know that Mann was an ironist and must therefore discount these alarming statements. The question is: How much shall we subtract to the account of irony?

From the outset Mann was an antithetical or dialectical thinker; he saw thought developing from a confrontation between opposing views. The antithesis he chose to work with is that between life and spirit (*Geist*), which appears in his work under various synonyms: nature and mind, nature and culture, realism and idealism, *Bürger* and artist. A fundamental concept of his early thinking is the Rousseauistic notion of *Erkenntnisekel* (disgust with knowledge). This disgust is characteristic of the modern intellectual who, like Hamlet, believes that he "sees through" life and perceives his fellowmen not as they pretend to be but as they really are: greedy and grasping, bent on pleasure, cruel and unjust. Disgusted with this deeper insight, the intellectual withdraws from life and contemplates it objectively, like Schopenhauer's aesthete. He becomes an artist or scholar or, like Savonarola, an idealist-reformer. Standing apart from life, he becomes unfit for living in society; his instincts atrophy. When he does leave his observation post and descends into the arena of life, he is defeated by life, especially if the encounter involves an erotic experience.

The antithesis of the intellectual is the man of nature, common sense, instinct, the *Bürger*. He is the business or professional man, the soldier, civil servant, the representative of the establishment, the conventional man who accepts traditional values without questioning them. He strives for material success and is exhilarated by the struggle that life presents. Hans Hansen from the novella *Tonio Kröger* is the perfect example of the *Bürger*: in appearance, mentality, and in his aesthetic tastes. The *Bürger* accepts the restraints of natural and human laws; the artist-intellectual craves the freedom that intellect offers: the freedom to dream of Utopias in which the conditions of life are ideal, to create ideal beauty, to describe life as it *really* is (that is, as it might be), to strike out for uncharted regions. But he too imposes on himself certain necessary restraints: the discipline of work, taxing and rigorous to a degree the *Bürger* cannot conceive. This self-discipline makes the intellectual unfit for social life; he becomes slovenly, disreputable, maladjusted, deadened to life. He succumbs to the lure of death, if only on the metaphorical level: for, from the point of view of the *Bürger*, he is not living but at best observing, recording, or recreating life. But even on the physiological level there exists a German tradition that associates health with instinct and the common man, indeed with stupidity, and couples death with intellect. Thomas Mann worked within this tradition.

European romanticism created two different images of the artist. The first is that of the suffering, martyred genius: Alfred de Vigny's Moses or Chatterton, or Baudelaire's symbol of the poet as an albatross, an awkward, grotesque figure on earth but a "prince of the clouds," a "king of the azure sky." The second is that of the gay bohemian: Eichendorff's "god-for-nothing," waltzing through life, paying no heed to the practical chores over which the *Bürger* sweats. Both visions of the artist place him above bourgeois society.

But another tradition was developing. Kierkegaard condemned the aesthetic way of life. Dostoyevsky depicted the underground man as defeated at every step by the stupid *Bürger* types to whom he feels superior. Tolstoy passed severe judgment on the wasted life of Ivan Ilytch, the man of culture. Ibsen attacked "idealism" in *The Wild Duck* and took the side of the common man, who needs his illusions more than the hard truth. But more significant than all these was Nietzsche's drastic unmasking of the artist-intellectual, the most destructive picture of the artist since Plato exiled the poets from his ideal State because they tell lies. Nietzsche's position may be summed up in the following propositions: (1) One cannot be an artist without being sick. (2) The artist denies, or at least falsifies, reality. (3) Art is a compensation for failure in life (an anticipation of Freud). (4) The writer is an actor who pretends passion where he feels none. (5) The artist is a vampire, who shamelessly makes literature out of his own passions. Theodor Fontane, whom the young Thomas Mann read with admiration, wrote an essay, *The Social Position of the Writer*, in which he noted, without self-pity though with some resentment, that the artist stands lower in public esteem than the soldier, clergyman, civil servant or professional man. Finally, Paul Bourget, a conservative essayist and novelist of considerable reputation at the turn of the century, popularized this intellectual position in a radical Rousseauistic attack on progressive intellectualism. He was quoted with approval by Nietzsche and read by the young Mann brothers.

It is not surprising, therefore, to find these young scions of a conservative, patrician family of *Bürger* joining in the outcry against the bohemian, antiestablishment artist-intellectual. They were themselves infected with the virus of spirit, but had enough of the *Bürger* in them to be divided against themselves. Heinrich outgrew this dichotomy very quickly; Thomas evolved more slowly. In his early writings we find a regular pattern in theme: a man encounters "life" in some form and is defeated in the encounter. The protagonist is in most cases an intellectual, either physically deformed or grotesquely misshapen or eccentric in behavior and dress. He cannot stand up against crude but robust, self-confident, selfish, brutal life. In one early story the antagonist is actually referred to as "life." It is at least possible to interpret these stories as embodying a coarse form of social Darwinism: the representatives of intellect are defeated by life and well deserve to be.

From our story on, the antithesis of life versus spirit assumes the special form of a conflict between writer and *Bürger*: in *The Buddenbrooks, Tristan, Tonio Kröger, Schwere Stunde* (*The Difficult Hour*), *Der Tod in Venedig* (*Death in Venice*). A study of these more mature writings shows that the "Darwinian" interpretation of the early stages is inadequate. What is wrong with it is the omission of the ambivalent feeling about life and spirit that was present in Mann's mind at all times, and which grew stronger with time and experience. Mann's artist (and he is a distinct type in literature) feels both superior *and* inferior to the *Bürger*. He knows that he is better than the common run of men who make up and govern society; yet he feels that they look down on him and he is bothered by that contempt. In the words of Tonio, the artist yearns for the "bliss of ordinariness." He is an outsider who would like to get in, like Kafka's protagonists.

Mann's thinking on the life-spirit antithesis did not remain static. He had begun with a too sweeping generalization: *the* artist is or feels inferior to *the* Bürger. But *Tristan* already presents two different types of artist: the *Literat* or poetaster, represented by the pseudo-aesthete Detlev Spinell, and a genuine artist who is also half *Bürger*, portrayed by Frau Klöterjahn. In *Tonio Kröger* we meet three different artist types, each confronting the life-spirit antithesis in a different way. Tonio, who has Mann's mixed heritage and division, suffers from this dualism and yearns to be commonplace, like the happy *Bürger* Hans Hansen. He gives vent to some very harsh strictures about *the* artist. But in the end he comes to accept himself as he is; and he wonders whether he is not a better artist for this dichotomy in his psyche.

The subsequent development of this antithesis in Mann's writings is a long story that cannot be told here. It is enough to indicate that Mann radically altered his conception of the relationship between life and spirit, arriving at a synthesis that combines both into a harmonious whole. The different stages of this development are subtle and intricate. For instance, in *Death in Venice*, spirit is again defeated by life (in the shape of eros); but it is a tragic, heroic defeat, crowning a career devoted to the service of a noble ideal. This is a far cry from the coarse confrontations of the early stories, even from the more refined duel presented in *Tonio Kröger*.

The synthesis does not come until Mann had gone through the traumatic experience of the First World War, not as a combatant, but as a thinker agonizing over the philosophical issues involved in the devastating conflict. His final position, again the product of long and slow development, may be indicated by a brief quotation from the essay "Goethe and Tolstoy" (1922): "Effortless nature is crude. Effortless spirit is without root or substance. A noble encounter of nature and spirit, as they mutually yearn for each other, that is humanity."

THE WRITER

Thomas Mann was a writer of the reflective school. There is much philosophical discussion and massive erudition in his later fiction. But he never forgot that art derives from the play impulse; the games he introduces into literature are various types of symbolism: structural, verbal, the leitmotiv, different levels of communication, irony and humor. He is a writer "with long breath" as the French say: his stately periods, complex in structure and elegantly balanced, employ a wide and rich vocabulary. Mann is a master of montage; he is fond of weaving quotations into the fabric of a sentence without revealing the game; and he is a master of parody. He has the naturalist's love of detail and exact description of people and places; and he uses live models for his fictional characters. Much has been written about his irony and Mann himself referred to it frequently. The word has two distinct meanings: first, the common one of understatement and saying the opposite of what one means (Socratic irony); and second, a refusal to commit oneself wholly to any one position, keeping a distance from the matter at hand, mediating between antitheses, thinking with reservations, knowing that the whole truth is never on one side of an argument.

THE BUFFOON

Der Bajazzo* was written in 1897 and published that same year in the *Neue deutsche Rundschau*. It is the first of a series dealing with the conflict between the artist and *Bürger* in the same person. The story treats the whole psychological complex of *Erkenntnisekel* as described in this essay: "seeing through," alienation, dividedness, superiority plus inferiority. The cause of the buffoon's disarray is his loss of nerve, of his belief in himself and in what he is doing with his life. He has no more faith in the aesthetic existence than he had formerly in the lumber business. Our buffoon should have read *Werther* and Hugo von Hofmannsthal's *The Fool and Death*, which was published only four years before this document of despair was written. Kierkegaard too had dealt with this problem; but the Dane was as yet unknown in Europe.

The Buffoon does not have the substance of *Tonio Kröger* or *Death in Venice*. But it does reveal many of the features that we esteem in Thomas Mann's mature art. It is the first of the many changes that he rang on the basic theme of the problematic aspects of culture. It should prove a stimulus to an exploration of the later variations on this great theme.

---

*The word is a corruption of the Milanese *pajazz*, a dialect form of *pagliaccio*, clown. The German translation of Leoncavallo's opera *I Pagliacci* is *Der Bajazzo*.

The Buffoon

An end to the whole business and a dignified conclusion to it all, in fact, is the disgust which life — my life — which "all that," "the whole thing," inspires in me, a disgust that stifles me, pursues me, shakes me and prostrates me, and which may sooner or later give me the needed incentive to make short work of the whole absurd and contemptible affair and clear out and away. Very possibly, of course, I may carry on this way for another month or two; I may go on eating, sleeping, doing this or that for three or six months longer, in the quiet, orderly, mechanical way that my life has outwardly followed during the past winter, while in hideous contrast this devastating process of decay was going on within me all the time. It almost seems, does it not, that the calmer, the more detached, the more remote from the world a man's outward life is, the fiercer and the more exhausting are his inward struggles. There's no help for it: one must live; and if you refuse to lead a life of action and retire to the silence of the most peaceful desert, the vicissitudes of existence will still confront you in your soul, and compel you to test your character through them, to prove whether you are a hero or a fool.

I have procured this neat notebook to tell my "story" in it; but why, really? Perhaps to give me something to do — anything; perhaps because I have a weakness for psychological analysis, and to draw comfort from the conviction that it was all necessary. Necessity is so comforting! Perhaps also to enjoy a sort of momentary superiority over myself and something like indifference. For indifference, I know, could be a sort of happiness.

(1)

It has been left far behind, the little ancient town with its narrow, angular and gabled streets, its Gothic churches and fountains, its hard working, solid and simple people, and the large patrician house, gray with age, in which I grew up.

The house was situated in the middle of the city and had outlasted four generations of well-to-do and respected merchants. *Ora et labora** was written over the front door, and when you had mounted the wide staircase from the great stone-paved hall, around which ran a gallery of white enameled wood, you had to pass through another spacious vestibule and a little, dark, pillared anteroom before you entered, by one of the high white doors, the living room in which my mother was seated making music at the piano.

She sat in semidarkness, for the windows were draped with heavy, dark-red material and the white figures of gods on the tapestry seemed to stand out in plastic relief from a blue background, and to be listening to the heavy, deep opening notes of the Chopin nocturne that she loved most and always played so slowly that she might savor the sadness of every chord. The piano was old and had lost some of the fullness of its tone, but the soft pedal, veiling the high notes so that they reminded me of dimmed silver, could still produce the strangest effects.

Sitting on the massive straight-backed damask sofa, I watched my mother and listened to her playing. She was slight and delicately formed, and she generally wore a dress of soft, light-gray material. Her narrow face was not beautiful, but beneath the parted, gently waving hair of a modest fairness, it looked quiet, tender, dreamy and childlike; indeed, as she sat at the piano, with her head bent slightly to one side she resembled one of the touching little cherubs, often seen in old pictures, sitting at the feet of the Madonna and playing the guitar.

When I was small she often told me fairy tales that no one else could match, in her low, restrained voice; or she simply laid her hands on my head, as it lay in her lap, and sat there silent and motionless. I believe these were the happiest and most peaceful hours of my life. Her hair did not turn gray, and she did not seem to grow

*"Pray and work."

older; only her form became more and more delicate and her face narrower, quieter and dreamier.

My father, on the other hand, was tall and broad. He wore a coat of fine black tweed and a white vest on which hung gold eyeglasses. His chin, clean-shaven like his upper lip, emerged round and firm from between his short, iron-gray side whiskers, and there were always two deep vertical folds between his eyebrows. He was a man of some weight and influence in public affairs; I have seen people leave him with quickened breath and flashing eyes, and there were others who went out broken and despairing. For it happened at times that I and my mother and my two older sisters were witnesses of such scenes, perhaps because my father hoped thereby to inspire me with the ambition to achieve as much in life as he had; perhaps, as I suspect, because he needed an audience. The way he leaned back in his chair with one hand thrust into the breast of his coat and gazed after the fortunate or ruined man, planted this suspicion in me, even in childhood.

I would sit in a corner contemplating my father and mother as if I were choosing between them, and I pondered whether it would be better to pass one's own life in dreamy reflection or in activity and power. But in the end my eyes would always return to the quiet countenance of my mother.

(2)

Not that I resembled her in my outward behavior; my occupations were for the most part neither quiet nor noiseless. I recall one of them, which I passionately preferred to any game or activity indulged in by companions of my own age, and which even now that I am already thirty years old fills me with serene contentment.

This was a large and well-stocked puppet show with which I used to lock myself in my room alone and stage the most remarkable musical dramas. My room, which was on the third floor, with two dark ancestral portraits in Van Dyck beards, was darkened and a lamp placed near the theater, for artificial light seemed to me an indispensable requisite for heightening the atmosphere. I sat down directly in front of the stage, for I was conductor of the orchestra, and my left hand rested on a large round cardboard box which constituted the only visible orchestral instrument.

Then the assisting artists appeared, whom I had myself drawn with pen and ink, cut out and fixed upon sticks of wood so that they would stand upright. There were gentlemen in topcoats and silk hats and ladies of great beauty.

"Good evening, ladies and gentlemen," I would say, "How are you all? I came early because there were still a few details to be arranged. However, it is time to proceed to the dressing rooms."

They would proceed to the dressing rooms which lay behind the stage and soon return transformed into gay theatrical figures, to ascertain, by means of the hole that I had cut in the curtain, whether the audience was satisfactory. The house being fairly well filled, I rang the bell that gave me the signal that the performance might begin. Raising my baton, I paused to enjoy the profound silence this motion imposed. Then, in response to another movement, there was heard the portentous hollow roll of the drum with which the overture opened and which I executed with my left hand upon the cardboard box. The trumpets, clarinets, and flutes, the timbre of which I imitated in an incomparable manner, joined in and the music played on until, at a mighty crescendo, the curtain rose and the drama began in a dark wood or a glittering hall.

The plot had already taken shape in my mind, though the details had to be improvised, and the sweet, passionate strains that were heard, to which the clarinets trilled and the cardboard box rumbled, were bold, sonorous verses, full of great and stirring words that rhymed occasionally but seldom yielded an intelligible meaning. Nevertheless the opera proceeded, while I drummed with my left hand, sang or made music with my mouth, and with my right hand directed not only the puppet actors but everything else with such skill that at the end of each act the applause was enthusiastic, the curtain had to part again and again, and at times it was even necessary for the proud and flattered conductor to turn in his seat and thank the audience.

Truly, as I packed up my theater with burning cheeks after one of these strenuous performances, I felt a happy weariness such as must be known by a great artist who has just completed a work on which he has expended all the forces of his genius. This game remained my favorite occupation until my thirteenth or fourteenth year.

(3)

How did the years of my childhood and adolescence pass in that great house, where my father carried on his business in the lower rooms, while upstairs my mother sat dreaming in an easy chair or played softly and meditatively upon the piano, while my two sisters, who were two and three years older than I, busied themselves about the kitchen and linen cupboards? I remember so little of all that.

This much is clear, that I was an enormously lively boy, who was able to gain the respect and affection of my schoolfellows because of my social status, my exemplary powers of impersonating our teachers, a sort of superior turn of speech, and the thousand histrionic bits I could perform. My learning, however, was lamentably little, for I was too much engaged in studying the comic behavior of the teachers to pay attention to anything else; and at home my head was too full of the texts of new operas, verses and motley nonsense to leave room for any serious work.

"Shame," said my father, and the lines between his brows deepened when I brought my report into the living room after dinner and he had read the sheet through, his free hand thrust into his coat front. "It's little credit I get through you, that's certain. What is to become of you, will you kindly tell me that? You'll never amount to anything in life."

This saddened me, but it did not keep me from reading aloud to my parents and sisters after the evening meal a poem I had written that afternoon. It made my father laugh till his pince-nez bobbed up and down on his vest. "What tomfoolery!" he exclaimed over and over again. But my mother drew me to her, pushed my hair out of my eyes and said, "It isn't at all bad, my dear; I think there are a few nice passages in it."

Later, when I was a little older, I taught myself to play the piano after my own fashion. I began by striking the F-sharp major chords, because I thought the black keys especially intriguing and, since I spent many hours at the grand piano, I found transitions to other keys and gradually acquired a certain skill in going from one harmony to the next without changing rhythm or melody, putting as much expression as I could into the mystical surge of sound.

My mother said, "He has a good touch; his taste shows through." And she saw to it that I received instruction, which lasted for half a year. But I never learned either proper fingering or timing.

Well, the years passed and, in spite of the anxiety that school caused me, I grew up an uncommonly cheerful lad. I moved gaily and easily in the circle of my relatives and acquaintances, behaving gracefully and with charm, because I liked to play the part of the charming youth, although I was beginning to despise all these people instinctively as dull and devoid of all imagination.

(4)

One afternoon, when I was about eighteen and ready to enter the upper classes at school, I overheard a short conversation between my parents, who were sitting at the round sofa-table in the living room, unaware that I was lolling idly in the window seat in the adjoining dining room, looking out at the pale sky above the gabled roofs. Hearing my name, I went softly up to the white folding doors, which stood half open.

My father was leaning back in his chair with his legs crossed, holding the financial paper on his knee with one hand while the other slowly caressed his chin between the side whiskers. My mother sat on the sofa, bending her calm face over some embroidery. The lamp stood between them.

My father was saying, "My opinion is that we should take him away from school now and put him into some large business house for training."

"Oh," said my mother sadly, looking up. "But he is such a gifted child."

My father was silent for a moment, during which he carefully blew a speck of dust from his coat. Then he shrugged his shoulders and spread his arms, showing the palms of his hands to my mother, and said, "If you suppose, my dear, that the calling of a merchant demands no sort of gifts, you are quite mistaken. At all events, he is achieving nothing at school, as I am more and more compelled to recognize, to my sorrow. The gift of which you speak is a kind of buffoon's talent, though I hasten to add that I in no way underestimate that sort of thing. He can be charming when he wants to; he knows how to handle people, to amuse and flatter them; he has the need to please and to be successful. With such a character many a man has made his fortune, and as he is not especially interested in any other career, he is likely enough to become a good businessman on a large scale."

At this point my father leaned back in his chair complacently, took a cigarette from his cigarette case and lit it slowly.

"I'm sure you are right," said my mother, and looked unhappily around the room. "Only I have often thought and somehow hoped that he would one day become an artist . . . It is true we can't attach much weight to his talen for music, which has remained undeveloped; but have you noticed that recently, since he went to that little art exhibition, he has taken to sketching? He doesn't do at all badly, it seems to me . . ."

My father blew out the cigarette smoke, settled himself in his chair and said curtly, "All that is buffoonery and humbug! Anyhow, we can ask him what his own wishes are, that's only fair."

Well, what sort of wishes was I to express? The prospect of a change in my way of living certainly seemed very pleasing; with a grave face I declared that I was ready to leave school and enter a business, and I was enrolled as an apprentice in the large lumber works of Herr Schlievogt down at the riverside.

(5)

The change was entirely an outward one; that goes without saying. My interest in Herr Schlievogt's lumber business was of the slightest, and I sat in my revolving chair beneath a gas jet in a small, dark office feeling as indifferent to it all as I had formerly done in the schoolbenches; I now had fewer worries, that was the only difference.

Herr Schlievogt, a corpulent individual with a red face and the bristly gray beard of a seaman, took little notice of me, since he was mostly in the sawmill, which was some distance from the office and lumberyard, and the employees treated me with respect. I had personal relations with only one of them, a cheerful, able young man of good family, whom I had known at school and whose name was Schilling. Like myself, he made fun of everything, but at the same time he showed quite a lively interest in the lumber trade, and hardly a day passed that he did not express his firm intention of, somehow or other, becoming a rich man.

For my own part, I mechanically discharged the duties that fell to me and spent the rest of my time strolling about the yard among the stacks of lumber and the workmen, gazing through the high wooden fence at the river, where a freight train would roll by now and again, and thinking of a play I had seen, a concert I had attended or a book I had read.

I read much, devouring everything I could lay my hands on, and my ability to absorb impressions was great. I entered emotionally into the personality of every character in turn, recognizing myself in him and ordering all my thoughts and experience in the key of one book until I fell under the influence of another. In my room, where I had once set up my puppet theater, I now sat with a book on my knee and gazed at the two portraits of my ancestors, in order to recapture the cadence of the diction that had engrossed me, while a futile jumble of half-formed thoughts and images filled my mind . . .

My sisters had married in quick succession, and when I was not at the office I often went down into the living room, where my mother, whose health was not all it should have been and whose face was gradually more and more growing childlike and calm, now mostly sat by herself. After she had played some Chopin for me and I had shown her a new combination of chords I had discovered, she would ask me if I were contented and happy in my work . . . Of course I was happy.

I was not much more than twenty, and my position was only a temporary one, for the thought that nothing compelled me to spend all my life with Herr Schlievogt, or with some bigger lumber business still, was no stranger to my mind. Any day I might strike out for freedom and leave the gabled city to live somewhere in the great world according to my inclinations, reading good and well-written novels, going to the theater and making a little music . . . Happy? Why, I dined extremely well and was well dressed; even early, in my school days, when I saw how poorer and shabbier boys habitually recognized my superiority and deferred to my wishes and to those of my peers with a sort of flattering diffidence as gentlemen and tone setters, I had been serenely conscious that I belonged to the upper classes, the rich and envied ones who have a natural right to look down with kindly contempt on the poor, the unhappy and the envious. Why should I not be happy? Let things take their course. In the meantime, it was delightful to move serenely and with a calm and distant superiority among those relatives and friends whose limitations I made fun of, even while I exercised my charm upon them out of a mere desire to please. I basked complacently in the ambiguous respect that all those people showed for my person and character, recognizing vaguely that there was something antagonistic and extravagant in them.

(6)

A change began to take place in my father. When he came in to dinner at four o'clock in the afternoon, the lines between his eyebrows seemed to grow deeper from day to day and he no longer thrust his hand into the front of his coat with an imposing gesture, but appeared nervous, oppressed, and uneasy.

One day he said to me: "You are old enough now to share the anxiety which is undermining my health. Besides, it is my duty to acquaint you with the facts so that you do not entertain any false expectations as to your future position in life. You know that the marriages of your two sisters have exacted considerable sacrifices. Recently the firm has suffered losses of such a nature as to reduce our capital substantially; I am an old man and I have become discouraged; I cannot see any prospect of material improvement. I beg you to realize that you will be thrown upon your own resources . . ."

He told me this about two months before his death. One day he was found in his armchair in the private office, waxen, paralyzed and babbling incoherently; a week later the whole city attended his funeral.

My mother sat on the sofa beside the round table in the living room, quiet and delicate, her eyes for the most part closed. When my sisters and I performed little services for her, she would perhaps nod and smile; but she remained silent and motionless, gazing sadly with

wide, absent eyes at some divinity on the tapestry, her hands folded
in her lap. When the black-coated gentlemen appeared to report to
her about the liquidation of the estate, she only nodded and again
closed her eyes.

She no longer played Chopin, and when she gently patted her hair,
the pale, delicate and tired hand trembled. Less than six months
after my father's death she lay down and passed away without a
moan, making no attempt to fight for her life...

Now that all was over, what was there to keep me in the place? Our
affairs had been settled, for better or worse; it was found that an inheritance of about a hundred thousand marks had fallen to my
share, enough to make me independent — the more so since, for some
inconsequential reason, I had been rejected as unfit for military
service.

Nothing bound me any longer to the people among whom I had
grown up, who regarded me with even stranger and more astonished
eyes, and whose view of life was too narrow for me to share. Granted
that they knew me for what I was, in their eyes a totally useless being;
this is how I saw myself. And though I was enough of a cynic and
fatalist to accept my father's description of my "mountebank talent"
with serenity, I was wholly satisfied with myself and cheerfully prepared to enjoy life in my own way.

I gathered up my small fortune and left the city, saying good-bye
to hardly a soul; my immediate goal was to travel.

(7)

The three years that now followed, in the course of which I was
eagerly receptive to a thousand rich and changing impressions, I remember like a beautiful, far-off dream. How long ago is it since I
celebrated New Year's Eve with the monks among the snow and ice of
the Simplon? Since I strolled over the Piazza Erbe in Verona? Since I
walked for the first time beneath the colonnades of St. Peter's from
the Borgo San Spirito, and my awestruck eyes lost themselves in the
distances of that enormous square? Since I looked down upon
Naples, white and shimmering, from the Corso Vittorio Emanuele
and saw the graceful silhouette of Capri dissolving in the blue vapor
of the distant sea?... It is in reality just six years and no more.

Oh, I lived most carefully, in accordance with my means, in simple private rooms and cheap pensions; but expenses were unavoidable, it seemed, what with the constant change of scene and because I found it difficult at first to give up my good bourgeois style of living. I had set aside fifteen thousand marks of my capital for traveling expenses, but of course I exceeded that sum.

For the rest, I felt at ease among the people whom I met here and there in my travels, often casual and very interesting folk; to be sure, they paid me no particular respect, such as I had been accustomed to receive in my former environment, but on the other hand I had to fear no questions or disapproving looks from them.

My special type of social gifts sometimes gained for me a real popularity among the other guests in the pensions—I remember in particular one scene in the salon of the Pension Minelli in Palermo. Before a circle of French people of various ages I had begun to improvise on the upright piano a music drama "by Richard Wagner," making lavish use of tragic pantomime, recitative, and rolling harmonies. I had just brought it to an end amid great applause, when an old gentleman, almost completely bald, with white whiskers straggling down over his gray traveling jacket hurried up to me. He seized both my hands and cried with tears in his eyes:

"Why, that's astounding! It's astounding, my dear sir! I swear I have not heard anything so delightfully entertaining in thirty years. Permit me to thank you from the bottom of my heart. But you must, you absolutely must, become a musician or an actor!"

On such occasions, I confess I felt something of the exalted pride of a great painter who has allowed himself to be persuaded to sketch some clever absurdity for his friends on a table top. But after dinner I returned to the salon by myself and spent a lonely, melancholy hour in drawing sustained chords from the instrument, into which I tried to put the feelings that the view of Palermo had awakened in me.

From Sicily I made a hasty trip to Africa, and from there went on to Spain where, near Madrid, on a dull rainy winter afternoon in the country, I felt for the first time a desire to return to Germany, and something of a necessity as well. For, apart from the fact that I was beginning to long for a regular and peaceful life, it was not hard for me to calculate that, with the strictest economy, I would have spent twenty thousand marks before I managed to return.

I did not delay long in setting out on the leisurely journey through

France, spending nearly six months in lengthy sojourns in different cities; and I remember with melancholy distinctness the summer evening on which I arrived in the railway station in the capital of the central German state which I had selected before setting out on my travels — somewhat better informed now, equipped with some experience and knowledge, and filled with a childlike joy at the prospect of leading an undisturbed, contemplative existence there, of being carefree and independent, secured by my modest competence.

At that time I was twenty-five years old.

(8)

The place was not ill chosen. It is a sizable city, free from the noise and confusion of the great centers and the objectionable features of the industrial towns, containing a few quite handsome old squares and a street life lacking neither liveliness nor a certain degree of elegance. The area around the town has a number of pleasant spots, but my preference was always for the tastefully laid out promenade leading to the Lerchenberg — a long narrow hill that forms a background for much of the city, and from which one can enjoy a distant view of the open country, the churches, houses and the gently winding river. At certain points, especially when a military band is playing on fine summer afternoons, while pedestrians and carriages move in and out, one is reminded of the Pincio. But we shall return to this promenade later . . .

It would hardly be believed with what elaborate satisfaction I arranged the spacious room which I had rented, along with an adjacent bedroom, in a lively central part of the city. The parental furniture had mostly passed to the homes of my sisters, but I had acquired as much as I needed — handsome, substantial pieces which arrived together with my books and the two ancestral portraits and, chief of all, the old grand piano, which my mother had bequeathed to me.

Indeed, when everything had been set in order, when the photographs that I had collected on my travels adorned the walls, the heavy mahogany secretary and the bow-front chest of drawers were in their place, and when I sank down in an armchair by the window, settled and secure, allowing my gaze to alternate between the streets outside and my new apartment, my satisfaction was not small. And yet — I have not forgotten this moment — besides contentment and confidence, there was something else stirring in me, a slight, vague feeling of anxiety and uneasiness, the faint consciousness of a sort of revolt and rebellion on my part against some threatening force . . . the slightly depressing thought that my position, which had never been more than a temporary matter, must now, for the first time, be accepted as final and permanent . . .

I will not conceal the fact that these and similar feelings recurred from time to time. But then, is there any way of avoiding these inevitable afternoon hours when one looks out into the growing darkness, perhaps into a slowly falling rain, and yields to the inroads of pessimism? In any event my future was secure. I had entrusted the round sum of eighty thousand marks to the care of the local bankers, and the interest — heavens, how bad the times are! — amounted to about six hundred marks quarterly, on which I could live respectably, provide myself with books, visit the theater now and then — and not deny myself some of the lighter pastimes.

My days, thenceforth, really passed according to the ideal that I had set as my goal. I got up about ten o'clock, breakfasted, and passed the time till noon, perhaps at the piano, perhaps in reading a literary journal or a book. Then I strolled up the street to the little restaurant I regularly patronized, had my dinner, and walked through the streets to an art gallery, or out into the surrounding country, or to the Lerchenberg. When I returned home I took up my morning occupations again: I read, played, toyed with a sketch or wrote a letter with due care. In the evening, if I did not attend a concert or a play, I sat in the cafe and read the newspapers till bedtime. But the day had been good and agreeable, and if I had succeeded in evoking from the piano some motif that seemed to me new and beautiful, if I had carried away from a book or picture some tender and enduring impression, that was enough to fill the day with a happy content . . .

But I must confess frankly that I set about all my occupations with the deliberate object of giving my days as great a degree of content as possible; I strove earnestly to achieve this. I regulated my bodily needs carefully, eating frugal meals and usually possessing but one suit of clothes, so as to be able to afford a good seat at the opera, to attend an expensive concert, buy the latest books or visit this or that art exhibit . . .

But as the days passed into weeks and months—boredom? I do not deny it. There is not always at hand the book that will provide content for a series of hours; you may have tried unsuccessfully to improvise at the piano, and irresistibly there creeps over you, as you sit by the window smoking cigarette after cigarette, a feeling of distaste for the world and for yourself; anxiety attacks you again, the familiar anxiety, and you jump up, dash off down the street, looking about you with the careless shrug of those fortunate ones at the professional or working men who have not the intellectual or material gifts for leisure and enjoyment.

(9)

Can a person of twenty-seven really believe seriously that his life is irrevocably settled and unchangeable, even though it appears only too plainly to be so? The twittering of a bird, a glimpse of blue sky, some half-forgotten dream of the night—any of these is sufficient to set a stream of vague hope suddenly welling in the heart, to fill it with a festal expectation of great and unpremeditated happiness... I drifted from one day to the next, pensive and aimless, full of some petty expectations that might be nothing more weighty than the date on which some entertaining journal was to appear, energetically convinced that I was happy, but at times a little wearied by my loneliness.

Yes, there were not a few hours in which I gave way to a peevish discontent at the lack of intercourse and society—a lack that I need not explain further. I was not in contact with good society, with the first or second social circles in that town; I lacked the financial means to introduce myself as a *fêtard** among the golden youth. And as for the bohemians—well, I am a man of breeding, I wear clean linen and good clothes and I simply have no taste for talking anarchy with disheveled young people in the cafés at tables sticky with absinthe. In short, there was no particular social group into which I naturally fitted, and the casual friendships that I formed from time to time in one way or another, were few, superficial and cool. This was my own fault, I am willing to admit, for on these occasions I held myself back out of a feeling of insecurity, with a disturbing consciousness that I

*"Reveller," "playboy."

could not give a clear, concise statement of who or what I really was, even to a shabbily dressed painter, in a way that would win me recognition.

Besides, had I not broken with "society," renounced it, when I allowed myself to take the liberty of going my own way, without paying any attention to its demands? If I had needed society in order to be happy, would I not in that case have been busying myself acquiring a fortune as a captain of industry, thereby serving the common good and gaining universal envy and respect?

And yet, and yet — the fact remained that my philosophical isolation was far too irksome and that, finally, it simply became incompatible with my conception of happiness, my belief and conviction that I was happy, since it was impossible — there was no doubt of that — that I should be anything else. That I was not happy, that I was unhappy — that was unthinkable, surely? Of course it was unthinkable, which settled the matter — until once more I was sitting at the window, apart and withdrawn, unable to convince myself that this was as it should be, and getting alarmingly peevish over it.

Peevishness — was that the mood of a happy man? I recalled my life at home in the narrow circle in which I had moved, happy in the consciousness of my superior artistic gifts, sociable, charming, my eyes filled with gaiety, mockery, and good-natured superiority toward all the world; a little odd in the opinion of people, but still popular. I had been happy then, even when I had to work in Herr Schlievogt's lumber firm; but now? now? . . .

But then an unusually interesting book would appear, a new French novel that I allowed myself to buy, and I would settle comfortably in my armchair to enjoy it at my leisure. Once more, three hundred pages of good taste, humbug and choice artistry. Yes, I have achieved the life that truly satisfies me. Am I unhappy? The question is ridiculous, simply ridiculous . . .

(10)

Once again a day has passed; a day in which, thank heaven, I have certainly found content; it is evening, the window curtains have been drawn, on the secretary the lamp is burning and it is already near midnight. I could go to bed, but I linger, reclining in my armchair,

with folded hands, gazing up at the ceiling, while following intently
the gnawing and boring of an ill-defined pain I have not been able to
banish.

Only a few hours before I had been in the grip of a great work of
art, one of those tremendous and monstrous creations that can shake,
stun, torment, enrapture and crush us by the decadent pomp of their
ruthless but brilliant dilettantism. My nerves are still quivering, my
imagination is stirred; strange moods surge within me, moods of
longing, of religious fervor, of triumph, of mystical peace, and there
is a need within me that constantly drives them to the surface, that
would like to drive them right out of me: the need to express them, to
communicate them, to exhibit them, to "make something of them."

Suppose I were really an artist, able to express myself in music, in
words or on canvas — preferably, if the truth must be told, in all three
at once! Well, after all, I can do many of these things. I can, for
example, sit down at the piano and evoke beautiful feelings here in
my little room, and that ought to be sufficient for me; for if I needed
people to be happy — I admit all that! But assuming that I did place
some slight value upon success, fame, recognition, praise, envy, love?
By heaven! The mere memory of that scene in the drawing room at
Palermo shows me that if something of that kind were to happen at
this moment, it would be an incomparable benefit and encouragement for me.

Thinking the matter over, I cannot help feeling that there is a distinction between inner and outward happiness, however sophistical
and absurd it may appear. "Outward happiness" — what does that
really mean? There is a certain class of people, favorites of heaven, it
seems, whose happiness is their genius and their genius, happiness.
Children of light they are, who trip through life, lightly, gracefully,
charmingly, with the light of the sun reflected in their eyes, while the
whole world crowds around them, admiring, praising, envying,
loving them, because even envy is incapable of hating them. But they
accept it all like children, with a sunny friendliness, mocking,
spoiled, whimsical, high-spirited, secure in their happiness and their
genius, as if it could not conceivably be otherwise . . .

As for myself, I do not deny that I am weak enough to wish to be
one of these people and, rightly or wrongly, the conviction keeps
forcing itself on me that once I actually was one of them. Rightly or
wrongly; for let us be honest: what you are is altogether a question of

how you look upon yourself, the image you project, the image you
are confident you can project.

Perhaps the real situation is that I have renounced this "outward
happiness" by withdrawing from "society" and arranging my life
without taking account of "other people." That I am content to do so
goes without saying, it is beyond doubt, cannot be doubted and must
not be doubted — for to repeat, and to repeat with desperate emphasis, I will, and must, be happy! The conception of "happiness" as a
sort of merit, genius, distinction and charm; the conception of "unhappiness" as something ugly, darkness loving, despicable and, in a
word, ridiculous, is too profoundly rooted in my mind to let me retain any self-respect if I should ever become unhappy.

How could I permit myself to be unhappy? What sort of role would
I be allowing myself to play? Would I not be compelled to crouch in
darkness, like a sort of bat or owl, blinking enviously at the "children
of light," those charming, happy ones? I should be obliged to hate
them, with that hatred which is only envenomed love, and to despise
myself!

"To crouch in the darkness!" Ah, now I know what it is that I have
been thinking and feeling off and on for months, about my "position
as an outsider" and my "philosophical isolation." And my anxiety returns, the old enemy, the consciousness of some sort of rebellion
against a threatening power . . .

Of course, on this occasion and the next and the next after that, I
was able to find relief in some numbing diversion. But it came back,
all this, it returned a thousand times in the course of the months and
years.

(11)

There are autumn days that are like a miracle. The summer is
past; outside, the leaves have long begun to turn yellow, and in the
city the wind has been blowing for days about all the street corners,
while muddy streams have been bubbling in the gutter. You have resigned yourself and, sitting by the stove, are prepared, so to speak, to
let winter descend on you; but one morning on waking, you notice
with incredulous eyes that a narrow streak of brilliant blue is shining
into your room between the curtains. Astonished, you leap out of bed

and open the window; a wave of flickering sunlight bathes you and at the same moment you hear, through all the street noises, a gay chattering and twittering of birds; as you breathe the light, fresh air of an early october day, you seem to find in it that matchless sweetness and fragrant promise that belongs to the winds of May. It is spring, it is quite unmistakably spring in spite of the calendar, and you pull on your clothes to hurry through the streets and out into the open beneath that shimmering sky.

Such an unexpected and unusual day occurred about four months ago — it was about the beginning of February — and on that day I saw an exceptionally pretty sight. I had set out before nine o'clock in the morning; filled with a gay and joyful mood, vaguely expectant of changes, surprises and good fortune, I took the road to the Lerchenberg. I ascended the hill from the right and walked the whole length of the ridge, always keeping to the edge of the main boulevard with its low stone parapet, so as to command, throughout the stroll, which took about half an hour, a constant view of the terraced city and of the river, whose windings gleamed in the sun, while behind it the landscape with its hills and verdure faded in the sunny haze.

Hardly a soul was up there yet. The benches on the other side of the road stood empty, and here and there a statue, shimmering white in the sun, gleamed from between the trees, while a withered leaf occasionally settled slowly down upon it. The silence to which I was listening as I walked, with my eyes fixed on the bright panorama by my side, was unbroken until I reached the end of the hill, and the road began to decline between old chestnut trees. But then there sounded behind me the trampling of horses and the rolling of carriage wheels; a vehicle was approaching at a swift trot and I had to make way for it about halfway down the hill. I stepped aside and waited.

It was a small, quite light, two-wheeled dogcart, drawn by two large, glossy chestnut horses, frisking and snorting. The reins were held by a young lady of nineteen or perhaps twenty, and beside her sat an old gentleman of stately and dignified appearance, with a white mustache brushed up *à la russe* and thick white eyebrows. A groom in a simple black and silver livery adorned the back seat.

At the beginning of the descent the pace of the horses had been slackened, since one of them seemed to be nervous and restive. It was pulling away from the shaft and held its head against its breast, setting down its slender legs with such trembling unwillingness that the old gentleman was slightly concerned and bent forward to help the young lady pull on the reins with his elegantly gloved left hand. The driving had apparently been entrusted to her only temporarily and half in fun, for she seemed to be treating it with a sort of childlike importance and inexperience. She made a slight, earnest and indignant movement of her head as she sought to calm the stumbling and shying animal.

She was dark and slender. On her hair, which was drawn to a firm knot at the nape of the neck and lay loosely about brow and temples, so that light-brown threads could be distinguished in it, was perched a round, dark straw hat, whose only trimming was a simple arrangement of ribbons. For the rest, she wore a short, dark-blue jacket and a plainly made skirt of light-gray cloth.

In her finely formed oval face, its delicate brunette coloring heightened by the morning air, the most attractive feature was certainly the eyes, narrow almond-shaped eyes whose half-hidden irises were flashing black, and above them rose arched brows of an extraordinary regularity, as if drawn with a pen. Her nose was perhaps a trifle long and the mouth might have been smaller, though the lips were clear and fine. At the moment, however, its charm was enhanced by the white, widely spaced teeth, which the young girl was pressing firmly against her lower lip in the effort to hold in the horse, and they seemed to draw the childlike rounded chin slightly upwards.

It would be quite untrue to say that this face was of a striking and admirable beauty. It possessed the charm of youth and joyous freshness, and this charm was, as it were, smoothed, subdued and ennobled by the freedom from anxiety that prosperous circumstances, aristocratic upbringing, and luxurious care bestow; it was certain that those narrow flashing eyes, which now regarded the stubborn horse with a petulant vexation, would in the next minute be filled once more with a proud and unquestioning ease. The sleeves of her coat, wide and flaring at the shoulders, fitted tightly around her slender wrists, and never have I received a more ravishing impression of high-bred elegance than was conveyed by the way in which those small, ungloved white hands held the reins.

I stood by the roadside without receiving a glance while the carriage passed, and I continued my course when it set off again at a trot and swiftly disappeared. My feeling was one of delight and admiration; but it was mixed, at the same time, with a vague, stinging pain, a keen, distressing sense of — envy? love? (I did not dare to pursue the thought) or of self-depreciation?

As I write now, I have a vision of a poor beggar staring into a jeweler's window at the glitter of a costly diamond. He will never have the self-assurance to desire to possess the gem; merely to think of forming such a wish would be so absurdly impossible as to make him an object of ridicule to himself.

(12)

I have now to narrate that, as the result of an accident, I saw this lady for a second time in the course of that week, at the opera Gounod's *Faust* was being performed, and I had scarcely stepped into the brightly lit theater to take my seat in the orchestra when I saw her, seated in a stage box on the opposite side, on the old gentleman's left. At this same moment I became aware that a slight terror had seized me, accompanied by something akin to confusion, which, ridiculous though it was, for some unknown reason caused me to avert my eyes at once and to let them wander over the other tiers of boxes. Not until the overture began did I attempt to study the pair more intently.

The old gentleman, in a tightly buttoned frock coat and black tie, was leaning back in his chair with quiet dignity, resting one of his brown-gloved hands lightly on the velvet-covered front of the box, while the other from time to time slowly stroked his mustache or the short-cropped gray hair. The young girl, on the other hand — his daughter no doubt — was leaning forward with an air of lively interest, resting her hands, which held a fan, on the padded velvet railing before her. At intervals she tossed her head lightly to shake back the loose light-brown hair from her brow and temples.

She was wearing a blouse of bright colored silk with a bunch of violets at the waist, and, in the dazzling light, her narrow eyes flashed even more darkly than they did when I saw her a week before. I noticed further that the set of the mouth, which I had noticed then, was characteristic; at every other moment she pressed her gleaming white teeth, which were widely but regularly spaced, on her lower lip, tilting her chin slightly upward. This ingenuous expression, in which there was no trace of coquetry; the quiet but cheerfully roving

glance of her eyes; her delicate white throat, which was bare except
for the narrow silk ribbon that encircled it, of the same color as her
sash; the occasional movement with which she turned to the old
gentleman to call his attention to something in the orchestra, on the
curtain or in one of the loges — all this produced the effect of an inde-
scribably tender and childlike charm, which yet had nothing notice-
ably touching about it, nothing that would excite "sympathy" in
itself. It was an aristocratic, controlled youthfulness, which had been
rendered secure and superior by easy material circumstances, and
the happiness it revealed expressed no arrogance but rather a serenity
that could not possibly be questioned.

Gounod's clever and tender music was, it seemed to me, an apt accompaniment for this picture, and I listened without paying any attention to the stage, completely absorbed in a gentle, pensive mood;
its sadness might perhaps have been more painful but for the music.
But in the interval that followed the first act a gentleman of some
twenty-seven to thirty years of age rose from his seat in the orchestra
and vanished, to reappear in the box that I was observing. As he entered, bowing gracefully, the old gentleman immediately stretched
out a hand to him, and the young lady gave him hers with a friendly
nod; he raised it to his lips with dignity and was promptly urged to be
seated.

I am ready to confess that this cavalier wore the most incomparable shirt front it has ever been my privilege to see. It was completely visible, this shirt front, for the vest was nothing but a narrow
black strip, and the tailcoat, held together by a single button placed
low at the waist, swept from his shoulders in an unusually broad
curve. The shirt front was terminated at the high, sharply turned
down collar by a wide black bow tie and also showed two large,
square black studs mathematically spaced; it was dazzlingly white,
this shirt front, and had been admirably starched without losing its
flexibility, for in the region of the stomach it fell into a gentle decliv-
ity, rising again in an agreeable, gleaming convexity.

It goes without saying that the gentleman's shirt front claimed the
greater part of one's attention; his head, however, was perfectly
round and his skull covered with a coat of short-cropped, pale blond
hair; it was further adorned with a rimless and ribbonless pair of eyeglasses, a not too vigorous, fair and slightly curling mustache, and
with a host of small dueling scars on one cheek, stretching up to the

temple. For the rest, his figure was flawless and he moved with assurance.

In the course of the evening—for he remained in the box—I observed him in two attitudes that seemed especially characteristic of him. Whenever the conversation lapsed he would sit with crossed legs, his opera glasses in his lap, leaning back comfortably, while his head was bent forward and his lips projected abnormally so that he could lose himself in contemplation of the two ends of his mustache; he seemed to be completely hypnotized by them as he turned his head slowly from one side to the other in silence. On the other hand, when he was conversing with the young lady, he altered the position of his legs out of respect for her, but leaned back still farther, grasping his chair with both hands and raising his head as far as possible, to smile down upon his young companion, his mouth opened quite wide, in an amiable and slightly superior fashion. This gentleman must have been filled with a marvelously happy sense of his own importance...

Seriously, I can appreciate something like that. None of his movements, though daring in their nonchalance, caused any painful embarrassment; he was buoyed up by his self-confidence. And why should it be otherwise? It was clear that, without any undue presumption, he had taken a path that was the right one, and one that he would follow to a clear and useful goal; he was living in the shade of universal harmony and in the sunshine of general esteem. Meanwhile, he was sitting there in the loge, chatting with a young girl to whose exquisite and innocent charm he was perhaps not impervious, and to whose hand he could, in that case, unhesitatingly aspire. I certainly feel no wish to utter a disrespectful word against this gentleman.

And what of myself? I was sitting down there below them, able to observe gloomily from a distance and out of the darkness how that precious and unattainable creature was chatting and laughing with the unworthy fellow. Excluded, unnoticed, without rights, a stranger, *hors ligne*,* *déclassé*, a pariah, pitiful in my own eyes.

I stayed to the end and I met the party again in the cloakroom, where they lingered awhile, donning their furs and exchanging a casual word with a lady here and an officer there. The young gentleman left the theater in the company of the father and daughter, and I followed them through the foyer at a short distance.

*"A misfit."

It was not raining; there were a few stars in the sky, and they did not call a carriage. Chatting leisurely, the three walked on ahead of me and I followed at a respectful distance, depressed and haunted by a tormenting feeling of wretchedness, at once stinging and humiliating . . . They had not far to go; scarcely had they traversed one block when they stopped before a stately house with a simple facade, into which the father and daughter disappeared, taking a cordial leave of their escort, who also strode swiftly away.

On the heavy carved door of the house I read the name, "Counselor of Justice Rainer."

(13)

I am determined to complete my entries in this diary, although some inward resistance urges me every minute to rise and run away. I have dug and bored into this business to the point of exhaustion. I am utterly sick of it all, to the point of nausea! . . .

It is not quite three months since the newspapers announced that a charity bazaar would be held in the city hall, with the participation of the fashionable world. I read the announcement attentively and determined immediately to attend the bazaar. She will be there, I thought, perhaps as a salesgirl at one of the booths, and in that case there will be nothing to prevent me from approaching her. Calm reflection tells me that I am a man of culture and good family; if this Fräulein Rainer attracts me, I have as much right as the gentleman in the astonishing shirt front to take advantage of such an opportunity to address her, to exchange a few amusing words with her . . .

It was a windy and rainy afternoon when I set out for the city hall, at the entrance of which was a crowd of people and vehicles. I elbowed my way into the building, paid the admission fee, checked my hat and coat, mounted the crowded staircase with some difficulty, and reached the banquet hall on the second floor; I was met by a heavy atmosphere of mingled wine, food, perfume and pine wood, by the confused noise of laughter, conversation, music, barkers' shouting and bell ringing.

The immensely wide and lofty room was decorated with multi-colored flags and garlands; along the walls and down the center stood the booths, both open and enclosed, a visit to which was loudly recommended by gentlemen in fantastic masks, shouting at the top of their lungs. The ladies were selling flowers, fancywork, tobacco and refreshments all over the place, and were likewise wearing costumes of various sorts. On a platform, filled with plants, at the upper end of the hall a band was playing loudly, while in the narrow passages between the booths a compact mass of human beings moved slowly forward.

Somewhat overcome by the noise of the music, the lottery booths and the merry barkers, I joined the stream of humanity and a minute later caught sight of the face I was seeking, four feet to the left of the entrance. In a small booth adorned with pine branches she was selling wine and lemonade; her costume was Italian: brightly colored skirt, white rectangular headdress and the short bodice of Albanian women, the lawn sleeves of which left her delicate arms bare to the elbow. A little flushed, she was leaning sideways against the counter, playing with her gay fan and chatting with a number of gentlemen who stood about the booth smoking, and among whom I instantly spied my acquaintance; he was standing nearest to her at the table, four fingers of each hand thrust into the pockets of his jacket.

I forced my way slowly past, determined to approach her as soon as an opportunity offered, when she would be less occupied. Ah, now we would see whether I still commanded a remnant of cheerful self-confidence and proud ease of manner, or whether the moroseness and half-despairing gloom of the last few weeks had been justified! What had come over me, anyway? What was the cause of this wretched, tormented feeling at the sight of this girl — a feeling made up of envy, love, bashfulness and irritated bitterness? It was, I had to confess, already suffusing my face with blood. The devil! Where was my openness and charm, my serene and graceful composure, befitting a gifted and happy man? And with nervous eagerness I prepared the *bon mot*, the Italian speech that I proposed to address to her . . .

It took a long time to traverse the entire length of the hall among this slowly moving throng, and when I once more stood before the little wine booth, the semicircle of men had indeed vanished and only my acquaintance was still leaning against the counter, conversing with the young barmaid in lively tones. Well then, I must take the liberty of interrupting this conversation. And with a sharp turn I drew out of the stream and stopped before the counter.

What happened? Oh, nothing! Practically nothing! The conversation broke off, my acquaintance stepped aside a pace, and holding his rimless and ribbonless eyeglasses with all five fingers, regarded me through his hand, while the young lady sent a calm, appraising glance over me, over my suit and down to my boots. The suit was by no means new and the boots were soiled by the mud of the streets, I knew that. Moreover, my face was flushed and possibly my hair was in disorder. I was not cool, nor at ease, nor master of the situation. The feeling came over me that I, a stranger, an outsider without rights, was a nuisance here, was making myself ridiculous. Insecurity, helplessness, wretchedness and hatred blurred my vision; in a word, I carried out my gay intentions by uttering the curt, almost crude order in a hoarse voice and with brows knitted grimly:

"A glass of wine, please."

It is of no consequence at all whether I was or was not right in believing that I saw a rapid mocking glance pass from the young girl to her friend. In total silence she handed me the wine; flushed and confused with pain and rage, I stood there with downcast eyes between these two, an unhappy and ridiculous figure; after taking a few sips I laid down the money, bowed awkwardly, and precipitately left the hall for the street.

From that moment I was finished, and it makes precious little difference that I read a few days later in the newspaper the announcement, "Counselor of Justice Rainer has the honor to announce the engagement of his daughter Anna to Dr. Alfred Witznagel, Assistant Judge."

(14)

From that moment I was finished. My last remnant of happiness and self-confidence has collapsed, hounded to death—I can take no more. Yes, I am unhappy, I admit it, and I see in myself a wretched and ridiculous figure! But this I cannot endure. It will destroy me. I shall shoot myself, it may be today or it may be tomorrow.

My first impulse, my first instinct, was to make a furtive attempt to infuse a literary element into the affair and interpret my pitiful malaise as "unhappy love"; a piece of stupidity, as anyone can see. One is not destroyed by an unhappy love affair. Unhappiness in love is a not unpleasant pose. The victim of unhappy love can still like himself. But I am being destroyed because the power to take any pleasure in myself is beyond all hope.

Was I in love—if this question is permitted—was I really in love with this girl? Perhaps—but how and why? Was it not a love that was merely the outgrowth of my irritated and sick vanity, awakened long before and arising to torment me at the first sight of this unattainable treasure, producing feelings of envy, hatred and self-loathing, for which love became merely a pretext, a subterfuge and an escape?

Yes, all that is vanity. Did not my father once call me a buffoon?

Ah, I of all people had no justification for sitting on the sidelines and ignoring society; I, who am too vain to ignore its indifference and contempt; I, who cannot exist without society or its approval. But perhaps it is not a question of justification but of necessity? And my useless buffoonery has no social value? Well, it was this buffoonery of mine that was destined to bring about my destruction.

Indifference, I know, is a kind of happiness. But I cannot be indifferent toward myself; I cannot look at myself with other eyes than those of my fellowmen, and I am being destroyed, innocent as I am, by an uneasy conscience. Is a bad conscience, I wonder, ever anything but a festering vanity?

There is only one kind of unhappiness: to lose pleasure in oneself. No longer to like oneself, that is unhappiness; yes, I have always known that well. All else is play and enrichment of life; in any other kind of suffering one can still remain altogether satisfied with oneself, cut a fine figure in one's own eyes. Only discord with yourself, suffering with a bad conscience, the spasms of vanity, only these can turn you into a wretched and repulsive spectacle...

An old acquaintance appeared on the scene, one by the name of Schilling, with whom I once served society in Herr Schlievogt's wholesale lumber business. He was passing through the city on business and came to see me—a "skeptical individual," his hands in his trouser pockets, wearing a black-rimmed pince-nez and shrugging his shoulders with realistic tolerance. He appeared one evening and said, "I'm staying a few days." We went to a wine house.

He talked to me as though I were still the happy, self-satisfied person he had once known, and in the sincere belief that he was merely presenting me with my own opinion of myself, he said, "By George, you've arranged things very snugly for yourself, my lad! Independent,

eh? Free! Damn it, you're quite right! We only live once, what? What
do we really care about the rest? You're smarter than I, I must admit.
But then, you always were a genius." As before, he was ready to
accord me a perfectly spontaneous recognition and to flatter me
without suspecting that I was secretly torn with anxiety lest I should
fail to please him.

Desperately I strove to retain the place I occupied in his judgment,
to appear still, as I had always done, at the pinnacle of happiness and
self-contentment. In vain! I lacked the stamina, the poise, the bearing. I faced him with a weary, embarrassed air, submissive and uncertain—and he grasped the situation with incredible speed. It was
horrible to see how he, who had been quite prepared to accept me as
a fortunate and superior person, began to see through me, to stare at
me in astonishment, to grow first cool, then superior, then impatient
and resentful, and finally to show his contempt for me in every feature. He left early, and the next day a few hasty lines informed me
that he had been obliged to leave the city after all.

The fact is that the whole world is far too urgently occupied with
itself to have time to form a serious opinion about anyone; the degree
of self-respect which you have the self-confidence to reveal is accepted
with a slothful acquiescence. Be what you will, live as you will, but
show a bold front and never betray a bad conscience; no one will be
moral enough to despise you. On the other hand, once you lose harmony with yourself, lose your self-complacence, and show that you
despise yourself, people will blindly agree with your estimate of yourself. As for me, I am lost.

I cease writing; I throw down my pen—full of disgust, full of disgust! Make an end of it! But would that not be too heroic for a "buffoon"? The result will be, I fear, that I shall continue to live—to eat,
sleep and occupy myself somehow, and gradually become dully
reconciled to being an unhappy and ridiculous figure.

Good heavens, who would have thought, who *could* have thought,
that it is such a misfortune, such a fatal destiny to be born a
"buffoon"?

Gerhart Hauptmann

1862 — 1946

Gerhart Hauptmann was born and raised in a small Silesian summer resort, where his father owned and managed a hotel. He was an undisciplined, confused and unhappy boy, who could make no progress in school and who lived in a dream world of his own. A year spent on a farm during adolescence did not make a farmer out of him, so he was sent to Breslau to study art. After a brief taste of student life at Jena and Zurich he went to Rome, where he tried his hand at sculpture. He also thought of becoming an actor, but finally decided to write. His first marriage was unhappy and ended in divorce. Though he married again, his relationship with his first wife played an important role in his writings and he remained deeply affected by it even as an old man.

Hauptmann became a celebrity overnight with the performance in 1889 of his naturalist tragedy *Vor Sonnenaufgang* (*Before Sunrise*). From then on he unflaggingly produced work after work: tragedies, comedies, novels, novellas, verse epics, autobiography, essays, lyric poetry. His dramas were performed throughout the Western world and his writings translated into many languages. He won many honors and distinctions, including the Nobel prize for literature in 1912. Under the Weimar Republic he was acclaimed as the representative poet of liberal, democratic Germany, and his sixtieth and seventieth birthdays were celebrated as official national events. He lived through the National Socialist regime and the Second World War, suffering official disapproval, but enjoying popularity as the Nestor of German letters. Before he died, at the age of eighty-three, he saw his beloved Dresden destroyed by Allied bombs and his native Silesia invaded by Polish and Russian troops at the end of World

War II. His last important work, and one of his best, was a tetralogy in verse on the Iphigenia theme.

Hauptmann's artistic range is extraordinary, embracing all the principal genres and including works of striking originality and varied mood and style. His novellas constitute only a fraction of his total output; among the eight that he wrote, several were distinguished contributions to the form. His most outstanding novella is undoubtedly *Der Ketzer von Soana* (*The Heretic of Soana*, 1918) which deals with a theme that is central to Hauptmann's work: the conflict in our culture between pagan or Dionysian and ascetic, Christian values. The affirmation of life through the acceptance of Eros, the generative principle, as the source and support of all life, and the acceptance of it without that sense of guilt which puritanical Christianity has instilled in us — this is the meaning of his tale. Yet it is no vulgar rebellion against a restrictive, strait-laced morality that Hauptmann depicts, but a philosophical, Nietzschean challenge thrown down by one way of life to another.

The central experience in *The Heretic of Soana* is Francesco's gradual realization that he has been living an unnatural life, deprived of an appreciation of nature and art, a life steeped in fanatical spiritual zeal which, as events show, perhaps disguised a strong erotic impulse that could be repressed only temporarily. The innocent agent who brings about this transformation is a child of sin, indeed of the most horrifying sin known to man. And yet Hauptmann succeeds in making the reader accept this transformation as something natural. For it takes place amidst a superb natural setting, the wild, remote region of the Italian Alps, where, surrounded by modern life, a vestige of primitive culture still exists. We enter into the world in which the zealous priest has lived all his life and see him awakening, under the spell of the wild child of nature, to the beauty of the surrounding landscape. We see ascetic guilt yielding to pagan joy in life, remorse vanishing before the pure innocence of sensuous enjoyment. The beauty of nature, the rhythm of God's mute creatures carrying on the quiet, steady business of life, the relics of devotion and art which dot the countryside, the idyllic remnants of primitive life on the mountain slopes, the bestial superstition of the incestuous couple and the implacable hatred of the good Christian villagers below — all this is presented with quiet power and great beauty of language. Moreover, Hauptmann wholly succeeds in persuading us of the innocence of this beautiful girl by contrasting her with her depraved parents on the one hand, and the self-righteous Christians of Soana on the other.

The descriptions of Alpine nature are superb; but still more remarkable is the atmosphere of serenity and of a relentless erotic urge that finds expression despite every obstacle, disguises itself with various masks and penetrates even the holiest traditional sanctuaries. For Eros, Hauptmann affirms again and again, is the oldest and most powerful of the gods, greater even than Zeus himself and antedating him. Nothing can withstand him.

In most of Hauptmann's work Fate appears as a destructive force; here, however, it directs two creatures toward permanent happiness. Agata ("the good"), the child of sin, is able to stir the zealous ascetic Francesco to an appreciation of the beauty of this world. It is small wonder that the narrator looks at her in awe, as a sublime, almost frightening, being whose spell grows incessantly, embracing the whole scale of human emotion, from voluptuous bliss to death.

The Heretic of Soana

Tourists can set out for the summit of Mount Generoso in Mendrisio or take the rack railway in Capolago or start from Melida by way of Soana, which is the most difficult road of all. The whole region belongs to Ticino, a Swiss canton with an Italian population.

At a great height mountain climbers not infrequently met the figure of a bespectacled goatherd, whose appearance was striking in other ways too. His face bespoke the man of culture in spite of his tanned skin. He looked not unlike the bronze statue of John the Baptist by Donatello in the cathedral of Siena. He had dark hair which hung in curls over his brown shoulders. His dress consisted of a goatskin.

Whenever a group of strangers came near this man, the mountain guides began to laugh. When the tourists saw him, they often burst into crude roars of laughter or into loud, provocative cries. They felt justified in doing so because of the strange sight he presented. The goatherd paid no heed to them; he did not even turn his head.

All the mountain guides seemed to be on basically good terms with him. They often climbed over to him and entered into confidential conversations with him. When they returned and were asked by the strangers what sort of a weird saint this was, the guides tended to act mysterious until he was out of sight. Those tourists whose curiosity was still alive learned that this man had a dark history, was popularly called "the heretic of Soana" and enjoyed a dubious esteem mingled with superstitious fear.

When the editor of these pages was still young and fortunate enough to spend frequent glorious weeks in beautiful Soana, it was inevitable that he should now and then climb Mount Generoso and one day come face to face with the so-called "heretic of Soana." He could not forget the man's appearance. After gathering all sorts of contradictory impressions about him, he resolved to see him again, in fact simply to visit him.

The editor was strengthened in his intention by a German Swiss, the doctor of Soana, who assured him that the eccentric was not averse to receiving visits from educated people. He had visited him once himself. "I should really be angry with him," he said, "because the fellow is an unauthorized competitor of mine. But he lives very high up and far away and is, thank Heaven, only consulted in secret by those few who would not stop at being cured by the devil himself." The doctor continued, "You must know there is a belief among the people that he has sold his soul to the devil, a view that is not contested by the clergy, because it originated with them. Originally, they say, the man was under an evil spell, until he himself became a hardened villain and infernal sorcerer. As far as I am concerned, I've noticed neither claws nor horns on him."

The editor remembers his visits to the strange man very clearly. The nature of the first meeting was remarkable. A special circumstance gave it the character of an accident. At a steep spot on the road the visitor found himself face to face with a helpless mother goat which had just thrown a kid and was in the process of giving birth to a second. The distress of the lonely mother, who looked at him fearlessly as if she expected his help, and the profound mystery of birth in that vast rocky wildness, made the deepest impression on him. But he hastened his ascent, for he had concluded that this animal probably belonged to the herd of the eccentric, and wanted to summon him to help. He found him among his goats and cattle, told him what he had observed and led him to the mother in labor. Behind her the second kid was already lying in the grass, damp and bloody.

With the sure touch of a physician, with the tender love of the merciful Samaritan, the owner cared for the animal. After waiting a certain amount of time, he took each of the newborn creatures under an arm and slowly began the way back to his home, followed by the mother, whose heavy udder almost dragged on the ground. The visitor was not only rewarded with the most friendly thanks, but invited in an irresistible manner to accompany him.

The eccentric had erected several buildings on the mountain

meadow that was his property. From the outside, one of these resembled a crude pile of stones. Inside it was a dry, warm stable.
There the goat and her young were housed, while the visitor was led
higher up to a whitewashed square building leaning against the wall
of Mount Generoso and situated on a terrace overgrown with grapevine. Not far from the little gate a stream of water as thick as an arm
shot out of the mountain and filled a huge stone basin which had
been hewn out of the rock. Near the basin a mountain cave was
locked off by an iron-bound door; this soon revealed itself to be a
vaulted cellar.

This place, which, when viewed from the valley, seemed to hang at
an inaccessible height, offered a splendid view; but the editor does
not wish to speak about that. To be sure, when he enjoyed it for the
first time, he fell from speechless astonishment into loud exclamations of rapture and back again into speechless astonishment. But his
host, who at this moment emerged from the house (where he had
been looking for something), suddenly seemed to be walking on
softer soles. This, as well as his generally quiet, calm conduct, did
not escape the visitor. It was an admonition to him to be sparing of
words and chary of questions. He already liked the odd goatherd too
much to run the risk of estranging him by even a hint of curiosity or
importunity.

The visitor still sees the round stone table which stood on the terrace, surrounded by benches. He sees it with all the good things the
"heretic of Soana" had spread on it: the most wonderful *stracchino di
lecco*, delicious Italian wheat bread, salami, olives, figs and medlars,
besides a jug full of red wine which he had fetched fresh from the
grotto. When they sat down, the goatskin-clad, bearded host, with
his long flowing locks, looked warmly into the eyes of the visitor,
grasping the latter's right hand as if to indicate affection.

It is difficult to remember all that was said at this first meeting;
only some of it has remained in the memory. The goatherd wished to
be called Ludovico. He related many things about the Argentine. At
one point, when the ringing of the angelus bells penetrated to us
from below, he remarked about this "ubiquitous irritating noise."
Once the name of Seneca was mentioned. We also talked casually
about Swiss politics. Finally the eccentric wanted to know some
things about Germany, because it was the visitor's native land. When

the time came for the visitor to depart, according to a prearranged plan, the host said, "You will always be welcome here."

Although the editor of these pages was eager for this man's story, as he frankly admits, he avoided betraying any interest in it even on subsequent visits. In chance conversations he had in Soana, he gathered some of the external reasons for Ludovico's being called the "heretic of Soana"; but the visitor was much more concerned with finding out in what sense this designation was justified, and in what peculiar inner destinies, in what special philosophy, Ludovico's way of life was rooted. But he refrained from putting questions and was richly rewarded for this.

Mostly he met Ludovico alone, either among the animals of his herd or in his cell. A few times he came upon him milking the goats with his own hands, like Robinson Crusoe, or forcing a rebellious mother to suckle her kids. At such times he seemed to merge completely with his calling of Alpine shepherd; he rejoiced in the mother goat who dragged her swollen udder on the ground, and in the ram when it was in active heat. Of one goat he said, "Doesn't he look like the Evil One himself? Just look at his eyes. What power, what flashing anger, what rage and malice! And yet what a sacred fire!" His smile took on a hard, grim character; he showed his splendid white teeth and fell into a dreamy state when he watched, with the eye of an expert, one of his demonic matadors going about his useful work.

At times the "heretic" played the pipes of Pan, and the visitor could hear their simple scale even as he approached. On one such occasion the conversation naturally turned to music, about which the shepherd unfolded strange views. When he was among his herd Ludovico never spoke of anything except the animals and their habits, of the goatherd's vocation and its customs. Not infrequently he pursued the subject of animal psychology and traced the goatherd's way of life into the remotest past, betraying a scholar's knowledge of no common range. He spoke of Apollo tending the herds of Laomedon and Admetus as a servant and shepherd. "I would like to know on what instrument he made music to his flocks then." And he concluded, as if he were talking about something real, "By Heaven, I would have enjoyed listening to him." Those were the moments in which the shaggy anchorite might perhaps have created the impression that his mental powers were not quite intact. On the other hand, his thoughts received a certain justification when he demonstrated in what varied ways a herd could be influenced and guided by music. He brought them to their feet with one note and brought them to rest with another. With music he fetched them from distant places, with music he made the animals scatter or follow close on his heels.

There were also visits at which almost nothing was said. Once, when the oppressive heat of a June afternoon had penetrated to the meadows of Mount Generoso, Ludovico was lying in a blissful state of somnolence beside his cud-chewing herds. He merely gave his visitor a flashing look and motioned to him to stretch out in the grass too. When this was done and both of them had been lying there for a while in silence, he said in a drawling voice, without any introduction, something to this effect:

"You know that Eros is older than Cronus and mightier too. — Do you feel this silent fire about us? Eros! — Do you hear the cricket chirping? Eros!" — At this moment two lizards which were chasing each other shot over the prostrate shepherd with lightning speed. He repeated, "Eros! Eros!" — And, as if obeying an order he had issued, two strong bucks now got up and locked horns. He did not interfere, although the combat became more and more heated. The clang from the thrusts became louder and louder, and the number of attacks increased. And again he said, "Eros! Eros!"

And now for the first time the visitor heard words which made him listen with special attention, because they shed, or at least seemed to shed, light on the question why Ludovico was known to the people as the "heretic." "I prefer," he said, "to worship a living goat or a living bull to a man who was hanged on the gallows. I am not living in an age that does this. I hate and despise this age. Jupiter Ammon was represented with the horns of a ram. Pan has the legs of a goat; Bacchus, the horns of a bull. I mean the Bacchus Tauriformis or Tauricornis of the Romans. Mithra, the sun god, is represented as a bull. All the peoples revered the bull, the goat, the ram, and shed their sacred blood in sacrifice. To this I say: yes! — for the procreative power is the highest power, the procreative power is the creative power, procreation and creation are the same thing. Of course, the cult of this power is not the frigid bleating of monks and nuns. I once dreamed of Sita, the wife of Vishnu, who assumed human shape under the name of Rama. Priests died in her embraces. During that moment I knew something of all sorts of mysteries; of the mystery of black procreation in the green grass, of procreation in mother-of-pearl-colored lust; of raptures and stupors; of the mystery of yellow maize kernels, of all fruits, all sizes, all colors. I could have bellowed in the frenzy of pain when I caught sight of the merciless almighty Sita. I thought I would die of desire."

During this revelation the writer of these lines felt like an involuntary eavesdropper. He stood up with a few words, which were designed to give the impression that he had not heard the monologue but had concentrated his thoughts on other matters. Then he tried to take his leave. But Ludovico would not permit it. And so once more, on that mountain terrace, there began a banquet, and this time its course became significant and unforgettable.

The visitor was introduced into the dwelling, the interior of the cabin described above. It was square shaped, clean, had a fireplace and resembled the simple study of a scholar. It contained ink, pen, paper and a small library, chiefly of Greek and Latin authors. "Why should I conceal the fact from you," said the shepherd, "that I am of good family and enjoyed a misguided youth and the education of a scholar? Of course you will want to know how I changed from an unnatural to a natural man, from a prisoner into a free man, from a disturbed and morose man into a happy and contented one. Or how I excluded myself from bourgeois society and Christianity." He gave a loud laugh. "Perhaps I shall write the history of my transformation some day." The visitor, whose suspense had reached its peak, found himself once more thrown far from his goal. It did not help much when his host finally declared that the cause of his regeneration lay in the fact that he worshiped natural symbols.

In the shadow of the rock, on the terrace, at the edge of the overflowing basin, in the delicious coolness, a more sumptuous meal than the first was spread: smoked ham, cheese and wheat bread, figs, fresh medlars and wine. There had been much talk, not high-spirited but full of quiet gaiety. Finally the stone table was cleared. And now there came a moment which lives in the editor's mind as if it were yesterday.

The bronzed goatherd, as we know, created a savage impression with his long, unkept locks and beard and his goatskin. He has been compared to Donatello's Saint John the Baptist. His face did in fact have much in common with John's in fineness of line. Upon close inspection, Ludovico was really handsome, if one could forget his spectacles. To be sure, these spectacles gave his whole appearance, apart from a slightly comical expression, a strange, enigmatic and arresting quality. At the moment which I am describing, his whole person underwent a transformation. If the bronzelike quality of his body had found expression in a certain immobility, this now vanished to the extent that his features became mobile and rejuvenated. One might say that he smiled with a tinge of boyish bashfulness. "What I now ask of you," he said, "I have never proposed to anyone else. I really don't know myself where I get the courage to do it. From an old habit I still read from time to time, and even play with ink and pen. So I've written down, in the winter hours of my leisure, a simple tale which is supposed to have happened here, in and around Soana, long before my time. You will find it extremely simple, but it attracted me for all sorts of reasons, which I will not discuss now. Tell me briefly and frankly: Do you want to go back into the house with me, and do you feel inclined to forfeit some of your time to this story, which has already cost me, too, many a fruitless hour? I don't want to urge you, I would rather dissuade you. Moreover, if you say so, I will take the pages of the manuscript and throw them down into the depths right now."

Of course this did not happen. He took the wine jug, went into the house with his visitor and the two men sat facing each other. From a case made of the finest goat leather, the mountain shepherd had unfolded a manuscript, written in a monkish hand on strong paper. As though to give himself courage, he once more raised his glass to his visitor before he cast away from shore to plunge into the stream of narration. Then he began in a soft voice.

THE MOUNTAIN SHEPHERD'S TALE

On a mountain slope above Lake Lugano one may find a small hamlet among many others, which may be reached after about an hour's journey from the lake shore by way of a steep highway that winds about the mountain.

The houses of the hamlet, which, like most of the Italian places of that region, are one single gray ruin of brick and mortar, emerging like a series of boxes out of each other, front on a gorgelike valley of meadows and terraces behind the mighty slope of the towering giant Mount Generoso.

Into this valley, at the point where it really ends as a narrow gorge, a waterfall pours from the bottom of a valley situated about a hundred yards higher up. The power of the waterfall varies with the time of day and year and with the prevailing air currents; its roar constitutes perpetual music in the hamlet.

A long time ago a priest named Raffaele Francesco, who was then about twenty-five years old, was transferred to this community. He had been born in Ligornetto, which is in the canton of Ticino, and could boast that he was a member of the same family, long established there, which had produced the most significant sculptor of united Italy, who had also been born in Ligornetto and had eventually died there too.

The young priest had spent his childhood with relatives in Milan, and his student days in various theological seminaries of Switzerland and Italy. From his mother, who was descended from a noble family, he inherited the serious side of his character, which impelled him, at a very early age and without the slightest hesitation, to embrace the religious vocation.

Francesco, who wore spectacles, was distinguished from the host of his fellow pupils by exemplary industry, a strict way of life, and piety. Even his mother had to urge on him tactfully that, as a future secular priest, he might well permit himself a little joy in life, since he was not really bound to the most stringent monastic rules. However, as soon as he had received holy orders, his sole wish was to find a most remote parish, where he might dedicate himself to his heart's desire, even more than hitherto, as a sort of hermit, to the service of God, the Son and the Holy Mother.

When he came to little Soana and moved into the parsonage that adjoined the church, the mountain-dwellers soon noticed that he was an entirely different type from his predecessor. Even in appearance; for his predecessor had been a massive, bull-like peasant who used means other than ecclesiastical penances and penalties to keep the pretty women and girls of the place obedient to him. Francesco, by contrast, was pale and delicate. His eyes were deep-set. Hectic spots glowed on the impure skin that covered his cheekbones. To this were added the spectacles, which to simple folk are still a symbol of preceptorial severity and learning. After a period of from four to six weeks he had, in his own way, brought the somewhat rebellious wives and daughters under his power, and indeed to an even greater degree than the other priest.

As soon as Francesco stepped into the street through the little gate of the tiny parish yard adjoining the church, he was surrounded by children and women, who kissed his hand with genuine reverence. And the number of times in the course of the day when he was called into the confessional by the tinkling of the little church bell, mounted up, by the time evening came, to a total which elicited from his newly hired housekeeper, a woman almost seventy years old, the exclamation that she had never realized how many angels were hidden in the normally rather corrupt Soana. In short, the reputation of the young pastor Francesco Vela echoed far and wide in the region, and he soon acquired the name of saint.

Francesco did not allow any of this to affect him and was far from harboring any consciousness of doing more than discharging his duties in a tolerably competent manner. He said Masses, performed all the ecclesiastical functions of the divine Service with undiminishing zeal and in addition carried out the duties of secular instruction, for the little schoolroom was in the parsonage.

One evening at the beginning of the month of March there was a violent tug at the bell of the parish yard. When the housekeeper opened the door and shone her lantern out into the bad weather, she was confronted by a somewhat savage-looking fellow, who asked to speak to the pastor. After locking the gate the old housekeeper went in to her young master to announce the late visitor, not without visible anxiety. But Francesco, who had made it a point of duty, among others, to reject no one who needed him, whoever he might be, looked up from reading some church father and said shortly, "Go, Petronilla, bring him in."

Soon afterwards there stood before the priest's table a man of about forty, whose outward appearance was that of the people of the region, but much more neglected, indeed ragged. The man was barefoot. His threadbare, rain-soaked trousers were fastened about his hips by a belt. His shirt stood open. Above his tanned, hairy chest rose a bushy throat and a face that was overgrown with thick, black hair, out of which two dark, glowing eyes burned.

The man had hung a tattered, rain-soaked jacket over his left shoulder, as shepherds do, and he nervously twirled a small felt hat, shrunk and discolored by the wind and weather of many years, in his brown, hard fists. He had set down a long cudgel at the door.

When he was asked what he wished, the man poured out a flood of raw, unintelligible sounds and words, accompanied by wild grimaces. He spoke in the dialect of the district, to be sure, but deviated from it so much that it sounded like a foreign language even to the housekeeper, who had been born in Soana.

The young priest, who had attentively studied his visitor as he stood in the light of the small burning lamp, tried in vain to grasp the sense of his request. With much patience and by means of numerous questions, he was finally able to get this much out of him: that he was the father of seven children, some of whom he would like to send to the young priest's school. Francesco asked, "Where are you from?" And when the answer came tumbling out, "I'm from Soana," the priest was astonished and said at once, "That isn't possible! I know everyone in this place but I don't know you or your family."

The shepherd or peasant or whatever he was, now described the location of his home in excited tones, accompanying his description with many gestures; but Francesco could make no sense of it. He merely said, "If you are an inhabitant of Soana and your children have reached the legal age, they should have been in my school long ago. And I must surely have seen you or your wife or your children at a church service, at Mass or confession."

At this point the man opened his eyes wide and pressed his lips together. Instead of replying, he exhaled as though his heaving chest were congested.

"Well then, I'll write down your name. I think it's good of you to come of your own accord to take steps to prevent your children from remaining ignorant and possibly godless." At these words the ragged creature began to utter strange, croaking, animal-like sounds, so that his brown, sinewy, almost athletic body was shaken by them. "Yes," Francesco repeated in embarrassment, "I'll write down your name and look into the matter." One could see tear upon tear roll out of the stranger's reddened eyes and down his shaggy face.

"Very well, very well," said Francesco, who could not account for his visitor's excitement and was, besides, more disturbed than moved by it. "Very well, very well, your case will be investigated. Just tell me your name, my good man, and send me your children tomorrow morning." The man grew silent at this point, and looked at Francesco for a long time with a restless and tortured expression on his face. The priest asked once more, "What is your name? Tell me your name."

He had noticed, from the very beginning, a fearful, hunted quality

in the movements of his guest. Now, when he was supposed to state
his name and Petronilla's step became audible on the stone floor outside, he ducked down and displayed that pervasive fearsomeness that
we associate mostly with the insane or the criminal. He appeared to
be persecuted. He seemed to be in flight from the police.

However, he took a piece of paper and the priest's pen, walked
away from the light into the darkness, toward the window sill, where
the sounds of a nearby brook below and of the more distant waterfall
of Soana penetrated into the room; with some effort he managed to
scrawl something legible on the paper and handed it resolutely to the
priest. The latter said, "Good," and, making the sign of the Cross,
added, "Go in peace." The savage went, leaving behind him a cloud
of odors compounded of salami, onions, charcoal smoke, goats and
cow stables. As soon as he was gone the priest threw the windows wide
open.

The next morning Francesco said Mass as usual, rested a while and
then ate his frugal breakfast. Soon after, he was on his way to the
mayor, who had to be visited early if he was to be found at home. For
every day he went to Lugano, taking a train at the railway station far
below on the lakeshore; he had a wholesale and retail business in
Ticino cheese on one of the busiest streets of the town.

The sun shone down on the little square close to the church, which
formed, so to speak, the agora of the village, surrounded by old chestnut trees, which were as yet bare of leaves. Children sat around and
played on some of the stone benches, while the mothers and older
daughters washed their linen at an antique marble sarcophagus overflowing with the cold mountain water which it was copiously fed, and
carried the laundry away in baskets to dry. The ground was wet from
rain mingled with snowflakes that had fallen the previous day; on the
other side of the gorge, the mighty rocky slope of Mount Generoso,
covered with newly fallen snow, towered in its own shadow, and from
its inaccessible crags blew fresh mountain air toward them.

The young priest walked past the washerwomen with downcast
eyes, returning their loud greetings with a nod. He briefly held out
his hand to the children who pressed about him, looking at them over
his spectacles like an old man; they wiped their lips on his hand with
zeal and haste. The village, which began behind the square, was
made accessible by a few narrow lanes. But even the main street

could only be used by small vehicles, and then only at its front end. Toward the exit from the village the street became narrower and so steep that one could just about squeeze through and make one's way with a loaded mule. On this little street stood a small grocery store and a branch of the Swiss post office.

The postmaster, whose relations with Francesco's predecessor had been those of a comrade, greeted Francesco and was greeted by him in turn, but in such a way that due distance was maintained between the gravity of the consecrated priest and the casual friendliness of the layman. Not far from the post office the priest turned into a wretched little side lane which led down hazardously by means of stairways large and small, past open goat stables and all manner of dirty, windowless, cellarlike caves. Hens cackled; cats sat on rotten galleries under clusters of suspended corncobs. Here and there a goat bleated, or a cow, which for some reason had not been taken out to pasture, lowed.

It was astonishing, coming from this neighborhood, to pass through a narrow gate to the mayor's house and find oneself in a suite of small, vaulted rooms, whose ceilings craftsmen had elaborately decorated with figures in the style of Tiepolo. Tall windows and glass doors, hung with long red drapes, led from these sunny rooms to an equally sunny terrace, which was decorated with very ancient box-trees cut in conical shape and by wonderful laurel trees. Here, as everywhere, one heard the beautiful music of the waterfall and saw before one the wall of the wild mountain.

The mayor, Sor Domenico, was a well-dressed, sedate man in his middle forties, who had taken a second wife less than three months before. The beautiful, blooming woman of twenty-two, whom Francesco had found busy preparing breakfast in the gleaming kitchen, led him into the garden. When the mayor had heard the priest's story about the visit of the previous evening and had read the slip of paper which bore the name of the savage visitor in his clumsy scrawl, a smile passed over his face. After inviting the young priest to sit down, he retailed the desired information about the mysterious visitor, who was indeed a citizen of Soana, until now unknown to the priest. The mayor's narration was wholly factual and the masklike indifference of his features was never disturbed.

"Luchino Scarabota," said the mayor—it was the name which the priest's visitor had scribbled on the piece of paper—"is by no means a poor man, but for years his domestic affairs have given me and the whole community a headache, and it isn't really possible to see at this point where the whole thing is going to end. He belongs to an old family, and it is very probable that he has in his veins some of the blood of the famous Luchino Scarabota da Milano, who built the nave of the cathedral down in Como between fourteen hundred and fifteen hundred. As you know, Father, we have a number of such old, famous names in our little place."

The mayor had opened the glass door and, as he was talking, led the priest out to the terrace, where he showed him with slightly up-raised hand one of the square huts in which the peasants of the region live, in the steep, funnel-shaped area which forms the source of the waterfall. But this property, hanging at a great height above all the others, differed from them not only by its isolated, seemingly inaccessible location but also by its smallness and poverty.

"Do you see, there, where I am pointing with my finger? That's where this Scarabota lives," the mayor said.

"I am surprised, Father," the speaker continued, "that you haven't heard anything about that mountain pasture and its inhabitants before this. For a decade and more these people have constituted the most disgusting nuisance in this region. Unfortunately there is no way of getting at them. The woman has been brought to court and has claimed that the seven children she has borne are not those of the man she is living with—is there anything more absurd than that? —but from Swiss summer tourists who have to pass the pasture to climb Mount Generoso. And the hag is lousy and caked with dirt and as frighteningly ugly as the night, besides.

"No, it's common knowledge that the man who called on you yesterday, and with whom she is living, is the father of her children. But this is the point: this man is also her blood brother."

The young priest turned pale.

"Of course, this incestuous couple is avoided and outlawed by everyone. In this respect the vox populi seldom errs." With this ex-planation the mayor continued his narrative. "Whenever one of the children has appeared here or in Arogno or in Melano, he has nearly been stoned. Where these people are known any church is regarded as desecrated if the infamous brother and sister have set foot in it, and the two outlaws, whenever they thought they might dare to make such an attempt, were made to feel this in such a terrible way that for years now they have lost all desire to attend church.

"And can we permit," the mayor continued, "such children, such cursed creatures, who are the abomination and horror of everyone, to attend our school here below, and sit on the schoolbenches among the children of good Christians? Can we be expected to allow everyone in our village, big and small, to be infected by these products of moral disgrace, these wicked, mangy beasts?"

The pale face of the priest Francesco in no way betrayed to what extent he had been moved by the narrative of Sor Domenico. He thanked him and went away with the same dignified seriousness with which he had appeared.

Soon after the conversation with the mayor, Francesco reported to his bishop concerning the case of Luchino Scarabota. A week later the bishop's answer was in his hands; it charged the young clergyman to take personal cognizance of the general situation on the so-called mountain pasture of Santa Croce. In the same letter the bishop praised the ecclesiastical zeal of the young man and confirmed that he had good cause for feeling oppressed in hs conscience because of these aberrant and outlawed souls, and for being concerned about their salvation. No sinner, however far he had strayed, could be excluded from the blessings and consolation of Mother Church.

It was not until the end of the month of March that official duties and the snow conditions on Mount Generoso permitted the young clergyman of Soana to undertake the ascent to the mountain pasture of Santa Croce, with a peasant as his guide. Easter had almost come and although constant avalanches were descending the steep wall of the giant mountain and falling like muffled thunder into the gorge below the waterfall, spring had set in with full force wherever the sun was able to penetrate freely.

However little of a nature worshiper Francesco was, unlike his namesake the saint of Assisi, he could not help being affected by the tender, juicy sprouts that he saw, green and blooming about him. Though the young man did not have to become clearly aware of it, the subtle fermentation of spring was in his blood, and he was enjoying his share of that inner swelling and throbbing in all of nature which is heavenly in origin, and in all the joys that blossom from it, despite its delightful, sensuous, earthy manifestations.

The chestnut trees on the square, which the priest first had to cross with his guide, had stretched out tender, green little hands from brown, sticky buds. The children were noisy, and so were the sparrows that nested under the church roof and in countless hiding places offered by the many corners in the village. The first swallows flew in broad arcs from Soana over the abyss of the gorge, where they apparently swerved aside close to the fantastically towering, inaccessible rock massif of the mountain wall. Up there on promontories or in holes in the rock, where the foot of man had never trod, the osprey nested. These big brown couples embarked on glorious flights, and floated, for the pure fun of floating, above the mountain peaks for hours on end, circling higher and higher, as though they sought to forget themselves and move majestically into the infinite freedom of space.

Everywhere, not only in the air, not only on the brown earth, which was either plowed up or clothed in grass and narcissi, not only in everything nature permitted to rise through stalks and stems into leaves and blossoms, but in human beings also, there was a festive air, and the brown faces of the peasants who were working on the terraces between the rows of grapevine with mattock or curved knife, shone with a Sunday glow. Most of them had already slaughtered the so-called Easter lamb, a young kid, and hung it up, with its hind legs tied together, on the doorpost of their home.

The women, who were assembled about the overflowing marble sarcophagus with their filled laundry baskets, were especially numerous and noisy; when the priest and his companion walked past, they interrupted their shrill merriment. At the exit from the village there were washerwomen too; here, beneath a small statue of the Madonna, a stream of water gushed out from the rock and likewise emptied into an antique marble sarcophagus. Both basins, this sarcophagus and the one that stood on the square, had been lifted quite some time ago out of an orchard full of thousand-year-old holm oaks and chestnuts, where they had stood since time immemorial, hidden under ivy and wild laurel, jutting only slightly out of the ground.

As he passed the spot, Francesco Vela crossed himself; in fact, he interrupted his walk for a moment to pay homage on bent knee to the small Madonna above the sarcophagus, who was charmingly surrounded by the gifts of wild flowers that the country folk had brought her. It was the first time he had seen this lovely little shrine, about which the bees buzzed, since he had never visited this upper part of the village before. The lower part of Soana, with its church and a few attractive middle-class homes, adorned with green shutters and

placed about the chestnut square with its terrace-like pavement, gave
the appearance of almost bourgeois prosperity; gardens large and
small displayed blossoming almond and orange trees, tall cypresses,
in short, a vegetation rather southern in character. Here, some hundred feet up, it was nothing but a poor Alpine shepherds' village,
which gave out an odor of goats and cow stables. Here, too, an extremely steep mountain road began, paved with tap rock, which had
been smoothed down by the large communal herd of goats going out
to graze in the morning and returning at night. For this road led up
and out to the communal meadow in the kettle-shaped spring region
of the little Savaglia River, which forms the splendid waterfall of
Soana further down and, after a brief, roaring passage through the
deep gorge, disappears into Lake Lugano.

After the priest had climbed this mountain road for a short while,
still guided by his companion, he stopped to catch his breath. Taking
his big black plate-shaped hat from his head with his left hand, he
drew a large colored handkerchief from his soutane with his right, to
mop the beads of perspiration on his forehead. On the whole, an appreciation of nature, a feeling for the beauty of landscape, is not par
ticularly well developed in an Italian priest. But the spaciousness
afforded by a great height, from the so-called bird's eye view, is after
all a delight which at times affects even the naïvest person and evokes
a certain degree of astonishment in him. As he looked down far
below him, Francesco saw his church and the whole village that went
with it as no more than a miniature picture, while round about him
the mighty mountain world seemed to rise ever higher to heaven.
The feeling of spring was now joined by a sense of the sublime, which
may perhaps arise from a comparison of one's own smallness with the
oppressively powerful works of nature and their threatening, mute
proximity, and which may be tied to the partial realization that we,
too, in some way share in this tremendous power. In short, Francesco
felt himself sublimely great and minutely small at one and the same
moment, and this caused him to make the accustomed sign of the
Cross on brow and chest to protect himself against aberrations and
demons.

As he climbed higher, religious questions and the practical church
affairs of his diocese soon occupied the zealous young cleric's mind
again. And when he stopped once more, this time at the entrance to
a high rocky valley, and turned around, he caught sight of a badly

neglected saint's shrine, built of stone, that had been erected here for the shepherds. This gave him the idea of seeking out all the extant shrines of his diocese, even the remotest, and restoring them to a condition that was worthy of God. He allowed his eyes to roam freely, seeking a point from which he might possibly survey all the existing shrines.

As his starting point he took his own church and the parsonage that was attached to it. It was situated, as was said, on the village square, and its outside walls merged with the steep walls of rock, past which a merry mountain brook rushed downward. This mountain brook, which crossed the square of Soana underground, emerged in a stone arch, where it watered orchards and flowering meadows, though it was badly muddied by sewage. Beyond the church, a little higher up, the oldest shrine of the region stood on a round, flat-terraced hill, although it could not be seen from this spot; it was a small chapel dedicated to the Virgin Mary, whose dusty image on the altar was surmounted by a vaulted Byzantine mosaic in the apse. This mosaic, which was well preserved in both golden background and design, in spite of its thousand or more years, depicted Christus Pantokrator. The distance from the main church to this shrine was not more than three stones' throws. Another handsome chapel, this one dedicated to Saint Anne, was located at an equal distance from it. Above Soana and behind it rose a sharply pointed mountain cone, which was of course surrounded by broad valleys and by the flanks of the Generoso chain towering above it. This mountain, shaped almost like a cone of sugar, covered with growth to its very summit and seemingly inaccessible, was called Sant' Agata, because at its peak it harbored a little chapel for this saint for use in cases of emergency. Thus there were a church and three chapels within the very narrowest circumference of the village, to which were added three or four more chapels within the larger radius of the diocese. On every hill, at every pretty turn in the road, on every peak that looked out into the distance, here and there on picturesque, rocky precipices, near and far, over gorge and lake, the pious centuries had established houses of God, so that in this respect one could still feel the profound and general piety of paganism, which, in the course of millennia, had originally consecrated all these points and had thus procured for itself divine allies against the threatening, fearful powers of this wild nature.

The young zealot contemplated with satisfaction all these institutions of Roman Catholic Christianity, which distinguish the whole canton of Ticino. At the same time, he had to admit to himself, with the pain felt by the true champion of God, that an active and pure faith was not everywhere alive in them, nor even an adequately loving concern on the part of his ecclesiastical associates to safeguard all these scattered heavenly dwelling places against neglect and oblivion.

After some time they turned into the narrow footpath that leads to the summit of Generoso after a difficult ascent that took them three hours. Moreover, the bed of the Savaglia had to be crossed very soon over a dilapidated bridge; and very close by was the reservoir of the little river, which plunged down from it to a depth of a hundred yards or more in a fissure formed by its own erosion. Here Francesco heard, from various heights, depths and directions, the roaring of the wild water rushing to the reservoir and the tinkling of herd bells, and saw a man of rude exterior — it was the communal shepherd of Soana — stretched out full length on the ground, supporting himself with his hands on the bank, his head bent down to the surface of the water, slaking his thirst quite like an animal. Behind him several mother goats were grazing with their kids, while an Alsatian dog was waiting with pointed ears for odors and for the moment when his master would be finished with his drinking. "I am a shepherd too," Francesco thought, and when the other man got up from the ground and produced a piercing whistle through his fingers — a whistle that echoed from the cliffs — and threw stones a great distance at his widely scattered flocks to frighten them, to drive them on, to call them back and in general to save them from the danger of falling into the depths, Francesco thought how difficult and heavy with responsibility this task was, even with animals, to say nothing of human beings, who are always a prey to the temptations of Satan.

With redoubled zeal the priest now began to climb higher, as if there were cause to fear that the devil might possibly get to the stray sheep first. Still accompanied by his guide, whom Francesco did not consider worth conversing with, he climbed the steep and difficult ascent for an hour and more, higher and higher into the rocky wilderness of Generoso, when suddenly he saw the mountain pasture of Santa Croce lying fifty feet before him.

He refused to believe that this heap of stones and the wall in the midst of it, made of flat stones piled on each other without mortar,

was the place he was looking for, as the guide assured him it was.
What he had expected from the words of the mayor was a certain
prosperity, whereas this dwelling could at best be regarded as a sort
of refuge for sheep and goats during a sudden squall. Since it was
situated on a steep slope of stone rubble and jagged blocks of rock,
and as the path to it was concealed in its zigzag course, the cursed
place seemed to be inaccessible. Only after the young priest had overcome his astonishment and a certain horror that took possession of
him and had moved closer, did the picture of the infamous and
shunned homestead take on a somewhat friendlier aspect.

Indeed, the ruin actually became transformed before the eyes of
the approaching priest into sheer loveliness; for it seemed as if an
avalanche of blocks and rubble which had been released from a great
height had been piled up and held fast by the rudely constructed
square of the homestead, so that beneath it there remained a slope of
lush green free of stones, from which charming yellow marigolds
climbed in delightful abundance to the ramp in front of the house
door and, as though they were curious, up over the ramp and literally through the front door into the disgraceful cave-house.

At this spectacle Francesco was taken aback. This assault of yellow
field flowers against the degraded threshold, and luxuriant trains of
long-stemmed blooming forget-me-nots, which likewise sought to
overrun the door with their blue reflection of the sky, and under
which veins of mountain water trickled away, seemed to him to be
almost an open protest against human outlawry, bans and popular
courts. In his astonishment, which was followed by a certain confusion, Francesco had to sit down in his black soutane on a granite
boulder that was warmed by the sun. He had spent his youth in the
valley, and besides, mostly indoors, in churches, lecture halls or
study rooms. His feeling for nature had not been awakened. He had
never before carried out an enterprise like this, into the sublime,
severe loveliness of the high mountains, and he would perhaps never
have undertaken it if chance, combined with duty, had not forced
the ascent of the mountain upon him. Now he was overwhelmed by
the novelty and grandeur of his impressions.

For the first time the young priest Francesco Vela felt the clear and
truly grand sensation of existence course through him, making him
forget for moments that he was a priest and why he had come here.
All his notions of piety, which were intertwined with a host of ecclesi-

astical rules and dogmas, had not only been displaced by this sensation, but extinguished by it. Now he even forgot to cross himself. Below him lay the beautiful Lugano region of the Upper Italian Alpine
world; Sant' Agata with the little pilgrims' chapel, over which the
brown ospreys were still circling; the mountain of San Giorgio; the
emerging peak of Mount San Salvatore; and finally, below him, at a
depth that made one dizzy, lay the arm of Lake Lugano that was
known as Capolago, carefully set in the valleys of the mountain relief
like a longish glass plate, with a fisherman's sailboat on it, looking
like a tiny moth on a hand mirror. Behind all this, in the distance,
were the white peaks of the lofty Alps, which seemed to have climbed
up and up with Francesco. From among them rose Mount Rosa with
its seven white points, gleaming out of the silken blue sky like a dia-
dem and a phantom.

If one is justified in speaking of mountain sickness, then one is
equally entitled to speak of a state that overcomes people on mountain heights and which may best be designated as incomparable
health. This health the young priest now felt in his blood like a re-
juvenation. Near him, among stones in the still withered heather,
was a little flower, the like of which Francesco had never seen before.
It was a wonderfully lovely species of blue gentian, whose petals were
an astonishingly exquisite flaming blue. The young man in the black
soutane, who had wanted to pluck the little flower in his first joy of
discovery, left it unmolested in its modest spot, and merely bent the
heather aside to look in extended rapture at the miracle. Everywhere
young bright-green leaves of dwarf beech looked out among the
stones, and from a certain distance, across the slopes of hard, gray
rubble and delicate green, the flock of poor Luchino Scarabota announced itself by the tinkling of bells. This entire mountain world
possessed pristine individuality, the youthful charm of extinct ages of
mankind, of which there was no trace left in the valleys below.

Francesco had sent his guide home, since he wanted to make his
way back undisturbed by the presence of another person and did not
wish to have a witness for what he planned at Luchino's hearth.
Meanwhile he had already been noticed, and a number of dirty and
greasy children's heads kept looking out curiously from the smoky
black door-hole of the Scarabota stone castle.

Slowly the priest began to approach it and moved into the area of
the property, which revealed its owner's large stock of cattle and was

dirtied by the droppings of a big herd of cows and goats. Into Francesco's nose the odor of cattle and goats rose more and more acridly, mingled with the rare, invigorating mountain air; its increasing pungency at the entrance of the dwelling was only made bearable by the charcoal smoke that issued from the interior. When Francesco appeared in the frame of the door and blocked the light with his black soutane, the children retreated into the darkness, where the priest could not see them, and they met his greeting and all that he said to them with silence. Only an old mother goat came up to him, bleated gently and sniffed at him.

Gradually the interior of the room had become brigher to the eyes of the messenger of God. He saw a stable filled with a high pile of manure, deepening towards the back into a natural cave, which had been there originally in the nagelfluh, or whatever type of rock it was. In a thick stone wall at the right, a passage had been opened up, through which the priest caught sight of the family hearth, which was now abandoned; a mountain of ashes, still burning at the center, was piled up on the floor of exposed natural rock. From a chain with a thick covering of soot on it hung a battered copper pot, which was also sooty. At this fireplace of paleolithic man stood a bench without a back, whose fist thick, broad seat rested on two posts, of the same breadth, anchored in the rock. This seat had been worn down and polished by a century and more of tired shepherds, their wives and their children. The wood no longer seemed to be wood but a yellow, polished marble or soapstone with countless scars and cuts in it. The square room really looked more like a cave, its naturally undecorated walls consisting of strata of rude blocks and slate, from which the smoke passed through the door into the stable and from there again through the door into the open air outside, having no other way of escape, except perhaps through cracks in the walls. The room was blackened by the smoke and soot of decades, so that one might almost gain the impression of being in the interior of a chimney coated with thick soot.

Francesco had just noticed the peculiar glow emanating from a pair of eyes in a corner of the hut, when the rolling and sliding of stone rubble became audible outside, and immediately afterwards the figure of Luchino Scarabota stepped into the doorway and, like a noiseless shadow, shut out the sun, causing the room to become even darker. The savage mountain shepherd was breathing heavily, not only because he had hurried down the long distance from a higher pasture soon after he had seen the priest approach, but also because this visit was an event for the outlawed fellow.

The greeting was brief. After he had cleared the soapstone bench with his coarse hands, removing the stones and plucked marsh marigolds which his cursed brood of children had used as toys, Francesco's host urged him to sit down.

The mountain shepherd blew up the fire with puffed cheeks, and this made his feverish eyes shine even more wildly in the reflected light. He nourished the flame with logs and dry twigs, so that the pungent smoke almost drove the priest out. The shepherd's behavior was of a cringing submissiveness characterized by an anxious zeal, as if everything now depended on his not losing the grace of the Higher Being who had entered his wretched dwelling. He brought over a large dirty bucket full of milk, with a layer of thick cream at its top; unfortunately it was unbelievably foul, for which reason alone Francesco would not touch it. But he also declined to eat the fresh cheese and bread, in spite of the fact that he had become hungry, because, in his superstitious fear, he was afraid of committing a sin by doing so. Finally, when the mountain shepherd had calmed down somewhat and stood facing him with a timid, expectant look, his arms hanging from his sides, the priest began to talk as follows:

"Luchino Scarabota, you shall not lose the consolation of our Holy Church, and your children shall no longer be cast out from the community of Catholic Christians if it is proved that the evil rumors about you are untrue, or if you will confess sincerely, show remorse and contrition and be prepared, with God's help, to remove the obstacle from your path. So open your heart to me, Scarabota, let me know frankly in what respect you are being maligned, and confess with complete honesty the sinful guilt which may be weighing on you."

After this speech the shepherd was silent. But suddenly a brief, wild note struggled out of his throat, a sound betraying no emotion whatever but having something gurgling and birdlike about it. Francesco proceeded in his customary way to represent to the sinner the frightful consequences of his stubbornness, and the conciliatory kindness and love of God the Father, who had shown it through the sacrifice of His only Son, the sacrifice of the Lamb that took the sins of the world upon itself. Through Jesus Christ, he concluded, every sin can be forgiven, provided that a complete confession, combined with repentance and prayer, proves to the Heavenly Father the contrition of the poor sinner.

Only after Francesco had waited a long time and had stood up, shrugging as though to go away, did the shepherd begin to choke out an unintelligible confusion of words: a sort of clucking, such as one hears from a bird of prey. With strained attention the priest sought to grasp what was comprehensible in this confusion. But this intelligible material seemed to him just as strange and wonderful as the obscure part. Only this much became clear from the frightening and oppressive host of imaginary things: that Luchino Scarabota wanted to secure his aid against all sorts of devils that lived in the mountains and were persecuting him.

It would have been unsuitable for the believing young priest to doubt the existence and activity of evil spirits. Was not Creation filled with all sorts and degrees of fallen angels from the company of Lucifer, the rebellious one, whom God had cast out? But here he felt a horror; he did not know whether it was in the face of the darkness arising from the incredible superstition he met here, or before the hopeless blindness resulting from ignorance. He decided to form, by means of specific questions, a judgment on the mental state and intellectual powers of his parishioner.

It soon became evident that this wild, demoralized creature knew nothing of God, even less about Jesus Christ the Savior, and least of all about the existence of a Holy Ghost. On the other hand, it appeared that he felt himself surrounded by demons and was possessed by a sinister persecution mania. And to him the priest was not the authorized servant of God, but rather a mighty magician, or God himself. What could Francesco do except cross himself, while the shepherd threw himself humbly on the ground and idolatrously licked his shoes and showered them with kisses from his moist, thick lips?

The young priest had never been in a situation like this. The rare mountain air, the spring, his separation from the stratum of civilization proper, caused his mind to become slightly clouded. He fell into a dreamlike trance, in which reality dissolved into floating, airy forms. This change was combined with a slight fearfulness, which counseled him several times to flee hastily down into the sphere of consecrated churches and church bells. The devil was powerful; who

could know how many means and ways he had for seducing the unsuspecting, most faithful Christian and hurling him from the edge of
a giddy precipice?

Francesco had not been taught that the idols of the heathen were
mere empty creatures of the imagination and nothing more. The
Church recognized their power explicitly, except that it represented
this power as hostile to God. They were still contending with almighty
God for the world, though the struggle was hopeless. For this reason
the pale young priest was not a little frightened when his host fetched
a wooden object from a corner of his dwelling, a horrible piece of
carving which, beyond a doubt, represented a fetish. In spite of his
priestly horror at the obscene object, Francesco could not help looking at the thing intently. With abhorrence and astonishment he had
to admit to himself that in this place the most abominable pagan horror, namely that of a rural cult of Priapus, was still alive. It was evident that this primitive icon could represent none other than Priapus.

Francesco had scarcely taken the little innocent god of procreation
in his hand, the god of agricultural fertility, who stood in such
frankly high esteem among the ancients, when his strange feeling of
oppressiveness was transformed into holy wrath. Instinctively he
threw the shameless little mandrake into the fire, from which, however, the shepherd retrieved it immediately with the swift movement
of a dog. It glowed in one spot, burned in another, but was promptly
restored to its former condition of safety by the rude hands of the
heathen creature. But now the object and its rescuer had to suffer a
flood of reproachful words.

Luchino Scarabota did not seem to know which of the two gods he
should regard as the stronger; the one made of wood or the god of
flesh and blood. However, he kept his eyes, in which terror and
horror mingled with malicious rage, fixed on the new deity, whose
impious daring at any rate did not indicate a state of weakness. Once
he was in full swing, the emissary of the One and Only God refused to
be intimidated in his sacred zeal by the dangerous glances which the
benighted idolator cast in his direction. And now, without beating
about the bush, he began to talk about the vile sin to which, as was
generally asserted, the mountain shepherd owed his crop of children.
Into these loud words of the young priest Scarabota's sister erupted,
so to speak, but without uttering a word; she merely cast stealthy
glances at the zealot and busied herself here and there in the cave.

She was a pallid, repulsive woman, to whom water seemed to be an unknown commodity. One could catch unpleasant glimpses of her naked body through the tears in her tattered clothing.

When the priest had finished and had, for the moment, exhausted his stock of reproachful accusations, the woman sent her brother outside with a brief, barely audible word. The savage creature disappeared at once without contradiction, like the most obedient dog. Then the sinful woman, who was encrusted with dirt, and whose greasy black hair hung down over her broad hips, kissed the priest's hand with the words "Praised be Jesus Christ."

The next moment she burst into tears.

She said the priest was perfectly right in condemning her in harsh words. She had indeed sinned against God's commandment, though not at all in the manner which slander attributed to her. She alone was the sinner; her brother was completely innocent. She swore, and indeed by all the saints, that she had never committed that fearful sin of which she was accused, namely incest. True, she had lived unchastely, and since she was now confessing, she was prepared to describe the fathers of her children, though not to name them all. For she knew very few names, since, as she said, she had often sold her favors to passing strangers out of necessity.

For the rest, she had brought her children into the world in pain without help, and some of them she had had to bury here and there in the debris of Mount Generoso soon after their birth. Whether or not he could now give her absolution, she knew that God had forgiven her, for she had atoned enough through privation, suffering and anxiety.

Francesco could not but regard the tearful confession of the woman as a tissue of lies, at least as far as the crime was concerned. He felt, to be sure, that there were acts which absolutely defied confession before a human being, and which God alone learns of in the lonely silence of prayer. He respected this bashfulness in the degenerate woman, and in general could not conceal from himself the fact that in many respects she was a higher type than her brother. In the manner of her justification there lay a clear resoluteness. Her eye confessed, but neither kind persuasion nor the hangman's fiery tongs would have torn from her a confession in words. It turned out that it was she who had sent the man to Francesco. She had seen the pale young priest one day when she went to market in Lugano, where she sold the products of her pasture, and at the sight of him she had gained confidence and had hit upon the idea of commending her outlawed children to him. She alone was the head of the family and cared for her brother and children.

"I will not discuss the question," Francesco said, "whether you are guilty or not. One thing is clear: if you don't want your children to grow up like animals, you must separate from your brother. As long as you live with him, it will never be possible for you to live down the fearful reputation you have acquired. People will always assume that you are guilty of this terrible sin."

After these words obduracy and defiance seemed to gain control of the woman's mind; at any rate she made no answer, but devoted herself for some time to domestic activity, as if there were no stranger present. During this time a girl of about fifteen came in, driving some goats through the opening of the stable and then helping the woman in her work, again as if Francesco were not there. The young priest realized at once, when he merely saw the girl's shadow glide through the depth of the cave, that she must be of extraordinary beauty. He crossed himself, for a slight feeling of inexplicable terror passed through him. He did not know whether he should resume his exhortations in the presence of the youthful shepherdess. She was beyond doubt thoroughly depraved, since Satan had awakened her to life by way of the vilest sin; but there might still be a remnant of purity in her, and who could tell whether she had any inkling of her dark origin.

Her movements, at any rate, showed a great serenity, which certainly did not permit one to draw any conclusions about emotional disturbance or a burdened conscience. On the contrary, everything about her bespoke a modest self-confidence, which was not affected by the presence of the pastor. So far, she had not as much as cast a glance at Francesco, at least not in such a way as to meet his eye or in any other discernible fashion. In fact, while he himself was looking at her stealthily through his glasses, he was compelled to doubt more and more whether a child of sin, a child of such parents, could look like this. She finally vanished by way of a ladder into a sort of attic, so that Francesco was able to continue his difficult work of spiritual ministration.

"I can't leave my brother," the woman said, "for the very simple reason that he is helpless without me. He can, when necessary, write his name, and I've taught him to do so with the greatest difficulty. He can't distinguish coins and is afraid of trains, cities and people. If I leave him, he will pursue me as a poor dog pursues his lost master. He will either find me or perish miserably; and what will then happen to the children and our property? If I stay here with the children, I'd like to see the man who could get my brother away from here; they'd have to put him in chains and lock him behind iron bars in Milan."

The priest said, "This may yet happen, if you do not follow my good advice."

At that the woman's anxiety turned to rage. She had sent her brother to Francesco that he might take pity on them, not make them miserable. She preferred in that case to continue living as she had till now, hated and rejected by the people below. She was a good Catholic, but when the Church rejected someone, he had a right to give himself to the devil. And she might then perhaps really commit that great sin she was accused of but of which she was as yet innocent.

Mingled with these strained words and lone shrieks that came from the woman, Francesco heard, from above, where the girl had vanished, a sweet singing, first like the most gentle breathing, then swelling with power, and his mind was influenced more by this melodious spell than by the furious outbursts of the degenerate woman. A hot wave rose within him, mingled with an anxiety he had never felt before. The smoke-filled hole of this animal-human dwelling stable seemed to be transformed, as if by magic, into the loveliest of all crystalline grottoes of Dante's Paradise, full of angelic voices and the sounding pinions of laughing doves.

He went. It was impossible for him to endure such confusing influences any longer without trembling visibly. When he reached the hollowed-out pile of stones outside, he inhaled the freshness of the mountain air and was at once filled like an empty vessel with the immense impression of the mountain world. His spirit passed, as it were, into the farthest range of his eyes and consisted of the colossal masses of the earth's crust, from distant, snowy peaks to adjacent fearful abysses, under the royal brightness of the spring day. He still saw brown ospreys drawing their unselfconscious circles over the cone-shaped Sant' Agata. The idea came to him to hold a private service there for the outlawed family, and he revealed this thought to the woman, who had stepped dejectedly across the threshold of the

cave, luxuriant in the yellow marigolds. "You dare not come to
Soana, as you yourself know," he said. "If I invited you to do so, we
would all be equally ill advised."

The woman was again moved to the point of tears, and promised
to appear on a certain day before the chapel of Sant' Agata with her
brother and the older children.

When the young priest had gotten far enough away from Luchino
Scarabota's home and his curse-laden family so that he could no
longer be seen from there, he chose a stone block that had been
warmed through by the sun as a resting place in which to reflect on
what he had just experienced. He told himself that while it was true
he had climbed the mountain with a morbid interest, he had still
done so in a sober frame of mind and with a sense of duty, and without any thought of what was disturbing him now with such foreboding. And what was this disturbance? He tugged, stroked, and
brushed his soutane for a long time, as if by doing so he could rid
himself of it.

When, after some time, he still did not feel the desired clarity, he
took his breviary out of his pocket with an habitual movement; but
even though he immediately began reading aloud, he was not freed
from a certain strange indecision. He felt as if he had forgotten to
attend to something, some important aspect of his mission. For this
reason he kept looking back at the road from under his spectacles
with a certain expectancy, and lacked the strength to continue the
descent which he had begun.

So he fell into a strange reverie, out of which he was awakened by
two slight incidents which his imagination, wrenched out of its accustomed groove, saw with considerable exaggeration: first of all, the
right lens of his spectacles cracked with a bang under the impact of
the cold mountain air, and almost immediately after that he heard a
fearful panting above his head and felt a strong pressure on his
shoulders.

The young priest leaped up. He laughed aloud when he recognized
the cause of his panic in a spotted he-goat, which had given him
proof of his unbounded confidence by planting his forehooves on his
shoulders without any regard for his clerical garb.

But this was only the beginning of the animal's most intimate
importunity. The shaggy goat with the strong, beautifully curved

horns and flashing eyes had, it seemed, the habit of begging from passing mountain-climbers and did so in such a droll, firm and irresistible manner that one could ward him off only by taking flight. Standing above Francesco, he kept putting his hooves on the priest's chest and seemed determined to nibble at his hair, nose and fingers, after forcing the harassed victim to submit to having his pockets sniffed at and devouring a few bits of bread with incredible greed.

An old, bearded she-goat, whose bell and udder dragged on the ground, had followed the highwayman and, encouraged by him, began to harass the priest too. She was especially impressed by the breviary with its cross and gilt edges and, when Francesco was busy defending himself against a curved goat horn, she succeeded in getting possession of the little book. Taking its black-printed leaves for green ones, she began eating the sacred truths literally and greedily, according to the prescription of the prophet.

On this scene of distress, aggravated by the gathering of other animals that had been grazing by themselves, the shepherdess suddenly appeared as a rescuer. It was the very same girl of whom Francesco had first caught a fleeting glimpse in Luchino's hut. When the slim, strong girl, after driving the goats away, stood before him with her fresh cheeks flushed and her laughing eyes, he said, "You have saved me, my good girl." And, taking his breviary from the hands of the young Eve, he added, laughing too, "It is really strange that, in spite of my shepherd's office, I am so helpless against your flock."

A priest may not converse with a young girl or woman any longer than his ecclesiastical duty demands, and the congregation notices it at once if he is seen holding such a conversation outside the church. And so Francesco, mindful of his stern calling, continued his way back without delay; and yet he felt as if he had detected himself in a sinful act and had to purify himself through a remorseful confession at the earliest opportunity. He had not yet got beyond the range of the herd bells when the sound of a woman's voice penetrated to him, suddenly making him forget all his meditations again. The voice was of such quality that it did not occur to him that it could belong to the shepherdess he had just left. Francesco had not only heard the church singers of the Vatican in Rome but had formerly listened to secular singers in Milan with his mother, so the coloratura and bel canto of the prima donnas were not unknown to him. He stopped involuntarily and waited. No doubt they are tourists from Milan, he thought, and hoped that he might, if possible, catch a passing glimpse of the owner of this glorious voice. But since she did not seem willing to appear, he continued to set foot before foot, cautiously descending into the giddy depths.

What Francesco had experienced on this professional visit, as a whole and in detail, was superficially not worth mentioning, if one excludes the abominations that had as their breeding ground the hut of the poor Scarabotas, brother and sister. But the young priest felt at once that this mountain trip had become for him an event of great importance, though for the present he had not even a remote idea of the entire scope of its significance. He felt that a transformation had taken place in him, working from the inside out. He found himself in a new state, which became minute by minute more strange to him, and he grew suspicious, but by no means so suspicious as to scent the presence of Satan or to wish perhaps to throw an inkwell at him, even if he had had one in his pocket. The mountain world lay below him like a paradise. For the very first time, folding his hands involuntarily, he congratulated himself on having been entrusted by his superior with the care of this very parish. Compared with this precious valley, what was the cloth of St. Peter, which came from heaven, held by angels at its three corners? Where could the human mind find a greater majesty than in these inaccessible crags of Mount Generoso, from which one could hear continuously the muffled spring thunder of melting snow descending in avalanches?

From the day of his visit to the depraved family, Francesco, to his astonishment, could no longer find his way back into the unthinking peace of his former existence. The new countenance which Nature had assumed for him refused to fade, and she would not permit herself to be forced back in any way into her former lifeless state. The character of her influence, which plagued him not only in the daytime but in his dreams too, he recognized at once and named it temptation. And since the faith of the Church is fused with pagan superstition through the mere fact of combating it, Francesco in all seriousness traced his transformation back to the touching of that wooden object, that little mandrake which the ragged shepherd had rescued from the fire. Beyond doubt a relic still remained alive, a fragment of those abominations to which the ancients paid homage under the name of phallic worship, that shameful cult which had been suppressed in the world by the holy war of the Cross of Jesus.

—Up to the moment when he had caught sight of the loathsome object, the Cross alone had been burned into Francesco's soul. He had been branded with the brand of the Cross, precisely as the sheep of a herd are marked with a white-hot stamp, and his stigma had become the essential symbol of his self, present in him in both his waking and dreaming life. Now the accursed Satan incarnate looked down at him from the crosspiece of the crucifix; this most unclean, dreadful, satyr symbol was gradually usurping the place of the Cross and was in constant rivalry with it.

Francesco had reported the success of his pastoral mission to the mayor and especially to the bishop. The answer he received from the bishop was approval of his procedure. "Above all," the bishop wrote, "we must avoid any flagrant scandal." He thought it was exceedingly shrewd that Francesco had instituted a special secret service for the poor sinners on Sant' Agata, in the chapel of the Holy Mother of Mary. But the endorsement of his action by his superior could not restore Francesco's peace of mind; he could not get rid of the idea that he had come down from up there with a sort of enchantment clinging to him.

In Ligornetto, where Francesco was born and where his uncle, the famous sculptor, had spent the last ten years of his life, there still lived the same old priest who had introduced him as a boy to the saving truths of the Catholic faith and shown him the way of grace. One day, walking from Soana to Ligornetto in about three hours, he called on the old priest, who welcomed him and was visibly touched at being asked to hear the young man's confession. Of course he granted him absolution.

Francesco's scruples of conscience are expressed approximately in the following revelation which he made to the old man. He said: "Since I visited the poor sinners on the mountain pasture of Soana, I have been in a sort of possessed state. I shudder! I feel as if I had put on, not merely another coat, but actually another skin. When I hear the waterfall of Soana roar, I want most of all to climb down into the deep gorge and stand for hours under the falling masses of water, as if to purify myself both outside and in and to regain my health. When I see the crucifix in the church or the crucifix over my bed, I laugh. I can no longer weep and sigh as I used to do, or imagine the sufferings of our Savior. On the other hand, my eyes are attracted by all sorts of objects which resemble the little mandrake belonging to

Luchino Scarabota. Sometimes they are quite unlike it, but I see a resemblance nevertheless. I had made curtains for the windows of my little room, so that I might work, steep myself in the study of the Church Fathers. Now I have removed these curtains. The singing of the birds, the murmur of the many brooks that run through the meadow past my house after the snow has melted, yes, even the fragrance of the narcissi used to disturb me. Now I open my windows wide, so that I may drink it all in greedily.

"All this alarms me," Francesco continued, "but this is perhaps not the worst. Still worse, perhaps, is the fact that I have fallen into the orbit of unclean devils, as though under the spell of black magic. Their pinching and clawing, their impudent tickling and provocation to sin, at every hour of the day and night, is terrible. I open my window and their magic power makes it seem as if the song of the birds in the blossoming cherry tree under my window were charged with unchastity. I am challenged by certain shapes in the bark of trees and they, yes, even certain lines of the mountains, remind me of parts of the *corporis femini*. It is a terrifying assault of crafty, malicious, ugly demons to which I am being delivered up in spite of all my prayers and chastisements. All nature, I say it to you with a shudder, sometimes murmurs, roars and thunders a tremendous phallic song into my terrified ears, thus—as I am compelled to believe against my better judgment—paying homage to the shepherd's wretched little wooden idol.

"All this," Francesco continued, "naturally increases my alarm and mental anguish, the more so because I recognize it as my duty to enter the field as a champion against the focus of infection up there on the mountain pasture. But even this is not the worst part of my confession. What is worse: something like an ineradicable poison, mingled with a sort of devilish sweetness, has penetrated the very basic duties of my calling, spreading confusion everywhere. I was at first moved with a pure and holy power by the words of Jesus about the lost sheep and the shepherd who leaves his flock to bring it back from the inaccessible rocks. But now I doubt whether this purpose still exists in its pristine purity. It has increased in passionate zeal. I awaken at night, my face bathed in tears, and I dissolve into a sobering compassion for the fate of the lost souls up there. But when I say 'lost souls,' this is perhaps the point at which a sharp line must be drawn between truth and falsehood. For the fact is that the sinful

souls of Scarabota and his sister appear before my mind's eye solely
and uniquely as the image of the fruit of their sin, that is, their
daughter.

"Now, I ask myself whether the cause of my seemingly worthy zeal
may not be a forbidden desire for her and whether I am doing right
and not running the risk of eternal death by continuing my seemingly
meritorious labors."

The old, experienced priest had listened to most of the youth's
pedantic confession with a serious look on his face, but he smiled at
several points. This was Francesco as he knew him, with his conscien-
tious sense of outer and inner order and his need of clear accuracy
and cleanliness. He said: "Francesco, do not be afraid. Just keep on
the road you have always walked. You must not be surprised that the
machinations of the evil enemy reveal themselves most powerfully
and most dangerously when you proceed to snatch victims from him
which he felt to be securely his, so to speak."

His mind set at ease, Francesco stepped out of the priest's house
into the street of the little village of Ligornetto, in which he had
spent his earliest youth. It is a small village, lying fairly flat on a
broad valley floor surrounded by fertile fields; the vineyards wind in
and out from mulberry tree to mulberry tree like solidly twisted
ropes, between vegetable and grain plots. This place, too, is dominated by the mighty jagged crags of Mount Generoso, whose majesty
is visible here from the west side of its broad base.

It was around midday and Ligornetto appeared to be in a state of
somnolence. Francesco was barely greeted on his walk by a few cack-
ling hens, some children at play, and at the end of the village by a
barking little dog. Here, at the end of the village, his uncle's home,
built with the resources of a wealthy man, was thrust forward like a
bolt on a door, the *buen retiro* of that Vincenzo, the sculptor. It was
now uninhabited and had gone over into the possession of the canton
of Ticino as a kind of memorial foundation. Francesco walked up the
steps leading to the abandoned and neglected garden and then
yielded to a sudden desire to see the interior of the house. Peasants
who lived nearby, old acquaintances of his, gave him the key to the
house.

The relation of the young priest to the arts was one that is common
to his class. His famous uncle had been dead about ten years, and
Francesco had not seen the rooms of the celebrated artist's home

since the day of the funeral. He could not have said what suddenly moved him to visit the empty house, in which he had until now for the most part shown only a passing interest. The uncle had never been more than a celebrity to him, and his sphere of activity was alien and meaningless.

As Francesco turned the key in the lock and entered the hall through the door, which creaked on its rusty hinges, he shuddered slightly at the dusty stillness that was wafted toward him from the staircase and from all the open rooms. To the right of the entrance hall was the deceased artist's library, which revealed at once that a culturally active man had lived here. The low bookcases contained, apart from Vasari, the complete works of Winckelmann, while the Italian Parnassus was represented by the sonnets of Michelangelo, the works of Dante, Petrarch, Tasso, Ariosto and others. A collection of drawings and etchings was stored in cabinets which had been especially built for the purpose; medals of the Renaissance and all sorts of valuable rarities, among them painted Etruscan clay vases and some other antiquities of bronze and marble, were set up in the room. Here and there a particularly beautiful print of Leonardo or Michelangelo hung framed on the wall, depicting a male or female nude. The small adjoining room was practically filled from top to bottom with such objects on three of its walls.

From there you entered a room with a cupola, which was several stories high and lighted from above. Here Vincenzo had worked with modeling wood and chisel, and the plaster casts of is best works filled this almost churchlike room, forming a crowded and silent collection.

Constrained, indeed alarmed, and frightened by the echo of his own footsteps, Francesco had come this far almost with a bad conscience, and now proceeded to subject this and that work of his uncle's to a first real inspection. Beside a statue of Michelangelo a Ghiberti could be seen. There was a Dante there and works covered with stippling dots, as the models had been executed in marble in enlarged form. But these world-famous figures could not long hold the attention of the young priest. Beside them stood the statues of three young girls, the daughters of a marchese who had been broadminded enough to allow the master to portray them completely unclothed. To judge from the statues the youngest of the three ladies was not more than twelve, the second not more than fifteen and the third not

over seventeen years old. Francesco came to himself only after he had
contemplated the slender bodies for a long time in complete absorption. Unlike the works of the Greeks, these figures did not display
their nudity as a natural nobility and image of divinity, but one experienced it as an indiscretion of the boudoir. In the first place, the
copies had not been dissociated from the originals but were distinctly
recognizable as copies; and these originals seemed to say: we have
been indecently exposed and undressed by a brutal order against our
will and our sense of modesty. When Francesco awoke from his
revery, his heart was pounding and he looked fearfully in every direction. He was doing nothing that was evil but he felt it was a sin just to
be alone with such figures.

He resolved to go away as quickly as possible, so that he might not
actually be caught there. But when he reached the front door,
instead of going out, he put the door latch into the lock from the
inside and turned the key, so that he was now locked in the spectral
house of the deceased and could not be surprised. After this he returned to the plaster scandal of the three graces.

His heart beating more violently, he was overcome by a wan and
fearful madness. He felt a compulsion to stroke the hair of the oldest
of the marchionesses as if she were alive. Although this act obviously
bordered on insanity, as he himself realized, it was still in a sense
commensurate with his priestly calling. But the second marchioness
had to suffer being stroked on the shoulder and arm: an opulent
shoulder and arm, which led to a soft, delicate hand. Soon Francesco
had become a hopelessly confused and contrite sinner, through further acts of tenderness toward the third, the youngest, marchioness,
finally planting a shy, criminal kiss under her left breast. He felt no
better than Adam when he heard the voice of the Lord after he had
eaten of the apple from the tree of knowledge. He fled. He ran as if
pursued.

The following days Francesco spent partly in church in prayer,
partly in his parsonage chastising himself. His contrition and remorse
were great. In a fervor of devotion such as he had not known hitherto, he dared hope in the long run to triumph over the temptations of
the flesh. At any rate the conflict between the principles of good and
evil had broken out in him with undreamed-of frightfulness, so that
it seemed that God and the devil had for the first time transplanted

their theater of war into his breast. Even sleep, that part of his activity for which he was not responsible, no longer offered the young cleric any peace; for this unguarded period at night seemed especially welcome to Satan for inducing seductive and destructive delusions into the young man's normally innocent soul. One night, towards morning — he did not know whether it had happened while he was asleep or awake — in the white light of the moon, he saw the three white figures of the marchese's beautiful daughters come into his room and up to his bed. When he looked more closely, he recognized that each figure had become magically fused with the image of the young shepherdess on the pasture of Santa Croce.

Beyond a doubt a thread led from the small, toylike homestead of Scarabota to the priest's room, whose window permitted the pasture to look into it; and this thread had not been spun by angels. Francesco knew enough about the celestial hierarchy, and the infernal one too, to recognize at once whose brainchild this work was. Francesco believed in sorcery. Learned in many branches of scholastic science, he assumed that evil demons made use of the influence of the stars to accomplish certain destructive ends. He had learned that, as regards the body, man belongs to the celestial spheres; his intelligence has placed him on a level with the angels, and his will is subordinate to God; but God has permitted fallen angels to turn his will away from Him, and the realm of the demons is increased by their bond with such perverted humans. Besides, a temporal, physical emotion, exploited by the spirits of hell, can often be the cause of a man's eternal destruction. In short, the young priest trembled to the very marrow of his bones and feared the poisonous bite of the *diaboli*, the demons that smell of blood, the beast Behemoth and especially Asmodeus, the specific demon of whoring.

At first he could not bring himself to believe that the cursed brother and sister were guilty of the sin of witchcraft and sorcery. True, he had one experience that threw him into a state of deep suspicion. Every day he undertook a spiritual purification with holy zeal and all the resources of religion, in order to purify himself of the image of the shepherd girl, but every time he did so it stood more clearly, more firmly and more plainly before him. What sort of painting was this, what sort of indestructible wooden tablet stood under it, or what sort of canvas was it that water or fire did not affect it at all?

The way this picture thrust itself forward everywhere became at times the subject of his silent and astonished observation. He would read a book; when he saw the soft face, framed by the strangely reddish, earth-brown hair, looking at him with big, dark eyes from a page, he inserted a blank leaf, which was intended to cover and conceal it. But when he turned the leaf he found that the picture penetrated every page as if there were no leaf, as indeed it penetrated drapes, doors and walls in the house and church.

Amid such anxieties and inner dissensions, the young priest was perishing with impatience because the time set for the special service on the peak of Sant' Agata would not come fast enough. He wished to perform the duty he had undertaken as quickly as possible, because he might perhaps in that way snatch the girl from the claws of the prince of hell. He wished even more to see the girl again; but what he longed for most of all was liberation from his tormented enchantment, a liberation he definitely hoped to achieve. Francesco ate little, spent the greater part of his nights awake and, growing paler and more haggard daily, acquired in the eyes of his parishioners an even greater reputation for exemplary piety.

The morning had finally come on which the priest had arranged with the poor sinners to meet in the chapel that was situated high on the cone of Sant' Agata. The extremely difficult ascent to it could not be made in less than two hours. At nine o'clock Francesco appeared on the village square, ready for the walk, serene and refreshed in his heart and viewing the world with newborn eyes. May was approaching, and a day had dawned, more exquisite than could be imagined; but the young man had already often experienced days equally beautiful, without, however, finding in nature a Garden of Eden as he did today. Today he was surrounded by paradise.

As at most other times, women and girls were standing about the sarcophagus, which was overflowing with mountain rain water; they greeted the priest with loud cries. Something in his manner and face, and the festive freshness of the young day, had given the laundresses spirit. Their skirts wedged in between their legs, so that some of them revealed their brown calves and knees, they stood bent over, working vigorously with powerful, naked arms that were tanned too. Francesco went up to the group. He found himself moved to say all sorts of friendly words that had nothing to do with his spiritual office, but concerned the good weather, good spirits and hopes for a good vintage. For the first time, probably stimulated by his visit to the house of his uncle the sculptor, the young priest condescended to study the ornamental frieze on the sarcophagus, which depicted a procession of bacchantes and prancing satyrs, dancing girls playing the flute, and Dionysos, the god of wine, wreathed in grapes, in his panther-drawn chariot. At this moment it did not seem strange to him that the ancients had covered the stone receptacle of death with figures that represented exuberant life. The women and girls, some of whom were of uncommon beauty, chattered and laughed away with him during this inspection, and at times it seemed to him that he himself was surrounded by joyful, shouting, intoxicated maenads.

This second ascent into the mountain world was like that of a man who walks with open eyes in contrast to one who is blind from birth. Francesco felt with a compelling clarity that he had suddenly re gained his sight. Accordingly, the contemplation of the sarcophagus seemed to him no accident but of deep significance. Where was its dead occupant? The living water of life filled the open stone and coffin, and eternal resurrection was proclaimed on the surface of the marble in the language of the ancients. This is how the gospel had to be interpreted.

To be sure, this was a gospel that had little in common with the one he had once studied and taught. It had no relation to the leaves or letters of a book, but rather, it came welling out of the earth through the grass, plants and flowers or flowing down with the light from the center of the sun. All nature took on, as it were, a speaking life. She who had been dead and mute became alive, intimate, direct and communicative. Suddenly she seemed to tell the young priest everything she had been silent about till now. He seemed to be her favorite, her chosen son, whom she was initiating, like a mother, into the sacred mystery of her love and motherhood. All the abysses of terror, all the anxieties of his disturbed soul were no more. There was nothing left of all the darkness and fear of a supposed stormy course to hell. The whole of Nature radiated kindness and love and Francesco, rich in kindness and love, could return kindness and love to her.

Strange: as he laboriously climbed upwards through broom, beech and thickets of bramble, often sliding down from jagged stones, the spring morning enveloped him like a joyful and tremendous symphony of nature, which spoke more about the process of creating than about the created world. The mystery of a creative activity that was forever exempt from death was openly revealed. Anyone who did not hear this symphony, so it seemed to the priest, was deceiving himself when he ventured to sing with the psalmist the hymns "*Jubilate Deo omnis terra*" or "*Benedicite coeli Domino.*"

The waterfall of Soana rushed down in satiate abundance into its narrow gorge. Its roar sounded full and luxurious. Its speech could never fail to be heard. Muffled at one moment, becoming clear the next, the voice of satiety sounded in perpetual variation. A thundering avalanche broke loose from the gigantic shadow-wall of Mount Generoso, and when it became audible to Francesco, the avalanche itself had already poured down in noiseless streams of rolling snow into the bed of the Savaglia. Where was there anything in nature that was not in the grip of the metamorphosis of life and that was without soul? anything in which a driving will was not active? Word, writing, song and coursing heart's blood were everywhere. Did not the sun place a warm, pleasant hand on his back between his shoulders? Did the leaves of the laurel and beech thickets not whisper and sway when he touched them in passing? Did the water not flow everywhere and, softly babbling, sketch everywhere the meandering and tangled script of its channel?

Didn't he, Francesco Vela, and didn't the fiber roots of myriads of growing things, small and large, read it, and was it not its mystery that was depicted in myriads of flowers and calyxes? The priest picked up a tiny stone and found a reddish net of lines running through it; here, too, a miraculous world—spoken, painted, written —a forming form that bore testimony everywhere to the creative power of life in pictures.

And didn't the voices of the birds bear the same testimony as they united in a network of infinitely delicate, invisible threads above the eaves of the mighty valley of rock? This audible network seemed to Francesco at times to be tranformed into visible threads of a silver splendor, which an inner and speaking fire caused to glitter. Was it not love made audible and visible in forms and a revelation of nature's bliss? And was it not delightful, the way this web, as often as it was dissolved or torn, was tied together again, as though by tiny weavers' shuttles, swiftly, tirelessly flying back and forth? Where were the small feathered weavers? One did not see them, except possibly when a little bird swiftly and silently changed its place; the tiniest throats poured out this speech that carried into space, drowning everything in its jubilation.

With everything welling forth, everything throbbing both within him and around him, Francesco did not know how to determine the place of death in the scheme of things. He touched the trunk of a chestnut tree and felt that he was pressing the nourishing juices upward within it. He drank in the air like a living soul and knew at once that it was this air to which he owed the breathing and hymning of his own soul. And was it not this air alone that made a speaking instrument of revelation out of his throat and tongue? Francesco stopped for a moment before a teeming, zealously active swarm of ants. A tiny dormouse had been almost wholly stripped down to its graceful skeleton by the mysterious little creatures. Did not the precious little skeleton and the dormouse that had perished and vanished in the warmth of the ant state testify to the indestructibility of life, and had not Nature, in her urge or compulsion to create, merely sought a new form? The priest saw the brown ospreys of Sant' Agata again, this time not below but high above him. Their winged and plumed bodies bore the miracle of the blood, the miracle of the pulsating heart, in majestic bliss through space. But who could fail to recognize that the changing curves of their flight delineated, on the blue silk of the sky, a clear, unmistakable writing, whose meaning and beauty were most intimately bound up with life and love? Francesco was convinced that the birds were inviting him to read it. And though they wrote by means of the path of their flight, the power of reading was not denied them. Francesco thought of the keen vision that was vouchsafed these winged fishermen. And he thought of the countless eyes of humans, birds, mammals, insects and fish, by means of which Nature views herself. With an astonishment that grew deeper and deeper, he recognized her in her infinite maternity. She saw to it that nothing in her whole maternal realm should remain hidden from her children's enjoyment; not only had she endowed them with the senses of sight, hearing, smell, taste and touch, but, Francesco felt, she was still other, countless new senses in readiness for the transformation of the aeons. What a vastness of seeing, hearing, smelling, tasting and touching there was in the world! And over the ospreys hung a white cloud. It resembled a radiant pleasure-tent. But it, too, went away and was visibly transformed.

They were profound and mystical powers that had opened the eyes of the priest Francesco. But, though he would not admit this to himself, the background for this experience was the happy circumstance that he saw four delightful hours ahead of him, including another meeting with the poor, outlawed shepherd girl. This awareness made him secure and rich, as if the time that was filled with such precious content could not come to an end. Up there, yes, up there where the little chapel stood, above which the ospreys were circling — up there, there awaited him a happiness which, so he thought, the angels must envy him. He climbed and climbed, and the most blissful zeal gave him wings. What he planned up there in unmoored proximity to heaven must surely transfigure him and put him almost on a plane with the good Eternal Shepherd Himself. *"Sursum corda! Sursum corda!"* He kept repeating to himself the greeting of St. Francis, while alongside him walked Sant' Agata, the martyr to whom the little chapel above had been dedicated and who had walked to her death at the hands of the hangman as if to a gay dance. And behind her and him, so it seemed to Francesco in his zealous ascent, there followed a procession of holy women, all of whom wanted to be present at the miracle of love on the festive summit. Mary herself, with her exquisite ambrosial flowing hair and her graceful feet, strode far ahead of the priest and his procession of sainted women, so that the earth might be covered with flowers for all those under her eye, her breath, her feet. *"Invoco te! Invoco te!"* Francesco whispered in rapture under his breath. *"Invoco te nostra benigna stella."*

Without feeling tired, the priest had reached the peak of the mountain cone, which was scarcely wider than the little church that stood on it. There was just room left for a narrow ledge and a tight little square in front of the church; in the middle of this square stood a young chestnut tree that was still without leaves. The blue gentian had spread so thickly about the sanctuary that a piece of the sky or of Mary's blue gown seemed to be strewn around the little church in the wilderness. Or one could also imagine that the mountain had simply dipped its peak in the azure of the sky.

The choirboy and the Scarabotas, brother and sister, were already there and had made themselves comfortable under the chestnut tree. Francesco turned pale, for his eyes had looked fleetingly but in vain for the young shepherdess. But he put on a stern look and opened the chapel door with a big rusty key, without showing his disappointment and the turbulent struggle that was going on in his heart. He entered the small church, in which the choirboy at once began to make some preparations behind the altar for celebrating the Mass. A little holy water was poured into the dry fountain from a bottle that had been brought up, so that the Scarabotas could dip their hard and sinful fingers in it. They sprinkled and crossed themselves and fell to their knees just inside the threshold of the door in timid reverence.

Meanwhile Francesco, driven by uneasiness, went out once more into the open, where, after walking about a little, with a sudden mute but deep emotion, he came upon the girl he was seeking; she was resting a little below the platform formed by the mountain peak, on a starry sky of gleaming blue gentian. "Come in, I'm waiting for you," the priest said. She got up with apparent indolence and looked at him calmly from under lowered lashes. At the same time she seemed to be smiling gently with a soft charm but this was merely an illusion produced by the natural shape of her sweet mouth, the lovely light in her blue eyes and the delicate dimples in her full cheeks.

At this moment the picture Francesco had cherished in his heart was fatefully renewed and enhanced. He saw a childlike, innocent Madonna face, whose maddening charm was combined with a very gentle, painful severity. The rather pronounced red of her cheeks lay on a white, not brown, skin, from which the moist red of the lips shone with the glow of the pomegranate. Every strain in the music of this childlike head was at once sweetness and bitterness, melancholy and serenity. In her eyes one could read shy retirement and at the same time a delicate challenge: both without the violence of animal impulse but artless and flowerlike. If her eyes seemed to bear in them the riddle and the fairy tale of the flower, the girl's whole appearance resembled rather a beautiful and ripe fruit. This head, as Francesco realized with astonishment, was still altogether that of a child, insofar as it expressed her soul; only a certain grapelike, swelling opulence indicated that she had crossed the boundary of childhood and had attained the state of womanhood. Her hair, which was partly earth brown in color, with lighter strands running through it, was tied around her forehead and temples to form a heavy crown. A heavy, inwardly fermenting, nobly ripe sleepiness seemed to draw the girl's eyelashes downward and gave her eyes a certain moist, overpowering tenderness. But the music of the head modulated below the ivory neck into another, whose eternal notes expressed another meaning. At the shoulders, the woman began. She was a woman of youthful and yet mature fullness, almost tending toward an opulence that did not seem to belong to the childlike head. The bare feet and strongly tanned calves wore a fruitlike fullness which, it seemed to the priest, was almost too heavy for them. This head possessed the hot, sensuous mystery of its Isis-like body unconsciously, or at most with a gentle awareness. But for this very reason Francesco realized that he had fallen a hopeless victim, for life and death, to this head and to this omnipotent body.

But whatever the young priest saw, realized and felt at this moment of reunion with this creature of God, who was so heavily burdened by her heritage of sin, he did not reveal except by a slight trembling of his lips. "What is your name?" he merely asked the innocent sinner. The shepherdess gave her name as Agata and did this in a voice that seemed to Francesco like the cooing of a paradisial ring dove. "Can you read and write?" he asked. She replied, "No." "Do you know anything about the meaning of the Holy Mass?" She looked at him but did not reply. He then told her to go into the little church and went in ahead of her. Behind the altar the choirboy helped him into his vestments. Francesco put the biretta on his head and the sacred service began; never before had the young man been moved to such a solemn fervor.

He felt as if all-bountiful God had only now called him to His service. The road to priestly consecration which he had traveled now seemed to him to be nothing more than a dry, empty, deceptive precipitancy that had nothing in common with the truly divine. But now the divine hour, the sacred season, had been born within him. The Savior's love was like a heavenly rain of fire in which he stood and through which all the love in him was suddenly liberated and kindled. His heart expanded with infinite love into the whole of creation and was united with all creatures in a harmonious, rapturous pulsebeat. Out of this intoxication, which almost stupefied him, compassion for every creature, zeal for the divinely good, broke out with redoubled strength, and he believed that only now did he fully understand Holy Mother Church and her service. He now wanted to become her servant with a renewed but very different zeal.

How the journey, the ascent to this mountain peak, had unlocked to him the mystery whose meaning he had inquired from Agata! Her silence, which had made him mute too, signified for him, though he did not show it, a common knowledge through the revelation that had come to them both. Was not the Eternal Mother the essence of

all transformations, and had he not lured the forsaken, lost children
of God, groping about in the dark, to this peak, raised high above
the ground, to reveal to them the miracle of the transubstantiation of
the Son, the eternal flesh and blood of the Godhead? Thus the youth
stood and raised the cup, his eyes overflowing with joy. It seemed to
him as if he himself were becoming God. In this state, in which he
felt himself to be one of the elect, a sacred instrument, he seemed to
expand with invisible organs into all the heavens with a joy and omnipotence that lifted him, he believed, infinitely above the whole teeming spawn of the churches and their clerics. They should see him,
should lift their eyes to him with astonished reverence, on the dizzy
heights of the altar at which he stood. For he was standing at the
altar in a very different and higher sense than the Pope, the holder of
Peter's keys, does after his election. With a convulsive ecstasy he held
the cup of the Eucharist and the transubstantiation, as a symbol of
God's body renewing itself perpetually in the whole of creation into
the infinity of space, where it shone like a second, brighter sun. And
while he stood there with the raised sacrament for what seemed to
him an eternity but was in reality two or three seconds, it appeared to
him that the cone of Sant' Agata was covered from top to bottom
with listening angels, saints and apostles. But even more beautiful
was a muffled drumbeat and a round dance performed by beautifully dressed women, wearing garlands of flowers and clearly visible
through the walls as they moved about the chapel. Behind them
whirled the maenads of the sarcophagus in ecstatic frenzy; the goat-
footed satyrs danced and skipped, some of them carrying Luchino
Scarabota's wooden symbol of fertility in joyful procession.

The descent to Soana brought Francesco to that brooding disenchantment felt by a person who has drunk to the last drop from the
cup of intoxication. The Scarabota family had left after the Mass:
the brother, sister and daughter had kissed the young priest's hand in
gratitude when they departed. As he now descended deeper and
deeper, the state of mind in which he had said the Mass up above
became more and more an object of suspicion to him. The peak of
Sant' Agata had surely, in former times, been the seat of a pagan
cult, consecrated to some idol; what had possessed him up there, apparently with the murmuring sound of the Holy Ghost, was perhaps
the demonic work of that dethroned theocracy which Jesus Christ

had overthrown, but whose destructive power was still tolerated by
the Creator and Director of the world. Upon arriving at his vicarage
in Soana, the priest was overwhelmed by the consciousness that he
had been guilty of a grievous sin, and his anxiety on this account became so heavy that he entered the church, which stood wall to wall
with his residence, even before taking his midday meal, to entrust
himself in passionate prayer to the Highest Mediator and, if possible,
to purify himself in His grace.

Feeling his own helplessness, he begged God not to deliver him up
to the assaults of demons. He was aware, he confessed, that they were
attacking his soul in all sorts of ways, either constricting it or extending it beyond its accustomed salutary boundaries and transforming it
in a terrible way. "I was a small garden, carefully cultivated in Your
honor," Francesco said to God. "Now it has been destroyed by a
flood, which will perhaps rise and rise under the influence of the
planets and on whose boundless waters I am drifting about in a tiny
bark. Formerly I knew my way precisely. It was the same way which
Your Holy Church prescribes for her servants. Now I am drifting, no
longer certain of the goal and the way.

"Grant me," Francesco implored, "my former narrowness and my
certainty, and command the evil angels to desist from their dangerous assaults on Your helpless servant. Lead, oh, lead us not into
temptation. I went up to the poor sinners in Your service; grant that
I may find my way back into the firm, restricted sphere of my sacred
duties."

Francesco's prayers no longer possessed their former clarity and
sharpness of contour. He asked for things that were mutually incompatible. At times he was unsure himself whether the stream of passion that bore his requests came from Heaven or from another
source. That is, he did not really know whether he was not fundamentally imploring Heaven to grant him a hellish prize. His inclusion
of the Scarabotas, brother and sister, in his prayers might indeed
have had its origin in Christian compassion and priestly care. But
was this true when he implored Heaven fervently, to the point of
scalding tears, for the salvation of Agata?

For the present he could still answer this question affirmatively, for
the clear stirring of the mightiest impulse, which he felt when he saw
the girl again, had been transformed into a romantic feeling for
something infinitely pure. This transformation prevented Francesco

from noticing that the fruit of mortal sin was forcing its way into the place of Mary, the Mother of God, and was, so to speak, the incarnation of the Madonna in his prayers and thoughts. On the first of May there began in the church of Soana, as everywhere, a special service for the Virgin Mary, the observance of which lulled the young priest's alertness still more. Day after day, at about the hour of twilight, he gave a short talk, chiefly to the women and daughters of Soana, on the theme of the virtues of the Blessed Virgin. Before and after the talk the nave of the church echoed with the hymns of praise in honor of Mary; they passed through the open doors into the spring air. And the old, exquisite airs, so lovely in both words and music, mingled outside with the cheerful noise made by the sparrows and with the sweetest lament of the nightingales which came from the damp gorges nearby At such moments Francesco, apparently absorbed in the service of Mary, was wholly given up to the service of his idol.

If the mothers and daughters of Soana had suspected that they formed for the priest a congregation which he drew into the church day after day for the glorification of this hated fruit of sin, or to have himself carried aloft, on the pious strains of the hymns to Mary, to the distant little meadow that was stuck high up on the rock, they would certainly have stoned him; but as things stood, it seemed to the astonished eyes of the whole congregation that the piety of the young cleric increased with every day. Bit by bit, young and old, rich and poor, in short, everyone from the mayor to the beggar, from the most fervent churchgoer to the most indifferent, was drawn into Francesco's sacred May-madness.

Even the long, solitary walks which he now frequently took were interpreted in the young saint's favor. And yet they were only undertaken in the hope that chance might lead Agata into his path. For in his fear that he might betray himself, he had set an interval of more than a week till the next special service for the Scarabota family; and this period of time now became unbearably long to him.

Nature still spoke to him in that open way he had first experienced on his walk to Sant' Agata, on the heights where the little sanctuary stood. Every blade of grass, every flower, every tree, every vine and ivy leaf were merely words of a language that welled up from the very base of existence, which spoke to him with a mighty roaring even in the deepest silence. Never had music penetrated his whole being like this and, as he believed, filled it with holy spirit.

Francesco had forfeited the deep, calm sleep of his nights. The mystical call which had come to him seemed, so to speak, to have slain Death and banished his brother Sleep. Each of these creative nights, pulsating with life of every sort, became a sacred period of revelation for Francesco's young body, so much so in fact that it sometimes seemed to him that the last veil was being removed from the mystery of divinity. Often, when he made the transition from the passionate dreams, which almost represented a waking state, into the waking of the senses, and outside the waterfall of Soana roared twice as loud as it did in the daytime, and the moon struggled with the darkness of the mighty abysses, and the black clouds, with a gigantic surliness, darkened the highest points of Mount Generoso, Francesco's body trembled as it never had before with fervent prayers, as a thirsty tree whose top is watered by the spring rain shudders in the wind. In this state he wrestled with God, filled with yearning to be initiated into the sacred miracle of creation as into the burning core of life, into this most holy, most inward something which permeates all Being from within. He said: "From there, O You, my almighty God, Your strongest light comes; from this core, radiating out in inexhaustible waves of fire, spreads all the bliss of existence and the mystery of the profoundest pleasure. Do not lay a finished creation into my lap, O God, but make me Your creative partner. Let me participate in Your uninterrupted work of creation; for only in this way and no other can I share in Your paradise." In order to cool the passion of his body Francesco walked back and forth in his room before open windows, so that the night air might penetrate his naked form. At the same time it seemed to him that the black storm above the gigantic rocky ridge of Mount Generoso resembled a huge bull over a heifer, snorting rain from its nostrils, grunting, shooting darting flashes out of its darkly flaming eyes and performing the generative act of fertility with its heaving haunches.

Such images were wholly pagan in nature, and the priest knew it but was no longer disturbed by it. He was already too deeply absorbed in the general numbness produced by the fermenting spring juices. The narcotic breath which filled him dissolved the limits of his narrow self and expanded him into the sphere of the general. Everywhere gods were being born in early, still lifeless nature, and the depths of Francesco's soul likewise opened and sent up images of things that lay buried in the abyss of the millions of years.

One night, in a state of half-wakefulness, he fell into a deep and, in a sense, terrible dream, which threw him into a gruesome sort of devotion. He became, as it were, the witness of a mystery from which emanated a terrible weirdness and at the same time something like the consecration of an ancient, irresistible power. Hidden somewhere in the rocks of Mount Generoso there seemed to be monasteries, from which dangerous stairways and rock steps led down into inaccessible caverns. Down these rock steps bearded men and old men in brown cowls descended in a solemn procession, one behind the other; the raptness of their movements and the withdrawn expression on their faces made him shudder; they seemed to be condemned to practice a frightful cult. These well-nigh gigantic, wild figures were venerable in an oppressive way. They descended very erectly, their hair and beards fused, mighty, shaggy, bushy. And these celebrants of a mirt- ilrss and beastly worship were followed by women covered only by the opulent billows of their hair, forming heavy golden or black cloaks. While these dream monks were held rigidly and insensibly captive under the yoke of fearful instinct as they mutely descended the steps, the women displayed the humility of sacrificial animals offering themselves voluntarily to a terrible deity. In the eyes of the monks there lay a silent, senseless fury, as if the poisonous bite of a crazed animal had wounded them and infused a madness into their blood, which might be expected to erupt. On the brows of the women, on their eyelashes, which were lowered in pious devotion, there lay a sublime solemnity.

After the monks of Mount Generoso had, like living idols, finally taken their individual positions in the shallow caves formed by the wall of rock, a phallic worship began, at once ugly and sublime. Ghastly as it was—and Francesco was terrified to the depths of his soul—it was equally thrilling in its utter seriousness and fearful holiness. Near the falling water and in the magic light of the immense moon, owls circled the rocky walls with piercing shrieks, but the powerful cries of the great night birds were drowned out by the blood-congealing, anguished cries of the priestesses as they expired amid the torments of lust.

The day of the divine service for the poor outlawed Alpine shepherds had finally come again. Even the early morning, when the priest Francesco Vela awoke, was unlike any other he had ever expe-

rienced. So in the life of every superior person days break, unexpected and unbidden, like dazzling revelations. On this morning the
youth did not wish to be either a saint or an archangel or even a god.
Rather, he was overcome by a slight fear that saints, archangels and
gods might become his enemies out of envy, for on this morning he
felt himself to be exalted above saints, angels and gods. But up on
Sant' Agata a disappointment was in store for him. His idol, who
bore the name of the saint, had excluded herself from the church
service. Questioned by the pale priest, the rude animal-like father
could only produce rude, animal-like sounds, while his wife, who was
at the same time his sister, excused their daughter on the score of
domestic duties. Thereupon Francesco carried out his holy office
with such apathy that he did not know at the end of the Mass whether
he had begun it yet. Mentally, he experienced the torments of hell,
and indeed entered a state of mind which could be likened to a real
descent into hell and which made of him a poor damned soul.

After dismissing the ministrant as well as the Scarabotas, he descended at random one side of the steep mountain cone, still completely dazed, unaware of a goal and even less of any danger. Again
he heard the nuptial cries of circling ospreys. But they sounded to
him like mockery, which poured down out of a deceptively shining
ether. Amidst the rubble of a dried-out rivulet he slid down, panting
and running, whimpering confused prayers and curses. He felt the
torments of jealousy. Although nothing had happened beyond the
fact that the sinner Agata had been detained by something on the
pasture of Soana, it seemed certain to the priest that she had a lover
and was spending the time she had stolen from church in his villainous arms. While her absence made him suddenly aware of his great
dependence on her, his feelings alternated between anxiety, dismay
and rage, the urge to punish her and to beg for deliverance from his
distress, that is, for the return of his love. He had by no means lost
the pride of the priest yet — the wildest and most unbending pride —
but had been most severely wounded. The sinner had rejected him as
a man, as a servant of God and as a giver of His Sacrament. The
man, the priest, the saint writhed in the convulsions of trampled
vanity and foamed at the thought that she had probably preferred
some beastly fellow, a shepherd or a woodcutter, to him.

His soutane torn and covered with dust, his hands bleeding and his
face scratched, Francesco spent some hours climbing about wildly

and blindly, up and down gorges, among broom bushes, over roaring mountain streams, and arrived at a region of Mount Generoso where the sound of cowbells reached his ear. He did not for a moment doubt what place he had reached. He looked down on forsaken Soana, on his church, which could be seen clearly in the bright sun, and recognized the crowd that was now streaming in vain to the sacred place. At this very moment he ought to have been putting on his vestments in the sacristy. But he could much more easily have put a rope about the sun and pulled it down than broken the invisible bonds that drew him powerfully to the Alpine pasture.

The young priest was on the point of attaining some measure of reason when a fragrant smoke, carried by the fresh mountain air, reached his nostrils. Instinctively he looked about him searchingly and noticed, not very far away, a seated male figure; he seemed to be tending a little fire, at the edge of which a tin vessel was steaming, probably with minestrone. The seated man did not notice the priest, for he had his back turned to him. So the priest in turn could distinguish only a round head covered with blond, woolly hair, a strong, brown neck, and shoulders draped in a loose-fitting jacket which age, weather and wind had turned earth brown. The peasant, shepherd, woodcutter or whatever he was, sat bent over the little fire, whose scarcely visible flames, held down by the mountain wind, shot out horizontal tongues along the earth and flat billows of smoke into the air. He was, it soon appeared, preoccupied with some work, some carving, and was silent most of the time like someone who has forgotten God and the world in the work that engages him. When Francesco had stood there for a while, for some reason anxiously avoiding any movement, the man or boy beside the fire began to whistle softly; having swung into the rhythm of music, he suddenly sent broken fragments of some song into the air in a melodious voice.

Francesco's heart pounded wildly. It was not because he had been climbing so vigorously up and down the gorges, but for reasons which derived partly from the strangeness of his situation, partly from the peculiar impression made on him by the presence of the man beside the fire. This brown neck, this curly, yellow-white hair, the youthful physique, bursting with vigor, that could be divined behind the shabby clothes, the palpable freedom and satisfied well-being of the mountain dweller — everything together entered Francesco's mind in a flash and established a relationship in which his morbid and groundless jealousy flared up even more tormentingly.

Francesco went up to the fire. He could not have remained hidden in any case; and he was, moreover, impelled forward by irresistible forces. The mountaineer turned round, revealing a face full of youth and strength, the like of which the priest had never seen before, jumped up, and looked at the newcomer.

It was now clear to Francesco that he had a cowherd before him, since the object he was carving was a sling. He kept his eye on the brown-and-black-spotted cattle that were visible here and there, but on the whole were far away and hidden from view, climbing about among the rocks and bushes, betrayed only by the tinkling of the bells which the bull and this or that cow wore on their necks. He was a Christian; what else could he have been among all these mountain chapels and Madonna images of the region? But he also seemed to be a most devoted son of Holy Church, for, immediately recognizing the priest's gown, he kissed Francesco's hand with timid fervor and humility.

But Francesco recognized at once that the shepherd resembled the other parish children in no other respect. He was more powerfully and heavily built, his muscles were those of an athlete, his eyes seemed to have come from the blue lake down in the depths, and were equal in visual power to those of the brown ospreys who were, as always, circling about Sant' Agata. He had a low brow, his lips were thick and moist, his look and smile were of a coarse frankness. That secretive, furtive air that is common among people of the South was alien to him. All this Francesco took in as he stood eye to eye with the fair young Adam of Mount Generoso and agreed that he had never seen such a primitively beautiful peasant before.

In order to conceal the true reason for his coming and at the same time to make his presence intelligible, he told a lie: he said that he had given the sacrament to a dying man in a remote hut and had returned home with his ministrant. He had lost his way, had slid down the mountain and now wished to be shown the right way after he had taken a short rest. The shepherd believed this lie. With a coarse laugh that revealed his healthy teeth, yet with embarrassment, he followed the cleric's account and prepared a seat for him, throwing the jacket from his shoulders and spreading it out near the edge of the fire. This act bared his brown, gleaming shoulders, in fact his whole upper body down to his belt, since he wore no shirt.

To begin a conversation with this child of nature was a matter of considerable difficulty. It seemed embarrassing to him to be alone with the ecclesiastical gentleman. After he had been on his knees for a while, blowing into the fire, adding twigs, lifting the lid of the pot from time to time, uttering words in an unintelligible dialect, he suddenly gave a tremendous shout of joy which reverberated from the rocky bastions in a manifold echo.

Scarcely had this echo died away when someone could be heard approaching with loud laughter and screaming. It was a group of voices, the voices of children, from among which one could distinguish a woman's voice alternately laughing and calling for help. At the sound of this voice Francesco felt his arms and legs grow numb, and at the same time he sensed a power announcing itself which, compared with that which had produced his natural existence, contained the secret of true and real life. Francesco burned like the bush of the Lord, but outwardly he betrayed nothing of his condition. For a few seconds he lost consciousness; he felt an unfamiliar liberation, and at the same time a captivity that was as sweet as it was hopeless.

Meanwhile the feminine cries of distress, stifled by laughter, had been approaching until, at the turn of a precipitous path, a bucolic picture became visible, as innocent as it was unusual. That very spotted goat which had molested the priest on his first visit to the mountain pasture was leading a little bacchantic procession, puffing and resisting, carrying the sole bacchante of the troop astride on his back, followed by the noisy children. The beautiful girl whom, it seemed to Francesco, he was seeing for the first time, held the curving horns of the goat in a firm grip; but, however powerfully she pulled back, forcing the animal's neck toward her, she was neither able to make it stop nor to get off its back. Some prank, which she might perhaps have played for the sake of the children, had brought the girl to this helpless situation; she was not really sitting on the unsuitable mount, but touched the ground with her bare feet, so that she was not being carried but was walking, and yet could not leave the unruly, fiery billy goat without falling. Her hair had come loose, the straps of her coarse shirt had slipped from her shoulders, so that an exquisite sphere became visible, and her short skirts, which even normally scarcely reached down to her calves, were now not even adequate to cover her gorgeous knees.

It was some time before the priest realized the identity of the bacchante and that he had before him the object of his tormented yearning, whom he had been seeking so avidly. The girl's shrieks, her laughter, her involuntary wild movements, her loose, flying hair, her open mouth, her full heaving bosom, the insane character of the ride —in a sense an act of compulsion and yet deliberate—had completely altered her outward appearance. A rosy glow covered her face, where pleasure and anxiety were mingled with bashfulness, which expressed itself with droll charm, as when she lifted one of her hands from the goat's horn and directed it momentarily to the dangerously high hem of her skirt.

Francesco stood there spellbound, captivated by this picture, as if it had the power to paralyze him. Its beauty was such that the obvious similarity with a witches' ride did not even occur to him. However, it did bring back to him impressions of classical antiquity. He thought of the carvings he had recently studied on the marble sarcophagus that stood, constantly overflowing with clear mountain water, on the village square of Soana. Was it not as if this world of stone, which was nevertheless so alive, of the wreath-crowned god of wine, the dancing satyrs, the panther-drawn triumphal chariot, the girl flute players and bacchantes, was it not as if they had hidden in the stony wastes of Mount Generoso, and as if one of the divinely inspired women had suddenly torn herself away from the raging mountain cult of the maenads and amazingly stepped into the life of the present?

If Francesco had not immediately recognized Agata, the goat had indeed recognized the priest, and dragged his burden, shrieking and resisting in vain, straight towards him; by planting his two deft forehooves abruptly on the priest's lap, he enabled his rider, finally released, to glide gently from his back.

When the girl became aware of the fact that there was a stranger present, and when she recognized Francesco in this stranger, her laughter and her gaiety suddenly ended, and her face, which had just been glowing with merriment, assumed an almost defiant pallor.

"Why did you not come to church today?" Francesco asked this question, standing erect, in a tone and with an expression on his pale face that could only be interpreted as anger, although it was caused by a different emotion. Whether it was because he wanted to conceal this emotion or because he was embarrassed, indeed helpless, or whether the spiritual mentor in him had been aroused to indignation —his anger increased and came to the surface in a way that made the cowherd look up in astonishment, while the girl's face showed in turn the flush and pallor of dismay and shame.

But while Francesco was speaking and punishing with words, words that were familiar to him but did not involve his soul, his emotions were at peace, and while the veins on his alabaster brow swelled, he experienced the bliss of deliverance. The sense of utter deprivation that had assailed him only a short time before was transformed into a feeling of plenty, his tormenting hunger became satiety, and the infernal world which he had cursed but a moment earlier was now dripping with the splendor of paradise. And as his wrath flowed stronger and stronger, his bliss grew and grew. He had not forgotten the desperate state in which he had just been, but the jubilation he now felt, he had to bless, bless over and over. For this desperate state had been the bridge to happiness. Francesco had already gone so far into the magic spheres of love that the mere presence of the beloved object brought with it that enjoyment which stupefies one with happiness and does not permit one to think of deprivation, however near it may be.

With all this the young priest felt, and no longer concealed from himself, the change that had taken place within him. The true state of his being had, as it were, come to the surface naked. The mad chase he had behind him was, he well knew, not prescribed by the Church and ran outside the consecrated network of roads that clearly and strictly delineated his activity. For the first time, not only his foot but his soul, too, had left the highway, and it seemed to him that he had reached the spot on which he now stood, not so much as a human being, but rather, as a falling stone, a falling drop of water, a leaf driven by the storm.

Every one of his angry words showed Francesco that he was no longer in control of himself but was, on the contrary, compelled to seek and exercise power over Agata at any price. He took possession of her with words. The more he humiliated her, the more sonorously the harps of bliss resounded within him. Every pain he inflicted on her as a punishment awakened ecstasy within him. In fact, if the cowherd had not been there, Francesco might easily have lost his last shred of self-control in this ecstasy and, falling at the girl's feet, have betrayed the true beating of his heart.

Although she had grown up in a degenerate household, Agata had nevertheless retained to this day the innocence of a flower. Like the mountain gentian which they resembled, her blue eyes had never been seen at the lake in the valley below. She had the most limited sphere of experience. And yet, although the priest was for her not a human being at all, but rather a creature halfway between God and man, a sort of strange magician, she nevertheless suddenly divined what Francesco was trying to conceal and recorded it with a look of astonishment.

The children had led the billy goat away over the gravel and upward. The woodcutter had begun to feel uncomfortable in the presence of the priest. He took the pot from the fire and with great effort climbed up with it, probably to a comrade, who was sending bundles of brushwood down over a precipice into the depths below by means of a seemingly endless wire. From time to time one of these dark bundles traveled along the rocky bastions with a scraping sound, not unlike a brown bear or the shadow of a gigantic bird. Moreover, since the wire was invisible, the bundle seemed to fly down. When the cowherd had vanished from view after giving a powerful yodel, which echoed from the battlements and bastions of Mount Generoso, Agata kissed the hem of the priest's gown and then his hand, as though in contrition.

Francesco had mechanically made the sign of the Cross over the girl's head, and in doing so his hands had touched her hair. But now his arm trembled convulsively as if something wanted to keep another something in its power with its last ounce of strength. But the tense, resisting something could not prevent the blessing hand from extending slowly and bringing its palm closer and closer to the head of the repentant sinner, or from suddenly resting firmly and fully on it.

Francesco looked about him fearfully. He was far from fooling himself at this moment and justifying the position he was in by connecting it to the duties of his sacred office; yet all sorts of phrases came from him about confession and confirmation. and his almost unbridled passion, ready to leap, was so fearful of arousing horror and abomination when it was discovered, that it, too, sought cowardly refuge again behind the mask of the Church.

"You will come down to my school at Soana, Agata," he said. "You will learn to read and write there. I will teach you a morning and evening prayer, God's commandments too, and how you may recognize and avoid the seven cardinal sins. Then you will confess to me every week."

But Francesco, who had torn himself away after these words and descended the mountain without looking around, decided next morning, after a painful, sleepless night, to go to confession himself. When he revealed his tormented conscience, not without playing the game of hide-and-seek, to a snuff-taking archpriest in the nearby mountain town, he was most readily absolved. It was obvious that the devil was opposing the young priest's attempt to lead stray souls back into the bosom of the Church, especially since woman is always man's most direct opportunity for committing sin. After breakfasting with the archpriest in the parsonage beside an open window which admitted gentle air, sun and the song of birds, and hearing some frank words about the frequent conflict between human and ecclesiastical affairs, Francesco yielded to the delusion that he was carrying away a relieved heart.

This transformation had probably been aided in part by a few glasses of that heavy dark-violet wine which the peasants of Arogno press and of which the priest possessed a few hogsheads. At the completion of the meal the priest even led the priest and confessant to the vaulted cellar under mighty, tender-leaved chestnut trees, where this treasure was stored on beams, since he was accustomed at about this time to fill a flask, which he took with him for the further needs of the day.

But Francesco had scarcely said farewell to his confessor on the flower-studded, wind-swept meadow before the ironbound gate of the rocky vault, and, walking briskly around a bend in the road, had hardly put enough hilly land, with trees and bushes, between them, when he began to feel an inexplicable repugnance toward his colleague's consolation and to regret all the time he had spent with him.

This grimy peasant, whose shabby soutane and sweaty underwear gave off an obnoxious odor, whose scurvy head and raw, dirt-encrusted hands demonstrated that soap was an alien commodity to him, seemed rather an animal, a block of wood, than a priest of God. Clergymen, Francesco said to himself, are, according to the Church, consecrated persons who have through their consecration received a supernatural dignity and power, so that even angels bow to them. This cleric could only be described as a travesty of this teaching. What a shame it was to see the priestly omnipotence put into such bumpkin hands, since even God was subject to such omnipotence and was compelled through the words *hoc est enim meum corpus* to descend upon the altar on which the Mass was celebrated.

Francesco hated, indeed despised, him. Then again he felt a profound regret. But finally it seemed to him that the stinking, ugly, obscene Satan had assumed his form. And he thought of those births which had taken place with the help of an incubus or succubus.

Francesco himself was astonished at such stirrings of his psyche and at the course of his thoughts. His host and confessor had hardly given him cause for them, except through his very existence; for his words at breakfast were entirely in the spirit of propriety. But Francesco was already swimming once more in such an emotion of exaltation and believed he was inhaling air of such celestial purity that, compared with this sanctified element, the everyday world seemed to him to be chained down in a state of damnation.

The day had arrived on which Francesco expected the sinful girl from the Alpine pasture in his parsonage at Soana for the first time. He had directed her to ring the bell not far from the church door, by which he could be summoned to give confession. But midday was already approaching and the bell had not stirred and, as he instructed some half-grown girls and boys in the schoolroom, he became more and more absentminded. Through the open window he could hear the roar of the waterfall, now swelling, then subsiding, and the priest's excitement grew whenever the sound increased. At such times he feared that he might miss the sound of the bell. The children were perplexed by his restlessness and absentmindedness. That his mind was not on his business and not with them either, escaped the girls least of all, for they feasted on the young saint with their earthly as well as their heavenly senses. Tied to the stirrings of his youthful nature by a profound instinct, they even shared the tension that dominated him at the moment.

Shortly before the twelve o'clock bell rang, there arose a murmur of voices on the village square, which till then had lain quietly in the light of the sun, the tops of its chestnut trees covered with May blossoms. A mob of people was approaching. One could hear calmer, throaty male sounds, apparently protesting. But an irresistible stream of female words, shrieks, curses and protests suddenly drowned these out and made them inaudible. Then a fearful silence ensued. Suddenly muffled voices reached the priest's ears, but the source of these voices remained at first unintelligible to him. It was May and yet it sounded as if a chestnut tree, under the weight of a gust of wind, were suddenly shaking off its autumnal burden of fruit. The hard chestnuts were falling to the ground and bursting like drumbeats.

Francesco leaned out of the window.

With horror he saw what was going on in the square. He was so alarmed, indeed so filled with dismay, that he was brought to his senses only by the shrill, ear-piercing peal of the confession bell, which was being tugged with desperate doggedness. He hurried into the church and to the church door, and pulled the penitent — it was Agata — away from the bell into the church. Then he stepped out in front of the portal.

This much was clear: the entrance of the outlaw into the village had been noticed and the usual thing had happened. They had tried to drive her out of the abode of human beings with stones, as if she were some mangy dog or wolf. The children and mothers had soon banded together and pursued the outcast, curse-laden creature; the beauty of the girl did not in the least disturb their conviction that their stones were aimed at a dangerous animal, a monster, which spread pestilence and destruction. Meanwhile Agata, feeling certain of the priest's protection, had not allowed herself to be deflected from her goal. And so the resolute girl, persecuted and hunted, had arrived at the church door, which was still being pelted with a few stones thrown by the children.

The priest did not need to bring the agitated members of his congregation to their senses by a sermon; as soon as they saw him they scattered.

In the church Francesco had motioned to the mute, heavily breathing fugitive to follow him into the parsonage. He, too, was agitated and so they heard each other breathing fitfully. On a narrow staircase of the parsonage, between white-washed walls, stood the dismayed housekeeper, now somewhat calmer, to receive the hunted game. One could see from her face that she was prepared to help if help were needed. Only the sight of the old woman seemed to make Agata aware of the humiliating aspect of her present state. Alternating between laughter and anger, she uttered strong imprecations and so gave the priest the first opportunity to hear her voice, which,

it seemed to him, sounded full, sonorous and heroic. She did not
know why she was being persecuted. She regarded the town of Soana
the way one would regard a nest of mud wasps or an ant heap. Furious and indignant as she was, it still did not occur to her to reflect on
the cause of such dangerous malice. For she had known this condition since her childhood and assumed it to be something natural. But
one fights off wasps and ants too. Even though it is animals that are
attacking us, we are roused by them to hatred, to rage, to despair,
according to the circumstances, and relieve our feelings by threats,
tears or the stirrings of the deepest contempt. Agata did so too, while
the housekeeper put the girl's ragged clothes in order and she herself
pinned up the astounding mass of her hair, ranging in color from
rust to ochre, which had fallen down in her hasty running.

At this moment young Francesco was suffering as never before
under the compulsion of his passion. The presence of the woman who
had matured in the mountain wilderness like an exquisite wild fruit,
the intoxicating fire that streamed from her warm body, the fact that
she, who had been distant and unattainable, was now enclosed in the
narrow confines of his own dwelling—all this made Francesco clench
his fists, tense his muscles and gnash his teeth, merely to keep on his
feet in a situation which for some seconds threw him into total darkness. When the darkness lifted, there was an enormous commotion of
images, thoughts and feelings within him: landscapes, people, the
most distant memories, living moments of his domestic and professional past, fused with present ideas. As though he were fleeing from
these, an inescapable future rose up before him, sweet and terrible,
to which he knew he would wholly succumb. Thoughts flashed over
this chaos of mental pictures, countless, restless, impotent thoughts.
His conscious will, Francesco realized, had been dethroned in his
mind; another will reigned, which brooked no contradiction. With
horror the youth confessed to himself that he was delivered up to it
for slavation or damnation. This state of mind was a sort of obsession.
But if he was overcome by his fear of falling unavoidably into the
crime of mortal sin, he felt at the same time like bellowing with
boundless joy. His hungry eyes looked with a hitherto unknown,
amazed satiety. More than that: here hunger *was* satiety and satiety,
hunger. The cursed thought shot through his mind that here alone
was the imperishable, divine food by which the sacrament gives heavenly nourishment to believing Christian souls. His emotions were

idolatrous in nature. He condemned his uncle in Ligornetto as a bad
sculptor. And why had he himself never painted? Perhaps he might
still become a painter. He thought of Bernardino Luini and his great
painting in the old monastery church in nearby Lugano and of the
exquisite blond holy women his brush had created there. But then
they were as nothing compared to this hot, most living reality.

Now Francesco did not know what to do. A warning impulse at
first made him want to flee from the girl. All sorts of reasons, not all
of them equally pure, moved him to seek out the mayor at once and
inform him of the incident before others could do so. The mayor listened to him calmly — Francesco had fortunately found him at home
— and shared the priest's view of the matter. It was but Christian and
good Catholic practice not to let the bad situation on the Alpine pasture continue indefinitely, and to take an interest in the degenerate
people who were enmeshed in sin and shame. As to the villagers and
their conduct, he promised to take stern measures against them.

When the young priest had gone, the mayor's pretty wife, who had
a quiet, taciturn way of observing people, said:

"This young priest could go so far as to become a cardinal, even
Pope. I believe he is consuming himself with fasting, praying and
sleepless nights. But the devil pursues saints especially, with his hellish tricks and with the most secret wiles and stratagems. May the
young man, with God's help, always be protected against them."

When Francesco walked back to the parsonage, as slowly as he
could, he was followed by many desirous but also evil female eyes. It
was known where he had been and they were resolved to submit to
this pestilence of Soana only if they were compelled to do so. Girls
walking upright, carrying bundles of wood on their heads, met him
on the square near the marble sarcophagus; they did, it is true, greet
him with submissive smiles, but afterwards they exchanged disdain-
ful looks behind his back. Francesco strode along as though in a
fever. He heard the confused song of the birds, the swelling and restrained roar of the eternal waterfall; but it was as if his feet were not
on the ground, as if he were being pulled forward without a rudder,
in a whirlpool of sounds and images. Suddenly he found himself in
the sacristy of his church, then in the nave before the main altar,
praying to the Virgin Mary on his knees for help in his emotional turmoil.

But his prayers did not express the desire that she free him from

Agata. Such a desire would have found no nourishment in his heart. They were, rather, a cry for mercy. He wanted the Mother of God to understand, to forgive, if possible to approve. Francesco interrupted his prayer abruptly and broke away from the altar when the idea suddenly shot through his head that Agata might have gone away. But he found the girl still there, in the company of Petronilla.

"I have cleared everything up," Francesco said. "The way to the church and to the priest is open to everyone. Trust me, what has happened will not recur." He was overcome by a firmness and sureness, as if he once again stood on the right path and on solid ground. Petronilla was sent to the neighboring parish with an important ecclesiastical document. The errand could unfortunately not be postponed. Moreover, the housekeeper was to report the incident to the priest there. "If you meet any people, tell them," he stated emphatically, "that Agata has come down here to the parsonage from the Alpine pasture and is receiving instruction from me in the teachings of our religion, our sacred faith. Let them come and prevent it and draw the punishment of eternal damnation down on their heads. Let them make a scene in front of the church and maltreat their fellow Christian. The stones will not strike her but me. If need be, I will personally take her back at twilight to the pasture."

When the housekeeper had gone, a lengthy silence ensued. The girl had folded her hands in her lap and still sat on the same rickety chair that Petronilla had placed near the white-washed wall for her. There were still flashes of fire in Agata's eyes, injury was mirrored in these lightning bolts of indignation and secret rage; but her full Madonna face had assumed more and more a helpless expression, until finally a silent, copious stream bathed her cheeks. Francesco had meanwhile turned his back to her and was looking out of the open window. As he let his eyes roam over the gigantic mountain wall of the Soana valley, from the fateful Alpine pasture to the lakeshore, with the everlasting murmur of the waterfall, the song of a single, sweet boy's voice penetrated to him from the luxuriant vine terraces; he was compelled to doubt that he now really held the fulfillment of his superterrestrial desires. Would Agata still be there when he turned around? And if she were there, what would happen when he turned around? Would this turning not be decisive for his whole earthly existence, even beyond that, in fact? These questions and

doubts persuaded the priest to remain in his present position as long
as possible, in order to pass judgment on himself, or at least take
counsel with himself once more before he arrived at a decision. This
was a matter of seconds, not minutes; but in these seconds, not only
the entire history of his entanglement, beginning with Luchino Scarabota's first visit, but his whole conscious life became the immediate
present to him. In these seconds a whole tremendous vision of the
Last Judgment, with Father, Son and Holy Ghost in heaven, spread
out before him over the ridge of the peak of Mount Generoso and terrified him with the blare of trumpets. One foot on Generoso, the
other on a mountain peak on the other side of the lake, in his left
hand the scale, in his right, his naked sword, the Archangel Michael
stood like a terrible threat, while behind the Alpine pasture of Soana
abominable Satan had descended with horns and claws. But almost
everywhere the priest's eyes strayed there stood a woman, dressed in
black and wearing a black veil, wringing her hands; she was none
other than his despairing mother.

Francesco closed his eyes and then pressed both hands against his
temples. When he turned around slowly, he looked for a long time
with an expression of horror at the girl, who was swimming in tears,
her dark, red mouth trembling painfully. Agata became frightened.
Francesco's face was distorted as if it had been touched by the finger
of death. Without a word he staggered over to her. And with a
hoarse cry, like that of someone who has been defeated by an inexorable power, a cry that was at the same time a savage, life-hungry
groan and a moan for mercy, he sank to his knees before her, a
crushed man, and wrung his clasped hands.

Francesco might not perhaps have succumbed to his passion in this
degree for a long time if the crime committed by the villagers against
Agata had not infused a nameless, ardent element of human compassion into it. He realized what must lie in store for this creature in her
future life and in a world without a protector, she who was so endowed by God with aphrodisiac beauty. Circumstances had made
him her protector today; perhaps he had saved her from death by
stoning. He had thereby won a personal claim on her: a thought that
was not clear to him, but which nevertheless influenced his actions;
working unconsciously, it swept away all sorts of inhibitions, fear and
timidity. And in his mind he saw no possibility of ever again withdrawing his hand from the outcast. He would stand at her side, even

if the world and God stood on the other. Such considerations, such currents, combined unexpectedly with the stream of passion, and so this stream overflowed its banks.

For the present his conduct was not yet a turning away from the right path and the consequence of a resolve to sin; it was merely a state of impotence and helplessness. He could not have said why he did what he did. In reality he did nothing. Something was happening to him. And Agata, who should now really have been terrified, was not, but seemed to have forgotten that Francesco was a stranger to her and a priest. He seemed all at once to have become her brother. And as her weeping turned into sobbing, she not only permitted him, who was likewise shaken by dry sobs, to embrace her as if to comfort her, but she lowered her tear-drenched face and hid it on his breast.

Now she had become a child and he her father, insofar as he sought to calm her in her suffering. But he had never felt a woman's body so close to his and his caresses and tendernesses soon became more than paternal. To be sure, he felt clearly that the girl's sobbing pain concealed something akin to a confession. He realized that she knew to what an ugly love she owed her existence, and was submerged in the same sorrow as he was because of it. He bore her distress, her pain, with her. In this way their hearts were united. But he soon raised her sweet Madonna face to his, putting his hand to the nape of her neck and drawing her to him, bending her white brow back with his right hand; and after feasting his greedy eyes for a long time on the object he held clasped in this way, with the fire of madness in his eye, he suddenly swooped down like a hawk on her hot, tear-salted mouth and remained inseparably fused with her.

After some moments of earthly time, but eternities of numbing bliss, Francesco suddenly tore himself loose and stood firm on both feet, tasting blood on his lips. "Come," he said, "you can't go home alone without protection, so I will accompany you."

A changeable sky lay over the Alpine world when Francesco and Agata stole out of the parsonage. They turned off into a meadow path, on which they climbed down unseen from terrace to terrace between mulberry trees, through garlands of vines. Francesco knew very well what lay behind him and what boundary he had now crossed; but he could feel no remorse. He was changed, sublimated, liberated. It was a sultry night. In the plain of Lombardy, it seemed,

storms were gathering, whose distant flashes of lightning spread out
like a fan behind the gigantic silhouette of the mountains. The fragrance from the giant lilac tree under the windows of the parsonage
floated down with the water from the network of brooks that trickled
by, mingled with cool and warm currents of air. The intoxicated
couple did not speak. He supported her in the dim light whenever
they climbed down the wall to a lower-lying terrace, caught her in his
arms too, on which occasions her breast heaved on his, his thirsty lips
clung to hers. They did not really know where they wanted to go, for
from the depth of the gorge of the Savaglia no road led up to the Alpine pasture. But on this point they were agreed, that they must
avoid the ascent to it through the village. But their aim was not to attain some external, distant goal but to enjoy to the full what had
been attained.

How full of dross, how dead and empty the world had been till
now, and what a transformation it had undergone! How it had
changed in the eyes of the priest and how he had changed in it! All
the things that had until now meant everything to him were erased
and of no worth. His father and mother, as well as his teachers, had
been left behind like worms in the dust of the old, rejected world;
while for him, the son of God, the new Adam, the gate of paradise
had been opened again by the cherub. In this paradise, in which he
now took his first enraptured steps, timelessness prevailed. He no
longer felt himself to be a man of some special time or age. Equally
timeless was the nocturnal world about him. And because the time of
his expulsion, the world of banishment and of original sin lay behind
him outside the guarded gate of paradise, he no longer felt even the
slightest fear of it. No one out there could harm him in any way. It
was not in the power of his superiors, nor in the power of the Pope
himself, to prevent his enjoyment of even the most trivial fruit of
paradise or to rob him of the smallest trifle of the highest bliss that
had now become his as a gift of grace. His superiors had become in-
feriors. They lived forgotten in an extinct earth of wailing and gnash-
ing of teeth. Francesco was no longer Francesco; he had just been
awakened by the Divine Breath as the First Man, the only Adam, sole
lord of the Garden of Eden. There lived no second man beside him in
the plenitude of sinless creation. Constellations quivered with bliss,
making a divine music. Clouds lowed like luxuriantly grazing cows,
dark-red fruits radiated sweet rapture and delicious refreshment,

tree trunks sweated fragrant resin, blossoms strewed out precious spices; but all this depended on Eve, whom God had placed among all these miracles as the fruit of fruits, the spice of spices, upon her who was herself the highest miracle. The fragrance from all the spices, their most delicate essence, the Creator had placed into the hair, skin and the fruit-flesh of her body; but her form, her substance, had no equal. Her form, her substance, was God's secret. The form moved of itself and remained exquisite alike at rest or in change. Her substance seemed to be made of the same mixture as lily and rose leaves, but it was chaster in its coolness and hotter in its fire, it was both more delicate and tougher. In this fruit there was a living, vibrant kernel; precious, trembling pulses hammered within it and, when one tasted of it, it yielded new blisses that were rarer and even more exquisite, without any loss of heavenly abundance occurring in the process.

And what was most precious in this creation, in this paradise regained, could indeed be deduced from the presence of the Creator. Here God had neither completed His work and left it alone, nor laid Himself to rest in it. On the contrary, His creative hand, His creative Spirit, His creative power were not withdrawn, they remained at the work of creating. And each of all the parts and members of paradise remained creative, Francesco-Adam, who had just emerged from the potter's workshop, felt himself a creative person within the whole sphere of his activity. With a rapture that was not of this world he felt and saw Eve, the daughter of God. The love that had formed her still clung to her, and the most precious of all the substances which the Father had employed to form her body still had an unearthly beauty that was not sullied by even a speck of earthly dust. But this creation, too, still quivered, swelled and shone from the heavenly fire of active, creative power and yearned to be fused with Adam. Adam in turn was impelled toward her, to enter with her into a new perfection.

Agata and Francesco, Francesco and Agata, the priest, the youth of good family, and the outlawed, despised child of the shepherd, were the first human pair as they climbed down into the valley hand in hand on the secret, nocturnal bypaths. They sought the deepest seclusion. Silently, their hearts filled with a nameless astonishment, with a rapture that almost caused both their hearts to burst, they descended deeper and deeper into the precious miracle of the cosmic hour.

They were moved. Because of the grace, the election they felt to be resting on them, their boundless happiness was tinged with an earnest solemnity. They had felt each other's body, had been united in a kiss, but they sensed the unfamiliar destiny to which they were moving. It was the final mystery. It was that for the sake of which God created, and for which He had put death into the world and had accepted it as part of the bargain, so to speak.

In this way the first human pair reached the narrow gorge below, sawed through by the little Savaglia River. It was very deep, and only an unfrequented footpath led upwards along the edge of the brook bed to the reservoir into which the mountain water poured from a dizzy height. At a considerable distance from it the brook was divided into two arms, which were united again by a little green island that Francesco loved and often visited because it was very lovely with its few young apple trees that had struck root there. And Adam took off his shoes and carried his Eve to it. "Come, or I shall die," he said to Agata several times. And they trampled down narcissi and Easter lilies with their heavy, almost intoxicated lovers' steps.

Even here in the gorge there was summer warmth, though the course of the brook brought coolness with it. How brief a time had passed since the turning point in the life of the pair, and how far behind them everything before the turning point lay. Since the little island was rather remote from the village, the peasant who owned it had built a hut out of stones, twigs and earth to afford some shelter against accidental storms; this provided a bed of leaves that was tolerably secure against the rain. It was this hut perhaps that had been in Adam's mind when he had headed toward the valley rather than up the mountain. The hut seemed to have been prepared to receive the lovers. Mysterious hands seemed to have been forewarned of the impending celebration of the secret creation of man; for there were clouds of light about the hut, clouds of sparks, June bugs, glowworms, worlds, Milky Ways, which sometimes rose in tremendous sheaves as if they wanted to populate empty space. They flowed and floated through the gorge at such a height that one could no longer distinguish them from the stars in the sky.

Although this spectacle was familiar to them, this silent magic nevertheless produced wonder in Francesco and Agata, and their astonishment made them hesitate a moment. Is this the place, Francesco thought, which I so often sought out and contemplated with

pleasure, not dreaming what it would one day mean to me? It seemed
to me a place to which I might retreat as a hermit from the misery of
the world and steep myself in God's word through renunciation. But
what it really was — an island on the Euphrates River or the Hiddekel,
the secret, most blissful place in paradise — I would not have recognized. And the mystical, flaming spark-clouds, nuptial fires, sacrificial fires, or whatever they might be, freed him completely from the
earth. When he did not forget the world altogether, he knew that it
lay powerless before the gates of paradise like the seven-headed
dragon, the seven-headed beast that came out of the sea. What had
he in common with those who worshiped the dragon? Let him blas-
pheme against God's hut. His venom could not reach this spot. Never
had Francesco, the priest, felt such proximity to God, such security
in Him, such selfforgetfulness; and in the murmuring of the mountain brook the mountains gradually seemed to resound melodiously,
the crags of rock to peal like an organ, the stars to make music with
myriads of golden harps. Choirs of angels shouted in jubilation
through infinity, the harmonies roared down from above like tem-
pests, and bells, bells, ringing bells, wedding bells, small and large,
deep and high, powerful and gentle, spread an oppressive, blissful
solemnity through world space. — And so they sank down on the bed
of leaves, entwined in each other.

There is no moment that endures, and even when one wants to
cling with anxious haste to those instants that afford the highest bliss,
one finds no way of holding onto them, strive as he will. His whole
life, Francesco felt, consisted of steps leading to the summit of the
mystery he was now experiencing. Where would one breathe in the
future if one could not hold onto it? How was one to endure a
damned existence if one were cast out again from the raptures of
one's innermost heaven? In the midst of the superhuman intoxication
of enjoyment, the youth experienced transitoriness with a stinging
pain; in the enjoyment of possession he felt the torment of loss. He
felt as if he must empty a cup of delicious wine and quench an
equally delicious thirst; but the cup never became empty, and his
thirst was never quenched. And the drinker did not want his delicious
thirst to be satisfied nor the cup to be emptied; yet he sucked at it
with greedy frenzy, tormented because he could never reach bottom.
Surrounded by the rushing brook, flooded by it, with glowworms

dancing around them, the young couple rested in the rustling leaves, while the stars twinkled through the roof of the hut. He had taken trembling possession of all of Agata's secrets, which he had admired as unattainable treasures. He had immersed himself in her flowing hair, clung with his lips to hers. But his eye was immediately filled with envy of his mouth, which had robbed it of the sight of the sweet maiden's mouth. And bliss, more and more inconceivable, flowing, benumbing, welled up from the mysteries of her young body. What he had never hoped to possess, when it was mirrored before his eyes on hot nights, was as nothing compared to what he now had as a boundless possession.

And as he reveled, he became incredulous over and over again. The excess of his fulfillment caused him repeatedly to assure himself insatiably of his possession. For the first time his fingers, his quivering hands and palms, his arms, his chest, his hips felt woman. And she was more than woman to him. He felt as if he had regained something that he had lost, something he had wantonly thrown away, without which he had been a cripple, and with which he had now formed a bond of unity. Had he ever been separated from these lips, this hair, these breasts and arms? She was a goddess, not a woman. And she was not something that existed in itself; he burrowed his way into the core of the world, and, his ear pressed under the virginal breasts, he heard, with a shudder of bliss, the heart of the world beating away.

That numbness, that half-sleep, descended on the pair, in which the raptures of exhaustion merge with the charms of waking sensation and the charms of waking sensation merge with the raptures of the numbness produced by oblivion; in this state Francesco fell asleep in the arms of the girl, and then Agata in his. How strangely and with what confidence the shy, wild girl had yielded to the caressing compulsion of the priest, how submissively and happily she had served him! And when she fell asleep in his arms, it was with the trusting smile of the satiated infant who closes its eyes at the breast and in the arms of its mother. But Francesco contemplated the sleeping girl in amazement and loved her. Through her body passed waves of trembling, like those produced by the relaxation of life. Sometimes the girl cried out in her dream. But when she opened her languishing eyelids, she always had the same intoxicating smile, and the same dying in ultimate abandonment. Whenever the youth fell asleep it seemed to him that some power was gently, gently withdrawing from him the body he held in his embrace and which he felt with his whole body. But every time upon waking, this brief withdrawal was followed by a sensation of the highest, most gratefully experienced sweetness, an ineffable dream with a blissful, live sensation of the sweetest reality.

This was it, the fruit of paradise, from the tree that stood in the middle of the garden. He held it in the embrace of his whole body. It was the fruit from the tree of life, not from that of the knowledge of good and evil, with which the serpent had tempted Eve. It was, rather, that fruit, the enjoyment of which made one as God. In Francesco every wish for a higher, for another happiness, had died. Neither on earth nor in heaven were there raptures that could compare with his. There was no king, no god whom the youth, rioting in his extravagant excess, would not have felt to be a starving beggar. His speech had sunk to a stammer, to a convulsive breathing. He sucked in the intoxicating breath that came from between Agata's open lips. He kissed away the tears of ecstasy, hot on the girl's lashes and on her cheek. With eyes closed, looking at each other only sparingly, they both enjoyed themselves in the other, their gaze turned inward, feeling passionately and clearly. But all this was more than enjoyment — it was something that human speech cannot adequately express.

Next morning Francesco celebrated early Mass punctually. His absence had been noticed by no one, his return home, not even by Petronilla. The precipitous haste with which, after making a summary toilet, he had to rush to the sacristy to join the waiting ministrants, and to the altar before the small, waiting congregation, prevented him from coming to his senses. Reflection came when he was in the parsonage again, in his little room, where the housekeeper set the customary breakfast before him. But this reflection did not immediately yield the clarity of disenchantment. Rather, his old environment and the advancing day gave to what he had experienced the resemblance of something unreal, which faded before him like a past dream. But it was reality after all. And although it surpassed in fantastic incredibility any dream that Francesco had ever dreamed, he nevertheless could not disavow it. He had had a fearful fall, there was no quibbling about this fact; the question was whether it was at all possible to lift himself from this fall, from this fearful lapse into sin. The plunge was so deep and from such a height that the priest was compelled to despair of it. This terrible fall was without example, not only in the ecclesiastical, but also in a worldly sense. Francesco thought of the mayor and how he had talked to him about the possibility of saving the outcasts of the Alpine pasture. Only now, secretly, in his profound humiliation, did he recognize the extent of the priestly arrogance, the whole overbearing conceit with which he had been puffed up at that time. He ground his teeth in shame, he squirmed, as it were, like a vain, unmasked swindler, in his dishonor, in his naked helplessness. Had he not been a saint only a moment ago? Had not women and virgins of Soana looked up to him almost idolatrously?

And had he not succeeded in lifting the ecclesiastical spirit of the place to such an extent that attending church and Masses had become popular even among the men? Now he had become a traitor to God, a deceiver and betrayer of his congregation, a traitor to the Church, a traitor to the honor of his family, a traitor to himself, yes, even a traitor to the despised, cursed, reprobate, wretched Scarabotas, whom he had really ensnared into damnation under the pretext of saving their souls.

Francesco thought of his mother. She was a proud, almost masculine woman, who had protected and guided him with a firm hand when he was a child, and whose unbending will had prescribed for him the course of his future life. He knew that her harshness towards him was nothing but ardent mother-love, that even the slightest cloud on her son's honor would wound her pride most deeply, and that a serious lapse on his part would certainly cause an incurable wound in the very seat of her life. It was strange that, in relation to her, what had really happened, what had been experienced intimately and clearly, could not even be thought about.

Francesco had sunk into the most disgusting mire, into the filth of final depravity. In it he had left behind his vows as a priest, his essence as a Christian, as his mother's son, as a human being in fact. He would have been reduced to a werewolf, that stinking, demonic beast, in the opinion of his mother and of people in general, if they had known of his crime. The youth jumped from his chair and from the breviary on the table, in which he had seemed to be absorbed. It had seemed to him as if a hail of stones had rattled against the house;

not like yesterday, when they had attempted the stoning, but with a hundredfold, thousandfold power, as if the parsonage was to be destroyed or at least turned into a heap of rubble, and he buried under it like the corpse of a poisonous toad. He had heard strange sounds, fearful cries, frantic shouts, and knew that among the raging mob who tirelessly hurled stones there was not only the whole of Soana, the mayor and his wife, but also Scarabota and his family and, indeed, at the head of them all, his mother.

But after some hours had passed, such fantasies and stirrings were displaced by very different ones. Everything that had been born out of his stock-taking, out of his horror at the deed, his contrition, now seemed as if it had never existed. Francesco was desiccated by a distress he had never known, by a burning thirst. His spirit cried out as someone who is rolling about in anguish in the burning desert sand cries for water. The air seemed to be without those substances we require in order to breathe. The parsonage became a cage to the priest, and he paced restlessly between its walls like a beast of prey with aching knees, resolved, if they would not liberate him, to bang his head against the wall and smash it rather than live on like this. How is it possible to live as a dead man? he asked himself, observing the inhabitants of the village through the window. How is it that they want to breathe, how can they breathe? How can they endure their wretched existence, since they do not know what I have enjoyed and now miss? And Francesco grew within himself. He looked down on popes, emperors, princes and bishops, in short, on everyone, as people commonly look down on ants. He did so even in his thirst, his misery, his deprivation. To be sure, he was no longer master of his life. An overpowering magic had made him into a completely will-less and, without Agata, completely lifeless victim of Eros, the god who is older and mightier than Zeus and the rest of the gods. He had read in the writings of the ancients about such sorcery and about this god, and had dismissed both with a superior smile. Now he felt clearly that one had to believe even in the arrow and the deep wound with which, according to the ancients, the god poisoned the blood of his victims. This wound was indeed burning, piercing, flaming, eating and gnawing within him. He felt terrible piercing pains until, when it grew dark, he set out, inwardly shouting with happiness, on the road to the same small island world that had united him yesterday with his beloved and on which he had arranged a new meeting with her.

The mountain shepherd Ludovico, known to the inhabitants of the region as "the heretic of Soana," fell silent when he had read to the point where his manuscript broke off. The visitor would have liked to hear the end of the tale. But when he was frank enough to express this wish, his host revealed to him that his manuscript went no further. He was also of the opinion that the story could, in fact must, break off here. The visitor did not share this opinion.

What had become of Agata and Francesco, of Francesco and Agata? Did the affair remain a secret or had it been discovered? Did the lovers find a permanent or merely fleeting attraction for each other? Did Francesco's mother learn of the affair? And finally, the listener wanted to know, was the tale based on a real incident or was it a complete fiction?

"I have already told you," Ludovico replied, turning slightly pale, "that a real incident was the occasion for my scribbling." After this he was silent for a long time. "About six years ago," he continued, "a clergyman was literally driven from the altar of his church with sticks and stones. At least, when I returned to Europe from the Argentine and came to this region, this was told to me by so many people that I have no doubt of the incident itself. Moreover, the incestuous Scarabotas lived here on Mount Generoso, though not under that name. The name Agata is fictitious too; I simply took it from the chapel of Sant' Agata, above which, as you see, the brown ospreys are still circling. But the Scarabotas really did have, among other fruits of their sins, a grown daughter, and the priest was accused of having illicit relations with her. People say that he did not deny the fact nor did he ever show the slightest remorse, and the Pope, it is said, excommunicated him because of it. The Scarabotas had to leave the region. They—the parents, not the children—are supposed to have died in Rio from yellow fever."

The wine and the excitement aroused in the listener by the place, the hour, the company and especially by the work of fiction that had been read to him, combined with all sorts of mystical circumstances, made him still more importunate. He asked once more about Francesco's and Agata's fate. The shepherd could tell him nothing about this. "They are said to have been an annoyance to the region for a

long time, because they desecrated and profaned the solitary shrines
that are scattered about everywhere and misused them as an asylum
for their wicked lust." At these words the anchorite broke into loud,
unrestrained laughter that was wholly without cause and which he
was unable to control for a long time.

Thoughtful and strangely moved, the reporter of this travel adventure set out on his way home. His diary contains descriptions of this
descent, but he does not wish to insert them here. The so-called blue
hour that appears when the sun has sunk beneath the horizon was in
any case especially beautiful on that occasion. One could hear the
waterfall of Soana roar. Just so, Francesco and Agata had heard it
roar. Or did they really still hear its sound at that very moment? Was
that spot not the location of the Scarabotas' pile of stones? Could one
not hear sounds of merry children coming from there, mingled with
the bleating of goats and sheep? The wanderer drew his hand across
his face as if he wanted to wipe away a veil of confusion: had the little
tale that he had heard really gorwn, like a tiny gentian flower or its
like, on a meadow of this mountain world, or had this glorious, primitively powerful mountain relief, this petrified gigantomachy
emerged out of the frame of this little novella? He was thinking this
and similar thoughts when the sonorous sound of a woman's singing
reached his ears. Was it not said that the anchorite was married? The
voice carried, as in a spacious, acoustic hall, when people hold their
breath to listen. Nature, too, was holding her breath. The voice
seemed to be singing in the wall of rock. Sometimes, at least, it
seemed to be streaming out from there, in broad waves full of the
sweetest mellowness and fiery nobility. But the singer came, it turned
out, from the very opposite direction, climbing up the path to Ludovico's square hut. She bore an earthenware vessel on her head, holding it lightly with her uplifted left hand, while she led her little
daughter by the right hand. In this way the full and yet slender figure
assumed that straight, exquisite bearing which strikes us as being so
solemn, indeed sublime. At this sight a vague surmise shot through
the spectator's mind like an illumination.

He had probably been discovered by this time, for the song suddenly grew silent. One could see the mounting woman come closer,
completely irradiated by the splendor of the western sky. One could
hear the voice of the child, and the mother replying in calm, deep
tones. Then one could hear the bare soles of the woman striking the

rough-hewn steps resoundingly. She had to step firmly and securely because of her burden. For the waiting wanderer these moments before meeting her possessed a tension and mystery that he had never experienced before. The woman seemed to grow. One saw her dress, tucked up high, saw a knee peeping out for a moment with every step she took, saw naked shoulders and arms emerge, saw a round, feminine face, sweet in spite of a proud self-confidence, surrounded by luxuriant hair, the color of red-brown earth, like some pristine being. Was this not the man-woman, the virago, the Syrian goddess, the sinner who fell out with God to yield herself wholly to man, her husband?

The returning wanderer had stepped aside and the resplendent canephore, returning his greeting almost imperceptibly, because of her burden, strode past him. She turned both her eyes toward him while her head remained fixed ahead of her. At the same moment a proud, self-confident, knowing smile glided over her countenance. Then she lowered her eyes to the road once more, while at the same time an unearthly sparkle seemed to run through her eyelashes. The observer may have been overheated by the warmth of the day, the wine and everything else he had experienced, but this much is certain: before this woman he felt himself grow quite, quite small. These full lips, curled almost in scorn for all their enchanting sweetness, knew that there was no resisting them. There was no protection, no armor against the claims of this neck, these shoulders and this breast, which was blessed and stirred by the breath of life. She rose up out of the depth of the world and past the astonished man — and she rises and rises into eternity, as the one into whose merciless hands heaven and hell have been delivered.

Arthur Schnitzler

1862 — 1931

Arthur Schnitzler lived in Vienna throughout his uneventful life. Trained as a physician, he was at first assistant to his father, a prominent throat specialist, but gradually moved into the field of psychiatry, which was then entering its golden age under the impact of Sigmund Freud. Schnitzler was also interested in parapsychological phenomena, such as mental telepathy and spiritism. He began publishing his literary works around 1890 and soon devoted all his energies to writing.

Schnitzler was acknowledged to be a writer of stature, with a voice all his own; yet throughout his life he suffered vicious attacks by reactionary intellectuals and government officials. But the advanced and discriminating Viennese public appreciated him as an artist of rare quality.

Schnitzler began writing in the naturalistic era, to which he belonged by his cast of mind and temperament. He saw man as a pawn of external forces and his own libido. Heroic gestures he believed to be futile; we may dream of them, but we do not carry them into reality; we submit or escape into pleasure, conventional restraint, deception, neurosis or death.

This much is orthodox naturalism; but Schnitzler offered more. He reflected one side of the Viennese "myth": the sophisticated, tired skepticism that was both gay and melancholy at the same time. Schnitzler's grace, wit and urbanity were a perfect medium for expressing this spirit of the *fin de siècle* that prevailed in Europe at the turn of the century.

Tragedy can be suggested by the rueful smile as effectively as by the cry of anguish. Schnitzler depicts a wide variety of situations, conflicts and problems which express man's groping for the meaning of life. It is a mark of his modernity that his cultured men and women rarely emerge from the labyrinth into the light, but wander about aimlessly, fighting loneliness and disillusionment, unable to hold on to fixed values, unable even to distinguish clearly between reality and dream. His people do not understand each other or life. Their best intentions go awry; their clearest judgments lead them into defeat and catastrophe. They are placed in situations in which they must choose between alternatives that are unfair or downright impossible. Or he shows what the literature of a later day has shown repeatedly: a destiny that fulfills itself by playing tricks on humans, suggesting that life is in the power of a demiurge who delights in making sport at man's expense. "As flies to wanton boys, are we to the gods; they kill us for their sport."

These theses are not presented in the tragic vein but through a genre that Schnitzler himself called his "melancholodies" (*Melancholödien*). Elemental, atavistic passions are there, but in subdued form, always covered over by a veneer of civilization and breeding.

Schnitzler's work is divided equally between drama and fiction; he was most successful in the shorter forms: the one-act play and the novella. In the latter he was a pioneer in the use of the stream-of-consciousness technique. Early in his career he wrote *Leutnant Gustl*, and toward the end of it, the novella *Fräulein Else*, both employing the stream-of-consciousness device. *Fräulein Else* appeared at about the same time as Joyce's *Ulysses*. Virtually the entire novella is a record of Else's thoughts, and through them we learn her story. We see and interpret all the characters through her mind and study her own character through the self-revelation that she provides in this record of her thoughts. A careful examination of the story will reveal the depth and subtlety with which Schnitzler has described the society in which Else moves. Else herself is a very complex character. Her reaction to Herr von Dorsday's offer is not to be taken on the surface, but must be analyzed carefully in the light of the revelations she makes about herself before he presents the proposal to her. There is a conflict in her character between elements of decadence (narcissism, exhibitionism, oedipal attachment, sensuality, perhaps even a lesbian component) on the one hand, and an innate dignity, which is mortally insulted by the repeated attempts of her parents to treat her as a chattel and commodity by exploiting her beauty in order to recoup their sagging fortunes.

Her dilemma is a typical Schnitzlerian one. Shall she act amorally like her father and her friends, get out of life what she can, and thus save her father from disgrace and prison, and so be a "good" daughter? Or should she maintain her integrity and dignity and thereby ruin her parents? This conflict is subtly but clearly revealed in her interior monologues and in the hysterical dream she has in the garden after Dorsday has left her. Her decision to show herself in public rather than to Dorsday alone, is testimony to Schnitzler's profound insight into the conflicting ideals that are at war within her. Freudian symbols proliferate in the novella, though never obtrusively

The artistic problem that Schnitzler faced was to convince the reader that this girl, who had most of the good things that life can offer, could be lured to her death. He has succeeded brilliantly by creating a profound and moving study of human misery amid the splendor of modern civilization.

The opening sentence sets the tone for the psychological drama that ensues. Else is too tired to play. This game is the symbol of the game of life as it is played in the social set in which she moves, by the aristocratic society in the summer resort, by her gambling father, by Cissy and Paul, by her friend Bertha, by her flighty brother. She is no match for the wholly uncomplicated, sensual Cissy, who can live the normal life of a mother while having an affair with Paul and not go to pieces. It is a stroke of masterful irony that the end of the action shows the "normal" Cissy making love to Paul over the very bed on which the "corrupt" Else is dying because of her sense of decency.

A work like *Fräulein Else* poses special problems for the translator. The literary level on which it moves is difficult to transpose into an American environment. Its language is that of everyday speech among the upper middle class of Vienna — a highly specialized language. Else clips her verb endings, omits pronoun subjects, even introduces some colloquialisms and slang into her speech. But with all that, she speaks beautiful classical German. It would be a falsification of the German text to render her speech in colloquial American, to translate "papa" and "mama" by "dad" and "mom." And what is one to do with the deferential titles and apostrophes that abound in Viennese society talk, with the scraps of French and Italian which Else mixes naturally into her conversation and her soliloquies? An attempt has been made to preserve them, even though it entails some stiffness. The reader must simply bear in mind that he is reading about Vienna in the twenties and not about the America of our day.

Fräulein Else

"*You really don't want to play any more, Else?*" — "No, Paul, I can't play any more. Adieu. — Good-by, madam." — "*But Else, why don't you call me Frau Cissy? Or better still, just Cissy.*" — "Good-by, Frau Cissy." — "*But why are you going already, Else? There are still two full hours before* dîner." — "Why don't you play your singles with Paul, Frau Cissy? It's really no fun playing with me today." — "*Leave her alone, madam, today is her ungracious day. — But it really suits you superbly, this ungraciousness, Else. — And the red sweater even better.*" — "I hope you'll win more favor from blue, Paul; adieu."

That was quite a good exit. I hope the two of them don't think I'm jealous. I could swear there's something between them, between Cousin Paul and Cissy Mohr. Nothing in the world could concern me less. — Now I'll turn round again and wave to them. Wave and smile. Do I look gracious now? Oh Lord, they're already playing again. I really play better than Cissy Mohr, and Paul isn't exactly a crack player either. But he does look good—with his open collar and his naughty boy's face. If only he were less affected. You need have no fear, Aunt Emma . . .

What a wonderful evening! This would have been the right weather for the trip to the Rosetta Hut. How splendidly the Cimone towers up into the sky! — We would have started out at five o'clock in the morning. Of course I would have felt ill at first, as usual. But that passes. — There's nothing more delightful than hiking at dawn. — That one-eyed American on the Rosetta looked like a prize fighter. Perhaps someone poked his eye out in a fight. I'd like to marry someone from America, but not an American. Or I'll marry an American and we'll live in Europe. A villa on the Riviera. Marble steps leading down to the sea. I'll lie naked on the marble. — How long ago is it since we were in Menton? Seven or eight years. I was thirteen or fourteen. Ah yes, we were still well off then. —It was really stupid to postpone the party. We certainly would have been back by now. —At four, when I went to the tennis game, the special-delivery letter from mama, which had been announced by the telegram, hadn't arrived yet. Who knows if it's here now? I could have played another set quite comfortably. —Why do these two young people bow to me? I don't even know them. They've been living in the hotel since yesterday; they sit at the left of the dining room by the window, where the Dutchmen used to sit. Did I return their greeting ungraciously? Or even haughtily? I'm not like that at all. How did Fred put it on the way home from *Coriolanus?* Gay-spirited. No, high-spirited. You are high-spirited, Else, not arrogant. —A beautiful word. He always finds beautiful words. —Why am I walking so slowly? Am I really afraid of mama's letter? Well, I don't imagine it will contain pleasant news. Special delivery! Perhaps I'll have to go back home. Oh dear! What a life, in spite of my red silk sweater and silk stockings. Three pairs! The poor relation, invited by the rich aunt. I'm sure she regrets it already. Shall I put it in writing for you, dear Aunt, that I'm not thinking of Paul in my dreams? Ah, I'm not thinking of anyone. I'm not in love. With anyone. And I've never been in love yet. I wasn't in love with Albert either, though I thought so for a whole week. I don't believe I can fall in love. Really strange. For I'm certainly sensual. But high-spirited, too, and ungracious, thank Heaven. At thirteen I was perhaps really in love for the only time in my life. With the Vandyke—or rather with Abbé des Grieux and with that Renard girl too. And when I was sixteen, at Lake Wörther. —Oh no, that was nothing. Why think back? After all, I'm not writing my memoirs. Not even a diary, like Bertha. I like Fred, it's nothing more than that. Perhaps if he were more elegant. I really am a snob. Papa thinks so, too, and makes fun of me. Oh, dear Papa, you worry me so. I wonder if he ever deceived mama? Of course. Often. Mama is rather stupid. She has no suspicion about me. Nor have other people. Fred?—a mere suspicion. —Heavenly evening. How festive the hotel looks. You can feel it: they're all people who are well off and have no cares. I, for instance. Ha, ha! Too bad. I was really born for a carefree life. It could be so beautiful. Too bad. —There's a red glow on the Cimone. Paul would say 'alpine glow.' But that's far from being an alpine glow. It's beautiful enough to draw tears. Oh, why must I go back to the city?

"*Good evening, Fräulein Else.*" —"My respects, madam."

—*"Coming from tennis?"* —Can't she see? Why does she ask? "Yes, madam. We played almost three hours. And you are taking a walk, madam?" —*"Yes, my usual evening walk. Along the Rollweg. It runs so beautifully between the meadows, in the daytime it's almost too sunny."* —"Yes, the meadows here are glorious. Especially in the moonlight from my window."

"Good evening, Fräulein Else. —My respects, madam." —"Good evening, Herr von Dorsday." —*"Coming from tennis, Fraulein Else?"* —"What keen perception, Herr von Dorsday." —*"Don't make fun of me, Else."* —Why doesn't he say "Fräulein Else"? —*"When one looks so attractive with a racket, one may in a sense carry it as an ornament."* —Ass, I won't even answer that one. "We played all afternoon. Unfortunately there were only three of us. Paul, Frau Mohr and I." —*"I used to be a fanatical tennis player."* —"And you aren't any more?" —*"I'm too old for that now."* —"Oh, old. In Marienlyst there was a sixty-five-year-old Swede; he played every evening from six to eight. And the year before he even played in a tournament." —*"Well, thank Heaven I'm not sixty-five yet, but unfortunately I'm not a Swede either."* —Why unfortunately? I suppose he intends that to be a joke. It will be best if I laugh politely and go. "My regards, madam. Adieu, Herr von Dorsday." What a deep bow he makes and what eyes! Calf-eyes. Did I offend him with the sixty-five-year-old Swede? No matter. Frau Winawer must be an unhappy woman. She's certainly close to fifty. Those bags under her eyes—as if she had cried a lot. Oh, how terrible to be so old. Herr von Dorsday is showing an interest in her. Now he's walking at her side. He still looks quite good with that Vandyke of his peppered with gray. But I don't care for him. Puts on artificial airs. What use is your first-class tailor to you, Herr von Dorsday? Dorsday! I'm sure you used to have some other name. —Here comes Cissy's sweet little girl with her nursemaid. —"Good day, Fritzie. Bon soir, mademoiselle. Vous allez bien?" —*"Merci, mademoiselle. Et vous?"* "What do I see, Fritzie, why, you have an alpenstock. Are you going to climb the Cimone?" —*"Oh no, I'm not allowed to go up so high yet."* —"You will next year, you may be sure. Bye, Fritzie. A bientôt, mademoiselle." —*"Bon soir, mademoiselle."*

An attractive girl. I wonder why she's a nursemaid? And for Cissy at that. A bitter lot. Oh Lord, it might happen to me too. No, I could always get something better. Better? —A delightful evening.

'The air is like champagne,' Dr. Waldberg said yesterday. The day before yesterday someone said it too. — Why do the people sit in the lobby in this wonderful weather? Inconceivable. Or is everyone waiting for a special-delivery letter? The porter has seen me; if there were a special-delivery letter for me, he would have brought it to me at once. So there isn't any. Thank Heaven. I'll lie down for a bit before dinner. Why does Cissy say *dîner?* Stupid affectation. They belong together, Cissy and Paul. — Oh, I'd prefer it if the letter were here. Perhaps it will come during *dîner.* And if it doesn't come, I'll have a restless night. I slept so miserably last night too. Of course it's one of those days. That's why I have that drawing pain in my legs. Today is the third of September. So perhaps on the fifth. I'll take Veronal today. Oh, I won't make a habit of it. No, dear Fred, you needn't worry. In my thoughts I always address him as *du.* One should try everything, even hashish. Naval Ensign Brandel brought some hashish back with him, from China I believe. Do you drink hashish or smoke it? It's supposed to give you magnificent visions. Brandel invited me to drink — or smoke — hashish with him. An impertinent fellow. But good-looking –

"*Excuse me, Fräulein, a letter.*" The porter! So it is here! — I'll turn around quite naturally. It might be a letter from Caroline or Bertha or from Fred or Miss Jackson? "Thank you." It is from mama after all. Special delivery. Why didn't he say: a special-delivery letter? — "Oh, special delivery!" — I won't open it till I get to my room, where I can read it in peace. — The marchesa. How young she looks in the semi-darkness. Forty-five for sure. Where will I be at forty-five? Perhaps dead. I hope so. She gives me such a nice smile, as usual. I'll let her pass, give a slight nod — not as if it were a special honor for me to be smiled at by a marchesa.

"*Buona sera.*" — She's saying buona sera to me. Now I must at least bow to her. Was that too deep? She's so much older than I am. How superbly she walks. Is she divorced? I walk beautifully too. But — I know it. Yes, that's the difference. — An Italian man could become dangerous for me. Too bad the handsome dark fellow with the Roman head has gone. "He looks like a *filou,*" Paul said. Lord, I have nothing against rogues, on the contrary. — There — here we are. Number seventy-seven. A lucky number, really. Nice room. Cembra pine. There stands my virginal bed. — Now it has become a real alpine glow. But I'll deny it before Paul. Paul is really shy. A doctor, a

woman's doctor! Perhaps for that very reason. Day before yesterday
in the forest, when we were so far ahead of the rest, he might really
have been a little more enterprising. But I would have given him a
bad time. No one has been really enterprising with me yet. Perhaps
at Lake Wörther, three years ago, in the pool. Enterprising? No, he
was just indecent. But handsome. Apollo of Belvedere. I didn't really
quite understand, that time. Well — at sixteen. My heavenly meadow!
Mine — ! If I could take it back with me to Vienna. Delicate mists.
Autumn? Well, yes, it's September the third, high in the mountains.

Well, Fräulein Else, couldn't you decide once and for all to read
the letter? Maybe it doesn't refer to papa at all. Couldn't it be something about my brother? Perhaps he has become engaged to one of
his flames? A chorus girl or a glove salesgirl. Oh, no, he's really too
sensible to do that. Actually, I don't know much about him. When I
was sixteen and he twenty-one, we were really friends for a while. He
told me a lot about a certain Lotte. Then he suddenly stopped. This
Lotte must have done something to him. And since then he has told
me nothing. — Now the letter is open and I didn't even notice that I
had opened it. I'll sit down on the window sill and read it. Be careful
not to fall out. It is reported from San Martino that a regrettable accident has occurred in the Hotel Fratazza there. Fräulein Else T., a
strikingly beautiful girl of nineteen, daughter of the well-known
lawyer. . . . Of course, they would say I had committed suicide because of unhappy love or because I was pregnant. Unhappy love, ah
no.

"My dear child" — I'll look at the end first. — "So, once more, don't
be angry, my dear, good child, and a thousand. . . ." — For Heaven's
sake, they can't have committed suicide! No, in that case there would
be a telegram from Rudi. — "My dear child, you may believe me
when I say how sorry I am that I must burst into your beautiful vacation" — as if I weren't on vacation always, unfortunately — "with such
unpleasant news." — What a terrible style mother has. "But upon
mature reflection there is nothing left for me to do. Well, to put it
briefly, papa's situation has become acute. I don't know where to get
advice or help." — Why all these words? — "The sum involved is a
relatively ridiculous one — thirty thousand gulden" — ridiculous? —
"which must be produced in three days, or all is lost." — For Heaven's
sake, what does that mean? — "Just imagine, my dear child, Baron
Höning. . ." — What, the district attorney? — "sent for papa this

morning. You know how much the baron thinks of papa, really
adores him. A year and a half ago, that time when things also hung
by a thread, he spoke personally to the principal creditors and settled
the affair at the last moment. But this time absolutely nothing can be
done if the money is not produced. And apart from the fact that we
will all be ruined, there will be a scandal—unprecedented. Just
imagine, a lawyer, a famous lawyer—who—no, I just can't write it
down. I keep fighting back my tears. You know, child, you're a clever
girl, we've been in a similar situation several times before this,
Heaven help us, and the family always helped us out. The last time it
involved as much as a hundred and twenty thousand. But then papa
had to sign an agreement that he would never again appeal to his
relatives, especially to Uncle Bernhard." —Well, get on, get on,
where is this leading to? What can I do about it? "The only person
we could possibly still think of would be Uncle Victor, but he is unfortunately away on a journey to the North Cape or Scotland"—yes, he's
well off, the disgusting fellow—"and is absolutely beyond reach, at
least for the moment. His colleagues, especially Dr. Sch., who has
often helped papa out"—Good Lord, what have we come to?—"he's
out of the question, since he has married again." —Well, so what? so
what? What do you want from me? —"And now your letter has
come, my dear child, in which you mention, among others, Dorsday,
who is also staying in the Fratazza, and this seemed to us like a nod
from Fate. You know of course how often Dorsday used to visit us
years ago." —Well, yes quite often. —"It is sheer chance that for the
last two or three years he has shown up less frequently; he is said to be
in someone's firm clutches—between you and me it's nothing very
nice—" —Why "between you and me?" —"In the Royal Club, papa
still plays whist with him every Thursday, and last winter he saved
him a pretty sum of money in his lawsuit against another art dealer.
For the rest, why shouldn't you know it? He helped papa out once before." —I thought so. —"At that time it involved a trifle, eight
thousand gulden, but after all—thirty doesn't mean anything to
Dorsday either. That's why I wondered if you might do us a favor and
talk to Dorsday." —What? —"You know he's always liked you especially." —Never noticed it. He stroked my cheek when I was twelve or
thirteen years old. "A regular young lady." —"And as papa fortunately has never approached him again since the eight thousand,
he will not refuse him this service of love. Recently he's supposed to

have made eighty thousand from one Rubens alone that he sold to
someone in the United States. Of course you mustn't mention this."
—Do you take me for a silly goose, Mama? —"Otherwise, you can
talk to him quite frankly. If the occasion should warrant it, you may
also mention the fact that Baron Höning has sent for papa. And that
the thirty thousand will prevent the worst from happening, not only
for the moment but, God be willing, forever." —Do you really believe that, Mama? —"The Erbesheimer case, which is going splendidly, will certainly bring papa a hundred thousand, but of course at
this stage he can't ask the Erbesheimers for anything. So please,
child, speak to Dorsday. I assure you it doesn't mean anything. Papa
could, of course, simply have telegraphed him. We considered it seriously, but after all, it's something quite different, child, to talk to a
man personally. The money must be here at twelve on the fifth: Dr.
F. —" Who is Dr. F.? Oh yes, Fiala. —"is inexorable. Of course, personal grudge is also involved in the matter. But since it unfortunately
concerns trust money"—For Heaven's sake, Papa, what have you
done?—"nothing can be done. And if the money is not in Fiala's
hands by noon on the fifth, the warrant will be issued, or rather,
Baron Höning is managing to restrain him till then. Well then, Dorsday would have to wire the money to Dr. F. through his bank. Then
we'll be saved. Otherwise God knows what will happen. Believe me,
you are not compromising yourself in the least, my beloved child.
Papa at first had his doubts. He even made efforts in two different
directions. But he came home in utter despair." —Can papa possibly
be in despair? —"Perhaps not so much because of the money, as because people are behaving so disgracefully toward him. One of them
was once papa's best friend. You can imagine whom I mean." —I
can't imagine anything. Papa has had so many best friends, but in
reality not one. Warnsdorf perhaps? —"Papa came home at one
o'clock, and now it's four in the morning. He's asleep at last, thank
Heaven." —If he never woke at all, that would be the best thing for
him. —"I'll take the letter to the post office first thing in the morning, special delivery, then you'll be sure to get it on the morning of
the third." —How did mama work this out? She's always lost in such
matters. —"So talk to Dorsday at once, I implore you, and wire us at
once how it turns out. For Heaven's sake, don't let Aunt Emma
notice anything; it's sad enough, of course, that in such a case one
can't turn to one's own sister, but you might as well talk to a stone.

My dear, dear child, I'm so sorry that you have to experience such things at your young age, but believe me, papa is to blame for it least of all." — Who else, then, Mama? — "Well, let us hope to God that the Erbesheimer case marks a turning point in our existence in every respect. We must just get beyond these few weeks. It would really be a true mockery if some misfortune should occur because of the thirty thousand gulden." — Surely she doesn't mean seriously that papa would take. . . . But would — the other thing not be worse still? — "Now I close, my child, I hope that at all events" — at all events? — "you will be able to stay in San Martino over the vacation, at least till the ninth or tenth. You musn't come back on our account. Give my regards to aunt, keep on being nice to her. So, once again, don't be angry, my dear, good child, and a thousand . . ." — yes, I know all that.

So I'm to solicit Dorsday . . . insane. How does mama imagine this? Why didn't papa simply get on the train and come here? — This would have been just as fast as the special-delivery letter. But perhaps they would have — at the station on suspicion of flight — terrible, terrible! Of course the thirty thousand won't help us either. Always the same business! For seven years! No — longer. Who would suspect anything from looking at me? No one can tell anything from looking at me, nor even at papa. And yet everyone knows it. It's a puzzle how we can still keep our heads up. How you get used to everything. And with it all we live quite well. Mother is really an artist. The supper for fourteen last New year's Day — incredible. But on the other hand, my two pairs of ballroom gloves, they were a major effort. And when Rudi recently needed three hundred gulden, mama almost wept. And papa is always in good spirits in spite of it all. Always? No. Oh no. Recently at the opera, *Figaro,* the look in his eyes — suddenly quite vacant — I was frightened. Then he was like a totally different person. But afterward we had supper in the Grand Hotel and he was in as splendid a mood as ever. And here I'm holding the letter in my hand. The letter is of course insane. I'm to speak to Dorsday? I'd die of shame. — I? Feel ashamed? Why? It isn't my fault, after all. — Suppose I did speak to Aunt Emma? Nonsense. She probably hasn't that much money at her disposal. Uncle is a miser. Oh Lord, why don't I have money? Why haven't I earned anything for myself yet? Why haven't I learned anything? Oh, I have learned something! Who would dare say I've learned nothing? I play the piano, I know

French, English, a little Italian too, I've attended lectures on art history. —Ha ha! And suppose I'd learned something more sensible,
what good would it do me? I couldn't have saved up thirty thousand
gulden under any circumstances. —

The alpine glow is gone. The evening is no longer marvelous. The
countryside is sad. No, not the countryside, but life is sad. And I am
sitting here calmly on the window ledge. And papa is to be locked
up. No. Never, never. That must not happen. I'll save him. Yes,
Papa, I'll save you. Why, it's quite simple. A few words quite noncha-
lantly, that's just my meat, "high-spirited"—haha, I'll treat Herr
Dorsday as if it were an honor for him to lend us money. And it really
is. —Herr von Dorsday, have you a minute for me? I've just received
a letter from mama, she's temporarily embarrassed—or rather, papa
is. —"But of course, miss, with the greatest of pleasure. How much is
it?" —If only I didn't dislike him so much. Including the way he looks
at me. No, Herr Dorsday, I'm not taken in by your elegance or your
monocle or your aristocratic manner. You could just as well deal in
old clothes as in old paintings. —But Else! Else, how can you? —Oh,
I have a right. No one notices that about me. I'm even blond, reddish
blond, and Rudi looks absolutely like an aristocrat. In mama, of
course, you notice it at once, at least in her speech. But then with
papa, you don't at all. For that matter, let them notice it. I don't
deny it at all and Rudi even less. On the contrary. What would Rudi
do if papa were locked up? Would he shoot himself? What nonsense!
Shooting yourself and prison, all these things just don't exist, you
only read about them in the newspapers.

The air is like champagne. Dinner-*dîner* is in an hour. I can't
stand Cissy. She doesn't care a bit about her little girl. What shall I
wear? The blue or the black? Perhaps the black would be more correct today. Too low a neckline? *Toilette de circonstance* they call it in
French novels. In any case I must look enchanting when I talk to
Dorsday. After *dîner*, nonchalant. His eyes will bore into my *décol-
leté*. Repulsive fellow. I hate him. I hate all people. Must it be Dorsday of all people? In the whole world is there really only this Dorsday
who has thirty thousand gulden? Suppose I spoke to Paul? Suppose
he told aunt that he has gambling debts—the money could certainly
be produced.

Almost dark now. Night. Night of the grave. Best of all, I'd like to
be dead. —But it isn't true at all. Suppose I went down right now

and spoke to Dorsday before dinner? Oh, how horrible! — Paul, if
you get me the thirty thousand, you may have whatever you want
from me. But there, I'm quoting from a novel again. The noble
daughter sells herself for her beloved father, and even gets some fun
out of it. Bah! No, Paul, even for thirty thousand you can't have anything from me. No one can. But for a million? — For a palace? For a
string of pearls? If I ever marry, I'll probably do it more cheaply. Is it
really so bad? After all, Fanny sold herself too. She told me herself
that her husband fills her with horror. Well, how would it be, Papa,
if I sold myself at auction tonight? To save you from prison? Sensa-
tional—! I have a fever, I'm sure. Or am I already feeling unwell?
No, it's a fever. Perhaps from the air. Like champagne. — If Fred
were here, could he advise me? I don't need advice. There's really
nothing to advise. I'll talk to Herr Dorsday from Presov, I'll touch
him for a loan, I, the high spirited one, the aristocrat, the marchesa,
the beggar, the daughter of the embezzler. How did I get into this
situation? How did I get into this situation? No one can climb like
me, nobody has so much spunk—sporting girl, I should have been
born in England, or a countess.

My dresses hang there in the wardrobe. Is that green loden paid
for yet, Mama? Only a down payment, I believe. I'll put on the black
one. They all stared at me yesterday. Even the pale little man with
the gold pince-nez. I'm not really beautiful, but I'm interesting. I
should have gone on the stage. Bertha has already had three lovers
and no one thinks anything of it. In Düsseldorf it was the bank president. In Hamburg she lived with a married man and had an apartment in the Atlantic, with a bath. I really believe she's proud of it.
They're all stupid. I'll have a hundred lovers, a thousand, why not?
The neckline isn't low enough; if I were married, it could be lower.
— It's a good thing I ran into you, Herr von Dorsday, I've just received a letter from Vienna . . . I'll take the letter along in case of
emergency. Shall I ring for the chambermaid? No, I'll dress myself. I
don't need anyone for the black dress. If I were rich, I'd never travel
without a lady's maid.

I must turn on the lights. It's getting cool. Shut the window. Pull
down the shade? — superfluous. There's no one on the mountain over
there with a telescope. Too bad. — I've just received a letter, Herr
von Dorsday. — Perhaps it would be better after *diner* after all. One
is in a lighter mood. Dorsday too— and I could drink a glass of wine

first. But if the matter were settled before dinner, I would enjoy the
meal more. Pudding à la merveille, fromage et fruits divers. But if
Herr von Dorsday says no? — Or if he even gets fresh? Oh no, no one
has ever got fresh with me yet. Well, Brandel the naval lieutenant,
but he meant nothing by it. — I've got a little slimmer again. It's becoming. — The twilight is staring in. It stares like a ghost. Like a
hundred ghosts. The ghosts rise up from my meadow. How far away
is Vienna? How long have I been away? How alone I am here. I
haven't a friend, male or female. Where are they all? Whom will I
marry? Who will marry the daughter of a swindler? — I've just received a letter, Herr von Dorsday. — "But really, Fräulein Else, it
isn't even worth mentioning. Only yesterday I sold a Rembrandt.
You embarrass me, Fräulein Else." And now he tears a check out of is
checkbook and signs with his gold fountain pen; and tomorrow
morning I go to Vienna with the check. I'll go anyway, even without
the check. I won't stay here any longer. I really couldn't; I really
mustn't. I'm living here as an elegant young lady and papa is standing with one foot in the grave — no, in prison. My next to last pair of
silk stockings. No one will notice the little tear just below the knee.
No one? Who knows? Don't be frivolous, Else. — Bertha is just a slut.
But is Christine the least bit better? Her future husband may look
forward to something. I'm sure mama was always a faithful wife. I
shall not be faithful. I'm high-spirited but I shall not be faithful.
Filous are a danger to me. I'm sure the marchesa has a *filou* for a
lover. If Fred really knew me, his admiration for me would vanish.
— "You could have become anything, Fräulein, a pianist, a bookkeeper, an actress, there is so much potential in you. But you've
always had too easy a time of it." Too easy a time. Ha ha. Fred over-
estimates me. I really have no talent for anything. — Who knows? I
could have got as far as Bertha anyway. But I lack energy. Young
lady of good family. Ha, good family. The father embezzles trust
money. Why do you do this to me, Papa? If you at least got something out of it! But to lose it on the stock exchange! Is it worth the
effort? And the thirty thousand won't help you either. For three
months perhaps. In the long run he'll have to abscond. A year and a
half ago it almost came to that. But then help came. But some day it
will not come — and what will happen to us then? Rudi will go to
Rotterdam to Vanderhulst's bank. But I? A wealthy marriage. Oh, if
I could make that my goal! I am really beautiful today. That's prob-

ably because of my excitement. For whom am I beautiful? Would I
be happier if Fred were here? Oh, Fred is really not for me. Not a
filou! But I would take him if he had money. And then a *filou* would
appear and my undoing would be certain. — You'd really like to be a
filou, Herr von Dorsday? — From a distance you sometimes look like
one. Like a *roué vicomte*, like a Don Juan — with your stupid monocle
and your white flannel suit. But you are still far from being a *filou*.
— Have I everything? Ready for *dîner?* — But how will I spend a
whole hour in case I don't meet Dorsday? If he goes for a walk with
the unhappy Frau Winawer? Oh, she isn't unhappy at all, she doesn't
need thirty thousand gulden. So, I will sit down in the lobby, magnificently in a *fauteuil*, look at the *Illustrated News* and the *Vie pari-
sienne*, cross my legs — they won't see the tear below the knee. Perhaps a millionaire has just arrived. It's you or no one. — I'll take
the white shawl, it suits me well. Carelessly I put it about my superb
shoulders. Who are these superb shoulders for? I could make a man
very happy. If only the right man were here. But I won't have children. I'm not the mother type. Marie Weill is the mother type.
Mama is the mother type, Aunt Irene is the mother type. I have a
noble brow and a beautiful figure. — "If I were allowed to paint you
as I would like to, Fräulein Else." — Yes, you'd like that. I don't even
remember his name any more. It certainly wasn't Titian, so it was a
piece of insolence. — I've just received a letter, Herr von Dorsday.
— A little more powder on the back of my neck and throat, a drop of
verveine on my handkerchief, close the chest, open the window
again, oh, how wonderful! It could draw tears. I'm nervous. Oh, how
can one help being nervous in these circumstances? The box of Veronal is among my chemises. I need new chemises too. That will be a
nuisance again. Oh Lord!

The Cimone is uncanny, gigantic, as if it wanted to fall on me. Not
a star in the sky yet. The air is like champagne. And the fragrance
from the meadows! I'll live in the country. I'll marry a landed propri-
etor and have children. Dr. Froriep was perhaps the only man with
whom I could have been happy. How beautiful those two evenings
were, one after the other, the first at Kniep, and then the one at the
artists' ball. Why did he suddenly vanish — at least as far as I was concerned? Perhaps because of papa? Probably. I'd like to shout a greeting into the air before I go down again among that mob. But to
whom should the greeting go? I'm all alone here. I'm so terribly

alone, no one can imagine how much...Greetings, my beloved.
Who? Greetings, my bridegroom! Who? Greetings, my friend! Who?
— Fred? — Not a bit of it. There, the window will remain open. Even
if it gets cool. Turn out the light. There. — Yes, that's right, the
letter. I must have it with me in case of emergency. The book on the
bedside table, I'll continue reading *Notre Coeur* tonight, absolutely,
no matter what happens. Good evening, most beautiful lady in the
mirror, don't forget me, good-by...

Why do I lock the door? Nothing is ever stolen here. I wonder if
Cissy leaves her door open at night. Or does she unlock it for him
when he knocks? But is it quite certain? Of course it is. Then they lie
together in bed. Disgusting. I won't share a bedroom with my husband and my thousand lovers. — The stairway is completely empty.
Always at this time. My steps echo. I've been here for three weeks. On
the twelfth of August I left Gmunden. Gmunden was boring. Where
did papa get the money to send mama and me to the country? And
Rudi even went away on a four weeks' trip. Lord knows where. He
didn't write twice all that time. I'll never understand our way of life.
True, mama has no more jewelry left. — Why was Fred in Gmunden
only two days? I'm sure he has a girl friend too! Though I can't
imagine that. I can't imagine anything at all. He hasn't written me
for a week. He writes beautiful letters. — But who is that sitting at the
small table? No, it isn't Dorsday, thank Heaven. Now, before dinner,
I really couldn't tell him anything. — Why is the porter looking at me
so strangely? Could he possibly have read mama's special-delivery
letter? I think I'm crazy. I must give him another tip soon. — That
blonde there is dressed for *dîner* too. How can anyone be so stout!
— I'll go outside for a bit and walk up and down in front of the hotel.
Or into the music room? Isn't someone in there playing? A sonata by
Beethoven! How can anyone play a Beethoven sonata here? I'm
neglecting my piano. In Vienna I'll go back to regular practice
again. And begin a different life altogether. We must all do that.
Things must not go on like this. I'll have a serious talk with papa
someday — if there is still time. There will be, there will be. Why have
I never done it before? Everything in our house is settled by a joke
and yet no one feels like joking. Everyone is really afraid of the
others, everyone is alone. Mama is alone because she isn't bright
enough, and knows nothing about anyone, not about me, not about
Rudi, nor about papa. But she doesn't feel it and Rudi doesn't feel it

either. He's really a nice, elegant lad, but at twenty-one he promised more. It will be good for him to go to Holland. But where will I go? I'd like to go away and be able to do what I want to do. If papa absconds to America, I'll go with him. I'm already quite confused. . . . The porter will think I'm mad, the way I'm sitting here on the arm of the chair, staring out into space. I'll light a cigarette. Where's my cigarette case? Upstairs. But where? The Veronal is among my underwear. But where is the cigarette case? Here come Cissy and Paul. Yes, she must get dressed for *diner* at last, otherwise they would have continued to play in the dark. — They don't see me. I wonder what he's saying to her? Why does she laugh so damn stupidly? Would be fun to write an anonymous letter to her husband in Vienna. Could I do such a thing? Never. Who knows? Now they've seen me. I'll nod to them. She's annoyed because I look so attractive. How embarrassed she is.

"*What, Else, you're dressed for dinner already?*" — Why does she say dinner now and not *dîner*? She's not even consistent. — "As you see, Frau Cissy." — "*You really look enchanting, Else, I have a great desire to court you.*" — "Save yourself the trouble, Paul, and give me a cigarette instead." — "*Delighted.*" — "Thank you. How did the singles come out?" — "*Frau Cissy beat me three times in succession.*" — "*He wasn't concentrating, you know. By the way, do you know, Else, that the Crown Prince of Greece is arriving here tomorrow?*" — What do I care about the Crown Prince of Greece? "Oh, really?" O Lord — Dorsday with Frau Winawer! They're bowing. They go on. I returned their bow too courteously. Yes, not the way I usually do. Oh, what sort of person am I! — "*But your cigarette isn't burning, Else?*" — "Well, give me another match then. Thanks." — "*Your shawl is very pretty, Else, it matches your black dress like a dream. But I must change now too.*" — I'd rather she didn't go away, I'm afraid of Dorsday. — "*And the hairdresser is coming at seven. She's wonderful. She's in Milan in winter. Well, adieu, Else, adieu, Paul.*" — "*My respects, madam.*" "Adieu Frau Cissy."

She's gone. Good thing that at least Paul is here. — "*May I sit down beside you for a moment, or am I disturbing your dreams?*" — "Why my dreams? Perhaps my realities." That doesn't really mean anything. I wish he'd go away. For I really must speak to Dorsday. He's still standing there with the unhappy Frau Winawer, he's bored, I can see it on his face, he'd like to come over to me. — "*But are there any realities in which you don't want to be disturbed?"* —What's that he's saying? Let him go to the devil. Why do I smile at him so coquettishly? I don't mean him at all. Dorsday is peering in my direction. Where am I? Where am I? —*"What's wrong with you today, Else?"* —"What do you expect to be wrong?" —*"You're mysterious, demonic, seductive."* —"Don't talk nonsense, Paul." —*"One could really go mad looking at you."* —How dare he? In what sort of tone is he talking to me? He's attractive. The smoke from my cigarette gets caught in his hair. But he's no use to me now. —*"You're sort of looking over my head. But why, Else?"* —I won't answer him at all. He's no use to me now. I'll put on my most insufferable face. Above all, no conversation now. —*"Your thoughts are somewhere else altogether."* —"Could be." He doesn't exist for me. Does Dorsday notice that I am waiting for him? I won't look over in his direction, but I know that he's looking over here. —*"Well, good-by, Else."* —Thank Heaven. He's kissing my hand. He never does that. "Adieu, Paul." Where did I get that melting voice? He's going, the *filou*. Probably he still has to make arrangements with Cissy for tonight. Hope you have a good time. I'll drape the shawl around my shoulders and stand up and go out in front of the hotel. Of course it's probably a little cool by now. Too bad I didn't bring my coat. —Oh, I hung it up in the porter's room this morning. I feel Dorsday's eyes on the back of my neck, through the shawl. Frau Winawer is going up to her room now. How do I know that? Telepathy. "Please, porter." —*"You wish your coat, Fräulein?"* —"Yes, please." —*"It gets a little cool these evenings, Fräulein. It comes so suddenly here."* —"Thank you." Shall I really go out in front of the hotel? Of course, what else? At least as far as the door. Now they're coming one after the other. The gentleman with the gold pince-nez. The tall, blond man with the green vest. They're all looking at me. The little woman from Geneva is pretty. No, she's from Lausanne. It really isn't so cool at all.

"*Good evening, Fräulein Else.*" —For Heaven's sake, it's he. I'll say nothing about papa. Not a word. Not till after dinner. Or I'll go to Vienna tomorrow. I'll go to Dr. Fiala personally. Why didn't this occur to me at once? I'll turn around with a look as if I didn't know who is standing behind me. "Ah, Herr von Dorsday." —*"You want to go for a walk, Fräulein Else?"* —"Oh, not exactly a walk, just up and down a little before dinner." —*"It's almost an hour till then."* —"Really?" It isn't cool at all. the mountains are blue. It would be gay if he suddenly proposed to me. — *"There really isn't a more beautiful spot in the world than this."* — "Do you think so, Herr von Dorsday? But please don't say that the air is like champagne." — *"No, Fräulein Else, I say that only when it's above six thousand feet. And here we are scarcely two thousand above sea level."* — "Does it make that much difference?" — *"But of course. Have you ever been at Engadine?"* — "No, never. But the air is really like champagne there?" — *"One could almost say so. But champagne is not my favorite drink. I prefer this region. If only because of the wonderful forests."* — How boring he is. Doesn't he realize it? He obviously doesn't really know what to talk to me about. It would be simpler with a married woman. You tell her something slightly indecent, and the conversation is launched. — *"Are you staying here in San Martino a while longer, Fräulein Else?"* — Idiotic. Why do I look at him so coquettishly? And he's already smiling in that certain way. Really, how stupid men are! "That depends partly on aunt's plans." Isn't true at all. Of course I can go to Vienna by myself. "Probably till the tenth." — *"I suppose your mama is still in Gmunden?"* — "No, Herr von Dorsdays. She's back in Vienna. Has been for three weeks now. Papa is in Vienna too. He took scarcely a week's vacation this year. I believe the Erbesheimer case is giving him a lot of work." — *"I can believe that. But your papa is probably the only man who can free Erbesheimer. . . . The fact that the thing has become a civil action is a success in itself."* — That's good, that's good. "It's pleasant for me to hear that you, too, have such a favorable premonition." — *"Premonition? How do you mean?"* — "Well, that papa will win the case for Erbesheimer." — *"I didn't mean to say that with any certainty."* — What, he's retreating already? He's not going to succeed. "Oh, I place some value on premonitions and forebodings. Just imagine, Herr von Dorsday, only today I received a letter from home." That wasn't very skillful. He has a slightly puzzled look on his face. Keep going, don't gag. He's a good old friend of papa's. On. On. Now or never. "Herr von Dorsday, you've just spoken so warmly of papa, it would really be mean of me if I weren't altogether frank with you." What sort of calf's eyes is he making? Oh dear, he notices something. Keep going, keep going. "I mean, the letter mentions you, too, Herr von Dorsday. I mean the letter is from mama." — *"Really."* — "Really a very sad letter. Of course you know the situation in our home, Herr von Dorsday." — For Heaven's sake, I actually have tears

in my voice. Keep going, keep going, there's no turning back now.
Thank Heaven. "In short, Herr von Dorsday, we've come to *that*
point again." —Now he would most of all like to vanish. "It's a—
trifle. Really only a trifle, Herr von Dorsday. And yet, as mama
writes, everything is at stake." I'm talking away as stupidly as a cow.
—"*But do calm yourself, Fräulein Else.*" —He said that nicely. But
he needn't touch my arm. —"*Well then, Fräulein Else, what's really
wrong? What does mama's sad letter say?*" —"Herr von Dorsday,
papa"—my knees are trembling. "Mama writes me that papa—"
—"*But for Heaven's sake, Else, what's wrong with you? Won't you—
here's a bench. May I put your coat about your shoulders? It's a bit
cool.*" —"Thank you, Herr von Dorsday; oh, it's nothing, nothing
special at all." There, now I'm suddenly sitting here on the bench.
Who is that lady who's passing there? Don't know her. If only I didn't
have to go on talking. The way he looks at me! How could you ask
this of me, Papa? That wasn't right, Papa. But now it's done. I
should have waited till after dinner. —"*Well, Fräulein Else?*" —His
monocle is dangling. It looks stupid. Shall I answer him? But I must.
Well then, quickly, and get it over with. What can happen to me,
after all? He's a friend of papa's. "Oh Lord, Herr von Dorsday,
you're an old friend of the family, aren't you?" I said that very well.
"And you will probably not be surprised if I tell you that papa finds
himself once more in a really unpleasant situation." How strange my
voice sounds. Is this me talking? Am I dreaming perhaps? I'm sure I
now have a very different face from my usual one. —"*Of course I'm
not excessively surprised. You're quite right about that, dear Fräulein Else—though I regret it profoundly.*" —Why do I look up to him
so imploringly? Smile, smile. You'll manage it. —"*I feel such a sincere friendship for your papa, for all of you.*" —He must not look at
me like that, it's indecent. I'll talk to him in a different way and not
smile. I must behave with more dignity. "Well, Herr von Dorsday,
you could now have an opportunity to demonstrate your friendship
for my father." Thank Heaven, I have my old voice again. "You must
know, Herr von Dorsday, it seems that all our relatives and acquaintances—the majority of them are not back in Vienna yet—or mama
would not have hit on the idea. —Recently, I must tell you, I casually
mentioned your presence here in San Martino in a letter to mama—
among other things, of course." —"*I gathered, Fräulein Else, that I
don't constitute the sole theme of your correspondence with your*

mama." —Why is he pressing his knees against mine while he's standing here before me? Oh, I'll put up with it. What does it matter?
Once you've sunk this low. "This is the way things are. It's Dr. Fiala,
who seems to be making special difficulties for papa this time."
—"*Ah, Dr. Fiala.*" —Obviously he, too, knows what he ought to
think of this Fiala. "Yes, Dr. Fiala. And the sum in question is to be
in his hands by noon on the fifth, that is the day after tomorrow, or
rather it must be in his hands if Baron Höning is not to—why, just
think, the baron asked papa to come and see him in private, for he
loves him very much." Why am I talking about Höning, that
wouldn't have been necessary at all. —"*You mean, Else, that otherwise an arrest will be inevitable?*" —Why does he say that so harshly?
I won't answer, I'll merely nod. "Yes." Now I've said yes after all.
—"*Hm, that's really—bad, that's really very—this highly gifted, brilliant man. —And what is the sum involved, Fräulein Else?*" —But
why is he smiling? He thinks it's bad, and he smiles. What does he
mean by that smile? That it doesn't matter how much the amount is?
And suppose he says no! If he says no, I'll kill myself. Well then, I'm
to mention the sum. "What, Herr von Dorsday? I haven't said how
much yet? A million." —Why do I say that? Surely this is no time for
joking? But when I tell him later how much less it really is, he'll be
glad. How his eyes open! Does he actually think it's possible that papa
would ask him for a million? —"Excuse me, Herr von Dorsday, for
joking at such a moment. I really don't feel like joking." Yes, yes,
keep pressing your knees, you have a right to take that liberty. "Of
course it isn't a million that's involved, all in all it's thirty thousand
gulden, Herr von Dorsday, which must be in Dr. Fiala's hands by
noon the day after tomorrow. Yes, mama writes me that papa has
made every possible effort, but, as I said, the relatives who might be
approached are not in Vienna." —Oh Lord, how I'm humiliating
myself. —"Otherwise papa would naturally never have dreamed of
appealing to you, Herr von Dorsday, that is to say, to ask me to do
so." —Why is he silent? Why doesn't he move a muscle? Why doesn't
he say yes? Where is the checkbook, and the fountain pen? For Heav-
en's sake, he's not going to say no! Shall I fall on my knees before
him? Oh Lord! Oh Lord!—

"*You said the fifth, Fräulein Else?*" —Thank Heaven, he's speaking. "Yes, the day after tomorrow, Herr von Dorsday, at twelve noon.
So it would be necessary—I believe it could hardly be settled by letter

this late." — "*Of course not, Fräulein Else, we'd certainly have to do it by telegraphing.*" — We, that's good, that's very good. — *Well, that's the least important part of it. How much did you say, Else?*" — But he heard me, why then does he torture me? "Thirty thousand, Herr von Dorsday. Really a ridiculous amount." Why did I say that? How stupid! But he's smiling. Stupid girl, he's thinking. He's smiling quite amiably. Papa is saved. He would have loaned him fifty thousand too, and we could have gotten all sorts of things for ourselves ...I would have bought myself new chemises. How cheap I am! That's what you turn into. — "*Not so utterly ridiculous, dear child—*" — Why does he say "dear child"? Is that good or bad?— "*— as you imagine. Even thirty thousand gulden have to be earned.*" — "Pardon me, Herr von Dorsday, I didn't mean it that way. I only thought, how sad it is that papa should—for such an amount, such a trifle—" Oh Lord, I'm getting entangled again. "You just can't imagine, Herr von Dorsday—even though you have some insight into our situation, how terrible it is for me, and especially for mama." He's putting one foot on the bench. Is that supposed to be elegant—or what? — "*Oh, I can imagine it all right, dear Else.*" — How his voice sounds, quite different, strange! — "*And I have sometimes thought to myself: a pity, a pity about this brilliant man.*" — Why does he say: a pity? Won't he let me have the money? No, he only means it in a general way. Why doesn't he say yes once and for all? Or does he take that for granted? How he looks at me! Why doesn't he go on talking? Oh, because the two Hungarian women are passing. Now he's at least standing once more in a decent posture, no longer with his foot on the bench. His tie is too loud for an elderly gentleman. Does his mistress choose them for him? Not especially refined, "between you and me," mama writes. Thirty thousand gulden! But I'm smiling at him! But why am I smiling? Oh, I'm a coward! — "*And if one could at least assume, my dear Fräulein Else, that this sum would really accomplish anything? — But, you're such a clever creature, Else, what would these thirty thousand gulden be? A drop of water on a hot stone.*" — For Heaven's sake, he won't advance the money? I must not show such a frightened face. Everything is at stake. Now I must say something sensible and say it energetically. "Oh no, Herr von Dorsday, this time it would not be a drop of water on a hot stone. The Erbesheimer case is impending, don't forget that, Herr von Dorsday, and it is as good as won this very day. Why, you yourself thought so,

Herr von Dorsday. And papa has other cases too. And apart from that, I intend—you mustn't laugh, Herr von Dorsday—to talk to papa, very seriously. He thinks something of me. I dare say if anyone is in a position to exercise a certain influence on him, I'm the most likely person—" —"*You really are a touching, a delightful creature, Fräulein Else.*" His voice is ringing again. How disgusting it is when their voices begin to ring, these men. I don't like it in Fred either. —"*A delightful creature indeed.*" —Why does he say "indeed"? That's absurd. That's really said only in the Burgtheater. —"*But, however much I should like to share your optimism—once the cart has gone that far—*" —"It isn't that, Herr von Dorsday. If I didn't have faith in papa, if I weren't wholly convinced that these thirty thousand gulden—" I don't know what more I should say. After all, I can't beg from him outright. He's considering. Obviously. Perhaps he doesn't know Fiala's address? Nonsense. The situation is impossible. I'm sitting here like a poor sinner. He stands before me in silence, boring his monocle into my forehead. I'll stand up now, that'll be best. I will not let anyone treat me like this. Let papa kill himself. I'll kill myself too. This life is a disgrace. The best thing would be to throw myself off that rock over there and it would all be over. It would serve you right, all of you. I'll stand up. —"*Fräulein Else.*" —"Pardon me, Herr von Dorsday, for troubling you at all under these circumstances. Of course, I can completely understand your negative attitude." There, it's over, I'm going. —"*Stay, Fräulein Else.*" —Stay, he says? Why should I stay? He'll give the money. Yes, quite definitely. He must, of course. But I will not sit down again. I'll remain standing as if it were only for half a second. I'm a bit taller than he. —"*You haven't waited to hear my answer, Else. Once before, pardon me, Else, for mentioning it in this connection—*" —He doesn't have to say Else so often— "—*I was in a position to help your papa out of an embarrassing situation. To be sure, with a—still more ridiculous amount than this time, and I did not really flatter myself that I would ever see that sum again—and so there is really no ground for refusing you my help this time. And especially when a young girl like you, Else, when you yourself come before me as an intermediary.*" —What is he driving at? His voice no longer "rings." Or it has a different "ring." How is he looking at me? He'd better be careful!! —"*Well, Else, I'm ready—Dr. Fiala shall have the thirty thousand gulden at noon the day after tomorrow—on one condition.*" — He must not go on talking, he must not. "Herr von Dorsday, I, I personally, will guarantee that my father will repay this sum as soon as he has received his fee from Erbesheimer. The Erbesheimers haven't paid a cent so far. Not even a retainer — mama herself writes me —" — "*Never mind, Else, one should never take over a guarantee for another person, not even for oneself.*" — What does he want? His voice is "ringing" again. Never has a man looked at me that way. I suspect what he's driving at. He'll be sorry! — "*Would I have thought it possible, an hour ago, that I would permit myself to even think of stipulating a condition in an affair of this sort? Yet now I'm doing it. Yes, Else, I'm only human after all, and it isn't my fault that you're so beautiful, Else.*" — What does he want? What does he want? — "*Perhaps I would have asked the same thing of you today or tomorrow that I'm going to ask now, even if you hadn't asked me for a million, pardon me, thirty thousand gulden. But of course, under different circumstances you would hardly have granted me the opportunity to talk to you in private for so long.*" — "Oh, I've really taken too much of your time already, Herr von Dorsday." I said that well. Fred would be satisfied. What's that? He's taking my hand? How dare he? — "*Haven't you really known it for a long time, Else?*" — He must let go of my hand! Well, thank Heaven, he's letting go. Not so close, not so close. — "*You couldn't be a woman, Else, if you hadn't noticed it. Je vous désire.*" — He could have said it in German just as well, M. le vicomte. — "*Must I say more?*" — "You have said too much already, Herr von Dorsday." And I'm still standing here. But why? I'll go, go without a good-by. — "*Else! Else!*" — Now he's beside me again. — "*Pardon me, Else. I too was only joking, just as you were about the million. I don't make my demand as high either—as you feared, I must unfortunately use that expression—so that the lesser demand will perhaps be a pleasant surprise to you. Please stop, Else.*" — I'm really stopping. Why? Here we stand facing each other. Shouldn't I simply have slapped his face? Isn't there still time to do so? The two Englishmen are passing. This would be the right moment. For that very reason. Then why don't I do it? I'm a coward, I'm crushed, I'm humiliated. What will he want in return for the million? A kiss perhaps? That could be discussed. A million is to thirty thousand as—there are some funny equations. — "*If you should ever really need a million, Else—though I'm not a rich man— we'll see about it. But this time I'll be modest, like you. And this time, I want nothing else, Else, except—to see you."* —Is he crazy? But he is seeing me. Oh, that's what he means, that! Why don't I slap his face, the scoundrel? Did I turn red or pale? You want to see me naked? Many would like that. I'm beautiful when I'm naked. Why don't I slap his face? His face is as big as a giant's. Why so close, you scoundrel? I don't want your breath on my cheeks. Why don't I simply leave him standing here? Am I held spellbound by his eyes? We're looking into each other's eyes like mortal enemies. I would like to call him a scoundrel, but I can't. Or is it that I don't want to? —*"You look at me, Else, as if I were insane. Perhaps I am a little, for there is a magic emanating from you, Else, which you yourself probably do not suspect. You must feel, Else, that my request implies no insult. Yes, I say request, although it looks desperately like black mail. But I am no blackmailer, I'm only a human being who has had much experience—and, among other things, I have learned this: that everything in the world has its price and that a man who gives away his money when he is in a position to receive value for it is an utter fool. And—what I want to buy for myself this time, Else, though it's much, won't make you any poorer for selling it. And it will remain a secret between you and me, Else, I swear it to you by— by all the charms through the revelation of which you would make me happy."* —Where did he learn to talk like this? It sounds as if it came out of a book. —*"And I swear to you, too, that I—shall make no use of the situation not provided for in our contract. I ask nothing more of you than to be permitted to stand in devotion before your beauty for a quarter of an hour. My room is on the same floor as yours, Else, number sixty-five, easy to remember. The Swedish tennis player you talked about today was just sixty-five years old, wasn't he?"* —He's crazy! Why do I let him talk on? I'm paralyzed. —*"But if, for some reason, it doesn't suit you to visit me in room number sixty-five, Else, I propose a little walk after dinner. There's a clearing in the forest, I discovered it quite by chance recently, scarcely five minutes away from our hotel. —It will be a wonderful summer night tonight, almost warm, and the starlight will make a glorious gown for you."* —He talks to me as to a slave. I'll spit in his face. —*"Don't give me an immediate answer, Else. Think it over. After dinner you will kindly impart your decision to me."* —Why does he say "impart"? What a stupid word: impart. —*"Think it over quite calmly. You will perhaps feel that it is not simply a bargain that I propose to you."* —What else, you unequivocal rascal! —*"Possibly you realize that you are talking to a man who is rather lonely and not especially happy and who perhaps deserves a little indulgence."* —Affected scoundrel. Talks like a bad actor. His well-manicured fingers look like claws. No, no, I will not. Then why don't I say so? Take your life, Papa! What does he want with my hand? My arm is quite limp. He raises my hand to his lips. Hot lips. Phew! My hand is cold. I feel like knocking his hat off. Ha, how funny that would be. Through with your kissing soon, you scoundrel? —The arc lamps in front of the hotel are already lit. Two windows on the fourth floor are open. The one where the curtain is stirring is mine. Up on the clothespress there is something shining. There's nothing up there, it's only the brass edging. —*"Well then, good-by, Else."* —I'll make no reply. I stand here motionless. He looks into my eyes. My face is impenetrable. He knows nothing. He doesn't know whether I'll come or not. I don't know either. I only know that everything is finished. I'm half dead. There he goes. Slightly bowed. Scoundrel! He feels my eyes on the back of his neck. Whom is he greeting? Two ladies. As if he were a count, that's how he greets them. Paul must challenge him to a duel and kill him. Or Rudi. What does he think, anyway? Shameless fellow! Never, no never. There's no other way for you, Papa, you must take your life. —Those two are obviously coming from an excursion. Both attractive, he and she. Will they still have time to change before dinner? I'm sure they're on their honeymoon, or perhaps not even married. I'll never go on a honeymoon. Thirty thousand gulden. No, no, no! Aren't there thirty thousand gulden in the world? I'll go to Fiala. I'll manage it somehow. Mercy, mercy, Dr. Fiala. "With pleasure, dear lady. Will you please go to my bedroom?" —Please do me a favor, Paul, ask your father for thirty thousand gulden. Tell him you have gambling debts, otherwise you'll have to shoot yourself. "Gladly, dear cousin. My room is number so and so, I'll be expecting you at midnight." Oh, Herr von Dorsday, how modest you are. For the present. Now he's changing. Dinner jacket. Well then, let's decide. Meadow in the moonlight or room No. 65? Will he accompany me to the woods in his dinner jacket?

There's still time before dinner. Go for a little walk and think the matter over calmly. I'm a lonely old man, ha ha. Heavenly air, like champagne. Not cool at all now—thirty thousand . . . thirty thousand . . . I must look very attractive now against this spacious landscape.

Too bad there are no more people outside. That gentleman over there at the edge of the forest obviously likes me very much. O sir, I am far more beautiful naked, the price is ridiculously small, thirty thousand gulden. Perhaps you'll bring your friends along, then it will be cheaper. I hope you have only good-looking friends, more attractive and younger than Herr von Dorsday? Do you know Herr von Dorsday? He's a scoundrel—a rascal with a "ringing" voice...

So think it over, think it over.... There's a human life at stake. Papa's life. But no, he won't take his life, he'd rather let himself be locked up. Three years of hard labor, or five. He's been living in this permanent anxiety for five or ten years now...trust funds...and mother in the same state. And I too, as a matter of fact. —Before whom will I have to strip next time? Or shall we, for the sake of simplicity, stick to Herr von Dorsday? His present mistress is not refined, you know—"between you and me." He would certainly prefer me. It's by no means so certain that I'm much more refined. Don't put on airs, Fräulein Else, I could tell tales about you...a certain dream, for instance, which you have had three times already—you didn't even tell your friend Bertha about it. And she can really take a lot. And then, how was it this year in Gmunden, at six o'clock in the morning on the balcony, my superior Fräulein Else? Perhaps you didn't notice the two young people in the canoe who were staring at you? True, they couldn't make out my face clearly from the lake, but they certainly noticed that I was in my chemise. And I was glad of it. Oh, more than glad. I was as though intoxicated. I stroked my hips with both hands and pretended to myself that I wasn't being watched. And the canoe did not stir from the spot. Yes, that's the way I am, that's the way I am. A tramp, yes. They all feel it, of course. Paul feels it too. Of course—he's a woman's doctor, isn't he? And the naval lieutenant felt it too, and the painter too. Only Fred, the stupid fellow, doesn't feel it. That's why he loves me, of course. But I wouldn't be naked before him of all people, never, never. I would find no pleasure in it at all. I'd feel ashamed. But before the *filou* with the Roman head—I'd love it. Before him best of all. Even if I had to die right after it. But of course, it isn't necessary to die right after it. One can survive it. Bertha has survived even more. I'm sure Cissy lies naked with Paul when he steals to her through the hotel corridors, as I shall steal to Herr von Dorsday tonight.

No, no. I don't want to. To anyone else—but not to him. To Paul, for all I care. Or I'll pick out a man at dinner tonight. It doesn't matter, after all. Only I really can't tell everyone that I want thirty thousand gulden for it. For then I'd be like a woman from the Kärntnerstrasse. No, I will not sell myself. Never. I'll never sell myself. I'll give myself. Yes, if I ever find the right man, I'll give myself. But I will not sell myself. I'll be a tramp, but not a whore. You have miscalculated, Herr von Dorsday. And papa too. Yes, he has miscalculated. He must have foreseen it. For he does know people. And he certainly knows Herr von Dorsday. He must surely have been able to figure out that Herr von Dorsday wouldn't give anything away. — Otherwise, he could have telegraphed or come here himself. But this way was more convenient and more certain, wasn't it, Papa? If one has such a pretty daughter, why go to prison? And mama, in her stupidity, sits down and writes the letter. Papa did not dare. If he had, it would have struck me immediately. But you won't succeed. No, you speculated too confidently with my affection as a child, Papa, counted too securely on the fact that I would rather put up with any baseness than let you suffer the consequences of your criminal irresponsibility. For you are a genius. Herr von Dorsday says so, everyone says so. But what good is that to me? Fiala is a nonentity, but he doesn't embezzle trust funds; even Waldheim cannot be mentioned in the same breath as you.... who was it that said that? Dr. Froriep. 'Your papa is a genius.' — And I've only heard him speak once! Last year in jurors' court — for the first and last time! Marvelous! The tears ran down my cheeks. And the wretched fellow he was defending was acquitted. Perhaps he wasn't such a wretched fellow at all. At any rate, he merely stole, he didn't embezzle trust funds to play baccarat and speculate in stocks. And now papa himself will stand before the jurors. People will read about it in all the newspapers. Second day of the trial, third day of the trial; the counsel for the defense rose for the rebuttal. I wonder who will be his counsel? Not a genius. Nothing will save him. Unanimous verdict of guilty. Sentenced to five years. Stones, prison dress, hair cropped close. We may visit him once a month. I'll ride out with mama, third class. For, of course, we'll have no money. No one will lend us any. A small flat in Lerchenfelderstrasse, like the one I visited the seamstress in ten years ago. We'll bring him some food. But where will we get it? We have nothing ourselves. Uncle Victor will settle an annuity on us. Three hundred gulden per month. Rudi will be in Holland with

Vanderhulst — if they still have any interest in him. The children of a jailbird! A novel by Temme, in three volumes. Papa receives us in a striped convict's suit. He doesn't look angry, merely sad. He just can't look angry. — Else, if you had got the money for me that time, that's what he'll think, but he will say nothing. He won't have the heart to reproach me. He's a kind soul, only irresponsible. His evil fate is a passion for gambling. He can't help it, of course, it's a kind of insanity. Perhaps they'll acquit him because he's insane. He didn't think of the consequences of the letter either. Perhaps it didn't even occur to him that Dorsday might use the opportunity to request such a vile thing from me. He's a good friend of the family, he has loaned papa eight thousand gulden once before. How can you suspect such a thing of a man? I'm sure papa tried everything else first. What he must have suffered before he asked mamma to write this letter! He went from one person to the next, from Warsdorf to Burin, from Burin to Wertheimstein and Heaven knows to whom else. I'm sure he went to Uncle Karl too. And they all left him in the lurch. All his so-called friends. And now Dorsday is his hope, his last hope. And if the money doesn't appear, he'll kill himself. Of course he'll kill himself. He certainly will not let himself be locked up. Imprisonment pending trial, hearing, jury court, prison, prison dress. No, no! When the warrant is sworn out, he'll shoot or hang himself. He'll hang from the window sash. They'll send someone over from the house across the street, the locksmith will have to open the door, and it will be my fault. And he's sitting with mama, smoking a Havana cigar, in the same room in which he will be hanging the day after tomorrow. Where does he get those Havana cigars? I hear him talking as he soothes mama. "You may depend on it, Dorsday will remit the money. Just remember, I saved him a large sum of money this winter through my intervention. And then the Erbesheimer case is coming up. . . ." Really! — I hear him talking. Telepathy! Remarkable. I see Fred at this moment too. He's walking with a girl past the casino in the city park. She's wearing a light blue blouse and light-colored shoes and has a slightly husky voice. I know all this very precisely. When I get to Vienna I'll ask Fred if he was with his girl in the city park on the third of September between seven-thirty and eight o'clock in the evening.

Where to now? What's wrong with me? Almost total darkness. How beautiful and quiet. Not a soul far and wide. By now they're all

sitting at dinner. Telepathy? No, this is no telepathy. I heard the
gong before, didn't I? Where's Else? Paul will think. They will all be
surprised if I don't appear for the hors d'oeuvres. They'll send someone up to my room. What's wrong with Else? She's usually so punctual. The two gentlemen beside the window will think: Where is that
beautiful young girl with the reddish-blond hair today? And Herr
von Dorsday will be frightened. I'm sure he's a coward. Calm yourself, Herr von Dorsday, nothing is going to happen to you. You know
how much I despise you. If I wished it, you'd be a dead man tomorrow night. — I'm convinced that Paul would challenge him to a duel
if I told him about it. I grant you your life, Herr von Dorsday.

How immensely broad the meadows are and how terribly black the
mountains. Almost no stars. Yes there are—three, four—they're already increasing. And the woods behind me are so silent. Beautiful
to sit here on the bench at the edge of the forest. The hotel so far
away, so far, and it casts such a fairylike glow in this direction. And
what rogues live in it. Oh no, human beings, poor humans, I feel so
sorry for them all. I feel sorry for the marchesa too, I don't know
why, and for Frau Winawer and the nurse of Cissy's little girl. She
doesn't sit at the table d'hôte, she has had dinner earlier, with Fritzie.
"What's wrong with Else?" Cissy asks. "What, she's not in her room
either?" They're all frightened for me, I'm sure of that. Only I am
not frightened. Yes, here I am in Martino di Castrozza, sitting on a
bench at the edge of the forest, and the air is like champagne and I
really believe I'm crying. Yes, but why am I crying? There's really no
reason for crying. It's my nerves. I must control myself. I must not let
myself go like this. But crying isn't at all unpleasant. Crying always
makes me feel better. When I visited our old French woman in the
hospital, the one who died later, I cried too. And at grandmama's
funeral, and when Bertha went to Nuremberg, and when Agatha's
little child died, and in the theater at *Camille*. Who will cry when
I'm dead? Oh, how beautiful it would be to be dead. I'm lying in
state in the drawing room. Candles are burning. Long candles.
Twelve long candles. Downstairs the hearse is already waiting. People stand in front of the house. How old was she? Only nineteen.
Really, only nineteen? —Just imagine, her papa is in prison. But
then why did she take her life? Because of an unhappy love for a
filou. Oh, what nonsense! She was going to have a baby, No, she fell
down from the Cimone. It was an accident. Good day, Herr von

Dorsday, you're paying your last respects to little Else too? Little Else, the old woman says. —But why? Of course I must pay her my last respects. It was I who inflicted the first disgrace on her. Oh, it was worth it, Frau Winawer, I've never seen so beautiful a body before. It only cost me thirty millions. A Rubens costs three times as much. She poisoned herself with hashish. She only wanted to have beautiful visions, but she took too much and didn't wake again. But why does he have a red monocle, that Herr von Dorsday? Whom is he waving at with his handkerchief? Mama is coming down the steps and is kissing his hand. Shame, shame. Now they are whispering together. I can understand nothing, because I'm lying in state. The wreath of violets about my forehead is from Paul. The ribbons reach down to the floor. No one dares enter the room. I think I'd do better to get up and look out the window. What a large blue lake! A hundred boats with yellow sails. —The waves glitter. So much sun. Regatta. All the gentlemen are wearing rowing sweaters. The ladies are in bathing suits. That's indecent. They think I'm naked. How stupid they are! I'm wearing deep mourning because I'm dead. I'll prove it to you. I'll lie right down on the bier again. But where is it? It's gone. They've taken it away. They've absconded with it. That's why papa is in prison. But they've put him on three years' probation! All the jurors have been bribed by Fiala. I will now go to the cemetery on foot, in that way mama will save the funeral expenses. We must be economical. I'll walk so fast that no one can follow me. Oh, how fast I can walk! They all stop in the streets, wondering. How dare anyone look that way at someone who is dead? It's very annoying. I'll go across the field, it's all blue with forget-me-nots and violets. The naval officers are forming a lane. Good morning, gentlemen. Open the door, Sir Matador. Don't you recognize me? Why, I'm the dead girl.... You don't have to kiss my hand because of that.... But where is my grave? Have they absconded with that too? Thank Heaven, it isn't the cemetery at all. Why, that's the park in Menton. Papa will be glad that I'm not buried. I'm not afraid of snakes. If only they don't bite my foot. Oh dear!

But what is going on? Where am I? Have I been asleep? Yes. I've been asleep. I must have dreamed too. My feet feel so cold. My right foot feels cold. But why? There's a small tear in my stocking at the ankle. But why am I still sitting in the forest? The dinner bell must have sounded long ago. The *diner* bell.

Oh Lord, where was I? I was so far away. What was it I dreamed, anyway? I think I was already dead. And I had no worries and didn't have to torment myself. Thirty thousand, thirty thousand . . . I don't have them yet. I must earn them first. And here I'm sitting alone at the edge of the forest. You can still see the hotel lights from here. I must go back. It's frightful that I must go back. But there's no more time to lose. Herr von Dorsday is awaiting my decision. Decision. No. No, Herr von Dorsday; short and sweet—no. You were joking of course, Herr von Dorsday. Yes, that's what I'll tell him. Oh, that's excellent. Your joke was not very elegant, Herr von Dorsday, but I will forgive you. I will telegraph papa tomorrow morning, Herr von Dorsday, that the money will be in Dr. Fiala's hands punctually. Wonderful. That's what I'll tell him. There'll be no way out for him, he'll have to send the money. Have to? Does he have to? But why does he have to? And if he did it, he would take vengeance in some way. He would arrange matters in such a way that the money would arrive too late. Or he would send the money and tell everyone that he had had me. But he won't send the money at all. No, Fräulein Else, that wasn't our agreement. You may wire your papa whatever you please, I won't send the money. You are not to believe, Fräulein Else, that I'm going to let myself be outwitted by some little girl, I, vicomte de Presov.*

I must walk carefully. The road is quite dark. Strange, I feel better than I did before. Nothing has really changed, yet I feel better. What was it I dreamed, anyway? About a matador? What sort of matador? It's really farther to the hotel than I thought. I'm sure they're all still sitting at dinner. I will sit down quietly at the table and say that I had had a migraine, and order late. Herr von Dorsday will eventually come to me himself and tell me that the whole thing was only a joke. "Excuse me, Fräulein Else, pardon the bad joke, I have already wired to my bank." But he will not say it. He hasn't wired. Everything is still exactly as it was before. He's waiting. Herr von Dorsday is waiting. No, I don't want to see him. I can't see him any more. I don't want to see anyone any more. I don't want to go to the hotel any more, I don't want to go home any more, I don't want to go to Vienna, I don't want to go to anyone, not to a single person, not to papa, or mama, or Rudi, or Fred, or Bertha, or to Aunt Irene.

*Prešov, a town in eastern Slovakia, originally founded by Germans and containing a German minority. Else implies that Dorsday's patent of nobility is spurious.

She's the best of them all, she would understand everything. But I'll have nothing more to do with her, or with anyone else. If I could practice magic, I would be in an entirely different part of the world. On some splendid ship in the Mediterranean—but not alone. With Paul, for example. Yes, I could picture that quite well. Or I would live in a villa by the sea, and we would lie on the marble steps leading down to the water, and he would hold me close in his arms and bite my lips, as Albert did two years ago at the piano, the shameless fellow. No. I'd like to lie alone on the marble steps by the sea and wait. And finally one man would come, or several men, and I could choose, and the ones I spurned would throw themselves into the sea in despair. Or they would have to be patient till the next day. Oh, what a delightful life that would be. Why else do I have my glorious shoulders and my beautiful slender legs? And what am I in the world for anyway? And it would serve them quite right, all of them, for they have merely brought me up to sell myself, in one way or another. They would not hear of my becoming an actress. They laughed at me. And they would have found it quite acceptable last year if I had married Wilomitzer, the theater director who will soon be fifty. Only they didn't urge me. So papa really must have been embarrassed. But mama threw out some plain hints.

How gigantic it stands there, the hotel, like an immense, illuminated magic castle. Everything is so gigantic. The mountains too. They could make you feel afraid. They've never been so black before. The moon isn't out yet. It will appear only for the performance, for the great performance on the meadow, when Herr von Dorsday orders his slave girl to dance naked. What do I care for Herr von Dorsday? Well, Mademoiselle Else, what a fuss you're making. Weren't you prepared to run off, to become the mistress of strange men, one after the other? And the trifle that Herr von Dorsday demands means so much to you? You are prepared to sell yourself for a pearl necklace, for beautiful clothes, for a villa at the sea? And your father's life isn't worth that much to you? This would be just the right beginning. It would be at the same time the justification for everything else. It was you, I could say, you who brought me to it, all of you are responsible for the fact that I have turned out this way, not merely papa and mama. Rudi, too, is responsible, and Fred, and all of them, all of them, because no one cares. A little bit of tenderness when you look attractive, and a bit of concern when you have a fever,

and they send you to school, and at home you learn piano and
French, and in the summer you go to the country, and for your birthday you get presents, and at dinner they talk about all sorts of things.
But what goes on inside me and what stirs within me and is afraid,
have you ever worried about that? Sometimes there was a suspicion of
it in papa's eyes. But a very fleeting one. And then his profession occupied him at once, and cares, and gambling on the stock exchange
— and probably some woman very much on the quiet, "not very refined, between you and me" — and I was alone again. Well, what
would you do, Papa, what would you do today if I weren't here?

Here I stand, yes, here I stand in front of the hotel. — Terrible to
have to go in there, to see all those people, Herr von Dorsday, my
aunt, Cissy. How beautiful it was before on the bench at the edge of
the forest, when I was already dead. Matador — if only I could remember what — it was a regatta — right — and I was watching it from
the window. But who was the matador? — If only I weren't so tired,
so terribly tired. And I'm supposed to stay up till midnight and then
slip into Herr von Dorsday's room? Perhaps I'll meet Cissy in the corridor. Does she wear anything under her dressing gown when she goes
to him? It's hard if you're not well versed in such matters. Shouldn't I
ask her advice, Cissy's advice? Of course I wouldn't tell her that it's
Dorsday, but she'd have to suppose that I have a rendezvous at night
with one of the attractive young men here in the hotel. For instance,
the tall blond one with the glowing eyes. But he's no longer here. He
vanished suddenly. Why, I haven't even thought of him till this
moment. But unfortunately it isn't the tall blond one with the glowing eyes; it isn't Paul either, it's Herr von Dorsday. Well, how shall I
do it? What shall I say to him? Simply yes? But I really can't go to
Herr von Dorsday's room. I'm sure he has lots of elegant bottles on
his washstand and the room smells of French perfume. No, not to his
room for all the world. Better outside. There he doesn't concern me
at all. The sky is so high and the meadow is so big. I don't have to
think of Herr von Dorsday at all. I don't even have to look at him.
And if he should dare to touch me he would get a kick from my
naked feet. Oh, if only it were another man, any other man. He
could have everything, everything from me tonight, any other man,
except Dorsday. And he's the one! He's the one! How his eyes will
pierce and bore. He will stand there with his monocle and grin. But
no, he won't grin. He will put on an aristocratic face. Elegant. He's

used to such things, of course. How many times has he done such a
thing? A hundred or a thousand? But was there one like me among
them? No, certainly not. I'll tell him that he is not the first man to see
me like that. I'll tell him that I have a lover. But only when the thirty
thousand gulden have been dispatched to Fiala. Then I'll tell him
that he's a fool, that he could have had me, too, for the same money.
— That I have already had ten lovers, twenty, a hundred. — But of
course he won't believe all that. — And if he does believe it, what
good is that to me? — If only I could spoil his fun in some way . . . Suppose another man were present? Why not? He didn't say that he must
be alone with me. Ah, Herr von Dorsday, I'm so afraid of you. Won't
you kindly permit me to bring an old friend along? Oh, it's in no way
contrary to our agreement, Herr von Dorsday. If I felt like it, I could
invite the whole hotel to watch, and you'd still be obliged to send the
thirty thousand gulden. But I am satisfied to bring my cousin Paul
along. Or would you perhaps prefer another man? The tall blond
one is unfortunately no longer here and neither is the *filou* with the
Roman head. But I'll find someone else, don't worry. You fear an
indiscretion? That doesn't really matter. I place no value on discre-
tion. When a person has reached my stage, nothing really matters.
For this thing today is merely the beginning, of course. Or do you
think that, after this adventure, I'll go home as a decent girl of good
family? No, neither a good family nor a decent girl. That's over with.
I shall now stand on my own feet. I have beautiful legs, Herr von
Dorsday, as you and the other participants in the festivities will soon
have occasion to observe. So everything is in order, Herr von Dorsday. At ten o'clock, when everyone is still sitting in the lobby, we'll
stroll in the moonlight over the meadow, through the forest, to the
famous clearing you discovered yourself. You will bring the telegram
to the bank with you, just to make sure. For I certainly have a right to
demand security from a scoundrel like you. And at midnight you
may go home again, and I will stay on the meadow with my cousin or
someone else. You've no objection, have you, Herr von Dorsday? You
have no right to object, you know. And if I should happen to be dead
tomorrow morning, don't be astonished. In that case, Paul will send
the telegram. It will be taken care of, no fear. But don't imagine, for
Heaven's sake, that it was you, wretched fellow, who drove me to my
death. I've known a long time that I would end this way. Just ask my
friend Fred if I didn't tell him so often. Fred, you must know, is Herr

Friedrich Wenkheim, incidentally the only decent human being I
have come to know in my life. The only man I would have loved, if he
had not been such a decent person. Yes, what a depraved creature I
am. I wasn't made for a bourgeois life, and I have no talent either. In
any case, it would be best for our family if it became extinct. Rudi,
too, will be involved in some misfortune. He will go into debt for
some Dutch chanteuse and embezzle money from Vanderhulst.
That's the way it is in our family. And my father's youngest brother
shot himself when he was fifteen years old. Nobody knows why. I
didn't know him. Ask them to show you his photograph, Herr von
Dorsday. We have it in an album . . . I'm supposed to look like him.
No one knows why he took his life. And no one will know in my case
either. Certainly not because of you, Herr von Dorsday. I won't do
you that honor. Whether at the age of nineteen or twenty-one, it's all
the same, really. Or shall I become a French nursemaid or a tele-
phone operator or marry a Herr Wilomitzer or let you keep me? It's
all equally disgusting, and I won't go with you to the meadow at all.
No, all that is much too strenuous and too stupid and too repulsive.
When I'm dead you will surely be good enough to send off the few
thousand gulden to papa, for it would really be too sad if he were
arrested the very day they take my body to Vienna. But I will leave
behind a letter with the authority of a will: Herr von Dorsday has the
right to see my body. My beautiful, naked, virginal corpse. So you
can't complain, Herr von Dorsday, that I put one over on you. You
will get something for your money. It doesn't say in our contract that
I must still be alive. Oh no. That's nowhere in writing. Well then, I
bequeath the viewing of my corpse to the art dealer Dorsday, and to
Herr Fred Wenkheim I bequeath my diary of my seventeenth year of
life — I never kept one beyond that — and to Cissy's girl I bequeath the
five twenty-franc coins I brought back from Switzerland years ago.
They are lying in my desk with the letters. And to Bertha I bequeath
my black evening gown. And to Agatha, my books. And to my cousin
Paul I bequeath a kiss on my pale lips. And to Cissy I bequeath my
racket, because I'm generous. And I'm to be buried right here in San
Martino di Castrozza, in the beautiful little cemetery. I don't want to
go back home again. Even in death I don't want to go back again.
And papa and mama are not to grieve, I'm better off than they are.
And I forgive them. No one need pity me. — Ha ha, what a funny
will. I'm really touched. When I think that tomorrow at this time,

when the others are sitting at dinner, I shall be dead. —Aunt Emma will, of course, not come down to dinner, nor will Paul. They will take their dinner in their rooms. I'm curious to know how Cissy will behave. But unfortunately I'll never find out. I'll never find out anything more, ever. But perhaps you still know everything as long as you're not buried? And really I'll only be in a trance. And when Herr von Dorsday steps up to my corpse, I'll come to life and open my eyes, and he'll drop his monocle in fright.

But unfortunately none of this is true. I will not be in a trance and not dead either. I won't take my own life at all, I'm far too cowardly for that. Even though I'm an intrepid mountain climber, I'm still a coward. And perhaps I don't even have enough Veronal. How many powders are necessary? Six, I believe. But ten are more certain. I think there are still ten left. Yes, that will be enough.

How many times have I walked around this hotel? and what now? Here I am standing in front of the gate. There's no one in the lobby yet. Of course—they're all still sitting at dinner. The lobby looks strange like this, without people. On that easy chair there's a hat, a tourist's hat, quite smart. Pretty chamois brush. An old gentleman is sitting in the *fauteuil* there, probably lost his appetite. Reading a newspaper. He's lucky. He has no worries. He reads his newspaper calmly and I have to rack my brain how to get thirty thousand gulden for papa. But no. I know how, don't I? Why, it's so terribly simple. What do I want, anyway? What do I want, anyway? What am I doing here in the lobby? They'll all be here from dinner in a moment. What shall I do? Herr von Dorsday is sitting on pins and needles, I'm sure. Where is she? he's thinking. Can she possibly have committed suicide? Or is she hiring someone to kill me? Or is she stirring up her cousin Paul against me? Have no fear, Herr von Dorsday, I am not such a dangerous person. I'm a little slut, no more. For the anxiety you have endured you shall have your reward. Midnight, room No. 65. It would really be too cool for me outside. And from your room, Herr von Dorsday, I'll go straight to my cousin Paul. You've no objection, have you, Herr von Dorsday?

"*Else! Else!*"

What? What? Why, that's Paul's voice. Dinner over already? —"*Else!*" —"Oh, Paul, what is it, Paul?" I'll act quite innocent. —"*Why, where have you been, Else?*" —"Where do you suppose I've been? I went for a walk." —"*Now, during dinnertime?*" —"Well, when else? That's the most beautiful time for a walk." I'm talking nonsense. — *"Mama has been imagining all sorts of things. I was at the door of your room, I knocked."* — "I didn't hear a thing." — *"But seriously, Else, how can you cause us so much worry! You could at least have told mama that you weren't coming to dinner."* — "You're right, of course, Paul, but if you had any idea what a headache I had." I'm talking quite ingratiatingly. Oh, what a slut I am! — *"Do you feel better now?"* — "I can't really say. No, not really." — *"I'll tell mama."* — "Wait, Paul, not yet. Give my apologies to aunt, I just want to go up to my room for a few minutes to fix myself up a bit. Then I'll come right down and have a late bite." — *"You're so pale, Else. Shall I send mama up?"* — "Oh, don't make such a fuss over me, Paul, and don't look at me like that. Haven't you ever seen a woman with a headache before? I'll come down again, for sure. In ten minutes at the latest. Good-by, Paul." — *"Well good-by, Else."* — Thank Heaven, he's going. Stupid boy, but nice. What does the porter want with me? What, a telegram? "Thank you. When did the wire come, porter?" — *"Fifteen minutes ago, Fräulein."* — Why does he look at me like that, so — pityingly? For Heaven's sake, what can there be in it? I won't open it till I get upstairs, otherwise I may faint. Possibly papa has. . . . If papa is dead, then everything is all right, then I no longer have to go to the meadow with Herr von Dorsday. . . . Oh, what a wretched creature I am. Dear God, don't let the telegram bring bad news, let papa still be alive. Under arrest, for all I care, but not dead. If there is no bad news in it, I'll make a sacrifice. I'll become a French nursemaid, I'll take a job in an office. Don't be dead, Papa. I'm really ready. I'll really do anything you wish . . .

Thank Heaven, I'm upstairs. Put on the lights, put on the lights. It's turned cool. The window was open too long. Courage, courage. Ha, perhaps it says that the matter has been arranged. Perhaps Uncle Bernhard gave the money and they are wiring me: "Don't speak to Dorsday." I'll see at once. But of course if I look at the ceiling, I can't read what's in the telegram. Trala, trala, courage. It must be done. "Repeat urgent request talk Dorsday. Sum not thirty, but fifty. Otherwise all in vain. Address remains Fiala." — But fifty. Otherwise all in vain. Trala, trala. Fifty. Address remains Fiala. But, of course, whether it's fifty or thirty doesn't matter. Not to Herr von Dorsday either. The Veronal is lying under my linen, as a last resort. Why didn't I say fifty in the first place? I did think of it. Otherwise all

in vain. Well then, downstairs, quick, don't sit here on the bed. A
slight mistake, Herr von Dorsday, pardon me. Not thirty but fifty,
otherwise all in vain. Address remains Fiala. —"I suppose you take
me for a fool, Fräulein Else?" By no means, M. le vicomte, why
should I? "For fifty I must of course ask correspondingly more, Fräulein." Otherwise all in vain. Address remains Fiala. As you wish,
Herr von Dorsday. Just command me, please. But first of all, you will
write out the telegram to your bank, naturally, otherwise I have no
guarantee. —

Yes, that's how I'll do it. I'll come to his room, and only after he
has written out the telegram before my eyes —I'll undress. And I'll
keep the telegram in my hand. Oh, how unappetizing. And where
am I to put my clothes? No, no, I'll undress right here and put on my
big black coat, which will cover me completely. That's most convenient for both parties. Address remains Fiala. My teeth are
chattering. The window is still open. Close it. Outside! It could be my
death. Scoundrel! Fifty thousand. He can't say no. Room No. 65. But
first I'll tell Paul to wait for me in his room. From Dorsday I'll go
directly to Paul and tell him everything. And then Paul will slap his
face. Yes, this very night. A full program. And then comes the Veronal. No, what for? Why should I die? Not a bit of it. Gay, gay, now
life is really beginning. You shall have your joy of me. You shall be
proud of your precious daughter. I'll turn into a slut such as the
world has never known. Address remains Fiala. You shall have your
fifty thousand gulden, Papa. But the next I earn after that, I'll spend
on new chemises trimmed with lace, quite transparent, and expensive silk stockings. We only live once. What does one have a face like
mine for? Turn on the lights, I'll turn on the lamp over the mirror.
How beautiful my blond-red hair is, and my shoulders. My eyes
aren't bad either. Whew, how big they are. It's really a pity about
me. It's never too late for the Veronal. —But I must go down, of
course. Way down. Herr von Dorsday is waiting and he doesn't know
yet that the amount has meanwhile become fifty thousand. Yes, my
price has risen, Herr von Dorsday. I must show him the telegram,
otherwise he won't really believe me and think I want to earn something on the side in the transaction. I'll send the wire to his room and
write a note on it. To my deep regret the amount has now become
fifty thousand, Herr von Dorsday, but that doesn't make any difference to you. And I am convinced that your counter-demand was not

meant seriously at all. For you are a vicomte and a gentleman. Tomorrow morning you will send Fiala the fifty thousand on which the life of my father depends, without any further question. I'm counting on it. — "Of course, my dear young lady, just to play safe I'll send a hundred thousand right off, without asking for anything in return, and, moreover, I assume the responsibility from this day on to support your whole family, to pay your papa's gambling debts and to replace all the trust money he embezzles." Address remains Fiala. Ha ha ha! Yes, that's precisely the way he is, the vicomte of Presov. But that's all nonsense. What then is left for me? It must be done, of course I must do it, of course, I must do everything, everything that Herr von Dorsday requests, so that papa may have the money tomorrow — so that he won't be locked up, so that he won't take his own life. And I will do it too. Yes, I will do it, although it's all for the birds. Half a year from now we'll be back where we are today. Four weeks from now! — But then it will no longer be my concern. I'll make this one sacrifice — and then no more. Never, never, never again. Yes, that's what I'll tell papa as soon as I get back to Vienna. And then away from that house, no matter where. I'll get advice from Fred. He's the only one who really likes me. But I haven't got to that point yet. I'm not in Vienna, I'm still in Martino di Castrozza. Nothing has happened yet. So how, how, what? There's the telegram. What am I to do with the telegram? I knew it at once. I must send it to his room. But what else? I must write a note too. Well then, what shall I write him? Expect me at twelve. No, no, no! He shall not have that triumph. I don't want to, don't want to, don't want to. Thank Heaven, I have the powders here. That's my only salvation. Where are they, anyway? For Heaven's sake . . . has someone . . . stolen them? But no, there they are. There in the box. Are they still all there? Yes, there they are. One, two, three, four, five, six. I just want to look at them, the precious powders. There's no obligation whatever. Even emptying them into the glass puts me under no obligation. One, two — but I will certainly not take my life. Wouldn't even think of it. Three, four, five — not enough to kill anyone. It would be terrible if I didn't have the Veronal with me. Then I'd have to jump out of the window and I really wouldn't have the courage to do that. But the Veronal — you fall asleep slowly, don't wake up again, no torment, no pain. You lie down in bed; you drink it off at one draught, dream and it's all over. The day before yesterday I took a powder too, and recently even two. Sh, don't tell anyone, today it'll just be a bit more. It's only in case of emergency. In case I should feel too much horror. But why should I feel horror? If he touches me, I'll spit in his face. Just like that.

But how shall I get the letter to him? I certainly can't send a letter to Herr von Dorsday by the chambermaid. The best thing will be if I go down and talk to him and show him the telegram. I must go down in any event. I can't stay up here in my room. I couldn't stand it for three whole hours—till the moment comes. I must go down because of aunt, too. Ha, what does my aunt matter to me? What do these people matter to me? Do you see, ladies and gentlemen, here's the glass with the Veronal. There, now I take it in my hand. There, now I raise it to my lips. Yes, at any moment I can be over there, where there are no aunts and no Dorsday and no father who embezzles trust funds . . .

But I won't kill myself. I don't need to do that. I won't go to Herr von Dorsday's room either. Wouldn't think of it. I certainly will not, for fifty thousand gulden, stand naked before an old roué, to save a scoundrel from prison. No, no; either—or. How did Herr von Dorsday ever hit upon such an idea? He, of all people? If one man is to see me, then others shall see me too. Yes! —Splendid idea! —They shall all see me. The whole world shall see me. And then the Veronal. No, not the Veronal—what for? Then comes the villa with the marble steps and the handsome young men and freedom and the big world! "Good evening, Fräulein Else, that's the way I like you." Ha ha. Downstairs they'll think I've become crazy. But I was never so rational. For the first time in my life I am really rational. All, all, shall see me! —Then there will be no turning back, no going home to papa and mama, to my uncles and aunts. Then I'll no longer be the Fräulein Else whom they want to sell to some Director Wilomitzer; that way I'll make fools of them all—above all, that rogue Dorsday—and will be born a second time . . . otherwise it's all in vain. —Address remains Fiala. Ha ha!

Lose no more time, don't become a coward again. Off with my dress. Who will be first? Will it be you, Cousin Paul? You're lucky that the Roman head is no longer here. Will you kiss these beautiful breasts tonight? Ah, how beautiful I am. Bertha has a black silk chemise. Subtle. I will be far more subtle still. A splendid life. Off with my stockings, that would be indecent. Naked, quite naked. How

Cissy will envy me! And others too. But they don't dare. They'd all like to—so much. Profit by my example. I, the virgin, dare. I will die laughing at Dorsday. Here I am, Herr von Dorsday. To the post office, quick. Fifty thousand. Surely it's worth that much?

I'm beautiful, beautiful! Behold me, Night! Behold me, Mountains! Behold me, Heaven, how beautiful I am. But of course you're blind. What use are you to me? Those below have eyes. Shall I let my hair down? No. Then I'd look like a madwoman. But you're not to think I'm crazy. You shall merely consider me shameless. A baggage. Where's the telegram? In Heaven's name, where is that telegram? Why, here it is, lying peacefully near the Veronal. "Repeat urgent request—fifty thousand—otherwise all in vain. Address remains Fiala." Yes, that's the telegram. That is a piece of paper and there are words on it. Sent from Vienna at four-thirty. No, I'm not dreaming, it's all true. And at home they are waiting for the fifty thousand guldens. And Herr von Dorsday is waiting too. Just let him wait. We have time. Ah, how nice it is to walk up and down the room naked like this. Am I really as beautiful as I look in the mirror? Ah, please come closer, beautiful Fräulein. I want to kiss your blood-red lips. I want to press your breasts to my breasts. What a pity that the glass is between us, the cold glass. How well we would get along together. Wouldn't we? We wouldn't need anyone else. Perhaps there are no other people. There are telegrams and hotels and mountains and railway stations and forests, but there are no people. We merely dream them. Only Dr. Fiala exists, with his address. Nothing changes. Oh, I'm by no means insane. I'm only a little excited. That's quite understandable, after all, before you come into the world for the second time. For the former Else has already died. Yes, quite definitely, I am dead. You need no Veronal for that. Shouldn't I pour it out? The chambermaid might drink it by mistake. I will put a slip of paper beside it and write on it? Poison; no, better still: Medicine, so that the chambermaid will come to no harm. How noble I am! There, Medicine, underlined twice, with three exclamation marks. Now nothing can happen. And when I come back upstairs and have no wish to kill myself and merely want to sleep, I just won't drink the whole glass but only a quarter of it or even less. Quite simple. I have everything under control. The simplest thing would be if I ran—just as I am, through the hall and down the steps. But no, I might be stopped before I got downstairs—and I must of course be

certain that Herr von Dorsday is present! Otherwise he will of course
not send the money, the dirty beast. — But I must still write to him.
That's the most important thing, of course. Oh, the arm of the chair
is cold, but pleasant. When I have my villa beside the Italian lake, I
will always walk about naked in my park . . . I bequeath my fountain
pen to Fred, when I die some day. But for the present I have more
sensible things to do than to die. "Dear Vicomte" — well now, be sensible, Else, no salutation, neither dear nor despised. "Your condition, Herr von Dorsday, is fulfilled" — — — "The moment you read
these lines, Herr von Dorsday, your condition will be fulfilled, if not
quite in the manner foreseen by you." — "My, how well the girl
writes," papa might say. — "And so I count upon it that you, for your
part, will keep your word and send the fifty thousand gulden by wire
to the said address without delay. Else." No, not Else. No signature
at all. There My beautiful yellow stationery. Got it for Christmas.
Too bad. There — and now telegram and letter in the envelope.
— "Herr von Dorsday, Room No. 65." Why the number? I'll just put
the letter in front of his door as I pass. But I don't have to. I don't
have to do anything. If I feel like it, I can lie down in bed now and
sleep and not concern myself with anything. Not about Herr von
Dorsday and not about papa. A striped prison suit can be quite elegant too. And many have killed themselves before this. And we must
all die.

But you don't need all that for the time being, Papa. For you have
your gorgeously beautiful daughter, and the address remains Fiala. I
will take up a collection. I'll pass the plate. Why should only Herr
von Dorsday pay? That would be unfair. Each according to his
means. How much will Paul put on the plate? And the gentleman
with the gold pince-nez? Only don't imagine that the fun will last
long. I will wrap my coat around me at once, run upstairs to my
room, lock myself in and, if I feel like it, drink the whole flask at one
draught. But I won't feel like it. It would only be cowardice. They
don't deserve that much respect, the rogues. Ashamed of you? I feel
ashamed of anyone? I really don't need to. Let me look at your eyes
again, beautiful Else. What enormous eyes you have when they are
seen from close up. I would like someone to kiss me on my eyes, on
my blood-red lips. My coat scarcely reaches over my ankles. They will
notice that my feet are bare. What does it matter, they'll see even
more! But I'm not committed. I can turn around again at once, even

before I get downstairs. I can turn around on the second floor. I don't need to go down at all. But I do want to, of course. I'm looking forward to it. Haven't I wished for something like this all my life?

What am I still waiting for? I'm ready. The show can begin. Don't forget the letter. An aristocratic handwriting, Fred says. Good-by, Else. You look beautiful in that coat. Florentine women have had themselves painted like that. Their portraits hang in the galleries and it is an honor for them. — You don't have to notice anything if I pull my coat about me. Only my feet, only my feet. I'll put on my black patent leather shoes, they'll think I have flesh-colored stockings on. I will go through the lobby like that and no one will suspect that under the coat there is nothing but me, me, I, myself. And then I can always go back . . . — Who is that playing the piano so beautifully down there? Chopin? — Herr von Dorsday will be a little nervous. Perhaps he's afraid of Paul. Just patience, patience, everything will come out all right. I know nothing yet, Herr von Dorsday, I'm in terrible suspense myself. Turn out the light. Is everything in the room all right? Farewell, Veronal, see you again. Farewell, my passionately beloved mirror image. How you shine in the dark. I have already become quite used to being naked under my coat. Quite pleasant. Who knows, perhaps many people sit in the lobby like that and no one knows it? Perhaps many a lady goes to the theater like that and sits in her loge like that — for fun, or for other reasons.

Shall I lock the door? What for? Nothing is stolen here. And even if it were — I don't need anything more. The End . . . Where's No. 65? There's no one in the corridor. They're all still at dinner. Sixty-one . . . sixty-two . . . Why, those are huge mountain boots standing in front of that door. There's a pair of trousers hanging on a hook. How vulgar. Sixty-four, sixty-five. There. That's where he lives, the vicomte . . . I'll stand the letter up against the door. There, he'll have to see it at once. Will no one steal it? There, it's lying there . . . no matter . . . I can still do what I please. I've simply made a fool of him . . . If only I don't meet him on the stairs now. Why, that's . . . no, it isn't he! . . . He's much more attractive than Herr von Dorsday, very elegant, with his little black mustache. When did that one arrive? I could have a little rehearsal — lift my coat just a tiny bit. I've a great desire to do it. Just look at me, sir. You have no idea whom you're passing. Too bad you're going upstairs just now. Why don't you stay in the lobby? You're missing something. A grand performance. Why

don't you stop me? My destiny is in your hands. If you greet me, I'll
turn around again. So do greet me. I'm looking at you so invitingly
...He doesn't greet me. He's passed me. He's turning around, I can
feel it. Call me, greet me! Save me! You may be responsible for my
death, sir! But you will never find it out. Address remains Fiala...

Where am I? In the lobby already? How did I get here? So few people and so many strangers. Or do my eyes deceive me? Where is Dorsday? He's not here. Is this a hint from fate? I'll go back. I'll write a
different letter to Dorsday. I'm expecting you in my room at midnight. Bring the telegram to your bank with you. No. He might consider it a trap. Could be one too. I could have Paul hidden in my
room and he might force him at gunpoint to give us the telegram.
Blackmail. A couple of crooks. Where is Dorsday? Dorsday, where
are you? Is it possible he killed himself from remorse for my death?
He must be in the game room. Of course. He must be sitting at a
card table. In that case I'll signal him from the doorway with my
eyes. He'll stand up at once. "Here I am, Fräulein." His voice will
ring. —"Shall we go for a little walk, Herr Dorsday?" —"As you
please, Fräulein Else." We walk toward the forest by way of the
Marienweg. We're alone. I open my coat. The fifty thousand are
due. The air is cold, I catch pneumonia and die.... Why are the
two ladies looking at me? Do they notice anything? But why am I
here? Am I insane? I'll go back to my room, dress quickly, my blue
dress, my coat over it, just like now, but open, then no one will think
that I had nothing on before...I can't go back any more. I don't
want to either. Where's Paul? Where's Aunt Emma? Where's Cissy?
Where are they all? No one will notice it.... It can't be noticed at
all. Who is playing so beautifully? Chopin? No, Schumann.

I'm flitting about the lobby like a bat. Fifty thousand! Time is passing. I must find this cursed Herr von Dorsday. No, I must go back to
my room...I will drink Veronal. Only a little sip, then I'll sleep well
...When work is done rest is sweet...But the work is not done yet...
If the waiter serves the black coffee to the old gentleman over there,
everything will turn out well. But if he brings it to the young couple
in the corner, all is lost. Why is that? What does that mean? He's
bringing the coffee to the old gentleman. Triumph! Everything will
turn out well. Ha, Cissy and Paul! They're strolling up and down outside the hotel. They're talking to each other quite happily. He's not
especially disturbed by my headache. Cheat!...Cissy's breasts are

not as beautiful as mine. Of course not, because she has a child . . .
What are those two talking about? If only I could hear them! What
do I care what they're talking about? But I could go out in front of
the hotel too, say good evening to them and then walk on, flutter on
over the meadow, into the forest, mount, climb, higher and higher,
to the top of Cimone, lie down, fall asleep, freeze to death. Mysterious suicide of a young lady from Viennese society. Wearing only a
black evening cloak, the beautiful girl was found dead at an inaccessible spot on Cimone della Pala. . . . But perhaps they won't find me.
. . . Or not till next year. Or later still. Decomposed. As a skeleton.
Better stay here in the heated lobby and not freeze to death. Well,
Herr von Dorsday, where are you anyway? Do I have to wait? It's you
who ought to be looking for me, not I for you. I'll take a look in the
game room. If he isn't there, he has forfeited his right. And I'll write
to him: you were not to be found, Herr von Dorsday, you have renounced your rights voluntarily; but this does not absolve you from
the obligation to send the money at once. The money. But what
money? What do I care about that? Really, it's a matter of utter indifference to me whether he sends the money or not. I no longer feel
the slightest sympathy for papa. I feel sympathy for no one. Not even
for myself. My heart is dead. I believe it has actually stopped beating. Perhaps I have already drunk the Veronal. . . . Why does that
Dutch family look at me like that? It isn't possible to notice anything,
is it? The porter is looking at me very suspiciously too. Perhaps
another telegram has come? Eighty thousand? A hundred thousand?
Address remains Fiala. If there were a telegram, he would tell me so.
He's looking at me with great respect. He doesn't know that I have
nothing on under my coat. Nobody knows. I'm going back to my
room. Back, back, back! If I should stumble over a step, it would
make a pretty story. Three years ago on Lake Wörther a lady went
swimming quite naked. But she left that same afternoon. Mama said
she was a singer from the Comic Opera in Berlin. Schumann? Yes,
Carnival. He or she plays quite beautifully. But the card room is to
the right. Last chance, Herr von Dorsday. If he's there, I'll motion to
him with my eyes and tell him I'll be with him at midnight. No, I
won't say scoundrel to him. But I'll say it to him afterwards. . . .
Someone is following me. I'm not going to turn around. No, no. —
"*Else!*" — For Heaven's sake, my aunt. On, on! — "*Else!*" — I must
turn around, it's no use. "Oh, good evening, Aunt." — "*But, Else,*

what's wrong with you? I was just going to look in your room. Paul told me— Why, but you look—" "How do I look, Aunt? I'm feeling all right again. I ate a little too." She notices something, she notices something. —*"Else—you've—you've no stockings on."* —"What are you saying, Aunt? Upon my soul, I have no stockings on. Really—!" —*"Don't you feel well, Else? Your eyes—you have a fever."* —"Fever? I don't think so. I've had the most awful headache, I've never had a headache like that in my life." —*"You must go to bed at once, child, you're as pale as death."* —"That's just the lighting, Aunt. Everyone looks pale here in the lobby." She looks down at me so strangely. Surely she can't notice anything? Now I must keep my head. Papa is lost if I don't keep my head. I must say something. "Do you know, Aunt, what happened to me this year in Vienna? I once went out on the street in one yellow and one black shoe " Not a word of truth in it. I must keep on talking. What shall I say? "Do you know, Aunt, after my migraines I sometimes have such attacks of absent-mindedness. Mama used to have them too, once." Not a word of truth. —*"I'm going to send for the doctor, anyhow."* —"But please, Aunt, there isn't one in the hotel. They'd have to get one from another place. He would have a good laugh at being called because I have no stockings on. Ha ha." I shouldn't laugh so loudly. Aunt's face is distorted with anxiety. The thing seems weird to her. Her eyes are popping. —*"Tell me, Else, have you by any chance seen Paul?"* —Ah, she wants to get help. Keep your head, everything is at stake. "I believe he's walking up and down in front of the hotel with Cissy Mohr, if I'm not mistaken." —*"In front of the hotel? I'll call them both in. We'll all drink a cup of tea together, won't we?"* —"Gladly." What a stupid face she makes. I'll nod to her in a quite friendly and innocent way. She's gone. Now I'll go up to my room. No, what would I do in my room? It's high time, high time. Fifty thousand, fifty thousand. Why am I running so? Slowly, slowly.... What do I want, anyway? What is the man's name? Herr von Dorsday. Funny name.... Why, here's the game room. Green curtain in front of the door. You can't see a thing. I'll stand on my tiptoes. Game of whist. They play every evening. Over there two gentlemen are playing chess. Herr von Dorsday isn't here. Victoria! Saved! But how? I must go on looking. I'm condemned, Herr von Dorsday, to keep looking to the end of my life. I'm sure he's looking for me too. We keep missing each other. Perhaps he's looking for me upstairs. We'll meet on the steps. The

Dutch people are looking at me again. The daughter is quite attractive. The old gentleman wears spectacles, spectacles, spectacles.... Fifty thousand. Why, that isn't so much. Fifty thousand, Herr von Dorsday. Schumann? Yes, *Carnival*...I learned it too, once. She

plays beautifully. But why she? Maybe it's a he. Perhaps it's a virtuoso, I'll take a look in the music room.

Why, here's the door. —Dorsday! I'm going to fall. Dorsday! There he is, standing at the window, listening. How is this possible? I'm eating my heart out — I'm going crazy — I'm dead — and he's listening to a strange lady playing the piano. Two gentlemen are sitting on the sofa over there. The blond one just arrived today. I saw him get out of the carriage. The lady is no longer young. She has been here a few days. I didn't know she played the piano so beautifully. She's well off. Everyone is well off...only I am condemned...Dorsday! Dorsday! Is that really him? He doesn't see me. Now he looks like a respectable man. He's listening. Fifty thousand! Now or never. Open the door

softly. Here I am, Herr von Dorsday! He doesn't see me. I'll merely give him a signal with my eyes, then I'll raise my coat slightly, that's enough. For, after all, I'm a young girl, a respectable young girl of good family. I'm not a prostitute...I want to go away. I want to take Veronal and sleep. You were mistaken, Herr von Dorsday, I'm not a prostitute. Adieu, adieu!...Ha, he looks up. Here I am, Herr von Dorsday. What eyes he makes. His lips are trembling. His eyes bore into my forehead. He doesn't suspect that I am naked under my coat. Let me go, let me go! His eyes are glowing. His eyes are threatening.

What do you want with me? You're a scoundrel. No one sees me
except him. You're listening. Well then, come on, Herr von Dorsday!
Don't you notice anything? There in the *fauteuil*—Lord God, in the
fauteuil—why, that't the *filou!* Heaven, I thank you. He's here again,
he's here again! He was only away on a trip! Now he's back again.
The Roman head is here again. My bridegroom, my lover! But he
doesn't see me. Nor shall he see me. What do you want, Herr von
Dorsday? You look at me as if I were your slave. I'm not your slave.
Fifty thousand! Does our agreement stand, Herr von Dorsday? I'm
ready. Here I am. I'm quite calm. I'm smiling. Do you understand
the look in my eyes? His eyes speak to me: "Come!" His eyes speak: "I
want to see you naked." Well, you scoundrel, I am naked. What
more do you want? Send off the wire...immediately...my skin is
tingling. The lady goes on playing. A delightful ripple runs over my
skin. How wonderful it is to be naked. The lady plays on, she doesn't
realize what is happening here. No one realizes it. No one has seen

me yet. *Filou, filou!* Here I stand, naked, Dorsday opens his eyes
wide. Now, at last, he believes it. The *filou* stands up. His eyes are
shining. You understand me, handsome youth. "Ha ha!" The lady
isn't playing any more. Papa is saved. Fifty thousand! Address
remains Fiala! "Ha, ha, ha!" Who is that laughing? Me? "Ha, ha,
ha!" What sort of faces are these around me? "Ha, ha, ha!" Too
stupid, my laughter. I don't want to laugh, I don't want to. "Ha ha!"

—"*Else!*" Who's calling Else? That's Paul. He must be behind me. I feel a draught of air on my naked back. There is a roaring in my ears. Perhaps I'm already dead? What do you want, Herr von Dorsday? Why are you so big, why do you fall over me? "Ha, ha, ha!" What have I done? What have I done? What have I done? I'm falling. It's all over. Why is there no more music? An arm is encircling my neck. That's Paul. But where's the *filou?* I'm lying here. "Ha, ha, ha!" The coat flies down to cover me. And I'm lying here. Everyone thinks I'm unconscious. No, I'm not unconscious. I'm fully conscious. I am awake a hundred times, a thousand times. But I must keep on laughing. "Ha, ha, ha!" Now you have your wish, Herr von Dorsday, you must send the money to papa. Immediately. "Haaaah!" I don't want to scream, but I have to keep screaming. But why must I scream? —My eyes are closed. No one can see me. Papa is saved. —"*Else!*" —That's aunt. —"*Else! Else!*" —"*A doctor! A doctor!*" —"*Quick! to the porter.*" —"*But what's happened?*" —"*But that isn't possible!*" —"*The poor child.*" —What are they saying there? I'm not a poor child. I'm happy. The *filou* saw me naked. Oh, I feel so ashamed. What have I done? I'll never open my eyes again. —"*Please shut the door.*" —Why should they shut the door? All that murmuring! There are a thousand people around me. They all think I'm unconscious. I'm not unconscious. I'm only dreaming. —"*Calm yourself, madam.*" —"*Has the doctor been sent for yet?*" —"*It's a fainting spell.*" —How far away they all are. They're all talking down from the top of Cimone. —"*But we can't leave her lying on the floor.*" —"*Here's a plaid.*" —"*A blanket.*" —"*Blanket or plaid, what's the difference?*" —"*Please be quiet.*" —"*On the sofa.*" —"*Will you please shut the door!*" —"Don't be so nervous, it's closed." —"*Else! Else!*" —If only aunt would keep quite! —"*Do you hear me, Else?*" —"*Don't you see, Mama, that she's unconscious?*" —Yes, thank Heaven, for you I'm unconscious. And I'll stay unconscious too. —"*We must take her to her room.*" —"*What has happened here? For Heaven's sake!*" —Cissy. How did Cissy get to the meadow? Oh, it isn't the meadow, of course. —"*Else!*" —"*Quiet, please.*" —"*Please step back a little.*" —Hands, hands under me. What do they want anyway? How heavy I am. Paul's hands. Away, away. The *filou* is near me, I feel it. And Dorsday has gone. He must be looked for. He must not take his life before he has sent the fifty thousand. Ladies and gentlemen, he owes me money. Arrest him.

—*"Have you any idea who the telegram was from, Paul?"* —*"Good evening, ladies and gentlemen."* —*"Else, do you hear me?"* —*"Do leave her alone, Frau Cissy."* —*"Oh, Paul."* —*"The manager says it may be four hours before the doctor arrives."* —*"She looks as if she were asleep."* — I'm lying on the sofa, Paul is holding my hand, he's feeling my pulse. Right. He's a doctor, of course. —*"There's no question of danger, Mama. An—attack."* —*"I won't stay in the hotel a day longer."* —*"Please, Mama."* —*"We're leaving tomorrow morning."* —*"Simply, by the service stairway. The stretcher will be here at once."* —Stretcher? Wasn't I on a bier earlier today? Wasn't I dead already? Do I have to die again? —*"Herr Director, will you please get the people away from the door?"* —*"Just don't get excited, Mama."* —*"It's most inconsiderate of these people."* —Why are they all whispering? As though in the bedroom of a dying person. The bier will be here at once. Open the door, matador! —*"The hall is clear."* —*"These people might have at least this much consideration."* —*"I beg of you, Mama, calm yourself."* —*"Please, madam."* —*"Won't you look after my mother, Frau Cissy?"* —She's his mistress, but she isn't as beautiful as I am. What is it now? What's happening here? They're bringing the bier. I see it with my eyes closed. That's the stretcher on which they carry accident victims. It's the one on which Dr. Zigmondi lay when he fell from the Cimone. And now I will lie on the stretcher. I too fell. "Ha!" No, I won't scream again. They're whispering. Who's bending over my head? There's a pleasant smell of cigarettes. His hand is under my head. Hands under my back, hands under my legs. Away, away, don't touch me. Because I'm naked. Shame, shame. What do you want, anyway? Leave me in peace. It was only for papa. —*"Please be careful—that's it, slowly."* —*"The plaid?"* —*"Yes, thanks, Frau Cissy."* —Why is he thanking her? What has she done? What's happening to me? Ah, how good, how good, I'm floating. I'm floating. I'm floating over there. They're carrying me, they're carrying me, they're carrying me to my grave. —*"But we're used to 't, Doctor. We've had heavier folks layin' on it. Oncet last fall two of 'em at the same time."* —*"Sh, sh."* —*"Will you be good enough to go ahead, Frau Cissy, and see if everything is all right in Else's room."* —What business has Cissy in my room? The Veronal, the Veronal! If only they don't pour it out. Then I'd have to jump out of the window. —*"Thanks very much, Herr Director, don't go to any more trouble."* —*"I'll take the liberty of inquiring again later on."* — The stairs creak, the bearers have heavy mountain boots on. Where are my patent leather shoes? Left in the music room. They'll be stolen. I wanted to bequeath them to Agatha. Fred gets my fountain pen. They're carrying me, they're carrying me. Funeral procession. Where is Dorsday, the murderer? He's gone. The *filou* is gone too. He went right off on a hike again. He only came back to have one look at my white breasts. And now he's off again. He's walking on a precipitous road between rocks and depths — farewell, farewell. — I'm floating, I'm floating. Let them carry me up, higher and higher, up to Heaven. That would be so comfortable. — *"You Know I saw it coming, Paul."* — What did aunt see coming? — *"For the last few days I've seen something like this coming on. She's not normal at all. Of course, she must go to an institution."* — *"But, Mama, this is not the time to talk about it."* — Institution — ? Institution — ?! — *"You surely don't think, Paul, that I'm going to ride back to Vienna in the same compartment with this creature. It might lead to some pretty experiences."* — *"Not the slightest thing will happen, Mama. I guarantee you that you won't have the slightest trouble."* — *"How can you guarantee that?"* — No, Aunt, you'll have no trouble. No one will have any trouble. Not even Herr von Dorsday. But where are we? We're stopping. We're on the third floor. I'll blink my eyes. Cissy is standing in the doorway talking to Paul. — *"This way, please. That's it. That's it. Thanks. Move the stretcher quite close to the bed."* — They're lifting the stretcher. They're carrying me. How nice. Now I'm home again. Ah! — *"Thanks. There, that's all right. Please shut the door. — If you'll be good enough to help me, Cissy."* — *"Oh gladly, Doctor."* — *"Slowly, please. Here, please, Cissy, take hold of her. Here by the legs. Careful. And then—Else—? Do you hear me, Else?"* — But of course I hear you, Paul. I hear everything. But what business is it of yours? It's really wonderful to be unconscious. Ah, do what you wish. — *"Paul!"* — *"What?"* — *"Do you really think she's unconscious, Paul?"* — Du? She says du to him. Now I've caught you. She says du to him! — *"Yes, she's completely unconscious. This generally happens after such attacks."* — *"Really, Paul, you make me sick laughing when you act so grown-up like a doctor."* — I've caught you, you cheats, I've caught you. — *"Quiet, Cissy."* — *"But why, if she hears nothing?"* — But what's happened? I'm lying naked in bed under the blanket. How did they do it? — *"Well, how are you? Better?"* — That's aunt. What does she want here? — *"Still unconscious?"* —She's stealing over here on tiptoe. Let her go to the devil. I'm not going to let them send me to an institution. I'm not insane. —*"Can't she be brought back to consciousness?"* —*"She'll soon regain consciousness, Mama. Right now she needs nothing but rest. For that matter, you too, Mama. Won't you please go to bed? There's absolutely no danger. I'll sit up all night at Else's bedside with Frau Cissy."* —*"Yes, madam, I'll be the chaperone. Or Else, as you wish . . ."* —Horrid woman. I lie here unconscious and she's joking. —*"And can I count on you, Paul, to wake me as soon as the doctor comes?"* —*"But Mama, he won't come until morning."* —*"She looks as though she were asleep. Her breathing is quite regular."* —*"It really is a kind of sleep, Mother."* —*"I still can't collect myself, Paul. Such a scandal! —You'll see, it will get into the papers."* —*"Mama!"* —*"But she can't hear a thing if she's unconscious. And we're talking quite softly."* *"In this condition the senses are sometimes uncannily sharpened."* —*"You have such a learned son, madam."* —*"Please, Mama, go to bed."* —*"Tomorrow we leave here, no matter what . . . and in Bozen we'll get a nurse for Else."* —What? A nurse? But you'll find you're wrong. —*"We'll discuss all that tomorrow, Mama. Good night, Mama."* —*"I'll have a cup of tea sent up to my room and in fifteen minutes I'll look in again."* —*"But that's absolutely not necessary, Mama."* —No, it isn't necessary. May you go to the devil altogether. Where is the Veronal? I must wait awhile yet. They're accompanying aunt to the door. Now no one sees me. It must be on the bedside table, the glass with the Veronal. When I drink it, it will be all over. I'll drink it at once. Aunt is gone. Paul and Cissy are still standing beside the door. Ha. She's kissing him. She's kissing him. And I'm lying naked under the blanket. Aren't you ashamed at all? She kisses him again. Aren't you ashamed? —*"See, Paul, now I know that she's unconscious. Or she'd certainly have leaped at my throat."* —*"Would you please do me a favor and keep quiet, Cissy?"* —*"But what's bothering you, Paul? Either she is really unconscious and hears and sees nothing. Or she's making fools of us. Then it would serve her right."* —*"Someone knocked, Cissy."* —*"I thought so too."* —*"I will open the door softly and see who it is. —Good evening, Herr von Dorsday."* —*"Excuse me, I merely wanted to inquire how the patient—"* —Dorsday! Dorsday! Would he really dare? All the wild beasts have been let loose. Where is he? I hear them whispering at the door. Paul and Dorsday.

Cissy is going to the mirror. What are you doing in front of that mirror? That's my mirror. Isn't my image still in it? What are they saying out there at the door, Paul and Dorsday? I feel Cissy's eyes. She's looking at me from the mirror. What does she want? Why is she coming over to me? Help! Help! I'm screaming but no one hears me. What do you want beside my bed, Cissy?! Why do you bend down over me? Do you want to strangle me? I can't move. — *"Else!"* — What does she want? — *"Else! Do you hear me, Else?"* — I hear, but I'll be silent. I'm unconscious, I must be silent. — *"Else, you've given us a pretty fright."* — She's speaking to me. She's speaking to me as if I were awake. What does she want? — *"Do you know what you've done, Else? Think of it, you went into the music room wearing only your coat. You suddenly stood there naked before everyone, and then fell down unconscious. They say it's a hysterical attack. I don't believe a word of it. I don't believe that you're unconscious, either. I bet you hear every word I'm saying."* — Yes, I hear, yes, yes, yes. But she doesn't hear my yes. But why not? I can't move my lips. That's why she doesn't hear me. I can't move. What is really wrong with me? Am I dead? Am I in a trance? Am I dreaming? Where is the Veronal? I'd like to drink my Veronal. But I can't stretch out my arm. Go away, Cissy. Why are you bending over me? Away, away! She'll never know that I heard her. No one will ever know. I'll never speak to a human being again. I'll never wake up again. She's going to the door. She's turning around to me once more. She opens the door. Dorsday! He's standing there. I saw him with my eyes closed. No, I really see him. For my eyes are open. The door is ajar. Cissy, too, is outside. Now they're all whispering. I'm alone. If I could move now.

Ha, I can, can indeed! I'm moving my hand, I stretch my fingers, I stretch out my arm, I open my eyes wide. I see, I see. My glass is standing there. Quick, before they come back into the room. Are there enough powders?! I must never wake again. What I must do in the world, I have done. Papa is saved. I could never go among people. Paul is peering in through the crack in the door. He thinks I'm still unconscious. He doesn't see that I've almost stretched out my arm to its full length. Now all three of them are out there in front of the door, the murderers! — They're all murderers. Dorsday and Cissy and Paul, Fred is a murderer too, and mama is a murderess. They've all murdered me and act as if they knew nothing. "She took her own life," they'll say. You have taken my life, all of you, all of you! My glass! Have I got it at last? Quick, quick! I must. Don't spill a drop. There. Quick. It tastes good. More, more. It isn't poison at all. Never has anything tasted so good to me. If you knew how good death tastes. Good night, my glass. Clink, clink! What's that? The glass is lying on the floor. It's lying down there. Good night. — *"Else! Else!"* — What do you want? — *"Else!"* — Are you here again? Good morning. Here I lie unconscious with my eyes closed. You shall never see my eyes again. — *"She must have moved, Paul. How else could it have fallen?"* — *"An involuntary movement, that could certainly be possible."* — *"If she isn't awake!"* — *"What do you mean, Cissy? Just look at her."* — I have taken Veronal. I'll die. But I feel no different. Perhaps it wasn't enough . . Paul is taking my hand. — *"Her pulse is quiet. Don't laugh, Cissy. The poor child."* — *"I wonder if you would have called me a poor child if I had turned up in the music room naked?"* — *"Do be quiet, Cissy."* "*As you please, sir. Perhaps I should go away and leave you alone with the naked young lady. Oh, please, don't mind me, act as if I weren't here."* — I took Veronal. It's good. I'll die. Thank Heaven. — *"Besides, you know what I think? This Herr von Dorsday is in love with the naked young lady. He was as agitated as if the matter concerned him personally."* — Dorsday, Dorsday! Why that's — fifty thousand! Will he send it? For Heaven's sake, suppose he doesn't send it? I must tell them. They must force him. For Heaven's sake, suppose it was all in vain? But they can still save me now. Paul! Cissy! Why don't you hear me? Don't you know that I'm dying? But I feel nothing. I'm only tired. Paul! I'm tired. Don't you hear me? I'm tired, Paul. I can't open my lips. I can't move my tongue, but I'm not dead yet. That's the Veronal. Where are you? I'm going to fall asleep any moment. Then it will be too late! I don't hear them speaking at all. They're talking but I don't know what they're saying. Their voices roar so. Why don't you help me, Paul! My tongue feels so heavy. — *"I think she'll wake soon, Cissy. She seems to be making an effort to open her eyes. But Cissy, what are you doing?"* — *"Why, I'm embracing you. And why not? She wasn't embarrassed either."* — No, I wasn't embarrassed. I stood there naked before everyone. If I could only talk, you would understand why. Paul! Paul! I want you to hear me. I took Veronal, Paul, ten powders, a hundred. I didn't want to do it. I was crazy. I don't want to die. You must save me, Paul. You're a doctor, aren't you? Save me! — *"Now she seems quite calm again. The pulse—the pulse is fairly regular."* —Save me, Paul. I implore you. Don't let me die. There's still time. But then I'll fall asleep and you won't know it. I don't want to die. So do save me. It was only for papa. Dorsday demanded it. Paul! Paul! —*"Look here, Cissy, don't you think she's smiling?"* —*"Why shouldn't she smile, Paul, when you keep holding her hand tenderly?"* —Cissy, Cissy, what have I done to you that you're so mean to me? Keep your Paul—but don't let me die. I'm still so young. Mama will grieve. I want to climb many more mountains. I want to dance some more. I want to get married, too, someday. I want to travel more. Tomorrow we'll go up to Cimone as a group. Tomorrow will be a beautiful day. The *filou* must come with us. I invite him most humbly. Do run after him, Paul, he's walking on such a precipitous road. He'll meet papa. Address remains Fiala, don't forget. It's only fifty thousand, and then everything will be all right. There they are, all marching in their convicts' clothes, singing. Open the door, Herr Matador! Why, all this is only a dream. There's Fred too, walking with the hoarse young lady, and the piano is standing under the open sky. The piano tuner lives in Bartensteinstrasse. Mama! Why didn't you write to him, child? But you forget everything. You should practice more scales, Else. A girl of thirteen should be more diligent. —Rudi was at the masquerade and didn't get home till eight o'clock in the morning. What did you bring me, Papa? Thirty thousand dolls. Then I'll need a house of my own for them. But they can also go for a walk in the garden. Or to the masquerade with Rudi. Good day to you, Else. Oh, Bertha, are you back from Naples? Yes, from Sicily. Allow me to introduce my husband to you, Else. Enchanté, Monsieur. —*"Else, do you hear me, Else? It's me, Paul."* —Ha, ha, Paul. Why are you sitting on the giraffe on the merry-go-round? —*"Else, Else!"* —Don't ride away from me. You can't hear me if you ride so fast down the main avenue. You're supposed to save me, you know. I've taken Veronal. There's something running over my legs, right and left, like ants. Yes, catch him, that Herr von Dorsday. He's running over there. Don't you see him? There, he's jumping over the pond. He killed papa, you know. So do run after him. I'll run with you. They've strapped the stretcher on my back but I'll run along too. My breasts quiver so. But I'll run along too. Where are you, Paul? Fred, where are you? Mama, where are you? Cissy? Why do you let me run alone through the desert? I'm afraid, so by myself. I'd rather fly. I knew I could fly.

"*Else!*" . . .

"*Else!*" . . .

Where are you? I hear you, but I don't see you.

"*Else!*" . . .

"*Else!*" . . .

"*Else!*" . . .

What is that now? A whole choir? And an organ too? I'm singing with them. What sort of song is it? Everyone is singing. The forests, too, and the mountains and the stars. I've never heard anything so beautiful. I've never seen such a bright night. Give me your hand, Papa. We'll fly together. The world is so beautiful when you can fly. But don't kiss my hand. I'm your child, Papa, don't you know?

"*Else! Else!*"

They call from so far away. What do you want? Don't wake me. I'm sleeping so well. Tomorrow morning. I'm dreaming and flying. I fly . . . fly . . . sleep . . . and dream . . . and fly . . . don't wake . . . tomorrow morning . . .

"*El . . .*"

I fly . . . I dream . . . I sleep . . . I dr . . . dr . . . I fl . . . . . .

Franz Kafka

1883 — 1924

Franz Kafka was born of Jewish parents in Prague, at that time part of the Austro-Hungarian Empire. His father was a self-made businessman, of domineering temperament. Franz took a law degree at the German University of Prague in 1906, after which he entered the service of a large accident insurance company, where he was employed until 1917, when he developed tuberculosis and was retired on a pension. Three times he became engaged to be married, twice to the same girl; he broke all three engagements. He spent the last year of his life in Berlin in the company of a young woman who looked after him and gave him the happiest days of his life. He died from tuberculosis at the age of forty-one.

Kafka began writing for publication while he was employed by the insurance firm. He kept in touch with other Prague writers, and for two decades lived in close friendship with Max Brod, himself a distinguished writer. Brod became Kafka's literary executor, edited and published Kafka's manuscripts after his death, and wrote a biography of his friend. In undertaking this labor of love Brod was acting contrary to Kafka's wish that all his unpublished manuscripts be burned after his death. Fortunately Brod had enough moral courage to disregard the dying man's behest.

Kafka had developed an anxiety neurosis toward his father. The *Letter to My Father* (1917), which analyzes their relationship, is one of the extraordinary documents in psychology and literature. The father-son conflict, as it was then called, is a common theme in German Expressionist literature; it is, of course, a forerunner of the "generation gap" of the sixties. Kafka treated it not only in the famous letter but in the novellas *Das Urteil* (*The Judgment*) and *Die Verwandlung* (*The Metamorphosis*) as well. His inability to carry through a normal relationship with a woman, paralleled in the life of Kierkegaard, is yet another aspect of his neurotic behavior pattern. And yet those who knew him personally testified to his apparent outer serenity, orderly life style and good humor. The fact that he held a post in a large business organization for ten years points in the same direction. But that there was much inner turmoil is beyond doubt.

This turmoil, anxiety and suffering is expressed in Kafka's work symbolically, often parabolically, sometimes in the form of allegory. Kafka's fiction calls compellingly for a deciphering of the symbols, and the call has been heeded; but the enterprise has proved a Sisyphean task for the interpreters because of the multiplicity of readings that it invites. There seem to be as many interpretations as there are interpreters. Some of Kafka's symbols are extremely baffling, and the stories he tells even more so; others appear to be transparent enough but turn out to be as baffling as the hermetic ones. Not only do the individual stories and parables present this ambiguity of interpretation, but the basic approach to his work has aroused discord among his readers. Some see him as a theological-metaphysical writer, others believe he is dealing with ontological problems; there are psychoanalytic interpretations of his work; he has been interpreted sociologically; the Marxists have declared him a Fascist. Even the aesthetic critics have claimed him, seeing his work as a collection of images, an assemblage of linguistic configurations.

Kafka creates situations in which many aspects of human existence are explored: family and social relationships; specific human needs and institutions, such as the state, religion, art; questions of ethics, such as the problem of evil, the nature of justice; ontological concerns of the kind that Heidegger, Jaspers, Sartre and the other existentialists deal with; and aspects of art in its relation to society. Kafka does not supply answers or solutions the way the older writers did. He poses questions and states problems; he gives case histories. But his presentation of cases is so ambiguous and mutli-faceted that Max Brod could characterize him as a firm believer in God and an optimist, while other interpreters see him as one of the progenitors of the absurd universe that the existentialists invented. The latter have a mass of textual evidence to support them. For the universe that Kafka presents to us seems to be the most disorderly that any major writer has created. It is a world filled with frustration, mismanage-

ment, injustice, irrationality. Those in authority are always wrong
but convey to their victims the impression that they are always right.
Men (Kafka's central figures are always men) feel estranged, excluded, alienated, ignored, while their most intense desire is to
belong, to be admitted, to be ordered about. They run from freedom
to servitude. They are, writes Günter Anders, negative prisoners: not
locked in but locked out. They live in ignorance of ultimate goals
and do not know how to attain the goals that they do recognize.
Cause and effect are reversed: because a man is accused of some
crime whose nature he does not even suspect, he becomes guilty (of
what? he doesn't know), acknowledges his guilt, and is executed for it
(*Der Prozess, The Trial*). In most cases there is not even this negative
certainty; man goes through life in a state of uncertainty feeling
both guilty and not guilty, so that neither submission nor rebellion is
a solution to his problem. Thus existence is a halfway house between
"not yet" and "no longer." This irrationality is taken for granted as
perfectly normal by the people surrounding the main character; he
alone feels bewildered by the senselessness of life. Sometimes even the
hero-victim is unaware that there is something wrong. The story tells
us so; then the critics miss the point and judge that Kafka is pro-
moting some specific ideology. This in itself is a Kafkaean situation.

Kafka seems to offer his readers various metaphysical options to
choose from: (1) There is no order in the universe; all is absurdity.
(2) There is a God but he is a cruel joker, an Aristophanes who is
having fun directing or just watching the crazy antics of his creatures.
(3) There is a malevolent God, whose aim is to frustrate man and
make him suffer. (4) God is just inefficient. In the words of Peer
Gynt: "God is a Father to me after all, but economical he is not."
These theologies contradict each other, of course; but Kafka records
them, like the scientific researcher who builds various models to test
out the validity of different hypotheses.

Some of Kafka's heroes are questers, humble knights of the Grail,
in search of happiness or peace of mind, a meaning in life, justice or
grace or vindication from a groundless accusation, or absolution
from a sense of guilt whose cause they cannot fathom. They nearly
always fail; but even when they succeed, it is because the system is
fundamentally irrational. In *Die Prüfung* (*The Examination*), for
instance, the candidate cannot answer the examiner's questions; that
is why he passes the test.

Kafka's works, like Hoffman's but much more drastically, mix the
real and the unreal, the finite and the infinite. Much of his writing
gives the impression of being a record of dreams or nightmares.
Friedrich Beissner has suggested that the whole action of *The Trial*
takes place in the hero's mind. At other times Kafka delights in playing with intellectual and verbal paradoxes. Yet his style is simple,
matter of fact, rendering in minute detail the commonplace sur-
roundings in which the characters move. His diction is of a classical
purity and lucidity; the difference between content or spirit and form
is drastic.

Kafka was not discovered until the thirties. He became *the* fashionable author during the heyday of the existentialist movement after
the Second World War. The existentialist fashion has passed; but a
writer of such striking originality, such mythopoeic power, who
grasped the spirit of his time so profoundly, will surely survive
beyond his time.

Ein Hungerkünstler (*A Hunger Artist*) was written in 1922 and
published that year in *Die Neue Rundschau*. It appeared in book
form two years later as the title piece of a collection of four stories. At
first reading it appears to be the most realistic of Kafka's novellas. In
content it is a straightforward, completely logical, human account of
an episode from circus life, a tale of rivalry between the various
attractions in the big organization, of the decline and fall of one circus man from great prestige and popular acclaim to neglect and
finally death, and his replacement by a new attraction. There are no
crazy dreams, no flights from reality, no sudden breakdowns of logic
or continuity.

But the experienced Kafka reader knows that this surface clarity is
deceptive. He finds himself asking the standard Kafka question:
What do all these people and events "really stand for?" The interpreters are eager to help him. They are generally agreed that Kafka is
depicting the life of the artist who is so fanatically devoted to his art
that he neglects to live and becomes an ascetic. It is the old romantic
topos of the *poète maudit*, a version of which we found in Thomas
Mann's *The Buffoon*. But why did Kafka choose this unusual symbol
—a professional faster—to stand for the artist? For Kafka's protagonist hungering is the goal of his existence; his profession is to demonstrate the glory of his unworldliness by breaking his record from fast
to fast. One would expect that, as he sat out his forty days in the

cage, he would keep busy painting pictures or sculpting or composing a symphony or writing a poem. Nothing of the sort; his cage is bare except for a clock. Our hero is not a hungering artist at all but an artist in hungering. The suffering of the artist at the hands of an indifferent public is a by-product either of his social position or of his psychological makeup. A great artist may prefer to starve rather than betray or compromise his artistic vision; but that is very different from saying that the *goal* of his art is to promote starvation to the visiting public.

We are told that the hunger artist lived for the hours during which the public visited his cage. Some have inferred from this that Kafka is telling the story of a false artist, who lives for the publicity he can gain. Does the story lend itself to such an interpretation? Is it not clear, rather, that the hunger artist is set off from his whole environment: the hungfer guards, the impresario, the society ladies, the milling crowds making for the other attractions, with the children alone (symbols of innocence) showing some genuine sympathy for the lonely figure in the cage? If, however, the hunger artist is a noble man, as most interpreters maintain, what is the meaning of the statement that the public visits were the fulfillment of his purpose in life? We will concede that even the most idealistic artist is human enough to wish approbation from the public for whom he creates; but his life goal? Then there is the historic change in the hunger artist's fortunes; to what event in the history of art or in the social history of the artist does this refer? And the panther who takes the place of the hunger artist in the cage—what does he represent? Is the final paragraph a condemnation of the hunger artist or is it poignant irony that links the flesh-eating beast with the butcher guards at the opening of the parable and signals the tragic defeat of nobility by brutal materialism? A comparison between this ending and that of Kafka's most famous story, *Die Verwandlung* (*The Transformation*), is enlightening. In the parable of the hunger artist Kafka raises the old question: If one of the great spiritual leaders of the past—Moses, Jesus, the Buddha, St. Francis—were to return to our world, how would he be received? A crucial factor in interpreting Kafka's answer to this question is the narrator's attitude toward the central character: is he a hero or anti-hero? Some have argued that the hunger artist is portrayed as a ridiculous figure, who deserves the fate that befalls him. They point to the comic touches that are scattered throughout the narrative. Others find the mood of the narrator to be a mixture of sympathy and irony. Now comic touches there undoubtedly are; the question is, what is the source of the irony; does the narrator create it or does life itself mock the hunger artist? The judgment expressed by the narrator toward the end of the story— "It was not the hunger artist who was cheating, the world was cheating him of his reward" — supplies a definitive answer to this question. And it is in the light of this statement that the ambiguous passages should be read.

The basic symbols of the story are food and abstention from food, which symbolize respectively the life of the senses and spirituality, asceticism. Another of Kafka's stories, *Forschungen eines Hundes* (*Investigations of a Dog*), uses the same symbols.

If we think of the hunger artist as an ascetic idealist or religious saint, who devotes his life to the glorification of the spirit, it becomes clear that his mission in life is to *demonstrate* to humanity that the unworldly life is admirable and easy to achieve. The last puzzling interchange between the hunger artist and the circus manager, in which the hunger artist seems to contradict himself almost in the same breath, now takes on sense. The behavior of the other characters becomes intelligible; all the symbols, even the lone clock in the cage, become transparent. Everything points to the conclusion that Kafka is writing not about a hungering artist, but about an artist in hungering.

A Hunger Artist

In the last decades the interest in hunger artists has greatly declined.
It used to be quite profitable to produce fasting spectacles on a grand
scale under one's own management: today this is quite impossible.
Those were different times. The hunger artist would attract the
attention of a whole city, and the interest grew from fast day to fast
day; everyone wanted to see him at least once every day. In the later
stages of the fast there were holders of season tickets who sat for days
before the little barred cage. Exhibitions were held at night too, in
torchlight, to enhance the effect. In fine weather the cage was taken
out-of-doors and a special exhibition was arranged for children.
While for the elders the hunger artist was often no more than a joke,
in which they participated because it was fashionable, the children
would gaze at him in open-mouthed astonishment, holding each
other by the hand for security. Here he sat on his bed of straw, even
scorning to use a chair, pallid, dressed in a black tricot through
which his ribs stuck out grotesquely, occasionally nodding politely,
answering questions with a strained smile, or stretching his arm
through the bars of the cage to let someone feel how skinny it was,
then plunging once more into deep abstraction, conscious of nothing, not even of the ticking clock—so important to him—the sole
furnishing in the cage, gazing before him with eyes almost closed,
and now and then sipping water from a tiny glass to moisten his lips.

Besides the changing stream of spectators a guard of three men,
chosen by the public, was always present; strangely enough, these
were usually butchers, whose duty it was to watch the hunger artist
day and night, lest he should somehow contrive to take nourishment
in secret. But this was a mere formality, introduced to appease the
masses, for the initiated were well aware that the hunger artist would

never, under any circumstances, have touched food during a fast, not even under compulsion; the honor of his art forbade it. Of course, not all his guards could grasp this fact; often there were guards on the night shift who carried out their duties in a very perfunctory way, deliberately retiring into a distant corner and becoming absorbed in a game of cards, with the obvious intention of giving the hunger artist an opportunity of taking a little snack from a secret store which they imagined he must have somewhere. Nothing was more agonizing to the hunger artist than such guards; they saddened him, they made fasting horribly difficult for him. Sometimes he overcame his weakness and sang as long as he could during such watches, to show these people how unfounded their suspicions were. But that did not help much; they merely wondered at his skill in being able to eat and sing at the same time. He much preferred the guards who sat close to the cage, were not satisfied with the dim night-lighting in the hall but focused on him the rays of the electric torches supplied by the impresario. The harsh glare did not disturb him in the least; sleep was of course out of the question, and he could always doze off, in any light, at any time, even in the noisy, overfilled hall. He was quite prepared to sit up all night with such guards, joke with them, tell them tales of his wanderings and listen to their stories, merely to keep them awake and prove to them over and over again that he had no food in his cage and that he was fasting as none of them could fast. He was happiest when morning came and a lavish breakfast was brought to them at his expense, which they attacked with the appetite of healthy men who had spent an arduous night of watching. There were, to be sure, people who purported to see in these breakfasts an improper attempt to influence the guards; but this was really going too far, and when they were asked if they were willing to take over the night watch without breakfast, just to serve the cause, they faded away; but their suspicions were not allayed.

Of course, such suspicions were part and parcel of the art of fasting. For no one could spend all his days and nights keeping an uninterrupted watch on the hunger artist; and so no one could know from personal observation whether the fasting had been continuous and uninterrupted; only the hunger artist himself could know that, he alone could be the completely satisfied spectator of his fast. But he too was never satisfied—for another reason; if he had grown so thin that many people had to stay away from his performances because they could not bear to look at him, it was perhaps not because of his fasting but because of his dissatisfaction with himself. For he alone knew, as not even the initiated could know, how easy it was to fast. It was the easiest thing in the world. He made no secret of this, but no one believed him. Those who were most kindly disposed toward him called it modesty, but most people said he was publicity mad or even a swindler, who found it easy to fast because he knew how to make it easy and was even brazen enough to half admit it. He had to accept all this, and in the course of the years he had got used to it; but inwardly this dissatisfaction consumed him, and—this much everyone had to admit—he had never yet willingly left his cage at the end of a fast. The impresario had set a maximum of forty days for a fasting period; he never allowed a fast to exceed this limit, not even in the great metropolitan centers of the world, and for a good reason. Experience showed that, by carefully controlled advertising, the interest of a city could be increasingly stimulated for about forty days, but beyond that the public failed to respond and a marked decrease in attendance could be noted. Of course, there were minor variations between cities and different countries, but as a rule the maximum period was forty days. On the fortieth day the cage was draped in flowers and the door was opened. The amphitheater was filled with enthusiastic spectators, a military band played, two physicians entered the cage to make the necessary tests on the hunger artist, the results were announced to the audience through a megaphone, and finally two young ladies, feeling happy that they had been chosen for the honor, came to escort the hunger artist down the few steps that led from the cage to a small table where a carefully selected invalid's meal had been set out. And at this moment the hunger artist invariably put up a resistance. He was willing enough to place his bony arms into the outstretched hands of the ladies who were bending over him, but he refused to stand up. Why stop fasting just now, after forty days? He could have held out for a long time yet, for an indefinite time; why stop just now, when he was at his peak, when in fact he had not yet reached his peak? Why did they want to cheat him of the fame that would be his if he continued to fast, if he became not merely the greatest hunger artist of all time—he felt he was that already—but if he broke his own record beyond human imagination, for he felt that there were no limits to his power of fasting. Why did this mob, which pretended to admire him so much, have so little

patience with him; if he could endure to go on fasting, why couldn't
they endure it? Besides, he was tired, felt comfortable in the straw,
and now he was supposed to stand up to his full height and partake of
that food the mere thought of which made him feel sick; it was only
out of consideration for the ladies that he was able, with an effort, to
suppress his nausea. And he looked up into the eyes of the ladies,
apparently so kind but really so cruel, and shook his head, which
hung heavy on his feeble neck. And then there happened what
always happened. The impresario approached and raised his arms
silently above the hunger artist's head (the music made talking
impossible), as if inviting heaven to look down at its handiwork here
on the straw, this abject martyr — which the hunger artist indeed was,
but in a very different sense. The impresario grasped the hunger
artist around the emaciated waist, seeking through exaggerated caution to convey an impression of the fragility of the object he was
handling; then he covertly shook the hunger artist slightly, so that his
legs and body swayed uncontrollably in the air, and handed him to
the ladies, who had by this time turned deathly pale. Now the hunger
artist endured everything; his head lay limp on his chest as if it had
rolled away and hung on by some inexplicable means; his body
formed a hollow curve; his legs were pressed firmly against the knees
as if in an effort of self-preservation, yet they scraped the floor as if it
were not solid ground, which they were still seeking; and the whole
weight of the body — a very slight one to be sure — rested on one of the
ladies, who was panting (this was not how she had pictured her pres-
tigious duties), seeking help, first stretching her neck to the limit to
avoid contact with the hunger artist's face; but since this effort failed
and her more fortunate companion did not come to her aid but,
quivering and trembling, was content to hold the hunger artist's
hand, that little bundle of bones, extended in front of her, she then
burst into tears, to the delighted laughter of the whole auditorium,
and was finally replaced by an attendant, who had been waiting
there for a long time in anticipation of this development. Then came
the meal, a small portion of which was administered by the impresario while the hunger artist sat in a trancelike state, to the accompaniment of a stream of cheerful patter designed to divert attention
from his condition. Then the public was favored by a toast, osten-
sibly whispered into the impresario's ear by the hunger artist; the
orchestra underlined the whole proceedings by a grand flourish; the

crowd dispersed, and no one had any cause to be dissatisfied with the
event, no one except the hunger artist, always he alone.

In this way he lived on for many years, with regular short intervals
of rest, in seeming splendor, honored by the world, yet in spite of
everything in a depressed state of mind, which was aggravated by the
fact that no one had the wit to take it seriously. For what comfort
could be offered him? What was there left for him to wish for? And
when an occasional good-natured person turned up, who pitied him
and tried to explain to him that his melancholy could probably be
traced to his fasting, it could happen—especially if the fasting had
reached an advanced stage—that the hunger artist would reply with
an outburst of fury and begin to shake the bars of the cage like an
animal, to the terror of the bystanders. However, to handle such
scenes the impresario had devised a favorite punishment. He would
apologize to the assembled public for the hunger artist's conduct,
explaining that it could only be excused by the irritation caused by
the fasting, something that well-fed people simply could not grasp.
Then he went on to offer the same explanation for the hunger artist's
assertion that he could fast much longer still; praised the lofty aspira-
tion, the good will, the great self-denial implied by this claim. But
then he sought to refute the assertion by the simple device of producing photographs—which were sold to the public—showing the
hunger artist on the fortieth day of a fast, lying on his bed in a state
of almost utter exhaustion. This perversion of the truth, though it
was familiar to the hunger artist, never failed to unnerve him anew,
it was too much for him to take. The consequence of a premature
ending of the fast was here represented as its cause! How could one
combat such obtuseness, such monumental stupidity? Once again he
had eagerly listened to the impresario in good faith; but when the
photographs appeared, his fingers released the bars of the cage, he
sank back into the straw with a sigh, and the public, restored to calm,
could once more come forward to inspect him.

Looking back on such scenes a few years later, the spectators were
often at a loss to understand themselves. For in the interval the
change mentioned above had taken place; it had come about quite
suddenly; there may have been deep-seated reasons for it, but who
cared enough to look for them? At all events, one day the pampered
hunger artist saw himself abandoned by the pleasure-seeking mob,
which preferred to surge toward other spectacles. Once more the

impresario raced with him through half of Europe, to see whether
they could uncover the old interest here or there; but it was all in
vain; as if by secret agreement, an actual dislike of exhibition fasting
had sprung up everywhere. Of course, the change could not really
have come about so suddenly; and now, after the event, people recalled many indications which, in the intoxication of success, had not
been properly heeded nor adequately dealt with, and now it was too
late to do anything about the situation. No doubt the time would
come again when fasting would return to favor; but that was small
comfort for those living in our age. What was the hunger artist to do
now? He who had received the homage of thousands could not
exhibit himself in booths at minor country fairs, and as for adopting
another profession, not only was the hunger artist too old for that,
but he was too fanatically devoted to fasting. So he dismissed the
impresario, the companion of an unparalleled career, and entered
the service of a large circus; in order not to offend his sensitivity, he
did not even glance at the contract he signed.

A big circus, with its multitude of people, animals and instruments, counterbalancing and supplementing each other, can always
use everyone, even a hunger artist, provided of course that his
demands are appropriately modest; moreover, in this particular instance, it was not the hunger artist alone who was engaged but his old
and famous name as well; indeed, considering the peculiar nature of
this art, which is not adversely affected by the age of the performer,
one could not even say that a worn-out artist who had passed the
peak of his powers was taking refuge in a quiet nook of the circus
world. On the contrary, the hunger artist assured the circus people
that he could fast as well as ever, which was quite believable; in fact,
he asserted that, if he were allowed to have his way — which he was
granted without argument — he would now really astonish the world;
an assertion, to be sure, that merely provoked a smile on the lips of
the circus experts, who knew the spirit of the times, which the hunger
artist, in his zeal, easily forgot.

But in reality even the hunger artist did not lose sight of the true
state of affairs; he assumed as a matter of course that he and his cage
would not be featured as a main attraction of the circus but placed
near the stables, though in a spot that was quite accessible to the
viewers. Large signs in bright colors surrounded the cage and announced what was to be seen there. During the intermissions of the

main performance, when the public thronged to the stables to see the animals, it was almost unavoidable that they should pass the hunger artist and make a brief pause before his cage; they might have stayed longer if the stream of people through this narrow passage, who were unable to grasp what was blocking their progress to the popular stables, had not made it impossible to indulge themselves in leisurely, calm contemplation. And that was the reason why the hunger artist trembled at these intermission visits, though he looked forward to them as the fulfillment of his purpose in life. At first he had hardly been able to wait for these intermissions; he had anticipated the surging mass with delight; but only too soon — even the most stubborn, almost deliberate self-deception could not stand up against the weight of experience — he became convinced that these were mostly, over and over again, almost without exception, people who wished to get to the stables. And this view from afar was still the best part of the experience. For when the crowds reached his cage, he was surrounded by the turmoil of shouting and abuse, coming from the cliques that kept forming, consisting of those who wanted to see the hunger artist in a leisurely way — and these came to be the more annoying of the two groups — not out of a spirit of understanding, if you please, but through whim and stubborness, and those who only wished to get to the stables at once. When the big mob had passed, the stragglers followed, and these latter, who were no longer prevented from staying there as long as they wished, hurried past with long strides, hardly casting a side-glance at him, so that they might reach the animals in time. And none too often a lucky accident brought a father and his children to the cage; the father would point his finger at the hunger artist, explain in detail what this was all about, tell of years gone by when he had been present at similar performances but on an incomparably grander scale; then the children would still be puzzled about it, for neither life nor school had prepared them for it — what did fasting mean to them? — yet the gleam in their searching eyes betrayed something of new, more favorable times to come. Perhaps, the hunger artist would sometimes say to himself, things would improve slightly if his cage were not so close to the stables. This made the odds against him too great, to say nothing of the fact that he was hurt and permanently depressed by the stench from the stables, the restlessness of the animals at night, the chunks of raw meat that were carried past his cage for them, their roaring at feeding time. But he did not dare complain to the management; for after all, it was the animals that brought him the crowds of visitors, among whom there might be an occasional one who was interested in him. And who could tell into what corner they might thrust him if he reminded them of his existence and that, in point of fact, he was merely an obstruction on the way to the stables?

A slight obstruction, to be sure, and one that kept getting slighter. In these times people were becoming accustomed to the fact that it was an anomaly to show interest in a hunger artist and it was this habituation that sealed his doom. He might—and he did—fast as well as he had ever done, but nothing could save him, people simply passed him by. Try to explain the art of fasting to someone! If he doesn't feel it, he will never be made to grasp it. The beautiful signs became dirty and illegible, they were torn down; and it occurred to no one to replace them. The little tablet announcing the number of days the fast had lasted, which in early times had been carefully changed, remained the same day after day, for after the first weeks the attendants had grown tired of performing even this trifling duty; and so the hunger artist kept on fasting, as he had once dreamed of doing; and he succeeded without effort, as he had predicted he would, but no one counted the days; no one, not even the hunger artist himself, knew how great was the feat he had achieved; and his heart grew heavy. And when occasionally an idler stopped before his cage and made fun of the number on the tablet and talked of fraud, it was the most stupid lie that apathy and innate malice could invent, for it was not the hunger artist who was cheating, the world was cheating him of his reward.

However, many more days went by and this too came to an end. Once the cage caught a manager's eye and he asked the attendants why this good, serviceable cage was standing there unused, filled with rotted straw; no one knew the answer until one man looked at the tablet and remembered the hunger artist. "You're still fasting?" asked the manager, "When will you finally stop?" "Pardon me, all of you," whispered the hunger artist; only the manager, who had his ear to the bars, could make out what he was saying. "Of course we pardon you," said the manager, tapping his forehead with his finger to indicate to the attendants the hunger artist's mental state. "I have always wanted you to admire my fasting," said the hunger artist. "We do admire it," said the manager obligingly. "But you shouldn't admire it," said the hunger artist. "Well then, we don't admire it," said the manager; "but why shouldn't we admire it?" "Because I have to fast, I can do nothing else," said the hunger artist. "Imagine that," said the manager, "why can't you do anything else?" "Because," said the hunger artist, raising his little head slightly and pursing his lips as if for a kiss, and speaking right into the manager's ear so that not a word would be lost, "because I could not find the food I like. If I had found it, believe me, I wouldn't have made a fuss but eaten my fill like you and anyone else." These were his last words, but his dimmed eyes still shone with the firm, though no longer proud conviction that he would continue to fast.

"Clean up now," said the manager, and they buried the hunger artist and his straw. Into the cage they put a young panther. Even the dullest wit felt refreshed at the sight of the wild beast ranging around the cage that had stood desolate so long. He lacked nothing. The food he liked was brought to him by the guards, who did not have to beat their brains out looking for it. He did not seem to mind his loss of freedom; this noble body, equipped with everything it needed to the bursting point, seemed to carry its freedom with it; somewhere in the region of its jaws it seemed to lie; and the joy of life emanated from its jaws with such fiery power that the spectators did not find it easy to retain their equanimity. But they made an effort, crowded about the cage, and refused to budge.

Werner Bergengruen

1892 — 1964

The preamble to Bergengruen's novel *Der Grosstyrann und das Gericht* (*The Arch Tyrant and the Court,* 1935) states: "This book reports on the temptations of the mighty and the susceptibility of those who are powerless and threatened in the face of seduction. The report shall be of such a nature that our faith in human perfection will be shaken: for our perfection can of course exist in nothing but this faith."

This statement epitomizes Bergengruen's program as a writer. The themes that concern him are: power, justice, the human condition and faith in a world order which it is man's duty to maintain in the perfection it had when it came from the hands of God. A man who thinks in such terms is religious and conservative; Bergengruen is both. A convert to Roman Catholicism, he reveres tradition and traditional Christian values. But he is not a reactionary; he does not want to conserve that which should yield to juster and better social forms. He is not for anarchic freedom, but for an independence that is self-imposed restraint. Proceeding from this view of life, Bergengruen feels justified in speaking of our world as fundamentally sound. By this he means that the evil, corruption, baseness and absurdity in it are man's fault, not God's. In the things that matter, however, the conservative Christian Bergengruen proclaims the same values as the avant-garde atheists Sartre and Camus: political commitment, ethical choice, the subordination of self to the common good, the "authentic" existence. Bergengruen showed his commitment during the Nazi regime, when he wrote subversive poetry which was circulated surreptitiously in multigraphed form or was published outside Germany.

Bergengruen is a writer with a message, but the message is not trivial, nor is it presented didactically. Nature and history, human life and the destiny of nations are for him a pledge of eternal order. To reveal this order is the mission of the poet; not to advocate, nor to proclaim, but to reveal through art. For Bergengruen, the core of fiction, which is his principal concern, is a "metaphysical point": an ethical, social or religious motif.

The "metaphysical point" of *Die Feuerprobe* (*Ordeal by Fire*) is St. Paul's message to the Corinthians, "For the letter killeth, but the spirit giveth life." Barbara is unharmed by the glowing iron because her repentance is sincere. At the time of the ordeal she is pure of soul; the "righteous God who trieth the heart and reins" knows this and therefore abides by His covenant with man to accept genuine remorse for sin and crime and restore the erstwhile sinner to his former state of grace within the human community. For Barbara's transgression is not like the gross misdeeds of the irresponsible rabble whose antics are described in the story's opening paragraphs. She is a woman with a high sense of duty and responsibility, even in her sin. Her passion for Schwenkhusen is a noble, though tragically illicit, love, like that of Tristan and Isolde. Its flame is fanned by the Pharisaical coldness of her husband, that automaton of bourgeois virtue and self-righteousness. Under the shock of exposure she becomes aware of the enormity of her crime against one of the basic taboos of mankind. She is not a rebel against social laws, as Tristan and Isolde are, but a woman who accepts traditional sanctions and is therefore prepared to live by the standards of society. Schwenkhusen is a person of different caliber. He is no Tristan, but closer to the rabble whose licentious doings are mentioned at the outset. Or maybe he *is* a Tristan, a genuine disciple of *amour passion*, a believer in the doctrine that love permits everything. And do not events confirm him in this belief? Why did God save him from destruction in the Finnish forests, why did He permit the miracle of the ordeal, except to demonstrate the principle that love conquers all? So he renews his pursuit of Barbara and rekindles in her the illicit passion from which she had temporarily freed herself. Consequently God, whom she had compelled by her sincere repentance, punishes her through a second miracle: she is burned by a *cold* iron. For it is the paradox of the miracles in this tale that they do not cancel out nature, but confirm it, if by nature we understand the true essence of things, rather than their external appearance. The iron is by nature cold; heat applied to it externally does not alter its nature. It is still cold to those who are innocent, like the repentant, and therefore pure, Barbara. At the second ordeal the iron is physically cold; but to the guilty Barbara it feels hot. The harmless physical condition of the iron cannot save her from the retribution she deserves in a well-ordered universe. By the time the story ends, her husband Tidemann has been punished adequately for his coldness. The closing paragraph suggests that retribution will now come for Schwenkhusen too. This is a moral tale.

So much for the "metaphysical point." The novella is also a powerful study of character, depicting the development of three principal persons and delineating briefly but sharply the inner profiles of peripheral figures. The transformation of Barbara, under Schwenkhusen's influence, from a humble and contrite Christian into an arrogant, self-righteous, self-indulgent pagan, is depicted with consummate mastery. The style is terse, cold, controlled, objective—until the ordeal itself is described. Here the author goes into minute detail, giving us a series of close-ups, training his camera on the principal actors in the tense drama, then upon the bystanders in the church.

Bergengruen believed that the modern novella should tell of an extraordinary event, as fiction had done from the very beginning. Of the stories in this collection, only Kleist's *Michael Kohlhaas* can rival *Ordeal by Fire* for sheer excitement. Both stories combine cold factualness with excursions into the supernatural. And both aim at a "metaphysical point" which is ethical in character.

Werner Bergengruen was a Baltic German, born into the German minority of Riga, Lithuania, when that country was a province of the Russian Empire. He was educated in Germany and fought on the German side in the First World War. During the Russian Revolution he joined the Baltic militia in its unsuccessful war against the Red Army. Later he traveled extensively and lived from journalism for some years, until he decided to devote himself to creative literature. He wrote lyric poetry and fiction, but the latter is the most characteristic product of his genius. His writings have been translated into various European languages. In 1936 he became a convert to Roman Catholicism, and the following year incurred the displeasure of the National Socialist hierarchy, which expelled him from the National Chamber of Letters as "one unsuited to co-operate in the promotion of German culture through his literary publications." He lived in Germany, Switzerland and Italy, a country he loved dearly. He died in 1964.

Ordeal by Fire

(1)

In those strife-torn times it was decided that there should be two councilmen in the city hall every night, to receive messages and, when necessary, to make quick decisions of limited importance. The plan demanded that every councilman should spend about one night each week away from home; this was possibly of benefit to the city, but it was detrimental both to the domestic situation of the councilmen and to the security of order and morals. In the house of Henning von Warendrop, a widower of advanced years, the servants treated themselves to a party at which the best china was damaged. Lubert Mistenborch's maid ran around in the suburbs all night and later drowned her child under the ice in the Dvina River. Gottfried von Radenow's young son, who attended St. Peter's School, consorted with women in Ellenbrook; one morning he was brought home with a wound in his skull. Tidemann Gripen, finally, was taken aside on the street by a cousin: annoying rumors were circulating; he could not test their accuracy, but was duty-bound to call his relative's attention to them.

Tidemann Gripen went home to call his wife to account. When he had left his cousin, he was still smarting from the silly piece of gossip; by the time he had reached the door of his home he believed that his disgrace and Barbara's guilt had been proved.

His wife stood in the kitchen, supervising the cleaning and shredding of the cabbage which was to be pickled for the winter. She looked up in surprise when her husband came in; she was not accustomed to seeing him in the kitchen. The servants, too, raised their eyes in astonishment and stopped their singing.

Gripen took Barbara by the hand and led her silently into the drawing room. As he let her hand go, it was almost as if he were thrusting it away.

"Has Schwenkhusen been here?" he asked.

His wife looked with fear into his angry face.

"Schwenkhusen? When? Today?" she asked in return.

Gripen began to pant.

"You know precisely what I'm asking," he said threateningly. "I want to know whether Schwenkhusen lay in my bed while I was at city hall."

His wife parted her lips, which were trembling.

"Who said so?" she shrieked.

"It doesn't matter who said so, but whether it happened. Answer; yes or no?"

"No," his wife said angrily, and, turning away, left the room with heaving shoulders.

The councilman went to see Schwenkhusen, a young and passionate person, who was considered to be frivolous and was popular. He belonged to the Black Heads company, lived lavishly and hospitably and, as an unmarried man, had his mother with him.

Gripen found the mother in a troubled state. That very morning a military unit had departed for war; as they said in Riga, it was a quick thrust against the Bishop of Dorpat and the Vitalian Brothers, who had landed in northern Livonia at the bishop's request. The Black Heads company had had to supply fourteen horsemen and their esquires for the levy; Schwenkhusen was one of them.

Gripen wished the mother the happy return of her son and left.

From that day on, husband and wife ate their meals in silence; nor did they sleep together any more. The councilman spent little time at home. It was at this point that he assumed the habit of turning his head around with a jerk as if he were trying to catch some slanderer or someone laughing at him in secret. His severe taciturnity was noticed without causing surprise; everyone knew about the rumor, and in these unsettled times every rumor had its power over the minds of men.

His wife did not think of hiding. She went to church, to market and to social events still erect and beautiful. Some people deduced from this a stubborn insolence to which guilt might also be ascribed; others deduced the security given by an innocent conscience; and still others, leaving aside the question of guilt or innocence, found in her bearing merely a confirmation of that proud, hard will which everyone knew she possessed.

Gripen spent another night at the city hall. A messenger was led in. He brought the report of a military catastrophe.

Gripen asked about this and that. Finally he asked about Schwenkhusen.

"Schwenkhusen is dead," was the reply.

When day dawned, many people mourned for their relatives, others for the horses and armor with which they had had to equip their servants and substitutes. Schwenkhusen's mother was sought out by many and comforted.

Gripen did not come home from the city hall until noon. During luncheon he began: "Do you know about it yet?"

"What?" asked Barbara, who had not been out of the house that day. It struck Gripen that he was hearing her voice for the first time in days.

"Schwenkhusen has been killed in battle," he said, and watched her face.

"But surely he wasn't the only one?" she cried vehemently, and pulled at her amber necklace.

He quoted numbers and names.

They were silent. The maid served a new course.

"Perhaps not even his mother waited for his return as eagerly as I have," Gripen began again. "Perhaps not even you."

She did not speak; she merely looked stonily into his face with her big, beautifully shaped eyes. For a while each endured the other's glance.

"What does this mean?" she asked.

Gripen bent forward over the table and shouted: "Now it must be brought to light in another way!"

She was silent.

"Why don't you speak? How do you intend to cleanse yourself?"

"I?" she asked in astonishment.

"You know what I reproach you with. But perhaps you don't know that the city is talking about it."

"I shouldn't like to have to worry about that!" his wife replied. "When I married I believed that my husband would protect me against slander."

"Very well," he said. "It may have been unjust for me to mention the idle talk, although my position prohibits me from offending the common man or even from providing him with an example of domestic ambiguity. But it's for my own sake. We have lived together for four years and we are to continue to do so till one of us dies. But I cannot go on with you this way."

"You must settle that with yourself," replied Barbara. "It is your guilt and strikes at you personally if you think lightly of your wife. What do you want of me?"

"Hold the iron!" he whispered.

She moved the upper part of her body backwards against the back of her chair. At the same time, she bent her head down toward the table so that Gripen could not look into her face. She felt his panting breath at the nape of her neck.

"Do I know the municipal ordinances better than you?" she asked.

The citizens of Riga, aristocrats and commoners alike, enjoyed the privilege of immunity from compulsion to undergo any test or to fight a duel arranged by the courts.

"The law cannot compel you, I know that. That's why I want you to do it voluntarily. If you refuse, I shall consider you convicted and I will sue for adultery. Whether the suit will be valid, now that Schwenkhusen is dead, I can't say; but bringing the suit will in itself indicate my opinion to the city and condemn you as an adulteress."

"Or you as a madman."

"You are afraid of the iron. If you were innocent, you would not need to be afraid."

"Where the law demands a test it should be complied with. To submit to a test when one doesn't have to would be to challenge God. It is God's privilege to test human beings. But it is not permitted to humans to emulate Him in this way."

"Don't refuse, Barbara. I will make you live a life that you will not like."

"And do you think that if I withstand the test I shall be able to live with you as before?"

"Can you do so now?" he asked softly, and received no answer.

Gripen supported himself on the back of her chair. "Don't give me an answer yet," he said bending forward. "I'll ask you again tomorrow."

She stood up. The swift movement of her chair backwards forced

the man almost violently aside. She went out without looking at him,
her head held erect.

Next morning he repeated his question. She replied briefly, with
reasons that were undeniably valid. It was guilt that should be
proved, not innocence. The mere existence of the privilege, which
could not possibly have been created for the protection of the guilty,
testified to the insanity of his request. Would he perhaps be willing to
hold a glowing iron in his hand to demonstrate his innocence in the
slaying of Abel by Cain, in the boiling over of the breakfast soup or
the frost of last night? He felt innocent about these, so what did he
have to fear?

"I am not accused, Barbara," he replied. "You are. What you say
is right. But don't think that it has weight because of that. You don't
believe this yourself."

In this Gripen was right, more than he realized. No, the grounds
which his wife produced had no weight in her own mind. The
moment she expressed them she felt disgust at their indisputable
rightness. Schwenkhusen was dead; this alone had weight, but this
one fact she dared not confess.

The husband asked again. She refused, but again declined to produce grounds. He left her for a time, then asked again; she gave no
reply. For hours she sat huddled at the hearth, without light, first in
the twilight, then in darkness, paying no heed to the servants who
came with questions, or to her husband when he came home. And he
no longer put the question. She tried to picture Schwenkhusen as if
she could question him, but Schwenkhusen was not there. There was
no one in the world but herself. She tried to picture her husband
bringing the accusation; the attempt led nowhere, except that she
noticed how honor and shame in the eyes of human beings were a
matter of indifference when measured by the degree of her despair.
She tried to imagine how things would go at the ordeal by fire but her
thoughts could not go beyond Schwenkhusen's death.

Gripen came into the dark room.

"Is anyone here?" he asked harshly.

"I."

"You've had time to consider," he said. "I'll ask you tomorrow for
the last time. After that there will be no more talk of the matter one
way or another."

Her eyes were accustomed to the dark, so she saw the outline of his
figure. He's like that iron, she thought, and I have held that iron. It

is as cold as stone at its core, yet it glows like fire when it has under-gone heating from without. The fire does not cancel out the cold nature of the iron, but neither can the cold nature of the iron destroy the fire.

Gripen called the maid and ordered her to bring him blankets and pillows for his night at city hall. He went without saying good-by.

Barbara did not go to bed. When dawn came she got up from her easy chair and studied the last red glow on the hearth. She was almost tempted to put her hand into the coals.

The servants were still sleeping; there was a deathlike silence in the house. She went into the kitchen and washed her face. "The fact that Schwenkhusen has lost his life," she told herself, "must not sway my judgment in any way. It would be foolish if I wished to see in this a sign for myself, for after all, many others who had nothing to do with the affair were also killed!"

But at the same time she felt the clarity and strength of her nature shaken. This clarity and strength did not now reach beyond the recognition that there was nothing left that could still have value for her. She thought of her tiny son, who lay in St. Peter's Church be-neath a huge stone slab carved with the family coat of arms. A week after being baptized, he had become ill, and had died ten days later. Schwenkhusen had presented a baptismal gift in the name of the Black Heads and had spoken the traditional words: "We wish that the child may some day become a councilman of Riga, or at least king of Denmark."

Barbara interrupted her pacing and said aloud: "I place myself in the hands of God, who has brought Schwenkhusen to his death."

When Gripen came home, Barbara was no longer in the house. The head maid informed him what she had been told to say: the lady was prepared to fulfill the master's wish. Would he let her know the time and place? Until then she would be living in the Convent of St. Mary and Jacob.

(2)

Barbara spent the days in the Convent of the Virgin in seclusion, not even associating with the nuns, among whom she had relatives and schoolmates. Once she received a message from her husband and replied by declaring her willingness to hear it. When, soon after that,

a visit was announced, she declined to see him. This was on a Saturday, the day on which the inmates of the convent usually made confession. The woman searched her conscience according to the prescriptions of the Church, stirred remorse and suffering in herself and
waited patiently till her turn came. She confessed, received absolution and carried out the penance imposed on her earnestly and with
faith.

From then on she no longer left her cell, nor did she utter a word
to anyone, in order not to endanger, even through a venial sin, the
state of grace she had attained. On Sunday morning she took the
Sacrament.

For High Mass she went to St. Peter's Church. The church was
fuller than usual, and when she went through the nave toward the
pews reserved for the councilmen, a sort of tidal wave swept through
the throng. People nudged each other, whispered, craned their
necks. Barbara did not notice, so completely had she turned in upon
herself, with all the powers of her proud and passionate soul. She
walked slowly, dressed all in white, her head erect, her hair and face
under a white veil. Tidemann entered the pew soon after her. They
did not greet each other.

High Mass was ended, but the church did not empty. The throng
increased. In the streets around St. Peter's the people stood pressed
together: burghers, servants, non-German peasants from the surrounding country, members of the German Order from the castle,
vassals of the religious order of the land. What was to take place in
the vestry seemed monstrous, partly because of its rarity, but even
more because it had been undertaken voluntarily. Most excited of all
were the country folk, both peasants and nobles, because they lacked
that privilege accorded to the townspeople.

When the husband and wife stepped into the vestry, the basin was
already piled high with coals, filled with glowing cubes of fuel. Beside it stood the sacristan in his robes of office, and beside him, in
their Sunday clothes, stood an official master smith and the sacristan's half-grown son—a saddler's apprentice—holding a pair of
tongs in his hand. All three raised their heads quickly and tried to
look into the woman's face, but their eyes could not penetrate the
dense white of the veil. Behind the Gripens the officiating priest had
entered, an aged and serene man. As people pressed in, the sacristan
hastened forward. He allowed a few distinguished people whom the

councilman had summoned against their will, as witnesses, to enter, then bolted the door.

The priest beckoned to the sacristan's son with a motion of his chin. The young boy handed him the iron, a rectangular object the size of a child's hand. The priest studied it carefully, held it out to the official master smith and asked whether he recognized it under oath as being true iron, untampered with and suitable for the test. The smith affirmed this. Then the priest showed it to the councilman and the witnesses. They nodded silently.

The priest sprinkled the piece of iron with holy water and said: "I bless you in the name of the Father and the Son and the Holy Ghost, thus you are elevated above all other objects of your kind." He placed it on the charcoal; it hissed.

The priest said: "Lord Jesus, Thou Initiator and Completer of all justice we beg Thee to grant this iron Thy grace, that we may recognize justice from it."

In a softer voice he asked Barbara for her hand. She stepped up to him; they stood facing each other in the center of the circle. The woman's hands had hitherto been hidden in her white garment. Now she stretched her right hand out of the ample sleeve, which hung loose at the wrist, thus exposing half of her lower arm. The hand was beautiful, shapely and strong, the only part of the body that stood bared to view. About the wrist there was a simple golden bracelet, an heirloom from her mother's family. The rings that had been given her by Gripen were not on her fingers.

The priest took her hand carefully, turned it and tested the palm. He washed the hand in consecrated water and dried it with a new linen towel, which he first held out to those present to test.

"I have been able to find neither salve nor powder on it," he said. "He who would see may see. He who would object, let him speak now or keep his peace forever after."

No one stirred. Slowly Barbara let her hand fall. Now she remained in her former position, white, erect and motionless.

The smith studied the coal basin. He cleared his throat, then said in an undertone: "As far as the iron is concerned, we need wait no longer."

The priest did not trust himself to speak. He made a sign to Barbara and to the sacristan's boy.

Barbara stretched out her open hand. Her elbow rested on her hipbone. Her hand and lower arm stood out at right angles from her body. Then her fingers curved slightly like those of a child eager to get hold of a gift it had obtained after much yearning and begging.

Gripen distorted his mouth and groaned. This was the first sound that was heard from him. The sacristan's son took the red-hot iron from the coal basin with the tongs and handed them to the priest; the latter drew a deep breath and stretched out his right hand, holding the tongs. The sacristan drew a sand-glass from his pocket and held it up. The head of the tongs clasping the iron was above the woman's palm, only a finger's breadth away from it.

The priest took hold of the left arm of the tongs with his left hand and suddenly pulled it aside. The sacristan turned the sand-glass over in his raised hand, and sand began to trickle down, visible to everyone; but no one looked. The piece of iron lay on Barbara's palm; the golden bracelet shone reddish in its reflection.

The hand did not stir, the arm did not stir, her whole figure remained motionless. Gripen lost the power to endure the sight of this immobility. His eyes sought help in the running white sand. But the sand ran slowly. It was not the slight quantity of sand filling the space of the glass that had to run through the narrow strait between the upper and lower containers. It was hundredweights of sand, wagonloads of sand, all the sand from the Baltic shore, from Danzig to Pernau; this sand trickled through eternities.

The priest's eyes moved swiftly from the sand to the iron, from the iron to the sand. The open tongs wavered close to the slowly graying metal. At the moment when the flow of sand ceased, after the last little grain had fallen, the tongs closed in. When the iron clanged on the brick floor, Barbara's hand retained its position, as if what had just been removed had been a snowflake.

All eyes darted to the same spot in the vestry; here they lingered awhile, then drew away, met each other shyly and dropped as though they had been blinded. The spot was the outstretched white hand below the golden bracelet and silken sheen of the sleeve. Nothing could be seen on the hand except a few blackish spots from coal soot. The priest passed the towel carefully over it and they were gone.

The first person to stir was Henning von Warendrop, the aged councilman, who was among the invited witnesses. He bowed deeply and kissed the open hand without daring to touch it with his own.

Then he cast an angry look at Gripen's face, drew back the bolt and went out without saying goodby. He was followed by the other witnesses.

During all this time, those in the vestry had heard the voices of the throng outside like the distant murmuring of treetops. Now that the door stood open until the last witness had gone, cries, questions and wild shouting echoed in the church. The roar of human voices swelled, moved from the church into the streets and filled the vestry even after the door had been closed again.

Barbara dropped her unscathed hand and turned as if she, too, wanted to go. The priest and the smith, the sacristan and his son did not dare look into Gripen's face, which had sunk onto his chest. Suddenly Gripen uttered a cry, fell at his wife's feet and kissed her shoes. The man turned away; only the sacristan's boy stared open mouthed at the couple. As the councilman pressed his eyes into the white hem of her dress, the sacristan's son thought he heard in the stifled stammering an imploring cry for forgiveness.

Barbara bent down to Tidemann, placed both her hands on his head and drew him upright. "God forgives us all, however sinful we are," she said. "Forgive me, too, for whatever I may have done to you."

Together they left the vestry and the church. Barbara had thrown back her veil. Before the portal stood the city constables, pushing the crowd back with the shafts of their spears. It was of little use. the Gripens were able to leave the spot only inch by inch. Women and peasants were on their knees, thrusting each other aside in order to kiss the hem of Barbara's dress. Fists and insults were hurled at the councilman; if the police had not been there, he would have been thrown to the ground. In Sinner's Lane, not far from Gripen's house, a stone was thrown at him; Barbara darted forward and the stone struck her chin, a thin line of blood trickled down her white dress.

In the entrance hall the councilman began: "Everything shall be according to your will. If you ask for it, I will give over to you my house and everything that I bequeathed to you in our marriage contract in case of survival. If you ask for it, my country estate belongs to you. If you ask for it, I will leave the city and go begging on a white cane. I know well that you will not be able to live with me any more."

"I will try, Tidemann," his wife replied.

(3)

Tidemann Gripen had ordered two Masses at St. Peter's Church to be read in perpetuity on the anniversary of the ordeal: one in grateful memory of the event and one for the soul of the dead Schwenkhusen. The iron, it was stipulated in the deed, should be exhibited on the altar steps during these Masses.

In the city the opinion prevailed that Councilman Gripen would, as much as possible, live in retirement in his house. But this expectation was not realized. Rather, it was as if he had condemned himself to exposure. He suffered patiently every look of anger or horror, every deliberate avoidance of a meeting, every insult that was hurled at him from houses and gateways. He showed himself to the world on every occasion where his presence was necessary or even justified.

Barbara, however, kept herself hidden from human beings. A few ladies from the council families had come to visit her, but Barbara had excused herself courteously. On holidays she did not go to High Mass in St. Peter's Church, as the patrician ladies did, letting their maids carry their prayer books and warming stones wrapped in cloths for their feet. Instead, she went, unaccompanied and unnoticed, to one of those poor little churches and chapels visited by the humble city folk or by peasants who had come in from the country; musty interiors in which mendicant monks preached in the Lettish language, and from which you brought back home a bad odor and lice and fleas in your clothes. On one of these morning walks she met Schwenkhusen's mother. Barbara wanted to turn aside, but the old woman crossed the street and embraced her with grief and warmth, repeating: "Poor child! Good child!" Barbara suffered the embrace in silence.

That she wanted to avoid all social life, the people could well understand. Their sympathy and affection turned into reverence but also into fear, for she was a person who had stood under God's judgment. To speak with such a person about servants, market prices, salmon-catching and poultry-feeding did not seem possible. It was not possible to inquire from such a person about her opinion of a new embroidery pattern, or to invite such a person to admire an altar painting that had been imported from Germany and had just been set up, enabling one to read the latest Burgundian fashion. All this, in fact, no longer seemed possible to Barbara either.

The servants reported about her strict brooding, her reticent seriousness; her forbidding, indeed almost arrogant, mien. This, too,
was accepted.

The evening after Epiphany, Gripen met old Henning von Warendrop at the Schaal Gate. Gripen had grown used to having people,
and especially Councilman Warendrop, say little to him, except on
municipal or business matters. So he greeted the old man without
interrupting his walk. But Warendrop came up to him and said:
"This concerns you more than other people, so I am telling it to you
in case you don't know it yet. Schwenkhusen returned home yesterday."

Schwenkhusen sat with his mother, let her fondle him and had difficulty in preventing her from cooking all his favorite dishes simultaneously. He told her of his experiences, not for the first time, and
was compelled to interrupt himself frequently because of her sobs.

"They wanted to take my armor, so they knew that I was still alive.
They dragged me into a peasant house and later onto a ship. Knowing quite well how much a Black Heads brother is worth, they feared
they would lose a large ransom if I died. For that reason they cared
for me better than for their own wounded. If one of them dies, it is
no great misfortune; they get enough recruits. They even had Masses
said and vowed candles, as thick as trees, for my recovery. But I was
not in my right mind for a long time because of fever and weakness,
so they could not negotiate with me about my ransom."

The ship, so he reported, had had to sail away, for vessels from
Riga and Lübeck had been reported. Since they were pursued by
these, anyone who could not fight had to be thrown overboard. Thus
they brought him to the home of friendly fisherfolk, in the rock
islands near Abo, where the thousand islands are, and where there
were many hideaways. Here he lay a long time, cared for and
guarded; one night he escaped, while his wounds were still unhealed,
and suffered distress at sea, losing his mast and rudder.

He shook with horror as he told of those days in the stolen fishing
boat, between cliffs and rocky islands. His mother's tears trickled
through the fingers with which she covered her face. She could not
believe that this man, who had been her little child, could ever again
lead a dance and plan a party. It was a pity, for on such occasions he
had enjoyed much admiration, and this had given her heartfelt satisfaction.

On the morning after his arrival Schwenkhusen had asked his mother at breakfast what had happened in Riga in the meantime. She reported on this or that circumspectly, and considered while she talked whether to tell him about the ordeal by fire. Finally she did so; he would soon learn about it from others. Schwenkhusen at first listened earnestly to her and seemed to his mother to be frightened. But when she had finished, he began to laugh, loud, harshly and long, the way peasants and sailors laugh, and the old woman had the impression that her son had formerly laughed in a different way. But at the same time she was astonished that he had found something to laugh at in this story.

He kissed her hand absent-mindedly and said: "Don't be astonished; I've lived among pirates and fishermen, so occasionally I laugh at inappropriate times."

Schwenkhusen occupied himself with his business, his horses and his hunting dogs. He visited people and gave banquets in the house of the Black Heads company. He received more invitations than he could accept. His house was never empty of congratulatory visitors, especially people from the younger set, who had seen in Schwenkhusen their leader. Women and girls surrounded his mother, kissed her hand and begged her to tell them about her son's experiences. She did so more readily than he. Tirelessly she reported again and again about the drifting fishing boat, which had finally gained firm land in a miraculous way; about Schwenkhusen's beggar life in the Finnish forests, among the peasants of the wilderness, whose language he did not understand; about sickness and hunger, about wandering and snowstorms and monastic hospitals; and how he had finally reached business friends at Reval, who cared for him and advanced him money so that he could supply himself with clothes and undertake the journey home in a sled with a servant. He had been away for fifteen months.

After that meeting with old Warendrop, Gripen had immediately gone to see Schwenkhusen. But the coming and going of the many visitors frightened him back home. He did not see Barbara again that day; she had furnished a separate room for herself and often had her meals brought to her there.

Early next morning the councilman announced himself to Schwenkhusen, who received him in his business room. Schwenkhusen looked at his face in astonishment, for Gripen had had his

broad, reddish beard removed; it was said that when he was looking
in the mirror the quivering candlelight had fallen on his beard, and
Gripen had been frightened, thinking he saw it glow like a coal fire.

Gripen bowed and asked whether Schwenkhusen knew what he
had suspected him of. Schwenkhusen made a deprecatory movement, to characterize the matter as a trifle that was past.

Gripen said: "No, that won't do. I have come to beg your pardon.
If you wish, I will do so in public."

"My dear fellow, for Heaven's sake!" cried Schwenkhusen with a
slight and not quite audible laugh. "Did I escape the pirates and the
Finnish wastes only to die of embarrassment in Riga? Leave well
enough alone, and may God protect us against unpleasantness."

Then he described his adventures and with a smile thanked Gripen
for the Mass he had established for his soul; the donor would no
doubt be kind enough to have it changed from a Mass for the dead
into one for the living.

Gripen waited until he met Barbara in the house. For he only
dared go to her room when she summoned him. He wanted to inform
her of Schwenkhusen's return in a guarded manner; but she interrupted him indifferently with the words: "Is it that? You are telling
me nothing new. I saw him yesterday from my window crossing the
street."

Gripen reported to her about his visit. He had asked Schwenkhusen to come to the Gripen house as he had done in former times.

"You should not have done that, Tidemann," said Barbara coldly.
"I don't want to see him any more."

"Forgive me, but I have been unjust not only to you but to him
too," he replied. "For that reason I believe I owe him public satisfaction; I mean, he should have the opportunity to decline an invitation."

This was the first time he had contradicted her in anything.

However, it was not his protest that finally moved her to yield; it
was the night that preceded this conversation and the night that followed it. She had seen Schwenkhusen walk down the street, give a
beggar a coin, nod to a street urchin and clap a merchant, who stood
in front of his shop, on the shoulder; he had met a constable, who
may have been with him on that swift military thrust, and had gone
on with him, chatting, putting his arm over the constable's in a natural way. These were his movements, this was his behavior. An intoxi-

cating terror rushed into the woman at the window like a stream of white light, dazzled her and brought confusion into the thoughts she had lived with since the day of her great and miraculous trial.

At night she had brought her thoughts to order again, though in a strange way: namely, she commanded herself to believe that it would not do for Schwenkhusen, as a guilty man who had not atoned, ever to come into her presence — the presence of one who had been vindicated, indeed elevated above human essence. From this point of view she gained the strength to tell her husband: "I don't care to see him." But scarcely had Gripen left her when she once more fell a prey to that intoxicating terror, for now a meeting with Schwenkhusen had been brought very close, indeed he was almost an immediate presence. To attain this presence, she realized, would cost her only one word, a word of yielding permission to her beseeching husband.

For a long time Barbara had not enjoyed the vigorous and clear sleep of former years. For many hours of the following night she remained a prisoner of her divided, tormented heart. But in the morning she went to Gripen and said: "I will not put any obstacle in your path. If you wish, send the invitation."

(4)

Schwenkhusen declined an invitation from the head of the Order so that he might accept the one given by Gripen. It was the first time since the ordeal that they had had guests. There were four of them at the table: the Gripens, husband and wife, Schwenkhusen and his mother. They spoke to each other courteously and with constraint. As always, Schwenkhusen was questioned and had to tell his story; this time he did so without that slighting of his experiences to which he had been driven by the frequent need to report on them.

At dessert Gripen was called away. It is possible that he had planned this summons or at least wished for it to come; in his humiliation, prompted by hatred of self, he may have believed that he had no right to keep his place at this table any longer than was dictated by propriety.

Schwenkhusen's mother fell asleep. Schwenkhusen looked penetratingly at Barbara and did not know whether his heart was being cooled by fire or burned by ice. She had long given up wearing gay

and bright dresses and had little jewelry on. She wore dark, nunlike
clothes, which gave her sparse jewelry a powerful, almost threatening, effect. Schwenkhusen felt both seduction and horror, as he had
experienced horror and seduction in the infinite Finnish forest
wastes, where the old heathen gods Ukko and Akka were still invoked. The first moment they were alone, so he had resolved, he
would ask her the question—the only question to be asked; and this
question had seemed to him to be inseparable from a winking laughter, a vulgar familiarity. But now he merely took her hand, which
was bare of jewelry except for the golden bracelet at the wrist, looked
at the palm which had remained spotless and kissed it. Full of shyness, without taking his glance from Barbara's face, he whispered:
"Tell me now. How did it happen?" And an inexplicable shame
oppressed him as he added, almost involuntarily: "What sort of art
did you practice? Who gave you the salve?"

Barbara looked nobly beyond him; he could not remember this
look from former times. She was silent a while longer. The wind,
caught in the hearth, roared. The old woman snored rhythmically in
her sleep. From outside came a subdued chiming of the hours: one
tower bell began after the other, each with its peculiar tone, and the
last notes of the dying chimes combined with the beginning notes of
the belated ones into a mysterious polyphony. The candles on the
table burned silently over the shining wine tankards, fruit bowls and
candy dishes.

Barbara talked as if she were talking to herself. Schwenkhusen
could not understand everything. Her whispered words came more
swiftly; sometimes they had the dark sound of imploring; in between
she shouted a sentence, and it was weird, for even this shouting remained a whisper. Her face seemed pale, she flushed. There was
something she was afraid of. He shuddered, but what do we desire
more than that which makes us afraid?

Barbara spoke of the despair of that period; her voice trembled;
and this trembling communicated itself to Schwenkhusen. His heart
passed it on to his lips, his hands and the wings of his nose. But Barbara had already raised herself above the misery of her affliction, her
eyes blazed big and triumphant, for now she was speaking of the
great mystery of her faith.

It had been Schwenkhusen's custom to sit in church in satin and
furs in the pew of the Black Heads, and to follow with a respectable

seriousness the ministrations of the six priests whose living the company provided, so that they might care for its members in St. Peter's. He had conscientiously burned wax candles for the Knight Mauritius, who was associated with the Black Heads, for protection and intercession. Schwenkhusen's faith had been a polite faith. But Barbara's faith had been the faith of strong and bold souls, which is capable of storming the mysteries of Heaven.

It has been said that remorse and resolution, confession and absolution take away sin. Barbara had awakened remorse and suffering in herself, she had made resolutions earnestly and with her total will, she had confessed and received absolution and had done penance. That is why there was no sin in her when she went to the ordeal. God had had to take it from her for the sake of His own truth and promise, for He is of course Lord, not only over the future and the present but also over the past. And because she possessed this faith that can move mountains, that can turn blood-red into snow-white, and make the cold glowing hot and the glowing heat cold, she feared not and was found pure and guiltless; pure and guiltless according to the law, for the sacrament of atonement had made her pure. She had compelled God in His own law. Be comforted, my daughter, your faith has helped you.

Barbara grew silent; Schwenkhusen stood up, pale as death, and held onto the back of his chair. He asked nothing; it was as if he feared making Barbara speak once more, for what more could a person who has uttered such things say?

Schwenkhusen had listened to her with horror. His faith was, to be sure, no longer a polite faith, as it had been before that expedition, and in many things Schwenkhusen had acquired new thoughts; this happens to a man who has had to live for more than a year among pirates and heathens versed in magic, and to wander in great loneliness, poverty and danger. Nevertheless, he would have liked to deny the woman her faith, but he felt that she was pulling his faith toward her.

The mother raised her head, her face reddened by sleep. She blinked her eyes in the yellow candlelight and its metallic reflection and sank back into her sleep with a sigh. A few slight candle flames still flickered a little from the current of air caused by this sigh, then the old lifelessness returned again.

Schwenkhusen went up to Barbara cautiously, took her hand

again and kissed the palm. It was as if his lips could no longer free themselves from the lines of this hand. Barbara, however, did not feel the kisses on her hand, any more than she had felt the hot iron on that hand.

Suddenly she stood up and motioned Schwenkhusen to his chair. Schwenkhusen obeyed.

"I must tell you something else," she whispered. "I have had a great desire for this hour ever since I saw you cross the street. For can you understand the meaning of a life such as mine has been since the day of the ordeal? I lived in a mystery. And I live in the perfect solitude of this mystery. I have been able to speak to no one, do you understand? To no one. And I know that I have become a mystery to everyone, for no one can suspect what I was deemed worthy to experience. When I saw you I was horrified. Not that I feared temptation; I can no longer be tempted by you. But I was horrified at the thought that now a door might be opened into which I might shout my secret —a door such as every person in the world has, every servant, every beggar child, all those who have nothing to lock away. Before one person, at least — before the man who is most closely concerned with it — I want to be known and revealed, revealed by the sign with which God has marked me, marked and distinguished me above all other human beings."

She dropped her voice, so that Schwenkhusen had difficulty in understanding the words that followed, although her head moved slowly toward him across the table.

Barbara whispered: ". . . as a vessel of divine selection, whose rigor is placed upon me."

Schwenkhusen jumped from his chair. He looked wild and handsome at this moment of highest emotional turmoil.

Barbara leaned back. Her face had again assumed its mask of stern imperturbability. Stretching her right arm slightly forward, she made a movement that left no room for even the slightest hope.

"I have had the strength to compel God," said Barbara. "I have had the strength to prevent the two of us from experiencing this hour together. I have told you all this. We'll have nothing further to do with each other."

Gripen's steps became audible on the stairway leading up from the ground floor. He made a noisy appearance, cleared his throat and banged doors to give warning of his return.

Schwenkhusen realized that he had only a few more moments left.

"You will listen to me, Barbara," he shouted, but without raising his voice above a whisper. "I will not leave you in the belief that I have no more share in your life. I will not permit myself to be thrust aside, and I will not . . ."

Barbara struck one of the table knives against a tin plate. The tone it gave off was clear and full, like the peal of a bell. Schwenkhusen's mother started out of her sleep and looked anxiously and stupidly about her.

"Children," she said, "oh, children, I suppose it's late? I'm an old woman."

Schwenkhusen, who had stood there with his legs wide apart, let his head droop between his shoulders. His clenched fists opened and he returned to his place. Soon after that Gripen came in. The old woman asked for the servant, who accompanied her and her son home through the dark streets, carrying a smoking torch in his hand.

(5)

Barbara had been to early Mass, and after returning home had given some orders to her servants. After that she sat by the window working at the gold embroidery for a surplice. In former times she had had little inclination for female work of this sort. Only since she had been leading her hermit-like, introspective life did she find pleasure in such labors, which are, of course, tasks for the thoughtless or the brooding.

Outside in the rising street mist, that merchant whom Schwenkhusen had clapped on the shoulder stood in front of his shop, his legs spread wide.

Was it the right shoulder or the left? Barbara thought; unconsciously she began to force every detail out of her memory. The street urchin had stood at that curb, in the brownish soft snow. Before that door, where the barefoot crippled girl was now sweeping together the horse manure, Schwenkhusen had met the constable. The turned-up fur collar of his cloak had displayed silver embroidery, tendrils and leaves. Barbara did not remember noticing it then, but now it was so clear to her that she could have repeated the lines of it in the surplice she was working on. But her hands had long ago stopped working without her noticing; they were lying between her knees, the palms pressed against each other.

Tidemann, who had just left the house, appeared on the street, pulling on his left glove as he walked. He did not dare to look up at Barbara's window. She gazed after him. His walk still had the imperious swiftness of former times, but this swiftness was now out of tune with the curvature in his back below his neck.

This had been a difficult thing to bear since the ordeal: the self-humiliation of this man, which was almost a doglike devotion. A hundred times Barbara had been weighed down by the temptation to sink down before him, to embrace his knees and shriek out to him the confession she had made to the father confessor in the Convent of the Virgin. She avoided Tidemann from fear of him, indeed from a fear of herself; but he thought he could recognize in this an aversion stemming from horror, and accepted it as a due punishment.

Perhaps it would not have been possible for Barbara to endure if her nature had not, without her knowledge, provided her with a measure of self-protection; for through her ordeal all her thoughts and all her emotions had been given a dominant center of incomparable radiance. What had formerly occupied space in Barbara's life had forfeited its rights. A miracle of grace had happened to her; every future hour of her existence had to be nourished from its light. But the nature of this miracle was not such as to lead her into a believing communion with human beings; it was one that shut her off into an inexorable loneliness.

With this miracle she lived as with a child that had been born in secret. From her fervent, incessant contemplation of it there slowly grew in her a secluded pride; God's connivance flooded her with ice-cold light. Yes, was it not right that Tidemann should bow before her, abject like a condemned man, that he did not dare take her hand or seek out her eyes? He was a human being like all the others. But she had exercised power over God.

It was this that had made Schwenkhusen shudder that evening. On the way home he guided his mother, the torch shedding a reddish glow in front of them. They walked in the middle of the road, for masses of snow, which had been loosened by the warm thaw wind, tumbled down from the many-pointed, projecting roofs.

Suddenly anger arose in Schwenkhusen, so strong that he pressed his mother's arm, then unconsciously let it go and stopped.

"What's wrong?" she asked in sleepy astonishment.

He made no reply, took her arm again and led her silently on. She did not notice that his arm, on which her fur-clad hand lay, was seized with trembling.

Anger always causes the person who is overcome by it to consider himself just and a steward of God, in whose name he is duty-bound to avenge some impropriety and thereby restore the order which God has put into the world. Schwenkhusen felt with boundless bitterness that a human being — no matter what had happened to her — was laying claim to a superhuman dignity out of the confusion of her secluded religiousness. He suddenly felt embittered by Tidemann Gripen's humiliation and by his own, which he had been forced to experience this evening.

His anger did not wholly abate in the next few days, during which he observed the Gripen house very intently and cautiously. For he was vehemently resolved to encounter Barbara. Within a short time he learned about her church attendance.

When Schwenkhusen left his house in the wintry dawn, wearing a peasant's sheepskin coat, whose upturned collar hid his face up to his eyes, his anger still burned within him, but it could not have endured in him by itself. For only the stored-up passion that sought its goal in Barbara endured in Schwenkhusen; and passion exists, of course, in excess, since it does not know whether it is attracted by its object for good or for evil. Thus in Schwenkhusen's passion anger had a place too; but added to it was his earlier desire now transfigured into a savage sublimity; it was a greed to participate in the somber, fateful splendor of the beloved person, the greed for a union that had received its perfect seal from an unearthly mystery. In this way Schwenkhusen grasped at what his heart and body had formerly possessed and which was now elevated, surrounded by the light and darkness of shudders and emotional turmoils of a new kind. And in a miraculous way he believed that he could not separate Barbara from all the terrors and powers to which he had fallen prey among the heathen, in their primeval forests and swamps, and on the rocky islands where the wind had shrieked like the poor souls in purgatory and blown as if it wanted to kindle all the flames of hell so that they might finally melt away the lethal winter.

A few altar candles were burning in the church; the low vaulted nave lay in darkness. A sourish and heavy smell pervaded the place. No incense was as strong as this smell of the burdened and poor. Peasants and old women shuffled forward into the sanctuary. Barbara had taken her customary place at the side, in the gloom of the cluster of pillars.

The priest was praying as he washed his hands: "Among the innocent I wash my hands . . . Let not, O God, my soul be destroyed with the impious, nor my life with the bloodstained, in whose hands are misdeeds and in their right hand iniquitous possessions . . ."

The significance of these words had penetrated Barbara's mind for the first time during that High Mass at St. Peter's before she had entered the vestry. From then on they appeared to her as the mightiest element in the liturgy of the Mass. She always repeated them after the priest in an undertone.

The priest had concluded and returned to the middle of the altar.

"Barbara!"

Schwenkhusen's voice sounded behind her; his lips could not be far from her ear, and again it was that shouting in a whisper.

She felt her heart grow cold.

"Barbara!"

Far out in front of her, in the light of the candles, she saw the priest, who was bending forward toward the altar, touch the embroidered altar cloth with his folded hands and pray silently. She perceived the nape of his neck and the place where his hair began, the stole which stood out stiffly under it, and the flaming large golden crucifix on the back of the chasuble. At such moments it seemed difficult for her to feel that this frame could house a human being.

"Barbara!"

She made a sudden movement, as though she wanted to leave and flee into the candlelight, into the region of the altar, among the people from whom a confused, peasantlike groaning and murmuring emanated.

"Barbara!"

She stopped, leaning back against the pillar. She did not turn her head. Her face remained motionless, facing the altar.

Schwenkhusen seemed to feel a need to satiate himself by uttering her name before he began talking.

He had wanted to beseech, beseech and demand. But if one demands, one admits the possibility that the demand may be refused.

Schwenkhusen did not beseech, Schwenkhusen did not demand; Schwenkhusen knew, with sudden enlightenment: there really cannot be a division between Barbara and me, this is a situation, irrevocable and indubitable, like breathing, like the morning chill and the darkness of the pillars. I need do nothing except arouse this situation in Barbara's consciousness.

From the recognition of this inviolability came the calm that stood behind his words, but also the penetrating, indeed the imploring, vehemence with which he uttered his words. He was in the situation of a person who strives to make clear to his beloved but stubbornly uncomprehending child that four times five is twenty. He is just as certain of the inviolability of his assertion as of the impending moment when the child will grasp and accept it — but how is it possible that this child, my child, the child I love, can resist this insight even for minutes?

Schwenkhusen felt himself being carried deeper and deeper into an enchanted world by the breath of his own words, which became progressively swifter and more passionate. Before him he saw the motionless half-silhouette of the black figure, whose right side projected just beyond the pillar. Around him was the morning-chilled, dark church, which he had never before set foot in; far in front, in the light of the altar candles, people were pressed together like bald willow stumps, and from there came the monotonous, plaintive murmur like a distant roar. Incessantly, much more frequently than ecclesiastical custom demanded, or indeed permitted, they crossed themselves with crude, clodhopper-like movements, as if their workers' hands did not permit them to endure the resting position of folded hands for more than moments at a time.

Almost without interruption the hot, shouting whisper penetrated to Barbara. She wanted to escape it by repeating the prayers of the Mass, but Schwenkhusen's voice was stronger. The woman was tied to the spot, condemned to listen without replying.

She, she wanted to tear herself from him? they had been forged to each other in the glow of the iron. For had not the miracle that occurred been his miracle too?

His voice hissed like the sprinkled iron in the vestry when it had touched the fire.

"You all thought I was dead. Good. You took it as a sign. Good. But isn't it a sign that I have brought back my life unscathed? I was able to retain it in spite of everything that happened to me. That is a miracle, Barbara, no less significant than the ordeal."

That evening in the Gripen house when Barbara had done the talking, Schwenkhusen had had to listen and accept. Now it was he who was talking. He talked as he knelt, he talked as he stood, almost without pause. He stopped only for the few moments of the transubstantiation, but in these moments Barbara thought she could feel his burning breath through her fur collar.

When the priest blessed himself with the Host, Barbara heard Schwenkhusen's steps retreating softly. He had left the church without waiting for the end of the Mass.

(6)

In the city people noticed and discussed the fact that the Schwenkhusens had been guests in the Gripen house. This was seen as the end of that series of events which had begun with the first rumors. Now everyone was suddenly inclined to see in Barbara's withdrawal from the world something like a limited period of mourning, which, however, had now run its course. It was the opinion of society that in the near future the Gripens would probably accept a return invitation from the Schwenkhusens, and after that gradually revert to their former social habits. Both men and women were equally excited at the prospect of meeting Barbara Gripen once again at dinners, weddings, baptisms and other parties. The thought was in many minds: "I'll talk to her, touch her hand, dance with her!"

All this brought about a change in the attitude of the men toward Councilman Gripen. Here and there one heard that he had atoned enough. If his guilt had been annulled by Barbara and Schwenkhusen, no one had a right to exact greater strictness.

Henning von Warendrop took the decisive step. He spoke to Gripen on the street as if nothing had happened, and asked him what he thought of the horse-breeding of one of his cousins; he, Warendrop, was thinking of buying his daughter-in-law a hunting horse for her name day.

Gripen gave him the information with a reserved face, on which, however, one could see astonishment.

But Warendrop, looking at him with his bright eyes, which had

tiny folds of skin around them, chattered about this and that; as he
warmed to the conversation, he took hold of Gripen's belt buckle,
and continued talking until he felt that the incident had been observed by a sufficient number of people. Then he took his leave,
shaking hands with Gripen.

The rest happened as society expected. Tidemann and Barbara
visited the Schwenkhusens and found a fairly large number of guests
there; for Schwenkhusen had told himself that he had less possibility
of talking to Barbara when the four of them sat alone at dinner.

Schwenkhusen found the opportunity to say a few words when they
stood in the hall after the meal, in a heavy vapor of wine, food, odors
and conversation.

"How can that which God Himself covered up have been a sin?" he
suddenly asked, and since he could not talk loudly because of the
people around him, they were both for the moment once more in the
magic circle of that penetrating and dangerous whispering.

"God did not cover it up," replied Barbara without looking at him.
"He took it away because, having recognized it as guilt myself, I
repented and confessed."

"Then your account is squared," said Schwenkhusen angrily. "You
are free to begin a new one."

It was the custom when the great, gray-white chunks of ice in the
river began to move, for people of all classes to go to the shores of the
Dvina River to watch the ice going out. The Gripens, too, appeared
on the bulwark that protected the shores and the city fortification
from the weight of the advancing ice. It was the first time they had
appeared together before a broad public.

The day was windy and bright. From the direction of the river
came a dull pounding. A few children shouted with joy. A hunch-
back was selling warm beer and hot wine. The crowd was shoving
and pushing toward the lime kilns. The sun came out intermittently,
faint between mother-of-pearl clouds. All this Barbara perceived; for
moments she was able to wonder about it.

There was a crowding about Tidemann and Barbara. Some
people acted importunately, others were embarrassed; but everyone
wanted to greet the Gripens, everyone wanted to have contact with
them, everyone wanted to see Barbara at close range.

We know that there is a necessity of things and that the actions of
people, too, take place by virtue of this necessity. For Barbara a new

chain of necessities had begun the moment she realized that Schwenkhusen was alive and present in the city. And now she, who after all had held a red-hot iron in her hand, stood among wholly polite and sympathetic and familiar faces, and all around her there was talk of engagements and the birth of twins, of an expected rise in the water level and the coming navigation season and the illness of the mayor, who was related to Barbara.

Schwenkhusen forced his way through the group. Barbara felt that she had no relationship with anyone but him.

After greetings and courtesies had been exchanged, Schwenkhusen took part in the conversation like everyone else. Barbara hastily sought his glance. In this alone she found confirmation of the extraordinary character of her existence. The ordeal by fire had irrevocably separated her from him, but this separation had irrevocably chained her to him.

Not long after the ice thaw came Easter, and with it the end of Lent; the festive and social weeks began again, and the Gripens now shared in them like other married people. Barbara had lost the habit of going to the churches attended by the lower classes; she appeared on Tidemann's arm in the councilman's pew at St. Peter's. It was the first time since the ordeal, so it caused a stir; and since it lessened the distance that lay between Barbara and the others, it increased the respectful affection she had won for herself.

"I agreed for your sake that the Schwenkhusens should come to our house," she said to him. "Now it is proper that I should no longer live like a widow."

He treated her tenderly and timidly, yet they hardly spoke to each other; indeed they scarcely saw each other except in company.

"She has forgiven him," people said. "They are living together as before."

The men thronged around her. Every individual believed he had to spread his devotion before her like homage to prove that she was pure. The women, too, sought her presence, but later on began to give her a wide berth; she was proud, they said; her pride was very cold; no one dared believe she could be satisfied. Perhaps this was understandable.

They were willing to allow her an eccentricity that they would have permitted no one else. Barbara could suddenly say: "One must have stood where I stood to be able to pass judgment on such matters."

Sometimes she spoke as if she were standing at the center of something, elevated, visible to all; as if what had occurred in her heart
and in her thoughts must be as important for everyone as what had
occurred in the hearts and thoughts of the saints of whom legends
and altar pictures gave account. This, too, many were willing to
grant her; but Schwenkhusen's angry flame of love fed on this most of
all.

They met frequently but never alone; every meeting was a goad.
Schwenkhusen desired the pain from this goad; Barbara split into
desire and resistance, as she had done in those days after Schwenkhusen's return.

In May a visit from Schwenkhusen was announced to her. Tidemann was away. Barbara wanted to refuse to see him but nevertheless gave orders to show him in.

They looked at each other, each the enslaved enemy and lord of
the other.

"Why have you come here?" she asked.

"Why didn't you refuse to see me?" he countered.

"Because I must remind you of what happened then. Don't you
realize I have made a resolution that is harder than any other in my
life? Don't you realize that it was only the power of this resolution
with which I compelled God?"

Schwenkhusen replied: "You made your resolution in the belief
that I was dead. Your belief was false. What meaning has the resolution now?"

"Do you think the resolution concerned only you?" she asked vehemently. "Do you regard yourself as a unique man?"

Schwenkhusen's reply, Schwenkhusen's voice and face betrayed a
surprising fervor; they possessed religious certainty that was free from
all arrogance, all self-seeking. He said softly: "Almost, Barbara, I
believe that. I know that you loved me. I know that you love me now.
I know that no other man can tempt you."

Barbara stood with averted face.

Schwenkhusen began anew: "I have said: tempt you. But that's not
right. You say you have compelled God, and I know that you have
compelled God. But for that reason you are free to do what you wish.
For you have found your place in a sphere where commandments are
no longer valid. This is a lonely place and it is an icy place, more
lonely and icy than the wastes in which I experienced loneliness and

cold. And this alone can therefore be your temptation, your temptation to sin: that your power is forsaking you, your power to endure
such a place, that you are taking flight into the warm atmosphere of
the other realm, which is hedged about by commandments and pro-
hibitions. That you may crawl under the commandments, above
which God Himself permitted you to rise. I have learned that there is
still another Divine Majesty than that which dwells in monstrances
and on altars. You sin against this majesty if you consider yourself
subject, as a weak human creature, to the laws that are given for the
weak. This is your temptation, Barbara, this alone: to want to be
smaller than God."

Barbara had turned back to Schwenkhusen. Suddenly a boundless
hatred broke out on her face.

"Go away!" she shrieked. "Go away!"

Schwenkhusen looked into her eyes, into her face, which was now
white, even to the twitching nostrils and lips.

Barbara lowered her head a little. "Go away!" she repeated softly,
and with the look of a frightened person Schwenkhusen went.

(7)

Not long after this conversation Barbara left the city and moved to
Gripenhof, her husband's family estate, which was situated upon the
Dvina River, far from the city. This had not happened for a series of
summers; for Tidemann, whose business and official duties did not
allow him to be absent from the city, would not gladly have suffered
such a separation; in the past year, when his will no longer had
validity, Barbara had been too little concerned about her external
life to make the decision and preparations for such a change.

Gripenhof is situated among the great forests; neighbors are distant; on the farms of the Order of Knights and of the Cistercian
monks there are no women to associate with. Tidemann came for
Pentecost and returned to the city after the holiday. Barbara was
lonely; she wanted this. At first she spent much time in the garden,
then she developed the habit of walking through the woods, glades
and hunting paths, always alone. In Gripenhof there were a few German people: the manager and his wife, the miller, several artisans.
They had not seen Barbara for a long time, but they had probably

heard something: that great and holy things had happened to her in
Riga. So they did not really dare to wonder at this strange situation —
that the lady walked through the woods this way—like a pilgrim, the
miller's wife said, who is afraid that he may die on the way; that's
why she is in such a hurry.

About this time Schwenkhusen left the city. He owned a few scattered estates somewhere along the Dvina; he wanted to look after
them, to talk over leases, to have wood cut down for mastheads and
to hunt. This could cause no astonishment to anyone.

He had taken no one along except one mounted servant, an obtuse
and taciturn man of advanced years.

Behind Uxkull the Cistercian monks had a little farm, on which a
few brothers of the Order lived with their servants. Here Schwenkhusen left his man behind, rode out at dawn and did not return before dark. He ate with the subprior, who took pleasure in Schwenkhusen's company and liked to hear about Finland. Schwenkhusen did
the same thing on the following days, waiting till after early Mass
only on Sunday, out of courtesy to his host.

He did not dare to appear in Gripenhof. But after grimly riding
through the Gripenhof forests for two weeks, he saw Barbara. She
was walking slowly in front of him at a great distance, between
swampy, glittering white and yellowish forest meadows. Behind the
log bridge she turned aside to the right. Schwenkhusen began to
gallop.

Barbara sat on a drift stone, bending forward, her hands on her
knees, her feet in the dense bilberry plants. The sun shone warmly
over the clearing; there was a smell of black alder blossom. Behind
the trees the thrushes were warbling.

Schwenkhusen jumped from his horse. She raised her head without
astonishment.

"You have been expecting me, Barbara?" Schwenkhusen asked,
and continued vehemently: "You've been expecting me."

"I heard you on the log bridge," she replied with a final evasion.

An hour later she suddenly returned to his question. "Yes, I've
been expecting you!" she shrieked. "Do you hear, God? Do you hear?"

Momentarily Schwenkhusen felt himself overcome once more by
that savage, abysmal shudder. He pulled Barbara to him.

She reminded him of their last meeting in the Gripen town house.
She said: "How did it happen that you knew my thoughts better than
I did myself?"

And Schwenkhusen replied: "Didn't I endure the ordeal with you? My heart lay on your right hand; that's why the iron could not burn it."

"Was it for that reason," the woman said, "that your heart could not freeze in the snowy wastes?"

"For that reason, Barbara. For it had taken on the glow of the iron."

Four, five times more they met in the forest. Then it was Sunday and Gripen came from the city.

"I'm going to return with you, Tidemann," Barbara declared.

"Oh," he said in surprise and with hesitant gratitude.

Schwenkhusen remained away from the city for a while longer and visited his farms with no thought for what he saw or attended to. This was the last concession he made to the rules of caution for Barbara's sake. He still possessed enough clarity of mind to realize that these forest rides to Barbara could not continue any longer without causing rumors to spread from the Cistercian farm. That is why Barbara's return to the city had been agreed upon.

When he entered Riga they had not seen each other for a week; the week had been more endless than his captivity and aimless wandering. On the following day Barbara paid a visit to Frau Schwenkhusen; after the visit the two found an hour together.

The summer blew away; autumn brought early darkness. The two remained intertwined, a burning hedge of thorns. Schwenkhusen went to the Gripen house without caring whether the councilman was there or not. Barbara went to the Schwenkhusens, indifferent to the time of day. Neither of them could think about prudence any longer. True, they did not need to: the whole city would have perceived what was happening if its opinion had not, like Gripen's, been unshakeably predetermined since the ordeal. But neither Schwenkhusen nor Barbara was capable of even this reflection. Of course, the change in Schwenkhusen struck people; but they were eager to find explanations: "He has experienced things unlike any other man; do you expect him to be as he was before?" And it was strange that no one thought of the objection that, after all, Schwenkhusen had shown nothing of this somnambulistic grimness, this morbid restlessness, this sudden glowing, in the first period after his return.

When the first anniversary of the ordeal arrived, Tidemann, deeply bowed, had been the only one to attend the Masses he had ordered in St. Peter's Church. Now, on the second anniversary, it was

as if the whole city had to share in celebrating the memory of a
miracle that had been vouchsafed it, indeed as if all these people who
had come out of courtesy, curiosity or for the sake of paying homage
to Barbara, had some share in the miracle. All those who had witnessed the event in the vestry were there: the witnesses, the sacristan
and his son, and the master smith, who was still wearing the same
Sunday coat. Right behind the Gripens stood Schwenkhusen's
mother on her son's arm, near her, old Warendrop in his brocaded
uniform with the broad golden chain under his trimmed white-gray
beard. Behind them in a dense throng was everyone of rank and importance, men and women from the noble families and from the
people. The Company of Black Heads was assembled in full force.

The Mass was celebrated at one of the side altars of the church. On
one of the altar steps lay the iron: gray, insignificant, watched by
everyone. In whispers, people called their neighbors' attention to the
wonderful metal; necks were craned, many a person tried to push his
way forward, a woman raised her child to her shoulder.

The memorial Mass was said by the same priest who had been
assigned to direct the ordeal and who seemed to have aged. After
that, the Mass for Schwenkhusen was to be said; one of the six clergymen supported by the Company of Black Heads had been selected
for it.

The priest read in a murmuring tone that portion of the gospel
which the Church reserves for votive masses. Neither he nor anyone
else understood the sense of the words—no one but Barbara and
Schwenkhusen.

"And Jesus, answering, saith unto them: Have faith in God.

"For verily I say unto you, that whosoever shall say unto this mountain, Be thou removed, and be thou cast into the sea, and shall not
doubt in his heart, but shall believe that those things which he saith
shall come to pass: he shall have whatsoever he saith."

Schwenkhusen felt a sudden cold in his shoulder blades. He shut
his eyes and believed he saw the angels and demons of the altar picture, which, hovering above Barbara and himself, let glowing roses
stream down on the ensnared couple like the flames of love and hell.

Barbara stood motionless before him, her head slightly bowed,
dressed in white and wearing a veil, to be seen by all the people as on
that Sunday two years ago.

The Mass was over, the altar abandoned. For a little while longer they all remained in the position of the last prayer. Then movements were heard, indistinct words; someone coughed; groups scattered and formed. Barbara turned around.

Councilman von Warendrop stepped up to her and kissed her hand, as he had done that time. Gripen, Schwenkhusen, many of the others thronged toward Barbara and pressed and kissed her hand; Schwenkhusen's mother embraced her, the sacristan's son let his lips glide swiftly along her hanging sleeve. She was greeted and congratulated. Many paid homage out of reverence, deep emotion, and heartfelt admiration, homage subdued in its expression only because of the special character of the solemnity. Barbara gave thanks with light inclinations of her head, which were often scarcely perceptible.

No one left the church, for now the second Mass was to be said, the one for Schwenkhusen· and everyone had the wish to reveal to him, as he had to the wife of Councilman Gripen, his share in this miraculous destiny. Meanwhile the second priest was already in the vestry, putting on his robes.

The movement of all those people pressing in on Barbara like a slow surge had made her step back a few paces. Thus she stood on the steps, with her back to the altar, her face turned towards the people, wonderfully erect, snow-white and tall.

One step below her, to the side, lay the piece of iron. Barbara pointed to it with a light motion of her hand. The bystanders guessed her wishes instantly, to touch the instrument in memory of the miracle. Gripen and Warendrop bent down at the same time to pick up the piece of iron. Schwenkhusen anticipated them and handed it to Barbara. He felt a chill at the cold touch. She slowly stretched out her open hand. The sleeve fell back and at her wrist appeared the simple golden bracelet. Her elbow rested on her hipbone. Hand and lower arm stood out from the body in a right angle. All eyes had turned to her.

At the moment when the priest stepped out of the vestry into the nave of the church filled with a deathly silence, he heard an inhuman cry: "I'm burning! I'm burning!" Immediately afterwards the muffled noise of a falling body could be heard.

The priest began to run with shaking knees. As he stumbled forward he made the sign of the Cross, his hand moving unsteadily over his face and breast.

For moments they all stood there, motionless and silent. Schwenkhusen turned away, staggered out. The people retreated before him, so that in seconds a lane of desolation had been created for him, through the whole length of the church, up to the exit.